# Introduction to the
# *Principles of Mechanics*

*To my parents*

This book is in the

**ADDISON-WESLEY SERIES IN PHYSICS**

# Introduction to the
# *Principles of Mechanics*

WALTER HAUSER

*Northeastern University*

ADDISON-WESLEY PUBLISHING COMPANY, INC.

READING, MASSACHUSETTS

**ADDISON-WESLEY PUBLISHING COMPANY, INC.**
PALO ALTO · READING, MASSACHUSETTS · LONDON
NEW YORK · DALLAS · ATLANTA · BARRINGTON, ILLINOIS

# *Preface*

This is a text for an intermediate mechanics course at the junior-senior level. It also contains sufficient material to make the book suitable for the first semester of an introductory graduate course in theoretical physics. The text has been written for students who have been exposed to a thorough introductory course in mechanics from a text such as Resnick and Halliday or Sears and Zemansky and who have had a course in differential and integral calculus. In addition, it is assumed that a course in differential equations will be taken concurrently with the intermediate mechanics course.

Classical mechanics has long been a basic course in the training of the physics and engineering student. This has in no small measure been due to the general applicability of classical mechanics to a vast number of familiar phenomena. Mechanics thus provides us with meaningful and readily visualizable examples with which to stimulate the student's interest in physics. It also provides him with a wealth of problems through the solutions of which he may become familiar with the mathematical tools that he will require for the efficient mastery of other fields of physics. Mechanics has long been and should be a mathematical training ground for the budding physicist.

The explosive rate at which the different fields of physics are growing has forced a revision of undergraduate physics curricula and a general upgrading of the level of the courses offered. This change in the educational program of the physics and engineering student justifies the addition of new books to an already long list of excellent texts even on such time-honored and seemingly closed subjects as classical mechanics.

We have long felt the need for an intermediate mechanics text which would fill the need of today's student of physics who is not permitted the luxury of a slow mastery of the subject. Today's student, more than ever before, must early in his career acquire the habit of mastering a great deal of mathematics and physics on his own initiative. It is therefore extremely important that intermediate physics texts stress the underlying unity of physics and strive to impart a deep understanding of the basic principles of their subject.

In writing the present text our principal concern has been the student. We have taken special care to try motivating the introduction of new concepts and mathematical methods in order to make them more palatable. On many occasions we did not hesitate to present an elementary (unsophisticated) approach if we felt that such a discussion added something to the understanding of the problem. New and important concepts are introduced slowly and antici-

v

pated long before full use is made of them. We also did not hesitate to include the details of the derivations in order to make the book more readable. This is not to say that the book is easy. Between its pages we have inserted a great deal of sophistication and advanced topics not customarily found in intermediate mechanics texts, sophistication which we consider indispensable to the student of today. Unfortunately, space did not permit us to include all the advanced topics we should have liked to. Originally, for example, we planned on including a chapter on variational principles. Perhaps we shall have the opportunity to rectify this and other omissions in future editions of this book. We hope that the serious student will not be satisfied with a mastery of just the material covered in class or with a single reading of the text. We hope that he will also find the time to consult other mechanics texts in his quest for an understanding of the subject. It is also extremely important that he struggle with the problems in order to strengthen this understanding.

Mechanics is an old and well-developed subject. The difference between ours and other presently available presentations of the subject lies solely in the order and mode of presentation of the material. We felt that we were sufficiently different in this respect to justify the publication of this book. To mention but a few innovations which we have introduced, in Chapter 1 we introduce the concept of linear independence of vectors and the representation of a three-dimensional vector as the linear sum of three linearly independent base vectors. This in turn leads us into a discussion of reciprocal base vectors, and quite naturally into a geometric definition of the covariant and contravariant components of a vector. At this point, we made a compromise in the notation. Having found the customary superscript notation for the contravariant components of a vector confusing to the average student, we consented, somewhat regretfully, to designate them by a star ($\star$) superscript. Anyone wishing to use the superscript notation should find no difficulty in replacing our $A_i^{\star}$ for the contravariant components of the vector $\mathbf{A}$ by the customary $A^i$. The introduction of this topic, we feel, is *most important*, for it in turn permits an early introduction of generalized coordinates and a very satisfying and readily understood geometric derivation of Lagrange's equations of motion. In our opinion this is a singularly important innovation. It was indeed the original stimulation for the writing of this book.

We also introduce the reader to the concept of the matrix representation of a vector and the Dirac ket and bras notation to distinguish between the vector represented by a column matrix and the vector represented by a row matrix. Until Chapter 10 only occasional use is made of matrices, matrix equations, and their equivalent operator equations. In Chapter 10, we present a discussion of the algebra of $n$-dimensional vectors and the basic elements of linear transformation theory which is required for the efficient handling of the theory of coupled oscillations (Chapter 11) and the special theory of relativity (Chapter 13).

Another innovation is the introduction of the Green function method for solving differential equations. In Chapter 4, we extend the usual discussion of the simple harmonic oscillator by expressing the general solution for the forced harmonic oscillator in terms of an integral involving a Green function. We also include a brief introduction to nonlinear oscillations, obtaining approximate iterative Fourier-series solutions to the problem of the anharmonic oscillator through the use of Green's function.

The book contains more material than can efficiently be covered in a two-semester course. This allows for a certain amount of flexibility in the choice of topics. We do not make any specific suggestions for a shorter or longer course. We have based a 72-hour mechanics course on the contents of the first nine chapters, varying the topics to suit the ability and mathematical background of the student. With mathematically weak students, who tend to tire with the development of the mathematical language presented in the first three chapters, we would omit Chapter 3 until such time as its contents was required. We would also feed such a group of weak students only a minimum of the advanced material which we have inserted from time to time for the benefit of the more able and serious student. The better students of an otherwise weak class we would encourage to attempt to master the material not covered in class on their own. In writing this book we were fully aware of this problem, and intended that a large part of the book be studied in this fashion by the more enthusiastic and able student.

I am grateful to a number of people for help and encouragement. First and foremost, I would like to thank my parents for their love, inspiration and sacrifice during my formative and later years. This book is as much theirs as it is mine. I would also like to thank my dear wife, Betty, for her help, patience and encouragement during the writing of the book. Her typing and editing of the material added immeasurably to its successful completion. I am grateful to my former teachers at Brooklyn College, especially Drs. Bernard Kurrelmeyer and Walter H. Mais, for their inspiring and clear lectures, which made physics such a delightful subject to me, and to Dr. Herman Feshbach for sustaining this inspiration for me during my stay at Massachusetts Institute of Technology.

I would like to thank my colleagues for many helpful discussions and suggestions. Specifically, I would like to thank Drs. Marving H. Friedman and Michael Glaubman, with whom I discussed many of the innovations which I have introduced. They were most helpful and encouraging. My thanks are also extended to Mr. Peter Gianino, who read the entire manuscript, correcting many errors and suggesting many improvements, and to Dr. Robert G. Arns, whose enthusiastic, understanding and helpful reviews I found most sustaining. I would also like to thank my students who suffered with me through the writing of this book. Finally, I would like to acknowledge the helpful cooperation I received from my publishers. Their staff was most congenial and a pleasure to work with, and I thank them for persuading me to write this book, a chore I enjoyed immensely. תושלב״ע

*Boston, Massachusetts*                                                                    W.H.
*March 1965*

# Contents

# 1

# *Vectors*

Physics is a science which concerns itself with observable (quantitatively measurable) physical quantities and the relationships which may exist between the experimentally determined values of the various physical quantities of interest. Some physical quantities require only the determination of a single number for their complete specification. Temperature, volume, time, path length, the speed of light, the frequency of a sound wave, and electric charge are examples of such physical quantities, which are referred to as *scalars*. On the other hand, there are physical quantities which require two or more numbers for their complete specification. To specify a rectilinear displacement for example, it is not sufficient merely to measure the magnitude of the displacement. To specify a rectilinear displacement in three-dimensional space, we require two more numbers from which we may determine the direction in which the displacement takes place. Any physical quantity which, like a rectilinear displacement, requires a magnitude and a direction for its specification, and which in addition may be added to another similar physical quantity in the same manner that two consecutive displacements are added (cf. Section 1–2) to form a unique physical quantity also with a magnitude and direction is referred to as a three-dimensional vector quantity or simply three-dimensional vector. In this chapter we shall acquaint the reader with the mathematical language and the fundamental mathematical manipulation of three-dimensional vectors. In a later chapter (Chapter 10) we shall generalize our results for three-dimensional vectors to $n$-dimensional vectors, which are quantities requiring $n$ numbers for their specification.

We shall use bold-faced letters to denote vectors to distinguish them from scalars, which will be indicated by light-faced italic letters. Thus **A** represents a vector, whereas its magnitude, being a pure number or scalar, is represented by $A$. At times we shall also utilize $|\mathbf{A}|$ to represent the magnitude $A$ of the vector **A**.

## 1–1 Geometrical representation of a vector

Graphically we can represent both the direction and the magnitude of a vector by a directed line segment or arrow drawn parallel to the vector and pointing in the direction of the vector. The length of the arrow is drawn to scale so that its length may be chosen to represent the magnitude of the vector.

1

In Fig. 1–1, for example, we represent graphically a vector **A** which is parallel to the $xy$-plane and which makes an angle $\phi$ with a line parallel to the $x$-axis. If the vector **A** has a magnitude of five units, then the length of the arrow representing it would be drawn five times the length chosen to represent a vector of unit magnitude.

The representation of the magnitude of a vector by the length of the arrow implies the definition that the multiplication of a vector **A** by a scalar $c$ yields a vector parallel to **A**, having a magnitude $c$ times the magnitude of **A**,

$$|c\mathbf{A}| = cA. \tag{1–1}$$

It follows from this that we should be able to express any vector as the product of a scalar and a vector of unit magnitude, called a *unit vector*. Indeed if $\mathbf{e}_A$ is the unit vector in the direction of **A**, the vector $A\mathbf{e}_A$ is a vector in the direction of **A** having magnitude $A$.

Two vectors **A** and **B** are said to be equal if they both have the same magnitude and direction. We can thus write

$$\mathbf{A} = A\mathbf{e}_A. \tag{1–2}$$

The *null vector* **O** is defined as a vector of zero magnitude. Its direction in any application is immaterial.

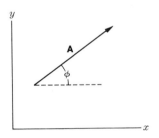

Fig. 1–1. Graphical representation of a vector.

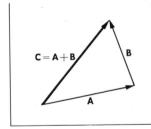

Fig. 1–2. Graphical representation of vector addition.

## 1–2 The addition and subtraction of vectors

The addition of two vectors **A** and **B** is represented graphically in Fig. 1–2. To add two vectors **A** and **B** graphically, we draw the arrow representing the vector **A**, and from its tip draw the arrow representing the vector **B**. The vector **C** which is the sum of the two vectors is then represented by the arrow drawn from the tail of the arrow representing **A** to the tip of the one representing **B**. This rule for vector addition is called the *parallelogram law of addition*.

From Fig. 1–3 it should be clear that vector addition is commutative:

$$\mathbf{A} + \mathbf{B} = \mathbf{B} + \mathbf{A}.$$

It is also associative (cf. Fig. 1–4):

$$\mathbf{A} + (\mathbf{B} + \mathbf{C}) = (\mathbf{A} + \mathbf{B}) + \mathbf{C}.$$

If the sum of the two vectors **A** and **B** equals a vector of zero magnitude,

$$\mathbf{A} + \mathbf{B} = \mathbf{0}, \tag{1–3}$$

then the two vectors **A** and **B** must obviously have equal magnitude and be oppositely directed. Equation (1–3) thus yields

$$\mathbf{B} = -\mathbf{A}, \tag{1–4}$$

which tells us that $-\mathbf{A}$ is a vector which has the same magnitude as the vector **A** but points in a direction opposite to that of **A**.

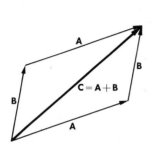

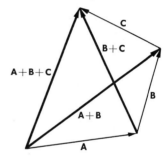

FIG. 1–3. Commutative nature of vector addition: $\mathbf{A} + \mathbf{B} = \mathbf{B} + \mathbf{A}$.

FIG. 1–4. Associative nature of vector addition: $(\mathbf{A} + \mathbf{B}) + \mathbf{C} = \mathbf{A} + (\mathbf{B} + \mathbf{C})$.

This permits us to define the subtraction of the vector **B** from the vector **A** as the addition of the vector **A** and the vector $(-\mathbf{B})$,

$$\mathbf{A} - \mathbf{B} = \mathbf{A} + (-\mathbf{B}). \tag{1–5}$$

## 1–3 Algebraic representation of a vector

Any vector **A**, as we shall show, may be represented algebraically by specifying its projections onto a set of coordinate axes or base vectors. The three base vectors of a three-dimensional coordinate system must be linearly independent; they must therefore satisfy the requirement that they be noncoplanar. The simplest choice, but by no means the only choice, for such a set of noncoplanar base vectors is a set of mutually perpendicular unit vectors.

In a cartesian coordinate system the three base vectors are chosen as the three unit vectors directed respectively along the positive $x$-, $y$-, and $z$-axes.

The unit vectors along the positive $x$-, $y$-, and $z$-coordinate axes are respectively designated by the symbols **i**, **j**, and **k** (Fig. 1–5). At times we shall also find it notationally convenient to designate them by the symbols $\mathbf{e}_1$, $\mathbf{e}_2$, and $\mathbf{e}_3$.

Graphically the projection of a vector **A** onto another vector **B** is represented by the length of the line segment between the intersection of any line parallel to **B** with the perpendiculars onto the direction of **B** drawn from the tail and tip of the arrow representing **A** (Fig. 1–6).

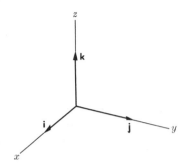

FIG. 1–5.  Cartesian unit base vectors.

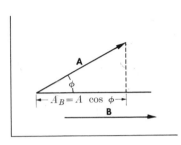

FIG. 1–6.  Projection of the vector **A** onto the vector **B**.

If the projection of the tip of the arrow representing **A** onto **B** lies in the direction of **B** with respect to the projection of the tail of the arrow representing **A** onto **B**, then the projection is considered to be positive. If it is oppositely directed, then it is considered to be negative. In terms of the smaller of the two angles, the angle $\phi$, which the arrow representing the vector **A** makes with any arrow drawn in the direction of **B** from the foot of the arrow representing **A**, the projection of **A** onto **B**, also called the **B**-component of **A** and designated by $A_B$, is given by the formula

$$A_B = A \cos \phi. \tag{1–6}$$

The angle $\phi$ will be referred to as the angle between the vectors **A** and **B**.

According to the rule by which we designate a projection to be positive or negative, we find that $A_B$ is positive for

$$0 < \phi. < \frac{\pi}{2}$$

and negative for

$$\frac{\pi}{2} < \phi < \pi.$$

From the addition law it follows that the vector **A** is expressible as the sum of the three vectors $A_x\mathbf{i}$, $A_y\mathbf{j}$, and $A_z\mathbf{k}$. That is,

$$\mathbf{A} = A_x\mathbf{i} + A_y\mathbf{j} + A_z\mathbf{k}, \tag{1–7}$$

where $A_x$, $A_y$, and $A_z$ are the components of **A** along the positive $x$-, $y$-, and $z$-axes. For example, consider a vector **A** which lies in the $xy$-plane ($A_z = 0$). In this case we can always consider the vector **A** to lie along the hypotenuse of a right triangle whose legs are parallel to the positive $x$- and $y$-axes. From Fig. 1–7 it should be evident that

$$A_x = A \cos \phi, \tag{1-8}$$

$$A_y = A \sin \phi, \tag{1-9}$$

$$A^2 = A_x^2 + A_y^2, \tag{1-10}$$

and that the relation

$$\mathbf{A} = A_x\mathbf{i} + A_y\mathbf{j} \tag{1-11}$$

is correct.

The extension to three-dimensional vectors is shown in Fig. 1–8. In terms of the angle $\theta$ which the vector **A** makes with the positive $z$-axis and the angle $\phi$ which the projection of **A** onto the $xy$-plane makes with the positive $x$-axis, it follows (cf. Fig. 1–8) that

$$A_z = A \cos \theta, \tag{1-12}$$

$$A_x = A \sin \theta \cos \phi, \tag{1-13}$$

$$A_y = A \sin \theta \sin \phi, \tag{1-14}$$

$$A^2 = A_x^2 + A_y^2 + A_z^2, \tag{1-15}$$

and that indeed

$$\mathbf{A} = A_x\mathbf{i} + A_y\mathbf{j} + A_z\mathbf{k}.$$

It should be clear from the definition of the equality of two vectors that the equality of their $x$-, $y$-, and $z$-components is a necessary and sufficient condition for them to be equal. It should also be clear that the $x$-, $y$-, and $z$-components of the sum of two or more vectors is equal to the sum of the respective com-

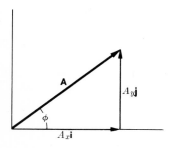

FIG. 1–7. Diagrammatic proof of **A** = $A_x\mathbf{i}$ + $A_y\mathbf{j}$ for a vector parallel to the $xy$-plane.

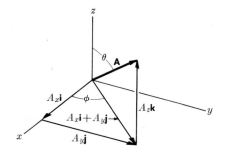

FIG. 1–8. Diagrammatic proof of **A** = $A_x\mathbf{i}$ + $A_y\mathbf{j}$ + $A_z\mathbf{k}$.

ponents of the vectors. That is, if the vector **C** is the sum of the vectors **A** and **B**,

$$\mathbf{C} = \mathbf{A} + \mathbf{B}, \tag{1-16}$$

then

$$C_x = A_x + B_x, \qquad C_y = A_y + B_y, \qquad \text{and} \qquad C_z = A_z + B_z, \tag{1-17}$$

whence we can obtain

$$C^2 = C_x^2 + C_y^2 + C_z^2 = A^2 + B^2 + 2(A_xB_x + A_yB_y + A_zB_z) \tag{1-18}$$
$$= A^2 + B^2 + 2AB \cos \phi.$$

The latter expression is the law of cosines. We note that the plus sign in front of the last term on the right-hand side of Eq. (1–18) is due to the fact that the angle between the vectors **A** and **B** is an exterior angle of the triangle formed by these vectors (Fig. 1–9).

The choice of the orientation of the $(x, y, z)$-coordinate system is, of course, quite arbitrary. Two equal vectors therefore have equal components along any direction, and the component of the sum of two or more vectors along any direction is equal to the sum of the components of the vectors being added along that direction,

$$C_D = A_D + B_D. \tag{1-19}$$

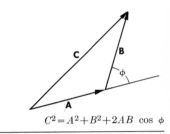

Fig. 1–9. The law of cosines.

## 1–4 Vector multiplication

Given the two vectors **A** and **B**, there exist two products of these vectors for which we shall find immediate use. The first product is called the scalar or dot product, since it is a scalar. We have already met this product in Eq. (1–18). It is denoted by **A** · **B**, and is defined by the equation

$$\mathbf{A} \cdot \mathbf{B} = AB \cos \phi, \tag{1-20}$$

where $\phi$ is the angle between the vectors **A** and **B**. As was seen, this expression occurs in the law of cosines from which we obtain (cf. Fig. 1–9) the relation

$$\mathbf{A} \cdot \mathbf{B} = \frac{C^2 - A^2 - B^2}{2} = A_xB_x + A_yB_y + A_zB_z. \tag{1-21}$$

From its definition the scalar product is obviously commutative,

$$\mathbf{A} \cdot \mathbf{B} = \mathbf{B} \cdot \mathbf{A}.$$

Since the projection of the sum of the vectors **A** and **B** along a vector **C** equals the sum of the projection of **A** along **C** plus the projection of **B** along **C**, the scalar product is found to satisfy the distributive law:

$$(\mathbf{A} + \mathbf{B}) \cdot \mathbf{C} = \mathbf{A} \cdot \mathbf{C} + \mathbf{B} \cdot \mathbf{C}.$$

The other product which we shall require is the vector or cross product of the two vectors **A** and **B**, indicated by **A** $\times$ **B**. In the next section we shall meet this product in the form

$$\mathbf{A} \times \mathbf{B} = \begin{vmatrix} \mathbf{i} & \mathbf{j} & \mathbf{k} \\ A_x & A_y & A_z \\ B_x & B_y & B_z \end{vmatrix} = \begin{aligned} &(A_y B_z - A_z B_y)\mathbf{i} \\ &+ (A_z B_x - A_x B_z)\mathbf{j} \\ &+ (A_x B_y - A_y B_x)\mathbf{k}, \end{aligned} \tag{1–22}$$

which we use as its definition.

It requires only a simple algebraic manipulation to show that

$$|\mathbf{A} \times \mathbf{B}|^2 = A^2 B^2 - (\mathbf{A} \cdot \mathbf{B})^2 = A^2 B^2 \sin^2 \phi,$$

or that the magnitude of the vector product of the vectors **A** and **B** is

$$|\mathbf{A} \times \mathbf{B}| = AB \sin \phi, \tag{1–23}$$

where $\phi$ is the angle between the vectors **A** and **B**.

The scalar product of **A** $\times$ **B** with either **A** or **B** is zero (Problem 1–1). The vector product **A** $\times$ **B** thus makes an angle of 90° with either of the vectors **A** or **B** and is therefore perpendicular to the plane of the vectors **A** and **B** as any plane parallel to the vectors **A** and **B** is referred to. For a complete specification of the vector product, we require a more precise specification of the direction of **A** $\times$ **B** along the perpendicular to the plane of **A** and **B**, there being two such directions. To find which it is, we choose the plane of **A** and **B** to be the $xy$-plane, with the positive $x$-axis lying along the vector **A**. For this choice of the coordinate axes, the vector product is given by

$$\mathbf{A} \times \mathbf{B} = \begin{vmatrix} \mathbf{i} & \mathbf{j} & \mathbf{k} \\ A_x & 0 & 0 \\ B_x & B_y & 0 \end{vmatrix} = A_x B_y \mathbf{k}.$$

Thus for positive $B_y$ the vector product of **A** and **B** lies along the positive **k**-direction, whereas for negative $B_y$ it lies along the negative **k**-direction. Choosing $\phi$ to represent the smaller of the two angles which the two vectors **A** and **B** make with each other, we find that we can set

$$\mathbf{A} \times \mathbf{B} = AB \sin \phi \mathbf{n}, \tag{1–24}$$

where **n** is the unit vector perpendicular to the plane of **A** and **B**, in the direction of the advance of a right-handed screw which is rotated about an axis perpen-

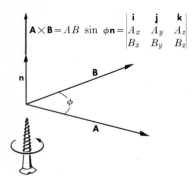

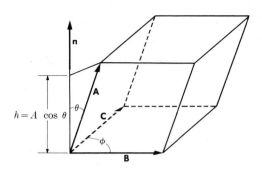

FIG. 1–10.  Definition of the vector product.

FIG. 1–11.  Volume of the parallelepiped of the three vectors **A**, **B**, and **C**: $V = (A \cos \theta)(BC \sin \phi) = |\mathbf{A} \cdot \mathbf{B} \times \mathbf{C}|$.

dicular to the plane of **A** and **B**, in the sense that would turn **A** into **B** through the smaller of the two angles which the two vectors make with each other (cf. Fig. 1–10).

From Eq. (1–22) it follows that the vector product is not commutative, but that

$$\mathbf{A} \times \mathbf{B} = -\mathbf{B} \times \mathbf{A}. \tag{1–25}$$

The distributive law,

$$\mathbf{A} \times (\mathbf{B} + \mathbf{C}) = \mathbf{A} \times \mathbf{B} + \mathbf{A} \times \mathbf{C}, \tag{1–26}$$

however, is valid.  This is readily verified through the use of the determinant definition of the vector product (Eq. 1–22).

The scalar product of the vector **A** with the vector product of the vectors **B** and **C** is referred to as a *scalar triple product*.  In terms of the cartesian components of these vectors, the scalar triple product is given by

$$\mathbf{A} \cdot (\mathbf{B} \times \mathbf{C}) = \begin{vmatrix} A_x & A_y & A_z \\ B_x & B_y & B_z \\ C_x & C_y & C_z \end{vmatrix}. \tag{1–27}$$

By interchanging the rows of the determinant, we find that

$$\mathbf{A} \cdot (\mathbf{B} \times \mathbf{C}) = (\mathbf{A} \times \mathbf{B}) \cdot \mathbf{C} = (\mathbf{C} \times \mathbf{A}) \cdot \mathbf{B}$$
$$= -\mathbf{A} \cdot (\mathbf{C} \times \mathbf{B}). \tag{1–28}$$

Because of the equivalence of the products $\mathbf{A} \cdot (\mathbf{B} \times \mathbf{C})$, $(\mathbf{A} \times \mathbf{B}) \cdot \mathbf{C}$ and $(\mathbf{C} \times \mathbf{A}) \cdot \mathbf{B}$, it is customary to omit the parentheses in the scalar triple product.

Geometrically, if the magnitudes of three vectors **A**, **B**, and **C** have the dimensions of length, their scalar triple product represents the volume of the parallelepiped formed by the three vectors (Fig. 1–11).  The volume of a parallelepiped equals the product of the area of its base and its altitude. For the parallelepiped of the vectors **A**, **B**, and **C** shown in Fig. 1–11, the area of the base, which is the area of the parallelogram formed by the vectors **B** and **C**, is given by the formula

$$\text{Area} = BC \sin \phi = |\mathbf{B} \times \mathbf{C}|. \tag{1–29}$$

The altitude $h$ can be seen to be expressed by

$$h = \mathbf{A} \cdot \mathbf{n} = A \cos \theta,$$

where **n** is a unit vector perpendicular to the base. Thus we have for the volume of the parallelepiped the formula

$$\text{Volume} = |\mathbf{B} \times \mathbf{C}| A \cos \theta = |\mathbf{A} \cdot \mathbf{B} \times \mathbf{C}|. \tag{1–30}$$

There exists another useful triple product, the triple vector product $\mathbf{A} \times (\mathbf{B} \times \mathbf{C})$. It is left as an exercise for the reader (Problem 1–5) to show that

$$\mathbf{A} \times (\mathbf{B} \times \mathbf{C}) = (\mathbf{A} \cdot \mathbf{C})\mathbf{B} - (\mathbf{A} \cdot \mathbf{B})\mathbf{C}. \tag{1–31}$$

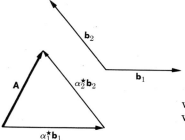

FIG. 1–12. Decomposition of a vector into the sum of two component vectors coplanar with the first.

## 1–5 Nonorthogonal coordinate systems

It is of course not necessary and not always the most convenient choice to represent a vector in terms of its components along three mutually perpendicular unit vectors. We therefore digress to discuss the representation of a vector **A** in terms of a linear sum of three noncoplanar vectors $\mathbf{b}_1$, $\mathbf{b}_2$, and $\mathbf{b}_3$ (Fig. 1–12).

If we set

$$\mathbf{A} = \alpha_1^\star \mathbf{b}_1 + \alpha_2^\star \mathbf{b}_2 + \alpha_3^\star \mathbf{b}_3, \tag{1–32}$$

where the $\alpha_i^\star$'s are constants, then by Eq. (1–17)

$$\begin{aligned}
A_x &= \alpha_1^\star b_{1x} + \alpha_2^\star b_{2x} + \alpha_3^\star b_{3x}, \\
A_y &= \alpha_1^\star b_{1y} + \alpha_2^\star b_{2y} + \alpha_3^\star b_{3y}, \\
A_z &= \alpha_1^\star b_{1z} + \alpha_2^\star b_{2z} + \alpha_3^\star b_{3z}.
\end{aligned} \tag{1–33}$$

Equations (1–33) are three simultaneous linear equations which we may solve for the three constants $\alpha_1^\star$, $\alpha_2^\star$, and $\alpha_3^\star$. The solutions may be expressed in determinant notation. Thus we obtain

$$\alpha_1^{\star} = \frac{\begin{vmatrix} A_x & A_y & A_z \\ b_{2x} & b_{2y} & b_{2z} \\ b_{3x} & b_{3y} & b_{3z} \end{vmatrix}}{\begin{vmatrix} b_{1x} & b_{1y} & b_{1z} \\ b_{2x} & b_{2y} & b_{2z} \\ b_{3x} & b_{3y} & b_{3z} \end{vmatrix}} = \frac{\mathbf{A} \cdot \mathbf{b}_2 \times \mathbf{b}_3}{\mathbf{b}_1 \cdot \mathbf{b}_2 \times \mathbf{b}_3}. \tag{1-34}$$

The last step follows from Eq. (1–27). Similarly, we obtain

$$\alpha_2^{\star} = \frac{\mathbf{A} \cdot \mathbf{b}_3 \times \mathbf{b}_1}{\mathbf{b}_1 \cdot \mathbf{b}_2 \times \mathbf{b}_3} \quad \text{and} \quad \alpha_3^{\star} = \frac{\mathbf{A} \cdot \mathbf{b}_1 \times \mathbf{b}_2}{\mathbf{b}_1 \cdot \mathbf{b}_2 \times \mathbf{b}_3}. \tag{1-35}$$

We realize, of course, that Eqs. (1–34) and (1–35) are uniquely soluble only if the scalar triple product of the three base vectors does not vanish,

$$\mathbf{b}_1 \cdot \mathbf{b}_2 \times \mathbf{b}_3 \neq 0.$$

This condition is satisfied if the three base vectors are noncoplanar.

Equations (1–34) and (1–35) may be expressed more concisely in terms of the vectors $b_1$, $b_2$, and $b_3$, which are defined by the equations

$$\begin{aligned} b_1 &= (\mathbf{b}_2 \times \mathbf{b}_3) \div (\mathbf{b}_1 \cdot \mathbf{b}_2 \times \mathbf{b}_3), \\ b_2 &= (\mathbf{b}_3 \times \mathbf{b}_1) \div (\mathbf{b}_1 \cdot \mathbf{b}_2 \times \mathbf{b}_3), \\ b_3 &= (\mathbf{b}_1 \times \mathbf{b}_2) \div (\mathbf{b}_1 \cdot \mathbf{b}_2 \times \mathbf{b}_3), \end{aligned} \tag{1-36}$$

and which satisfy the relations

$$b_1 \cdot \mathbf{b}_1 = b_2 \cdot \mathbf{b}_2 = b_3 \cdot \mathbf{b}_3 = 1$$

and $\tag{1-37}$

$$b_1 \cdot \mathbf{b}_2 = b_1 \cdot \mathbf{b}_3 = b_2 \cdot \mathbf{b}_1 = b_2 \cdot \mathbf{b}_3 = b_3 \cdot \mathbf{b}_1 = b_3 \cdot \mathbf{b}_2 = 0.$$

The scalar products of the vectors $b_1$, $b_2$, $b_3$ and the vectors $\mathbf{b}_1$, $\mathbf{b}_2$, $\mathbf{b}_3$ are concisely expressed by the equation

$$b_i \cdot \mathbf{b}_j = \delta_{ij}, \qquad i, j = 1, 2, 3, \tag{1-38}$$

where $\delta_{ij}$ is the *Kronecker delta* having the value zero when $i \neq j$ and the value one when $i = j$, or

$$\delta_{ij} = \begin{cases} 0 & i \neq j, \\ 1 & i = j. \end{cases} \tag{1-39}$$

In terms of the vectors $b_i$,

$$\begin{aligned} \alpha_1^{\star} &= \mathbf{A} \cdot b_1, \\ \alpha_2^{\star} &= \mathbf{A} \cdot b_2, \\ \alpha_3^{\star} &= \mathbf{A} \cdot b_3. \end{aligned} \tag{1-40}$$

The three vectors $b_1$, $b_2$, and $b_3$ are referred to as the *inverse* or *reciprocal* vectors of the three vectors $\mathbf{b}_1$, $\mathbf{b}_2$, and $\mathbf{b}_3$, and the coordinate system formed by the vectors $b_1$, $b_2$, and $b_3$ is referred to as the coordinate system reciprocal to the coordinate system formed by the vectors $\mathbf{b}_1$, $\mathbf{b}_2$, and $\mathbf{b}_3$ (Fig. 1–13). We note that a set of mutually orthogonal unit vectors is its own reciprocal set.

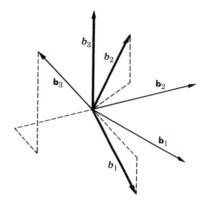

FIG. 1–13.   Reciprocal sets of base vectors:

$b_1 \perp \mathbf{b}_2, \mathbf{b}_3$;   $b_2 \perp \mathbf{b}_3, \mathbf{b}_1$;   $b_3 \perp \mathbf{b}_1, \mathbf{b}_2$;
$\mathbf{b}_1 \perp b_2, b_3$;   $\mathbf{b}_2 \perp b_3, b_1$;   $\mathbf{b}_3 \perp b_1, b_2$.

Through use of the definition of the inverse base vectors and Eq. (1–31), we obtain the important relation

$$b_1 \cdot b_2 \times b_3 = \frac{(\mathbf{b}_2 \times \mathbf{b}_3) \cdot [(\mathbf{b}_3 \times \mathbf{b}_1) \times (\mathbf{b}_1 \times \mathbf{b}_2)]}{(\mathbf{b}_1 \cdot \mathbf{b}_2 \times \mathbf{b}_3)^3}$$

$$= \frac{(\mathbf{b}_2 \times \mathbf{b}_3) \cdot [(\mathbf{b}_3 \times \mathbf{b}_1 \cdot \mathbf{b}_2)\mathbf{b}_1]}{(\mathbf{b}_1 \cdot \mathbf{b}_2 \times \mathbf{b}_3)^3} \tag{1–41}$$

$$= \frac{1}{\mathbf{b}_1 \cdot \mathbf{b}_2 \times \mathbf{b}_3} \, .$$

Those familiar with the multiplication of determinants could have obtained this same result through the product of the determinant

$$\mathbf{b}_1 \cdot \mathbf{b}_2 \times \mathbf{b}_3 = \begin{vmatrix} b_{1x} & b_{1y} & b_{1z} \\ b_{2x} & b_{2y} & b_{2z} \\ b_{3x} & b_{3y} & b_{3z} \end{vmatrix}$$

and the determinant

$$b_1 \cdot b_2 \times b_3 = \begin{vmatrix} b_{1x}^{\star} & b_{1y}^{\star} & b_{1z}^{\star} \\ b_{2x}^{\star} & b_{2y}^{\star} & b_{2z}^{\star} \\ b_{3x}^{\star} & b_{3y}^{\star} & b_{3z}^{\star} \end{vmatrix} = \begin{vmatrix} b_{1x}^{\star} & b_{2x}^{\star} & b_{3x}^{\star} \\ b_{1y}^{\star} & b_{2y}^{\star} & b_{3y}^{\star} \\ b_{1z}^{\star} & b_{2z}^{\star} & b_{3z}^{\star} \end{vmatrix} \, .$$

That is,

$$\begin{vmatrix} b_{1x} & b_{1y} & b_{1z} \\ b_{2x} & b_{2y} & b_{2z} \\ b_{3x} & b_{3y} & b_{3z} \end{vmatrix} \cdot \begin{vmatrix} b_{1x}^{\star} & b_{2x}^{\star} & b_{3x}^{\star} \\ b_{1y}^{\star} & b_{2y}^{\star} & b_{3y}^{\star} \\ b_{1z}^{\star} & b_{2z}^{\star} & b_{3z}^{\star} \end{vmatrix} = \begin{vmatrix} \mathbf{b}_1 \cdot b_1 & \mathbf{b}_1 \cdot b_2 & \mathbf{b}_1 \cdot b_3 \\ \mathbf{b}_2 \cdot b_1 & \mathbf{b}_2 \cdot b_2 & \mathbf{b}_2 \cdot b_3 \\ \mathbf{b}_3 \cdot b_1 & \mathbf{b}_3 \cdot b_2 & \mathbf{b}_3 \cdot b_3 \end{vmatrix} = 1$$

▶ As an example, we consider the vector

$$\mathbf{A} = 5\mathbf{i} - 3\mathbf{j} + 8\mathbf{k},$$

which we seek to express as a linear sum of the vectors

$$\begin{aligned}
\mathbf{b}_1 &= \phantom{-}3\mathbf{i} - 4\mathbf{j}, \\
\mathbf{b}_2 &= \phantom{-3\mathbf{i} - } 3\mathbf{j} + 4\mathbf{k}, \\
\mathbf{b}_3 &= -\mathbf{i} + \phantom{3}\mathbf{j} + 2\mathbf{k}.
\end{aligned}$$

We first verify that the three vectors $\mathbf{b}_i$ are noncoplanar by evaluating their scalar triple product,

$$\mathbf{b}_1 \cdot \mathbf{b}_2 \times \mathbf{b}_3 = \begin{vmatrix} 3 & -4 & 0 \\ 0 & 3 & 4 \\ -1 & 1 & 2 \end{vmatrix} = 22.$$

Since the scalar triple product does not vanish, we can find a unique solution for the $\alpha_i^\star$. It is

$$\alpha_i^\star = \mathbf{A} \cdot \boldsymbol{b}_i.$$

Through use of Eq. (1–36), the reciprocal vectors $\boldsymbol{b}_i$ are found to be the vectors

$$\boldsymbol{b}_1 = \frac{1}{22} \begin{vmatrix} \mathbf{i} & \mathbf{j} & \mathbf{k} \\ 0 & 3 & 4 \\ -1 & 1 & 2 \end{vmatrix} = \tfrac{1}{22}[2\mathbf{i} - 4\mathbf{j} + 3\mathbf{k}],$$

$$\boldsymbol{b}_2 = \frac{1}{22} \begin{vmatrix} \mathbf{i} & \mathbf{j} & \mathbf{k} \\ -1 & 1 & 2 \\ 3 & -4 & 0 \end{vmatrix} = \tfrac{1}{22}[8\mathbf{i} + 6\mathbf{j} + \mathbf{k}],$$

$$\boldsymbol{b}_3 = \frac{1}{22} \begin{vmatrix} \mathbf{i} & \mathbf{j} & \mathbf{k} \\ 3 & -4 & 0 \\ 0 & 3 & 4 \end{vmatrix} = \tfrac{1}{22}[-16\mathbf{i} - 12\mathbf{j} + 9\mathbf{k}],$$

yielding, by Eq. (1–40),

$$\alpha_1^\star = \mathbf{A} \cdot \boldsymbol{b}_1 = \frac{5 \times 2 + (-3) \times (-4) + 8 \times 3}{22} = \frac{23}{11},$$

$$\alpha_2^\star = \mathbf{A} \cdot \boldsymbol{b}_2 = \frac{5 \times 8 + (-3) \times (6) + 8 \times 1}{22} = \frac{15}{11},$$

$$\alpha_3^\star = \mathbf{A} \cdot \boldsymbol{b}_3 = \frac{5 \times (-16) + (-3) \times (-12) + 8 \times 9}{22} = \frac{14}{11}.$$

We have thus found that we can set

$$\begin{aligned}
\mathbf{A} &= \alpha_1^\star \mathbf{b}_1 + \alpha_2^\star \mathbf{b}_2 + \alpha_3^\star \mathbf{b}_3 \\
&= \tfrac{23}{11}\,\mathbf{b}_1 + \tfrac{15}{11}\mathbf{b}_2 + \tfrac{14}{11}\mathbf{b}_3.
\end{aligned}$$

Checking, we find that this indeed yields

$$\mathbf{A} = \tfrac{23}{11}(3\mathbf{i} - 4\mathbf{j}) + \tfrac{15}{11}(3\mathbf{j} + 4\mathbf{k}) + \tfrac{14}{11}(-\mathbf{i} + \mathbf{j} + 2\mathbf{k})$$
$$= 5\mathbf{i} - 3\mathbf{j} + 8\mathbf{k}. \blacktriangleleft$$

We could equally as well, of course, start our discussion with the reciprocal base vectors $\boldsymbol{b}_1$, $\boldsymbol{b}_2$, and $\boldsymbol{b}_3$, and set

$$\mathbf{A} = \alpha_1 \boldsymbol{b}_1 + \alpha_2 \boldsymbol{b}_2 + \alpha_3 \boldsymbol{b}_3. \tag{1-42}$$

This would quite analogously lead us to the definition of the set of vectors which are reciprocal to the vectors $\boldsymbol{b}_1$, $\boldsymbol{b}_2$, and $\boldsymbol{b}_3$. We find these to be the vectors (Problem 1-20)

$$\mathbf{b}_1 = \frac{\boldsymbol{b}_2 \times \boldsymbol{b}_3}{\boldsymbol{b}_1 \cdot \boldsymbol{b}_2 \times \boldsymbol{b}_3},$$

$$\mathbf{b}_2 = \frac{\boldsymbol{b}_3 \times \boldsymbol{b}_1}{\boldsymbol{b}_1 \cdot \boldsymbol{b}_2 \times \boldsymbol{b}_3}, \tag{1-43}$$

$$\mathbf{b}_3 = \frac{\boldsymbol{b}_1 \times \boldsymbol{b}_2}{\boldsymbol{b}_1 \cdot \boldsymbol{b}_2 \times \boldsymbol{b}_3}.$$

Analogously to the solution for the $\alpha_i^\star$, it follows that

$$\alpha_1 = \mathbf{A} \cdot \mathbf{b}_1, \qquad \alpha_2 = \mathbf{A} \cdot \mathbf{b}_2, \qquad \alpha_3 = \mathbf{A} \cdot \mathbf{b}_3. \tag{1-44}$$

▶Thus in the previous example we can also set

$$\mathbf{A} = \alpha_1 \boldsymbol{b}_1 + \alpha_2 \boldsymbol{b}_2 + \alpha_3 \boldsymbol{b}_3,$$

and obtain

$$\alpha_1 = \mathbf{A} \cdot \mathbf{b}_1 = 27, \qquad \alpha_2 = \mathbf{A} \cdot \mathbf{b}_2 = 23, \qquad \alpha_3 = \mathbf{A} \cdot \mathbf{b}_3 = 8.$$

That is,

$$\mathbf{A} = \tfrac{27}{22}(2\mathbf{i} - 4\mathbf{j} + 3\mathbf{k}) + \tfrac{23}{22}(8\mathbf{i} + 6\mathbf{j} + \mathbf{k}) + \tfrac{8}{22}(-16\mathbf{i} - 12\mathbf{j} + 9\mathbf{k}). \blacktriangleleft$$

We have thus arrived at the very important theorem that a three-dimensional vector is completely specified if its scalar products with three noncoplanar vectors is known.

It is interesting and extremely useful, as we shall see, to be able to compute the scalar and vector products of two vectors which are expressed in terms of their scalar products with three noncoplanar vectors. We find that the scalar product of two vectors **A** and **B** assumes its simplest form if we express one vector in terms of one set of noncoplanar base vectors and the other vector in terms of the reciprocal set of base vectors. If we thus set

$$\mathbf{A} = \alpha_1 \boldsymbol{b}_1 + \alpha_2 \boldsymbol{b}_2 + \alpha_3 \boldsymbol{b}_3 \tag{1-45}$$

and

$$\mathbf{B} = \beta_1^\star \mathbf{b}_1 + \beta_2^\star \mathbf{b}_2 + \beta_3^\star \mathbf{b}_3,$$

we obtain through use of Eq. (1–37)

$$\mathbf{A} \cdot \mathbf{B} = \alpha_1 \beta_1^\star + \alpha_2 \beta_2^\star + \alpha_3 \beta_3^\star, \tag{1–46}$$

or similarly,

$$\mathbf{B} \cdot \mathbf{A} = \beta_1 \alpha_1^\star + \beta_2 \alpha_2^\star + \beta_3 \alpha_3^\star. \tag{1–47}$$

▶ Thus, for example, consider the scalar product of the vector

$$\mathbf{B} = 2\mathbf{i} + \mathbf{j} - 4\mathbf{k}$$

with the vector $\mathbf{A}$ of the previous example. We find that the vector $\mathbf{B}$ is expressible in the form

$$\mathbf{B} = 2b_1 - 13b_2 - 9b_3,$$

where the $b_i$ are the reciprocal vectors of the previous example. Hence by Eq. (1–47) the scalar product of $\mathbf{A}$ and $\mathbf{B}$ is found to be

$$\mathbf{B} \cdot \mathbf{A} = \tfrac{23}{11} \times 2 + \tfrac{15}{11}(-13) + \tfrac{14}{11}(-9) = -25.$$

This result is in agreement with the scalar product found by using the cartesian components of the vectors $\mathbf{A}$ and $\mathbf{B}$,

$$\mathbf{A} \cdot \mathbf{B} = 5 \times 2 + (-3) \times (1) + 8 \times (-4) = -25. ◀$$

The vector product of two vectors $\mathbf{A}$ and $\mathbf{B}$ takes its simplest form when both vectors are expressed in terms of the same set of base vectors. Thus if we set

$$\mathbf{A} = \alpha_1^\star \mathbf{b}_1 + \alpha_2^\star \mathbf{b}_2 + \alpha_3^\star \mathbf{b}_3$$

and

$$\mathbf{B} = \beta_1^\star \mathbf{b}_1 + \beta_2^\star \mathbf{b}_2 + \beta_3^\star \mathbf{b}_3,$$

then we find that

$$\mathbf{A} \times \mathbf{B} = (\mathbf{b}_1 \cdot \mathbf{b}_2 \times \mathbf{b}_3) \begin{vmatrix} \mathbf{b}_1 & \mathbf{b}_2 & \mathbf{b}_3 \\ \alpha_1^\star & \alpha_2^\star & \alpha_3^\star \\ \beta_1^\star & \beta_2^\star & \beta_3^\star \end{vmatrix}. \tag{1–48}$$

Similarly, we find that

$$\mathbf{A} \times \mathbf{B} = (\mathbf{b}_1 \cdot \mathbf{b}_2 \times \mathbf{b}_3) \begin{vmatrix} \mathbf{b}_1 & \mathbf{b}_2 & \mathbf{b}_3 \\ \alpha_1 & \alpha_2 & \alpha_3 \\ \beta_1 & \beta_2 & \beta_3 \end{vmatrix}. \tag{1–48a}$$

▶ Utilizing once more the vectors $\mathbf{A}$ and $\mathbf{B}$ of the previous example,

$$\mathbf{A} = 27b_1 + 23b_2 + 8b_3$$

and

$$\mathbf{B} = 2b_1 - 13b_2 - 9b_3,$$

we find by Eq. (1–48a) that the vector product

$$\mathbf{A} \times \mathbf{B} = (\boldsymbol{b}_1 \cdot \boldsymbol{b}_2 \times \boldsymbol{b}_3) \begin{vmatrix} \mathbf{b}_1 & \mathbf{b}_2 & \mathbf{b}_3 \\ 27 & 23 & 8 \\ 2 & -13 & -9 \end{vmatrix}$$

$$= \tfrac{1}{22}(-103\mathbf{b}_1 + 259\mathbf{b}_2 - 397\mathbf{b}_3)$$

$$= 4\mathbf{i} + 36\mathbf{j} + 11\mathbf{k}.$$

This result checks with the vector product found by utilizing the cartesian components of the vectors **A** and **B**,

$$\mathbf{A} \times \mathbf{B} = \begin{vmatrix} \mathbf{i} & \mathbf{j} & \mathbf{k} \\ 5 & -3 & 8 \\ 2 & 1 & -4 \end{vmatrix} = 4\mathbf{i} + 36\mathbf{j} + 11\mathbf{k}. \blacktriangleleft$$

It should be apparent that we shall at times require some notation whereby we may recognize whether we expressed a vector in terms of the base vectors $\mathbf{b}_i$ or their reciprocal vectors $\boldsymbol{b}_i$. To distinguish the two ways of expressing the vector **A** we shall whenever necessary let **A** represent the vector **A** expressed in terms of one set of base vectors and $\mathbf{A}^\star$ the same vector **A** expressed in terms of the reciprocal base vectors. It does not matter how we choose the correspondence. The choice of the coordinate base vectors for the representation of **A** determines the representation of $\mathbf{A}^\star$. Thus if

$$\mathbf{A}^\star = \alpha_1^\star \mathbf{b}_1 + \alpha_2^\star \mathbf{b}_2 + \alpha_3^\star \mathbf{b}_3, \tag{1–49}$$

then

$$\mathbf{A} = \alpha_1 \boldsymbol{b}_1 + \alpha_2 \boldsymbol{b}_2 + \alpha_3 \boldsymbol{b}_3.$$

With this notation the scalar product of two vectors is most concisely represented by either

$$\mathbf{A} \cdot \mathbf{B}^\star = \alpha_1 \beta_1^\star + \alpha_2 \beta_2^\star + \alpha_3 \beta_3^\star \tag{1–50}$$

or

$$\mathbf{A}^\star \cdot \mathbf{B} = \alpha_1^\star \beta_1 + \alpha_2^\star \beta_2 + \alpha_3^\star \beta_3.$$

That is,

$$\mathbf{A}^\star \cdot \mathbf{B} = \mathbf{A} \cdot \mathbf{B}^\star.$$

---

Nonorthogonal base vectors are very important in physics. They are used extensively in problems dealing with the propagation of waves (electromagnetic, elastic, matter) in materials having a periodic structure as, for example, crystals.

An ideal crystal is a periodic structure, which is the same when viewed with respect to all points whose position is specified by

$$\mathbf{r} = \rho_1 \mathbf{b}_1 + \rho_2 \mathbf{b}_2 + \rho_3 \mathbf{b}_3,$$

where $\rho_1$, $\rho_2$, and $\rho_3$ are integers, as when viewed with respect to the point within the crystal chosen as origin. The vectors $\mathbf{b}_1$, $\mathbf{b}_2$, and $\mathbf{b}_3$ are referred to as the *crystal axes* or the *primitive translation vectors* of the crystal. The set of points defined by the above position vectors form what is referred to as the *crystal lattice* (Fig. 1–14). The reciprocal vectors $\mathbf{b}_i$ define the *reciprocal lattice*.

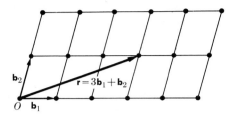

FIG. 1–14.  Example of a two-dimensional lattice.

As an example of their usefulness we consider the diffraction of x-rays by crystals. X-rays are electromagnetic radiations which have wavelengths comparable with the interatomic spacings within a crystal.  When x-rays strike a crystal, some of the incoming electromagnetic energy is scattered (absorbed and reradiated in all directions) by the electrons of the atoms in the crystal.  The radiation scattered from the periodically spaced atoms adds coherently to produce diffracted beams for certain incident directions.

W. L. Bragg was able to account for the angles at which the diffracted beams are observed.  His analysis showed that the diffracted beam and the incident beam make the same angle with a set of equally spaced parallel planes of crystal atoms.  (See Fig. 1–15.)  The different planes of the crystal thus act as a kind of partially reflecting mirrors.

The condition which must be met in order for the "reflected" beams which add constructively to yield an intense diffracted beam is that they all be in phase.  This condition, known as *Bragg's law*, is expressed by

$$2d \sin \theta = m\lambda, \qquad m = 1, 2, \ldots,$$

where $d$ is the spacing between the planes, $\theta$ the angle the incident beam makes with the planes and $\lambda$ the wavelength of the electromagnetic radiation.  We note that the

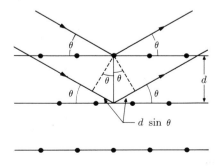

FIG. 1–15.  Bragg diffraction.

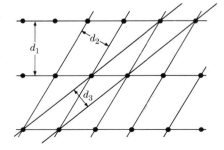

FIG. 1–16.  Bragg diffraction planes in a crystal.

index of refraction for x-rays is essentially unity. The transmitted beam therefore passes through the crystal unrefracted. From Fig. 1–15 we see that $(2d \sin \theta)$ represents the path difference between the rays "reflected" from neighboring planes.

Several sets of parallel planes exist within a crystal (Fig. 1–16). The location of the planes and the spacing between the planes are very efficiently represented in terms of the base vectors of the crystal lattice and the base vectors of the reciprocal lattice.

A plane is determined by three points. These three points are customarily chosen as the intercepts $\rho_1$, $\rho_2$, and $\rho_3$ of one of the planes on the three base axes of the crystal lattice (Fig. 1–17). In terms of the base vectors of the crystal lattice, these points are specified by the vectors

$$\mathbf{r}_1 = \rho_1 \mathbf{b}_1, \qquad \mathbf{r}_2 = \rho_2 \mathbf{b}_2,$$

and

$$\mathbf{r}_3 = \rho_3 \mathbf{b}_3.$$

For the plane nearest to the origin, the intercepts $\rho_1$, $\rho_2$, and $\rho_3$ will have no common integral factor. From these vectors we obtain the two vectors

$$\mathbf{A} = \mathbf{r}_1 - \mathbf{r}_2 = \rho_1 \mathbf{b}_1 - \rho_2 \mathbf{b}_2$$

and

$$\mathbf{B} = \mathbf{r}_1 - \mathbf{r}_3 = \rho_1 \mathbf{b}_1 - \rho_3 \mathbf{b}_3,$$

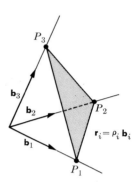

FIG. 1–17. A crystal plane.

which lie in the plane of the points $P_1$, $P_2$, and $P_3$. The vector

$$\mathbf{A} \times \mathbf{B} = \mathbf{b}_1 \cdot \mathbf{b}_2 \times \mathbf{b}_3 \begin{vmatrix} \mathbf{b}_1 & \mathbf{b}_2 & \mathbf{b}_3 \\ \rho_1 & -\rho_2 & 0 \\ \rho_1 & 0 & -\rho_3 \end{vmatrix}$$

$$= \rho_1 \rho_2 \rho_3 \, \mathbf{b}_1 \cdot \mathbf{b}_2 \times \mathbf{b}_3 \left( \frac{1}{\rho_1} \mathbf{b}_1 + \frac{1}{\rho_2} \mathbf{b}_2 + \frac{1}{\rho_3} \mathbf{b}_3 \right)$$

or the vector

$$\mathbf{C} = \frac{1}{\rho_1} \mathbf{b}_1 + \frac{1}{\rho_2} \mathbf{b}_2 + \frac{1}{\rho_3} \mathbf{b}_3$$

is thus normal to the set of planes. If $1/\rho_1$, $1/\rho_2$, and $1/\rho_3$ are not integers, then it is customary to multiply them by their lowest common denominator (lcd) and utilize the vector

$$\mathbf{n} = h\mathbf{b}_1 + k\mathbf{b}_2 + l\mathbf{b}_3,$$

where

$$h = \frac{\text{lcd}}{\rho_1}, \text{ etc.},$$

in order to specify the direction of the plane. The integers $h$, $k$, and $l$ are referred to as the *Miller indices* of the crystal plane.

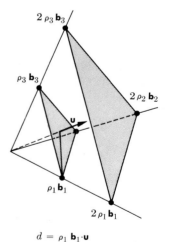

FIG. 1–18. Determination of the spacing between crystal planes.

The unit normal is of course the vector

$$\mathbf{u} = \frac{\mathbf{n}}{n}.$$

As can be seen from Fig. 1–18, the spacing between the planes is

$$d = \mathbf{u} \cdot \rho_1 \mathbf{b}_1 = \mathbf{u} \cdot \rho_2 \mathbf{b}_2 = \mathbf{u} \cdot \rho_3 \mathbf{b}_3$$

$$= \frac{h\rho_1}{n} = \frac{\text{lcd}}{n}.$$

From the location of different sets of planes and the spacing between them, the structure of the crystal may be determined.

## 1–6 Matrix representation of vectors

In the last section we found a vector $\mathbf{A}$ to be specified if its scalar products with three noncoplanar vectors are known. That is, the three scalar products $\alpha_1^\star$, $\alpha_2^\star$, and $\alpha_3^\star$ of the vector $\mathbf{A}$ and the vectors $\boldsymbol{b}_1$, $\boldsymbol{b}_2$, and $\boldsymbol{b}_3$ are sufficient to specify the vector, since then

$$\mathbf{A}^\star = \alpha_1^\star \mathbf{b}_1 + \alpha_2^\star \mathbf{b}_2 + \alpha_3^\star \mathbf{b}_3,$$

where $\mathbf{b}_1$, $\mathbf{b}_2$, and $\mathbf{b}_3$ are the vectors reciprocal to the vectors $\boldsymbol{b}_1$, $\boldsymbol{b}_2$, and $\boldsymbol{b}_3$. Notationally, arranging the three $\alpha_i^\star$'s in a matrix array is a very convenient way of expressing them.

The matrices

$$[\alpha_1^\star, \alpha_2^\star, \alpha_3^\star] \quad \text{and} \quad \begin{bmatrix} \alpha_1^\star \\ \alpha_2^\star \\ \alpha_3^\star \end{bmatrix}$$

are referred to respectively as the row and column matrix representations of the vector $\mathbf{A}^\star = \alpha_1^\star \mathbf{b}_1 + \alpha_2^\star \mathbf{b}_2 + \alpha_3^\star \mathbf{b}_3$. Analogously, the matrices

$$[\alpha_1, \alpha_2, \alpha_3] \quad \text{and} \quad \begin{bmatrix} \alpha_1 \\ \alpha_2 \\ \alpha_3 \end{bmatrix}$$

are the row and column matrix representations of the vector

$$\mathbf{A} = \alpha_1 \boldsymbol{b}_1 + \alpha_2 \boldsymbol{b}_2 + \alpha_3 \boldsymbol{b}_3.$$

Since both the column and row matrix representations of a vector are useful, we introduce an additional notation whereby we can, in referring to the vector $\mathbf{A}$, indicate specifically which matrix representation is being discussed. Thus if the vector $\mathbf{A}$ is to be represented by a column matrix, this fact will be indicated by inserting the $\mathbf{A}$ within the bracket |). If it is to be represented by a row matrix, it will be inserted within the bracket $(|$. That is,

$$|\mathbf{A}) \leftrightarrow \begin{bmatrix} \alpha_1 \\ \alpha_2 \\ \alpha_3 \end{bmatrix}, \tag{1–51}$$

$$(\mathbf{A}| \leftrightarrow [\alpha_1, \alpha_2, \alpha_3],$$

and similarly,

$$|\mathbf{A}^\star) \leftrightarrow \begin{bmatrix} \alpha_1^\star \\ \alpha_2^\star \\ \alpha_3^\star \end{bmatrix},$$

and

$$(\mathbf{A}^\star| \leftrightarrow [\alpha_1^\star, \alpha_2^\star, \alpha_3^\star]. \tag{1–52}$$

With this bracket notation, the scalar product of two vectors is very simply expressed by

$$\mathbf{A}^\star \cdot \mathbf{B} = (\mathbf{A}^\star \mid \mathbf{B}) = [\alpha_1^\star, \alpha_2^\star, \alpha_3^\star] \begin{bmatrix} \beta_1 \\ \beta_2 \\ \beta_3 \end{bmatrix} \tag{1–53}$$

$$= \alpha_1^\star \beta_1 + \alpha_2^\star \beta_2 + \alpha_3^\star \beta_3.$$

Equation (1–53) defines the multiplication of a column matrix by a row matrix. In this matrix multiplication the row matrix appears to the left of the column matrix. The multiplication in which the column matrix appears on the left we shall also find useful. It yields what is defined as the direct product of a column and a row matrix (cf. Chapter 10).

We note that our ability to represent a vector by an array and refer to the array as a matrix (not all arrays are matrices) is due to the fact that the rules for the equality and combination of matrices are satisfied by the arrays which we utilize for the representation of vectors. These rules are discussed in Chapter 10.

The fact that the matrix representations of $|\mathbf{A})$ and $(\mathbf{A}|$ have the same elements is expressed by stating that $(\mathbf{A}|$ is the transpose of $|\mathbf{A})$,

$$(\mathbf{A}| = \widetilde{|\mathbf{A})}, \tag{1–54}$$

and similarly,

$$|\mathbf{A}) = \widetilde{(\mathbf{A}|},$$

where the tilde above $|\mathbf{A})$ or any matrix indicates the transpose of the vector or matrix in question. Thus

$$\widetilde{\begin{bmatrix} \alpha_1 \\ \alpha_2 \\ \alpha_3 \end{bmatrix}} = [\alpha_1, \alpha_2, \alpha_3] \quad \text{and} \quad \widetilde{[\alpha_1, \alpha_2, \alpha_3]} = \begin{bmatrix} \alpha_1 \\ \alpha_2 \\ \alpha_3 \end{bmatrix}. \tag{1–55}$$

## 1–7 Differentiation of a vector with respect to a scalar

The vector **A** is said to be a single-valued function of the scalar $q$, if for every value of $q$ there exists only one value of the vector **A**. Similarly, if for every set of values of the scalars $q_1, q_2, \ldots$ there exists only one value of the vector **A**, then **A** is said to be a single-valued function of the scalars $q_1, q_2, \ldots$ We designate such a vector by

$$\mathbf{A} = \mathbf{A}(q_1, q_2, \ldots).$$

We shall restrict ourselves to continuous vectors for which

$$|\mathbf{A}(q + \Delta q) - \mathbf{A}(q)| < \epsilon$$

for all $|\Delta q| < \delta$, and

$$\epsilon \to 0 \quad \text{as} \quad \delta \to 0.$$

For example, the position vector

$$\mathbf{r} = x\mathbf{i} + y\mathbf{j} + z\mathbf{k}$$

is a continuous function of the scalars $x$, $y$, and $z$, and will therefore be designated, whenever appropriate, by

$$\mathbf{r} = \mathbf{r}(x, y, z).$$

In general we shall be interested in the position vector as a function of time. In such cases, letting $t$ represent time,

$$\mathbf{r} = \mathbf{r}[x(t), y(t), z(t), t] = \mathbf{r}(t).$$

An electric field vector is another example of a vector which is a function of the scalars $x$, $y$, $z$, and $t$,

$$\mathbf{E} = \mathbf{E}(x, y, z, t).$$

Following the definition of the derivative of a scalar function, we define the derivative of the vector function

$$\mathbf{A}(t) = A_x(t)\mathbf{i} + A_y(t)\mathbf{j} + Az(t)\mathbf{k}$$

($t$ in this case not necessarily representing time) by

$$\frac{d\mathbf{A}}{dt} = \lim_{\Delta t \to 0} \left[ \frac{\mathbf{A}(t + \Delta t) - \mathbf{A}(t)}{\Delta t} \right]. \tag{1–56}$$

From the rule for the addition or subtraction of two vectors we obtain

$$\frac{d\mathbf{A}}{dt} = \lim_{\Delta t \to 0} \left[ \frac{\Delta A_x}{\Delta t}\mathbf{i} + \frac{\Delta A_y}{\Delta t}\mathbf{j} + \frac{\Delta A_z}{\Delta t}\mathbf{k} \right]$$

$$= \frac{dA_x}{dt}\mathbf{i} + \frac{dA_y}{dt}\mathbf{j} + \frac{dA_z}{dt}\mathbf{k}. \tag{1–57}$$

The $x$-, $y$-, and $z$-components of the derivative of a vector are, respectively, the derivatives of the $x$-, $y$-, and $z$-components of the vector.

From the same rule it also follows that

$$\frac{d}{dt}(\mathbf{A} + \mathbf{B}) = \frac{d\mathbf{A}}{dt} + \frac{d\mathbf{B}}{dt}. \qquad (1\text{–}58)$$

The reader should have no difficulty utilizing the rule for the derivative of a product of two scalar functions to show that

$$\frac{d}{dt}(c\mathbf{A}) = \frac{dc}{dt}\mathbf{A} + c\frac{d\mathbf{A}}{dt}, \qquad (1\text{–}59)$$

where $c$ is a scalar function of $t$,

$$\frac{d}{dt}(\mathbf{A} \cdot \mathbf{B}) = \frac{d\mathbf{A}}{dt} \cdot \mathbf{B} + \mathbf{A} \cdot \frac{d\mathbf{B}}{dt}, \qquad (1\text{–}60)$$

and

$$\frac{d}{dt}(\mathbf{A} \times \mathbf{B}) = \frac{d\mathbf{A}}{dt} \times \mathbf{B} + \mathbf{A} \times \frac{d\mathbf{B}}{dt}. \qquad (1\text{–}61)$$

We note that in the last equation the order of the vectors $\mathbf{A}$ and $\mathbf{B}$ must be preserved.

It should be clear that the derivation of Eq. (1–57) reveals that in dealing with the matrix representation of a vector $\mathbf{A}$ whose elements are the scalar products of $\mathbf{A}$ with a set of three constant ($t$ independent) base vectors, the matrix whose elements are the derivatives of the elements of the matrix representing the vector $\mathbf{A}$ represents the derivative of $\mathbf{A}$. The derivative of a matrix is defined by

$$\frac{d}{dt}\begin{bmatrix} \alpha_1 \\ \alpha_2 \\ \alpha_3 \end{bmatrix} = \begin{bmatrix} \dfrac{d\alpha_1}{dt} \\[2mm] \dfrac{d\alpha_2}{dt} \\[2mm] \dfrac{d\alpha_3}{dt} \end{bmatrix}. \qquad (1\text{–}62)$$

We note that in general the derivative of the matrix representation of a vector does not yield the matrix representation of the derivative of the vector. This fact will become clear in subsequent sections.

## 1–8 Rotation of a vector

Equation (1–57) expresses the derivative of a vector in terms of the derivative of its $x$-, $y$-, and $z$-components. It is interesting and enlightening to consider the derivative of a vector which is expressed in terms of the product of its magnitude and the unit vector designating its direction,

$$\mathbf{A} = A\mathbf{e}_A.$$

By Eq. (1–59) we obtain

$$\frac{d\mathbf{A}}{dt} = \frac{d}{dt}\,(A\mathbf{e}_A) = \frac{dA}{dt}\,\mathbf{e}_A + A\,\frac{d\mathbf{e}_A}{dt}. \qquad (1\text{–}63)$$

We proceed to show that the first term on the right-hand side of Eq. (1–63) accounts for the change in the magnitude of the vector $\mathbf{A}$, whereas the second term accounts for the change in its direction. The change in the magnitude of a vector is within first-order infinitesimals given by

$$\Delta A = \frac{dA}{dt}\,\Delta t.$$

But

$$\frac{dA}{dt} = \frac{1}{2A}\,\frac{dA^2}{dt} = \frac{1}{2A}\,\frac{d}{dt}\,\mathbf{A}\cdot\mathbf{A}.$$

Hence

$$\frac{dA}{dt} = \frac{\mathbf{A}}{A}\cdot\frac{d\mathbf{A}}{dt} = \mathbf{e}_A\cdot\frac{d\mathbf{A}}{dt}. \qquad (1\text{–}64)$$

This latter relation tells us that the change in the magnitude of a vector $\mathbf{A}$ is produced by the component of $d\mathbf{A}/dt$ along $\mathbf{A}$. Applying this result to Eq. (1–63) in turn yields

$$\frac{dA}{dt} = \frac{dA}{dt}\,\mathbf{e}_A\cdot\mathbf{e}_A + A\mathbf{e}_A\cdot\frac{d\mathbf{e}_A}{dt} = \frac{dA}{dt} + A\mathbf{e}_A\cdot\frac{d\mathbf{e}_A}{dt} \qquad (1\text{–}65)$$

or that

$$\mathbf{e}_A\cdot\frac{d\mathbf{e}_A}{dt} = 0. \qquad (1\text{–}66)$$

We have thus succeeded in verifying that only the first term on the right-hand side of Eq. (1–63) contributes to the change in the magnitude of a vector $\mathbf{A}$.

The derivative of the square of the magnitude of $\mathbf{e}_A$ is

$$\frac{d}{dt}\,|\mathbf{e}_A|^2 = 2\mathbf{e}_A\cdot\frac{d\mathbf{e}_A}{dt}.$$

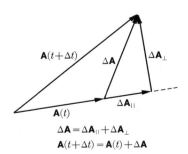

$\Delta\mathbf{A} = \Delta\mathbf{A}_{\|} + \Delta\mathbf{A}_{\perp}$

$\mathbf{A}(t+\Delta t) = \mathbf{A}(t) + \Delta\mathbf{A}$

FIG. 1–19. Variation of $\mathbf{A}(t)$ into $\mathbf{A}(t+\Delta t)$.

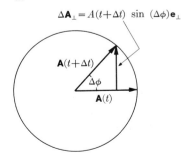

FIG. 1–20.    Rotation of a vector about a perpendicular axis.

Hence Eq. (1–66) expresses the fact that the magnitude of $\mathbf{e}_A$ does not change, and since $\mathbf{e}_A$ is a vector of unit magnitude, either $d\mathbf{e}_A/dt$ vanishes or it is perpendicular to $\mathbf{e}_A$. If $d\mathbf{e}_A/dt$ does not vanish, then $A\, d\mathbf{e}_A/dt$ is likewise perpendicular to $\mathbf{A}$. The component of $d\mathbf{A}/dt$ perpendicular to $\mathbf{A}$ has thus been shown not to affect the magnitude of the vector $\mathbf{A}$.

We could have come to the same conclusion by means of a geometric consideration of the change of the vector $\mathbf{A}(t)$ into the vector $\mathbf{A}(t + \Delta t)$ as $t$ changes by $\Delta t$. Consider the plane in which the vectors $\mathbf{A}(t)$ and $\mathbf{A}(t + \Delta t)$ lie (Fig. 1–19).

From Fig. (1–19) and through use of the Pythagorean formula it should be clear that

$$A(t + \Delta t) = \sqrt{(A + \Delta A_{||})^2 + (\Delta A_{\perp})^2}\,,$$

where $\Delta A_{\perp}$ and $\Delta A_{||}$ are the magnitudes of $\Delta \mathbf{A}_{\perp}$ and $\Delta \mathbf{A}_{||}$, the two vectors respectively perpendicular and parallel to $\mathbf{A}$ into which $\Delta \mathbf{A}$ can be decomposed.

To within first-order infinitesimals we find

$$A(t + \Delta t) = A + \Delta A_{||}.$$

This verifies what we have already concluded about the infinitesimal change in the magnitude of a vector, that it is produced only by the infinitesimal change parallel to the vector.

The other possible change in a vector, a change in its orientation, is accomplished by a rotation of the vector. We shall digress to show that the change of a vector produced by an infinitesimal rotation can be expressed in terms of the vector product of a rotation vector, to be defined, and the vector being rotated.

For simplicity, we consider at first the rotation of the vector $\mathbf{A}$ through an angle $\Delta \phi$ about an axis perpendicular to $\mathbf{A}$. This axis is thus also perpendicular to the plane of the initial and final directions of $\mathbf{A}$. As shown in Fig. 1–20, the head of the vector $\mathbf{A}$ moves under the rotation along a circle of radius $A$, since $\mathbf{A}$ remains constant in magnitude.

To first-order infinitesimals, it should be clear from this same figure that

$$\mathbf{\Delta A}_{\perp} = A(t + \Delta t) \sin \Delta \phi \mathbf{e}_{\perp} = A\, \Delta \phi \mathbf{e}_{\perp}, \tag{1–67}$$

where $\mathbf{e}_{\perp}$ is the unit vector perpendicular to $\mathbf{A}$ in the direction of the perpendicular change.

We now define the rotation vector (Fig. 1–21),

$$\mathbf{\Delta \phi} = \Delta \phi \mathbf{n}, \tag{1–68}$$

where $\mathbf{n}$ is the unit vector perpendicular to the plane of $\mathbf{A}(t)$ and $\mathbf{A}(t + \Delta t)$, pointing in the direction of $\mathbf{e}_A \times \mathbf{e}_{\perp}$. In fact, $\mathbf{n}$, $\mathbf{e}_A$, and $\mathbf{e}_{\perp}$ are three mutually orthogonal vectors for which

$$\mathbf{n} = \mathbf{e}_A \times \mathbf{e}_{\perp}, \quad \mathbf{n} \times \mathbf{e}_A = \mathbf{e}_{\perp}, \tag{1–69}$$

and

$$\mathbf{e}_{\perp} \times \mathbf{n} = \mathbf{e}_A.$$

In terms of $\Delta\boldsymbol{\phi}$, we can thus set

$$\Delta\mathbf{A}_\perp = \Delta\boldsymbol{\phi} \times \mathbf{A} = \Delta\phi A\mathbf{e}_\perp. \tag{1-70}$$

We have thus shown that the infinitesimal perpendicular change in a vector $\mathbf{A}$ can be thought of as being produced by an infinitesimal rotation of the vector $\mathbf{A}$, and as such it is expressible as the vector product of a rotation vector $\Delta\boldsymbol{\phi}$ and the vector $\mathbf{A}$.

Whereas Eq. (1–70) is correct only to within first-order infinitesimals, the equation for the component of the derivative of $\mathbf{A}$ along $\mathbf{e}_\perp$ times $\mathbf{e}_\perp$,

$$\left(\frac{d\mathbf{A}}{dt} \cdot \mathbf{e}_\perp\right)\mathbf{e}_\perp = \frac{d\boldsymbol{\phi}}{dt} \times \mathbf{A}, \tag{1-71}$$

is an exact equation.

The rotation vector which yields $\Delta\mathbf{A}_\perp$ is not unique, for

$$\Delta\boldsymbol{\phi}' = \Delta\boldsymbol{\phi} + c\mathbf{e}_A,$$

where $c$ is a constant, is another rotation vector which will give the same result as $\Delta\boldsymbol{\phi}$ of Eq. (1–68), since $\mathbf{e}_A \times \mathbf{A} = 0$.

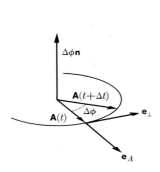

FIG. 1–21. The rotation vector.

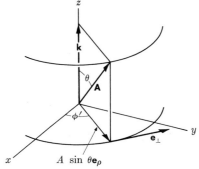

FIG. 1–22. Rotation of a vector about the $z$-axis.

In Fig. 1–22 we demonstrate that this is indeed so. There we represent graphically a vector $\mathbf{A}$ which makes an angle $\theta$ with the axis about which it is being rotated. We choose to call the axis of rotation the $z$-axis, and the direction of the progression of a right-handed screw rotated about the $z$-axis in the same sense as $\mathbf{A}$ we call the positive $z$-direction.

A rotation of the vector $\mathbf{A}$ about the $z$-axis causes the head of the arrow representing $\mathbf{A}$ to move in a circle of radius $A \sin \theta$ about the axis of rotation.

The change in the vector $\mathbf{A}$ is thus identical to the change in the vector $(A \sin \theta)\mathbf{e}_\rho$, where $\mathbf{e}_\rho$ is the unit vector in the $xy$-plane pointing along the positive direction of the projection of $\mathbf{A}$ onto the $xy$-plane. The infinitesimal change in

the latter vector and thereby the infinitesimal change in **A** are given by Eq.
(1–70),

$$\Delta\mathbf{A}_\perp = A \sin\theta \, \Delta\phi'\mathbf{k} \times \mathbf{e}_\rho = \Delta\boldsymbol{\phi}' \times \mathbf{A}, \tag{1–72}$$

where

$$\Delta\boldsymbol{\phi}' = \Delta\phi'\mathbf{k}.$$

We conclude our discussion of the infinitesimal rotation of vectors by verifying
that the infinitesimal rotation vector $\Delta\boldsymbol{\phi}$ to within first-order infinitesimals
also satisfies the parallelogram law of addition. The vector

$$\boldsymbol{\omega} = \frac{d\boldsymbol{\phi}}{dt} = \lim_{\Delta t \to 0} \frac{\Delta\boldsymbol{\phi}}{\Delta t},$$

on the other hand, will have been shown to be a vector to within all-order
infinitesimals.*

Consider two successive infinitesimal rotations $\Delta\boldsymbol{\phi}_1$ and $\Delta\boldsymbol{\phi}_2$. Performing
the first rotation, we obtain the new vector

$$\mathbf{A}' = \mathbf{A} + \Delta\mathbf{A} = \mathbf{A} + \Delta\boldsymbol{\phi}_1 \times \mathbf{A}. \tag{1–73}$$

The subsequent rotation $\Delta\boldsymbol{\phi}_2$ turns the vector $\mathbf{A}'$ into the vector

$$\begin{aligned}
\mathbf{A}'' &= \mathbf{A}' + \Delta\boldsymbol{\phi}_2 \times \mathbf{A}' \\
&= \mathbf{A} + \Delta\boldsymbol{\phi}_1 \times \mathbf{A} + \Delta\boldsymbol{\phi}_2 \times \mathbf{A} + \Delta\boldsymbol{\phi}_2 \times (\Delta\boldsymbol{\phi}_1 \times \mathbf{A}).
\end{aligned} \tag{1–74}$$

If we invert the order of the two rotations, we obtain first the vector

$$\overline{\mathbf{A}} = \mathbf{A} + \Delta\boldsymbol{\phi}_2 \times \mathbf{A}, \tag{1–75}$$

and subsequently the vector

$$\overline{\overline{\mathbf{A}}} = \mathbf{A} + \Delta\boldsymbol{\phi}_2 \times \mathbf{A} + \Delta\boldsymbol{\phi}_1 \times \mathbf{A} + \Delta\boldsymbol{\phi}_1 \times (\Delta\boldsymbol{\phi}_2 \times \mathbf{A}). \tag{1–76}$$

Since in general

$$\Delta\boldsymbol{\phi}_1 \times (\Delta\boldsymbol{\phi}_2 \times \mathbf{A}) \neq \Delta\boldsymbol{\phi}_2 \times (\Delta\boldsymbol{\phi}_1 \times \mathbf{A}),$$

we realize that finite rotations do not generally commute. If the rotations are
infinitesimal, however, the terms $\Delta\boldsymbol{\phi}_1 \times (\Delta\boldsymbol{\phi}_2 \times \mathbf{A})$ and $\Delta\boldsymbol{\phi}_2 \times (\Delta\boldsymbol{\phi}_1 \times \mathbf{A})$
are proportional to the product $\Delta\phi_1 \, \Delta\phi_2$ of the magnitudes of the two rotation
vectors, which is a second-order infinitesimal. To within first-order infinitesimals, therefore, we can set

$$\overline{\overline{\mathbf{A}}} = \mathbf{A}''.$$

Since the same result will be obtained by rotating the vector **A** by the rotation

---

* If $t$ represents time, then $\boldsymbol{\omega} = d\boldsymbol{\phi}/dt$ will be called the angular velocity of **A**.

specified by the vector $(\Delta\boldsymbol{\phi}_1 + \Delta\boldsymbol{\phi}_2)$, we have shown that to within first-order infinitesimals, infinitesimal rotations commute, and to within this approximation may be represented by rotation vectors.

The quantities

$$\boldsymbol{\omega} = \frac{d\boldsymbol{\phi}}{dt} = \lim_{\Delta t \to 0} \frac{\Delta\boldsymbol{\phi}}{\Delta t}, \qquad (1\text{--}77)$$

on the other hand, as noted above, are vectors to all-order infinitesimals.

## 1–9 Complex-number representation of plane vectors

Geometrically a complex number is representable in terms of a two-dimensional vector whose $x$- and $y$-components, respectively, represent the real and imaginary parts of the complex number. Thus the complex number

$$a + ib, \qquad (1\text{--}78)$$

where $a$ and $b$ are real numbers and $i$, the imaginary unit, is

$$i = \sqrt{-1}, \qquad (1\text{--}79)$$

may be represented by the two-dimensional vector

$$\mathbf{A} = a\mathbf{e}_x + b\mathbf{e}_y, \qquad (1\text{--}80)$$

where $\mathbf{e}_x$ and $\mathbf{e}_y$ are the unit vectors pointing along the coordinate axes (Fig. 1–23).

In such cases the $x$-axis is referred to as the real axis and the $y$-axis as the imaginary axis. The reason that such a representation is possible is that with each complex number there is associated a magnitude and a phase, the latter being the angle which its vector representation makes with the real axis. The magnitude of the complex number $a + ib$ is defined by

$$|a + ib| = \sqrt{(a + ib)(a - ib)} = \sqrt{a^2 + b^2} = A, \qquad (1\text{--}81)$$

and the phase of $a + ib$ by

$$\phi = \tan^{-1} \frac{b}{a}. \qquad (1\text{--}82)$$

The angle $\phi$ is the angle which $\mathbf{A}$ makes with the $x$-axis.

Complex numbers furthermore satisfy the rule for vector addition:

$$(a_1 + ib_1) + (a_2 + ib_2) = (a_1 + a_2) + i(b_1 + b_2). \qquad (1\text{--}83)$$

There is thus a one-to-one correspondence between the totality of vectors in the $xy$-plane and the complex numbers which they represent.

We shall find it convenient at times to reverse this process and think of the complex number $A_x + iA_y$ as the representation of the two-dimensional vector

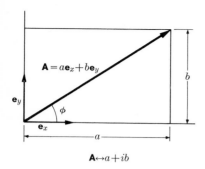

FIG. 1-23. Graphical representation of a complex number.

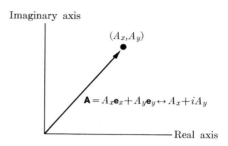

FIG. 1-24.    Complex-number representation of an $xy$-plane vector.

$[A_x, A_y, 0]$. We shall under such circumstances express this fact by setting

$$\mathbf{A} = A_x + iA_y. \tag{1-84}$$

In terms of the angle $\phi$ which $\mathbf{A}$ makes with the $x$-axis,* (cf. Fig. 1-24)

$$\mathbf{A} = A(\cos \phi + i \sin \phi) = Ae^{i\phi}. \tag{1-85}$$

Since $\mathbf{A}$ is a vector of magnitude $A$, it follows that $e^{i\phi}$ represents a unit vector indicating the direction of $\mathbf{A}$. Indeed we have

$$\mathbf{e}_A = \frac{\mathbf{A}}{A} = e^{i\phi}. \tag{1-86}$$

To complete the correspondence between the complex number $A_x + iA_y$ and the vector $\mathbf{A}$, we must be able to multiply two complex numbers and deduce from their product the scalar and vector products of the vectors which the complex numbers represent. We find that if we multiply the complex number $Ae^{i\phi_A}$ by the complex conjugate of $Be^{i\phi_B}$, we obtain

$$(A_x + iA_y)(B_x - iB_y) = (A_xB_x + A_yB_y) + i(A_yB_x - A_xB_y). \tag{1-87}$$

We recognize the real part of Eq. (1-87) as the scalar product of the vectors $\mathbf{A}$ and $\mathbf{B}$, and the imaginary part as the magnitude of the vector product $\mathbf{B} \times \mathbf{A}$.

---

* We can see that $e^{i\phi} = \cos \phi + i \sin \phi$ as follows: Consider $y = \cos \phi + i \sin \phi$ from which we obtain by differentiation

$$\frac{dy}{d\phi} = -\sin \phi + i \cos \phi = iy.$$

The solution of this equation is $y = e^{i\phi}$, which verifies Eq. (1-85).

That is,

$$\mathbf{A} \cdot \mathbf{B} = \text{Re } (\mathbf{B^*A}) = \text{Re } (\mathbf{A^*B})$$
$$= \text{Re } (ABe^{i(\phi_A - \phi_B)}) = AB \cos (\phi_A - \phi_B) \qquad (1\text{–}88)$$

and

$$|\mathbf{B} \times \mathbf{A}| = |\text{Im } (\mathbf{B^*A})| = |\text{Im } (ABe^{i(\phi_A - \phi_B)})|$$
$$= |AB \sin (\phi_A - \phi_B)|. \qquad (1\text{–}89)$$

The rotation of the vector $\mathbf{A} = Ae^{i\phi}$ about the $z$-axis through an angle $\theta$ is obtained by multiplying the vector $\mathbf{A}$ by $e^{i\theta}$. The multiplication by

$$e^{\pi i/2} = \cos \frac{\pi}{2} + i \sin \frac{\pi}{2} = i$$

rotates the vector $\mathbf{A}$ through 90° (cf. Fig. 1–25).

We note that the differentiation of the unit vector $\mathbf{e} = e^{i\phi}$ yields

$$\frac{d\mathbf{e}}{dt} = i \frac{d\phi}{dt} e^{i\phi} = i\omega e^{i\phi}.$$

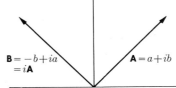

FIG. 1–25. Two perpendicular vectors in complex notation.

This shows that $d\mathbf{e}/dt$ is indeed a vector of magnitude $\omega$ perpendicular to the unit vector $\mathbf{e}$. This is in agreement with our discussion in the last section.

A very interesting and important example is the case when $\omega$ is a constant. Then

$$\phi = \omega t, \qquad (1\text{–}90)$$

and $e^{i\omega t}$ is a unit vector which rotates linearly with $t$ in a counterclockwise direction. On the other hand, the vector $e^{-i\omega t}$ is a unit vector which rotates linearly with $t$ in a clockwise direction. The combination of these two linearly

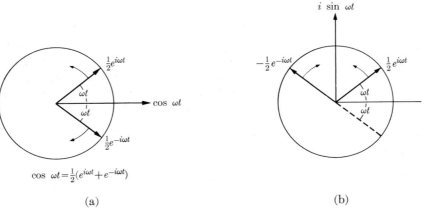

(a)          (b)

FIG. 1–26. A sinusoidally varying unidirectional vector expressed as a linear sum of two rotating vectors.

rotating vectors can lead to either the vector (Fig. 1–26a)

$$\mathbf{r}_1 = \tfrac{1}{2}(e^{i\omega t} + e^{-i\omega t}) = \cos \omega t \qquad (1\text{–}91)$$

or the vector (Fig. 1–26b)

$$\mathbf{r}_2 = \tfrac{1}{2}(e^{i\omega t} - e^{-i\omega t}) = i \sin \omega t. \qquad (1\text{–}92)$$

The first vector, being real, always lies along the $x$-axis, while the second vector is directed along the $y$-axis. Both vectors vary with $t$ in a simple harmonic fashion. This verifies the very important statement that a unidirectional vector varying sinusoidally with $t$ is expressible as the sum of a clockwise rotating vector and a counterclockwise rotating vector.

On the other hand, since

$$e^{i\omega t} = \cos \omega t + i \sin \omega t \qquad \text{and} \qquad e^{-i\omega t} = \cos \omega t - i \sin \omega t,$$

we conversely also have the fact that a uniformly rotating vector is expressible as the sum of two mutually orthogonal vectors which are simple harmonic functions of $t$.

We shall find the complex conjugate representation of rotating vectors to be extremely useful in our discussions of the polarization of harmonic transverse waves in Chapter 12 and of the effect of a magnetic field on an isotropic oscillator, and its use in the classical explanation of the *Faraday effect*, in Chapter 6.

## Problems

1–1. Given the three vectors

$$\begin{aligned}
\mathbf{A} &= \phantom{-}3\mathbf{i} + 4\mathbf{j} + 5\mathbf{k}, \\
\mathbf{B} &= -\mathbf{i} + 4\mathbf{j} - 2\mathbf{k}, \\
\mathbf{C} &= \phantom{-}2\mathbf{i} - \phantom{4}\mathbf{j} + \phantom{2}\mathbf{k}.
\end{aligned}$$

Find: (a) the vector sum $\mathbf{A} + \mathbf{B} - \mathbf{C}$; (b) the magnitude and direction cosines of the three vectors; (c) the unit vectors in the direction of the three vectors; (d) the scalar products $\mathbf{A} \cdot \mathbf{B}$, $\mathbf{A} \cdot \mathbf{C}$, and $\mathbf{B} \cdot \mathbf{C}$, and the angle between each pair of vectors; (e) the vector products $\mathbf{A} \times \mathbf{B}$, $\mathbf{A} \times \mathbf{C}$, and $\mathbf{B} \times \mathbf{C}$, and from their magnitude the angle between the pair of vectors; (f) the triple scalar product $\mathbf{A} \cdot (\mathbf{B} \times \mathbf{C})$ (are the vectors coplanar?); (g) $(\mathbf{A} \times \mathbf{B}) \cdot \mathbf{A}$ and $(\mathbf{A} \times \mathbf{B}) \cdot \mathbf{B}$.

1–2. Show that the three position vectors

$$\begin{aligned}
\mathbf{r}_1 &= 3\mathbf{i} + 2\mathbf{j} - \mathbf{k}, \\
\mathbf{r}_2 &= 3\mathbf{i} + 4\mathbf{j} - 5\mathbf{k}, \\
\mathbf{r}_3 &= c(\mathbf{i} + \mathbf{j} - \mathbf{k}),
\end{aligned}$$

are coplanar. What must be the magnitude of $c$ in order that the three vectors form the sides of a triangle?

1–3. What must be the value of $c$, the $z$-component of the vector

$$\mathbf{A} = 3\mathbf{i} + 4\mathbf{j} + c\mathbf{k},$$

in order that the vector $\mathbf{A}$ be perpendicular to the vector

$$\mathbf{B} = -2\mathbf{i} + 4\mathbf{j} + 5\mathbf{k}?$$

1–4. The position vectors of the points $P_1$ and $P_2$ with respect to the origin $O$ are

$$\mathbf{r}_1 = \mathbf{i} - 2\mathbf{j} + 3\mathbf{k} \quad \text{and} \quad \mathbf{r}_2 = 2\mathbf{i} - 4\mathbf{j} + 5\mathbf{k}.$$

Find the vectors which specify the points of the straight line joining the two points $P_1$ and $P_2$.

1–5. Prove Eq. (1–31) by expanding both sides in terms of the cartesian components of the vectors. Find the triple vector product $\mathbf{A} \times (\mathbf{B} \times \mathbf{C})$ of the three vectors of Problem 1–1.

1–6.  Find the position vector of the points which lie on the line passing through the point $(2, 0, 1)$ and which is perpendicular to the plane of the vectors

$$\mathbf{A} = \mathbf{i} - 2\mathbf{j} + \mathbf{k} \quad \text{and} \quad \mathbf{B} = 2\mathbf{i} + 3\mathbf{j} - \mathbf{k}.$$

1–7. Show that

(a) $\mathbf{A} \times (\mathbf{B} \times \mathbf{C}) = \mathbf{C} \times (\mathbf{B} \times \mathbf{A}) - \mathbf{B} \times (\mathbf{C} \times \mathbf{A})$,

(b) $(\mathbf{A} \times \mathbf{B}) \cdot (\mathbf{C} \times \mathbf{D}) + (\mathbf{B} \times \mathbf{C}) \cdot (\mathbf{A} \times \mathbf{D}) + (\mathbf{C} \times \mathbf{A}) \cdot (\mathbf{B} \times \mathbf{D}) = 0$,

(c) $(\mathbf{A} \times \mathbf{B}) \times (\mathbf{C} \times \mathbf{D}) = (\mathbf{A} \times \mathbf{B} \cdot \mathbf{D})\mathbf{C} - (\mathbf{A} \times \mathbf{B} \cdot \mathbf{C})\mathbf{D}$

$$= (\mathbf{A} \times \mathbf{C} \cdot \mathbf{D})\mathbf{B} - (\mathbf{B} \times \mathbf{C} \cdot \mathbf{D})\mathbf{A}.$$

1–8. Derive Eqs. (1–59) through (1–61).

1–9. Prove the following inequalities:

$$|\mathbf{A} + \mathbf{B}| \leq |\mathbf{A}| + |\mathbf{B}|,$$
$$|\mathbf{A} \cdot \mathbf{B}| \leq |\mathbf{A}| \, |\mathbf{B}|,$$
$$|\mathbf{A} \times \mathbf{B}| \leq |\mathbf{A}| \, |\mathbf{B}|.$$

1–10. Which of the following sets of vectors are noncoplanar?

(a) $\mathbf{b}_1 = 2\mathbf{i} + \mathbf{j} + 4\mathbf{k}$      (b) $\mathbf{b}_1 = \mathbf{i} + 2\mathbf{j} + 3\mathbf{k}$

$\quad\;\; \mathbf{b}_2 = \mathbf{i} \qquad + 3\mathbf{k}$          $\mathbf{b}_2 = -3\mathbf{i} - 4\mathbf{j} + 2\mathbf{k}$

$\quad\;\; \mathbf{b}_3 = -3\mathbf{i} - 4\mathbf{j} - \mathbf{k}$          $\mathbf{b}_3 = 2\mathbf{i} - \mathbf{j} - \mathbf{k}$

1–11. Obtain the reciprocal set of vectors for the noncoplanar set of vectors in Problem 1–10.

1–12. (a) Express the vectors

$$\mathbf{A} = 2\mathbf{i} - 4\mathbf{j} + 3\mathbf{k} \quad \text{and} \quad \mathbf{B} = -3\mathbf{i} + 2\mathbf{j} - \mathbf{k}$$

in terms of a linear sum of the noncoplanar vectors of Problem 1–10 and in terms of a linear sum of their reciprocal vectors.

(b) Evaluate $\mathbf{A} \cdot \mathbf{B}$ and $\mathbf{A} \times \mathbf{B}$, using the scalar products $\alpha_i$, $\beta_i$, $\alpha_i^\star$ and $\beta_i^\star$ of $\mathbf{A}$ and $\mathbf{B}$ with the noncoplanar set of vectors of Problem 1–10 and their reciprocal vectors. Compare your answer with the scalar and vector products of these vectors evaluated in terms of the cartesian components of $\mathbf{A}$ and $\mathbf{B}$.

1–13. Find the position vectors of the points which lie in the plane of the points $P_1$, $P_2$, and $P_3$ whose position vectors are

$$
\begin{aligned}
\mathbf{r}_1 &= \phantom{-}2\mathbf{i} - \phantom{4}\mathbf{j} + \mathbf{k}, \\
\mathbf{r}_2 &= \phantom{-}3\mathbf{i} + 4\mathbf{j} - \mathbf{k}, \\
\mathbf{r}_3 &= -\mathbf{i} + 2\mathbf{j}.
\end{aligned}
$$

1–14. Find the distance from the origin to the plane determined by the three points of the previous problem.

1–15. Show that the three vectors

$$
\begin{aligned}
\mathbf{b}_1 &= \phantom{-\sqrt{2}}\mathbf{i} - \sqrt{2}\mathbf{j} + \phantom{\sqrt{2}}\mathbf{k}, \\
\mathbf{b}_2 &= \phantom{-\sqrt{2}}-\mathbf{i} - \sqrt{2}\mathbf{j} - \phantom{\sqrt{2}}\mathbf{k}, \\
\mathbf{b}_3 &= -\sqrt{2}\mathbf{i} \phantom{- \sqrt{2}\mathbf{j}} + \sqrt{2}\mathbf{k},
\end{aligned}
$$

are mutually orthogonal.

1–16. The derivative of the vector $\mathbf{A}(t)$ of constant magnitude was shown to be expressible as a vector product,

$$
\frac{d\mathbf{A}(t)}{dt} = \boldsymbol{\omega} \times \mathbf{A}(t).
$$

However, $\boldsymbol{\omega}$ is not unique, since the addition of the term $c\mathbf{A}$ to $\boldsymbol{\omega}$ would yield the same result. The derivative of two vectors of constant magnitude, on the other hand, may determine a unique $\boldsymbol{\omega}$ in terms of which their derivatives are expressible in the form

$$
\frac{d}{dt} \mathbf{A}(t) = \boldsymbol{\omega} \times \mathbf{A} \qquad \text{and} \qquad \frac{d}{dt} \mathbf{B}(t) = \boldsymbol{\omega} \times \mathbf{B}.
$$

Consider the unit vectors

$$
\begin{aligned}
\mathbf{e}_1 &= \sin \alpha t \cos \beta t \mathbf{i} + \sin \alpha t \sin \beta t \mathbf{j} + \cos \alpha t \mathbf{k}, \\
\mathbf{e}_2 &= \cos \alpha t \cos \beta t \mathbf{i} + \cos \alpha t \sin \beta t \mathbf{j} - \sin \alpha t \mathbf{k}, \\
\mathbf{e}_3 &= -\sin \beta t \mathbf{i} + \cos \beta t \mathbf{j}.
\end{aligned}
$$

Find the angular velocity vector $\boldsymbol{\omega}$ which satisfies the equation

$$
\frac{d}{dt} \mathbf{e}_1 = \boldsymbol{\omega} \times \mathbf{e}_1 \qquad \text{and} \qquad \frac{d}{dt} \mathbf{e}_2 = \boldsymbol{\omega} \times \mathbf{e}_2.
$$

Show that the same $\boldsymbol{\omega}$ also yields

$$
\frac{d\mathbf{e}_3}{dt} = \boldsymbol{\omega} \times \mathbf{e}_3.
$$

1–17. For the kinematic description of the motion of a rigid body we require the relations which exist between a set of space coordinate axes, designated by the unit vectors $\mathbf{i}$, $\mathbf{j}$, and $\mathbf{k}$, and the axes of a coordinate system rotating with the rigid body designated by $\mathbf{i}'$, $\mathbf{j}'$, and $\mathbf{k}'$.

(a) Given the expressions for the three noncoplanar vectors

$$\mathbf{k} = \sin\theta\sin\psi\mathbf{i}' + \sin\theta\cos\psi\mathbf{j}' + \cos\theta\mathbf{k}',$$
$$\mathbf{k}' = \sin\theta\sin\phi\mathbf{i} - \sin\theta\cos\phi\mathbf{j} + \cos\theta\mathbf{k},$$
$$\mathbf{e}_\phi = \cos\phi\mathbf{i} + \sin\phi\mathbf{j} = \cos\psi\mathbf{i}' - \sin\psi\mathbf{j}' = \mathbf{e}'_\phi,$$

obtain their reciprocal vectors $\overline{\mathbf{k}}$, $\overline{\mathbf{k}}'$, and $\overline{\mathbf{e}}'_\phi$, expressed in terms of the base vectors $\mathbf{i}'$, $\mathbf{j}'$, and $\mathbf{k}'$ of the body coordinate system.

(b) Express the vectors $\mathbf{i}$ and $\mathbf{j}$ as a linear sum of the vectors $\mathbf{k}$, $\mathbf{k}'$, and $\mathbf{e}'_\phi$, and hence obtain the relations of $\mathbf{i}$ and $\mathbf{j}$ to the base vectors of the body coordinate system. [The angles $\theta$, $\phi$, and $\psi$ are known as the *Euler angles* (cf. Chapter 9).]

1–18. (a) Show that the scalar products $\alpha_i$ and $\alpha_i^\star$ of the vector $\mathbf{A}$ with the base vectors $\mathbf{b}_i$ and their reciprocal vectors $\boldsymbol{b}_i$ are linearly related, as expressed by

$$\alpha_i^\star = \sum_j g_{ij}^\star \alpha_j \quad \text{and} \quad \alpha_j = \sum_j g_{ij}\alpha_j^\star.$$

Express the scalars $g_{ij}$ and $g_{ij}^\star$ in terms of the base vectors $\mathbf{b}_i$ and the reciprocal vectors $\boldsymbol{b}_i$. (We note that the $g_{ij}$ are referred to as the covariant components of the metric tensor and the $g_{ij}^\star$ as the contravariant components of the metric tensor.)

(b) Show that the scalar product of two vectors $\mathbf{A}$ and $\mathbf{B}$ is expressible as

$$\mathbf{A} \cdot \mathbf{B} = \sum_{ij} g_{ij}^\star \alpha_i \beta_j = \sum_{ij} g_{ij}\alpha_i^\star \beta_j^\star.$$

1–19. (a) Show that the time-dependent position vector

$$\mathbf{r}(t) = A\cos\omega t\mathbf{i} + B\sin\omega t\mathbf{j}$$

moves along the points of the ellipse with semimajor axis $A$ ($A > B$) and semiminor axis $B$ rotating in a counterclockwise direction.

(b) Show that the sum of the complex vectors

$$\mathbf{r}_1 = Ae^{i\omega t} \quad \text{and} \quad \mathbf{r}_2 = Be^{-i\omega t}, \quad A \neq B,$$

represents a position vector moving along the points of an ellipse. Determine the direction of rotation of the vector in terms of the magnitudes of $A$ and $B$.

1–20. Verify Eq. (1–43) that the vectors $\boldsymbol{b}_1$, $\boldsymbol{b}_2$, $\boldsymbol{b}_3$ are reciprocal to the vectors $\boldsymbol{b}_1$, $\boldsymbol{b}_2$, and $\boldsymbol{b}_3$.

1–21. (a) Find the position vector of the points which lie in the plane perpendicular to the vector

$$A = 3i + 4j - k$$

which contains the points $(1, 2, 3)$.

(b) Find the position vector of the points which lie in the plane determined by the three points $(2, 1, 1)$, $(-1, 2, 2)$, and $(3, 2, 1)$.

1–22. (a) A rotation is a coordinate transformation which involves a change of base vectors. Consider the two sets of orthogonal unit base vectors $\mathbf{e}_1$, $\mathbf{e}_2$, $\mathbf{e}_3$ and

$\mathbf{e}'_1$, $\mathbf{e}'_2$, $\mathbf{e}'_3$ which are related by

$$\mathbf{e}'_i = \sum_{j=1}^{3} t_{ij}\mathbf{e}_j.$$

Show that

$$\mathbf{e}_j = \sum_{i=1}^{3} t_{ij}\mathbf{e}'_i.$$

(b) From the values of the scalar products between the vectors of either set show that

$$\sum_{j=1}^{3} t_{ij}t_{ik} = \delta_{ik}.$$

Such a transformation is referred to as an orthogonal coordinate transformation.

# 2

# *Kinematics of Particle Motion*

In this chapter, we shall proceed to develop the formalism which we require for the description of the motion of a particle. By a particle we mean a point body. In reality, of course, such bodies do not exist. The idea of a point body is a mathematical idealization of an object whose dimensions and orientation in space are negligible in the particular description of its motion of interest. For example, in the description of the motion of the planets about the sun, the planets may to a first approximation be treated as bodies of negligible dimensions; that is, as point bodies. On the other hand, an electron which ventures too close to another charged body may not be treated as a particle. We shall say more about this in a later chapter when we will be in a better position to understand and recognize the circumstances under which a body may or may not to a first approximation be treated as a particle.

The physical quantities required for the kinematic description of the motion of a particle are its position, velocity, and acceleration. The form which the description of these vector quantities takes depends on the coordinates in terms of which and the coordinate system with respect to which we choose to describe the motion of the particle. From the previous chapter, it should be clear that the choice of a coordinate system is quite arbitrary so long as the

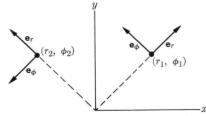

FIG. 2–1. Unit base vectors in the *xy*-plane for the polar coordinates *r* and *ϕ*.

three base vectors are not coplanar. The simplest choice with which to specify the coordinate axes is that of three mutually orthogonal unit vectors. Even with this choice, however, there is a great deal of flexibility. For example, for cylindrical and spherical coordinates we use three mutually orthogonal unit base vectors whose orientation in space depends on the position of the particle, (Fig. 2–1). The base vectors rotate as the particle changes its position. The coordinate base vectors which we shall use for any particular problem are determined, as we shall see, by the coordinates in terms of which we decide to describe the motion.

34

We shall proceed with the definition of the velocity and the acceleration of a particle and a description of them in cartesian, cylindrical, and spherical coordinates. We shall conclude with a discussion of them in generalized coordinates. It is strongly recommended that the reader make every effort to master the very important discussion on generalized coordinates.

## 2–1  Velocity and acceleration

The position vector of a particle is specified by the radius vector $\mathbf{r}$ from the origin of a fixed cartesian coordinate system to the point at which the particle is located. If the particle moves, then its position vector is a function of the time $t$, and is designated by

$$\mathbf{r} = \mathbf{r}(t). \tag{2-1}$$

The succession of points occupied by the particle will trace out a curve in space. A parametric representation of this curve is provided by the dependence of the $x$-, $y$-, and $z$-coordinates of the position vector of the particle on the time:

$$x = x(t), \qquad y = y(t), \qquad \text{and} \qquad z = z(t). \tag{2-2}$$

The instantaneous velocity of a particle at time $t$ is defined as the time derivative of its position vector:

$$\mathbf{v}(t) = \frac{d\mathbf{r}}{dt} = \lim_{\Delta t \to 0} \left[ \frac{\mathbf{r}(t + \Delta t) - \mathbf{r}(t)}{\Delta t} \right]. \tag{2-3}$$

The instantaneous velocity is thus the limit of the average velocity $\langle \mathbf{v} \rangle$ over the time interval $(t_2 - t_1)$,

$$\langle \mathbf{v} \rangle = \frac{\mathbf{r}(t_2) - \mathbf{r}(t_1)}{t_2 - t_1}, \tag{2-4}$$

as the time interval over which the average is defined approaches zero.

In terms of the cartesian components of the position vector, the velocity is given by

$$\mathbf{v} = \dot{x}\mathbf{i} + \dot{y}\mathbf{j} + \dot{z}\mathbf{k}, \tag{2-5}$$

where the dot over the $x$-, $y$-, $z$-components of the position vector represents the time derivative of the components. For example,

$$\dot{x} = \frac{dx}{dt}.$$

The acceleration of a particle is defined as the time derivative of its velocity,

$$\mathbf{a} = \frac{d\mathbf{v}}{dt} = \ddot{\mathbf{r}}. \tag{2-6}$$

The two dots above the position vector indicate the second time derivative of $\mathbf{r}$,

$$\ddot{\mathbf{r}} = \frac{d^2\mathbf{r}}{dt^2}.$$

Differentiation of Eq. (2–5) yields the description of the acceleration in cartesian coordinates,

$$\mathbf{a} = \ddot{x}\mathbf{i} + \ddot{y}\mathbf{j} + \ddot{z}\mathbf{k}. \tag{2–7}$$

▶ As an example, we obtain the velocity and acceleration of a particle whose position vector is specified by

$$\mathbf{r}(t) = A \cos \omega t \mathbf{i} + A \sin \omega t \mathbf{j} \tag{2–8}$$

or

$$x = A \cos \omega t, \qquad y = A \sin \omega t. \tag{2–9}$$

Equations (2–9) are parametric equations for a circle of radius $A$. For a particle moving along this circle, the velocity is found to be given by

$$\mathbf{v} = \dot{\mathbf{r}} = -A\omega \sin \omega t \mathbf{i} + A\omega \cos \omega t \mathbf{j}.$$

Since for a particle moving in a circle, the distance from the origin is fixed, or $r^2 = A^2$, $\mathbf{v} = \dot{\mathbf{r}}$ should be perpendicular to $\mathbf{r}$. This follows from our discussion in Section 1–8. We indeed find that $\mathbf{v} \cdot \mathbf{r} = 0$.

For the particular circular motion which we are considering in this example, the speed $v^2 = \omega^2 A^2$ is a constant. We should therefore also find $\mathbf{v} \cdot \mathbf{a} = 0$. Indeed, upon differentiating the velocity, we obtain

$$\mathbf{a} = -A\omega^2 \cos \omega t \mathbf{i} - A\omega^2 \sin \omega t \mathbf{j} = -\omega^2 \mathbf{r},$$

whence it follows that $\mathbf{a}$ is perpendicular to $\mathbf{v}$. ◀

## 2–2 Velocity and acceleration in cylindrical coordinates

The cylindrical coordinates $\rho$, $\phi$, and $z$ are defined by their relations to the cartesian coordinates $x$, $y$, and $z$. These relations are

$$\left. \begin{aligned} x &= \rho \cos \phi \\ y &= \rho \sin \phi \\ z &= z \end{aligned} \right\} \quad \text{or} \quad \begin{cases} x^2 + y^2 = \rho^2 \\ \tan^{-1}\left(\dfrac{y}{x}\right) = \phi. \end{cases} \tag{2–10}$$

It can be seen that $\rho$ is the projection of the radius vector $\mathbf{r}$ onto the $xy$-plane (Fig. 2–2), and that $\phi$ is the angle which $\rho$ makes with the $x$-axis. The coordinates are referred to as cylindrical coordinates, because the surfaces for which $\rho$ is a constant are circular cylinders parallel to the $z$-axis.

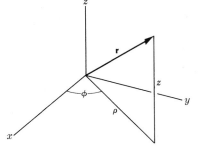

FIG. 2–2. Cylindrical polar coordinates.

The position vector may be expressed in terms of the cylindrical coordinates. From the relationship between the cartesian and cylindrical coordinates we obtain

$$\mathbf{r} = \rho \cos \phi \mathbf{i} + \rho \sin \phi \mathbf{j} + z\mathbf{k}. \qquad (2\text{–}11)$$

Successive differentiation of the position vector expressed in terms of the cylindrical coordinates yields for the velocity vector the result

$$\mathbf{v} = (\dot{\rho} \cos \phi - \rho\dot{\phi} \sin \phi)\mathbf{i} + (\dot{\rho} \sin \phi + \rho\dot{\phi} \cos \phi)\mathbf{j} + \dot{z}\mathbf{k}, \qquad (2\text{–}12)$$

and for the acceleration vector,

$$\mathbf{a} = (\ddot{\rho} \cos \phi - 2\dot{\rho}\dot{\phi} \sin \phi - \rho\dot{\phi}^2 \cos \phi - \rho\ddot{\phi} \sin \phi)\mathbf{i}$$
$$+ (\ddot{\rho} \sin \phi + 2\dot{\rho}\dot{\phi} \cos \phi - \rho\dot{\phi}^2 \sin \phi + \rho\ddot{\phi} \cos \phi)\mathbf{j} + \ddot{z}\mathbf{k}. \qquad (2\text{–}13)$$

These expressions are rather awkward. They appear somewhat simpler if expressed in terms of a new set of base vectors, which are found to be natural for the cylindrical coordinates.

The unit base vectors which should be employed whenever cylindrical coordinates are used for the kinematic description of the motion of a particle are the unit vectors $\mathbf{e}_\rho$, $\mathbf{e}_\phi$, and $\mathbf{k}$, which at any given point are, respectively, directed in the direction in which the position vector $\mathbf{r}$ changes when $\rho$, $\phi$, or $z$ are increased by infinitesimal amounts. These unit vectors are defined as follows*:

$$\mathbf{e}_\rho = \frac{\Delta\mathbf{r}_\rho}{|\Delta\mathbf{r}_\rho|} = \frac{\partial\mathbf{r}/\partial\rho}{|\partial\mathbf{r}/\partial\rho|} = \cos \phi \mathbf{i} + \sin \phi \mathbf{j}, \qquad (2\text{–}14)$$

$$\mathbf{e}_\phi = \frac{\Delta\mathbf{r}_\phi}{|\Delta\mathbf{r}_\phi|} = \frac{\partial\mathbf{r}/\partial\phi}{|\partial\mathbf{r}/\partial\phi|} = -\sin \phi \mathbf{i} + \cos \phi \mathbf{j}, \qquad (2\text{–}15)$$

and $\mathbf{k}$ is the unit vector in the positive $z$-direction. In Eqs. (2–14) and (2–15), $\Delta\mathbf{r}_\rho$ and $\Delta\mathbf{r}_\phi$ represent the changes in the position vector produced by changes in $\rho$ and $\phi$ respectively (cf. Fig. 2–3):

$$\Delta\mathbf{r}_\rho = \frac{\partial\mathbf{r}}{\partial\rho} \Delta\rho, \qquad \Delta\mathbf{r}_\phi = \frac{\partial\mathbf{r}}{\partial\phi} \Delta\phi.$$

It is readily verified that at any point the three unit vectors $\mathbf{e}_\rho$, $\mathbf{e}_\phi$, and $\mathbf{k}$ are a mutually orthogonal set of unit vectors forming a right-handed coordinate system at that point. The reader should prove to himself that indeed

$$\mathbf{e}_\rho \times \mathbf{e}_\phi = \mathbf{k}, \qquad \mathbf{e}_\phi \times \mathbf{k} = \mathbf{e}_\rho, \qquad \mathbf{k} \times \mathbf{e}_\rho = \mathbf{e}_\phi. \qquad (2\text{–}16)$$

---

* $\partial\mathbf{r}/\partial\rho$ and $\partial\mathbf{r}/\partial\phi$ are the partial derivatives of $\mathbf{r}$ with respect to $\rho$ and $\phi$. The partial derivative is defined by

$$\frac{\partial\mathbf{r}(u, v)}{\partial u} = \lim_{\Delta u \to 0} \left[ \frac{\mathbf{r}(u + \Delta u, v) - \mathbf{r}(u, v)}{\Delta u} \right].$$

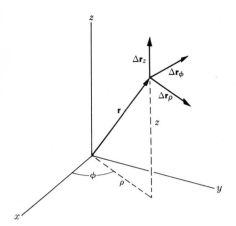

FIG. 2–3. Infinitesimal changes in the position vector produced by an infinitesimal change in the cylindrical coordinates $\rho, \phi, z$.

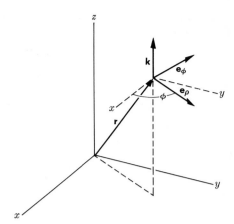

FIG. 2–4. The orthogonal unit base vectors $\mathbf{e}_\rho, \mathbf{e}_\phi, \mathbf{k}$ from a point in the cylindrical coordinates $\rho, \phi, z$.

Figure 2–4 shows the directions of the unit base vectors $\mathbf{e}_\rho$, $\mathbf{e}_\phi$, and $\mathbf{k}$. The unit vector $\mathbf{e}_\rho$ is in the $xy$-plane, making an angle $\phi$ with the $x$-axis. It lies along the projection of the position vector onto the $xy$-plane. The unit vector $\mathbf{e}_\phi$ also lies in the $xy$-plane. It is perpendicular to $\mathbf{e}_\rho$ and makes an angle $\phi$ with the positive $y$-axis.

In terms of the orthogonal set of unit base vectors $\mathbf{e}_\rho$, $\mathbf{e}_\phi$, and $\mathbf{k}$, the position vector is specified by $\mathbf{r} = (\mathbf{r} \cdot \mathbf{e}_\rho)\mathbf{e}_\rho + (\mathbf{r} \cdot \mathbf{e}_\phi)\mathbf{e}_\phi + (\mathbf{r} \cdot \mathbf{k})\mathbf{k}$, whence from Eq. (2–11) we obtain

$$\mathbf{r} = \rho\mathbf{e}_\rho + z\mathbf{k}. \tag{2–17}$$

Similarly, utilizing Eqs. (2–12) and (2–13), we find

$$\begin{aligned} \mathbf{v} &= (\mathbf{v} \cdot \mathbf{e}_\rho)\mathbf{e}_\rho + (\mathbf{v} \cdot \mathbf{e}_\phi)\mathbf{e}_\phi + (\mathbf{v} \cdot \mathbf{k})\mathbf{k} \\ &= \dot{\rho}\mathbf{e}_\rho + \rho\dot{\phi}\mathbf{e}_\phi + \dot{z}\mathbf{k}, \end{aligned} \tag{2–18}$$

and

$$\begin{aligned} \mathbf{a} &= (\mathbf{a} \cdot \mathbf{e}_\rho)\mathbf{e}_\rho + (\mathbf{a} \cdot \mathbf{e}_\phi)\mathbf{e}_\phi + (\mathbf{a} \cdot \mathbf{k})\mathbf{k} \\ &= (\ddot{\rho} - \rho\dot{\phi}^2)\mathbf{e}_\rho + (\rho\ddot{\phi} + 2\dot{\rho}\dot{\phi})\mathbf{e}_\phi + \ddot{z}\mathbf{k}. \end{aligned} \tag{2–19}$$

Equations (2–18) and (2–19) could have been obtained somewhat more readily by successively differentiating Eq. (2–17) directly. The first derivative of this equation leads us to the expression for the velocity,

$$\mathbf{v} = \dot{\mathbf{r}} = \dot{\rho}\mathbf{e}_\rho + \rho\dot{\mathbf{e}}_\rho + \dot{z}\mathbf{k}.$$

Differentiating Eq. (2–14) yields

$$\dot{\mathbf{e}}_\rho = \dot{\phi}(-\sin\phi\,\mathbf{i} + \cos\phi\,\mathbf{j}) = \dot{\phi}\mathbf{e}_\phi. \tag{2–20}$$

This result, when substituted into the previous equations, yields Eq. (2–18) for the velocity vector.

Similarly, from Eq. (2–15) we obtain

$$\dot{\mathbf{e}}_\phi = (-\cos\phi\mathbf{i} - \sin\phi\mathbf{j})\dot{\phi} = -\dot{\phi}\mathbf{e}_\rho, \tag{2–21}$$

a relation which we shall require to obtain the expression for the acceleration. Note that, as is to be expected, $\mathbf{e}_\rho \cdot \dot{\mathbf{e}}_\rho = \mathbf{e}_\phi \cdot \dot{\mathbf{e}}_\phi = 0$, and as discussed in Section 1–7 we can define an angular velocity vector

$$\boldsymbol{\omega} = \dot{\phi}\mathbf{k}, \tag{2–22}$$

in terms of which the time rate of change of the vectors $\mathbf{e}_\rho$ and $\mathbf{e}_\phi$ may be expressed as vector products,

$$\dot{\mathbf{e}}_\rho = \boldsymbol{\omega} \times \mathbf{e}_\rho \tag{2–23}$$

and

$$\dot{\mathbf{e}}_\phi = \boldsymbol{\omega} \times \mathbf{e}_\phi. \tag{2–24}$$

In terms of the angular velocity vector $\boldsymbol{\omega}$, the velocity is expressed by

$$\begin{aligned}\mathbf{v} &= \dot{\rho}\mathbf{e}_\rho + \rho\boldsymbol{\omega} \times \mathbf{e}_\rho + \dot{z}\mathbf{k} \\ &= \dot{\rho}\mathbf{e}_\rho + \rho\dot{\phi}\mathbf{e}_\phi + \dot{z}\mathbf{k}.\end{aligned} \tag{2–25}$$

Similarly, we obtain for the acceleration vector the expression

$$\begin{aligned}\mathbf{a} = \frac{d\mathbf{v}}{dt} &= \ddot{\rho}\mathbf{e}_\rho + 2\dot{\rho}\dot{\mathbf{e}}_\rho + \rho\ddot{\phi}\mathbf{e}_\phi + \rho\dot{\phi}\dot{\mathbf{e}}_\phi + \ddot{z}\mathbf{k} \\ &= (\ddot{\rho} - \rho\dot{\phi}^2)\mathbf{e}_\rho + (\rho\ddot{\phi} + 2\dot{\rho}\dot{\phi})\mathbf{e}_\phi + \ddot{z}\mathbf{k},\end{aligned} \tag{2–26}$$

which is in agreement with Eq. (2–19).

▶ As an illustration, we repeat the example of the last section, but obtain this time a description in cylindrical coordinates of the velocity and acceleration of a particle moving in a circle with constant speed. In cylindrical coordinates the position vector of the particle, $\mathbf{r} = A\cos\omega t\mathbf{i} + A\sin\omega t\mathbf{j}$, is given by

$$\mathbf{r} = \rho\mathbf{e}_\rho, \tag{2–27}$$

where $\phi$, the angle which $\mathbf{e}_\rho$ makes with the $x$-axis, varies linearly with time,

$$\phi = \omega t,$$

and $\rho = A$ remains constant in magnitude.

Thus we obtain

$$\mathbf{v} = A\dot{\mathbf{e}}_\rho = A\dot{\phi}\mathbf{e}_\phi \tag{2–28}$$

and

$$\mathbf{a} = A\omega\dot{\mathbf{e}}_\phi = -A\omega^2\mathbf{e}_\rho = -\omega^2\mathbf{r}. \tag{2–29}$$

The reader may recall from his first mechanics course that for a particle moving in a circle $\rho\dot{\phi}$ is the magnitude of the tangential velocity of the particle, $\rho\dot{\phi}^2$ its centripetal acceleration, and $\rho\ddot{\phi}$ the magnitude of its tangential acceleration. When the particle no longer moves in a circle, additional terms appear in the expressions for the velocity and the acceleration vectors, as can be seen from Eqs. (2–25) and (2–26). These additional terms are the radial component of the velocity $\dot{\rho}$, the radial acceleration $\ddot{\rho}$, and $2\dot{\rho}\dot{\phi}$. The last term appears in the tangential component of the acceleration, and is due to the rotation of the coordinate base vectors as the position vector changes. It is referred to as the *Coriolis acceleration.* ◀

## 2–3 Velocity and acceleration in spherical coordinates

Analogously to the way we obtained the expressions for the velocity and acceleration in cylindrical coordinates, we shall now obtain the expressions for the velocity and acceleration in spherical coordinates.

The spherical coordinates $r$, $\theta$, and $\phi$ are defined by the equations

$$r = \sqrt{x^2 + y^2 + z^2}, \tag{2–30}$$

$$\theta = \tan^{-1}\left(\frac{\sqrt{x^2 + y^2}}{z}\right), \tag{2–31}$$

$$\phi = \tan^{-1}\left(\frac{y}{x}\right); \tag{2–32}$$

or equivalently,

$$x = r \sin\theta \cos\phi, \tag{2–33}$$

$$y = r \sin\theta \sin\phi, \tag{2–34}$$

$$z = r \cos\theta. \tag{2–35}$$

Clearly $r$ is the magnitude of the position vector, $\theta$ the angle which the position vector makes with the $z$-axis, and $\phi$ the angle which the projection of the position vector onto the $xy$-plane makes with the $x$-axis (Fig. 2–5).

The unit base vectors which we should employ when we utilize spherical coordinates are defined by the equations

$$\mathbf{e}_r = \frac{\partial\mathbf{r}/\partial r}{|\partial\mathbf{r}/\partial r|}, \tag{2–36}$$

$$\mathbf{e}_\theta = \frac{\partial\mathbf{r}/\partial\theta}{|\partial\mathbf{r}/\partial\theta|}, \tag{2–37}$$

$$\mathbf{e}_\phi = \frac{\partial\mathbf{r}/\partial\phi}{|\partial\mathbf{r}/\partial\phi|}. \tag{2–38}$$

They are respectively the unit vectors pointing in the directions of the change in the position vector when the coordinates $r$, $\theta$, and $\phi$ are changed by in-

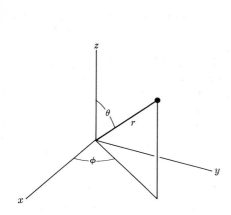

FIG. 2–5. Spherical coordinates $r$, $\theta$, and $\phi$.

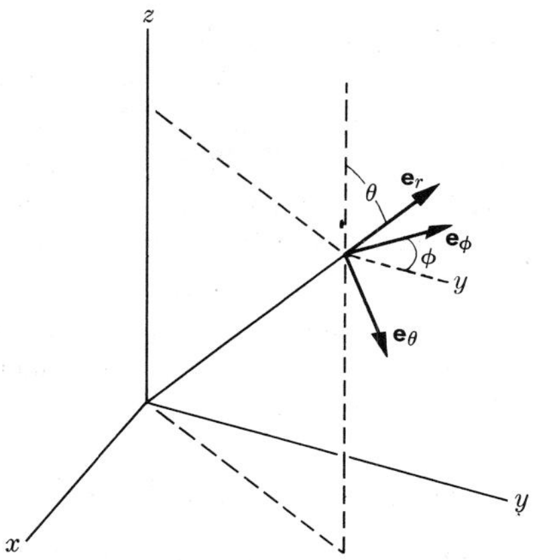

FIG. 2–6. Spherical unit base vectors.

finitesimal amounts (Fig. 2–6). From

$$\mathbf{r} = x\mathbf{i} + y\mathbf{j} + z\mathbf{k}$$
$$= r\sin\theta\cos\phi\,\mathbf{i} + r\sin\theta\sin\phi\,\mathbf{j} + r\cos\theta\,\mathbf{k}, \qquad (2\text{–}39)$$

and through the use of the equations defining the unit base vectors, we obtain the expressions

$$\mathbf{e}_r = \sin\theta\cos\phi\,\mathbf{i} + \sin\theta\sin\phi\,\mathbf{j} + \cos\theta\,\mathbf{k}, \qquad (2\text{–}40)$$

$$\mathbf{e}_\theta = \cos\theta\cos\phi\,\mathbf{i} + \cos\theta\sin\phi\,\mathbf{j} - \sin\theta\,\mathbf{k}, \qquad (2\text{–}41)$$

$$\mathbf{e}_\phi = -\sin\phi\,\mathbf{i} + \cos\phi\,\mathbf{j} \qquad (2\text{–}42)$$

for the unit base vectors at any point specified by a given set of $r$, $\theta$, and $\phi$. It is readily verified that these three unit base vectors are mutually orthogonal and define a right-handed coordinate system. They satisfy the relations

$$\mathbf{e}_r \times \mathbf{e}_\theta = \mathbf{e}_\phi, \qquad \mathbf{e}_\theta \times \mathbf{e}_\phi = \mathbf{e}_r, \qquad \mathbf{e}_\phi \times \mathbf{e}_r = \mathbf{e}_\theta. \qquad (2\text{–}43)$$

From Eqs. (2–40), (2–41), and (2–42), we note that, as was the case for the cylindrical coordinates, the unit base vectors for the spherical coordinates are likewise functions of position, changing their orientation as $\theta$ and $\phi$ vary. We shall therefore also require the use of their time derivatives, which we find to be

$$\dot{\mathbf{e}}_r = (-\sin\theta\cos\phi\,\dot\phi + \cos\theta\cos\phi\,\dot\theta)\mathbf{i} + (\sin\theta\cos\phi\,\dot\phi + \cos\theta\sin\phi\,\dot\theta)\mathbf{j} - \sin\theta\,\dot\theta\mathbf{k}$$
$$= \dot\theta\mathbf{e}_\theta + \sin\theta\,\dot\phi\mathbf{e}_\phi, \qquad (2\text{–}44)$$

$$\dot{\mathbf{e}}_\theta = (-\cos\theta\sin\phi\,\dot\phi - \sin\theta\cos\phi\,\dot\theta)\mathbf{i} + (\cos\theta\cos\phi\,\dot\phi - \sin\theta\sin\phi\,\dot\theta)\mathbf{j} - \cos\theta\,\dot\theta\mathbf{k}$$
$$= -\dot\theta\mathbf{e}_r + \cos\theta\,\dot\phi\mathbf{e}_\phi, \qquad (2\text{–}45)$$

$$\dot{\mathbf{e}}_\phi = -\cos\phi\,\dot\phi\mathbf{i} - \sin\phi\,\dot\phi\mathbf{j} = -\sin\theta\,\dot\phi\mathbf{e}_r - \cos\theta\,\dot\phi\mathbf{e}_\theta. \qquad (2\text{–}46)$$

We should suspect, from the fact that the three unit base vectors remain orthogonal to each other, that there exists a single angular velocity vector $\boldsymbol{\omega}$ in terms of which we can express the time rate of change of the unit vectors $\mathbf{e}_r$, $\mathbf{e}_\theta$, and $\mathbf{e}_\phi$. The base vectors change their orientation when the angles $\theta$ and $\phi$ change. A change in $\phi$ involves a rotation of the position vector about the $z$-axis, while a change in $\theta$ involves a rotation of the position vector about the $\mathbf{e}_\phi$ direction. We can therefore define an angular velocity vector

$$\begin{aligned}
\boldsymbol{\omega} &= \dot{\phi}\mathbf{k} + \dot{\theta}\mathbf{e}_\phi \\
&= \dot{\phi}\cos\theta\,\mathbf{e}_r - \dot{\phi}\sin\theta\,\mathbf{e}_\theta + \dot{\theta}\mathbf{e}_\phi \\
&= \dot{\phi}\mathbf{k} - \sin\phi\,\dot{\theta}\mathbf{i} + \cos\phi\,\dot{\theta}\mathbf{j},
\end{aligned} \tag{2-47}$$

where, to obtain the last two equalities, we have used the relations

$$\begin{aligned}
\mathbf{k} &= (\mathbf{k}\cdot\mathbf{e}_r)\mathbf{e}_r + (\mathbf{k}\cdot\mathbf{e}_\theta)\mathbf{e}_\theta + (\mathbf{k}\cdot\mathbf{e}_\phi)\mathbf{e}_\phi \\
&= \cos\theta\,\mathbf{e}_r - \sin\theta\,\mathbf{e}_\theta
\end{aligned}$$

and

$$\mathbf{e}_\phi = -\sin\phi\,\mathbf{i} + \cos\phi\,\mathbf{j}.$$

In terms of the angular velocity vector $\boldsymbol{\omega}$, the time derivatives of the unit base vectors are expressible as

$$\dot{\mathbf{e}}_r = \boldsymbol{\omega}\times\mathbf{e}_r, \tag{2-48}$$

$$\dot{\mathbf{e}}_\theta = \boldsymbol{\omega}\times\mathbf{e}_\theta, \tag{2-49}$$

$$\dot{\mathbf{e}}_\phi = \boldsymbol{\omega}\times\mathbf{e}_\phi. \tag{2-50}$$

---

We are now in a position to find the velocity and acceleration in spherical coordinates. Since $\mathbf{r} = r\mathbf{e}_r$, we obtain for the velocity the expression

$$\begin{aligned}
\mathbf{v} &= \dot{r}\mathbf{e}_r + r\dot{\mathbf{e}}_r \\
&= \dot{r}\mathbf{e}_r + r\dot{\theta}\mathbf{e}_\theta + r\sin\theta\,\dot{\phi}\mathbf{e}_\phi,
\end{aligned} \tag{2-51}$$

and subsequently for the acceleration,

$$\begin{aligned}
\mathbf{a} = \dot{\mathbf{v}} &= (\ddot{r}\mathbf{e}_r + \dot{r}\dot{\mathbf{e}}_r) + (\dot{r}\dot{\theta}\mathbf{e}_\theta + r\ddot{\theta}\mathbf{e}_\theta + r\dot{\theta}\dot{\mathbf{e}}_\theta) \\
&\quad + (r\sin\theta\,\dot{\phi}\dot{\mathbf{e}}_\phi + \dot{r}\sin\theta\,\dot{\phi}\mathbf{e}_\phi + r\cos\theta\,\dot{\theta}\dot{\phi}\mathbf{e}_\phi + r\sin\theta\,\ddot{\phi}\mathbf{e}_\phi) \\
&= (\ddot{r} - r\dot{\theta}^2 - r\sin\theta\,\dot{\phi}^2)\mathbf{e}_r + (r\ddot{\theta} + 2\dot{r}\dot{\theta} - r\sin\theta\cos\theta\,\dot{\phi}^2)\mathbf{e}_\theta \\
&\quad + (r\sin\theta\,\ddot{\phi} + 2\dot{r}\dot{\phi}\sin\theta + 2r\cos\theta\,\dot{\theta}\dot{\phi})\mathbf{e}_\phi.
\end{aligned} \tag{2-52}$$

## 2–4 Base vectors for generalized coordinates

Cylindrical and spherical coordinates are but two examples of generalized coordinates $q_1$, $q_2$, $q_3$, in terms of which one may desire to describe the motion of a particle. For the spherical coordinate system, for example,

$$q_1 = r, \qquad q_2 = \theta, \qquad \text{and} \qquad q_3 = \phi.$$

The steps which we took to obtain the expressions for the velocity and acceleration in cylindrical and spherical coordinates are generally applicable for any set of coordinates. Thus if

$$x = x(q_1, q_2, q_3) \qquad y = y(q_1, q_2, q_3), \qquad z = z(q_1, q_2, q_3) \qquad (2\text{–}53)$$

are the equations relating the cartesian coordinates to the generalized coordinates $q_1, q_2, q_3$, then the radius vector may be expressed as

$$\mathbf{r} = x(q_1, q_2, q_3)\mathbf{i} + y(q_1, q_2, q_3)\mathbf{j} + z(q_1, q_2, q_3)\mathbf{k}. \qquad (2\text{–}54)$$

We shall define the base vectors for the generalized coordinates analogously to Eqs. (2–14) and (2–15) for the cylindrical coordinates and the corresponding equations for the spherical coordinates. These base vectors, however, will not be normalized to be unit vectors.

The base vectors appropriate for the generalized coordinates $q_1, q_2, q_3$ are defined by

$$\mathbf{b}_1 = \frac{\partial \mathbf{r}}{\partial q_1} = h_1 \mathbf{e}_1, \qquad h_1 = \left| \frac{\partial \mathbf{r}}{\partial q_1} \right|, \qquad (2\text{–}55)$$

$$\mathbf{b}_2 = \frac{\partial \mathbf{r}}{\partial q_2} = h_2 \mathbf{e}_2, \qquad h_2 = \left| \frac{\partial \mathbf{r}}{\partial q_2} \right|, \qquad (2\text{–}56)$$

$$\mathbf{b}_3 = \frac{\partial \mathbf{r}}{\partial q_3} = h_3 \mathbf{e}_3, \qquad h_3 = \left| \frac{\partial \mathbf{r}}{\partial q_3} \right|. \qquad (2\text{–}57)$$

We note that the base vectors $\mathbf{b}_1$, $\mathbf{b}_2$, and $\mathbf{b}_3$ are not unit vectors. The reason for choosing them rather than the unit vectors

$$\mathbf{e}_i = \frac{\partial \mathbf{r}/\partial q_i}{|\partial \mathbf{r}/\partial q_i|}, \qquad i = 1, 2, 3, \qquad (2\text{–}58)$$

will become more apparent as the course develops. We shall generally find results to be expressible more concisely in terms of the base vectors $\mathbf{b}_i$. Where this is not the case, we shall utilize the unit vectors $\mathbf{e}_i$, which have other advantages.

In terms of their cartesian components, the base vectors defined above are specified by

$$\mathbf{b}_i = \frac{\partial x}{\partial q_i}\,\mathbf{i} + \frac{\partial y}{\partial q_i}\,\mathbf{j} + \frac{\partial z}{\partial q_i}\,\mathbf{k}. \qquad (2\text{–}59)$$

They have the magnitudes

$$h_i = \sqrt{\left(\frac{\partial x}{\partial q_i}\right)^2 + \left(\frac{\partial y}{\partial q_i}\right)^2 + \left(\frac{\partial z}{\partial q_i}\right)^2}. \qquad (2\text{–}60)$$

For the spherical coordinate system, for example, we find that

$$\mathbf{b}_1 = \mathbf{e}_r, \qquad \mathbf{b}_2 = r\mathbf{e}_\theta, \qquad \text{and} \qquad \mathbf{b}_3 = r \sin \theta \mathbf{e}_\phi.$$

That is, the base vectors have the magnitudes

$$h_1 = 1, \qquad h_2 = r, \qquad \text{and} \qquad h_3 = r \sin \theta.$$

The vector $\mathbf{b}_i$ points in the direction of the change in the position vector produced by an infinitesimal change in the generalized coordinate $q_i$, as can be seen from

$$\Delta \mathbf{r}_i = \frac{\partial \mathbf{r}}{\partial q_i} \, \Delta q_i.$$

Generally, the vectors $\mathbf{b}_i$ defined in Eq. (2–59) are not mutually perpendicular to each other. From our discussion of nonorthogonal base vectors, we realize that this is quite all right so long as the base vectors are not coplanar. The condition which assures us that they are not noncoplanar is the nonvanishing of their scalar triple product. That is,

$$\mathbf{b}_1 \cdot \mathbf{b}_2 \times \mathbf{b}_3 = \begin{vmatrix} \dfrac{\partial x}{\partial q_1} & \dfrac{\partial y}{\partial q_1} & \dfrac{\partial z}{\partial q_1} \\[2mm] \dfrac{\partial x}{\partial q_2} & \dfrac{\partial y}{\partial q_2} & \dfrac{\partial z}{\partial q_2} \\[2mm] \dfrac{\partial x}{\partial q_3} & \dfrac{\partial y}{\partial q_3} & \dfrac{\partial z}{\partial q_3} \end{vmatrix} \neq 0. \tag{2–61}$$

The determinant above is known as the *Jacobian* of the coordinates $x$, $y$, $z$ with respect to the generalized coordinates $q_1$, $q_2$, $q_3$. The Jacobian determinant is customarily designated by

$$\frac{\partial(x, y, z)}{\partial(q_1, q_2, q_3)} = \begin{vmatrix} \dfrac{\partial x}{\partial q_1} & \dfrac{\partial y}{\partial q_1} & \dfrac{\partial z}{\partial q_1} \\[2mm] \dfrac{\partial x}{\partial q_2} & \dfrac{\partial y}{\partial q_2} & \dfrac{\partial z}{\partial q_2} \\[2mm] \dfrac{\partial x}{\partial q_3} & \dfrac{\partial y}{\partial q_3} & \dfrac{\partial z}{\partial q_3} \end{vmatrix}. \tag{2–62}$$

Equation (2–61) is thus expressed by

$$\frac{\partial(x, y, z)}{\partial(q_1, q_2, q_3)} \neq 0.$$

This is also the necessary and sufficient condition that Eqs. (2–53) be soluble for the generalized coordinates $q_i$ as functions of the cartesian coordinates $x$, $y$, and $z$; in other words, that there be a one-to-one correspondence between the values of $x$, $y$, $z$, and the values of $q_1$, $q_2$, and $q_3$.

As we discussed in Section 1–5, in dealing with a set of nonorthogonal or unnormalized base vectors there is also a set of reciprocal base vectors which we must consider. When the base vectors $\mathbf{b}_i$ are orthogonal, that is, when we are utilizing a set of orthogonal curvilinear generalized coordinates, the reciprocal vectors are readily obtained. From Eq. (1–36) defining the reciprocal base vectors, we know that the reciprocal vectors of an orthogonal set of base vectors are parallel to the base vectors. From Eq. (1–37) it thus follows that, if for an orthogonal set of base vectors we set

$$\mathbf{b}_i = h_i \mathbf{e}_i, \tag{2–63}$$

where the $\mathbf{e}_i$ are unit vectors, then the reciprocal vectors are expressed by

$$\boldsymbol{b}_i = \frac{1}{h_i} \mathbf{e}_i = \frac{1}{h_i^2} \mathbf{b}_i. \tag{2–64}$$

When the base vectors are not orthogonal, the situation is somewhat more complicated. We nevertheless find that we can circumvent the use of Eqs. (1–36) which define the reciprocal base vectors. Equations (1–36) are the solutions to Eqs. (1–37). It should be clear that these solutions are unique and that therefore any set of vectors whose scalar products with the $\mathbf{b}_i$ satisfy Eqs. (1–37) must necessarily be the reciprocal vectors.

Now the generalized coordinates $q_1$, $q_2$, and $q_3$ are independent coordinates, whence it follows that

$$\frac{\partial q_1}{\partial q_1} = \frac{\partial q_2}{\partial q_2} = \frac{\partial q_3}{\partial q_3} = 1$$

and

$$\frac{\partial q_1}{\partial q_2} = \frac{\partial q_1}{\partial q_3} = \frac{\partial q_2}{\partial q_1} = \frac{\partial q_2}{\partial q_3} = \frac{\partial q_3}{\partial q_1} = \frac{\partial q_3}{\partial q_2} = 0,$$

or

$$\frac{\partial q_i}{\partial q_j} = \begin{cases} 0 & i \neq j, \\ 1 & i = j. \end{cases} \tag{2–65}$$

But considering the $q_i$'s to be functions of $x$, $y$, and $z$, and $x$, $y$, and $z$ in turn to be functions of the $q_j$'s, it follows that

$$\frac{\partial q_i}{\partial q_j} = \frac{\partial q_i}{\partial x} \frac{\partial x}{\partial q_j} + \frac{\partial q_i}{\partial y} \frac{\partial y}{\partial q_j} + \frac{\partial q_i}{\partial z} \frac{\partial z}{\partial q_j} = \delta_{ij}. \tag{2–66}$$

Comparing Eq. (2–66) with Eq. (1–38), we find that the reciprocal vectors are given by

$$\boldsymbol{b}_i = \frac{\partial q_i}{\partial x} \mathbf{i} + \frac{\partial q_i}{\partial y} \mathbf{j} + \frac{\partial q_i}{\partial z} \mathbf{k}. \tag{2–67}$$

The expression on the right-hand side of this equation is referred to as the gradient of $q_i$. It is denoted by $\boldsymbol{\nabla} q_i$; that is,

$$\operatorname{grad} q_i = \boldsymbol{\nabla} q_i.$$

In Section 2–6 we shall arrive at the identical result

$$\boldsymbol{b}_i = \boldsymbol{\nabla} q_i \tag{2–68}$$

on the basis of more fundamental geometric considerations.

▶ As an example, we consider the paraboloidal coordinates which are defined by the equations

$$x = \eta\xi\cos\phi, \qquad y = \eta\xi\sin\phi, \qquad \text{and} \qquad z = \tfrac{1}{2}(\xi^2 - \eta^2),$$

or

$$\xi^2 = \sqrt{x^2 + y^2 + z^2} + z, \quad \eta^2 = \sqrt{x^2 + y^2 + z^2} - z, \quad \text{and} \quad \phi = \tan^{-1}\frac{y}{x}.$$

Using Eq. (2–59) yields the base vectors

$$\mathbf{b}_1 = \frac{\partial \mathbf{r}}{\partial \xi} = \eta\cos\phi\,\mathbf{i} + \eta\sin\phi\,\mathbf{j} + \xi\mathbf{k},$$

$$\mathbf{b}_2 = \frac{\partial \mathbf{r}}{\partial \eta} = \xi\cos\phi\,\mathbf{i} + \xi\sin\phi\,\mathbf{j} - \eta\mathbf{k},$$

$$\mathbf{b}_3 = \frac{\partial \mathbf{r}}{\partial \phi} = -\eta\xi\sin\phi\,\mathbf{i} + \eta\xi\cos\phi\,\mathbf{j}.$$

These base vectors are mutually orthogonal and have the magnitudes $h_1 = h_2 = \sqrt{\eta^2 + \xi^2}$ and $h_3 = \eta\xi$. Equation (2–64) yields the reciprocal base vectors

$$\boldsymbol{b}^1 = \frac{\eta\cos\phi}{\eta^2 + \xi^2}\,\mathbf{i} + \frac{\eta\sin\phi}{\eta^2 + \xi^2}\,\mathbf{j} + \frac{\xi}{\eta^2 + \xi^2}\,\mathbf{k},$$

$$\boldsymbol{b}^2 = \frac{\xi\cos\phi}{\eta^2 + \xi^2}\,\mathbf{i} + \frac{\xi\sin\phi}{\eta^2 + \xi^2}\,\mathbf{j} - \frac{\eta}{\eta^2 + \xi^2}\,\mathbf{k},$$

$$\boldsymbol{b}^3 = -\frac{\sin\phi}{\eta\xi}\,\mathbf{i} + \frac{\cos\phi}{\eta\xi}\,\mathbf{j}.$$

These results for the reciprocal base vectors are also obtainable through the use of Eq. (2–67). For example, from

$$\boldsymbol{b}^1 = \frac{\partial\xi}{\partial x}\,\mathbf{i} + \frac{\partial\xi}{\partial y}\,\mathbf{j} + \frac{\partial\xi}{\partial z}\,\mathbf{k},$$

we obtain the same result, since

$$\frac{\partial\xi}{\partial x} = \frac{1}{2\xi}\frac{\partial\xi^2}{\partial x} = \frac{x}{2\xi\sqrt{x^2 + y^2 + z^2}} = \frac{\eta\cos\phi}{\xi^2 + \eta^2},$$

$$\frac{\partial\xi}{\partial y} = \frac{1}{2\xi}\frac{\partial\xi^2}{\partial y} = \frac{y}{2\xi\sqrt{x^2 + y^2 + z^2}} = \frac{\xi\sin\phi}{\xi^2 + \eta^2},$$

$$\frac{\partial\xi}{\partial z} = \frac{1}{2\xi}\frac{\partial\xi^2}{\partial z} = \frac{z}{2\xi\sqrt{x^2 + y^2 + z^2}} + 1 = \frac{\xi}{\xi^2 + \eta^2}. \ ◀$$

## 2–5 Velocity and acceleration in generalized coordinates

In terms of the base vectors $\mathbf{b}_i$ and their reciprocal vectors $\boldsymbol{b}_i$, the velocity of a particle may be expressed either as

$$\mathbf{v} = \sum_{i=1}^{3} (\mathbf{v} \cdot \boldsymbol{b}_i)\mathbf{b}_i = \sum_{i=1}^{3} v_i^{\star}\mathbf{b}_i \tag{2–69}$$

or

$$\mathbf{v} = \sum_{i=1}^{3} (\mathbf{v} \cdot \mathbf{b}_i)\boldsymbol{b}_i = \sum_{i=1}^{3} v_i\boldsymbol{b}_i, \tag{2–70}$$

where

$$v_i = \mathbf{v} \cdot \mathbf{b}_i \quad \text{and} \quad v_i^{\star} = \mathbf{v} \cdot \boldsymbol{b}_i.$$

In terms of the expressions for the vectors $\mathbf{b}_i$ we obtain for the $v_i$, referred to as the *covariant* components of the velocity, the expression

$$v_i = \dot{x} \frac{\partial x}{\partial q_i} + \dot{y} \frac{\partial y}{\partial q_i} + \dot{z} \frac{\partial z}{\partial q_i} . \tag{2–71}$$

From a knowledge of the functional dependence of the cartesian coordinates on the generalized coordinates, we may readily express the cartesian components of the velocity appearing in this latter equation in terms of the generalized coordinates and their time derivatives. We find that

$$\dot{x} = \sum_{i=1}^{3} \frac{\partial x}{\partial q_i} \dot{q}_i, \qquad \dot{y} = \sum_{i=1}^{3} \frac{\partial y}{\partial q_i} \dot{q}_i, \qquad \dot{z} = \sum_{i=1}^{3} \frac{\partial z}{\partial q_i} \dot{q}_i. \tag{2–72}$$

We note that in these equations $\dot{x}$, $\dot{y}$, and $\dot{z}$ are explicit functions of the generalized coordinates and their time derivatives. Hence we obtain from them the result

$$\frac{\partial \dot{x}}{\partial \dot{q}_i} = \frac{\partial x}{\partial q_i}, \qquad \frac{\partial \dot{y}}{\partial \dot{q}_i} = \frac{\partial y}{\partial q_i}, \qquad \frac{\partial \dot{z}}{\partial \dot{q}_i} = \frac{\partial z}{\partial q_i} . \tag{2–73}$$

Thus, replacing the partial derivatives in Eq. (2–71) by their equivalent partial derivative as furnished by Eq. (2–73), we find Eq. (2–71) to be expressible in the very concise form

$$v_i = \dot{x} \frac{\partial \dot{x}}{\partial \dot{q}_i} + \dot{y} \frac{\partial \dot{y}}{\partial \dot{q}_i} + \dot{z} \frac{\partial \dot{z}}{\partial \dot{q}_i} = \frac{\partial}{\partial \dot{q}_i} \left( \frac{1}{2}v^2 \right), \tag{2–74}$$

where $v^2 = \dot{x}^2 + \dot{y}^2 + \dot{z}^2$. Equation (2–74) tells us that the covariant components of velocity are equal to the partial derivatives of one-half the velocity squared with respect to the $\dot{q}_i$. Before we perform the differentiations, $\frac{1}{2}v^2$ is to be expressed as a function of the generalized coordinates $q_i$ and their time derivatives $\dot{q}_i$.

▶ For example, consider the spherical coordinates for which

$$\tfrac{1}{2}v^2 = \tfrac{1}{2}(\dot{r}^2 + r^2\dot{\theta}^2 + r^2 \sin^2 \theta \dot{\phi}^2),$$

and for which hence Eq. (2–74) yields the covariant components of velocity

$$v_1 = \frac{\partial}{\partial \dot{r}}\left(\frac{1}{2}v^2\right) = \dot{r}, \quad v_2 = \frac{\partial}{\partial \dot{\theta}}\left(\frac{1}{2}v^2\right) = r^2\dot{\theta}, \quad v_3 = \frac{\partial}{\partial \dot{\phi}}\left(\frac{1}{2}v^2\right) = r^2 \sin^2 \theta \dot{\phi}. ◀$$

The $v_i^\star$'s are referred to as the *contravariant components of the velocity*. Through the use of Eq. (2–67), we arrive at the result

$$v_i^\star = \mathbf{v} \cdot \mathbf{b}_i = \frac{\partial q_i}{\partial x}\dot{x} + \frac{\partial q_i}{\partial y}\dot{y} + \frac{\partial q_i}{\partial z}\dot{z} = \dot{q}_i. \tag{2–75}$$

The contravariant components of velocity are also referred to as the *generalized velocities*. In contradistinction, the covariant components of velocity multiplied by the mass of the particle (cf. Section 4–2) are referred to as the generalized particle momenta (cf. Section 5–2),

$$p_i = mv_i.$$

Analogously, we obtain the expression for the acceleration, which, however, we shall require only as expressed by

$$\mathbf{a} = \sum_{i=1}^{3} (\mathbf{a} \cdot \mathbf{b}_i)\mathbf{b}_i = \sum_{i=1}^{3} a_i \mathbf{b}_i, \tag{2–76}$$

where the *covariant components of the acceleration* are expressed as

$$a_i = \mathbf{a} \cdot \mathbf{b}_i = \ddot{x}\frac{\partial x}{\partial q_i} + \ddot{y}\frac{\partial y}{\partial q_i} + \ddot{z}\frac{\partial z}{\partial q_i}.$$

This last equation for the scalar product of $\mathbf{a}$ with the base vector $\mathbf{b}_i$ may be rewritten in an extremely useful form with the help of Eq. (2–73). Setting, for example,

$$\ddot{x}\frac{\partial x}{\partial q_i} = \frac{d}{dt}\left(\dot{x}\frac{\partial x}{\partial q_i}\right) - \dot{x}\frac{d}{dt}\frac{\partial x}{\partial q_i} = \frac{d}{dt}\left(\dot{x}\frac{\partial x}{\partial q_i}\right) - \dot{x}\frac{\partial \dot{x}}{\partial q_i},$$

and realizing once more that

$$\frac{\partial x}{\partial q_i} = \frac{\partial \dot{x}}{\partial \dot{q}_i},$$

we obtain

$$\ddot{x}\frac{\partial x}{\partial q_i} = \frac{d}{dt}\left(\dot{x}\frac{\partial \dot{x}}{\partial \dot{q}_i}\right) - \dot{x}\frac{\partial \dot{x}}{\partial q_i} = \frac{d}{dt}\frac{\partial}{\partial \dot{q}_i}\left(\frac{1}{2}\dot{x}^2\right) - \frac{\partial}{\partial q_i}\left(\frac{1}{2}\dot{x}^2\right). \tag{2–77}$$

With analogous expressions for $\ddot{y}(\partial y/\partial q_i)$ and $\ddot{z}(\partial z/\partial q_i)$, we can thus set

$$
\begin{aligned}
a_i &= \frac{d}{dt}\frac{\partial}{\partial \dot{q}_i}\left(\frac{\dot{x}^2 + \dot{y}^2 + \dot{z}^2}{2}\right) - \frac{\partial}{\partial q_i}\left(\frac{\dot{x}^2 + \dot{y}^2 + \dot{z}^2}{2}\right) \\
&= \frac{d}{dt}\frac{\partial}{\partial \dot{q}_i}\left(\frac{1}{2}v^2\right) - \frac{\partial}{\partial q_i}\left(\frac{1}{2}v^2\right).
\end{aligned}
\tag{2–78}
$$

▶ As an illustration of the use of Eq. (2–78), we shall once more obtain the components of the acceleration in cylindrical coordinates. From Eq. (2–12) or Eq. (2–18), we obtain

$$
v^2 = \dot{\rho}^2 + \rho^2\dot{\phi}^2 + \dot{z}^2,
$$

and hence

$$
\begin{aligned}
a_1 &= \mathbf{a}\cdot\mathbf{e}_\rho = \frac{d}{dt}\frac{\partial}{\partial \dot{\rho}}\left(\frac{\dot{\rho}^2 + \rho^2\dot{\phi}^2 + \dot{z}^2}{2}\right) - \frac{\partial}{\partial \rho}\left(\frac{\dot{\rho}^2 + \rho^2\dot{\phi}^2 + \dot{z}^2}{2}\right) \\
&= \ddot{\rho} - \rho\dot{\phi}^2, \\
a_2 &= \mathbf{a}\cdot(\rho\mathbf{e}_\phi) = \frac{d}{dt}(\rho^2\dot{\phi}) = \rho^2\ddot{\phi} + 2\rho\dot{\rho}\dot{\phi}, \\
a_3 &= \mathbf{a}\cdot\mathbf{k} = \frac{d}{dt}\dot{z} = \ddot{z},
\end{aligned}
$$

in agreement with the results obtained previously for

$$
\mathbf{a}\cdot\mathbf{e}_\rho = \mathbf{a}\cdot\mathbf{b}_1, \qquad \mathbf{a}\cdot\mathbf{e}_\phi = \frac{1}{\rho}\mathbf{a}\cdot\mathbf{b}_2, \qquad \mathbf{a}\cdot\mathbf{k} = \mathbf{a}\cdot\mathbf{b}_3. ◀
$$

The material of the last two sections is of such importance that we should like to summarize the steps to be taken for finding the base vectors, the velocity, and the acceleration of a particle in generalized coordinates.

Given the relations between the cartesian coordinates and the generalized coordinates, the base vectors are obtained through the use of Eqs. (2–59) as

$$
\mathbf{b}_i = \frac{\partial x}{\partial q_i}\mathbf{i} + \frac{\partial y}{\partial q_i}\mathbf{j} + \frac{\partial z}{\partial q_i}\mathbf{k},
$$

and for time-independent coordinate transformations, the reciprocal base vectors are obtained through use of Eq. (2–67) as

$$
\mathbf{b}_i = \frac{\partial q_i}{\partial x}\mathbf{i} + \frac{\partial q_i}{\partial y}\mathbf{j} + \frac{\partial q_i}{\partial z}\mathbf{k}.
$$

The contravariant velocities for time-independent coordinate transformations are simply the $\dot{q}_i$'s,

$$
\overset{\star}{v_i} = \dot{q}_i,
$$

and the covariant components of the velocity are given by

$$v_i = \frac{\partial}{\partial \dot{q}_i}\left(\frac{1}{2}\,v^2\right),$$

where $v^2$ should be expressed in terms of the generalized coordinates $q_i$ and the generalized velocities $\dot{q}_i$. This dependence may be obtained from

$$v^2 = \dot{x}^2 + \dot{y}^2 + \dot{z}^2.$$

In dealing with orthogonal curvilinear coordinates, $v^2$ may also be obtained very simply from the fact that

$$\mathbf{v} = \frac{d\mathbf{r}}{dt} = \sum_{i=1}^{3}\frac{\partial \mathbf{r}}{\partial q_i}\,\dot{q}_i = \sum_{i=1}^{3}\dot{q}_i\mathbf{b}_i = \sum_{i=1}^{3}\dot{q}_i h_i \mathbf{e}_i. \tag{2-79}$$

That is,

$$v^2 = \sum_{i=1}^{3} h_i^2(\dot{q}_i)^2. \tag{2-80}$$

The covariant components of acceleration are obtained through the use of the relation

$$a_i = \frac{d}{dt}\frac{\partial}{\partial \dot{q}_i}\left(\frac{1}{2}\,v^2\right) - \frac{\partial}{\partial q_i}\left(\frac{1}{2}\,v^2\right).$$

## 2–6 Differential geometry of curvilinear coordinates

Let $\phi(x, y, z)$ be a single-valued, continuous function having continuous partial derivatives. The equation

$$\phi(x, y, z) = \text{const} \tag{2-81}$$

then defines a surface in three-dimensional space. Similarly, the three equations

$$q_1(x, y, z) = c_1, \qquad q_2(z, x, y) = c_2, \qquad q_3(x, y, z) = c_3, \tag{2-82}$$

where the $q_i$'s are the generalized coordinates, define three surfaces which pass through the point whose cartesian coordinates are

$$\begin{aligned}
x_0 &= x(q_1 = c_1, q_2 = c_2, q_3 = c_3), \\
y_0 &= y(c_1, c_2, c_3), \\
z_0 &= z(c_1, c_2, c_3).
\end{aligned} \tag{2-83}$$

The intersection of the $q_1$- and the $q_2$-surfaces,

$$q_1(x, y, z) = c_1, \qquad q_2(x, y, z) = c_2,$$

defines a curve along which $q_3$ varies. This curve is referred to as the $q_3$-*curve*.

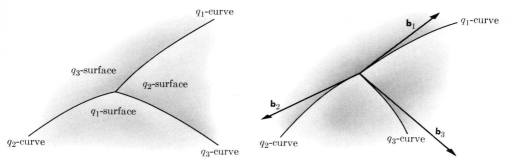

FIG. 2–7. Coordinate surfaces and curves.   FIG. 2–8. Generalized base vectors.

Analogously, there exist two other curves, the $q_1$-*curve* which is the intersection of the $q_2$- and $q_3$-surfaces, and the $q_2$-*curve* which is the intersection of the $q_1$- and $q_3$-surfaces. (See Fig. 2–7.)

The coordinate base vector $\mathbf{b}_i$ defined in Eq. (2–59) points in the direction of the change in the position vector produced by an infinitesimal change in $q_i$. It is thus tangent to the $q_i$-curve at the point $(x_0, y_0, z_0)$, as the head of the position vector remains on the $q_i$-curve while $q_i$ varies. (Fig. 2–8.)

The vectors $\boldsymbol{b}_i$ reciprocal to the base vectors $\mathbf{b}_i$ can be shown to be perpendicular to the $q_i$-surfaces (Fig. 2–9). For example, we know that the vector

$$\boldsymbol{b}_1 = \frac{\mathbf{b}_2 \times \mathbf{b}_3}{\mathbf{b}_1 \cdot \mathbf{b}_2 \times \mathbf{b}_3} \tag{2–84}$$

is perpendicular to the vectors $\mathbf{b}_2$ and $\mathbf{b}_3$. But both of these latter vectors are tangent to the $q_1$-surface. This follows from the fact that the vector $\mathbf{b}_2$, being tangent to the $q_2$-curve, which is the intersection of the $q_1$- and $q_3$-surfaces, is also tangent to these two surfaces. Similarly, the vector $\mathbf{b}_3$ is tangent to the $q_1$- and $q_2$-surfaces. Now, $\boldsymbol{b}_1$ is a vector perpendicular to the plane of the vectors $\mathbf{b}_2$ and $\mathbf{b}_3$ at the point $(x_0, y_0, z_0)$. But the plane of $\mathbf{b}_2$ and $\mathbf{b}_3$, like the vectors which determine it, is itself tangent to the $q_1$-surface at the point $(x_0, y_0, z_0)$. The vector $\boldsymbol{b}_1$ is thus normal to the $q_1$-surface.

The vector $\boldsymbol{b}_1$, defined by Eq. (2–84), may be directly related to the normal to the $q_1$-surface. To find this normal, consider the change in $q_1$, when $x$, $y$, and $z$ change by the infinitesimal amounts $\Delta x$, $\Delta y$, and $\Delta z$. The resulting infinitesimal change in $q_1$ is

$$\Delta q_1 = \frac{\partial q_1}{\partial x} \, \Delta x + \frac{\partial q_1}{\partial y} \, \Delta y + \frac{\partial q_1}{\partial z} \, \Delta z, \tag{2–85}$$

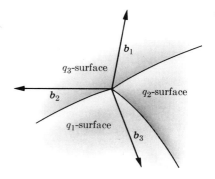

FIG. 2–9. Generalized inverse base vectors.

which is an expression that can be thought of as the scalar product of the vector

$$\Delta\mathbf{r} = \Delta x\mathbf{i} + \Delta y\mathbf{j} + \Delta z\mathbf{k} \qquad (2\text{--}86)$$

and the vector

$$\nabla q_1 = \frac{\partial q_1}{\partial x}\,\mathbf{i} + \frac{\partial q_1}{\partial y}\,\mathbf{j} + \frac{\partial q_1}{\partial z}\,\mathbf{k}. \qquad (2\text{--}87)$$

That is,

$$\Delta q_1 = \Delta\mathbf{r} \cdot \nabla q_1. \qquad (2\text{--}88)$$

The gradient $\nabla q_1$ of $q_1$ was defined once before. The del operator in cartesian coordinates is defined by

$$\nabla = \mathbf{i}\,\frac{\partial}{\partial x} + \mathbf{j}\,\frac{\partial}{\partial y} + \mathbf{k}\,\frac{\partial}{\partial z}. \qquad (2\text{--}89)$$

If we choose the new point $(x + \Delta x, y + \Delta y, z + \Delta z)$ to be one that also lies in the surface $q_1(x, y, z) = c_1$, that is, if

$$q_1(x + \Delta x, y + \Delta y, z + \Delta z) = c_1,$$

then obviously we have

$$\Delta q_1 = 0.$$

It follows, therefore, that in the limit as $|\Delta\mathbf{r}| \to 0$ along some curve in the $q_1$-surface, or as $\Delta\mathbf{r}/|\Delta\mathbf{r}|$ approaches the unit tangent to any curve in the $q_1$-surface,

$$\frac{\Delta q_1}{|\Delta\mathbf{r}|} \to \mathbf{e}_t \cdot \nabla q_1,$$

where $\mathbf{e}_t$ is that unit tangent. Since for all points in the surface

$$\frac{\Delta q_1}{|\Delta\mathbf{r}|} = 0,$$

we find that

$$\mathbf{e}_t \cdot \nabla q_1 = 0.$$

Hence it follows that $\nabla q_1$ is normal to the $q_1$-surface.

We have already shown that the reciprocal vectors are expressible as

$$\boldsymbol{b}_i = \nabla q_i$$

for time-independent coordinate transformations.

We conclude our present discussion of curvilinear coordinates by deriving some useful expressions for orthogonal curvilinear coordinate systems.

(a) *Arc length.* The arc length $\Delta s$ is defined by

$$\Delta s = |\Delta\mathbf{r}| = |\Delta x\mathbf{i} + \Delta y\mathbf{j} + \Delta z\mathbf{k}|.$$

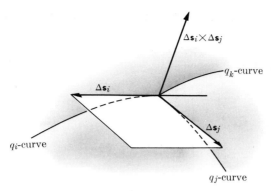

FIG. 2–10. Infinitesimal surface area.

For orthogonal curvilinear coordinates,

$$\Delta \mathbf{r} = \Delta q_1 \mathbf{b}_1 + \Delta q_2 \mathbf{b}_2 + \Delta q_3 \mathbf{b}_3$$
$$= h_1 \, \Delta q_1 \mathbf{e}_1 + h_2 \, \Delta q_2 \mathbf{e}_2 + h_3 \, \Delta q_3 \mathbf{e}_3, \tag{2–90}$$

whence

$$(\Delta \mathbf{r})^2 = (h_1 \, \Delta q_1)^2 + (h_2 \, \Delta q_2)^2 + (h_3 \, \Delta q_3)^2$$

or

$$(\Delta s)^2 = \sum_{i=1}^{3} h_i^2 (\Delta q_i)^2 \tag{2–91}$$

where $h_1$, $h_2$, $h_3$ are referred to as the *scale factors*.

(b) *Infinitesimal surface area.* In general, the area of the parallelogram defined by two vectors $d\mathbf{s}_1$ and $d\mathbf{s}_2$ is given by

$$\text{Area} = |d\mathbf{s}_1 \times d\mathbf{s}_2|.$$

Specifically, in many applications one is interested in an infinitesimal surface area which lies on one of the coordinate surfaces, say the $q_k$-surface, defined by the arc lengths $\Delta s_i$, $\Delta s_j$ directed along the tangents to the $q_i$- and $q_j$-curves, where $i \neq j \neq k$ (Fig. 2–10). The $\Delta \mathbf{s}_i$ and $\Delta \mathbf{s}_j$ are, respectively, the changes $\Delta q_i \, \mathbf{b}_i$ and $\Delta q_j \, \mathbf{b}_j$ in the position vector. The area of the parallelogram formed by the vectors $\Delta \mathbf{s}_i$ and $\Delta \mathbf{s}_j$ is given by

$$|\Delta \mathbf{S}_k| = |\Delta q_i \mathbf{b}_i \times \Delta q_i \mathbf{b}_j| = h_i h_j \, \Delta q_i \, \Delta q_j, \qquad i, j, k = 1, 2, 3, \quad i \neq j \neq k. \tag{2–92}$$

(c) *Infinitesimal volume.* Many a volume integral can be simplified if a proper choice of coordinates is made. For any curvilinear coordinate system, the infinitesimal volume element is given by the scalar triple product of the vectors $\Delta\mathbf{s}_i$. That is,

$$\Delta V = \Delta q_1\mathbf{b}_1 \cdot \Delta q_2\mathbf{b}_2 \times \Delta q_3\mathbf{b}_3$$

$$= \Delta q_1 \, \Delta q_2 \, \Delta q_3 \, \frac{\partial(x, y, z)}{\partial(q_1, q_2, q_3)} \cdot \tag{2-93}$$

For an orthogonal curvilinear coordinate system, this reduces to

$$\Delta V = h_1 h_2 h_3 \, \Delta q_1 \, \Delta q_2 \, \Delta q_3. \tag{2-94}$$

For example, the infinitesimal volume element in spherical coordinates is

$$dV = r^2 \sin\theta \, dr \, d\theta \, d\phi.$$

(d) *The gradient in orthogonal curvilinear coordinates.* The gradient of a scalar function was defined by Eq. (2–87) for cartesian coordinates. In orthogonal curvilinear coordinates it may be expressed in terms of the unit base vectors $\mathbf{e}_i$. That is,

$$\boldsymbol{\nabla}\phi = (\mathbf{e}_1 \cdot \boldsymbol{\nabla}\phi)\mathbf{e}_1 + (\mathbf{e}_2 \cdot \boldsymbol{\nabla}\phi)\mathbf{e}_2 + (\mathbf{e}_3 \cdot \boldsymbol{\nabla}\phi)\mathbf{e}_3.$$

Since

$$\mathbf{e}_i \cdot \boldsymbol{\nabla}\phi = \frac{1}{h_i} \, \mathbf{b}_i \cdot \boldsymbol{\nabla}\phi$$

$$= \frac{1}{h_i} \left( \frac{\partial\phi}{\partial x} \frac{\partial x}{\partial q_i} + \frac{\partial\phi}{\partial y} \frac{\partial y}{\partial q_i} + \frac{\partial\phi}{\partial z} \frac{\partial z}{\partial q_i} \right) = \frac{1}{h_i} \frac{\partial\phi}{\partial q_i},$$

it follows that for orthogonal curvilinear coordinates

$$\boldsymbol{\nabla}\phi = \sum_{i=1}^{3} \frac{1}{h_i} \frac{\partial\phi}{\partial q_i} \, \mathbf{e}_i. \tag{2-95}$$

In spherical coordinates the gradient of the scalar function $\Psi$ is found to be given by

$$\boldsymbol{\nabla}\Psi = \frac{\partial\Psi}{\partial r} \, \mathbf{e}_r + \frac{1}{r} \frac{\partial\Psi}{\partial\theta} \, \mathbf{e}_\theta + \frac{1}{r\sin\theta} \frac{\partial\Psi}{\partial\phi} \, \mathbf{e}_\phi.$$

## 2–7 Motion along a specified curve

The motion of a particle along a specified curve is a special case of what is called constrained motion, about which we shall have more to say in later sections. At present, we should like to analyze the motion along a specified curve in terms of the parameter $s$, where $s$ is the distance, measured along the curve, of the point at which the particle is located from a fixed point on the curve chosen as the origin. In parametric form, a curve may be specified by the three equations

$$x = x(s), \qquad y = y(s), \qquad \text{and} \qquad z = z(s),$$

or

$$\mathbf{r}(s) = x(s)\mathbf{i} + y(s)\mathbf{j} + z(s)\mathbf{k}. \tag{2-96}$$

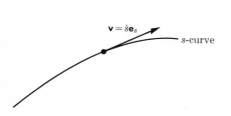

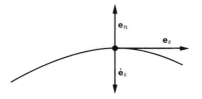

$\mathbf{e}_n$ =principal normal to the curve

FIG. 2–11. Motion along a specified          FIG. 2–12.  Unit tangent and principal
curve.                                        unit normal to a space curve.

Thus in terms of $s$ and its time derivative, the velocity is found to be given by

$$\mathbf{v} = \dot{\mathbf{r}} = \frac{\partial \mathbf{r}}{\partial s}\, \dot{s} = \dot{s}\left(\frac{\partial x}{\partial s}\,\mathbf{i} + \frac{\partial y}{\partial s}\,\mathbf{j} + \frac{\partial z}{\partial s}\,\mathbf{k}\right). \tag{2-97}$$

The vector

$$\frac{\partial \mathbf{r}}{\partial s} = \frac{\partial x}{\partial s}\,\mathbf{i} + \frac{\partial y}{\partial s}\,\mathbf{j} + \frac{\partial z}{\partial s}\,\mathbf{k} = \mathbf{e}_s$$

is the unit vector tangent to the curve at the point $[x(s),\, y(s),\, z(s)]$ (Fig. 2–11).
It points in the direction of increasing $s$.  That $\mathbf{e}_s$ is a unit vector follows from
the fact that

$$(\Delta s)^2 = (\Delta x)^2 + (\Delta y)^2 + (\Delta z)^2.$$

Differentiating the velocity expressed in the form $\mathbf{v} = \dot{s}\mathbf{e}_s$ yields the acceleration

$$\mathbf{a} = \ddot{s}\mathbf{e}_s + \dot{s}\dot{\mathbf{e}}_s. \tag{2-98}$$

Since $\mathbf{e}_s$ is a unit vector indicating the direction of $\mathbf{v}$, it follows from our discussion in Section 1–7 that $\dot{\mathbf{e}}_s$ is a vector perpendicular to $\mathbf{e}_s$.  Choosing $\mathbf{e}_n$ as the unit vector pointing in the direction $-\dot{\mathbf{e}}_s$ (Fig. 2–12) permits us to set

$$\dot{\mathbf{e}}_s = -\frac{\dot{s}}{\rho}\,\mathbf{e}_n, \tag{2-99}$$

where $\rho$, as yet undetermined, will be shown to be the radius of curvature of the curve at the point $[x(s),\, y(s),\, z(s)]$.  With this expression for $\mathbf{e}_s$, the acceleration of the particle is given by

$$\mathbf{a} = \ddot{s}\mathbf{e}_s - \frac{\dot{s}^2}{\rho}\,\mathbf{e}_n. \tag{2-100}$$

This equation tells us that the acceleration of a particle moving along a specified curve can be decomposed into a component $\ddot{s}$, tangential to the curve, and a normal component $-\dot{s}^2/\rho$ (Fig. 2–13).

In order to obtain a clearer understanding of $\rho$, we consider the motion of the particle at a time $t$ when the particle is located at the point $P$ specified by

$\mathbf{r} = \mathbf{r}(t)$, and is moving with a velocity $\mathbf{v}(t)$ and an acceleration $\mathbf{a}(t)$. The position of the point $Q$ at which the particle is located at a time $\Delta t$ later is approximately represented by the point $P'$, specified by

$$\mathbf{r}(t + \Delta t) = \mathbf{r}(t) + \mathbf{v}(t)\,\Delta t, \tag{2--101}$$

and the velocity of the particle at $Q$ is approximated by

$$\mathbf{v}(t + \Delta t) = \mathbf{v}(t) + \mathbf{a}(t)\,\Delta t. \tag{2--102}$$

The points $P$ and $P'$ and the approximate velocity vector given by Eq. (2–102) all lie in the plane of the vectors $\mathbf{v}(t)$ and $\mathbf{a}(t)$. Figure 2–14 shows the points $P$ and $P'$, the actual path followed by the particle, and point $Q$, the actual position of the particle at the time $t + \Delta t$.

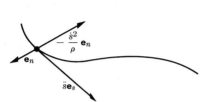

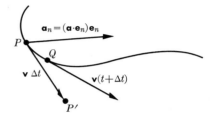

FIG. 2–13. Tangential and normal components of the acceleration.

FIG. 2–14. Approximate motion in the osculating plane.

In the plane of $Q$ and the velocity vector $\mathbf{v}(t)$ we can draw through the point $Q$ and tangent to $\mathbf{v}(t)$ at $P$ a circle which, in the limit as $\Delta t$ approaches zero, will naturally approach a limiting circle. The points $Q$ and $P'$ also approach each other as $\Delta t$ approaches zero. Furthermore, the actual velocity at the time $t + \Delta t$ and the approximate value given by Eq. (2–102), which is a vector lying in the plane of $\mathbf{v}(t)$ and $\mathbf{a}(t)$, do so likewise. It follows, therefore, that the limiting circle is a circle in the plane of $\mathbf{v}(t)$ and $\mathbf{a}(t)$.

The plane of $\mathbf{v}(t)$ and $\mathbf{a}(t)$ is known as the *osculating plane*, and the radius of the limiting circle as the *radius of curvature* of the curve at the point $P$.

To see that $\rho$ as introduced above is the radius of the limiting circle, let us choose the origin of the coordinate system to coincide with the center of the limiting circle. The origin thus lies along the principal normal to the curve which is the normal to the curve in the osculating plane. Utilizing cylindrical coordinates with the $z$-axis perpendicular to the osculating plane, we find $P$ to be specified by

$$\mathbf{r} = \rho\mathbf{e}_\rho, \tag{2--103}$$

where $\rho$ presently is the radius of the limiting circle (Fig. 2–15) and

$$\mathbf{e}_\rho = \mathbf{e}_n.$$

The velocity which is tangent to the curve lies obviously in the osculating plane and, being tangent to the limiting circle, is expressed by

$$\mathbf{v} = \rho\dot{\mathbf{e}}_\rho = \rho\dot{\phi}\mathbf{e}_\phi = \dot{s}\mathbf{e}_s, \qquad (2\text{--}104)$$

where $\rho\dot{\phi} = \dot{s}$ and

$$\mathbf{e}_\phi = \mathbf{e}_s. \qquad (2\text{--}105)$$

Similarly, since the acceleration has components only along $\mathbf{e}_s$ and $\mathbf{e}_n$, it follows that

$$\mathbf{a} = \ddot{s}\mathbf{e}_s + \dot{s}\dot{\mathbf{e}}_s = \ddot{s}\mathbf{e}_s - \dot{s}\,\dot{\phi}\mathbf{e}_\rho = \ddot{s}\mathbf{e}_s - \frac{\dot{s}^2}{\rho}\,\mathbf{e}_n.$$

$$(2\text{--}106)$$

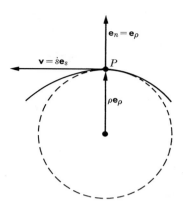

Fig. 2–15. Instantaneous motion in the osculating plane.

The choice of the radius of the limiting circle as the distance to the origin of the coordinate system from the point $P$ along the principal normal to the curve ensures that $\ddot{\rho}$ vanishes. We can thus understand Eq. (2–100) as the acceleration of a particle which for a fleeting moment is moving in a circle of radius $\rho$.

## Problems

2–1. Find the rectangular components of velocity and acceleration of the particle whose position vector is specified by the following:

(a) $\mathbf{r} = A \cos n\omega t\mathbf{i} + B \sin m\omega t\mathbf{j}$,     $n, m$ integers
(b) $\mathbf{r} = 3t\mathbf{i} - 4t\mathbf{j} + (t^2 + 3)\mathbf{k}$
(c) $\mathbf{r} = a(t - \sin \omega t)\mathbf{i} + a(1 - \cos \omega t)\mathbf{j}$
(d) $\mathbf{r} = (a_1 + b_1 t + c_1 t^2)\mathbf{i} + (a_2 + d_2 e^{-kt})\mathbf{j}$

2–2. Obtain the expressions for the polar components of the velocity and acceleration of the particle whose two-dimensional position vector is specified as below:

(a) $r = \dfrac{5}{2 - \cos \phi}$,     $\phi = \omega t$
(b) $r = A \cos \omega_1 t$,     $\phi = \omega_2 t$
(c) $r = a/t$,     $\phi = bt$

2–3. Find the velocity and acceleration of a particle whose motion along the circular spiral is specified in cylindrical coordinates by

$$\rho = a, \qquad \phi = bt, \qquad \text{and} \qquad z = -ct.$$

2–4. Find the spherical components of velocity and acceleration of the particle whose position vector is specified by

$$r = b, \qquad \theta = \theta_0 \cos \omega t, \qquad \text{and} \qquad \phi = \omega t.$$

2–5. Obtain the base vectors $\mathbf{b}_i$ and their reciprocal vectors $\mathbf{b}_i$, for the elliptic cylinderical coordinates defined by

$$x = \tfrac{1}{2}a \cosh q_1 \cos q_2,$$
$$y = \tfrac{1}{2}a \sinh q_1 \sin q_2,$$
$$z = z$$

or

$$\tfrac{1}{2}a(\cosh q_1 + \cos q_2) = \sqrt{(x + \tfrac{1}{2}a)^2 + y^2}$$

and

$$\tfrac{1}{2}a(\cosh q_1 - \cos q_2) = \sqrt{(x - \tfrac{1}{2}a)^2 + y^2}.$$

2–6. Obtain the expressions for the covariant components of the velocity and acceleration in (a) parabolic coordinates and (b) elliptic coordinates.

2–7. Given that the square of the velocity of a particle in terms of the generalized coordinates $q_1 = x$, $q_2 = \phi$ is

$$v^2 = ax^2 + bx\dot{x}\dot{\phi} \sin \phi + cx^2\dot{\phi}^2,$$

obtain the generalized covariant components of the velocity and the acceleration of the particle.

2–8. Repeat Problem 2–7 for $q_1 = \theta$, $q_2 = \phi$, given that

$$v^2 = a\dot{\theta}^2 + b\dot{\phi}^2 \cos^2 \theta + c\dot{\theta}^2 \sin^2 \theta + d\dot{\phi}\dot{\theta}.$$

2–9. Obtain the expressions for the acceleration of a particle in spherical coordinates through the use of Eq. (2–78).

2–10. Express the gradient of the scalar function $\Psi$ in (a) cylindrical coordinates, (b) spherical coordinates, (c) parabolic coordinates, and (d) elliptic coordinates.

2–11. Obtain the expressions for the radius of curvature of a plane curve in (a) rectangular coordinates and (b) polar coordinates.

2–12. Obtain the components of the velocity and acceleration which are tangential and normal to the curves followed by the particle of Problems 2–1(b) and 2–1(c).

2–13. Obtain the radius of curvature of the curves of Problems 2–1(b) and 2–1(c) at the point where the particle is located at time $t$.

2–14. Find the unit normal to the surface

$$\phi(x, y, z) = x^2 + 2xy - y^2 + yz + z^2 = 9$$

at the point $(2, 1, 1)$.

2–15. Obtain the unit tangent to the intersection of the surface of Problem 2–14 and the surface

$$\phi_2(x, y, z) = 3x^2 - xy + y^2 = 11$$

at the point $(2, 1, 1)$.

2–16. A particle moves along the intersection of the two surfaces of Problems 2–14 and 2–15 with constant speed $v_0$. Find the expression for the cartesian components of its velocity and acceleration at the point $(2, 1, 1)$.

2–17. (a) Show that

$$\frac{\partial \mathbf{b}_i}{\partial q_j} = \frac{\partial \mathbf{b}_j}{\partial q_i}$$

and

$$\mathbf{b}_k \cdot \frac{\partial \mathbf{b}_i}{\partial q_j} = \frac{\partial}{\partial q_j} (\mathbf{b}_k \cdot \mathbf{b}_i) - \mathbf{b}_i \cdot \frac{\partial \mathbf{b}_j}{\partial q_k} = \frac{\partial}{\partial q_j} (g_{ki}) - \mathbf{b}_i \cdot \frac{\partial \mathbf{b}_j}{\partial q_k},$$

where $g_{kj} = \mathbf{b}_k \cdot \mathbf{b}_j$. By continuing this process show that

$$\mathbf{b}_k \cdot \frac{\partial \mathbf{b}_i}{\partial q_j} = \frac{1}{2}\left[\frac{\partial g_{ik}}{\partial q_j} - \frac{\partial g_{ji}}{\partial q_k} + \frac{\partial g_{jk}}{\partial q_i}\right] = \Gamma_{ij,k},$$

where $\Gamma_{ij,k}$ is known as the *Christoffel symbol* of the first kind.    (b) The Christoffel symbol of the second kind is defined by the equation

$$\Gamma^l_{ij} = \sum_k g^{\star}_{lk}\Gamma_{ij,k}.$$

Show that

$$\frac{\partial \mathbf{b}_i}{\partial q_j} = \sum_k \Gamma^k_{ij}\mathbf{b}_k.$$

2–18. (a) The elements

$$A_{i,j} = \mathbf{b}_i \cdot \frac{\partial \mathbf{A}}{\partial q_j}$$

are referred to as the covariant derivatives of the covariant vector **A**. Show that

$$\mathbf{b}_i \cdot \frac{\partial \mathbf{A}}{\partial q_j} = \frac{\partial A_i}{\partial q_j} - \sum_k \Gamma^k_{ij}A_k,$$

where $A_i = \mathbf{A} \cdot \mathbf{b}_i$.

(b) The divergence of a vector is defined by

$$\mathrm{Div}\,\mathbf{A} = \nabla \cdot \mathbf{A} = \sum_{ij} g^{\star}_{ij} A_{i,j}.$$

Show that the divergence of a vector in orthogonal curvilinear coordinates is

$$\nabla \cdot \mathbf{A} = \frac{1}{h_1 h_2 h_3}\left[\frac{\partial}{\partial q_1}\left(\frac{h_2 h_3 A_1}{h_1}\right) + \frac{\partial}{\partial q_2}\left(\frac{h_1 h_3 A_2}{h_2}\right) + \frac{\partial}{\partial q_3}\left(\frac{h_1 h_2 A_3}{h_3}\right)\right].$$

# 3

# *Moving Coordinate Systems*

Frequently it is mathematically convenient to employ the kinematic description of the motion of a particle with respect to a moving coordinate system. The motion of the moving coordinate system may be translational, rotational, or a combination of both. In dealing with the problem of the bound motion of an electrically charged particle under the combined action of a central electric and weak magnetic field, for example, we shall find the kinematic description of the motion with respect to an appropriately rotating coordinate system to be approximately the same as the kinematic description of the motion of the charged particle with respect to a stationary coordinate system under the action of only the electric field, which is a much simpler problem. Furthermore, the description of the motion of a particle with respect to a coordinate system fixed on the surface of the earth involves quite naturally a coordinate system which is at the same time being translated and rotated in space. Since we shall postulate the fundamental laws of mechanics with respect to an inertial system which is a nonaccelerating, nonrotating coordinate system, we shall require for the application of these laws to specific problems a knowledge of the relationships between the kinematic descriptions of the motion of a particle with respect to coordinate systems which are in motion with respect to each other.

## 3–1 Translational motion

We consider first two coordinate systems whose orientations in space are observed to remain fixed. For simplicity we furthermore assume that their respective coordinate base vectors are parallel to each other. When this is not the case it requires only a transformation of one of them to a coordinate system which is parallel to the other. We shall consider such transformations in Section 3–4. The only motion these two coordinate systems can be observed to perform with respect to each other is the translational motion of one with respect to the other.

A single observer who sees the two coordinate systems is of course at liberty to describe the motion of a particle with respect to either of them, and he should be able to relate the two different descriptions thus obtained. We proceed to find this relation.

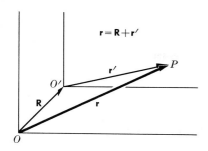

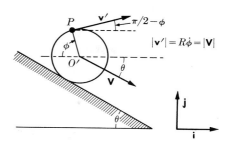

Fig. 3–1.    Relative position of a point $P$ with respect to two coordinate systems.

Fig. 3–2.    Wheel rolling down a fixed incline.

Designating the origins of the two coordinate systems by $O$ and $O'$, and assuming that the unprimed coordinate system remains fixed with respect to the observer, the position of any point $P$ with respect to $O'$ is known if its position with respect to $O$ and the position of $O'$ with respect to $O$ are known. The respective position vectors $\mathbf{r}'(t)$, $\mathbf{r}(t)$, and $\mathbf{R}(t)$ are, as can be seen from Fig. 3–1, related in the following way:

$$\mathbf{r}(t) = \mathbf{R}(t) + \mathbf{r}'(t). \tag{3–1}$$

Successive differentiations of Eq. (3–1) yield the relationships between the velocities and accelerations of point $P$ with respect to the two points $O$ and $O'$. For the velocities, we obtain

$$\dot{\mathbf{r}}(t) = \dot{\mathbf{R}}(t) + \dot{\mathbf{r}}'(t)$$

or

$$\mathbf{v}(t) = \mathbf{V}(t) + \mathbf{v}'(t), \tag{3–2}$$

where $\mathbf{v}(t)$ is the velocity of $P$ with respect to $O$, $\mathbf{V}(t)$ the velocity of $O'$ with respect to $O$, and $\mathbf{v}'(t)$ the velocity of $P$ with respect to $O'$. For the accelerations, we obtain

$$\mathbf{a}(t) = \mathbf{A}(t) + \mathbf{a}'(t), \tag{3–3}$$

where $\mathbf{a}(t)$, $\mathbf{A}(t)$, and $\mathbf{a}'(t)$ are respectively the accelerations of point $P$ with respect to point $O$, point $O'$ with respect to point $O$, and point $P$ with respect to point $O'$.

▶ Consider as an example the problem of finding the velocity and acceleration of a point $P$ on the rim of a wheel of radius $R$ which is rolling down an incline making an angle of $\theta$ with the horizontal (Fig. 3–2).

The velocity $\mathbf{v}$ of the point $P$ with respect to the incline is related to the velocity $\mathbf{v}'$ of the point $P$ with respect to the geometric center of the wheel and the velocity $\mathbf{V}$ of the center of the wheel with respect to the incline as can be seen from Eq. (3–2). From Fig. 3–2 we find that in component form

$$\mathbf{v'} = R\dot{\phi}\sin\phi\mathbf{i} + R\dot{\phi}\cos\phi\mathbf{j}$$

and

$$\mathbf{V} = R\dot{\phi}\cos\theta\mathbf{i} - R\dot{\phi}\sin\theta\mathbf{j},$$

thereby yielding

$$\mathbf{v} = R\dot{\phi}(\cos\theta + \sin\phi)\mathbf{i} + R\dot{\phi}(\cos\phi - \sin\theta)\mathbf{j}.$$

If the incline does not remain at rest, and we wish to find the velocity of the point $P$ with respect to the ground, we would subsequently have to add the velocity of the incline with respect to the ground to the velocity of the point $P$ with respect to the incline.

For the point of contact between the wheel and incline for which

$$\phi = \theta - \frac{\pi}{2},$$

we find that its velocity with respect to the incline vanishes,

$$\mathbf{v} = 0.$$

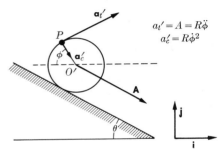

FIG. 3–3.   Wheel rolling down a fixed incline.

This equation expresses the condition of rolling. If one body rolls on a second body, then the relative velocity of the two points in contact with respect to each other vanishes.

The acceleration of point $P$ with respect to the incline is given by Eq. (3–3). From Fig. 3–3 we find that the acceleration $\mathbf{a'}$ of the point $P$ with respect to the center of the wheel about which it moves in a circle of radius $R$ is given by

$$\mathbf{a'} = (R\dot{\phi}^2\cos\phi + R\ddot{\phi}\sin\phi)\mathbf{i} + (R\ddot{\phi}\cos\phi - R\dot{\phi}^2\sin\phi)\mathbf{j}.$$

From the same diagram we also obtain for the acceleration of the center of the wheel with respect to the incline the result

$$\mathbf{A} = R\ddot{\phi}\cos\theta\mathbf{i} - R\ddot{\phi}\sin\theta\mathbf{j}.$$

Thus by Eq. (3–3) the acceleration of point $P$ with respect to the incline is found to be given by

$$\mathbf{a} = [R\dot{\phi}^2\cos\phi + R\ddot{\phi}(\sin\phi + \cos\theta)]\mathbf{i} + [R\ddot{\phi}(\cos\phi - \sin\theta) - R\dot{\phi}^2\sin\phi]\mathbf{j}. \blacktriangleleft$$

We should like to note once more that in our discussion we introduced only a single observer who describes the position, velocity, and acceleration of the points $P$ and $O'$ with respect to the origin of his coordinate system. The relative position, velocity, and acceleration of the point $P$ with respect to the point $O'$ represents merely a different kinematical bookkeeping system to this observer. Equations (3–1), (3–2), and (3–3) relate his entries for the different kinematical descriptions of the point $P$ to the observed relative position, velocity, and acceleration of $O'$ with respect to $O$. From this point of view we find the transformation equations which we have derived to be also quite generally applicable to the relativistic description of the motion of point bodies by a single observer.

Relativistic mechanics, with which we shall concern ourselves in Chapter 13, differs from classical mechanics in the kinematic description of the motion of a particle when a second observer enters the picture. It is only when $O$ and $O'$ represent the origins of the coordinate systems of two different observers moving respectively with these points and when $\mathbf{r}$, $\mathbf{v}$, and $\mathbf{a}$, and $\mathbf{r}'$, $\mathbf{v}'$, and $\mathbf{a}'$ are the kinematic descriptions of the motion of point $P$ with respect to the two inertial observers, that classical mechanics differs from relativitistic mechanics. Classical mechanics *assumes* that the equations which we have found above are the correct transformation equations for relating the different kinematical descriptions of the motion of point $P$ by the two observers. We find that for relative velocities of $O'$ with respect to $O$ whose magnitudes are small compared with the speed of light, the transformation equations which we obtained are good approximations to the correct relativistic relations which exist between the different kinematical descriptions of the motion of a point $P$ with respect to two observers moving respectively with the points $O$ and $O'$.

---

An interesting application of Eqs. (3–1) and (3–2) is the description of the propagation of a harmonic plane wave with respect to a moving coordinate system.

Consider the plane wave described by

$$\Psi = A \sin (kx - \omega t) = A \sin k(x - vt).$$

It is a plane wave of frequency $f = \omega/2\pi$ and velocity $v = \omega/k$, moving in the increasing $x$-direction, where $k$ is called the *wave number*. It is equal to $2\pi$ times the reciprocal of the wave length,

$$k = \frac{2\pi}{\lambda},$$

where $\lambda$ represents the wavelength of the wave.

Suppose that this is the description of the wave with respect to the transmitting medium. That is, it is the description of the wave with respect to an observer to whom the transmitting medium appears to be at rest. To a second observer who observes the transmitting medium moving in the direction of propagation of the wave with a speed $v_M$, the wave will be observed to move with a speed $v + v_M$. The second observer will thus describe the plane wave by the equation

$$\Psi = A \sin k(x' - v't) = A \sin (kx' - \omega't),$$

where $v'$ is defined as

$$v' = v + v_M = \frac{\omega'}{k}.$$

This latter description of the wave by the second observer can be obtained from the description of the first observer by replacing $x$ by $x' - v_M t$, where $x$ and $x'$ are respectively the positions of a wavefront at time $t$ with respect to the two observers (cf. Fig. 3–4).

The frequency $f'$ ascribed to the wave by the second observer differs from the frequency $f$ assigned to it by the first observer. The relation between the two frequencies is

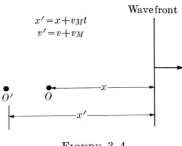

$$x' = x + v_M t$$
$$v' = v + v_M$$

FIGURE 3–4

$$f' = (v + v_M)\frac{k}{2\pi} = f\frac{v + v_M}{v}.$$

This formula is the classical *Doppler effect* for the frequency change produced by the motion of an observer, the transmitting medium, or both.

## 3–2 Rotational motion

In treating the case of two coordinate systems rotating with respect to each other, we take the origins of the two coordinate systems to be coincident. For simplicity, we also consider the respective base vectors of the two coordinate systems to be parallel to each other at time $t$. In that case the position of a point $P$ at time $t$ will be identically represented in the two coordinate systems. If

$$\mathbf{r} = x\mathbf{i} + y\mathbf{j} + z\mathbf{k}$$

and

$$\mathbf{r}' = x'\mathbf{i}' + y'\mathbf{j}' + z'\mathbf{k}' = x'\mathbf{i} + y'\mathbf{j} + z'\mathbf{k}$$

represent the position vectors of the point $P$ with respect to the two coordinate systems, we find that, at the time $t$, $\mathbf{r} = \mathbf{r}'$, since $O$ and $O'$ coincide. In matrix notation this fact is clearly expressed by the equation

$$\begin{bmatrix} x \\ y \\ z \end{bmatrix} = \begin{bmatrix} x' \\ y' \\ z' \end{bmatrix}.$$

To obtain the relationship between the different descriptions of the velocity and acceleration of the point $P$ with respect to the two coordinate systems, we recall our discussion in Section 1–8. There we decomposed the time derivative of a vector $\mathbf{A}(t)$ into two parts. The first part, $(d\mathbf{A}/dt)\cdot\mathbf{e}_A$, was found to account for the change in the magnitude of $\mathbf{A}(t)$, whereas the second part,

$$A\,\frac{d\mathbf{e}_A}{dt} = \frac{d\boldsymbol{\phi}}{dt} \times \mathbf{A}, \tag{3–4}$$

accounted for a change in the orientation of the vector $\mathbf{A}$. The quantity $d\boldsymbol{\phi}/dt = \boldsymbol{\omega}_A$ represents the instantaneous angular velocity of $\mathbf{A}$.

With respect to either of the two coordinate systems, the time derivative of a vector $\mathbf{A}$ should be expressed by an equation of the form

$$\frac{d\mathbf{A}}{dt} = \frac{dA}{dt}\,\mathbf{e}_A + \boldsymbol{\omega}_A \times \mathbf{A}. \tag{3–5}$$

If Eq. (3–5) represents the time rate of change of $\mathbf{A}$ with respect to the unprimed system, then a similar equation,

$$\frac{d\mathbf{A}'}{dt} = \frac{dA}{dt}\,\mathbf{e}_A + \boldsymbol{\omega}'_A \times \mathbf{A}' \tag{3–6}$$

is the equation which represents the time rate of change of $\mathbf{A}' = \mathbf{A}$ with respect to the primed coordinate system. Here $\boldsymbol{\omega}'_A$ is the angular velocity which the vector $\mathbf{A}$ has with respect to the primed system. Obviously,

$$\frac{d\mathbf{A}}{dt} \neq \frac{d\mathbf{A}'}{dt}.$$

The difference in the descriptions of the time derivative of $\mathbf{A}$ with respect to the two coordinate systems is due to the different relative angular velocities which $\mathbf{A}$ has with respect to the two systems. This difference in the angular velocities is due to the rotation of the primed coordinate system with respect to the unprimed coordinate system. If we let $\boldsymbol{\Omega}$ represent the angular velocity

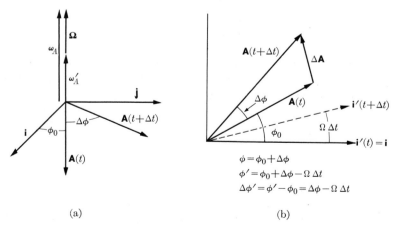

$$\phi = \phi_0 + \Delta\phi$$
$$\phi' = \phi_0 + \Delta\phi - \Omega\,\Delta t$$
$$\Delta\phi' = \phi' - \phi_0 = \Delta\phi - \Omega\,\Delta t$$

(a)                                         (b)

FIGURE 3–5

of rotation of the base vectors of the primed system with respect to the unprimed system, then, since angular velocities add like vectors, we find that the angular velocity which the vector **A** has with respect to the unprimed coordinate system is equal to the sum of the angular velocity which **A** has with respect to the primed system and **Ω**,

$$\boldsymbol{\omega}_A = \boldsymbol{\Omega} + \boldsymbol{\omega}'_A. \tag{3-7}$$

This, for example, is illustrated in Fig. 3–5 for the case when the three angular velocity vectors are parallel to each other, all being directed along the positive z-axis.

Inserting this result into Eq. (3–5) yields

$$\frac{d\mathbf{A}}{dt} = \left( \frac{dA}{dt} \, \mathbf{e}_A + \boldsymbol{\omega}'_A \times \mathbf{A} \right) + \boldsymbol{\Omega} \times \mathbf{A}'$$

$$= \frac{d\mathbf{A}'}{dt} + \boldsymbol{\Omega} \times \mathbf{A}'. \tag{3-8}$$

Equation (3–8) relates the descriptions of the time rate of change of the vector **A** with respect to the two coordinate systems. This equation is generally applicable to any vector **A**. It states that the description of the time rate of change of a vector **A** with respect to one (unprimed) coordinate system is equal to the sum of the description of the time rate of change of the same vector with respect to a second (primed) coordinate system, which is rotating with an angular velocity **Ω** with respect to the first, and the term **Ω** × **A**, which accounts for the different rotational change which the vector **A** has with respect to the two systems.

Applying this result to the position vector of point $P$, we obtain

$$\mathbf{v} = \frac{d\mathbf{r}}{dt} = \frac{d\mathbf{r}'}{dt} + \boldsymbol{\Omega} \times \mathbf{r}' = \mathbf{v}' + \boldsymbol{\Omega} \times \mathbf{r}', \tag{3-9}$$

where **v**′ is the description of the velocity of the point $P$ with respect to the primed coordinate system.

Equation (3–9) is an identity, the left-hand side of which obviously represents the description of the velocity of the point $P$ with respect to the unprimed coordinate system. The right-hand side, on the other hand, represents the description of this same velocity vector **v** in terms of the description of the velocity **v**′ of the point $P$ with respect to the primed system and its position vector $\mathbf{r}' = \mathbf{r}$. This fact can be grasped more readily if we express Eq. (3–9) in its matrix representation:

$$\begin{bmatrix} v_x \\ v_y \\ v_z \end{bmatrix} = \begin{bmatrix} v'_x + \Omega_y z' - \Omega_z y' \\ v'_y + \Omega_z x' - \Omega_x z' \\ v'_z + \Omega_x y' - \Omega_y x' \end{bmatrix}.$$

To find the relationship between the two descriptions of the accelerations, we apply Eq. (3–8) to the velocity vector $\mathbf{v}$ of Eq. (3–9). Setting

$$\mathbf{A} = \mathbf{v} \quad \text{and} \quad \mathbf{A}' = \mathbf{A} = \mathbf{v}' + \mathbf{\Omega}' \times \mathbf{r}',$$

where $\mathbf{\Omega}' = \mathbf{\Omega}$ is the description of $\mathbf{\Omega}$ in the primed system, we find that

$$\mathbf{a} = \frac{d\mathbf{v}}{dt} = \frac{d}{dt}(\mathbf{v}' + \mathbf{\Omega}' \times \mathbf{r}') + \mathbf{\Omega}' \times (\mathbf{v}' + \mathbf{\Omega}' \times \mathbf{r}')$$

$$= \frac{d}{dt}\mathbf{v}' + \left(\frac{d\mathbf{\Omega}'}{dt}\right) \times \mathbf{r}' + \mathbf{\Omega}' \times \frac{d\mathbf{r}'}{dt} + \mathbf{\Omega}' \times (\mathbf{v}' + \mathbf{\Omega}' \times \mathbf{r}')$$

$$= \mathbf{a}' + \boldsymbol{\alpha} \times \mathbf{r}' + 2\mathbf{\Omega} \times \mathbf{v}' + \mathbf{\Omega} \times (\mathbf{\Omega} \times \mathbf{r}'), \qquad (3\text{–}10)$$

where

$$\boldsymbol{\alpha} = \frac{d\mathbf{\Omega}'}{dt} = \frac{d\mathbf{\Omega}}{dt} - \mathbf{\Omega} \times \mathbf{\Omega} = \frac{d\mathbf{\Omega}}{dt} \qquad (3\text{–}11)$$

is the angular acceleration of the primed coordinate system with respect to the unprimed coordinate system.

Equation (3–10) relates the description of the acceleration $\mathbf{a}$ of the point $P$ with respect to the unprimed system to the description of its acceleration $\mathbf{a}'$ with respect to the primed system. The additional terms appear because of the rotation of the two systems with respect to each other. The term $2\mathbf{\Omega} \times \mathbf{v}'$ is known as the *Coriolis acceleration*, after G. Coriolis, who first discovered it. The term $\boldsymbol{\alpha} \times \mathbf{r}'$ is the acceleration produced by the angular acceleration of the primed coordinate system with respect to the unprimed. And finally $\mathbf{\Omega} \times (\mathbf{\Omega} \times \mathbf{r}')$ is known as the *centripetal acceleration*.

---

This same result could also have been obtained from the results of the previous chapter by considering the transformation from the coordinates $x$, $y$, $z$ to the coordinates $x'$, $y'$, $z'$ to be a time-dependent coordinate transformation expressed generally by

$$x = x(q_1, q_2, q_3, t), \quad y = y(q_1, q_2, q_3, t), \quad z = z(q_1, q_2, q_3, t). \quad (3\text{–}12)$$

For such transformations we are still at liberty to define the vectors

$$\mathbf{b}_i = \frac{\partial x}{\partial q_i}\mathbf{i} + \frac{\partial y}{\partial q_i}\mathbf{j} + \frac{\partial z}{\partial q_i}\mathbf{k} \qquad (3\text{–}13)$$

as our new base vectors at the point $(q_1, q_2, q_3)$. For such time-dependent transformations, however, the reciprocal base vectors $\boldsymbol{b}_i$ are not equal to the gradient of the generalized coordinates. This means that for time-dependent coordinate transformations,

$$\mathbf{v} \cdot \boldsymbol{b}_i \neq \dot{q}_i,$$

where $\dot{q}_i$ is nevertheless still referred to as a generalized velocity.

Since in this case, as in the case of the time-independent coordinate transformations, we still have the relation

$$\frac{\partial x}{\partial q_i} = \frac{\partial \dot{x}}{\partial \dot{q}_i},$$

the base vectors defined by Eq. (3–13) yield for the covariant velocities the relation

$$v_i = \mathbf{v} \cdot \mathbf{b}_i = \dot{x} \frac{\partial x}{\partial q_i} + \dot{y} \frac{\partial y}{\partial q_i} + \dot{z} \frac{\partial z}{\partial q_i} = \frac{\partial}{\partial \dot{q}_i} \left( \frac{1}{2} v^2 \right), \tag{3–14}$$

and for the covariant accelerations the expression

$$\begin{aligned} a_i = \mathbf{a} \cdot \mathbf{b}_i &= \ddot{x} \frac{\partial x}{\partial q_i} + \ddot{y} \frac{\partial y}{\partial q_i} + \ddot{z} \frac{\partial z}{\partial q_i} \\ &= \frac{d}{dt} \frac{\partial}{\partial \dot{q}_i} \left( \frac{1}{2} v^2 \right) - \frac{\partial}{\partial q_i} \left( \frac{1}{2} v^2 \right). \end{aligned} \tag{3–15}$$

For the problem under consideration we have, using Eq. (3–9),

$$\begin{aligned} \tfrac{1}{2} v^2 &= \tfrac{1}{2} (\mathbf{v}' + \boldsymbol{\Omega} \times \mathbf{r}') \cdot (\mathbf{v}' + \boldsymbol{\Omega} \times \mathbf{r}') \\ &= \tfrac{1}{2} [v'^2 + 2\mathbf{v}' \cdot (\boldsymbol{\Omega} \times \mathbf{r}') + (\boldsymbol{\Omega} \times \mathbf{r}') \cdot (\boldsymbol{\Omega} \times \mathbf{r}')]. \end{aligned}$$

Hence for the $x'$-component of the acceleration, since

$$\frac{\partial}{\partial \dot{x}'} \left( \frac{1}{2} v^2 \right) = \dot{x}' + (\boldsymbol{\Omega} \times \mathbf{r}')_{x'}$$

and

$$\frac{\partial}{\partial x'} \left( \frac{1}{2} v^2 \right) = (\mathbf{v}' \times \boldsymbol{\Omega})_{x'} - [\boldsymbol{\Omega} \times (\boldsymbol{\Omega} \times \mathbf{r}')]_{x'},$$

Eq. (3–15) yields

$$a_{x'} = \mathbf{a} \cdot \mathbf{i}' = \ddot{x}' + (\dot{\boldsymbol{\Omega}} \times \mathbf{r}')_{x'} + 2(\boldsymbol{\Omega} \times \mathbf{v}')_{x'} + [\boldsymbol{\Omega} \times (\boldsymbol{\Omega} \times \mathbf{r}')]_{x'}. \tag{3–16}$$

For the case to which we restricted ourselves at the beginning of this section, the instantaneous coincidence of the cartesian base vectors of the two coordinate systems,

$$\mathbf{i} = \mathbf{i}', \qquad \mathbf{j} = \mathbf{j}', \qquad \text{and} \qquad \mathbf{k} = \mathbf{k}',$$

we are able to set

$$\mathbf{a} = \mathbf{a}' + \boldsymbol{\alpha} \times \mathbf{r}' + 2\boldsymbol{\Omega} \times \mathbf{v}' + \boldsymbol{\Omega} \times (\boldsymbol{\Omega} \times \mathbf{r}'), \tag{3–17}$$

which is in agreement with Eq. (3–10).

---

▶ As an example, we consider the plane motion of a particle which in one coordinate system is observed to move in a straight line. In this coordinate system, choosing the $x$-axis as the axis along which the motion takes place, we find the motion to be described by

$$\mathbf{r} = x(t)\mathbf{i}, \qquad \mathbf{v} = \dot{x}(t)\mathbf{i}, \qquad \mathbf{a} = \ddot{x}(t)\mathbf{i}.$$

Such, for example, may be the motion of a particle in the earth's equatorial plane observed to be falling toward the center of the earth with respect to a coordinate system fixed at the center of the earth.

With respect to a coordinate system which the same observer observes to be rotating with an angular velocity $\boldsymbol{\Omega} = \Omega(t)\mathbf{k}$, however, the description of the motion in terms of the cylindrical coordinate $r$ and $\theta$ is given by

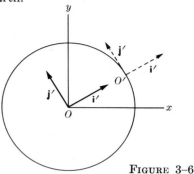

$$r(t) = x(t)$$

and

$$\theta(t) = -\int_{t_0}^{t} \Omega(t)\, dt.$$

FIGURE 3–6

For the special example mentioned, the rotating coordinate system would represent a coordinate system fixed at the center of the earth which is at all times parallel to the coordinate system of an observer who is fixed on the surface of the rotating earth (Fig. 3–6). In this case the angular velocity of rotation of the earth $\boldsymbol{\Omega}$ is a constant. A typical path which may generally be followed by such a particle with respect to the rotating coordinate system is shown in Fig. (3–7).

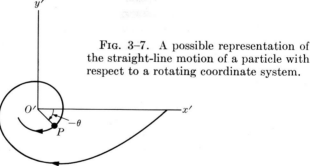

FIG. 3–7. A possible representation of the straight-line motion of a particle with respect to a rotating coordinate system.

In terms of the cartesian components along the base vectors, $\mathbf{i'}$ and $\mathbf{j'}$, of the rotating coordinate system, we have

$$\mathbf{r'}(t) = x(t)\cos\theta\mathbf{i'} + x(t)\sin\theta\mathbf{j'},$$

from which by successive differentiation we obtain

$$\mathbf{v'}(t) = \frac{d\mathbf{r'}}{dt} = \dot{x}(t)\cos\theta\mathbf{i'} + \dot{x}(t)\sin\theta\mathbf{j'} + \Omega(t)[x(t)\sin\theta\mathbf{i'} - x(t)\cos\theta\mathbf{j'}],$$

and

$$\mathbf{a'}(t) = \frac{d\mathbf{v'}}{dt} = [\ddot{x}(t)\cos\theta + 2\Omega\dot{x}\sin\theta - \Omega^2 x\cos\theta + \alpha x\sin\theta]\mathbf{i'}$$
$$+ [\ddot{x}\sin\theta - 2\Omega\dot{x}\cos\theta + \Omega^2 x\sin\theta - \alpha x\cos\theta]\mathbf{j'}.$$

At the time $t = t_0$ when the cartesian base vectors of the two coordinate systems coincide,

$$\mathbf{i}' = \mathbf{i} \quad \text{and} \quad \mathbf{j}' = \mathbf{j}, \quad \text{or} \quad \theta = 0,$$

we find that indeed

$$v'_x = v_x \quad \text{and} \quad v'_y = -\Omega x$$

or

$$\mathbf{v}' = \mathbf{v} - \mathbf{\Omega} \times \mathbf{r}.$$

Similarly, at the time $t = t_0$,

$$a'_x = \ddot{x} - \Omega^2 x, \qquad a'_y = -2\Omega \dot{x} - \alpha x,$$

or

$$\mathbf{a}' = \mathbf{a} - 2\mathbf{\Omega} \times \dot{\mathbf{r}} - \boldsymbol{\alpha} \times \mathbf{r} + \mathbf{\Omega} \times (\mathbf{\Omega} \times \mathbf{r}),$$

in agreement with Eq. (3–10) after replacing $\dot{\mathbf{r}}$ by $(\mathbf{v}' + \mathbf{\Omega} \times \mathbf{r})$. ◀

The time $t_0$ at which the cartesian base vectors of the two systems are chosen as coincident is a choice of the observer. It follows, therefore, that Eqs. (3–9) and (3–10) are correct at all times.

The results of this section play an important role in the description of the motion of a projectile or, for that matter, any particle with respect to an observer on our rotating earth. With respect to such an observer, the description of the acceleration and hence the motion of a projectile is much more complicated than the description of its motion with respect to a coordinate system whose orientation remains fixed in space. Neglecting the translational motion of the earth through space, the acceleration of a projectile with respect to a coordinate system at the center of the earth, which is parallel to the system of an observer on earth and rotating with the earth, is given by

$$\mathbf{a}' = \mathbf{a} + \mathbf{\Omega} \times (\mathbf{\Omega} \times \mathbf{r}) - 2\mathbf{\Omega} \times \mathbf{v},$$

where $\mathbf{a}$ is the radially directed acceleration of the projectile toward the center of the earth and $\mathbf{v}$ its velocity, both with respect to the fixed coordinate system. The vector $\mathbf{\Omega}$ represents the angular precessional velocity of earth, and hence of the coordinate system rotating with the earth.

As a result of this complication the resultant acceleration of a particle with respect to an observer on earth is not directed toward the center of the earth.

Other examples of the importance of these relations will be provided in the problems and in subsequent chapters.

## 3–3 Translational and rotational motion

If the origins of the two coordinate systems do not remain coincident, then the relationship between the two kinematic descriptions is provided by the sum of the results of the last two sections. This can be justified by considering three coordinate systems whose origins are represented by the three points $O$, $O'$, and $O''$. If the points $O'$ and $O''$ move together, then the relations between the velocity and acceleration of a point $P$ with respect to the primed and double-primed systems are as given in the last section:

$$\mathbf{v}'' = \mathbf{v}' + \boldsymbol{\Omega} \times \mathbf{r}' \quad \text{with} \quad \mathbf{r}' = \mathbf{r}'', \tag{3–18}$$

and

$$\mathbf{a}'' = \mathbf{a}' + 2\boldsymbol{\Omega} \times \mathbf{v}' + \boldsymbol{\alpha} \times \mathbf{r}' + \boldsymbol{\Omega} \times (\boldsymbol{\Omega} \times \mathbf{r}'), \tag{3–19}$$

where $\boldsymbol{\Omega}$ and $\boldsymbol{\alpha}$ are the angular velocity and angular acceleration of the primed coordinate system with respect to the double-primed system. If the orientation of the double-primed system does not change with respect to the unprimed system, then the relations between the velocities and accelerations of the point $P$ with respect to the double-primed and unprimed systems is as given in Section 3–1. Specifically, we have

$$\mathbf{v} = \mathbf{v}'' + \mathbf{V} = \mathbf{V} + \mathbf{v}' + \boldsymbol{\Omega} \times \mathbf{r}' \tag{3–20}$$

and

$$\begin{aligned}
\mathbf{a} &= \mathbf{a}'' + \mathbf{A} \\
&= \mathbf{A} + \mathbf{a}' + 2\boldsymbol{\Omega} \times \mathbf{v}' + \boldsymbol{\alpha} \times \mathbf{r}' + \boldsymbol{\Omega} \times (\boldsymbol{\Omega} \times \mathbf{r}').
\end{aligned} \tag{3–21}$$

Here $\mathbf{V}$ is the relative velocity of $O''$ (or $O'$) with respect to $O$, and $\mathbf{A}$ is the acceleration of $O''$ (or $O'$) with respect to $O$. Since the double-primed system does not change its orientation with respect to the unprimed system, $\boldsymbol{\Omega}$ and $\boldsymbol{\alpha}$ are also the angular velocity and angular acceleration of the primed coordinate system with respect to the unprimed system.

## 3–4 Coordinate transformation

In this section we shall consider the transformation of the cartesian description of a vector in one coordinate system to its cartesian description with respect to another whose origin coincides with the origin of the first but whose orthonormal base vectors are not parallel to those of the first. Such a transformation has to be performed in case the base vectors of the primed and unprimed coordinate systems are not coincident, and if we wish, for example, to relate the respective cartesian descriptions of each side of Eq. (3–20) or (3–21).

Referring to the two coordinate systems once more as the primed and unprimed coordinate systems (Fig. 3–8), the problem is to relate the cartesian components $(A_x, A_y, A_z)$ of a vector $\mathbf{A}$ in the unprimed system to the cartesian components $(A_x', A_y', A_z')$ of the same vector $\mathbf{A}$ with respect to the primed system. The relation between the two sets of cartesian components is readily obtainable if the scalar products between the base vectors of the two coordinate systems are known.

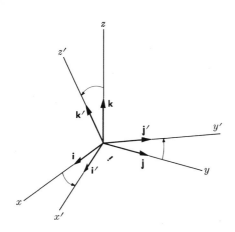

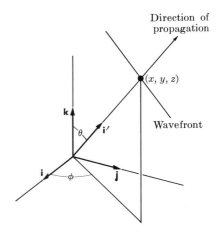

FIG. 3–8.  A general coordinate transformation.

FIG. 3–9.  Wavefront propagating in the direction specified by the angles $\theta$ and $\phi$.

Setting

$$\mathbf{i} \cdot \mathbf{i}' = t_{11}, \qquad \mathbf{j} \cdot \mathbf{i}' = t_{21}, \qquad \mathbf{k} \cdot \mathbf{i}' = t_{31},$$
$$\mathbf{i} \cdot \mathbf{j}' = t_{12}, \qquad \mathbf{j} \cdot \mathbf{j}' = t_{22}, \qquad \mathbf{k} \cdot \mathbf{j}' = t_{32}, \qquad (3\text{–}22)$$
$$\mathbf{i} \cdot \mathbf{k}' = t_{13}, \qquad \mathbf{j} \cdot \mathbf{k}' = t_{23}, \qquad \mathbf{k} \cdot \mathbf{k}' = t_{33},$$

we have

$$\mathbf{i}' = (\mathbf{i} \cdot \mathbf{i}')\mathbf{i} + (\mathbf{j} \cdot \mathbf{i}')\mathbf{j} + (\mathbf{k} \cdot \mathbf{i}')\mathbf{k}$$
$$= t_{11}\mathbf{i} + t_{21}\mathbf{j} + t_{31}\mathbf{k}, \qquad (3\text{–}23)$$

and similarly,

$$\mathbf{j}' = t_{12}\mathbf{i} + t_{22}\mathbf{j} + t_{32}\mathbf{k} \qquad (3\text{–}24)$$

and

$$\mathbf{k}' = t_{13}\mathbf{i} + t_{23}\mathbf{j} + t_{33}\mathbf{k}. \qquad (3\text{–}25)$$

The scalar products $t_{mn}$ of the two sets of base vectors are the *direction cosines* of the base vectors of the primed system with respect to the unprimed coordinate system.  They are also the direction cosines of the base vectors of the unprimed system with respect to the primed system, as we similarly find

$$\mathbf{i} = t_{11}\mathbf{i}' + t_{12}\mathbf{j}' + t_{13}\mathbf{k}',$$
$$\mathbf{j} = t_{21}\mathbf{i}' + t_{22}\mathbf{j}' + t_{23}\mathbf{k}', \qquad (3\text{–}26)$$
$$\mathbf{k} = t_{31}\mathbf{i}' + t_{32}\mathbf{j}' + t_{33}\mathbf{k}'.$$

With the help of Eqs. (3–26), we can obtain the relations we are seeking.  For example, we find that

$$A_x = \mathbf{i} \cdot \mathbf{A} = (t_{11}\mathbf{i}' + t_{12}\mathbf{j}' + t_{13}\mathbf{k}') \cdot \mathbf{A}$$
$$= t_{11}A'_x + t_{12}A'_y + t_{13}A'_z, \qquad (3\text{–}27)$$

where $A'_x = \mathbf{A} \cdot \mathbf{i}'$, etc.

Equation (3–21) can be simplified notationally by setting

$$\left.\begin{aligned} A_1 &= A_x, \\ A_2 &= A_y, \\ A_3 &= A_z, \end{aligned}\right\} \quad \text{and} \quad \left\{\begin{aligned} A'_1 &= A'_x \\ A'_2 &= A'_y. \\ A'_3 &= A'_z \end{aligned}\right.$$

With this change in notation, Eq. (3–27) is expressed by

$$A_1 = \sum_{m=1}^{3} t_{1m} A'_m. \tag{3–28}$$

Similarly, we obtain

$$A_2 = \sum_{m=1}^{3} t_{2m} A'_m \quad \text{and} \quad A_3 = \sum_{m=1}^{3} t_{3m} A'_m,$$

or in general,

$$A_n = \sum_{m=1}^{3} t_{nm} A'_m, \quad n = 1, 2, 3. \tag{3–29}$$

Analogously we also find that

$$\begin{aligned} A'_1 = \mathbf{A} \cdot \mathbf{i}' &= \mathbf{A} \cdot (t_{11}\mathbf{i} + t_{21}\mathbf{j} + t_{31}\mathbf{k}) \\ &= t_{11}A_1 + t_{21}A_2 + t_{31}A_3, \end{aligned}$$

with similar expressions for $A'_2$ and $A'_3$. All these are contained in the equation

$$A'_m = \sum_{n=1}^{3} t_{nm} A_n, \quad m = 1, 2, 3. \tag{3–30}$$

Equations (3–29) and (3–30) relate the cartesian components of the vector $\mathbf{A}$ with respect to the two coordinate systems in terms of the nine direction cosines $t_{nm}$.

▶As an example of the use of the transformation equations, we proceed to obtain the description of a plane harmonic wave whose direction of propagation is specified by $\theta$ and $\phi$, which are respectively the angle between the direction of propagation and the $z$-axis and the angle made by the projection of the direction of propagation of the wave onto the $xy$-plane with the $x$-axis (Fig. 3–9).

With respect to a primed coordinate system for which the direction of propagation is the $x'$-axis, the description of the wave is given by

$$\Psi = A \sin (kx' - \omega t).$$

By Eq. (3–30), the location $x'$ of a wavefront along the $x'$-axis may be re-expressed in terms of the projections $x$, $y$, $z$ of $x'\mathbf{i}'$ onto the $\mathbf{i}$-, $\mathbf{j}$-, and $\mathbf{k}$-axes.

This relation is

$$x' = (x\mathbf{i} + y\mathbf{j} + z\mathbf{k}) \cdot \mathbf{i}' = x \sin\theta\cos\phi + y\sin\theta\sin\phi + z\cos\theta,$$

where $\sin\theta\cos\phi$, $\sin\theta\sin\phi$, and $\cos\theta$ are respectively the direction cosines of the $\mathbf{i}'$-axis with respect to the $\mathbf{i}$-, $\mathbf{j}$-, and $\mathbf{k}$-axes (Fig. 3–9). Inserting this result into the description of the wave in the primed coordinate system yields its description in the unprimed system

$$\Psi = A \sin(kx\sin\theta\cos\phi + ky\sin\theta\sin\phi + kz\cos\theta - \omega t).$$

Defining the propagation vector $\mathbf{f}$ as a vector which has magnitude $k$ and which is directed along the path of propagation as expressed by

$$\mathbf{f} = k\mathbf{i}',$$

we find its $x$-, $y$-, and $z$-components to be given by

$$k_x = k\sin\theta\cos\phi, \qquad k_y = k\sin\theta\sin\phi, \qquad k_z = k\cos\theta.$$

Using this propagation vector $\mathbf{f}$, the description of a plane harmonic wave is very efficiently expressed by

$$\Psi = A\sin(\mathbf{f}\cdot\mathbf{r} - \omega t). \blacktriangleleft$$

Returning to the base vectors, we note that each set consists of mutually orthogonal unit vectors. We therefore conclude that the nine direction cosines $t_{mn}$ are not independent. From the scalar product of the base vectors of either system we obtain six relations between these nine direction cosines, which tell us that it should be possible to express the transformation equations in terms of only three parameters. We shall return to a discussion of three such independent parameters in Chapter 9 where we will discuss the kinematics of rigid-body motion.

The six relations between the nine direction cosines are obtained from the six scalar products between the base vectors of either set. Using Eq. (3–26) yields from the scalar products between the vectors $\mathbf{i}$, $\mathbf{j}$, and $\mathbf{k}$,

$$\sum_{n=1}^{3} t_{mn}t_{ln} = \delta_{ml}, \tag{3–31}$$

where the Kronecker delta $\delta_{ml}$ is defined as follows:

$$\delta_{ml} = \begin{cases} 0 & m \neq l, \\ 1 & m = l. \end{cases} \tag{3–32}$$

Equations (3–23), (3–24), and (3–25), on the other hand, yield the equivalent relations

$$\sum_{m=1}^{3} t_{mn}t_{ml} = \delta_{nl}. \tag{3–33}$$

## 3–5 Matrix representation of orthogonal coordinate transformations

Coordinate transformations are linear transformations, which are extremely important, since they occur frequently in physics. We shall meet them, for example, in our discussions of rigid-body motion, small-vibration theory and the special theory of relativity. They are also fundamental in the quantum mechanical description of physical phenomena. Their formal properties we shall study in Chapter 10. Here we should like to digress to give a brief discussion of the matrix representation of a coordinate transformation, in order to give the reader a first brief introduction to a most convenient mathematical way of handling linear transformations.

The representation of the scalar product of two vectors in matrix notation was introduced in Section 1–5. There we defined the matrix product of a row and column matrix by

$$[B_1, B_2, B_3] \begin{bmatrix} A_1 \\ A_2 \\ A_3 \end{bmatrix} = B_1 A_1 + B_2 A_2 + B_3 A_3. \tag{3–34}$$

The matrices

$$[B_1, B_2, B_3] \qquad \text{and} \qquad \begin{bmatrix} A_1 \\ A_2 \\ A_3 \end{bmatrix}$$

may, for example, be the row and column matrix representations of the vectors

$$\mathbf{B} = B_1 \mathbf{i} + B_2 \mathbf{j} + B_3 \mathbf{k}$$

and

$$\mathbf{A} = A_1 \mathbf{i} + A_2 \mathbf{j} + A_3 \mathbf{k}.$$

In terms of the row matrix representation $[t_{11}, t_{12}, t_{13}]$ of the vector

$$\mathbf{i} = t_{11} \mathbf{i}' + t_{12} \mathbf{j}' + t_{13} \mathbf{k}',$$

and the column matrix representation

$$(\mathbf{A}') = \begin{bmatrix} A_1' \\ A_2' \\ A_3' \end{bmatrix}$$

of the vector

$$\mathbf{A} = \mathbf{A}' = A_1' \mathbf{i}' + A_2' \mathbf{j}' + A_3' \mathbf{k}',$$

we obtain

$$A_1 = \mathbf{i} \cdot \mathbf{A} = [t_{11}, t_{12}, t_{13}] \begin{bmatrix} A_1' \\ A_2' \\ A_3' \end{bmatrix}. \tag{3–35}$$

Similarly, we obtain

$$A_2 = \mathbf{j} \cdot \mathbf{A} = [t_{21}, t_{22}, t_{23}] \begin{bmatrix} A'_1 \\ A'_2 \\ A'_3 \end{bmatrix}, \tag{3-36}$$

and

$$A_3 = \mathbf{k} \cdot \mathbf{A} = [t_{31}, t_{32}, t_{33}] \begin{bmatrix} A'_1 \\ A'_2 \\ A'_3 \end{bmatrix}. \tag{3-37}$$

The last three equations may be expressed as a single matrix equation by combining the nine elements of the three row matrix representations of the vectors $\mathbf{i}$, $\mathbf{j}$, and $\mathbf{k}$,

$$\mathbf{i} \leftrightarrow [t_{11}, t_{12}, t_{13}], \qquad \mathbf{j} \leftrightarrow [t_{21}, t_{22}, t_{23}], \qquad \mathbf{k} \leftrightarrow [t_{31, 32, 33}],$$

into the single $3 \times 3$ square matrix

$$(\mathbf{T}) = \begin{bmatrix} t_{11} & t_{12} & t_{13} \\ t_{21} & t_{22} & t_{23} \\ t_{31} & t_{32} & t_{33} \end{bmatrix}, \tag{3-38}$$

referred to as the *transformation matrix*.

Equations (3–35), (3–36), and (3–37) are thus expressible by the matrix equation

$$\begin{bmatrix} A_1 \\ A_2 \\ A_3 \end{bmatrix} = \begin{bmatrix} t_{11} & t_{12} & t_{13} \\ t_{21} & t_{22} & t_{23} \\ t_{31} & t_{32} & t_{33} \end{bmatrix} \begin{bmatrix} A'_1 \\ A'_2 \\ A'_3 \end{bmatrix}$$

$$= \begin{bmatrix} t_{11}A'_1 + t_{12}A'_2 + t_{13}A'_3 \\ t_{21}A'_1 + t_{22}A'_2 + t_{23}A'_3 \\ t_{31}A'_1 + t_{32}A'_2 + t_{33}A'_3 \end{bmatrix}$$

$$= \begin{bmatrix} \sum_{m=1}^{3} t_{1m}A'_m \\ \sum_{m=1}^{3} t_{2m}A'_m \\ \sum_{m=1}^{3} t_{3m}A'_m \end{bmatrix}, \tag{3-39}$$

or simply

$$(\mathbf{A}) = (\mathbf{T})(\mathbf{A}').$$

Equation (3–39) defines the matrix multiplication of a square matrix (**T**) and a column matrix (**A**). In a similar fashion we can express Eq. (3–30) by the matrix equation

$$\begin{bmatrix} A_1' \\ A_2' \\ A_3' \end{bmatrix} = \begin{bmatrix} t_{11} & t_{21} & t_{31} \\ t_{12} & t_{22} & t_{32} \\ t_{13} & t_{23} & t_{33} \end{bmatrix} \begin{bmatrix} A_1 \\ A_2 \\ A_3 \end{bmatrix} \tag{3–40}$$

or

$$(\mathbf{A}') = (\mathbf{S})(\mathbf{A}),$$

where

$$(\mathbf{S}) = \begin{bmatrix} s_{11} & s_{12} & s_{13} \\ s_{21} & s_{22} & s_{23} \\ s_{31} & s_{32} & s_{33} \end{bmatrix} = \begin{bmatrix} t_{11} & t_{21} & t_{31} \\ t_{12} & t_{22} & t_{32} \\ t_{13} & t_{23} & t_{33} \end{bmatrix}. \tag{3–41}$$

We note that the element $s_{mn}$ of the transformation matrix (**S**) of Eq. (3–41) is equal to the element $t_{nm}$ of the transformation matrix (**T**) of Eq. (3–38).

If the elements of two matrices (**S**) and (**T**) satisfy the condition

$$s_{mn} = t_{nm}, \tag{3–42}$$

then each matrix is said to be the *transpose* of the other. The transpose of a matrix (**T**) is designated by a tilde above the matrix. Thus we have

$$(\mathbf{S}) = (\widetilde{\mathbf{T}}) \qquad \text{or} \qquad (\mathbf{T}) = (\widetilde{\mathbf{S}}). \tag{3–43}$$

We can extend the usefulness of the matrix notation to represent still other equations. Suppose that we had two additional vectors, the vectors **B** and **C** whose components in the two coordinate systems were related to each other in the same fashion as those of **A**; that is, as expressed by the matrix equations

$$(\mathbf{B}) = (\widetilde{\mathbf{T}})(\mathbf{B}') \qquad \text{and} \qquad (\mathbf{C}) = (\widetilde{\mathbf{T}})(\mathbf{C}'), \tag{3–44}$$

where (**B**) and (**C**) represent the column matrix representations of the vectors |**B**) and |**C**),

$$|\mathbf{B}) \leftrightarrow (\mathbf{B}) = \begin{bmatrix} B_1 \\ B_2 \\ B_3 \end{bmatrix}$$

and

$$|\mathbf{C}) \leftrightarrow (\mathbf{C}) = \begin{bmatrix} C_1 \\ C_2 \\ C_3 \end{bmatrix}, \tag{3–45}$$

with similar matrix representation for the vectors |**B**′) and |**C**′). The equality of two matrices means that the elements of one matrix are equal to the corresponding elements of the other similar matrix. We can thus combine Eqs.

(3–39) and (3–44) into a single matrix equation by first defining the square matrix

$$(\mathbf{M}) = \begin{bmatrix} A_1 & B_1 & C_1 \\ A_2 & B_2 & C_2 \\ A_3 & B_3 & C_3 \end{bmatrix}. \tag{3–46}$$

In terms of the matrix $(\mathbf{M})$ and the similar matrix $(\mathbf{M}')$, Eqs. (3–39) and (3–44) are expressed by

$$(\mathbf{M}) = (\mathbf{T})(\mathbf{M}'), \tag{3–47}$$

which explicitly states that

$$\begin{bmatrix} A_1 & B_1 & C_1 \\ A_2 & B_2 & C_2 \\ A_3 & B_3 & C_3 \end{bmatrix} = \begin{bmatrix} t_{11} & t_{12} & t_{13} \\ t_{21} & t_{22} & t_{23} \\ t_{31} & t_{32} & t_{33} \end{bmatrix} \begin{bmatrix} A_1' & B_1' & C_1' \\ A_2' & B_2' & C_2' \\ A_3' & B_3' & C_3' \end{bmatrix}$$

$$= \begin{bmatrix} \sum_{1}^{3} t_{1m}A_m' & \sum_{1}^{3} t_{1m}B_m' & \sum_{1}^{3} t_{1m}C_m' \\ \sum_{1}^{3} t_{2m}A_m' & \sum_{1}^{3} t_{2m}B_m' & \sum_{1}^{3} t_{2m}C_m' \\ \sum_{1}^{3} t_{3m}A_m' & \sum_{1}^{3} t_{3m}B_m' & \sum_{1}^{3} t_{3m}C_m' \end{bmatrix}. \tag{3–48}$$

Equation (3–48) may be taken as the definition of the product of two square matrices. We note that it is the same as the multiplication rule for determinants.

An easy way to remember the general rule for the multiplication of any two matrices $(\mathbf{T})$ and $(\mathbf{M})$ is to remember how we constructed these two matrices. That is, consider the rows of the first matrix as the row matrix representation $(\mathbf{t}_i)$ of the vectors,

$$(\mathbf{t}_i| \leftrightarrow [t_{i1}, t_{i2}, t_{i3}],$$

and of the columns of the second matrix as the column matrix representations $(\mathbf{m}_j')$ of the vectors,

$$|\mathbf{m}_j') \leftrightarrow \begin{bmatrix} m_{1j}' \\ m_{2j}' \\ m_{3j}' \end{bmatrix}.$$

The element $m_{ij}$ of the product matrix

$$(\mathbf{M}) = (\mathbf{T})(\mathbf{M}')$$

is thus the scalar product of the vector $(\mathbf{t}_i|$ with the vector $|\mathbf{m}_j')$, $m_{ij} = (\mathbf{t}_i \mid \mathbf{m}_j')$.

If we multiply the transformation matrix $(\mathsf{T})$ of Eq. (3–38) by its transpose $(\widetilde{\mathsf{T}}) = (\mathsf{S})$, we obtain, through use of Eq. (3–31), the result

$$(\mathsf{T})(\widetilde{\mathsf{T}}) = \begin{bmatrix} \sum_{1}^{3} t_{1m}t_{1m} & \sum_{1}^{3} t_{1m}t_{2m} & \sum_{1}^{3} t_{1m}t_{3m} \\ \sum_{1}^{3} t_{2m}t_{1m} & \sum_{1}^{3} t_{2m}t_{2m} & \sum_{1}^{3} t_{2m}t_{3m} \\ \sum_{1}^{3} t_{3m}t_{1m} & \sum_{1}^{3} t_{3m}t_{2m} & \sum_{1}^{3} t_{3m}t_{3m} \end{bmatrix}$$

$$= \begin{bmatrix} 1 & 0 & 0 \\ 0 & 1 & 0 \\ 0 & 0 & 1 \end{bmatrix}$$

$$= (\mathbf{1}), \tag{3–49}$$

where $(\mathbf{1})$ is called the *unit matrix*. It has the property that its product with any square matrix $(\mathsf{U})$ yields the same matrix $(\mathsf{U})$,

$$(\mathsf{U})(\mathbf{1}) = (\mathbf{1})(\mathsf{U}) = (\mathsf{U}). \tag{3–50}$$

Two square matrices whose product is the unit matrix are said to be the *inverse* of each other.

The inverse of any matrix $(\mathsf{T})$ is indicated by $(\mathsf{T}^{-1})$. Thus

$$(\mathsf{T}^{-1})(\mathsf{T}) = (\mathsf{T})(\mathsf{T}^{-1}) = (\mathbf{1}). \tag{3–51}$$

For the transformation matrix of this section, the inverse is thus equal to the transpose of the matrix:

$$(\mathsf{T}^{-1}) = (\widetilde{\mathsf{T}}). \tag{3–52}$$

A coordinate transformation whose transformation matrix satisfies this relationship is referred to as an *orthogonal coordinate transformation*. We shall discuss these and other properties of transformation matrices more fully in Chapter 10.

For the moment we shall consider as an example a two-dimensional coordinate transformation. From Fig. 3–10 the reader should have no trouble inferring that

$$\mathbf{i}' = \cos \phi \mathbf{i} + \sin \phi \mathbf{j} \quad \text{and} \quad \mathbf{j}' = -\sin \phi \mathbf{i} + \cos \phi \mathbf{j}.$$

Similarly, from the same figure or by solving the previous equations, we obtain

$$\mathbf{i} = \cos \phi \mathbf{i}' - \sin \phi \mathbf{j}' \quad \text{and} \quad \mathbf{j} = \sin \phi \mathbf{i}' + \cos \phi \mathbf{j}.$$

The matrix which transforms the component description of a vector in the primed system into the component description of the same vector in the unprimed system is found to be,

$$(\mathbf{T}) = \begin{bmatrix} \cos \phi & -\sin \phi \\ \sin \phi & \cos \phi \end{bmatrix}.$$

Its transpose, which is also its inverse, is the matrix

$$(\widetilde{\mathbf{T}}) = (\mathbf{T}^{-1}) = \begin{bmatrix} \cos \phi & \sin \phi \\ -\sin \phi & \cos \phi \end{bmatrix}.$$

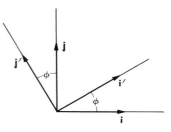

Fig. 3–10. Two-dimensional coordinate transformation.

The inverse matrix relates the component description of a vector in the unprimed system to its description in the primed system. Thus for the position vector $|\mathbf{r})$ which in the unprimed system is represented by $[\begin{smallmatrix} x \\ y \end{smallmatrix}]$ and in the primed system by $[\begin{smallmatrix} x' \\ y' \end{smallmatrix}]$, we have

$$\begin{bmatrix} x \\ y \end{bmatrix} = (\mathbf{T}) \begin{bmatrix} x' \\ y' \end{bmatrix} \quad \text{and} \quad \begin{bmatrix} x' \\ y' \end{bmatrix} = (\widetilde{\mathbf{T}}) \begin{bmatrix} x \\ y \end{bmatrix}.$$

The latter equations, in component form, state that

$$x = x' \cos \phi - y' \sin \phi, \qquad y = x' \sin \phi + y' \sin \phi,$$

and

$$x' = x \cos \phi + y \sin \phi, \qquad y' = -x \sin \phi + y \cos \phi.$$

We also find that

$$(\mathbf{T})(\widetilde{\mathbf{T}}) = \begin{bmatrix} \cos^2 \phi + \sin^2 \phi & \cos \phi \sin \phi - \cos \phi \sin \phi \\ \cos \phi \sin \phi - \cos \phi \sin \phi & \cos^2 \phi + \sin^2 \phi \end{bmatrix}$$

$$= \begin{bmatrix} 1 & 0 \\ 0 & 1 \end{bmatrix}.$$

verifying that

$$(\widetilde{\mathbf{T}}) = (\mathbf{T}^{-1}).$$

---

As a further example of a linear transformation and its matrix representation, we consider the time rate of change of a vector $\mathbf{A}$ of constant magnitude. The time derivative of such a vector was found to be expressible as the vector product of an angular velocity vector $\boldsymbol{\omega}$ with the vector $\mathbf{A}$ (Section 1–8),

$$\dot{\mathbf{A}} = \boldsymbol{\omega} \times \mathbf{A}.$$

The vector $\dot{\mathbf{A}}$ may be considered to be a linear vector function of the vector $\mathbf{A}$, as we can see by expressing the last equation in terms of its cartesian components,

$$\dot{A}_x = \omega_y A_z - \omega_z A_y, \qquad \dot{A}_y = \omega_z A_x - \omega_x A_z, \qquad \dot{A}_z = \omega_x A_y - \omega_y A_x.$$

These equations satisfy the properties of linear vector functions (cf. Chapter 10), and are therefore expressible in matrix notation. We find that

$$
(\dot{\mathbf{A}}) = \begin{bmatrix} \dot{A}_x \\ \dot{A}_y \\ \dot{A}_z \end{bmatrix} = \begin{bmatrix} 0 & -\omega_z & \omega_y \\ \omega_z & 0 & -\omega_x \\ -\omega_y & \omega_x & 0 \end{bmatrix} \begin{bmatrix} A_x \\ A_y \\ A_z \end{bmatrix}. \tag{3-53}
$$

In this sense the matrix

$$
(\mathbf{\Omega}) = \begin{bmatrix} 0 & -\omega_z & \omega_y \\ \omega_z & 0 & -\omega_x \\ -\omega_y & \omega_x & 0 \end{bmatrix} \tag{3-54}
$$

of Eq. (3–53) is considered to be the matrix representation of the linear operator $\mathbf{\Omega}$ which, operating on the vector $|\mathbf{A})$ as expressed symbolically by $\mathbf{\Omega} \, | \, \mathbf{A})$, yields the vector $|\dot{\mathbf{A}})$. Notationally, we write

$$
|\dot{\mathbf{A}}) = \mathbf{\Omega} \, | \, \mathbf{A}), \tag{3-55}
$$

and think of Eq. (3–53) as the matrix representation of this operator equation. We shall develop all these ideas more fully in Chapter 10.

## Problems

3–1. A helicopter landing on a moving ship in a crosswind is observed to be descending vertically at 10 knots by an observer on the ship. If the ship has a forward speed of 20 knots and the crosswind is blowing perpendicular to the ship's course at 20 knots, find the velocity of the helicopter through the air.

3–2. A child is riding a "horse" which moves up and down sinusoidally ($h = h_0 \sin \omega t$) relative to a merry-go-round which rotates about the vertical at the constant rate $\Omega$. If the child is at the distance $c$ from the axis of rotation, find an expression for his acceleration relative to the ground in terms of $\Omega$, $c$, $h_0$, $\omega$, and $t$.

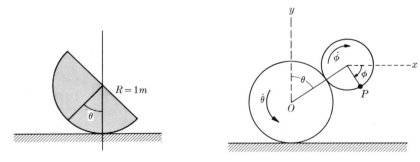

FIGURE 3–11                    FIGURE 3–12

3–3. A half-cylinder (Fig. 3–11) is rocking back and forth sinusoidally without slipping, as shown, such that $\theta = \sin 2t$. (a) As it goes through the neutral position $\theta = 0$, what is the acceleration of the point in contact with the stationary surface?

(b) When the half-cylinder is at the maximum angle of 1 rad, what is the acceleration of the point in contact with the stationary surface?

3–4. A cylinder of radius $r$ rolls on top of a larger cylinder of radius $R$ which is free to roll on a horizontal plane as shown in Fig. 3–12. (a) Find the velocity and acceleration of the point $P$ with respect to the point $O$. (b) Find the velocity and acceleration of the point $P$ with respect to the horizontal plane.

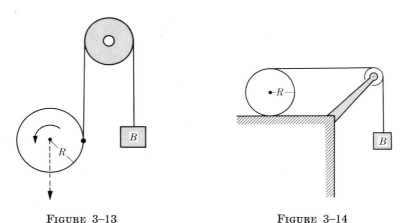

FIGURE 3–13                     FIGURE 3–14

3–5. A cylinder of radius $R$ is unwinding from a string wound about it. The string passes over a pulley and is attached to a body $B$ (Fig. 3–13). Relate the observed velocity and acceleration of the geometric center of the cylinder to its angular velocity and acceleration and to the velocity and acceleration of the body $B$.

3–6. A body $B$ is attached to the free end of a string wound about a cylinder of radius $R$. The cylinder is free to roll on a horizontal table and the body is allowed to descend as shown in Fig. 3–14. Relate the velocity and acceleration of the geometric center of the cylinder to the velocity and acceleration of the body $B$.

3–7. A particle is observed to perform simple harmonic motion along the $x$-axis, its position being given by

$$x = A \sin \omega t.$$

Find the description of its position, velocity, and acceleration with respect to a coordinate system rotating with the constant angular velocity $\boldsymbol{\Omega} = \Omega \mathbf{k}$.

3–8. Find expressions for the velocity and acceleration of a 24-hr satellite in a circular polar orbit as seen from the earth's surface. Let $r = 4000$ miles.

3–9. A body is dropped from a height $h$ above the surface of the earth. (a) Calculate the Coriolis acceleration as a function of time $t$, assuming that the distance $y$ of the body from the surface of the earth as a function of time is given by

$$y = h - \tfrac{1}{2}gt^2.$$

(b) Compute the net displacement $d$ of the point of impact due to the earth's rotation (Fig. 3–15). (Assume the initial velocity of the body to have been zero with respect to the center of the earth.)

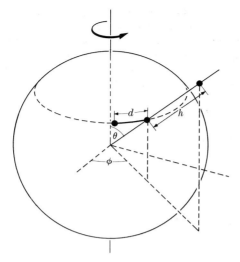

FIGURE 3–15

3–10. The point of support of a simple pendulum moves on a vertical circle of radius $a$ with constant angular velocity $\omega$, as shown in Fig. 3–16. (a) Obtain the expression for the cartesian components of the velocity and the acceleration of the mass $m$. (b) Obtain the generalized acceleration for the angle variable $\theta$.

3–11. Find the velocities and accelerations of particles $p_1$ and $p_2$ of the double pendulum shown in Fig. 3–17: (a) when the motion is confined to a vertical plane (express $\mathbf{v}$ and $\mathbf{a}$ in terms of $\theta_1$, $\theta_2$, $\dot{\theta}_1$, $\dot{\theta}_2$, etc.); (b) when the motion is unconstrained.

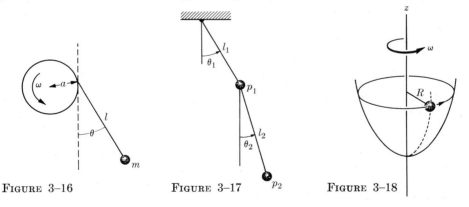

FIGURE 3–16          FIGURE 3–17          FIGURE 3–18

3–12. A bead is able to slide along a smooth wire in the shape of the parabola $z = cr^2$. When the parabola is rotating with an angular velocity $\omega$ about its vertical symmetry axis, the bead is observed to rotate in a circle of radius $R$ (Fig. 3–18). Find the magnitude of the gravitational acceleration $g$ as related to $R$, $\omega$, and $c$.

3–13. Find the product of the matrices

$$\begin{bmatrix} 3 & 0 & 1 \\ 2 & -1 & 2 \\ 0 & 4 & 6 \end{bmatrix} \quad \text{and} \quad \begin{bmatrix} 2 & 3 & -1 \\ 4 & 7 & 0 \\ 5 & 2 & 1 \end{bmatrix}.$$

3–14. By solving the equations

$$\begin{bmatrix} a_{11} & a_{12} & a_{13} \\ a_{21} & a_{22} & a_{23} \\ a_{31} & a_{32} & a_{33} \end{bmatrix} \begin{bmatrix} 1 & \phi_z & -\phi_y \\ -\phi_z & 1 & \phi_x \\ \phi_y & -\phi_x & 1 \end{bmatrix} = \begin{bmatrix} 1 & 0 & 0 \\ 0 & 1 & 0 \\ 0 & 0 & 1 \end{bmatrix},$$

find the inverse of the matrix

$$(\phi) = \begin{bmatrix} 1 & \phi_z & -\phi_y \\ -\phi_z & 1 & \phi_x \\ \phi_y & -\phi_x & 1 \end{bmatrix}.$$

Show that to within first order in the terms $\phi_x$, $\phi_y$, $\phi_z$, it is

$$(\phi^{-1}) = \begin{bmatrix} 1 & -\phi_z & \phi_y \\ \phi_z & 1 & -\phi_x \\ -\phi_y & \phi_x & 1 \end{bmatrix}.$$

3–15. Show that the element $a_{ij}^{-1}$ of the matrix $(a^{-1})$, which is the inverse of the matrix $(a)$, are given by

$$a_{ij}^{-1} = \frac{\text{cofactor } a_{ji}}{\det a_{ij}}.$$

3–16. (a) Show that the transformation matrices for a rotation through an angle $\theta$ about the $x$-, $y$-, and $z$-axes are, respectively,

$$(\mathbf{R}_x(\theta)) = \begin{bmatrix} 1 & 0 & 0 \\ 0 & \cos\theta & \sin\theta \\ 0 & -\sin\theta & \cos\theta \end{bmatrix},$$

$$(\mathbf{R}_y(\theta)) = \begin{bmatrix} \cos\theta & 0 & -\sin\theta \\ 0 & 1 & 0 \\ \sin\theta & 0 & \cos\theta \end{bmatrix},$$

$$(\mathbf{R}_z(\theta)) = \begin{bmatrix} \cos\theta & \sin\theta & 0 \\ -\sin\theta & \cos\theta & 0 \\ 0 & 0 & 1 \end{bmatrix}.$$

(b) Show that the product matrix

$$(\mathbf{R}) = (\mathbf{R}_x(\theta))(\mathbf{R}_z(\phi))$$

represents the transformation matrix for successive rotations about the $z$- and $x$-axes through the angles $\phi$ and $\theta$, respectively.  (c) Show that for this $(\mathbf{R})$

$$(\mathbf{R}^{-1}) = (\mathbf{R}_z(\phi)^{-1})(\mathbf{R}_x(\theta)^{-1}) = (\mathbf{R}_z(-\phi))(\mathbf{R}_x(-\theta)).$$

# 4

# *Particle Dynamics: One-Dimensional Motion*

Dynamics is the study of the motion of bodies and the relation between the motion and the forces determining it. There are several starting points for the study of the dynamics of point bodies. We develop our study of the subject by starting with Newton's three laws of motion.

## 4–1 Newton's first law of motion

Newton's first law of motion may seem obvious from our daily experience. It states that "Every body continues in its state of rest or uniform motion in a straight line unless it is compelled to change that state by forces acting on it."

This statement seems to be in good agreement with our daily observations that bodies change their velocity only by interacting with other bodies. This interaction we describe by saying that the bodies exert forces on each other. It is a logical conclusion that an isolated body which does not interact with any other body will have no forces exerted on it to change its motion. Thus the velocity will be observed to remain constant and the motion to take place in a straight line.

Having discussed moving coordinate systems, however, we should realize that this would not be the correct kinematic description of the motion of an isolated body in all coordinate systems. For example, an isolated body observed to be at rest in one coordinate system may be observed to move in a circle in a coordinate system rotating with respect to the first. Only in very special coordinate systems will the motion of an isolated noninteracting body be correctly described kinematically as stated in the first law of motion. These special coordinate systems are referred to as *inertial* coordinate systems. The first law of motion thus defines but does not identify an inertial system, a coordinate system in which the second law of motion will be assumed to hold.

We note that any coordinate system which moves with a constant velocity with respect to a coordinate system identified as inertial is also an inertial system. This follows from Eqs. (3–2), which tell us that if the velocity $\mathbf{v}'$ of a point in one (primed) coordinate system is a constant, then the velocity $\mathbf{v}$ in a second (unprimed) coordinate system moving with respect to the first with the constant velocity $-\mathbf{V}$ is also a constant, since

$$\mathbf{v} = \mathbf{v}' + \mathbf{V}. \tag{4–1}$$

The concept of inertial coordinate system is very important in physics, for it is with respect to an inertial coordinate system that the fundamental laws of physics are formulated. It is furthermore one of the basic assumptions of the special theory of relativity, which concerns itself with the relationship between the values of physical quantities measured by different inertial observers, that the fundamental laws of physics can be expressed in such a manner that they assume the same mathematical form in all inertial systems. That is to say, for example, that if **A**, **B**, and **C** are three physical vector quantities, functions of position and time, which are related in a relativistically invariant form in one inertial system by the equation

$$\mathbf{A} \times \mathbf{B} = \mathbf{C}, \tag{4-2}$$

then **A′**, **B′**, and **C′**, which are the descriptions of these same vector quantities in another inertial system, should be similarly related in that system by the equation

$$\mathbf{A'} \times \mathbf{B'} = \mathbf{C'}. \tag{4-3}$$

Another way of saying this is that the fundamental physical laws can be cast in a mathematical form which is invariant to a transformation of their description from one inertial coordinate system to another.

Unless otherwise indicated we shall always consider the motion of any particle under consideration to take place in an inertial coordinate system. The second law of motion below is formulated and assumed to hold only in an inertial system. As we shall see from our subsequent discussion on relativity (Chapter 13), the second law of motion as formulated here is not cast in a relativistically invariant form.

## 4–2 Newton's second law of motion: concepts of mass and force

The second law of motion relates the change in the motion of a body to its interaction with other bodies. This interaction is measured by the physical quantity called *force*.

Before stating the second law of motion, we shall inquire into the definition of the physical quantity called *mass*. An understanding of this concept is a prerequisite to an understanding of what is physically meant by a force.

In order to arrive at the concept of mass, we consider the hypothetical experiment of two interacting particles which are isolated from all other interactions. We call this a hypothetical experiment, because we are in no position to actually perform it. Any experiment which we do perform would be influenced by the presence of the earth's gravitational interaction with the particles. We could, however, imagine two particles on a frictionless horizontal plane where the presence of the plane makes the gravitational effect on the motion of the particles on the plane negligible. The interaction between the particles may, for example, be due to the fact that they carry electrical charge—and charged bodies are known to interact—or they may interact by being attached to the ends of a spring whose effect on the motion is small and negligible.

From our daily experience with the motion of bodies we expect that due to their interaction the bodies will receive oppositely directed accelerations along the line joining the two particles (Fig. 4–1). Furthermore, irrespective of the strength of their interaction, we expect the ratio of the magnitudes of the accelerations received by the two particles to be a constant.* That is,

$$a_1 = \lambda_{12}a_2. \tag{4–4}$$

The same experiment involving particle 1 and a third particle is expected to yield the similar result,

$$a_1 = \lambda_{13}a_3, \tag{4–5}$$

while a repetition of the experiment, this time using particles 2 and 3, in turn should yield

$$a_2 = \lambda_{23}a_3. \tag{4–6}$$

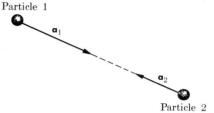

From our daily experience we expect to find $\lambda_{12}$, $\lambda_{13}$, and $\lambda_{23}$ to be related. That is, we expect as a result of an actual experiment to find

Fig. 4–1. Two interacting particles.

$$\lambda_{12}\lambda_{23} = \lambda_{13}. \tag{4–7}$$

This being so, it is possible to assign to each particle a number $m$ such that

$$\lambda_{12} = \frac{m_2}{m_1}, \quad \lambda_{13} = \frac{m_3}{m_1}, \quad \text{and} \quad \lambda_{23} = \frac{m_3}{m_2}. \tag{4–8}$$

This number $m$ is referred to as the *mass* of the particle. We note that once the number $m_1$ has been assigned as the mass of particle 1, the mass of any other particles is determined and can be obtained from an experiment such as the one described above, involving the latter particle and particle 1. The choice of the standard mass is of course quite arbitrary. In this text we shall use the kilogram mass of the mks system of units as the unit of mass.

In terms of the assigned masses of each of the particles, and remembering that the accelerations are oppositely directed, Eq. (4–4) may be rewritten as

$$m_1\mathbf{a}_1 = -m_2\mathbf{a}_2. \tag{4–9}$$

The quantity $m_1\mathbf{a}_1$ is taken as the quantitative measure of the interaction.

---

* That $\lambda_{12}$ of Eq. 4–4 is a constant independent of the velocities of the particles is an underlying assumption of classical mechanics. This assumption is found to be a good approximation for particles moving with velocities small compared to the velocity of light, as verified by the satisfactory results obtained on the basis of classical mechanics for such particles.

It is referred to as the *force* **F**, which particle 2 exerts on particle 1. The concept of force is thus defined by the equation

$$\mathbf{F} = m\mathbf{a}. \tag{4–10}$$

The force acting on a particle is the product of the mass of the particle times the acceleration which it attains due to its interaction with other bodies.

This is essentially Newton's second law of motion which, quoted more correctly, states: "The time rate of change of the momentum of a particle is proportional to the force applied to the particle and in the direction of the force."

The *momentum* **p** of a particle is defined as the product of the mass of the particle and its velocity,

$$\mathbf{p} = m\mathbf{v}. \tag{4–11}$$

In terms of **p**, Eq. (4–10) is expressed by

$$\mathbf{F} = \frac{d}{dt}(m\mathbf{v}) = \frac{d\mathbf{p}}{dt}, \tag{4–12}$$

which is the correct mathematical expression of the second law of motion.

The unit of force in the mks system of units may be determined from Eq. (4–10) in terms of the units of mass, length, and time. We define the unit of force, the *newton*, to be that force which gives a particle of mass one kilogram an acceleration of one meter per second, per second. Dimensionally,

$$1\text{ n} = 1\ \frac{\text{kg-m}}{\text{sec}^2}.$$

## 4–3 Newton's third law of motion

The third law of motion is expressed by Eq. (4–9). It states that "To every action there is always an equal and opposite reaction."

The third law of motion, we should like to point out, applies only to the interaction of two bodies. The forces which two bodies exert on each other are always equal in magnitude and oppositely directed.

Problems in which, due to the interaction between two particles, one or both of the particles radiate energy or other particles are created are not two-body problems. In such problems Newton's third law of motion is not satisfied. Nevertheless in any closed system of particles (cf. Chapter 8) we shall assume that the sum of the forces which the particles exert on each other vanishes,

$$\sum_{i \neq j} \mathbf{F}_{ij} = \sum_{i} \dot{\mathbf{p}}_{i} = \frac{d}{dt} \sum_{i} \mathbf{p}_{i} = 0, \tag{4–13}$$

where $\mathbf{F}_{ij}$ is the force which the $j$th particle exerts on the $i$th particle. In the special case of two interacting particles, this takes the form

$$\mathbf{F}_{12} + \mathbf{F}_{21} = m_1\mathbf{a}_1 + m_2\mathbf{a}_2 = 0 \tag{4-14}$$

or

$$\frac{d}{dt}(\mathbf{p}_1 + \mathbf{p}_2) = 0.$$

From Eq. (4–13) we obtain the important conservation theorem for the total linear momentum of an isolated system of particles:

$$\sum_i \mathbf{p}_i = \text{const.} \tag{4-15}$$

This important conservation theorem will be discussed in Chapter 8.

## 4-4 One-dimensional problems

In the usual mechanics problem the forces acting on a particle are specified, together with the initial values of the position and velocity of the particle. It is then desired to find the orbit traversed by the particle as a function of time. The orbit as a function of time is specified by the time dependence of the position vector:

$$\mathbf{r} = \mathbf{r}(t).$$

It represents the solution to the equation of motion. Equation (4–10) yields three simultaneous differential equations of motion of at least the second order, for which explicit solutions are not always available. For such cases one resorts to numerical or approximate solutions to the problem. We shall restrict ourselves essentially to the simpler problems, those for which exact or important explicit approximate solutions are available.

The decomposition of Eq. (4–10) into three component equations of motion may yield one or more differential equations, each involving only one of the coordinates utilized for the description of the motion of the particle. The solution of any such equation, which we call a one-dimensional equation of motion, is independent of the other two equations of motion. We consider it fortuitous if, through the proper choice of coordinates, we can obtain one or more such component equations.

Problems for which the separation of the equations of motion into one or more one-dimensional equations is not possible are problems for which in general explicit analytical solutions are not available.

The problems which we shall consider, therefore, will in general (with the proper choice of coordinates) be separable into one or more independent one-dimensional equations of motion. The solution of these equations will in turn permit us to solve the remaining equations which were not originally one-dimensional.

In this chapter we consider the solutions of various one-dimensional differential equations of motion, equations which we shall meet frequently and to which explicit solutions are readily available.

For simplicity in arriving at these equations of motion, we restrict ourselves in this chapter to the motion of a particle along a straight line. For such a problem there exists only one nontrivial component equation of motion. If the component of the force along this line is a function of the time, the position, and the velocity of the particle, then the equation of motion for the particle has the form

$$F(x, \dot{x}, t) = m\ddot{x}, \qquad (4\text{--}16)$$

where we have chosen the $x$-axis to lie along the line of motion. We proceed to consider solutions of Eq. (4–16) for various force functions.

## 4–5 Force as a function of time only

If the force is a function of time only, then the equation of motion is

$$F(t) = m\ddot{x}. \qquad (4\text{--}17)$$

This equation can be integrated to yield the velocity as a function of time. Integrating Eq. (4–17) with respect to time from the initial time $t_0$ to a final time $t$, we obtain

$$m(v - v_0) = \int_{t_0}^{t} F(\lambda)\, d\lambda, \qquad (4\text{--}18)$$

since

$$\int_{t_0}^{t} \ddot{x}\, dt = v(t) - v(t_0).$$

In Eq. (4–18) $\lambda$ is a dummy variable of integration, and $v_0 = v(t_0)$. The integral of the force with respect to time which appears on the right-hand side of Eq. (4–18) is referred to as the *impulse* which the force $F$ imparts to the particle. This equation is thus the *impulse-momentum theorem*, which states that the impulse imparted to a particle is equal to the change in its linear momentum.

A subsequent integration of Eq. (4–18) yields the desired solution:

$$x(t) - x(t_0) = v_0(t - t_0) + \frac{1}{m} \int_{t_0}^{t} dt \int_{t_0}^{t} F(\lambda)\, d\lambda. \qquad (4\text{--}19)$$

If the necessary integrations in Eq. (4–19) can be performed explicitly, then this equation yields an explicit solution for the position of the particle as a function of time. If the integrations cannot be performed explicitly, then we may still perform a numerical integration and obtain a numerical solution to the problem.

A special example of a force which may be considered as a function of time is the constant force.
For such a force, Eq. (4–18) yields, for the velocity
of the particle as a function of time, the result

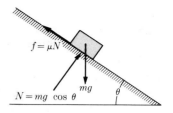

$$v = v_0 + a(t - t_0), \qquad (4\text{–}20)$$

where $a = F/m$ is the constant acceleration of
the particle. For the position of the particle we
obtain, upon integrating Eq. (4–20), the result

FIG. 4–2.    Particle sliding
down an incline.

$$x = x_0 + v_0(t - t_0) + \tfrac{1}{2}a(t - t_0)^2. \qquad (4\text{–}21)$$

Equations (4–20) and (4–21) should be familiar to the reader from his first
course in mechanics, which usually dwells at length on constant-force problems.
He may remember that the gravitational force acting on a particle moving near
the surface of the earth may for all practical purposes be considered to be
constant and equal to $mg$, where $g$ is the gravitational acceleration which a
particle receives when acted on by the constant gravitational force. Another
example is the equation of motion for a particle moving on an inclined plane
under the action of the constant gravitational force plus a frictional force. This
equation may be remembered by the reader (cf. Fig. 4–2) to be

$$mg \sin \theta - \mu mg \cos \theta = m\ddot{x}, \qquad (4\text{–}22)$$

where $\mu$ is the coefficient of sliding friction between the particle and the plane.

A constant force may also be considered as a special example of a force which
is a function of position only. This we shall consider in the next section.

As a second example of the solution of the equation of motion involving a
time-dependent force, we consider the problem of a particle which at time
$t = 0$ has the position $x_0$, the velocity $v_0$, and is being acted on by the sinusoidal
force

$$F = F_0 \sin \omega t.$$

The equation of motion

$$\ddot{x} = \frac{F_0}{m} \sin \omega t$$

can readily be integrated to yield the velocity as a function of time,

$$\dot{x} = v_0 + \frac{F_0}{m\omega} - \frac{F_0}{m\omega} \cos \omega t,$$

and by a subsequent integration the position as a function of time,

$$x = x_0 + \left(v_0 + \frac{F_0}{m\omega}\right) t - \frac{F_0}{m\omega^2} \sin \omega t.$$

This latter problem is of interest in connection with the scattering of electromagnetic radiation by free electrons, such as appear in the ionosphere. The scattering of an electromagnetic wave is produced by the electrons absorbing energy from the incoming electromagnetic wave and reradiating this energy in all directions.

An accelerated electron radiates electromagnetic energy, and the radiated electromagnetic field is a linear function of the electron's acceleration. Since only the sinusoidal term in the solution above contributes to the acceleration of the electron, it follows (neglecting the Doppler effect) that the radiated energy has the same frequency as the incoming electromagnetic wave. Furthermore, the radiated energy has a definite phase relationship to the incoming wave. This means that the radiation from all the electrons combines coherently. The net effect results in a reflected and a transmitted wave which is very much like the reflection and transmission which occurs when light goes from air into glass or vice versa (cf. Chapter 12). The amount of energy reflected is dependent on the phase velocity of propagation of the resultant electromagnetic wave within the ionosphere. This phase velocity turns out to be larger than the phase velocity of the wave in air,* and is a function of the frequency.

## 4–6 Force as a function of position: concepts of work and energy

Forces that are functions of position occur frequently in physics. Two examples with which we shall be especially concerned are the electrical and the gravitational forces.

The one-dimensional equation of motion for the rectilinear motion of a particle under the action of a force that is a function of position only is

$$F(x) = m \frac{dv}{dt}. \qquad (4\text{--}23)$$

We find that both sides of this equation are readily integrable with respect to the position variable $x$. The integral of the left-hand side of Eq. (4–23) is referred to as the *work* which the force $F$ performs on the particle while it moves from the initial position $x_0$ to its final position $x$,

$$\text{Work} = \int_{x_0}^{x} F(x)\, dx. \qquad (4\text{--}24)$$

---

* This does not introduce a contradiction to the theory of relativity, which states that energy cannot be transferred with a speed which exceeds the speed of light. For a discussion of this point, and for an illuminating derivation of the index of refraction of an electron gas from the response of the electrons to the electromagnetic wave, the reader is referred to *The Feynman Lectures on Physics*, Vol. I, Chapter 31. Reading, Mass.: Addison-Wesley, 1963.

The unit of work in the mks system of units is the *joule*; it is equivalent to one newton-meter. The work integral can always be evaluated, either explicitly or numerically. In either case we can define a function $U(x)$ such that

$$F(x) = -\frac{dU(x)}{dx} \tag{4–25}$$

or

$$U(x) = -\int^{x} F(x)\, dx.$$

This permits us to express the work as the difference in the value of $U(x)$ at the two endpoints,

$$W = \int_{x_0}^{x} F(x)\, dx = -U(x)|_{x_0}^{x} = U(x_0) - U(x). \tag{4–26}$$

The function $U(x)$ is referred to as the *potential energy* which the particle has when it is located at the point $x$. We have thus found the work performed by the force $F(x)$ to be equal to the difference between the initial and final values of the potential energy of the particle.

The right-hand side of Eq. (4–23) is also expressible as a perfect differential. Changing the variable of integration from $x$ to $t$—that is, letting $dx = v\, dt$—we obtain

$$\int_{x_0}^{x} m\frac{dv}{dt}\, dx = \int_{t_0}^{t} m\frac{dv}{dt} v\, dt = \int_{t_0}^{t} \frac{d}{dt}\left(\frac{1}{2}mv^2\right) dt$$

$$= \frac{1}{2}mv^2\bigg|_{t_0}^{t} = \frac{1}{2}mv^2 - \frac{1}{2}mv_0^2. \tag{4–27}$$

The quantity $\frac{1}{2}mv^2$ is referred to as the *kinetic energy* of the particle, for which we shall henceforth use the symbol $T$:

$$T = \tfrac{1}{2}mv^2. \tag{4–28}$$

The unit of kinetic energy in the mks system of units is like the unit of work, the joule.

We have thus found that, for any force $F(x)$,

$$W = \int_{x_0}^{x} F(x)\, dx = U(x_0) - U(x) = T(x) - T(x_0)$$

or

$$U(x) + T(x) = U(x_0) + T(x_0). \tag{4–29}$$

Equation (4–29) expresses the very important physical principle of the *conservation of total energy*:

$$T(x) + U(x) = E. \tag{4–30}$$

It is applicable in any one-dimensional problem in which the force is a function of position only. Equation (4–29) is also referred to as the *principle of work and energy*. It states that the work done on a particle by a force is equal to the change in its kinetic energy.

We note that the potential energy function defined by Eq. (4–25) is indeterminate to within a constant, the constant of integration. This does not matter, however, since only the difference in the potential energy appears in any application. This is a good point to remember, for it permits us to arbitrarily choose the point at which the particle has zero potential energy. It also permits us, at any time we find it convenient to do so, to add at all points the same constant value to the potential energy of a particle without affecting the results.

▶ As an illustration, we consider the vertical motion of a particle of mass $m$ under the action of a spring, to which it is attached, and the force of gravity (Fig. 4–3). This, it turns out, is a vexing problem to some students.

The gravitational force has a constant magnitude and acts in the downward direction, as shown. The force that the spring exerts on the particle, on the other hand, is a function of the change in the length of the spring. Its magnitude is given by

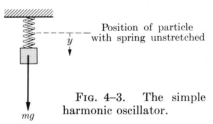

Position of particle with spring unstretched

$$F_s = ky,$$

FIG. 4–3.   The simple harmonic oscillator.

where $y$ represents the increase in the length of the spring. If $y$ is taken as positive in the downward direction, then the magnitude and direction of the force of the spring on the particle are given by

$$F_s = -ky.$$

The total vertical force on the particle of mass $m$ is thus given by

$$F = -ky + mg,$$

which yields the potential energy function

$$U(y) = -\int^y F \, dy = \frac{1}{2} ky^2 - mgy$$

$$= \frac{1}{2} k \left( y - \frac{mg}{k} \right)^2 - \frac{m^2 g^2}{2k}.$$

The coordinate transformation,

$$y = y' + \frac{mg}{k},$$

shifts the origin of coordinates to the point

$$y = \frac{mg}{k},$$

which is the equilibrium position of the system. In terms of $y'$ (the displacement of the particle from its equilibrium position), the potential energy is expressed by

$$U(y') = \frac{1}{2} ky'^2 - \frac{m^2 g^2}{2k}.$$

This potential energy function yields the same result for the motion of the particle as the potential energy function

$$U(y') = \tfrac{1}{2}ky'^2,$$

which in turn may be obtained from the previous expression for the potential energy by adding the constant value $m^2 g^2/2k$ to the value of the potential energy at all points. The principle of the conservation of total energy permits us to express the speed of the particle as a function of its position. For the example under discussion, we find that

$$\tfrac{1}{2}ky'^2 + \tfrac{1}{2}m\dot{y}'^2 = \text{const} = E,$$

or that the speed of the particle at the point $y'$ is given by

$$|\dot{y}'| = \sqrt{\frac{2E}{m} - \frac{k}{m} y'^2}.$$

The force acting on the particle when it is located at the point $y'$ is given by

$$F = -\frac{dU}{dy'} = -ky'.$$

As we shall show in Section 4–9, the displacement of the particle from the equilibrium point varies sinusoidally with time. A particle moving under the action of a restoring force proportional to the displacement is therefore referred to as a simple harmonic oscillator. ◀

Returning to the problem at hand, however, from Eq. (4–30) we obtain

$$T = \tfrac{1}{2}mv^2 = E - U(x)$$

or

$$v = \pm\sqrt{(2/m)[E - U(x)]}. \tag{4–31}$$

The choice of the plus or minus sign in front of the square-root sign depends on whether the particle is moving in the increasing or decreasing $x$-direction. This fact can be ascertained from the initial and subsequent values of $v$ as will be discussed in the next section. Equation (4–31), expressed as

$$\frac{dx}{\pm\sqrt{(2/m)[E - U(x)]}} = dt,$$

may be integrated to yield $t$ as a function of $x$:

$$t - t_0 = \int_{x_0}^{x} \frac{\sqrt{m}\, dx}{\pm\sqrt{2[E - U(x)]}}. \tag{4-32}$$

This latter equation, when subsequently solved for $x$ as a function of $t$, yields the required solution.

We should like to point out that time $t$ is a continuously increasing quantity. In performing the integration on the right-hand side of Eq. (4–32), we must therefore choose the plus sign when $x$ is increasing and the minus sign when $x$ is decreasing. The determination of the turning points at which the sign of the velocity changes is considered in the next section.

▶ Before discussing this more fully, let us consider once more the simple example of a constant force. For such a force, the potential energy is

$$U(x) = -\int^{x} F\, dx = -Fx,$$

whence, from the principle of work and energy, we obtain

$$\tfrac{1}{2}m(v^2 - v_0^2) = F(x - x_0)$$

or

$$v^2 = v_0^2 + \frac{2F}{m}\,(x - x_0) = v_0^2 + 2a(x - x_0). \tag{4-33}$$

The reader may remember the latter equation from his first physics course.

We may now proceed to determine $x(t)$ from Eq. (4–33). We find that

$$\frac{dx}{\pm\sqrt{v_0^2 - 2ax_0 + 2ax}} = dt,$$

which, when integrated (assuming $\dot{x} > 0$), yields

$$\frac{1}{a}\left.\sqrt{v_0^2 - 2ax_0 + 2ax}\,\right|_{x_0}^{x} = t - t_0. \tag{4-34}$$

Equation (4–34) can be solved for $x$ to yield the well-known solution

$$x = x_0 + v_0(t - t_0) + \tfrac{1}{2}a(t - t_0)^2,$$

which was also obtained in the previous section. ◀

## 4–7 Force as a function of position: bounded and unbounded motion

The problem of a force depending only on the position of the particle is a very important one. In this section we shall study the qualitative nature of the motion performed by a particle under the action of such a force. As mentioned in the last section, the force $F(x)$ is derivable from a potential energy function

$U(x)$, specifically

$$F(x) = -\frac{dU}{dx}.\qquad(4\text{--}35)$$

We also found that under the action of such a force the total energy, which is the sum of the potential and kinetic energies, is a constant of the motion:

$$T + U = E.\qquad(4\text{--}36)$$

Let us consider a graph of the potential energy function $U(x)$ as a function of $x$. Figure 4–4 represents some such arbitrary potential energy function plotted as a function of the position coordinate. If on the same graph we now draw a line representing the magnitude of the constant energy, the difference between the potential energy curve and the constant $E$ line at any point $x$ represents the kinetic energy which the particle has at the point in question. We indicated this fact for one specific point on the graph in Fig. 4–4. The kinetic energy, being proportional to the square of the particle velocity, must necessarily at all times be a positive quantity. It follows from this that the value $E$ of the total energy must, for all physical points—points at which the particle may be found—have a value which is larger than that of the potential energy at the physically accessible points. In other words, the total energy line must lie above the potential energy curve for all points physically accessible to the particle. Any region for which this is not the case we must conclude is not a physically accessible region for the problem under consideration.

For the potential energy and total energy curves depicted in Fig. 4–4, the regions between points $x_1$ and $x_2$ and the points $x_3$ and $x_4$, that is, regions II and IV, are two such inaccessible regions for the particle. All the other regions in the figure are physically accessible. In any problem, however, the particle will remain in the region in which it is initially located. For example, suppose that the particle is initially in region I and is moving in the increasing $x$-direction toward the point $x_1$. When it reaches point $x_1$ it will have zero kinetic energy,

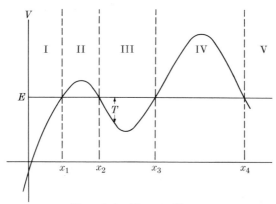

Fig. 4–4. Energy diagram.

since it is a point where the potential energy equals the total energy. This means that the particle will come to rest at the point $x_1$. An instant later it will once again be in motion going back whence it came. Since it cannot go on into region two, it must thus remain in region one.

Another way of recognizing that it will retrace its path is to note that the slope of the potential energy curve at the point $x = x_1$ is positive. A positive slope means that the force acting on the particle at that point, being the negative of the derivative of $U(x)$ with respect to $x$, points in the negative $x$-direction. The particle will therefore start to move in the negative $x$-direction.

The point $x = x_1$ at which $U(x) = E$ is called a *turning point*, since it is the point at which the particle will come to rest and instantly begin to move away in the direction from which it has come.

By a similar analysis we conclude that the points $x = x_2$, $x = x_3$, and $x = x_4$ are also turning points, and that a particle once located in any of the regions I, III, or V will remain in that region. We note that regions I and V each have only one turning point, extending on the other end to infinity. Such regions in which the particle can go to infinity are called *unbounded regions*, whereas region III which has two turning points in the finite part of space is called a *bounded region*.

A particle moving in a bounded region is said to perform bound motion. If the particle motion is one-dimensional, it is necessarily periodic. The motion will repeat itself after the lapse of a time $\tau$, called the period of the motion.

## 4–8 Stable and unstable equilibrium

For the potential energy function depicted in Fig. 4–4, there exist points for which its slope vanishes:

$$\frac{dU}{dx} = 0. \tag{4-37}$$

At such points the force is zero, and a particle placed at such a point with zero velocity will continue to remain at rest at that point.

When the force acting on a particle vanishes, the particle is said to be in equilibrium. There is a distinction, however, between the equilibrium points at which the potential energy has a minimum value and those at which it has a maximum value. At the former, a particle disturbed from equilibrium by receiving some kinetic energy or by being displaced slightly and subsequently released from rest will have a total energy which is larger than the minimum value of the potential energy (Fig. 4–5). It will move in a bounded region performing periodic motion. Such equilibrium points about which a particle will move in a bounded region, performing periodic motion when disturbed from equilibrium, are called points of *stable equilibrium*.

On the other hand, if the particle finds itself at a point of maximum potential energy, a slight displacement from equilibrium will result in the particle moving

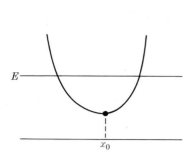

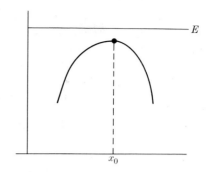

Fig. 4–5. Point of stable equilibrium.    Fig. 4–6. Point of unstable equilibrium.

further away from the equilibrium point when released. This can be understood from our analysis of the motion of a particle from a turning point (Fig. 4–6).

By the same token, if it were given some kinetic energy at a point of maximum potential energy it would also continue to move away from that point.

A point of maximum potential energy is for this reason referred to as a point of *unstable equilibrium*.

## 4–9 Motion about a point of stable equilibrium: the simple harmonic oscillator

The motion of a particle about a point of stable equilibrium is one of the most important problems in physics. We therefore proceed with a discussion of the one-dimensional motion of a particle about a point of stable equilibrium. We consider the motion for which the maximum displacement of the particle from the equilibrium position is small. By a small maximum displacement we mean a displacement for which, and naturally therefore also for all smaller displacements, the potential energy function may be approximated by retaining only the first important nonvanishing term of its Taylor-series expansion about the equilibrium point $x = x_0$.

The Taylor expansion of a function $f(x)$ is given by

$$f(x) = \sum_{n=0}^{\infty} \frac{1}{n!} f^{(n)}(x_0)[x - x_0]^n, \qquad (4\text{--}38)$$

where

$$f^{(n)}(x_0) = \frac{d^n f(x)}{dx^n}\bigg|_{x=x_0}. \qquad (4\text{--}39)$$

Remembering that at a point of stable equilibrium $dU/dx = 0$, it follows that

$$U(x) = U(x_0) + \frac{1}{2!} U^{(2)}(x_0)(x - x_0)^2 + \cdots. \qquad (4\text{--}40)$$

The first term $U(x_0)$ is a constant. It is the value of the potential energy at $x = x_0$. But we concluded earlier that we could always adjust the potential energy so that at one specific point its value may be made to vanish (cf. Section 4–6). We choose to do so at the point $x = x_0$, that is, we choose to make $U(x_0) = 0$. With this choice, and to a first approximation then,

$$U(x) = \tfrac{1}{2}k(x - x_0)^2, \tag{4–41}$$

where we have set

$$k = U^{(2)}(x_0). \tag{4–42}$$

Since, for a point of minimum potential energy,

$$\frac{d^2U}{dx^2} > 0, \tag{4–43}$$

the constant

$$k > 0. \tag{4–44}$$

The problem can be further simplified notationally by shifting the origin of the coordinate system to the point $x = x_0$. The point $x_0$ thus assumes the value zero and Eq. (4–42) becomes

$$U(x) = \tfrac{1}{2}kx^2. \tag{4–45}$$

For this potential energy function the force, being equal to the negative derivative of the potential energy with respect to $x$, has for any point $x$ the value expressed by

$$F = -\frac{dU}{dx} = -kx. \tag{4–46}$$

We should be cognizant of the fact that the motion about a point of stable equilibrium, being a bound motion, implies the existence of a maximum displacement from the equilibrium point which is obtained from the equation

$$U(x_{\max}) = E \quad \text{or} \quad \tfrac{1}{2}kx_{\max}^2 = E.$$

It has the solution

$$x_{\max} = \pm A = \pm\sqrt{2E/k}. \tag{4–47}$$

The equation of motion for a particle moving under the action of a restoring force proportional to the displacement of the particle from the equilibrium position is

$$m\ddot{x} = -kx. \tag{4–48}$$

To obtain its solution we choose to follow the procedure outlined in Section 4–6. We know that the potential energy is given by

$$U = \tfrac{1}{2}kx^2.$$

Inserting this into Eq. (4–31), which was obtained through use of the principle of the conservation of total energy,

$$E = \tfrac{1}{2}m\dot{x}^2 + U(x),$$

we obtain

$$\dot{x} = \pm\sqrt{(2E/m) - (kx^2/m)} = \pm\sqrt{\omega_0^2(A^2 - x^2)}. \qquad (4\text{–}49)$$

We have set

$$\frac{2E}{m} = \omega_0^2 A^2 \qquad (4\text{–}50)$$

and

$$k = m\omega_0^2, \qquad (4\text{–}51)$$

which leads us to the equation

$$\omega_0(t - t_0) = \int_{x_0}^{x} \frac{dx}{\pm\sqrt{A^2 - x^2}}. \qquad (4\text{–}52)$$

In performing the integration in Eq. (4–52), a little care must be exercised in the choice of the plus or minus sign, as mentioned in Section 4–6.

To perform this integration, we make the substitution

$$x = A \sin\theta, \qquad dx = A \cos\theta\, d\theta;$$

and to ensure that time is continuously increasing, we shall choose $\theta_0$ for positive initial velocities to have a value between $-\pi/2$ and $\pi/2$. On the other hand, for negative initial values of the particle velocity, we shall choose $\theta_0$ to have a value between $\pi/2$ and $3\pi/2$.

For this choice of $\theta_0$ we find that $\theta$ also increases continuously and that therefore we can set

$$\int_{x_0}^{x} \frac{dx}{\pm\sqrt{A^2 - x^2}} = \int_{\theta_0}^{\theta} \frac{A \cos\theta\, d\theta}{\sqrt{A^2(1 - \sin^2\theta)}} = \int_{\theta_0}^{\theta} d\theta.$$

Hence

$$\omega_0(t - t_0) = \theta - \theta_0 = \sin^{-1}\frac{x}{A} - \sin^{-1}\frac{x_0}{A},$$

yielding

$$x = A \sin[\omega_0(t - t_0) + \theta_0], \qquad (4\text{–}53)$$

where

$$\theta_0 = \sin^{-1}\frac{x_0}{A}. \qquad (4\text{–}54)$$

We have thus found, to a first approximation, the motion of a particle about a point of stable equilibrium to be a sinusoidal oscillation with a period

$$\tau = \frac{2\pi}{\omega_0}, \qquad (4\text{–}55)$$

and a maximum displacement or amplitude

$$A = \sqrt{2E/m\omega_0^2}. \qquad (4\text{--}56)$$

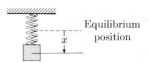

FIG. 4–7. A simple harmonic oscillator.

The motion of a particle which varies sinusoidally with time, as expressed by Eq. (4–53), is said to be simple harmonic. The reader should verify that (4–53) is a solution of the equation of motion, Eq. (4–48).

▶ As an example, we consider once more (cf. Section 4–6) a particle of mass $m$ attached to a spring of constant $k$, and free to move in a vertical direction (Fig. 4–7). The system consisting of the particle and spring has an equilibrium position at which the gravitational force acting on the particle is balanced by the force which the spring exerts on the particle.

Any displacement $x$ from this equilibrium position will change the magnitude of the force which the spring exerts on the particle, thereby leaving a net force

$$F = -kx$$

acting on the particle. This is exactly the type of force which will give the particle a simple harmonic oscillation with a frequency

$$f = \frac{1}{\tau} = \frac{1}{2\pi} \sqrt{\frac{k}{m}}. \qquad (4\text{--}57)$$

The amplitude of the motion in this problem depends on the initial position and velocity of the particle.

$$A = \sqrt{2E/m\omega_0^2} = \sqrt{(v_0^2/\omega_0^2) + x_0^2}. \qquad (4\text{--}58)$$

The phase $\theta_0$ of the motion is determined from the initial displacement amplitude and the initial velocity as discussed above. ◀

## 4–10 Motion under the action of a velocity-dependent force

Problems which involve a force which is a function only of the velocity lead to the equation of motion:

$$F(v) = m\ddot{x}. \qquad (4\text{--}59)$$

There exist several ways by which we can obtain a solution to this equation. For example, we can express Eq. (4–59) as either

$$F(v) = m\frac{dv}{dt} \qquad (4\text{--}60)$$

or

$$F(v) = mv\frac{dv}{dx}, \qquad (4\text{--}61)$$

where the latter equation was obtained by replacing $dv/dt$ in the equation preceding it by $(dv/dx)(dx/dt)$.

The last two equations are both first-order differential equations and, therefore, always have solutions. From the first equation we obtain time as a function of the velocity

$$t - t_0 = \int_{v_0}^{v} \frac{m\, dv}{F(v)}, \tag{4-62}$$

where $v_0$ is the particle velocity at the initial time $t_0$. The second equation when integrated yields the position as a function of the velocity,

$$x - x_0 = \int_{v_0}^{v} \frac{mv\, dv}{F(v)}. \tag{4-63}$$

Equations (4–62) and (4–63) together represent a parametric solution to the equation of motion. If we desire, we may eliminate the velocity between the two equations in order to obtain the position as a function of time directly.

Another approach toward finding $x$ as a function of $t$ is to integrate either of the last two equations, after first solving them for the velocity. From Eq. (4–62) we obtain $v$ as a function of $t$. A subsequent integration of $v$ with respect to time yields the desired solution,

$$x - x_0 = \int_{t_0}^{t} v\, dt. \tag{4-64}$$

From Eq. (4–63), on the other hand, we obtain $v$ as a function of $x$,

$$\frac{dx}{dt} = v(x). \tag{4-65}$$

The integration of this equation yields

$$t - t_0 = \int_{x_0}^{x} \frac{dx}{v(x)}. \tag{4-66}$$

To obtain $x$ as a function of $t$ we would have to invert the preceding equation, solving for $x$ as a function of time $t$.

▶ As an example, we consider the problem of a particle moving in a resistive medium. For low particle speeds we find the damping force which opposes the motion to be an approximately linear function of the velocity,

$$F_{\text{damping}} = -m\kappa v, \tag{4-67}$$

where $m\kappa$ is a constant, $m$ being used so that the solution will appear in a simpler form.

At higher particle speeds the damping force is found to be proportional to a higher power of the velocity.

For low speeds, then, we meet the equation of motion,

$$m \frac{dv}{dt} = -m\kappa v. \tag{4–68}$$

This first-order differential equation of motion may be integrated to yield

$$\kappa(t - t_0) = -\ln \frac{v}{v_0}$$

or

$$v = v_0 \exp\left[-\kappa(t - t_0)\right]. \tag{4–69}$$

A subsequent integration of the last equation yields the solution

$$x - x_0 = \frac{v_0}{\kappa} [1 - e^{-\kappa(t-t_0)}]. \tag{4–70}$$

We note that as time increases, the velocity decreases, approaching zero exponentially as the particle approaches the point

$$x_\infty = x_0 + \frac{v_0}{\kappa}. \tag{4–71}$$

It is of interest to compute the work performed by the damping force and to verify that it equals the kinetic energy lost by the particle.

The total work performed by the damping force is

$$W = \int_{x_0}^{x_\infty} F \, dx = -\int_{x_0}^{x_\infty} m\kappa v \, dx = -\int_{t_0}^{\infty} m\kappa v^2 \, dt.$$

Utilizing the value of $v$ given by Eq. (4–69), we obtain

$$W = -\int_{t_0}^{\infty} m\kappa v_0^2 e^{-2\kappa(t-t_0)} \, dt = -\frac{mv_0^2}{2},$$

as is to be expected. Similarly, we verify that the impulse

$$I = \int_{t_0}^{\infty} F \, dt,$$

which the damping force imparts to the particle, is equal to the change in its linear momentum. Indeed we find that

$$\int_{t_0}^{\infty} F_{\text{damping}} \, dt = -\int_{t_0}^{\infty} m\kappa v_0 e^{-\kappa(t-t_0)} \, dt = -mv_0. \blacktriangleleft$$

▶ Another interesting example, which together with the previous example describes the projectile motion of a particle under the action of the force of gravity and the damping produced by the air through which the particle must move, is the solution of the equation

$$m \frac{dv}{dt} = -mg - m\kappa v. \tag{4–72}$$

Equation (4–72) by itself represents the equation of motion of a particle moving in the vertical direction under the action of the gravitational force and the damping force. If the upward direction is taken as positive, the gravitational and damping forces will for positive velocities be directed in the negative direction; hence the minus signs in Eq. (4–72).

Equation (4–72) may be integerated and subsequently solved for $v$ as a function of $t$. We find that

$$t - t_0 = -\int_{v_0}^{v} \frac{dv}{g + \kappa v} = -\frac{1}{\kappa} \ln \frac{g + \kappa v}{g + \kappa v_0} ,$$

which when solved for $v$ yields

$$v = -\frac{g}{\kappa} + \left(\frac{g}{\kappa} + v_0\right)e^{-\kappa(t-t_0)} . \tag{4–73}$$

We note that as $t$ increases, the second term on the right-hand side of Eq. (4–73) decreases exponentially until, for sufficiently large values of $t$, it becomes negligible. The velocity of the particle will thus approach the limiting velocity $-g/\kappa$. For this limiting velocity the damping force just balances the gravitational force, permitting the body to continue to fall with the constant velocity $-g/\kappa$. In order to obtain the position of the particle at any time, we integrate Eq. (4–73) with respect to time, obtaining the solution

$$x = x_0 - \frac{g}{\kappa}(t - t_0) - \left(\frac{g}{\kappa^2} + \frac{v_0}{\kappa}\right)[e^{-\kappa(t-t_0)} - 1]. \blacktriangleleft \tag{4–74}$$

---

The macroscopic motion of charges in conductors, for which the relation between the current and the voltage across the conductor is given by Ohm's law, may be described in terms of motion of the charges under the action of a damping force proportional to the first power of the drift velocity of the charges. The constant of proportionality, $\kappa$, can be related to the d-c conductivity $\sigma$ of the conductor, where $\sigma$ is the reciprocal of the resistivity. The conductivity is also the ratio of the current density per unit area, $J$, to the applied d-c electric field $E$: $\sigma = J/E$. The current density is in turn related to the drift velocity, as expressed by $J = Nev$, where $N$ is the number of charged particles of charge $e$ per unit volume and $v$ is the average drift velocity of the charged particles.

Thus we find that

$$\sigma = \frac{Ne^2 v}{eE} .$$

From the above discussion we realize that the constant drift velocity is attained by the particles when the electric force $eE$ is balanced by the damping force, that is,

$eE = m\kappa v$, yielding the relation

$$\sigma = \frac{Ne^2}{m\kappa}$$

between the d-c conductivity of a metal and the damping constant $\kappa$.


## 4–11 Harmonic oscillator with damping

Our discussion of the simple harmonic oscillation of a particle about a point of stable equilibrium in Section 4–9 did not consider the effect of damping forces, which are ever present in any system.

We therefore reconsider the problem, assuming the presence of a dissipative force proportional to the first power of the velocity in addition to the restoring force proportional to the displacement from the equilibrium point. We shall restrict ourselves to damping forces proportional to the first power of the velocity in order to remain within the same order of approximation to which we restricted ourselves by using a restoring force proportional to the first power of the displacement. Furthermore, in so restricting our treatment we are led to an equation of motion which, besides being readily solvable, occurs frequently in physics. It is an equation which demands the reader's careful consideration.

The one-dimensional equation of motion for a particle moving about a point of stable equilibrium under the action of the restoring force $F = -kx$ and the damping force

$$F_{\text{damping}} = -2m\mu\dot{x} \qquad (4\text{--}75)$$

is

$$m\ddot{x} = -kx - 2m\mu\dot{x}. \qquad (4\text{--}76)$$

If in the equation of motion we set the restoring constant

$$k = m\omega_0^2, \qquad (4\text{--}77)$$

the equation of motion reduces to

$$\ddot{x} + 2\mu\dot{x} + \omega_0^2 x = 0, \qquad (4\text{--}78)$$

which is a homogeneous linear differential equation of the second order with constant coefficients. It is the simplest type of second-order linear differential equation, which always has at least one solution of the form

$$x = Ae^{\alpha t}. \qquad (4\text{--}79)$$

It is a simple matter to verify this fact for the equation which we are considering. Using Eq. (4–79) as a trial solution, we find that

$$\ddot{x} + 2\mu\dot{x} + \omega_0^2 x = Ae^{\alpha t}(\alpha^2 + 2\mu\alpha + \omega_0^2).$$

If the right-hand side of this equation is to vanish and yield a nontrivial solution, $\alpha$ must be a root of the characteristic equation

$$\alpha^2 + 2\mu\alpha + \omega_0^2 = 0. \tag{4-80}$$

In general, we find two values of $\alpha$ which satisfy Eq. (4-80). They are the values

$$\alpha = -\mu \pm \sqrt{\mu^2 - \omega_0^2}. \tag{4-81}$$

Thus for all $\mu \neq \omega_0$ we have two independent solutions,

$$x_1 = Ae^{-(\mu+\lambda)t} \tag{4-82}$$

and

$$x_2 = Be^{-(\mu-\lambda)t}, \tag{4-83}$$

where

$$\lambda = \sqrt{\mu^2 - \omega_0^2}. \tag{4-84}$$

It is a property of homogeneous linear differential equations that the linear sum of two linearly independent solutions of the equation is also a solution of the equation. Thus

$$x = x_1 + x_2 = e^{-\mu t}(Ae^{-\lambda t} + Be^{+\lambda t}) \tag{4-85}$$

is another solution of Eq. (4-78).

We can readily show that Eq. (4-85) is the general solution to Eq. (4-78) for $\mu \neq \omega_0$. That is, any solution to Eq. (4-78) is by a proper choice of the arbitrary constants $A$ and $B$ expressible in the form of Eq. (4-85).

To realize this we present another method for obtaining the solution to Eq. (4-78). We shall find that it will also yield the general solution for the case $\mu = \omega_0$. Equation (4-78) may be rewritten in operator form as

$$\left(\frac{d^2}{dt^2} + 2\mu\frac{d}{dt} + \omega_0^2\right)x = 0, \tag{4-86}$$

or

$$\left(\frac{d}{dt} + \mu + \lambda\right)\left(\frac{d}{dt} + \mu - \lambda\right)x = 0. \tag{4-87}$$

Equation (4-87) may now be expressed as two simultaneous first-order differential equations by setting

$$y = \left(\frac{d}{dt} + \mu - \lambda\right)x. \tag{4-88}$$

Then Eq. (4-87) becomes

$$\left(\frac{d}{dt} + \mu + \lambda\right)y = 0. \tag{4-89}$$

The solution to this latter first-order differential equation is

$$y = Ce^{-(\mu+\lambda)t}, \tag{4-90}$$

which means that $x$ is a solution of the first-order inhomogeneous differential equation

$$\frac{d}{dt} x + (\mu - \lambda)x = Ce^{-(\mu+\lambda)t}. \tag{4-91}$$

This first-order differential equation may be simplified by multiplying it by the integrating factor $e^{(\mu-\lambda)t}$, making the left-hand side of the equation the derivative of the function $xe^{(\mu-\lambda)t}$. We thus obtain

$$\frac{d}{dt} [xe^{(\mu-\lambda)t}] = Ce^{-2\lambda t},$$

which, for $\lambda \neq 0$, may be integrated to yield

$$xe^{(\mu-\lambda)t} = \frac{C}{-2\lambda} e^{-2\lambda t} + B,$$

where $B$ is the constant of integration. Setting $A = -C/2\lambda$, we obtain the solution found above for $\mu \neq \omega_0$ or $\lambda \neq 0$,

$$x = e^{-\mu t}(Ae^{-\lambda t} + Be^{\lambda t}). \tag{4-92}$$

The method we have used for obtaining Eq. (4–92) is very appropriate for finding the solution to Eq. (4–78) when $\mu = \omega_0$. Under these circumstances the characteristic equation yields only one root and therefore also only one solution,

$$x_1 = Ae^{-\mu t}.$$

A second-order homogeneous linear differential equation, however, has two linearly independent solutions. To obtain the second solution we proceed as before, expressing Eq. (4–78) in operator form. This time, however, the equation has the form

$$\left(\frac{d}{dt} + \mu\right) \left(\frac{d}{dt} + \mu\right) x = 0. \tag{4-93}$$

Once again setting

$$y = \left(\frac{d}{dt} + \mu\right) x, \tag{4-94}$$

we obtain the differential equation for $y$,

$$\frac{dy}{dt} + \mu y = 0. \tag{4-95}$$

This equation has the solution

$$y = Be^{-\mu t}. \tag{4-96}$$

With this solution for $y$, the equation satisfied by $x$ is

$$\left(\frac{d}{dt} + \mu\right) x = Be^{-\mu t}, \tag{4–97}$$

which may be simplified through multiplication by the integrating factor $e^{\mu t}$. Equation (4–97) then becomes

$$\frac{d}{dt} (xe^{\mu t}) = B, \tag{4–98}$$

which has the solution

$$xe^{\mu t} = Bt + A$$

or

$$x = e^{-\mu t}(A + Bt). \tag{4–99}$$

We have thus found that, in those problems where the two roots of the characteristic equation are equal, two linearly independent solutions to Eq. (4–80) are

$$x_1 = Ae^{-\mu t} \tag{4–100}$$

and

$$x_2 = Bte^{-\mu t}. \tag{4–101}$$

The general solution for the case $\mu = \omega_0$ is thus given by Eq. (4–99).

When $\mu \neq \omega_0$, we distinguish between the situations for which $\mu > \omega_0$ and those for which $\mu < \omega_0$, as the qualitative nature of the motion is different for these two cases. The two different situations are respectively referred to as the *overdamped* and the *underdamped* harmonic oscillator. The case where $\mu = \omega_0$ is called *critically damped*.

The values of the constants $A$ and $B$ which appear in Eqs. (4–85) and (4–99) are, of course, dependent on the initial values of the position and velocity of the particle.

We now proceed to investigate the motion expected for the three cases $\mu < \omega_0$, $\mu > \omega_0$, and $\mu = \omega_0$.

(a) *Underdamped case, $\mu < \omega_0$.* When $\mu < \omega_0$, the square root in Eq. (4–84) is imaginary. We therefore set

$$\lambda = -i\nu,$$

and find the solution to be expressible in the form

$$x = e^{-\mu t}(Ae^{i\nu t} + Be^{-i\nu t}). \tag{4–102}$$

Since the displacement of the particle from equilibrium is a real quantity, it follows that the constants $A$ and $B$, which in general will be complex numbers, are related. This must be so, since if $A$ and $B$ are complex, four constants of integration will appear in the general solution, whereas only two should appear. The relation between the constants $A$ and $B$ follows from the fact that $x$ is real, and hence $x = x^*$, where the asterisk designates the complex conjugate, or

$$e^{-\mu t}(Ae^{i\nu t} + Be^{-i\nu t})^* = e^{-\mu t}(A^*e^{-i\nu t} + B^*e^{i\nu t}).$$

This relation can be satisfied only if $B = A^*$.

From our brief discussion of complex numbers in Section 1–9 we realize that we can always set

$$A = \tfrac{1}{2}Ce^{i\phi}, \tag{4–103}$$

where $C$ and $\phi$ are real numbers.

In terms of these new constants the solution takes the form

$$x = \tfrac{1}{2}Ce^{-\mu t}[e^{i(\nu t+\phi)} + e^{-i(\nu t+\phi)}] = Ce^{-\mu t} \cos (\nu t + \phi). \tag{4–104}$$

We note that the underdamped harmonic oscillator still performs a kind of oscillatory motion. Its amplitude, however, decreases exponentially with time, as shown in Fig. 4–8.

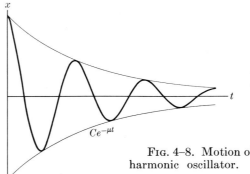

FIG. 4–8. Motion of the underdamped harmonic oscillator.

While the motion does not repeat itself, and is therefore not periodic in the usual sense, there still exists a time interval,

$$\tau = \frac{2\pi}{\nu} = \frac{2\pi}{\sqrt{\omega_0^2 - \mu^2}}, \tag{4–105}$$

between successive passages of the particle in the same direction past the equilibrium point. This same time interval also exists between successive maximum displacements on the same side of the equilibrium point.

It is of interest to consider the loss of energy of the oscillator in such a period of the motion. The instantaneous loss in energy is due to the damping force whose work per unit time is

$$\nu F_{\text{damping}} = -\dot{x}(m\ddot{x} + m\omega_0^2 x) = -\frac{dE}{dt},$$

where

$$E = \tfrac{1}{2}m\dot{x}^2 + \tfrac{1}{2}m\omega_0^2 x^2.$$

The instantaneous loss of energy is thus a function of time. The energy loss over a period $\tau$ of the motion, however, can be obtained by comparing the total energy at the two instants $t$ and $t + \tau$.

At any time $t$ the total energy is found to be given by

$$E = \tfrac{1}{2}mC_0^2 e^{-2\mu t}\{\omega_0^2 \cos^2(\nu t + \phi) + [\mu \cos(\nu t + \phi) + \nu \sin(\nu t + \phi)]^2\}$$
$$= \tfrac{1}{2}mC^2 e^{-2\mu t}f(t), \tag{4–106}$$

where $f(t)$ is the quantity in the braces. It happens to be periodic with period $\tau$. That is,

$$f(t + \tau) = f(t).$$

It follows, therefore, that

$$E(t + \tau) = E(t)e^{-2\mu\tau}. \tag{4–107}$$

The energy after a time interval $\tau$ has a value which is $e^{-2\mu\tau}$ times the energy at the beginning of the time interval. The energy over a period $\tau$ thus decays at twice the rate at which the amplitude decays.

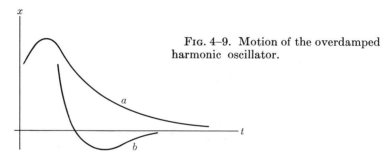

FIG. 4–9. Motion of the overdamped harmonic oscillator.

(b) *Overdamped case, $\mu > \omega_0$.* The displacement of the particle for the overdamped case, given by

$$x = Ae^{-(\mu+\lambda)t} + Be^{-(\mu-\lambda)t}, \tag{4–108}$$

is depicted in Fig. 4–9. Since $\mu > \lambda$, both terms in Eq. (4–108) decay exponentially. In terms of the initial displacement and velocity of the particle, taking the initial time $t_0$ as zero, we obtain the equations

$$A + B = x_0 \tag{4–109}$$

and

$$-(\mu + \lambda)A - (\mu - \lambda)B = v_0, \tag{4–110}$$

which upon solving for $A$ and $B$ yield

$$A = -\frac{v_0 + (\mu - \lambda)x_0}{2\lambda} \tag{4–111}$$

and

$$B = \frac{v_0 + (\mu + \lambda)x_0}{2\lambda}. \tag{4–112}$$

For positive values of $x_0$ and $v_0$, $B$ is positive and $A$ negative, and in magnitude $B$ is larger than $A$. Since the term in Eq. (4–108) which contains $A$ decays more rapidly than the term which contains $B$, and since $B > |A|$, it follows that the displacement will at all times remain positive, as depicted in curve (a) of Fig. 4–9.

For negative values of $v_0$ such that

$$v_0 < -(\mu + \lambda)x_0,$$

$B$ is negative while $A$ is positive. In magnitude $A$ is then larger than $B$. Since the $A$-term decays more rapidly than the $B$-term, it follows that for some value of $t$, and all values of $t$ thereafter, the $B$-term will be the dominant term. In other words, the displacement will eventually assume a negative value. The particle will thus pass the equilibrium position once and subsequently approach the equilibrium point, as depicted in curve (b) of Fig. 4–9.

(c) *Critically damped case*, $\mu = \omega_0$. In this case, too, the displacement is exponentially damped, having the form

$$x = e^{-\mu t}(A + Bt), \tag{4–113}$$

as found in Eq. (4–99).

The importance of this case lies in the fact that, for the same initial conditions, a system will in general return to its equilibrium position in the shortest time if it is critically damped. An exception to the rule is, for example, the case when $B$ in Eq. (4–108) happens to be zero.

As in the overdamped case one of the terms, $Bte^{-\mu t}$ in Eq. (4–115), decays less rapidly than the other. Depending on the relative magnitudes and signs of the constants $A$ and $B$, therefore, the particle once again either approaches the equilibrium position asymptotically or passes through it once before returning to it. The curves for this case are qualitatively similar to the curves depicted in Fig. 4–9 for the overdamped case.

## 4–12 The forced harmonic oscillator: resonance

The problem of the simple or the damped harmonic oscillator is interesting. In practice, however, it is the problem of the forced harmonic oscillator which is met and which is important in physics. For example, it is only through the action of additional forces that the damped harmonic oscillator can sustain its motion or, for that matter, obtain the initial values of position and velocity which determine the constants in terms of which the solutions of the last section are expressed.

The damped motion of a particle about a point of stable equilibrium, subject to an additional time-dependent force $F(t)$, is described by the differential equation

$$m\ddot{x} + 2m\mu\dot{x} + m\omega_0^2 x = F(t)$$

or

$$\ddot{x} + 2\mu\dot{x} + \omega_0^2 x = \frac{F(t)}{m}. \tag{4–114}$$

This is an inhomogeneous linear differential equation, represented symbolically by

$$Lx = \frac{F(t)}{m}.$$    (4–115)

The differential operator in this instance is

$$L\left(\frac{d}{dt}\right) = \frac{d^2}{dt^2} + 2\mu\frac{d}{dt} + \omega_0^2,$$    (4–116)

which, as we have done before, may be factored and expressed as

$$L = \left(\frac{d}{dt} + \mu + \lambda\right)\left(\frac{d}{dt} + \mu - \lambda\right),$$    (4–117)

where $\lambda = \sqrt{\mu^2 - \omega_0^2}$. A linear differential equation has the very convenient property that if $x_1$ is a solution of the equation

$$Lx_1 = f_1,$$

and if $x_2$ is a solution of the equation

$$Lx_2 = f_2,$$

then

$$x = x_1 + x_2$$

is a solution of the inhomogeneous equation

$$Lx = f_1 + f_2.$$

We noted this fact in the last section, when we were concerned with finding a solution for the homogeneous equation for which $f_1 = f_2 = 0$. Indeed we found the general solution of the homogeneous equation to be expressible as the sum of two linearly independent solutions of the homogeneous equation.

When we take into account this property of the solution of linear differential equations, we find that the general solution to an inhomogeneous differential equation is expressible as the sum of the general solution to its homogeneous equation ($f_1 = 0$) and a solution of the inhomogeneous equation ($f_2 = F(t)/m$). The solution to the homogeneous equation, $x_h$, is called the *homogeneous solution*, whereas the other, $x_p$, is referred to as the *inhomogeneous* or *particular solution*.

The different homogeneous solutions which we found in the last section were exponentially damped. This means that, given a sufficiently long period of time, their contribution to the general solution will be small and negligible. The homogeneous solutions to Eq. (4–114) are for this reason also referred to as *transient solutions*. The particular solution generally does not die out. It is therefore also referred to as the *steady-state solution*.

We shall consider the particular solution of Eq. (4–114) for two specific time-dependent forces $F(t)$. At first we shall consider the sinusoidal driving force,

$$F(t) = F_0 \sin (\omega t + \theta).$$

It is important to consider this type of force, because any function $F(t)$ which is periodic with period $2T$,
$$F(t + 2T) = F(t),$$

is expressible in terms of a linear sum of the sine and cosine terms. Such an expansion, or *Fourier series*,* is expressible in the form

$$F(t) = \frac{a_0}{2} + \sum_{n=1}^{\infty} a_n \cos \frac{n\pi t}{T} + \sum_{n=1}^{\infty} b_n \sin \frac{n\pi t}{T}, \qquad (4\text{–}118)$$

where the Fourier coefficients are

$$a_n = \frac{1}{T} \int_t^{t+2T} F(t) \cos \frac{n\pi t}{T} \, dt \qquad (4\text{–}119)$$

and

$$b_n = \frac{1}{T} \int_t^{t+2T} F(t) \sin \frac{n\pi t}{T} \, dt. \qquad (4\text{–}120)$$

Any periodic force $F(t)$ of period $2T$ is thus expressible as a sum of the sinusoidal forces $F_n(t)$,

$$F(t) = \sum_{n=0}^{\infty} F_n(t),$$

where

$$F_0(t) = \frac{1}{2T} \int_t^{t+2T} F(t) \, dt = F_0$$

and

$$F_n(t) = a_n \cos \frac{n\pi t}{T} + b_n \sin \frac{n\pi t}{T}$$

$$= \sqrt{a_n^2 + b_n^2} \sin \left( \frac{n\pi t}{T} + \theta_n \right).$$

The constants $a_n$ and $b_n$ are given by Eqs. (4–119) and (4–120) and the phase angle

$$\theta_n = \tan^{-1} \frac{a_n}{b_n}.$$

---

* I. S. Sokolnikoff and R. M. Redheffer, *Mathematics of Physics and Modern Engineering*. New York: McGraw-Hill, 1958.

From the property of the solution of a linear differential equation, it follows that if $x_n(\omega_n, t)$ represents the solution for the force

$$F_n(t) = C_n \sin (\omega_n t + \theta_n),$$   (4–121)

where

$$C_n = \begin{cases} F_0 & n = 0, \\ \sqrt{a_n^2 + b_n^2} & n \neq 0, \end{cases}$$   (4–122)

$$\theta_n = \begin{cases} \dfrac{\pi}{2} & n = 0, \\ \tan^{-1} \dfrac{a_n}{b_n} & n \neq 0, \end{cases}$$   (4–123)

$$\omega_n = \frac{n\pi}{T},$$   (4–124)

then the particular solution for the periodic driving force

$$F(t) = \sum_{n=0}^{\infty} F_n(t)$$

is given by

$$x(t) = \sum_{n=0}^{\infty} x_n(\omega_n, t).$$

By considering the solution for a sinusoidal driving force, we are thereby considering the solution for any periodic time-dependent driving force.

The second type of driving force we shall consider is an impulsive force of very short duration whose magnitude is sufficiently large, however, to impart a finite change in momentum to the particle. If this impulse occurs at a time $t'$ over a period $\Delta t$, then the change in the momentum of the particle is given by

$$\Delta p = \int_{t'}^{t'+\Delta t} F(t) \, dt.$$   (4–125)

For an impulsive force the time interval $\Delta t$ is assumed to be so short that the displacement of the particle from the position at which it found itself at the time $t = t'$ over the time interval $\Delta t$ may for all practical purposes be taken to be zero. Its importance will become clear when we show how the solution for any time-dependent driving force is expressible in terms of an integral involving the solution to the impulsive force problem.

(a) *Sinusoidal driving force.* The solution to Eq. (4–114) when

$$F(t) = F_0 \sin (\omega t + \theta)$$   (4–126)

is readily obtainable. The algebra simplifies, however, if we consider instead the force

$$F(t) = F_0 \cos (\omega t + \theta) + iF_0 \sin (\omega t + \theta) = F_0 e^{i(\omega t + \theta)}.$$   (4–127)

We note that if $x_1$ is the solution for the force

$$F_1(t) = F_0 \cos (\omega t + \theta),$$

and if $x_2$ is the solution for the force

$$F_2(t) = F_0 \sin (\omega t + \theta),$$

then the solution for the force

$$F(t) = F_0 e^{i(\omega t + \theta)}$$

is

$$x = x_1 + ix_2. \tag{4–128}$$

From this solution in turn we may obtain the solutions $x_1$ and $x_2$, for, since the differential operator $L$ in Eq. (4–114) is real, we have

$$x_1 = \text{Re } x \tag{4–129}$$

and

$$x_2 = \text{Im } x. \tag{4–130}$$

We can therefore proceed to find the solution to the equation

$$\ddot{x} + 2\mu \dot{x} + \omega_0^2 x = \frac{F_0}{m} e^{i(\omega t + \theta)}. \tag{4–131}$$

It is reasonable to assume that the inhomogeneous solution to this equation has the same exponential time dependence as $F(t)$. We thus assume a solution of the form

$$x = A e^{i(\omega t + \theta)}, \tag{4–132}$$

for which we find

$$\ddot{x} + 2\mu \dot{x} + \omega_0^2 x = A e^{i(\omega t + \theta)}(-\omega^2 + 2\mu\omega i + \omega_0^2). \tag{4–133}$$

In order that this expression equal $(F_0/m) \exp [i(\omega t + \theta)]$, we must have

$$A = \frac{F_0/m}{(\omega_0^2 - \omega^2) + 2i\mu\omega} = \frac{(F_0/m)(\omega_0^2 - \omega^2 - 2i\mu\omega)}{(\omega_0^2 - \omega^2)^2 + 4\mu^2\omega^2}. \tag{4–134}$$

Equation (4–134) can be simplified by setting

$$\frac{\omega_0^2 - \omega^2 - 2i\mu\omega}{\sqrt{(\omega_0^2 - \omega^2)^2 + 4\mu^2\omega^2}} = \cos \phi - i \sin \phi = e^{-i\phi}, \tag{4–135}$$

where

$$\cos \phi = \frac{\omega_0^2 - \omega^2}{\sqrt{(\omega_0^2 - \omega^2)^2 + 4\mu^2\omega^2}} \tag{4–136}$$

and

$$\sin \phi = \frac{2\mu\omega}{\sqrt{(\omega_0^2 - \omega^2)^2 + 4\mu^2\omega^2}}. \tag{4–137}$$

With this substitution, Eq. (4–134) assumes the form

$$A = \frac{(F_0/m)}{\sqrt{(\omega_0^2 - \omega^2)^2 + 4\mu^2\omega^2}}\, e^{-i\phi}, \tag{4–138}$$

whence we obtain the solution to Eq. (4–131) as

$$x(t) = \frac{(F_0/m)}{\sqrt{(\omega_0^2 - \omega^2)^2 + 4\mu^2\omega^2}}\, e^{i(\omega t + \theta - \phi)}. \tag{4–139}$$

The solution we seek is the response of the system to the force $F_0 \sin (\omega t + \theta)$. It is the imaginary part of the solution given by Eq. (4–139). That is,

$$x_2(t) = \operatorname{Im} x(t) = \frac{(F_0/m)}{\sqrt{(\omega_0^2 - \omega^2)^2 + 4\mu^2\omega^2}} \sin (\omega t + \theta - \phi). \tag{4–140}$$

We note that the steady-state solution for the driving force $F(t) = F_0 \sin (\omega t + \theta)$ has been found to be sinusoidal with the same frequency as the driving force. It differs, however, in phase from the driving force, lagging the driving force by $\phi$ radians. Since $\mu$ is a positive constant, the phase difference $\phi$ has a value between zero and $\pi$ (Fig. 4–10).

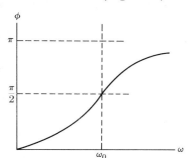

Fig. 4–10. Phase lag of the forced harmonic oscillator.

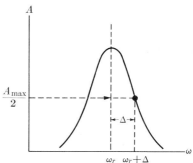

Fig. 4–11. The amplitude of the forced harmonic oscillator vs. the frequency of the driving force.

We also note that the amplitude of the steady-state solution

$$A = \frac{F_0/m}{\sqrt{(\omega_0^2 - \omega^2)^2 + 4\mu^2\omega^2}}$$

$$= \frac{F_0/m}{\sqrt{(\omega_0^2 - 2\mu^2 - \omega^2)^2 + 4\mu^2\omega_0^2 - 4\mu^4}} \tag{4–141}$$

is a function of the frequency $\omega$. For small $\mu$ the amplitude $A$ takes on the approximate maximum value of $F_0/2m\mu\omega_0$ at a frequency $\omega = \omega_r$ such that

$$\omega_r^2 = \omega_0^2 - 2\mu^2. \tag{4–142}$$

Whenever any physical quantity of interest, a function of another time-dependent physical quantity, takes on a maximum value as the frequency of the other physical quantity is varied, we have a situation referred to as *resonance*. The value of the frequency of the second physical quantity for which the first assumes its maximum value is called the resonance point. Thus $f_r = \omega_r/2\pi$ is the resonant frequency for the amplitude of the motion. It is also customary to refer to $\omega_r$ as the resonant frequency.

The amplitude-versus-frequency curve (Fig. 4–11) can be seen to be symmetric in the neighborhood of the resonant frequency. Since for large values of $\omega$ the amplitude is very small, there exists a frequency

$$\omega = \omega_r + \Delta$$

for which the amplitude will assume a value which is half its maximum value. The value

$$\Delta = |\omega_r - \omega| \tag{4–143}$$

for which this occurs is called the *half-width* of the resonance curve. From Eq. (4–141) it follows that for small values of $\mu$ the half-maximum value is assumed by $A$ at a frequency $\omega$ for which

$$\omega^2 = \omega_r^2 \pm 2\sqrt{3}\mu\sqrt{\omega_0^2 - \mu^2}$$

or

$$\omega \approx \omega_r \pm \frac{\mu\omega_0}{\omega_r}\sqrt{3} \approx \omega_0 \pm \mu\sqrt{3}. \tag{4–144}$$

This means that for small damping the amplitude curve has a half-width

$$\Delta = \mu\sqrt{3}. \tag{4–145}$$

We are thus able to obtain approximate values for the damping constant $\mu$ and the natural frequency of vibration of the undamped oscillator, $\omega_0$, from the steady-state amplitude-versus-frequency curve.

In many important problems as, for example, the forced oscillation of an electron about a point of stable equilibrium, it is not the displacement of the electron from equilibrium but the energy required to keep the oscillator in motion which is observed or measured. In dealing with electrons, we could not, even if we desired, observe their motion directly. It is of interest therefore to consider the average energy dissipated by the damping force per cycle of the steady-state solution, and to find the resonance point and the half-width of the average power dissipated-versus-frequency curve.

The average energy dissipated per cycle in the steady state should, of course (as the reader should verify), equal the average energy supplied by the driving force. In a time interval $\Delta t$, the magnitude of the energy dissipated is given by

$$\Delta W = 2m\mu\dot{x}^2 \, \Delta t.$$

From this we find the average power $\langle P \rangle$ dissipated per period $\tau$ to be given by

$$\langle P \rangle = \frac{1}{\tau} \langle W \rangle = \frac{1}{\tau} \int_t^{t+\tau} 2m\mu\dot{x}^2 \, dt$$

$$= \frac{2m\mu A^2\omega^2}{\tau} \int_t^{t+\tau} \cos^2(\omega t + \theta - \phi) \, dt$$

$$= m\mu A^2\omega^2.$$

Again we note that the physical quantity of interest here, which is the average power dissipated, is a function of the frequency $\omega$, for using Eq. (4–141) for the amplitude yields

$$\langle P \rangle = \frac{\mu F_0^2\omega^2}{m[(\omega_0^2 - \omega^2)^2 + 4\mu^2\omega^2]}. \qquad (4\text{–}146)$$

The maximum value of the average power dissipated, $(F_0^2/4m\mu)$, occurs at a frequency

$$\omega = \omega_0. \qquad (4\text{–}147)$$

Hence $\omega_0$ is the resonant frequency for the average absorbed power.

The half-width of the dissipated power-versus-frequency curve may be obtained by setting

$$\langle P \rangle = \frac{1}{2} \langle P \rangle_{\text{max}} = \frac{F_0^2}{8m\mu}$$

or

$$\frac{\mu\omega^2}{(\omega_0^2 - \omega^2)^2 + 4\mu^2\omega^2} = \frac{1}{8\mu}.$$

For small values of the dissipative constant $\mu$, this latter equation has the approximate solution

$$\omega = \omega_0 \pm \mu.$$

The dissipated power-versus-frequency curve therefore has a half-width

$$\Delta = \mu. \qquad (4\text{–}148)$$

Another term commonly used as a measure of the width of an energy-resonance curve is the $Q$ of the system. The $Q$ of a resonant circuit is defined as $2\pi$ times the ratio of the average energy stored in the system to the energy dissipated per cycle of the driving force. For the damped harmonic oscillator,

$$Q = 2\pi \frac{\langle \frac{1}{2}m\dot{x}^2 + \frac{1}{2}m\omega_0^2 x^2 \rangle}{\tau \langle 2m\mu\dot{x}^2 \rangle}$$

$$= 2\pi \frac{\frac{1}{2}m(\omega_0^2 + \omega^2)\langle x^2 \rangle}{(2\pi/\omega)2m\mu\omega^2\langle x^2 \rangle}$$

$$= \frac{\omega_0^2 + \omega^2}{4\mu\omega}. \tag{4–149}$$

Near resonance, when $\omega \approx \omega_0$, we obtain

$$Q = \frac{\omega_0}{2\mu}, \tag{4–150}$$

which is another definition given at times for the $Q$ of a system.

▶ The results of this section were applied by Drude and Lorentz in the classical derivation of the index of refraction of a medium. The early classical Lorentz theory of the electron considered the electrons in an atom to be located at points of stable equilibrium and thus to behave like harmonic oscillators. Interestingly, this crude classical model of the electrons in atoms, while incorrect, does lead to a remarkably good description of the optical properties of gases, dielectrics, and metals. Its continued use for explaining the optical properties of materials is justified by quantum mechanical results which indicated that the modification of an external electric field in a region due to the presence of atoms and their electrons is mathematically equivalent to its modification by a set of harmonic oscillators. We note that for high frequencies, $\omega \gg \omega_0$, and small damping, Eq. (4–140) for the response of a charged oscillator to a sinusoidal electric field yields

$$x(t) = -\frac{eE}{m\omega^2} \sin(\omega t + \theta),$$

which is identical to the sinusoidal term appearing in the solution for the response of a free electron to a sinusoidal electric field (Section 4–5). From this we realize that for the scattering of high-frequency electromagnetic radiation ($x$-rays or $\gamma$-rays) by the electrons of an atom, the electrons may be considered to be free particles. For a derivation of the index of refraction in terms of the parameters describing the oscillator, the reader is referred to books on electricity and magnetism or the Feynman lectures on physics.*

We further find that electrical circuits consisting of capacitors, inductances, and resistors in series with a time-dependent electromotive force satisfy a linear differential equation analogous to the differential equation satisfied by the

---

* Slater and Frank, *Electromagnetism*. New York: McGraw-Hill, Chapter 9.
*Feynman Lectures on Physics*, Vol. II. Reading, Mass.: Addison-Wesley, Chapter 32.

damped harmonic oscillator under the action of a time-dependent force. The results for the simple harmonic oscillator are therefore equally applicable to the problems of an a-c series circuit.

This analogy also extends to more complicated electrical circuits and mechanical vibrating systems, and is the basis of electrical analog computers, which permit the analysis of complicated mechanical problems in terms of the response of their easier to build and adjust analogous electrical circuits. ◄

(b) *Impulsive force, Green's function.* An impulsive force is a force of very short duration. So short is the time interval over which the force is acting on the particle that any change in the position of the particle occurring during this time interval may be neglected. The magnitude of the impulsive force is nevertheless sufficiently large to produce a finite change in the momentum of the particle during this very short time interval.

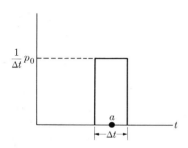
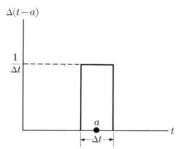

FIG. 4–12.  A constant impulsive force.

FIG. 4–13.  A constant unit impulsive force.

A unit impulsive force is a force which, over the short time interval $\Delta t$, produces a change of one unit in the particle momentum. If this unit impulse occurs at the time $t = t_1$, then

$$\int_{t_1}^{t_1+\Delta t} F(t)\, dt = 1. \tag{4–151}$$

The simplest impulsive force is a constant one. A constant unit impulsive force acting over the time interval $\Delta t$ has for that interval the magnitude

$$F = \frac{1}{\Delta t}.$$

We shall use the symbol $p_0 \Delta(t - a)$ for the constant impulsive force which, acting on the particle at the average time $t = a$ for an interval $\Delta t$ (Fig. 4–12), imparts to the particle a momentum $p_0$. Thus $\Delta(t - a)$ is the dimensionless impulse function having magnitude $1/\Delta t$ over the same interval (Fig. 4–13).

The smaller the time interval $\Delta t$ over which the impulsive force acts, the better of course will be the approximation, that for sufficiently small $\Delta t$ the particle displacement during that period is negligible.

In the limit as $\Delta t$ approaches zero, the maximum magnitude of any force referred to as an impulsive force necessarily approaches a very large number in order that $F \Delta t$ remain finite.   Figure 4–14 illustrates this fact for the unit impulsive force

$$F = \frac{1}{\Delta t \sqrt{\pi}} \exp\left[-\frac{(t-a)^2}{(\Delta t)^2}\right]. \tag{4-152}$$

For all the curves in Fig. 4–14, the area under the curve is equal to unity, with the main contribution to the integral coming from the region $[a - (\Delta t/2), a + (\Delta t/2)]$.

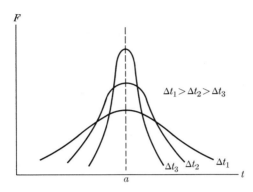

FIG. 4–14. The unit impulsive force

$$F = \frac{1}{\Delta t \sqrt{\pi}} \exp\left[\frac{-(t-a)^2}{(\Delta t)^2}\right].$$

One idealizes the limiting situation by saying that the unit impulsive force has a very large value at the point $t = a$ and the value zero at all other points. Whenever we have an impulsive force which can be thus represented, we shall use for it the symbol $p_0 \delta(t - a)$ if it imparts to the particle a momentum change of $p_0$. Thus $\delta(t - a)$ is the idealized unit impulse function defined by

$$\int_{t_1}^{t_2} \delta(t - a)\, dt = \begin{cases} 1 & t_1 < a < t_2, \\ 0 & \text{otherwise,} \end{cases} \tag{4-153}$$

and

$$\delta(t - a) = 0, \qquad t \neq a. \tag{4-154}$$

The function $\delta(t - a)$ which satisfies the above properties is called the *"Dirac delta function."**

---

* The Dirac delta function, though referred to as a function, is not a function in the usual sense, for any function which has a nonzero value at only one point does not have any area under its curve as a function should.   Texts in engineering refer to this function as the derivative of the Helmholtz or unit step function, which is defined by

$$H(t, a) = \begin{cases} 0 & t < a, \\ 1 & t > a. \end{cases}$$

We note that the constant impulsive function $\Delta(a - t)$, like the constant impulsive function $\Delta(t - a)$, has the magnitude $1/\Delta t$ for an interval $\Delta t$ about the point $t = a$. That is, $\Delta(t - a) = \Delta(a - t)$. Analogously, $\delta(t - a) = \delta(a - t)$, for $\delta[-t - (-a)]$ also satisfies Eqs. (4–153) and (4–154).

The importance of the unit impulse force lies in the fact that any time-dependent force is expressible as a sum of impulsive forces. By the superposition principle satisfied by the solutions to linear differential equations, the solution for any time-dependent force will thus be expressible as a sum of the solutions for impulsive forces.

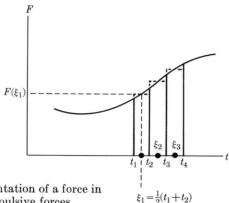

FIG. 4–15. Representation of a force in terms of a series of impulsive forces.

$$\xi_1 = \tfrac{1}{2}(t_1 + t_2)$$

For example, consider the force $F(t)$ depicted in Fig. 4–15. For any sufficiently small time interval $\Delta t$ between the times $t_1$ and $t_2$, a continuous force may be considered to vary linearly.

The value of $F(t)$ at the average time for this interval,

$$\xi_1 = \frac{t_1 + t_2}{2},$$

will thus represent the average value of $F(t)$ over the same interval. That is,

$$F(\xi_1) = \frac{1}{\Delta t} \int_{t_1}^{t_2} F(t) \, dt.$$

For small values of $\Delta t$ the effect of $F(t)$ on the motion of the particle can thus be approximated by the effect which the constant force $F(\xi_1)$ has on the motion of the particle over the same interval. The force $F(\xi_1)$ acting over the interval $\Delta t$ is represented by $F(\xi_1) \Delta(t - \xi_1) \Delta t$. By subdividing the range of time over which the force $F(t)$ acts on the particle into $N$ equally small time intervals $\Delta t$, we find by arguments similar to the one above that we can set

$$F(t) = \sum_{n=1}^{N} F(\xi_n) \Delta(t - \xi_n) \Delta \xi, \qquad (4\text{–}155)$$

where $\Delta(t - \xi_n)$ is the constant unit impulsive function defined above over the interval $\Delta t = \Delta \xi$. In the limit as $\Delta t$ or $\Delta \xi$ approaches zero, we have by the definition of the integral as the limit of a sum

$$F(t) = \int_{T_1}^{T_2} F(\xi) \, \delta(t - \xi) \, d\xi, \tag{4-156}$$

where we have used $\delta(t - \xi)$ to represent $\Delta(t - \xi)$ as $\Delta t \to 0$. Here $T_1$ and $T_2$ are the limits of the period over which the force $F(t)$ is acting on the particle.

Equation (4–156) could also have been obtained directly from the properties of the Dirac delta function. The interval about $\xi = t$ over which the Dirac delta function $\delta(t - \xi)$ is different from zero is so small that $F(\xi)$ in Eq. (4–156) will essentially have the constant value $F(t)$ over this interval. The contributions to the integral on the right-hand side of Eq. (4–156) thus come only from this interval, whence we obtain

$$\int_{T_1}^{T_2} F(\xi) \, \delta(t - \xi) \, d\xi = F(t) \int_{T_1}^{T_2} \delta(t - \xi) \, d\xi = F(t),$$

so long as the integral is evaluated over an interval which contains the point $\xi = t$, that is, so long as

$$T_1 < t < T_2.$$

By the superposition principle satisfied by the solutions to linear differential equations, if we let $g(t, \xi_n)$ represent the solution to the equation of motion for the unit impulsive force $\Delta(t - \xi_n)$, then we find the solution for the force $F(\xi_n) \, \Delta(t - \xi_n) \, \Delta \xi$ to be $g(t, \xi_n) F(\xi_n) \, \Delta \xi$, and the solution for the force of Eq. (4–155) to be given by

$$x(t) = \sum_{n=1}^{N} g(t, \xi_n) F(\xi_n) \, \Delta \xi. \tag{4-157}$$

In the limit as $\Delta \xi$ approaches zero we obtain

$$x(t) = \int_{T_1}^{T_2} g(t \mid \xi) F(\xi) \, d\xi, \tag{4-158}$$

where $g(t \mid \xi)$ is the solution to the equation of motion for the unit impulse function $\delta(t - \xi)$. It is called the *Green function* (usually referred to as the impulse response function in engineering textbooks).

Clearly at any time before the force begins to act on the particle it should have no effect on its motion. Up to the time $t = T_1$, therefore, the particle should be at rest at the equilibrium position. Equation (4–158) thus represents the solution which yields a zero displacement and zero velocity for the particle for all times less than $t = T_1$.

By the same reasoning it is to be expected that the Green function should vanish for all values of the time $t$ less than the time $\xi$ of the occurrence of the impulse; that is,

$$G(t \mid \xi) = 0, \quad t \leq \xi. \tag{4-159}$$

This fact ensures that the forces acting on the particle at times subsequent to $t$, at which we are observing the position of the particle, do not contribute to the solution $x(t)$ of Eq. (4–158) at the time $t$.

At times we shall be interested in the motion of the oscillator from the time $t = t_0$ and onward, where $t_0 > T_1$. In that case we shall seek the solution which will yield the observed values of position and velocity of the particle at time $t = t_0$.

We shall show how one may obtain the general solution to this problem for any initial conditions from a knowledge of the Green function. First, however, we must obtain the explicit expression for the Green function $G(t \mid \xi) = mg(t \mid \xi)$ which satisfies the equation

$$\left(\frac{d}{dt} + \mu + \lambda\right)\left(\frac{d}{dt} + \mu - \lambda\right) G(t \mid \xi) = \delta(t - \xi). \tag{4-160}$$

Making the substitution

$$y(t \mid \xi) = \left(\frac{d}{dt} + \mu - \lambda\right) G(t \mid \xi), \tag{4-161}$$

we obtain the first-order differential equation for $y(t \mid \xi)$,

$$\left(\frac{d}{dt} + \mu + \lambda\right) y(t \mid \xi) = \delta(t - \xi), \tag{4-162}$$

which through use of the integrating factor $e^{(\mu+\lambda)t}$ may be reduced to

$$\frac{d}{dt} [e^{(\mu+\lambda)t} y(t \mid \xi)] = e^{(\mu+\lambda)t} \delta(t - \xi). \tag{4-163}$$

The particular solution to Eq. (4–163) is

$$y(t \mid \xi) = \begin{cases} e^{-(\mu+\lambda)(t-\xi)} & t > \xi, \\ 0 & t < \xi. \end{cases} \tag{4-164}$$

Inserting this solution for $y$ into Eq. (4–161), we obtain the equation

$$\left(\frac{d}{dt} + \mu - \lambda\right) G(t \mid \xi) = \begin{cases} e^{-(\mu+\lambda)(t-\xi)} & t > \xi, \\ 0 & t < \xi, \end{cases}$$

which through multiplication by the integrating factor $e^{(\mu-\lambda)t}$ can be recast in the form

$$\frac{d}{dt} [e^{(\mu-\lambda)t} G(t \mid \xi)] = \begin{cases} e^{-2\lambda t} e^{(\mu+\lambda)\xi} & t > \xi, \\ 0 & t < \xi. \end{cases} \tag{4-165}$$

Integration of this latter equation yields, for $\mu \neq \omega_0$ or $\lambda \neq 0$, the Green function solution

$$e^{(\mu+\lambda)t}G(t \mid \xi) = \begin{cases} \dfrac{e^{(\mu+\lambda)\xi}}{2\lambda}\,(e^{-2\lambda\xi} - e^{-2\lambda t}) & t > \xi, \\ 0 & t < \xi, \end{cases}$$

or

$$G(t \mid \xi) = \begin{cases} \dfrac{1}{2\lambda}\,[e^{-(\mu-\lambda)(t-\xi)} - e^{-(\mu+\lambda)(t-\xi)}] & t \geq \xi, \\ 0 & t \leq \xi. \end{cases} \tag{4-166}$$

We note that the Green function $G(t \mid \xi)$ is a continuous function of $(t - \xi)$.

Thus for $\mu \neq \omega_0$ the solution for any driving force $F(t)$ as given by Eq. (4–158) for $t > T_1$ is expressed by

$$x(t) = \int_{T_1}^{t} \frac{F(\xi)}{2\lambda}\,[e^{-(\mu-\lambda)(t-\xi)} - e^{-(\mu+\lambda)(t-\xi)}]\,d\xi. \tag{4-167}$$

▶ As an example of the correctness of Eq. (4–167), we shall utilize it to obtain the particular solution for the sinusoidal driving force

$$F(t) = F_0 e^{i(\omega t+\theta)}.$$

The particular solution comes from the upper limit in the integral of Eq. (4–167). Thus since

$$\int^{t} e^{(\mu-\lambda)\xi} e^{i(\omega\xi+\theta)}\,d\xi = \frac{e^{(\mu+\lambda)t} e^{i(\omega t+\theta)}}{\mu - \lambda + i\omega}$$

and

$$\int^{t} e^{(\mu+\lambda)\xi} e^{i(\omega\xi+\theta)}\,d\xi = \frac{e^{(\mu+\lambda)t} e^{i(\omega t+\theta)}}{\mu + \lambda + i\omega},$$

we find the particular solution to be

$$\begin{aligned} x_p(t) &= \frac{F_0}{2m\lambda}\,e^{i(\omega t+\theta)}\left(\frac{1}{\mu - \lambda + i\omega} - \frac{1}{\mu + \lambda + i\omega}\right) \\ &= \frac{F_0 e^{i(\omega t+\theta)}}{m(\mu^2 - \omega^2 - \lambda^2 + 2i\mu\omega)} \\ &= \frac{F_0 e^{i(\omega t+\theta)}}{m(\omega_0^2 - \omega^2 + 2i\mu\omega)}, \end{aligned}$$

which is in agreement with Eq. (4–134) for the amplitude of $x_p(t)$. ◀

Equation (4–166) for the Green function for the damped harmonic oscillator equation could have been obtained from somewhat simpler considerations. We recall that the Green function is the solution of Eq. (4–160), which is the equation of motion of a damped harmonic oscillator of unit mass being acted on by the force $\delta(t - \xi)$. This force imparts to the oscillator a unit linear momentum or unit velocity at time $t = \xi$. Equation (4–166) should therefore represent the solution for a free damped harmonic oscillator which an instant after time $t = \xi$ had zero displacement and unit momentum or unit velocity. This follows from the fact that before the time $t = \xi$ the oscillator was at rest, and at time $t = \xi$ it received a unit impulse after which it performed damped simple harmonic oscillation. The solution of the problem for $\lambda \neq 0$ is given by Eq. (4–92). Explicitly for the initial conditions

$$x(\xi) = 0, \qquad v(\xi) = 1,$$

it takes on the form

$$x(t) = \frac{e^{-\lambda(t-\xi)}}{2\lambda} [e^{\lambda(t-\xi)} - e^{-\lambda(t-\xi)}]$$

for all $t > \xi$, in agreement with Eq. (4–166).

In conclusion we shall discuss how one can obtain the general solution for any initial conditions at time $t = t_0$ from a knowledge of the Green function.

In order to obtain the general solution with the help of the Green function we require the differential equation satisfied by the Green function $G(t \mid \xi)$ considered to be a function of $\xi$ for fixed $t$. This differential equation is readily obtainable, for we found $G(t \mid \xi)$ to be a function of $(t - \xi)$, and hence

$$\frac{\partial G(t \mid \xi)}{\partial t} = - \frac{\partial G(t \mid \xi)}{\partial \xi}$$

and

$$\frac{\partial^2 G(t \mid \xi)}{\partial t^2} = \frac{\partial^2 G(t \mid \xi)}{\partial \xi^2}. \tag{4–168}$$

We thus obtain the differential equation for $G(t \mid \xi)$ as a function of $\xi$,

$$\frac{\partial^2 G(t \mid \xi)}{\partial \xi^2} - 2\mu \frac{\partial G(t \mid \xi)}{\partial \xi} + \omega_0^2 G(t \mid \xi) = \delta(t - \xi). \tag{4–169}$$

Multiplying this equation by $x(\xi)$, and the equation

$$\frac{d^2}{d\xi^2} x(\xi) + 2\mu \frac{d}{d\xi} x(\xi) + \omega_0^2 x(\xi) = \frac{F(\xi)}{m}$$

satisfied by $x(\xi)$ by the Green function $G(t \mid \xi)$, we obtain upon subtracting the two resulting equations the result

$$x(\xi) \delta(t - \xi) - \frac{F(\xi)}{m} G(t \mid \xi) = \left( x(\xi) \frac{d^2 G(t \mid \xi)}{d\xi^2} - G(t \mid \xi) \frac{d^2 x(\xi)}{d\xi^2} \right)$$

$$- 2\mu \left( x(\xi) \frac{dG(t \mid \xi)}{d\xi} + G(t \mid \xi) \frac{dx(\xi)}{d\xi} \right)$$

$$= \frac{d}{d\xi} \left[ x(\xi) \frac{dG(t \mid \xi)}{d\xi} - G(t \mid \xi) \frac{dx(\xi)}{d\xi} - 2\mu x(\xi) G(t \mid \xi) \right]. \tag{4–170}$$

(We replaced the partial derivative $\partial/\partial\xi$ by the total derivatives $d/d\xi$. It is understood that $t$ is being held constant.) We can integrate Eq. (4–170) from time $t_0$ to any time $t+$, a little larger than $t$, and thus obtain

$$x(t) = \int_{t_0}^{t+} \frac{F(\xi)}{m} G(t \mid \xi) \, d\xi$$

$$+ \left[ x(\xi) \frac{dG(t \mid \xi)}{d\xi} - G(t \mid \xi) \frac{dx(\xi)}{d\xi} - 2\mu x(\xi) G(t \mid \xi) \right]_{\xi=t_0}^{\xi=t+}. \qquad (4\text{–}171)$$

But (cf. Eq. 4–166)

$$G(t \mid \xi) = 0 \qquad \text{for} \qquad \xi > t.$$

Hence so long as $\xi > t$ we similarly have

$$\frac{dG(t \mid \xi)}{d\xi} = 0, \qquad \xi > t.$$

The general solution is thus found to be given by

$$x(t) = \int_{t_0}^{t+} \frac{G(t \mid \xi) F(\xi)}{m} \, d\xi$$

$$+ \left\{ G(t \mid t_0)[\dot{x}(t_0) + 2\mu x(t_0)] - x(t_0) \frac{d}{dt_0} G(t \mid t_0) \right\}. \qquad (4\text{–}172)$$

We note that the first term of our solution is like the solution obtained previously. That is, it yields no displacement and zero velocity for the particle at time $t = t_0$. The quantity in the braces, on the other hand, is a solution to the homogeneous equation with the constants of integration adjusted so as to yield the correct initial conditions.

That the additional terms yield the correct initial conditions may be realized from the fact that $G(t \mid t_0)$ for $t > t_0$ is the solution of the homogeneous equation which satisfies the initial conditions

$$G(t_0+ \mid t_0) = 0$$

and

$$\left. \frac{\partial}{\partial t} G(t \mid t_0) \right|_{t=t_0+} = - \left. \frac{\partial}{\partial t_0} G(t \mid t_0) \right|_{t=t_0+} = 1,$$

where $t_0+$ represents a time infinitesimally larger than $t_0$. Hence Eq. (4–172) yields

$$x(t = t_0) = x(t_0)$$

and

$$\dot{x}(t = t_0+) = \dot{x}(t_0) + 2\mu x(t_0) - x(t_0) \left. \frac{\partial^2}{\partial t \, \partial t_0} G(t \mid t_0) \right|_{t=t_0+}$$

$$= \dot{x}(t_0) + 2\mu x(t_0) + x(t_0) \left. \frac{\partial^2}{\partial t^2} G(t \mid t_0) \right|_{t=t_0+} = \dot{x}(t_0).$$

The last step follows from

$$\frac{\partial^2}{\partial t^2}\, G(t \mid t_0)\bigg|_{t=t_0+} = -2\mu \frac{\partial}{\partial t}\, G(t \mid t_0)\bigg|_{t=t_0+} - \omega_0^2 G(t_0+ \mid t_0) = -2\mu.$$

## 4–13 Motion along a specified curve

The motion of a particle along a specified curve is an example of a problem which leads to a one-dimensional equation of motion for any coordinate whose values have a one-to-one correspondence with the points along the curve. One such coordinate is at all times the coordinate $s$, which represents the distance along the curve of the points of the curve from a fixed point of the curve. In terms of $s$, the component of Newton's equation of motion along the tangent to the curve is

$$F_s = m\ddot{s}, \tag{4–173}$$

where $F_s$ is the tangential component of the force, and $\ddot{s}$ is by Eq. (2–100) the tangential component of the acceleration.

If $F_s$ is a function of either the time, the coordinate $s$, or its time derivative $\dot{s}$, then, as has been discussed in the various sections of this chapter, a solution may readily be obtained. Specifically, if the force is a function of $s$ only, we can define a potential energy function $U(s)$ such that

$$F_s(s) = -\frac{dU}{ds}. \tag{4–174}$$

The work is expressible as the difference in the potential energy evaluated at the endpoints,

$$W_{12} = \int_{s_1}^{s_2} F_s(s)\, ds = \int_{s_1}^{s_2} \mathbf{F} \cdot d\mathbf{s} = U(s_1) - U(s_2). \tag{4–175}$$

Since the work equals the change in the kinetic energy,

$$W_{12} = \tfrac{1}{2}m\dot{s}_2^2 - \tfrac{1}{2}m\dot{s}_1^2,$$

we have for forces which are functions of the distance $s$ the conservation of the total energy

$$E = T + U, \tag{4–176}$$

where the kinetic energy is

$$T = \tfrac{1}{2}m\dot{s}^2.$$

As an example, we consider briefly the motion of a particle of mass $m$ moving in a vertical plane along a circular path. The forces acting on the particle are the gravitational force of magnitude $mg$ and the constraining force $\mathbf{R}$, which keeps the particle moving in a circle. From Fig. 4–16 we see that the distance along the circumference of the point $P$ from the lowest point on the circle is given by

$$s = l\theta, \qquad (4\text{--}177)$$

where $l$ is the radius of the circle and $\theta$ the angle in radians which the line $OP$ makes with the vertical. The constraining force, about which we shall have more to say in the next and subsequent chapters, acts in a direction normal to the circular path. The tangential component of the force acting on the particle thus comes solely from the gravitational force. From Fig. 4–16 we can see that the tangential component of the gravitational force is given by

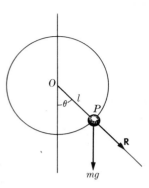

$$F_s = -mg \sin \theta = -mg \sin \frac{s}{l}. \qquad (4\text{--}178)$$

FIG. 4–16. Motion in a vertical circle.

The potential energy from which this tangential component of the force is derivable is given by

$$U(s) = -mgl \cos \theta = -mgl \cos \frac{s}{l}. \qquad (4\text{--}179)$$

It has a minimum at $s = 0$ or $\theta = 0$. For small values of $s$, the particle should thus perform simple harmonic motion about the equilibrium point. Indeed when we approximate $\sin \theta$ for small values of $\theta$ by $\theta = s/l$, the equation of motion becomes

$$m\ddot{s} = -\frac{mgs}{l}. \qquad (4\text{--}180)$$

This is the equation of motion for a simple undamped harmonic oscillator which oscillates with an angular frequency $\omega_0$, where

$$\omega_0^2 = \frac{g}{l}. \qquad (4\text{--}181)$$

If the displacements from equilibrium are not small, then we may obtain the solution following the method outlined in Section 4–6. We find that the total energy,

$$E = \tfrac{1}{2}m\dot{s}^2 - mgl \cos \frac{s}{l}, \qquad (4\text{--}182)$$

is a constant of the motion and in terms of $\theta$ has the form

$$E = \tfrac{1}{2}ml^2\dot{\theta}^2 - mgl \cos \theta. \qquad (4\text{--}183)$$

This equation may be solved for $\dot{\theta}$, which may subsequently be integrated to yield $\theta$ as a function of time. Thus we obtain

$$\dot{\theta} = \pm\sqrt{2/ml^2}\sqrt{E + mgl \cos \theta}, \qquad (4\text{--}184)$$

which yields the solution

$$\sqrt{\frac{2g}{l}}\,(t - t_0) = \int_{\theta_0}^{\theta} \frac{d\theta}{\pm\sqrt{a + \cos\theta}}, \qquad (4\text{–}185)$$

where $a = E/mgl$. The plus or minus sign in the integrand is to be chosen so as to yield an integral which is always increasing in magnitude, as discussed in an earlier section of this chapter.

The right-hand side of Eq. (4–185) is an elliptic integral. It may be integrated numerically by expanding the denominator in a binomial expansion. For example, for $a > 1$ we may set

$$(a + \cos\theta)^{-1/2} = a^{1/2} - \tfrac{1}{2}a^{-3/2}\cos\theta + \tfrac{3}{8}a^{-5/2}\cos^2\theta - \cdots, \qquad (4\text{–}186)$$

and integrate the resultant series term by term.

If $E > mgl$, no turning points exist. This situation occurs when the particle has sufficient energy to reach the top of the circle with some kinetic energy yet remaining. The particle will thus continue to move around the circle with $\theta$ increasing continuously in magnitude.

For $a < 1$ the motion is periodic. The period of the motion is found to be given by

$$\tau = 4\sqrt{\frac{l}{g}} \int_0^{\theta_{\max}} \frac{d\theta}{\sqrt{2}\sqrt{a + \cos\theta}}, \qquad (4\text{–}187)$$

where $\theta_{\max}$ is the maximum angular displacement of the particle. This maximum displacement occurs when the velocity of the particle (or $\dot{\theta}$) vanishes. We find that

$$\theta_{\max} = \cos^{-1}(-a.) \qquad (4\text{–}188)$$

## 4–14 The anharmonic oscillator

The motion of a particle for small displacements about a point of stable equilibrium was found to be simple harmonic. A displacement was considered to be small if the $x^3$ and higher terms in the Taylor-series expansion of the potential energy function about the equilibrium point were negligible. If this condition is not satisfied, then the motion is governed to within the next approximations by an equation of the form

$$m\ddot{x} = -kx - \alpha m x^2 - \beta m x^3 - \cdots. \qquad (4\text{–}189)$$

The motion about a point of stable equilibrium, being a bound motion, is still periodic, as discussed in Section 4–7; but it is no longer simple harmonic. It is said to be *anharmonic* motion. Equation (4–189) is not a linear differential equation. No general method for solving nonlinear differential equations exists. When only the $x^3$ and $x^4$ terms in the Taylor expansion of the potential energy function are retained, then we find that we can more readily obtain a numerical solution to the problem, since integrals of the form

$$\int \frac{dx}{\sqrt{E - \tfrac{1}{2}kx^2 - \tfrac{1}{3}m\alpha x^3 - \tfrac{1}{4}m\beta x^4}}$$

are expressible in terms of elliptic integrals for which complete and detailed tables can be found.

We shall concern ourselves with approximate solutions of the equation

$$\ddot{x} = -\omega_0^2 x - \alpha x^2 - \beta x^3. \tag{4-190}$$

The period of the motion of a particle moving about a point of stable equilibrium within the potential energy field

$$U(x) = \tfrac{1}{2}m\omega_0^2 x^2 + \tfrac{1}{3}m\alpha x^3 + \tfrac{1}{4}m\beta x^4 \tag{4-191}$$

is given by

$$\tau = 2\sqrt{\frac{m}{2}} \int_{x_1}^{x_2} \frac{dx}{\sqrt{E - U(x)}}. \tag{4-192}$$

Here $x_1$ and $x_2$ ($x_1 < x_2$) are the roots of the equation

$$U(x) = E,$$

and represent the maximum and minimum displacements from the equilibrium position located at the point $x = 0$.

As mentioned above, the integral in Eq. (4–192) for the potential energy function given by Eq. (4–191) is expressible in terms of elliptic integrals. If the terms $\alpha x^3$ and $\beta x^4$ are small, an approximate solution may be sufficient. Such approximate solutions are obtainable by several methods. We shall discuss two such equivalent methods below.

To simplify the algebra involved, thus making the methods clearer, we shall restrict ourselves to the case when $\alpha = 0$; that is, to a potential energy function which is symmetric about the equilibrium position. Since the motion which we are thus considering is bound and periodic, it is possible to express the solution in terms of a Fourier series,

$$x(t) = \frac{a_0}{2} + \sum_{n=1}^{\infty} a_n \cos n\omega t + \sum_{n=1}^{\infty} b_n \sin n\omega t, \tag{4-193}$$

where $\omega$ is the angular frequency of the motion. It is related to the period $\tau$ of the motion,

$$\omega = \frac{\tau}{2\pi}. \tag{4-194}$$

We can simplify the Fourier-series expansion for $x(t)$ by the following considerations. For a symmetric potential energy function the equilibrium position is also the average position of the oscillator. Hence it follows that

$$a_0 = 0.$$

Furthermore, by a proper choice of the initial time $t = 0$, we can find the motion to be also an even function of time, in which case only the cosine terms will appear in the Fourier expansion of the solution. Such would be the case if we choose $t$ to be zero when the particle is at a point of maximum displacement from equilibrium; that is, when its velocity is zero. We thus assume it possible to express the solution in the form

$$x(t) = \sum_{n=1}^{\infty} a_n \cos n\omega t. \tag{4–195}$$

Now since for $\beta = 0$ the solution is $x(t) = a_1 \cos \omega_0 t$, it follows that all the $a_n$'s in Eq. (4–195) are functions of $\beta$ and will, except for $a_1$, go to zero as $\beta$ goes to zero. The frequency $\omega$ is also a function of $\beta$. It approaches $\omega_0$ as $\beta$ approaches zero. For small values of $\beta$ it is thus reasonable to assume that all the $a_n$ for $n \neq 1$ are small compared with $a_1$. Using Eq. (4–195) as a trial solution, we find that

$$\ddot{x} + \omega_0^2 x = (\omega_0^2 - \omega^2)a_1 \cos \omega t + (\omega_0^2 - 4\omega^2)a_2 \cos 2\omega t$$
$$+ (\omega_0^2 - 9\omega^2)a_3 \cos 3\omega t + \cdots, \tag{4–196}$$

and that to a first approximation we can set

$$-\beta x^3 = -\beta a_1^3 \cos^3 \omega t$$
$$= -\tfrac{3}{4}\beta a_1^3 \cos \omega t - \tfrac{1}{4}\beta a_1^3 \cos 3\omega t. \tag{4–197}$$

If we now equate the last two equations, it follows that to a first approximation

$$(\omega_0^2 - \omega^2)a_1 = -\tfrac{3}{4}\beta a_1^3, \tag{4–198}$$

$$a_2 = 0,$$

and

$$(\omega_0^2 - 9\omega^2)a_3 = -\tfrac{1}{4}\beta a_1^3. \tag{4–199}$$

Equation (4–198) yields a first approximation for the change in the natural frequency of vibration. Assuming the change in this frequency to be small, we can set

$$\omega_0 + \omega \approx 2\omega_0 \quad \text{and} \quad \omega_0 - \omega = \Delta\omega.$$

With this approximation we obtain

$$\Delta\omega = -\frac{3\beta a_1^3}{8\omega_0},$$

or

$$\omega = \omega_0 + \frac{3\beta a_1^3}{8\omega_0}. \tag{4–200}$$

Indeed, since for positive $\beta$ the maximum amplitude of the oscillatory motion for a given total energy is less than the amplitude of the simple harmonic motion for which

$\beta = 0$ (cf. Fig. 4–17), we expect the frequency to increase. We note that the natural frequency of vibration of the anharmonic oscillator, unlike the case for the simple harmonic oscillator, is a function of the amplitude of the motion.

From Eq. (4–199) we obtain a first approximation for the coefficient $a_3$. Setting

$$\omega_0^2 - 9\omega^2 \approx -8\omega_0^2,$$

we obtain

$$a_3 = \frac{\beta a_1^3}{32\omega_0^2}, \qquad (4\text{–}201)$$

which thus gives us for a first approximation the solution

$$x(t) = a_1 \cos \omega t + \frac{\beta a_1^3}{32\omega_0^2} \cos 3\omega t. \qquad (4\text{–}202)$$

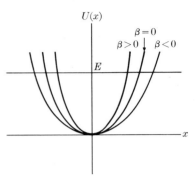

FIG. 4–17.    Plot of

$$U(x) = \tfrac{1}{2}kx^2 + \tfrac{1}{4}m\beta x^4.$$

We can continue this process, using the above values in the trial solution, thereby obtaining successively better approximations for the natural frequency of vibration $\omega$ and the coefficients in the Fourier expansion of the solution. This method is known as the *method of successive approximations.*

This same result could also be obtained by a somewhat more sophisticated approach to the method of successive approximations. In this approach the $\beta x^3$ term in the equation

$$\ddot{x} + \omega_0^2 x = -\beta x^3 \qquad (4\text{–}203)$$

is considered to be an inhomogeneous term of the otherwise linear differential equation. By Eq. (4–172) the inhomogeneous solution to this inhomogeneous equation is expressible in terms of the Green function, which for $\mu = 0$ is found to be [cf. (Eq. 4–166)]

$$G(t \mid \xi) = \begin{cases} \dfrac{\sin \omega_0(t - \xi)}{\omega_0} & t \geq \xi, \\[2ex] 0 & t \leq \xi. \end{cases} \qquad (4\text{–}204)$$

We are concerned only with the inhomogeneous solution to Eq. (4–203), since it is a nonlinear differential equation for which the general solution is not expressible as the sum of the solution of the equation for $\beta = 0$ plus the solution when $\beta \neq 0$.

The particular solution to Eq. (4–203) is

$$x(t) = -\int^t \beta x^3(\xi) \frac{\sin \omega_0(t - \xi)}{\omega_0} \, d\xi. \qquad (4\text{–}205)$$

Inserting into this equation the first approximation to the solution, the first term of the Fourier expansion for $x(\xi)$,

$$x_1(\xi) = a_1 \cos \omega \xi,$$

and using the trigonometric identity

$$\sin \omega_0(t - \xi) \cos^3 \omega\xi$$
$$= \tfrac{3}{8}\{\sin [\omega_0 t + (\omega - \omega_0)\xi] + \sin [\omega_0 t - (\omega + \omega_0)\xi]\}$$
$$+ \tfrac{1}{8}\{\sin [\omega_0 t + (3\omega - \omega_0)\xi] + \sin [\omega_0 t - (3\omega + \omega_0)\xi]\},$$

we obtain the new approximate solution

$$x(t) = -\frac{3\beta a_1^3}{8\omega_0}\left\{\frac{\cos \omega t}{\omega_0 - \omega} + \frac{\cos \omega t}{\omega_0 + \omega}\right\} - \frac{\beta a_1^3}{8\omega_0}\left\{\frac{\cos 3\omega t}{\omega_0 - 3\omega} + \frac{\cos 3\omega t}{\omega_0 + 3\omega}\right\},$$

or

$$x(t) = -\frac{3}{4}\frac{\beta a_1^3}{\omega_0^2 - \omega^2} \cos \omega t - \frac{1}{4}\frac{\beta a_1^3 \cos 3\omega t}{\omega_0^2 - 9\omega^2}. \tag{4–206}$$

In order for this solution to agree with the solution in the form

$$x(t) = a_1 \cos \omega t + a_2 \cos 2\omega t + a_3 \cos 3\omega t,$$

we must have, as previously found,

$$(\omega_0^2 - \omega^2)a_1 = -\tfrac{3}{4}\beta a_1^3, \qquad a_2 = 0, \qquad \text{and} \qquad a_3 = \frac{1}{32}\frac{\beta a_1^3}{\omega_0^2}.$$

If we subsequently insert the approximation

$$x(\xi) = a_1 \cos \omega t + \frac{1}{32}\frac{\beta a_1^3}{\omega_0^2} \cos 3\omega t$$

into the right-hand side of Eq. (4–205), we can obtain the next approximation to the solution of Eq. (4–203).

We note that Eq. (4–205) is referred to as an *integral equation*.

The importance of the anharmonic terms may be appreciated by considering, for example, the vibrational motion of the atoms of an isotropic crystal. Assuming each of the atoms of the crystal to be oscillating about a point of stable equilibrium, the motion in any direction is classically described as motion within the potential energy field

$$U = \tfrac{1}{8}kx^2 + \tfrac{1}{3}m\alpha x^3 + \tfrac{1}{4}m\beta x^4.$$

From our example we realize that, the average position of the oscillator for $\alpha = 0$ being zero, the terms in $kx^2$ and $\beta x^4$ will not account for the linear thermal expansion of the crystal. The linear thermal expansion of a crystal is accounted for by the $\tfrac{1}{3}m\alpha x^3$ term, which destroys the symmetry of the problem and hence yields an average position different from zero.

## 4–15 The forced anharmonic oscillator

The equation of motion of the anharmonic oscillator we are considering ($\alpha = 0$), whose motion is forced by the sinusoidal driving force

$$F = F_0 \cos \omega t,$$

is

$$\ddot{x} + \omega_0^2 x = \frac{F_0}{m} \cos \omega t - \beta x^3. \tag{4–207}$$

An approximate solution to this equation may also be obtained through the use of Eq. (4–172), which yields for the particular solution the integral equation

$$x(t) = \int^t \frac{F_0}{m} \cos \omega\xi \, \frac{\sin \omega_0(t - \xi)}{\omega_0} \, d\xi - \int^t \beta x^3(\xi) \, \frac{\sin \omega_0(t - \xi)}{\omega_0} \, d\xi. \tag{4–208}$$

Once again inserting the first approximation

$$x_1(\xi) = a_1 \cos \omega\xi$$

into this integral equation yields the second approximation to the solution,

$$x_2(t) = \frac{F_0}{m} \frac{\cos \omega t}{\omega_0^2 - \omega^2} - \frac{3}{4} \frac{\beta a_1^3}{\omega_0^2 - \omega^2} \cos \omega t - \frac{1}{4} \beta a_1^3 \frac{\cos 3\omega t}{\omega_0^2 - 9\omega^2}. \tag{4–209}$$

For this approximation the frequency $\omega$ is of course determined by the driving force. In order that this solution be equal to the trial solution

$$x(t) = a_1 \cos \omega t + a_2 \cos 2\omega t + a_3 \cos 3\omega t,$$

we must have

$$(\omega_0^2 - \omega^2)a_1 + \tfrac{3}{4}\beta a_1^3 - \frac{F_0}{m} = 0, \tag{4–210}$$

$$a_2 = 0, \tag{4–211}$$

and

$$a_3 = -\frac{1}{4} \frac{\beta a_1^3}{\omega_0^2 - 9\omega^2}. \tag{4–212}$$

So long as $\omega_0^2 - 9\omega^2$ is a large number such that $a_3$ is small,

$$x_1(t) = a_1 \cos \omega t \tag{4–213}$$

is a good first approximation to Eq. (4–208). The amplitude $a_1$ of this approximate solution is a root of Eq. (4–210).

We note that unlike the case for the undamped simple harmonic oscillator, the amplitude in this case does not increase without limit as $\omega$ approaches the natural frequency of oscillation of the anharmonic oscillator.

Another interesting phenomenon present in this problem but not in the harmonic oscillator is the fact that in this case, for some finite range of frequencies, Eq. (4–210) may have three real roots for $a_1$, whereas for all other values of $\omega$ it yields only one real root for $a_1$ (cf. Fig. 4–18). This means that, as $\omega$ increases from $\omega < \omega_1$, the amplitude $a_1$, which for small values of $\omega$ lies along the $e$-$f$ part of the curve of Fig. 4–18(a), will move along the $f$-$g$ part of the curve. When it reaches the value at $g$, any increase in the value of $\omega$ past the value of $\omega_2$ will necessarily bring it along the $h$-$j$ part of the curve. The amplitude of the forced anharmonic oscillator will thus show a discontinuity at $\omega = \omega_2$.

Similarly, as $\omega$ is decreased from the values $\omega > \omega_2$, which yield amplitudes lying along the $h$-$j$ part of the curve, the amplitude will jump discontinuously as $\omega$ passes through $\omega_1$.

We note that when $\omega = \tfrac{1}{3}\omega_0$ Eq. (4–212) yields a very large amplitude for the cos $3\omega t$ term. It should be clear, since we have used only the first term in the Fourier

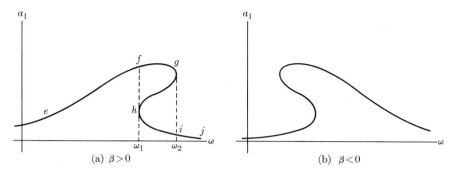

FIG. 4–18. Amplitude-vs.-frequency curve for the forced harmonic oscillator.

expansion of the solution to obtain Eq. (4–212), that when $\omega$ has a value close to $\frac{1}{3}\omega_0$, the $\cos 3\omega t$ term should be included in the first approximation to the solution (Problem 4–25).

The existence of new resonances in which the frequency of the driving force is not the same as the frequency of the oscillation excited in the oscillator is a further interesting and useful phenomenon present in the anharmonic oscillator. This phenomenon is at times used for generating electromagnetic waves at one frequency while driving the system at another frequency.

## Problems

4–1. A block is projected up an inclined plane with an initial velocity $v_0$. If the incline makes an angle $\theta$ with the horizontal and if the coefficient of sliding friction between the plane and the block is $\mu$, find the time it takes the block to return to the foot of the incline. For what minimum value of the static coefficient of friction will the block come to rest on the incline?

4–2. Find the position at any time $t$ of a particle of mass $m$ when the applied force is $F = 2m \cos \omega t$ and $x = 8$ at $t = 0$ and $x = -b$ at $t = \pi/2\omega$.

4–3. Find the motion of a particle of mass $m$ being acted upon by the force

$$\mathbf{F} = F_0 e^{-\alpha t} \sin \omega t \mathbf{i}.$$

4–4. (a) If the limiting velocity for an 80-kg man with a parachute is the same as his velocity after falling freely for 0.75 m, find the limiting velocity and the damping constant $\kappa$. (Assume $F_{\text{damping}} = -m\kappa v$.)

(b) Now suppose that the man falls freely from rest for 5 sec and then opens his 'chute. What will be his velocity after another 5 sec?

4–5. Find the expression for the velocity and displacement of a particle subject to a resistive force proportional to the square of its velocity.

4–6. Repeat Problem 4–5 with an additional constant force. If a particle has an initial velocity $v_0$ which is directed oppositely to the constant force, with what velocity will it return to the starting point? How far from the starting point is the turning point?

4–7. A particle of mass $m$ is acted on by a force $F = -kx^2$. If $\dot{x} = v_0$ at $x = 0$, find (a) the energy equation, (b) the turning point, and (c) the velocity at any position.

4–8. Find the rectilinear motion of a particle moving in a repulsive force field whose magnitude varies as the inverse cube of the distance of the particle from the force center.

4–9. A particle of mass $m$ moves in the potential energy field

$$U(x) = a \ln x + \frac{b}{x^2},$$

where $x$ is the distance of the particle from the origin (the force center), and $a$ and $b$ are positive constants. Find the expression for the force as a function of position. At what point does the force vanish? Is this a point of stable equilibrium? If so, find the period of small oscillations about the point of stable equilibrium.

4–10. Repeat Problem 4–9 for the following potential energy fields:

$$\text{(a)} \quad U(x) = a \cos x + \frac{b}{\sin^2 x}, \quad 0 \le x \le \pi$$

$$\text{(b)} \quad U(x) = -\frac{a}{x^6} + \frac{b}{x^{12}}$$

$$\text{(c)} \quad U(x) = ax^2 - bx^4$$

$$\text{(d)} \quad U(x) = -\frac{a}{x} + \frac{b}{x^2}$$

4–11. For what values of the energy will the motion of a particle of mass $m$ in the potential energy field

$$U(x) = -\frac{a}{x} + \frac{b}{x^2},$$

where $a$ and $b$ are positive constants, be bounded? unbounded? Find the period of the bounded motion. [*Hint:* Let $a = 2\alpha E$, $b = (\alpha^2 - \beta^2)E$.]

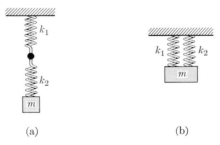

(a)                    (b)

FIGURE 4–19

4–12. Find the expression for the frequency of oscillation of a particle of mass $m$ being acted upon by two springs of constants $k_1$ and $k_2$, as shown in Fig. 4–19.

4–13. A particle of mass $m$ is moving under the combined action of the forces

$$F_1 = -kx, \qquad F_2 = F_0 t,$$

and a damping force proportional to the first power of the particle velocity,

$$F_{\text{damping}} = -2m\mu\dot{x}.$$

Express the solution in terms of the initial position and velocity of the particle.

4–14. Repeat Problem 4–14 for the forces

(a) $F_2 = F_0 e^{-at}$
(b) $F_2 = F_0 e^{-at} \cos \omega t$
(c) $F_2 = F_0 e^{-at} + F_0 e^{-at} \cos \omega t$.

4–15. Consider the motion of an electron in a conductor under the action of the complex sinusoidal driving force $F = F_0 e^{i\omega t}$. Obtain the expression for the frequency dependence of the complex conductivity. (Cf. Section 4–10.)

4–16. Find the general solution for the motion of a body subject to a linear repelling force $F = kx$. Show that this is the type of motion to be expected in the neighborhood of a point of unstable equilibrium.

4–17. Find the resonance point and the half-width of the velocity-versus-frequency curve for the damped harmonic oscillator under the action of a sinusoidal driving force.

4–18. Find the motion of a mass $m$ subject to a restoring force $-kx$ and to a damping force $(\pm)\mu mg$ due to dry sliding friction. Show that the oscillations are isochronous (period independent of amplitude), with the amplitude of oscillation decreasing by $2\mu g/\omega_0^2$ during each half-cycle until the mass comes to a stop.

4–19. Show that

(a) $\displaystyle\int_{t_1}^{t_2} F(t) \frac{d}{dt} \delta(t - a)\, dt = -\left.\frac{d}{dt} F(t)\right|_{t=a}, \qquad t_1 < a < t_2$

(b) $\displaystyle\int_{t_1}^{t_2} F(t)\, \delta(t^2 - a^2)\, dt = \int_{t_1}^{t_2} F(t) \left[\frac{\delta(t - a) + \delta(t + a)}{2a}\right] dt$

$$= \begin{cases} \dfrac{1}{2a} F(a) & t_1 < a < t_2 \\[2mm] \dfrac{1}{2a} F(-a) & t_1 < -a < t_2 \\[2mm] \dfrac{1}{2a} [F(a) + F(-a)] & \begin{cases} t_1 < -a \\ t_2 > a \end{cases} \end{cases}$$

(c) $\displaystyle\int F(t)\, \delta[b(t - a)]\, dt = \frac{1}{b} F(a)$

(d) $\displaystyle\int F(t)\, \delta(t - a)\, \delta(t - b)\, dt = \delta(a - b) F(a) = \delta(b - a) F(b)$

(e) $\dfrac{d}{dt} \delta(t - a) = -\dfrac{d}{dt} \delta(a - t)$

4-20. Find the Green function for the critically damped harmonic oscillator, $\mu = \omega_0$. Compare your solution with Eq. (4–99) for the case when the oscillator was located at time $t = t_0$ at $x = 0$ with a velocity $v_0 = 1/m$.

4-21. Use a Green function to obtain a solution for Problems 4–13 and 4–14. Consider both cases

$$\mu = \omega_0 \quad \text{and} \quad \mu \neq \omega_0.$$

4-22. Show that for $-\pi < x < \pi$,

(a)   $x = 2 \sum_{1}^{\infty} \dfrac{(-1)^{n+1}}{n} \sin nx$

(b)   $x^2 = \dfrac{\pi^2}{3} + 4 \sum_{1}^{\infty} \dfrac{(-1)^n}{n^2} \cos nx$

(c)   $x \sin x = 1 - \dfrac{\cos x}{2} + 2 \sum_{1}^{\infty} (-1)^n \dfrac{\cos (n+1)x}{n^2 + 2n}$

4-23. A particle of mass $m$ is moving in a vertical plane under the action of the gravitational force $mg$ along the curve

(a)   $y = -l \cos x$

(b)   $y = -b\sqrt{1 - x^2/a^2}$

Find the period of small oscillations about the lowest points of the curves.

4-24. Solve the equation

$$\ddot{x} + \omega_0^2 x - \alpha x^2 = 0$$

(a) by the method of successive approximations, (b) by the integral equation (Green's function) method. (c) Compare the approximate period found in (a) or (b) with the exact numerical value of the period obtained from Eq. (4–192).

4-25. Obtain an approximate solution of the equation of motion

$$\ddot{x} + \omega_0^2 x + \beta x^3 = \dfrac{F_0}{m} \cos \omega t$$

for the case where $\omega$ has a value close to $\tfrac{1}{3}\omega_0$.

4-26. Obtain an approximate solution to the equation

$$\ddot{x} + \omega_0^2 x - \alpha x^2 = \dfrac{F_0}{m} \cos \omega t$$

4-27. It is possible for subharmonics to be generated in an anharmonic oscillator. Consider the forced undamped anharmonic oscillator

$$m\ddot{x} + kx + m\beta x^3 = F_0 \cos \omega t.$$

Find the condition for which a solution of the form

$$x = a_1 \cos \omega t + a_{1/3} \cos \tfrac{1}{3}\omega t$$

is possible.

4-28. Consider the motion of the anharmonic oscillator whose potential energy is

$$U(x) \; = \; \tfrac{1}{2}kx^2 + \tfrac{1}{3}\beta x^3$$

under the combined action of two sinusoidal driving forces,

$$F \; = \; F_1 \cos \omega_1 t + F_2 \cos \omega_2 t.$$

Show that the solution contains sinusoidal terms whose frequencies are equal to the sum and difference of the driving frequencies. This phenomenon is known as intermodulation. What are possible values of $\omega_1$ and $\omega_2$ for resonance?

# 5

# *Lagrange's Equations of Motions*

In the preceding chapter, we formulated Newton's equations of motion. We subsequently applied them to the rectilinear motion of a particle, hoping that, through the proper choice of generalized coordinates, we might be fortunate enough to be able to reduce any problem to the solution of a number of one-dimensional differential equations of motion.

In this chapter, we shall discuss a general method for expressing the equations of motion in terms of generalized coordinates. The generalized equations of motion which we shall derive were first introduced by Lagrange in 1788 and are named after him.

## 5–1 Generalized forces

The method for representing a vector in terms of the base vectors of a generalized coordinate system was presented in Section 1–5; and in Section 2–5 we discussed the kinematic description of the motion of a particle in terms of generalized coordinates, obtaining general expressions for the velocity and acceleration of a particle.

The method for representing a vector in terms of generalized coordinates rests on the fact that any vector is specified if its scalar products with three noncoplanar vectors are known (cf. Section 1–5). Three such noncoplanar vectors at any point, specified by a set of values of the generalized coordinates $(q_1, q_2, q_3)$, are either the vectors

$$\mathbf{b}_i = \frac{\partial \mathbf{r}}{\partial q_i} = \frac{\partial x}{\partial q_i}\,\mathbf{i} + \frac{\partial y}{\partial q_i}\,\mathbf{j} + \frac{\partial z}{\partial q_i}\,\mathbf{k} \tag{5–1}$$

or their reciprocal vectors which, if the coordinate transformation from the cartesian coordinates to the generalized coordinates is time independent, are given by

$$\boldsymbol{b}_i = \boldsymbol{\nabla} q_i = \frac{\partial q_i}{\partial x}\,\mathbf{i} + \frac{\partial q_i}{\partial y}\,\mathbf{j} + \frac{\partial q_i}{\partial z}\,\mathbf{k}. \tag{5–2}$$

For orthogonal curvilinear coordinates, we found (cf. Sections 2–4 and 2–5) the reciprocal vectors to be

$$\boldsymbol{b}_i = \frac{1}{h_i}\,\mathbf{e}_i = \frac{1}{h_i^2}\,\mathbf{b}_i.$$

142

To represent a force vector we utilize the base vectors $\mathbf{b}_i$. The scalar products of $\mathbf{F}$ with the $\mathbf{b}_i$ are represented by

$$Q_i = \mathbf{F} \cdot \mathbf{b}_i = F_x \frac{\partial x}{\partial q_i} + F_y \frac{\partial y}{\partial q_i} + F_z \frac{\partial z}{\partial q_i}, \qquad (5\text{-}3)$$

and the $Q_i$'s are referred to as the *generalized forces*. In terms of the generalized forces and the inverse base vectors, a force $\mathbf{F}$ is expressed by

$$\mathbf{F} = \sum_{i=1}^{3} Q_i \mathbf{b}_i.$$

As an example, we consider the generalized forces which are obtained when we use the spherical coordinates $r$, $\theta$, and $\phi$, which were defined in Section 2–4.

The base vectors $\mathbf{b}_i$ for the spherical coordinate system were found to be the vectors (Fig. 5–1)

$$\mathbf{b}_1 = \frac{\partial \mathbf{r}}{\partial r} = \mathbf{e}_r,$$

$$\mathbf{b}_2 = \frac{\partial \mathbf{r}}{\partial \theta} = r\mathbf{e}_\theta = \mathbf{e}_\phi \times \mathbf{r}, \qquad (5\text{-}4)$$

$$\mathbf{b}_3 = \frac{\partial \mathbf{r}}{\partial \phi} = r \sin \theta \mathbf{e}_\phi = \mathbf{k} \times \mathbf{r}.$$

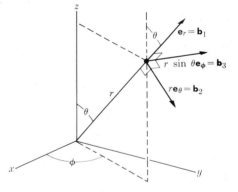

For the spherical coordinates we thus obtain the generalized forces,

$$Q_1 = \mathbf{F} \cdot \mathbf{b}_1 = \mathbf{F} \cdot \mathbf{e}_r = F_r, \qquad (5\text{-}5)$$

$$Q_2 = \mathbf{F} \cdot \mathbf{b}_2 = \mathbf{e}_\phi \cdot (\mathbf{r} \times \mathbf{F}), \qquad (5\text{-}6)$$

$$Q_3 = \mathbf{F} \cdot \mathbf{b}_3 = \mathbf{k} \cdot (\mathbf{r} \times \mathbf{F}). \qquad (5\text{-}7)$$

FIG. 5–1. Spherical base vectors at the point $(r, \theta, \phi)$.

We find $Q_1$ to be the component of the force $\mathbf{F}$ along the radial direction. On the other hand, $Q_2$ and $Q_3$ do not have the dimensions of force. These latter generalized forces are, respectively, the components of the vector $\mathbf{r} \times \mathbf{F}$ along the $\mathbf{e}_\phi$- and $\mathbf{k}$-directions.

The vector $\mathbf{r} \times \mathbf{F}$ is referred to as the *torque* about the origin which the force $\mathbf{F}$ exerts on the particle; $Q_2$ and $Q_3$ are thus specific components of this torque. In fact, the generalized force for any angle coordinate is always the component of the torque along the axis about which a change in the angle coordinate rotates the position vector. Since angular coordinates are frequently employed, the torque, defined by

$$\mathbf{N} = \mathbf{r} \times \mathbf{F}, \qquad (5\text{-}8)$$

is an important physical quantity of which we shall make frequent use.

We note that the work $\Delta W$ performed by the force $\mathbf{F}$ when $q_i$ is varied by the infinitesimal amount $\Delta q_i$ is

$$\Delta W = \mathbf{F} \cdot \Delta \mathbf{s}_i,$$

where

$$\Delta \mathbf{s}_i = \frac{\partial \mathbf{r}}{\partial q_i} \Delta q_i = \Delta q_i \mathbf{b}_i$$

is the change in the position vector when $q_i$ is varied. This yields

$$\Delta W = \mathbf{F} \cdot \mathbf{b}_i \, \Delta q_i = Q_i \, \Delta q_i. \tag{5–9}$$

The term $Q_i \, \Delta q_i$ thus has the dimension of work. For a general displacement for which

$$\Delta \mathbf{s} = \Delta \mathbf{r}_1 + \Delta \mathbf{r}_2 + \Delta \mathbf{r}_3 = \Delta q_1 \mathbf{b}_1 + \Delta q_2 \mathbf{b}_2 + \Delta q_3 \mathbf{b}_3, \tag{5–10}$$

the work is

$$\Delta W = \mathbf{F} \cdot \Delta \mathbf{s} = \left( \sum_{i=1}^{3} Q_i \mathbf{b}_i \right) \cdot \left( \sum_{j=1}^{3} \Delta q_j \mathbf{b}_j \right) = \sum_{i=1}^{3} Q_i \, \Delta q_i, \tag{5–11}$$

since

$$\mathbf{b}_i \cdot \mathbf{b}_j = \delta_{ij}.$$

## 5–2 Generalized particle momenta

Quite analogously, we represent the momentum vector $\mathbf{p} = m\mathbf{v}$ at any point $(q_1, q_2, q_3)$ in terms of its scalar products

$$p_i = \mathbf{p} \cdot \mathbf{b}_i, \tag{5–12}$$

with the three base vectors $\mathbf{b}_i$ defined at the point $(q_1, q_2, q_3)$. The scalar products $p_i$ are referred to as the *generalized particle momenta*.*

In terms of the definition of the linear momentum as the product of the mass and the velocity vector,

$$\mathbf{p} = m\mathbf{v},$$

we find that the generalized particle momenta are

$$p_i = m\mathbf{v} \cdot \mathbf{b}_i. \tag{5–13}$$

In Section 2–4 we found the covariant components of the velocities $v_i$ to be expressible as

$$v_i = \mathbf{v} \cdot \mathbf{b}_i = \frac{\partial}{\partial \dot{q}_i} \left( \tfrac{1}{2} v^2 \right).$$

---

* We should like to note that the generalized particle momenta defined here are not necessarily the same as the generalized or conjugate momenta which we shall introduce in Section 6–13. To avoid confusion, we refer to the $p_i$ introduced here as generalized *particle* momenta.

Hence we find that Eq. (5–13) may be rewritten in the form

$$p_i = \frac{\partial T}{\partial \dot{q}_i},\tag{5–14}$$

where $T = \frac{1}{2}mv^2$.

As an example, we obtain the generalized particle momenta for a particle whose motion is described in spherical coordinates. Analogous to the generalized forces which we found in the last section, we find

$$p_1 = \mathbf{p} \cdot \mathbf{e}_r = p_r\tag{5–15}$$

to be the component of the linear momentum along the radial direction, and

$$p_2 = \mathbf{p} \cdot (\mathbf{e}_\phi \times \mathbf{r}) = \mathbf{e}_\phi \cdot (\mathbf{r} \times \mathbf{p})\tag{5–16}$$

and

$$p_3 = \mathbf{p} \cdot (\mathbf{k} \times \mathbf{r}) = \mathbf{k} \cdot (\mathbf{r} \times \mathbf{p})\tag{5–17}$$

not to have the dimensions of linear momentum. The latter two generalized momenta are the components of the vector

$$\mathbf{L} = \mathbf{r} \times \mathbf{p}\tag{5–18}$$

along the $\mathbf{e}_\phi$- and $\mathbf{k}$-direction, respectively. The vector $\mathbf{L}$ is referred to as the *orbital angular momentum* of the particle. Once again we note that we shall meet the orbital angular momentum of a particle whenever we utilize angular coordinates. Since this is a frequent occurrence, the angular momentum is a very important physical quantity.

Explicit expressions for the generalized particle momenta may be obtained through the use of Eq. (5–14). In spherical coordinates the kinetic energy is

$$T = \tfrac{1}{2}m(\dot{r}^2 + r^2\dot{\theta}^2 + r^2\sin^2\theta\dot{\phi}^2),$$

whence we obtain

$$p_1 = \frac{\partial T}{\partial \dot{r}} = m\dot{r},$$

$$p_2 = \frac{\partial T}{\partial \dot{\theta}} = mr^2\dot{\theta},$$

$$p_3 = \frac{\partial T}{\partial \dot{\phi}} = mr^2\sin^2\theta\dot{\phi}.$$

The same expressions can also be obtained through the use of Eqs. (5–15) through (5–17), remembering that

$$\mathbf{p} = m\mathbf{v} = m(\dot{r}\mathbf{e}_r + r\dot{\theta}\mathbf{e}_\theta + r\sin\theta\dot{\phi}\mathbf{e}_\phi).$$

We recall that we referred to the contravariant components of the velocity

$$v_i^{\star} = \mathbf{v} \cdot \boldsymbol{b}_i = \dot{x}\,\frac{\partial q_i}{\partial x} + \dot{y}\,\frac{\partial q_i}{\partial y} + \dot{z}\,\frac{\partial q_i}{\partial z} = \dot{q}_i \qquad (5\text{–}19)$$

as the generalized velocities. In terms of the generalized velocities and the generalized particle momenta, we find the kinetic energy for time-independent coordinate transformations to be given by

$$T = \tfrac{1}{2} \sum_{i=1}^{3} p_i \dot{q}_i, \qquad (5\text{–}20)$$

since

$$T = \tfrac{1}{2}\mathbf{p} \cdot \mathbf{v}$$

and

$$\mathbf{p} \cdot \mathbf{v} = \left( \sum_{i=1}^{3} p_i \boldsymbol{b}^i \right) \cdot \left( \sum_{j=1}^{3} \dot{q}_i \boldsymbol{b}_i \right) = \sum_{i=1}^{3} p_i \dot{q}_i.$$

## 5–3 Generalized equations of motion

The generalized equations of motion are the scalar products of Newton's equation of motion, $\mathbf{F} = m\mathbf{a}$, with the three base vectors $\boldsymbol{b}_i$ of the generalized coordinate system. The scalar products of the force with the base vectors were defined in Section 5–1 as the generalized forces $Q_i$, and a generally very useful expression for the scalar products of the acceleration vector with the base vectors $\boldsymbol{b}_i$ was found in Section 2–4 to be

$$a_i = \mathbf{a} \cdot \mathbf{b}_i = \frac{d}{dt}\frac{\partial}{\partial \dot{q}_i}\,(\tfrac{1}{2}v^2) - \frac{\partial}{\partial q_i}\,(\tfrac{1}{2}v^2).$$

Using this result for the scalar products $\mathbf{a} \cdot \mathbf{b}_i$ yields the generalized equations of motion in the form

$$Q_i = \frac{d}{dt}\frac{\partial T}{\partial \dot{q}_i} - \frac{\partial T}{\partial q_i}, \qquad (5\text{–}21)$$

where $T = \tfrac{1}{2}mv^2$ is the kinetic energy.

The equations of motion expressed in this form are referred to as *Lagrange's equations of motion*.

We note that except for Eqs. (5–19) and (5–20), which are correct only for time independent coordinate transformations, all the other equations which we have obtained through use of the base vectors $\boldsymbol{b}_i$ are applicable also to the time-dependent coordinate transformations,

$$x = x(q_1, q_2, q_3, t),$$
$$y = y(q_1, q_2, q_3, t),$$
$$z = z(q_1, q_2, q_3, t).$$

▶As as example of the application of Lagrange's equations of motion, we consider the motion of a particle in a plane under the action of the central force

$$\mathbf{F} = -m\omega_0^2 \mathbf{r} = -m\omega_0^2(x\mathbf{i} + y\mathbf{j}). \tag{5–22}$$

In rectangular coordinates, the kinetic energy is

$$T = \tfrac{1}{2}m(\dot{x}^2 + \dot{y}^2),$$

and the base vectors are the cartesian base vectors

$$\mathbf{b}_1 = \mathbf{i} \quad \text{and} \quad \mathbf{b}_2 = \mathbf{j}.$$

We quite obviously should and do obtain, through the use of Eq. (5–21), Newton's equations of motion,

$$Q_1 = F_x = m\ddot{x} = -m\omega_0^2 x,$$
$$Q_2 = F_y = m\ddot{y} = -m\omega_0^2 y. \tag{5–23}$$

These equations are two independent one-dimensional equations of motion whose solutions were considered in Section 4–9. They are

$$x = A \cos (\omega_0 t + \phi) \tag{5–24}$$

and

$$y = B \cos (\omega_0 t + \theta), \tag{5–25}$$

where the constants $A$, $B$, $\phi$, and $\theta$ are functions of the initial values $x_0$, $y_0$, $\dot{x}_0$, and $\dot{y}_0$ of the components of the displacement and velocity along the coordinate axes. Depending on the values of the constants $A$, $B$, $\phi$, and $\theta$, the orbit of the motion (Problem 1–19) may be an ellipse, a circle or a straight line.

While this problem is readily soluble in cartesian coordinates, certain features of the motion are brought out more clearly when we solve the problem in cylindrical coordinates, for which the kinetic energy is given by

$$T = \tfrac{1}{2}m(\dot{r}^2 + r^2\dot{\phi}^2),$$

and the base vectors are

$$\mathbf{b}_1 = \mathbf{e}_r \quad \text{and} \quad \mathbf{b}_2 = r\mathbf{e}_\phi.$$

In cylindrical coordinates we thus obtain the equations of motion

$$Q_1 = F_r = -m\omega_0^2 r = \frac{d}{dt}(m\dot{r}) - mr\dot{\phi}^2 \tag{5–26}$$

and

$$Q_2 = \mathbf{k} \cdot (\mathbf{r} \times \mathbf{F}) = \frac{d}{dt}(mr^2\dot{\phi}). \tag{5–27}$$

Since for this problem the torque vanishes,

$$\mathbf{r} \times \mathbf{F} = \mathbf{r} \times (-m\omega_0^2 \mathbf{r}) = 0,$$

we immediately have one very simple equation of motion, which yields the solution that the $z$-component of the orbital angular momentum is a constant of the motion,

$$mr^2\dot{\phi} = p_2 = L_z = \text{const} = h. \qquad (5\text{--}28)$$

In this problem where the motion takes place in the $xy$-plane, the $z$-component of the orbital angular momentum happens to be the magnitude of the total orbital angular momentum as the latter lies along the $z$-axis. ◄

Generally we find the total orbital angular momentum of a particle to be a constant of the motion whenever the total torque acting on the particle vanishes. This is readily shown to be the case by taking the cross product of Newton's equations of motion with the radius vector $\mathbf{r}$. This yields

$$\mathbf{r} \times \mathbf{F} = \mathbf{r} \times \frac{d}{dt}\mathbf{p} = \frac{d}{dt}(\mathbf{r} \times \mathbf{p}) - \frac{d\mathbf{r}}{dt} \times \mathbf{p} = \frac{d}{dt}(\mathbf{r} \times \mathbf{p}), \qquad (5\text{--}29)$$

since

$$\frac{d\mathbf{r}}{dt} \times (m\mathbf{v}) = 0.$$

Thus whenever $\mathbf{r} \times \mathbf{F} = 0$,

$$\frac{d}{dt}(\mathbf{r} \times \mathbf{p}) = 0$$

or

$$\mathbf{L} = \mathbf{r} \times \mathbf{p} = \text{const.} \qquad (5\text{--}30)$$

If the torque does not vanish, Eq. (5–29) yields the equation of motion for the orbital angular momentum vector,

$$\mathbf{N} = \mathbf{r} \times \mathbf{F} = \frac{d}{dt}\mathbf{L}. \qquad (5\text{--}31)$$

We note that this equation contains a great deal more information than is contained within its specific components, which happen to appear among the generalized equations of motion. We shall therefore invariably check to see if any additional helpful information is furnished by this equation.

►Returning to our example, the other equation of motion, Eq. (5–26), is not a one-dimensional differential equation. Through the use of Eq. (5–28), however, remembering that $p_2 = mr^2\dot{\phi} = h$, and thus

$$\dot{\phi} = \frac{h}{mr^2}, \qquad (5\text{--}32)$$

Eq. (5–26) can be made one-dimensional. Using Eq. (5–32) permits us to express

Eq. (5–26) in the form

$$m\ddot{r} = -m\omega_0^2 r + \frac{h^2}{mr^3}.$$ (5–33)

This equation is now one-dimensional and may be solved by the methods outlined in Section 4–6.

We are thus led to a second integral of the motion, the energy integral

$$E = \tfrac{1}{2}m\dot{r}^2 + \tfrac{1}{2}m\omega_0^2 r^2 + \frac{h^2}{2mr^2},$$ (5–34)

which happens to be the total energy of the particle.

The force

$$\mathbf{F} = -m\omega_0^2 \mathbf{r}$$ (5–35)

in the problem just considered is an example of a central force, expressed by

$$\mathbf{F} = f(r)\mathbf{e}_r,$$ (5–36)

whose magnitude is a function of the radial coordinate $r$ only. The general features of central force field motion will be considered in Chapter 7. ◀

▶ As a second example we shall obtain the equations of motion in parabolic coordinates for an electron under the action of the attractive central force field

$$\mathbf{F} = -\frac{k}{r^2}\,\mathbf{e}_r = -\boldsymbol{\nabla}\left(-\frac{k}{r}\right)$$

and a uniform electric field directed along the positive $z$-axis. The influence of a uniform electric field on the motion and energy of the electrons in atoms is known as the *Stark effect*.

The parabolic coordinates were introduced in Section 2–4, where they were defined by the equations

$$\xi^2 = \sqrt{x^2 + y^2 + z^2} + z,$$
$$\eta^2 = \sqrt{x^2 + y^2 + z^2} - z,$$
$$\phi = \tan^{-1}\frac{y}{x}.$$

In terms of $\xi$, $\eta$, and $\phi$, through the use of Eq. (2–80) and the $h_i$'s found in Section 2–4, the kinetic energy is found to be given by

$$T = \tfrac{1}{2}m[(\eta^2 + \xi^2)(\dot{\eta}^2 + \dot{\xi}^2) + \eta^2\xi^2\dot{\phi}^2].$$

The force acting on the electron is expressed in terms of the parabolic coordinates by

$$\mathbf{F} = -\boldsymbol{\nabla}\left(-\frac{k}{r} + eEz\right) = -\boldsymbol{\nabla}\left[-\frac{2k}{\xi^2 + \eta^2} + \frac{eE}{2}(\xi^2 - \eta^2)\right],$$

which leads to the following generalized forces:

$$Q_\eta = \mathbf{F} \cdot \mathbf{b}_\eta$$

$$= -\left[\frac{\partial U}{\partial x}\frac{\partial x}{\partial \eta} + \frac{\partial U}{\partial y}\frac{\partial y}{\partial \eta} + \frac{\partial U}{\partial z}\frac{\partial z}{\partial \eta}\right] = -\frac{\partial U}{\partial \eta}$$

$$= -\frac{4k\eta}{(\xi^2 + \eta^2)^2} + eE\eta,$$

$$Q_\xi = -\frac{\partial U}{\partial \xi} = -\frac{4k\xi}{(\xi^2 + \eta^2)^2} - eE\xi,$$

and

$$Q_\phi = 0.$$

We thus obtain the generalized equations of motion

$$Q_\eta = \frac{d}{dt}\left[m\dot{\eta}(\xi^2 + \eta^2)\right] - m\eta(\dot{\xi}^2 + \dot{\eta}^2) - m\eta\xi^2\dot{\phi}^2,$$

$$Q_\xi = \frac{d}{dt}\left[m\dot{\xi}(\xi^2 + \eta^2)\right] - m\xi(\dot{\xi}^2 + \dot{\eta}^2) - m\xi\eta^2\dot{\phi}^2,$$

$$Q_\phi = \frac{d}{dt}\left(m\eta^2\xi^2\dot{\phi}\right).$$

The last equation is extremely simple, leading to a first integral of the motion

$$m\xi^2\eta^2\dot{\phi} = \text{const.}$$

As discussed above, $m\xi^2\eta^2\dot{\phi}$ should represent a component of the angular momentum. Indeed we find that

$$m\xi^2\eta^2\dot{\phi} = m(x^2 + y^2)\dot{\phi} = mr^2\sin^2\theta\dot{\phi},$$

which in Section 5–2 was found to represent the $z$-component of the orbital angular momentum. The reader should satisfy himself that $Q_\phi$ represents the vanishing $z$-component of the torque. In the next chapter we shall see that in this problem the total energy of the system, represented by

$$\mathcal{E} = T + \left(-\frac{k}{r} + eEz\right),$$

is also conserved. ◄

## 5–4 Constrained motion: holonomic constraints

Lagrange's equations of motion are especially appropriate for dealing with problems in which the motion of a particle is subject to constraints.

For example, a particle may be constrained to remain on a given surface or curve which may itself be a function of the time. Other constraints may impose restrictions on the generalized velocities of the particle.

In the present section, we shall restrict ourselves to constraints on the generalized coordinates, which are expressible in the form

$$\phi(q_1, q_2, q_3, t) = 0. \tag{5–37}$$

Such constraints are said to be *holonomic*.

Constraints necessarily imply reaction forces or forces of constraint. For example, a particle constrained to move on an inclined plane (Fig. 5–2) must have its $x$- and $y$-coordinates satisfy the condition

$$\phi(x, y, z, t) = y - x \tan \theta = 0,$$

where $x$ and $y$ are measured from the foot of the incline. The only way the particle will remain on the incline is for the incline to exert a force on the particle which balances the component of the resultant of the other forces pushing the particle against the incline.

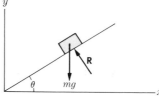

Fig. 5–2. Motion of a particle along an incline.

The reaction force **R** which a frictionless surface exerts on a particle is always in a direction which is normal to the constraining surface. At any time $t$ the constraining equation

$$\phi(q_1, q_2, q_3, t) = 0$$

defines such a frictionless constraining surface. Since two parallel vectors can differ only in magnitude, we can express the reaction force for a frictionless constraining surface in the form

$$\mathbf{R} = \lambda \nabla \phi, \tag{5–38}$$

since $\nabla \phi$ was shown in Section 2–6 to be a vector which is also normal to the surface defined by Eq. (5–37) for all values of $q_1$, $q_2$, and $q_3$ which satisfy Eq. (5–37) at time $t$. In general $\lambda$ is a function of the generalized coordinates, their time derivatives, and the time. Its explicit dependence on these variables, however, must come from the solution of the equations of motion.

We note that a constraining equation of the form (5–37) can be used to reduce by one the number of coordinates required for the description of the motion. We nevertheless still remain with three component equations of motion and three unknown variables, among which now is the unknown function $\lambda$ in place of the eliminated coordinate. Another way of looking at the problem is to consider it as a problem involving four unknown variables $q_1$, $q_2$, $q_3$, and $\lambda$, for which the three equations of motion together with Eq. (5–37) have to be solved.

If the particle is confined to move along the surface specified by Eq. (5–37), we find that its generalized constraining force is

$$R_i = \mathbf{R} \cdot \mathbf{b}_i = \lambda \left( \frac{\partial \phi}{\partial x} \frac{\partial x}{\partial q_i} + \frac{\partial \phi}{\partial y} \frac{\partial y}{\partial q_i} + \frac{\partial \phi}{\partial z} \frac{\partial z}{\partial q_i} \right) = \lambda \frac{\partial \phi}{\partial q_i}. \tag{5–39}$$

The generalized constraining force acting on the particle has to be added to the other generalized forces $Q_i$ acting on the particle. This yields the equation of motion

$$\frac{d}{dt}\frac{\partial T}{\partial \dot{q}_i} - \frac{\partial T}{\partial q_i} = Q_i + \lambda \frac{\partial \phi}{\partial q_i}. \tag{5-40}$$

If the particle is confined to motion along a certain path, then there exist two constraining equations relating the generalized coordinates:

$$\phi_1(q_1, q_2, q_3, t) = 0 \tag{5-41}$$

and

$$\phi_2(q_1, q_2, q_3, t) = 0. \tag{5-42}$$

The path along which the particle is constrained to move is the intersection of the two surfaces defined by the two constraining equations. The constraining force with which each of these two surfaces acts on the particle is, as before, directed normal to the constraining surface, and the constraining forces are thus expressible in the form

$$\mathbf{R}_1 = \lambda_1 \nabla \phi_1 \tag{5-43}$$

and

$$\mathbf{R}_2 = \lambda_2 \nabla \phi_2. \tag{5-44}$$

The equations of motion for a particle whose coordinates are required to satisfy the constraining Eqs. (5–41) and (5–42) are thus given by

$$\frac{d}{dt}\frac{\partial T}{\partial \dot{q}_i} - \frac{\partial T}{\partial q_i} = Q_i + \lambda_1 \frac{\partial \phi_1}{\partial q_i} + \lambda_2 \frac{\partial \phi_2}{\partial q_i}, \tag{5-45}$$

where $\lambda_1(\partial \phi_1/\partial q_i)$ and $\lambda_2(\partial \phi_2/\partial q_i)$ are the generalized constraining forces $\mathbf{R}_1 \cdot \mathbf{b}_i$ and $\mathbf{R}_2 \cdot \mathbf{b}_i$, respectively. The dependence of $\lambda_1$ and $\lambda_2$ on the coordinates, their velocities, and time is obtained from the solution of the equations of motion, Eq. (5–45), and the constraining equations, (5–41) and (5–42).

▶ As a first example, we consider the rather elementary problem of the motion of a particle along the surface of a frictionless inclined plane. Choosing the $x$- and $y$-axes, as indicated in Fig. 5–3, parallel and perpendicular to the inclined plane, and assuming the motion to take place in a vertical plane, the equations of constraint are

$$\phi_1(x, y, z) = y = 0$$

and $$\tag{5-46}$$

$$\phi_2(x, y, z) = z = 0.$$

Eliminating the $z$-dependence, the kinetic energy for this choice of generalized coordinates is given by

$$T = \tfrac{1}{2}m\dot{x}^2 + \tfrac{1}{2}m\dot{y}^2,$$

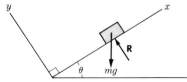

Fig. 5–3. Constrained motion of a particle along a smooth incline.

which by Eq. (5–45) yields the equations of motion

$$m\ddot{x} = -mg \sin \theta \qquad (5\text{–}47)$$

and

$$m\ddot{y} = -mg \cos \theta + \lambda. \qquad (5\text{–}48)$$

Since

$$y = \ddot{y} = 0,$$

the latter equation of motion yields the rather obvious result that the magnitude of the reaction force is

$$R = \lambda = mg \cos \theta. \qquad (5\text{–}49)$$

If the incline is not held fixed but moves to the right with an acceleration $A$, then, choosing the coordinates as shown in Fig. 5–4, the equation of constraint is

$$y - (x - V_0 t - \tfrac{1}{2}At^2) \tan \theta = 0, \qquad (5\text{–}50)$$

where $V_0$ is the initial velocity of the incline at time $t = 0$, and $x$ and $y$ are the cartesian components of the position of the particle as measured from the position of the foot of the incline at time $t = 0$.

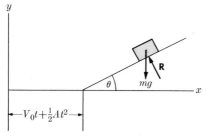

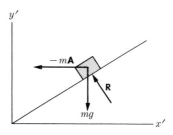

FIG. 5–4.   Motion along a moving incline.

FIG. 5–5.   The motion along a moving incline with respect to a coordinate system moving with the incline.

For this problem Eq. (5–40) yields the equations of motion

$$m\ddot{x} = -\lambda \tan \theta \qquad (5\text{–}51)$$

and

$$m\ddot{y} = -mg + \lambda. \qquad (5\text{–}52)$$

The $x$- and $y$-components of the reaction force, through the use of Eq. (5–38), are found to be

$$R_x = -\lambda \tan \theta \qquad (5\text{–}53)$$

and

$$R_y = \lambda, \qquad (5\text{–}54)$$

yielding

$$R = \lambda \sec \theta.$$

For this problem $\lambda$ turns out to be a constant which the reader should have no difficulty finding.

This problem could, of course, also be done by transforming the description of the motion to an accelerating system, specifically the coordinate system moving with the incline. In such an accelerating system, the equations of motion for the particle are identical to the equations of motion of a particle moving on a fixed incline under the action of the gravitational force plus the inertial force $-mA\mathbf{i}$ (cf. Fig. 5–5).

The equations of motion for this equivalent problem are

$$m\ddot{x}' = -R\sin\theta - mA \tag{5–55}$$

and

$$m\ddot{y}' = -mg + R\cos\theta. \tag{5–56}$$

These equations of motion are in agreement with Eqs. (5–51) and (5–52) if we realize that

$$\ddot{x}' = \ddot{x} - A \qquad \text{and} \qquad \ddot{y}' = \ddot{y}.$$

From this approach to the problem, it should be clear that $\lambda$, which we left for the reader to find, should yield a reaction force of magnitude

$$R = mg\cos\theta - mA\sin\theta. \blacktriangleleft \tag{5–57}$$

▶ As a second example, we consider the motion of a particle which is confined to move along the surface of a sphere of radius $l$ under the action of the gravitational force.

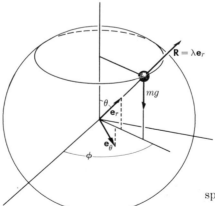

FIG. 5–6. Motion along a sphere of radius $l$.

The constraining equation, using spherical coordinates for this problem, is

$$r - l = 0. \tag{5–58}$$

In spherical coordinates the kinetic energy is given by

$$T = \tfrac{1}{2}m(\dot{r}^2 + r^2\dot{\theta}^2 + r^2\sin^2\theta\dot{\phi}^2), \tag{5–59}$$

and the gravitational force (cf. Fig. 5–6) by

$$\mathbf{F}_g = -mg\mathbf{k} = -mg\cos\theta\mathbf{e}_r + mg\sin\theta\mathbf{e}_\theta.$$

The equations of motion are found to be

$$m(\ddot{r} - r\dot{\theta}^2 - r\sin^2\theta\dot{\phi}^2) = -mg\cos\theta + \lambda, \tag{5–60}$$

$$\frac{d}{dt}(mr^2\dot{\theta}) - mr^2\sin\theta\cos\theta\dot{\phi}^2 = mgr\sin\theta, \tag{5–61}$$

$$\frac{d}{dt}(mr^2\sin^2\theta\dot{\phi}) = 0. \tag{5–62}$$

Equation (5–62) is extremely simple and yields a first integral of the motion which expresses the conservation of the $z$-component of the orbital angular momentum,

$$p_3 = mr^2\sin^2\theta\dot{\phi} = \text{const.} \tag{5–63}$$

This relation, when inserted into Eq. (5–61), in turn transforms the latter into the one-dimensional equation of motion

$$ml^2\ddot{\theta} = mgl\sin\theta + \frac{p_3^2\cos\theta}{2ml^2\sin^3\theta}. \tag{5–64}$$

Since the right-hand side of this equation is only a function of $\theta$, the method of Section 4–6 is applicable, yielding a second constant of the motion which happens to be the total energy,

$$E = \tfrac{1}{2}ml^2\dot{\theta}^2 + mgl\cos\theta + \frac{p_3^2}{2ml^2\sin^2\theta}. \tag{5–65}$$

That $E$ is a constant of the motion follows from Eq. (5–64), from which we find that

$$\frac{dE}{dt} = mr^2\dot{\theta}\ddot{\theta} - mgl\sin\theta\dot{\theta} - \frac{p_3^2\cos\theta\dot{\theta}}{ml^2\sin^3\theta} = 0.$$

Realizing that the motion takes place on a sphere of constant radius $r = l$, the reader should understand that $E$ indeed represents the total energy, since $\dot{r} = 0$.

We note that we could proceed to solve Eq. (5–65) for $\theta$, and subsequently by integrating obtain $\theta$ as a function of $t$. The solution to this problem cannot, however, be obtained in terms of elementary functions. It may be obtained in terms of elliptic integrals.

The case when $\dot{\phi} = 0$ was considered in Section 4–13. For $\dot{\phi} \neq 0$, the equation of motion for $\theta$ is a one-dimensional equation of motion,

$$m\ddot{\theta} = \frac{mg}{l}\sin\theta + \frac{p_3^2\cos\theta}{2ml^4\sin^3\theta},$$

which is the equation for the rectilinear motion of a particle in the effective potential energy field

$$U_{\text{eff}}(\theta) = \frac{mg}{l} \cos \theta + \frac{p_3^2}{2ml^4 \sin^2 \theta}. \qquad (5\text{-}66)$$

This effective potential energy function has a minimum point. The problem in question, therefore, has a point of stable equilibrium, or rather an angle $\theta = \theta_0$ which can remain fixed. For small displacements from this equilibrium point for which the particle moves in a circle, the particle will perform simple harmonic oscillation. The frequency of the oscillation about the stable circular orbit (Problem 4–10a) is given by

$$\omega = \sqrt{\frac{g}{l}} \sqrt{\frac{1 + 3 \cos^2 \theta_0}{|\cos \theta_0|}}. \qquad (5\text{-}67)$$

Using Eqs. (5–63) and (5–65), which express the conservation of the $z$-component of the orbital angular momentum and the total energy, and setting $\ddot{r} = 0$, the magnitude $R = \lambda$ of the reaction force can be obtained from Eq. (5–60). Specifically we obtain

$$R = \frac{2E - 3mg \cos \theta}{l}. \blacktriangleleft$$

We note that in this example, due to the choice of generalized coordinates, the reaction force appears in only one of the equations of motion. Such will be the case whenever the constraining equation is expressible in the form

$$q_i - \text{const} = 0.$$

That is, one of the generalized coordinates remains fixed. Even if this were not so, we could by a proper choice of new base vectors, two of which are tangent to the constraining surface, obtain two equations of motion which do not contain the reaction force. If these two tangential vectors are properly chosen, then the two resultant generalized equations of motion will be identical to the equations which would be obtained if the constraining equation were first solved for one of the coordinates, say $q_3$, in terms of the other two, and $q_3$ were completely eliminated from the problem. The position vector will thus be a function of the remaining two coordinates. If we do this for the coordinate $q_3$, then

$$\mathbf{r} = \mathbf{r}[q_1, q_2, f(q_1, q_2)], \qquad (5\text{-}68)$$

where

$$q_3 - f(q_1, q_2) = 0 \qquad (5\text{-}69)$$

is obtained from the constraining equation.

From Eq. (5–68) we define the two new base vectors

$$\bar{\mathbf{b}}_i = \frac{\partial \mathbf{r}}{\partial q_i} + \frac{\partial \mathbf{r}}{\partial f} \frac{\partial f}{\partial q_i} = \mathbf{b}_i + \frac{\partial f}{\partial q_i} \mathbf{b}_3, \qquad i = 1, 2. \qquad (5\text{-}70)$$

These new base vectors are tangent to the surface defined by Eq. (5–69), as can be seen by taking their scalar product with a normal to the surface. The gradient of the surface-defining function $\phi = q_3 - f(q_1, q_2)$ is such a normal. Since

$$\boldsymbol{\nabla}[q_3 - f(q_1, q_2)] = \boldsymbol{\nabla}q_3 - \boldsymbol{\nabla}f = \boldsymbol{\nabla}q_3 - \frac{\partial f}{\partial q_1}\boldsymbol{\nabla}q_1 - \frac{\partial f}{\partial q_2}\boldsymbol{\nabla}q_2, \qquad (5\text{–}71)$$

and remembering that $\boldsymbol{b}_i = \boldsymbol{\nabla}q_i$, we find that we indeed have

$$\bar{\boldsymbol{b}}_i \cdot \boldsymbol{\nabla}(q_3 - f) = \frac{\partial f}{\partial q_i} - \frac{\partial f}{\partial q_i} = 0. \qquad (5\text{–}72)$$

This verifies that the $\bar{\boldsymbol{b}}_i$ are tangent to the constraining surface. The scalar multiplication of Newton's equations with the $\bar{\boldsymbol{b}}_i$ leads us to the generalized equations of motion (cf. Problem 5–16)

$$Q_i + Q_3 \frac{\partial f}{\partial q_i} = \frac{d}{dt}\frac{\partial T}{\partial \dot{q}_i} - \frac{\partial T}{\partial q_i}, \qquad i = 1, 2, \qquad (5\text{–}73)$$

where the kinetic energy is now a function of $q_1$, $q_2$, $\dot{q}_1$, and $\dot{q}_2$. That is,

$$T = T[q_1, q_2, \dot{q}_1, \dot{q}_2, f(q_1, q_2), \dot{f}(q_1, q_2)],$$

where $f(q_1, q_2) = q_3$ and

$$\dot{f}(q_1, q_2) = \dot{q}_3 = \frac{\partial f}{\partial q_1}\dot{q}_1 + \frac{\partial f}{\partial q_2}\dot{q}_2.$$

▶As an example, we reconsider the problem of a particle of mass $m$ moving under the action of gravity on a frictionless accelerating incline (Fig. 5–4). The constraining equation

$$y - (x - V_0 t - \tfrac{1}{2}At^2)\tan\theta = 0$$

is in the form of Eq. (5–69). Eliminating the $y$-coordinate, we obtain the position vector as a function of $x$ and $t$,

$$\mathbf{r} = x\mathbf{i} + y\mathbf{j} = x\mathbf{i} + (x - V_0 t - \tfrac{1}{2}At^2)\tan\theta\mathbf{j}.$$

From this follows the new base vector

$$\bar{\mathbf{b}}_1 = \frac{\partial\mathbf{r}}{\partial x} = \mathbf{i} + \tan\theta\mathbf{j}.$$

The vector $\bar{\mathbf{b}}_1$ we note makes an angle $\theta$ with the $x$-axis. It is thus parallel to the surface of the incline. The kinetic energy as a function of $\dot{x}$ and $t$ is found to be given by

$$T = \tfrac{1}{2}m\dot{x}^2 + \tfrac{1}{2}m\dot{y}^2 = \tfrac{1}{2}m\dot{x}^2 + \tfrac{1}{2}m(\dot{x} - V_0 - At)^2\tan^2\theta.$$

We are thus led to an equation of motion which does not contain the reaction force,

$$(-mg\mathbf{j}) \cdot \mathbf{\bar{b}}_1 = \frac{d}{dt} \frac{\partial T}{\partial \dot{x}} - \frac{\partial T}{\partial x},$$

or more explicitly,

$$-mg \tan \theta = \frac{d}{dt} [m\dot{x} + m(\dot{x} - V_0 - At) \tan^2 \theta]$$

$$= m\ddot{x}(1 + \tan^2 \theta) - mA \tan^2 \theta$$

or

$$-mg \sin \theta = \frac{m\ddot{x}}{\cos \theta} - mA \frac{\sin^2 \theta}{\cos \theta}.$$

This equation is identical to the equation we would obtain from Eqs. (5–50), (5–51), and (5–52) if we were to utilize them for obtaining an equation involving only $x$. ◄

► As another illustration, we consider the motion of a bead of mass $m$ which is constrained to move along a frictionless wire in the form of the parabola (cf. Problem 3–12)

$$z = a\rho^2.$$

The wire lies in a vertical plane and is constrained to rotate with the constant angular velocity $\omega$ about the vertical symmetry axis of the parabola.

Since the bead is constrained to move along a specified curve, only one co-ordinate is required for the description of its motion. We choose this to be the $\rho$-coordinate. In terms of $\rho$, $\dot{\rho}$, and $\omega$, we thus find the kinetic energy

$$T = \tfrac{1}{2}m(\dot{\rho}^2 + \dot{z}^2 + \omega^2\rho^2)$$

to be expressed by

$$T = \tfrac{1}{2}m(\rho^2 + 4a^2\rho^2\dot{\rho}^2 + \omega^2\rho^2).$$

The gravitational force acting on the bead is given by

$$\mathbf{F} = -mg\mathbf{k}.$$

The base vector for the variable $\rho$ is

$$\mathbf{\bar{b}}_1 = \frac{\partial \mathbf{r}}{\partial \rho} = \mathbf{e}_\rho + \frac{\partial z}{\partial \rho} \mathbf{k} = \mathbf{e}_\rho + 2a\rho\mathbf{k}.$$

Since

$$\frac{\bar{b}_{1z}}{\bar{b}_{1\rho}} = 2a\rho = \frac{dz}{d\rho},$$

it follows that $\mathbf{b}_1$ is tangent to the parabola, yielding the generalized force

$$\bar{Q}_1 = \mathbf{F} \cdot \mathbf{\bar{b}}_1 = 2a\rho mg$$

and the generalized equation of motion

$$2a\rho mg = \frac{d}{dt}[m\dot{\rho}(1 + 4a^2\rho^2)] - m\dot{\rho}^2(4a^2\rho). \blacktriangleleft$$

## Problems

5-1. (a) Show that a force which is expressible as the negative gradient of the scalar function $U(x, y, z)$,

$$\mathbf{F} = -\mathbf{\nabla}U(x, y, z),$$

yields generalized forces which are given by

$$Q_i = -\frac{\partial U}{\partial q_i},$$

and that the generalized equations of motion are therefore

$$\frac{d}{dt}\frac{\partial T}{\partial \dot{q}_i} - \frac{\partial T}{\partial q_i} = -\frac{\partial U}{\partial q_i}.$$

(b) Show that for such forces

$$\Delta W = \mathbf{F} \cdot \Delta \mathbf{s} = -\Delta U,$$

and thus

$$dT = d[\tfrac{1}{2}m(\dot{x}^2 + \dot{y}^2 + \dot{z}^2)] = -dU,$$

or $T + U = \text{const.}$

5-2. Use the result of Problem 5-1 to obtain Lagrange's equations for a particle whose kinetic energy is

$$T = \tfrac{1}{2}a\dot{q}_1^2 + \tfrac{1}{2}b\dot{q}_2^2,$$

and whose scalar potential energy is

$$U = \tfrac{1}{2}k_1(q_1 + q_2)^2 + \tfrac{1}{2}k_2(q_1 - q_2)^2.$$

5-3. The point of support of a simple pendulum of length $l$ and mass $m$ is moved along a vertical line according to the equation

$$y = y(t).$$

The motion of the pendulum is confined to a vertical plane.

(a) Set up Newton's component equations of motion for the particle along the directions $\mathbf{e}_1$ and $\mathbf{e}_2$ shown in Fig. 5–7. [*Hint:* Consider the motion with respect to a coordinate system whose acceleration is $\mathbf{A} = \ddot{y}\mathbf{j}$.]
(b) Show that the kinetic energy of the particle is given by

$$T = \tfrac{1}{2}m(l\dot{\theta})^2 + \tfrac{1}{2}m\dot{y}^2 + ml\dot{\theta}\dot{y}\sin\theta.$$

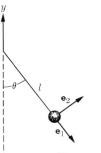

FIGURE 5–7

(c) Given that the scalar potential energy is

$$U = mgy - mgl \cos \theta,$$

show that Lagrange's equations derived from the kinetic energy of part (b) and this potential energy function (see Problem 5–1) for the variable $\theta$ are equivalent to Newton's equation along $\mathbf{e}_2$.   (d) Show that if we express the kinetic energy in the form

$$T = \tfrac{1}{2}m(\dot{r} \sin \theta + r\dot{\theta} \cos \theta)^2 + \tfrac{1}{2}m[-\dot{r} \cos \theta + r\dot{\theta} \sin \theta + \dot{y}]^2,$$

and constrain the motion by the equation

$$r - l = 0,$$

then Lagrange's equations for the variables $r$ and $\theta$ agree with Newton's equations found in part (a).

5–4. Consider the system depicted in Fig. 5–8. The spring is confined to move in a vertical line.  (a) Realizing that the force on the spring is equal to the vertical component of the tension in the string, set up Newton's equations of motion, taking components along the directions $\mathbf{e}_1$ and $\mathbf{e}_2$ shown.  (b) Show that the equations thus obtained are equivalent to Lagrange's equations for the variables $r$ and $\theta$ obtained from the kinetic energy of the particle

$$T = \tfrac{1}{2}m(\dot{r} \sin \theta + r\dot{\theta} \cos \theta)^2 + \tfrac{1}{2}m(-\dot{r} \cos \theta + r\dot{\theta} \sin \theta - \dot{y})^2$$

and the potential energy

$$U = \tfrac{1}{2}ky^2 - mg(r \cos \theta - y)$$

(note that the positive direction of $y$ is down) subject to the constraining equation

$$r - l = 0.$$

(c) Show that Lagrange's equation for the variable $y$ is equivalent to the equation

$$R \cos \theta = ky.$$

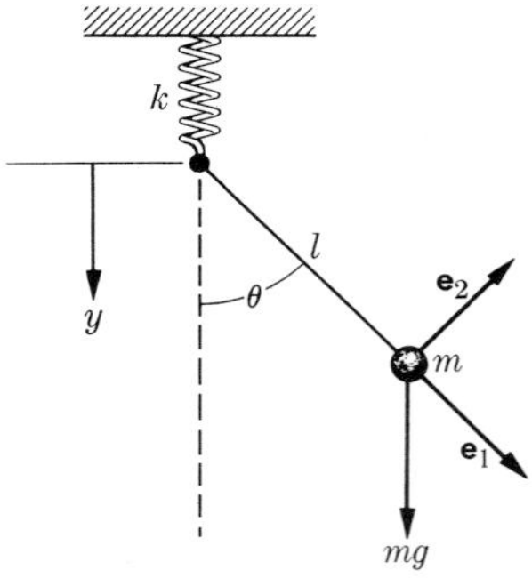

FIGURE 5–8

5–5. The point of support of a simple pendulum moves in a vertical circle of radius $R$, as shown in Fig. 5–9, with constant speed $v$. Obtain Lagrange's equation of motion for the pendulum. (Assume the motion to take place in the vertical plane of the circle.)

5–6. (a) Set up Newton's equations of motion for the simple pendulum whose point of support is attached to a spring free to move in the horizontal direction (Fig. 5–10). (b) Given that the potential energy for this problem is

$$U = \tfrac{1}{2}kx^2 - mgr \cos \theta, \qquad \text{where} \quad r - l = 0,$$

set up the expression for the kinetic energy of the particle and obtain Lagrange's equations of motion.  Compare the answers to Parts (a) and (b).

5–7. A particle of mass $m$ moves under the action of gravity on the surface of a smooth horizontal cylinder. (a) Obtain Lagrange's equations of motion for the particle. (b) If the particle slides in a vertical plane, having started from the top of the cylinder with a very small velocity, find the reaction force as a function of the position. (c) At which point will the particle leave the cylinder?

FIGURE 5–9                          FIGURE 5–10

5–8. Repeat Problem 5–7 for a particle moving on the smooth surface of the parabolic cylinder

$$y = -ax^2.$$

5–9. Under the action of gravity, a particle of mass $m$ slides on the smooth inner surface of the inverted cone (Fig. 5–11)

$$\rho = z \tan \alpha.$$

(a) Set up Lagrange's equations of motion for the particle.  (b) Show that circular orbits are possible, and find the speed of the particle in such an orbit.

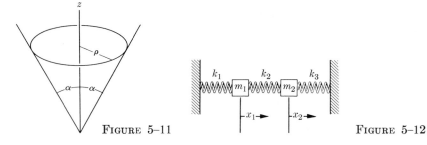

FIGURE 5–11                          FIGURE 5–12

5–10. Consider the system of particles shown in Fig. 5–12. (a) Write down Newton's equations of motion for each of the particles in terms of the displacement-from-equilibrium variables $x_1$ and $x_2$. (b) Show that, for any arbitrary displacements of the two particles, the potential energy stored in the springs is given by

$$U = \tfrac{1}{2}k_1 x_1^2 + \tfrac{1}{2}k_2(x_2 - x_1)^2 + \tfrac{1}{2}k_3 x_3^2.$$

(c) Using for the kinetic energy the expression

$$T = \tfrac{1}{2}m_1 \dot{x}_1^2 + \tfrac{1}{2}m_2 \dot{x}_2^2,$$

show that Lagrange's equations thus obtained for the variables $x_1$ and $x_2$ from this $T$ and the $U$ of part (b) agree with Newton's equations found in part (a). What do you surmise are Lagrange's equations for a system of particles?

5–11. (a) Obtain the total kinetic energy of the double pendulum shown in Fig. 5–13. (b) Using the kinetic energy found in part (a) and the potential energy

$$U = -m_1 l_1 g \cos \theta_1$$
$$- m_2 g(l_1 \cos \theta_1 + l_2 \cos \theta_2),$$

show that Lagrange's equations thus obtained for $\theta_1$ and $\theta_2$ agree with Newton's component equations along $\mathbf{e}_2$ and $\mathbf{e}_4$.

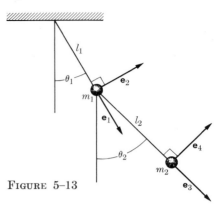

FIGURE 5–13

5–12. Coordinates $q_1$ and $q_2$ are defined in terms of plane polar coordinates $r$ and $\phi$ by the equations

$$q_1 = \ln\left(\frac{r}{a}\right) - \phi \cot \xi, \qquad q_2 = \ln\left(\frac{r}{a}\right) + \phi \tan \xi,$$

where $a$ and $\xi$ are constants. Sketch the curves of constants $q_1$ and $q_2$. Find the kinetic energy of a particle of mass $m$ in terms of $q_1, q_2, \dot{q}_1, \dot{q}_2$. Find expressions for $Q_1, Q_2$ in terms of the polar components $F_r$ and $F_\phi$ of the force, where $F_r = \mathbf{e}_r \cdot \mathbf{F}$ and $F_\phi = \mathbf{e}_\phi \cdot \mathbf{F}$. Find $p_1, p_2$. Find the forces $Q_1, Q_2$ required to make the particle move with constant speed $\dot{s}$ along a spiral of constant $q_1 = c$.

5–13. When forces act only during a short time interval, as in a collision, they are described as impulsive forces. The term impulse is given to the quantity

$$\mathbf{I} = \int_{\Delta t} \mathbf{F} \, dt,$$

where the integral is evaluated only over the infinitesimal time $\Delta t$ during which the impulsive force acts. Show that, if impulsive forces are present, Lagrange's equations may be transformed into

$$\Delta\left(\frac{\partial T}{\partial \dot{q}_i}\right) = \Delta \frac{\partial U}{\partial \dot{q}_i} + I_i,$$

where $I_i$ is the generalized impulsive force corresponding to $q_i$.

5–14. A bead of mass $m$ slides under gravity along a wire bent into the form of the parabola $y = 1 + x^2$. The coefficient of friction between bead and wire is $\mu$. Hence the frictional force acting on the bead is $\mu R$, where $R$ is the constraining force normal to the curve. This frictional force tends to oppose the motion. At the same time the plane of the wire rotates about $Oy$ at constant angular speed $\omega$. Obtain Lagrange's equations of motion for the bead.

5–15. (a) Set up the expression for the kinetic energy of a particle of mass $m$ in terms of the plane parabolic coordinates $q_1$, $q_2$, defined by

$$x = q_1 - q_2, \qquad y = 2(q_1 q_2)^{1/2}.$$

Find the generalized momenta $p_1$ and $p_2$. (b) Write out the Lagrange equations in terms of these coordinates for the case when the particle is not acted on by any force. (c) Find the generalized forces $Q_1$ and $Q_2$ required to make the particle move along a parabola $q_1 = c = $ constant, with constant generalized velocity $\dot{q}_2 = u_0$, starting from the point $q_1 = c$ and $q_2 = 0$ at $t = 0$. (d) Find the corresponding forces $F_x$ and $F_y$ relative to a cartesian coordinate system.

5–16. Show that the $\bar{\mathbf{b}}_i$'s defined by Eq. (5–70) yield the generalized equations of motion given by Eq. (5–73).

# 6

# *Conservative Motion*

## 6–1 Conservative forces

We are not always fortunate enough to be able to choose generalized coordinates in terms of which we may obtain three one-dimensional equations of motion. In general, the three equations of motion obtained through the use of Eq. (5–21) are simultaneous differential equations whose solution may be difficult to obtain. In problems dealing with forces which are functions of position only, we can come one step closer to a solution if the work which these forces perform on the particle as it moves from one point to another does not depend on the actual path taken by the particle. The work performed by a force **F** along a path joining two points $P_1$ and $P_2$ was previously defined (Section 4–13) by the equation

$$W_{12} = \int_1^2 \mathbf{F} \cdot d\mathbf{s} = \int_1^2 (F_x \, dx + F_y \, dy + F_z \, dz). \qquad (6\text{–}1)$$

In general the work performed by a force depends on the path along which the work is evaluated. For example, consider the force

$$\mathbf{F} = xy\mathbf{i} + 2z\mathbf{j} - (2x^2 - y^2)\mathbf{k}. \qquad (6\text{–}2)$$

The work which this force performs along two different paths joining the points $(0, 0, 0)$ and $(1, 1, 1)$ depends on the path.

The work along the straight line

$$x = y = z \qquad (6\text{–}3)$$

which joins these two points is found to be

$$W = \int xy \, dx + \int 2z \, dy - \int (2x^2 - y^2) \, dz$$

$$= \int_0^1 x^2 \, dx + \int_0^1 2y \, dy - \int_0^1 x^2 \, dx$$

$$= 1 \text{ unit of work.}$$

164

On the other hand, the work along the path

$$x = y^2 = z \qquad (6\text{–}4)$$

is found to be

$$W = \int xy\, dx + \int 2z\, dy - \int (2x^2 - y^2)\, dz$$

$$= \int_0^1 2y^4\, dy + \int_0^1 2y^2\, dy - \int (2y^4 - y^2)\, 2y\, dy$$

$$= \tfrac{9}{10} \text{ unit of work.}$$

The work along these two paths is obviously not the same. That is, the work performed by the force of Eq. (6–2) is dependent on the path along which it is evaluated.

The principle of work and energy, that the work performed by a force on a particle is equal to the change in the kinetic energy of the particle, is, of course, generally applicable to any force function. This follows quite readily from the derivation of the principle,

$$W = \int \mathbf{F} \cdot d\mathbf{s} = \int m\ddot{\mathbf{s}} \cdot \frac{d\mathbf{s}}{dt}\, dt = \int d(\tfrac{1}{2}m\dot{s}^2).$$

In dealing with a force whose work is dependent on the path, however, the principle of work and energy is really of no use to us unless the path followed by the particle is known. But this would reduce the problem to the one-dimensional problem of the motion of a particle along a specified curve, which we discussed in Section 4–13. This is not the problem we are presently considering, which is the unconstrained motion of a particle under the action of specified forces, where the path followed by the particle is one of the unknown bits of information sought. To say that we know the path would be to imply that we have found the solution, in which case there would be no further need for us to apply the principle of work and energy.

The forces for which the principle of work and energy is useful, even though the actual path followed by the particle is not known, are those for which the work they perform on a particle are independent of the path. For such forces we can evaluate the work along any path joining two points $P_1$ and $P_2$ through which the particle passes, and utilize the principle of work and energy,

$$W_{12} = \tfrac{1}{2}m(v_2^2 - v_1^2), \qquad (6\text{–}5)$$

as an equation auxiliary to the equations of motion. The use of the principle of work and energy generally simplifies the problem of finding a solution to the equations of motion. Forces whose work is independent of the path are referred to as *conservative forces*, and the motion under the action of such forces is known as conservative motion. The necessary and sufficient conditions by which a force may be recognized as conservative are discussed in Section 6–3.

## 6–2 Potential energy: conservation of energy

The work along a specified curve performed by a force which is a function of position was shown in Section 4–13 to be expressible in terms of the potential energy function $U(s)$. That is,

$$W_{12} = \int_1^2 \mathbf{F} \cdot d\mathbf{s} = \int_1^2 F_s \, ds = U(s_1) - U(s_2),$$

where

$$F_s(s) = - \frac{dU(s)}{ds},$$

and $s$ represents distance measured along the specified curve from a given point on the curve.

Since the work performed by a conservative force is independent of the path, it follows that once we assign a value of potential energy at one point in space, irrespective of the path chosen, the value of the potential energy at any other point is determined and given by

$$U(P_2) = U(P_1) - W_{12}. \tag{6–6}$$

A definite value of potential energy is thus assignable to every point in space. This value is, of course, dependent on the choice of potential energy at the first or reference point. The value of the potential energy at the reference point being arbitrary, it follows that the value of the potential energy at all other points in space has the same arbitrariness. This means that there will be no effect on the problem if we decide at any time to change the assigned value of the potential energy at all points in space by the same constant amount.

The potential energy, having a definite value at all points in space, is said to be a single-valued function of position, and is thus expressed by

$$U = U(x, y, z).$$

In terms of the potential energy function, the work for any infinitesimal displacement

$$\Delta \mathbf{s} = \Delta x \mathbf{i} + \Delta y \mathbf{j} + \Delta z \mathbf{k}$$

is given by

$$\Delta W = \mathbf{F} \cdot \Delta \mathbf{s} = -\Delta U$$

$$= - \frac{\partial U}{\partial x} \Delta x - \frac{\partial U}{\partial y} \Delta y - \frac{\partial U}{\partial z} \Delta z$$

$$= -\Delta \mathbf{s} \cdot (\boldsymbol{\nabla} U), \tag{6–7}$$

where

$$\boldsymbol{\nabla} U = \frac{\partial U}{\partial x} \mathbf{i} + \frac{\partial U}{\partial y} \mathbf{j} + \frac{\partial U}{\partial z} \mathbf{k}.$$

Equation (6–7) tells us that

$$(\mathbf{F} + \nabla U) \cdot \Delta \mathbf{s} = 0,$$

or, since $\Delta \mathbf{s}$ is arbitrary, that

$$\mathbf{F} = -\nabla U = -\frac{\partial U}{\partial x}\,\mathbf{i} - \frac{\partial U}{\partial y}\,\mathbf{j} - \frac{\partial U}{\partial z}\,\mathbf{k}. \tag{6–8}$$

Like the gradient of any scalar function of position (cf. Section 2–6), the force at the point $(x_0, y_0, z_0)$ points in a direction, normal to the surface, of constant potential energy,

$$U(x, y, z) = U(x_0, y_0, z_0),$$

which passes through that point. A conservative force is thus readily obtainable from its potential energy function. Conversely, given that a force is conservative, its potential energy is readily obtainable through the use of Eq. (6–6).

In order to obtain the potential energy for a conservative force, we choose for the path along which to compute the work it performs from the point $(x_0, y_0, z_0)$ to the point $(x, y, z)$ the broken straight line path shown in Fig. 6–1.

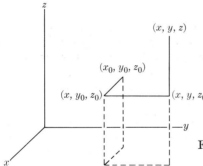

FIG. 6–1. A path of integration.

The work along the straight line from $(x_0, y_0, z_0)$ to the point $(x, y_0, z_0)$ is given by

$$W_a = \int_{x_0}^{x} F_x(x, y_0, z_0)\,dx.$$

The work along the straight line from the point $(x, y_0, z_0)$ to the point $(x, y, z_0)$ is given by

$$W_b = \int_{y_0}^{y} F_y(x, y, z_0)\,dy, \qquad x \text{ const},$$

and the work along the last part of the path by

$$W_c = \int_{z_0}^{z} F_z(x, y, z)\,dz, \qquad x \text{ and } y \text{ const}.$$

The total work is the sum of the work along each of the segments,

$$W = W_a + W_b + W_c = U(x_0, y_0, z_0) - U(x, y, z).$$

▶ As an example, we consider the conservative force

$$\mathbf{F} = xy\mathbf{i} + \tfrac{1}{2}(x^2 + z^2)\mathbf{j} + yz\mathbf{k},$$

for which we obtain

$$W_a = \int_{x_0}^{x} xy_0 \, dx = \tfrac{1}{2}y_0(x^2 - x_0^2),$$

$$W_b = \int_{y_0}^{y} \tfrac{1}{2}(x^2 + z_0^2) \, dy = \tfrac{1}{2}(y - y_0)(x^2 + z_0^2),$$

$$W_c = \int_{z_0}^{z} yz \, dz = \tfrac{1}{2}y(z^2 - z_0^2).$$

The total work is thus found to be

$$W = W_a + W_b + W_c = \tfrac{1}{2}(x^2 + z^2)y - \tfrac{1}{2}(x_0^2 + z_0^2)y_0,$$

whence we find that the potential energy function is

$$U(x, y, z) = -\tfrac{1}{2}(x^2 + z^2)y. \blacktriangleleft$$

Conservative forces are very important in physics, since such fundamental forces as electrical, gravitational, and nuclear forces are all of this kind. For such forces the principle of work and energy furnishes us with the important principle of the conservation of total energy,

$$E = T + U = \text{const.} \tag{6-9}$$

## 6–3 Necessary and sufficient conditions for a force to be conservative

The necessary condition for a force which is a function of position to be conservative follows readily from Eq. (6–8) and from the fact that it is immaterial in which order the partial derivatives of an $n$th-order partial derivative of a continuous function of several variables are taken. Specifically, for second-order partial derivatives we have

$$\frac{\partial^2 \phi}{\partial x \, \partial y} = \frac{\partial^2 \phi}{\partial y \, \partial x}, \tag{6-10}$$

with similar relations for the other second-order partial derivatives. For any conservative force expressible as the negative gradient of a potential energy function, the equations

$$\frac{\partial F_x}{\partial y} = -\frac{\partial^2 U}{\partial y\,\partial x} = \frac{\partial F_y}{\partial x},$$

$$\frac{\partial F_z}{\partial x} = -\frac{\partial^2 U}{\partial x\,\partial z} = \frac{\partial F_x}{\partial z}, \tag{6–11}$$

$$\frac{\partial F_y}{\partial z} = -\frac{\partial^2 U}{\partial z\,\partial y} = \frac{\partial F_z}{\partial y}$$

necessarily follow. These express the necessary conditions for a force to be conservative. They can also be shown to be sufficient conditions.

We can express these necessary and sufficient conditions more concisely in terms of the notation for the curl of a vector, defined by the equation

$$\operatorname{curl} \mathbf{F} = \nabla \times \mathbf{F} = \begin{vmatrix} \mathbf{i} & \mathbf{j} & \mathbf{k} \\ \dfrac{\partial}{\partial x} & \dfrac{\partial}{\partial y} & \dfrac{\partial}{\partial z} \\ F_x & F_y & F_z \end{vmatrix}. \tag{6–12}$$

Equations (6–11) express the fact that the curl of a conservative force vanishes:

$$\nabla \times \mathbf{F} = 0. \tag{6–13}$$

The proof that the vanishing of the curl of $\mathbf{F}$ is also a sufficient condition requires the use of Stokes' theorem.* This theorem relates the surface integral of the component of the curl of a vector function normal to the surface of integra-

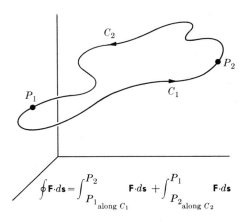

$$\oint \mathbf{F}\cdot d\mathbf{s} = \int_{P_1}^{P_2} \mathbf{F}\cdot d\mathbf{s} + \int_{P_2}^{P_1} \mathbf{F}\cdot d\mathbf{s}$$
$$\quad\text{along } C_1 \qquad\qquad \text{along } C_2$$

Fig. 6–2. Two paths joining the two points $P_1$ and $P_2$ forming a closed curve.

_____

* H. B. Phillips, *Vector Analysis*. New York: Wiley, 1933.

tion to the line integral of the tangential component of the vector function along the entire closed path which bounds the surface of integration. It is expressed by

$$\int (\boldsymbol{\nabla} \times \mathbf{F}) \cdot d\mathbf{S} = \oint \mathbf{F} \cdot d\mathbf{s}. \tag{6–14}$$

It follows from the vanishing of the curl of $\mathbf{F}$ that

$$\oint \mathbf{F} \cdot d\mathbf{s} = 0, \tag{6–15}$$

which is sufficient to ensure the independence of the work performed by $\mathbf{F}$ on the path.

Any two paths $C_1$ and $C_2$ joining the two points $P_1$ and $P_2$ will form a closed curve (see Fig. 6–2) for which Eq. (6–15) is expressible as

$$\int_{P_1 \text{ along } C_1}^{P_2} \mathbf{F} \cdot d\mathbf{s} + \int_{P_2 \text{ along } C_2}^{P_1} \mathbf{F} \cdot d\mathbf{s} = 0.$$

But along either path

$$\int_{P_1}^{P_2} \mathbf{F} \cdot d\mathbf{s} = - \int_{P_2}^{P_1} \mathbf{F} \cdot d\mathbf{s},$$

whence we find that for any given region wherein the curl of $\mathbf{F}$ vanishes,

$$\int_{P_1 \text{ along } C_1}^{P_2} \mathbf{F} \cdot d\mathbf{s} = \int_{P_1 \text{ along } C_2}^{P_2} \mathbf{F} \cdot d\mathbf{s}$$

along any two curves within that region joining the two points $P_1$ and $P_2$.

We have thus shown condition (6–13) to be necessary and sufficient for the work performed by a force to be independent of the path.

## 6–4 Lagrange's equations for conservative forces: the Lagrangian

For a conservative force which is derivable from a potential energy function, the generalized force defined in Section 5–1 assumes a very simple form. Specifically, we obtain

$$Q_i = \mathbf{F} \cdot \frac{\partial \mathbf{r}}{\partial q_i} = - \left( \frac{\partial U}{\partial x} \frac{\partial x}{\partial q_i} + \frac{\partial U}{\partial y} \frac{\partial y}{\partial q_i} + \frac{\partial U}{\partial z} \frac{\partial z}{\partial q_i} \right) = - \frac{\partial U}{\partial q_i}. \tag{6–16}$$

Lagrange's equations of motion for a particle under the action of a conservative force may thus be rewritten in the form

$$\frac{d}{dt} \frac{\partial T}{\partial \dot{q}_i} - \frac{\partial T}{\partial q_i} = - \frac{\partial U}{\partial q_i}. \tag{6–17}$$

For the potential energy functions defined above, which are functions of position only,

$$\frac{\partial U}{\partial \dot{q}_i} = 0.$$

We may therefore express Eq. (6–17) more symmetrically as

$$\frac{d}{dt} \frac{\partial (T - U)}{\partial \dot{q}_i} - \frac{\partial (T - U)}{\partial q_i} = 0,$$

or as

$$\frac{d}{dt} \frac{\partial L}{\partial \dot{q}_i} - \frac{\partial L}{\partial q_i} = 0, \qquad (6\text{–}18)$$

where we have set

$$L = T - U. \qquad (6\text{–}19)$$

The function $L(q_i, \dot{q}_i, t)$ is referred to as the *Lagrangian function* or simply the *Lagrangian*.

In addition to the conservative forces there may also be nonconservative forces acting on a particle. Their generalized forces are, of course, not included in Eq. (6–18). In such cases the generalized equations of motion are expressed by

$$\frac{d}{dt} \frac{\partial L}{\partial \dot{q}_i} - \frac{\partial L}{\partial q_i} = Q_i^n, \qquad (6\text{–}20)$$

where the $Q_i^n$ are the generalized nonconservative forces acting on the particle. The generalized conservative forces are accounted for by the potential energy function in the Lagrangian.

## 6–5 Examples of conservative forces: central, electric, and magnetic forces*

As examples of the motion of a particle in conservative force fields, we shall consider in this chapter a number of interesting and very important problems dealing with the motion of charged particles in time-independent electric and magnetic fields. In the next chapter we shall concentrate on the motion of a particle in a central force field, paying special attention to the motion of a particle in an inverse-square central force field.

When a charged particle finds itself in the neighborhood of other charged particles, depending on the motion performed by these other charged particles, there will be two kinds of forces acting on the particle whose motion is being investigated.

---

* We include magnetic forces in this section because, as we shall see, magnetic forces perform no work. Their presence therefore still permits us to compute the work done on the particle without knowing the path which it follows.

If the charged particles exerting forces on the particle of interest are all at rest, then the force which they exert on the particle is expressed by

$$\mathbf{F} = e\mathbf{E}(x, y, z), \tag{6-21}$$

where $e$ is the charge carried by the particle of interest and $\mathbf{E}(x, y, z)$ is a vector function of position, referred to as the electric field, produced by the other charges at the point $(x, y, z)$.

The force exerted on a point charge $e$ by another point charge $e'$ is given by Coulomb's law,

$$\mathbf{F}^{el} = \frac{ee'}{4\pi\epsilon_0 r^2}\left(\frac{\mathbf{r}}{r}\right), \tag{6-22}$$

where $r$ is the distance between the charges, $(\mathbf{r}/r)$ the unit vector pointing from the charge $e'$ to the charge $e$, and $1/4\pi\epsilon_0$ a dimensional constant. The electrical force between two charged particles is an example of a central force having the form

$$\mathbf{F} = f(r)\,\frac{\mathbf{r}}{r}. \tag{6-23}$$

Such a central force is expressible as the negative gradient of a potential energy function $U(r)$, which is a function of $r$ only:

$$\mathbf{F} = -\boldsymbol{\nabla}U(r) = -\frac{\partial U}{\partial r}\,\mathbf{e}_r, \tag{6-24}$$

where $f(r) = -\partial U/\partial r$ (cf. Section 2–6).

A central force of the form (6–23) is obviously conservative, since

$$\boldsymbol{\nabla}\times\mathbf{F} = \boldsymbol{\nabla}\times\boldsymbol{\nabla}U = 0. \tag{6-25}$$

In passing, we should also like to mention that, besides the principle of the conservation of the total energy, we find that for a central force for which the torque vanishes,

$$\mathbf{r}\times\mathbf{F} = 0,$$

there exists a second integral of the motion expressing the principle of the conservation of the orbital angular momentum [cf. Eqs. (5–29) and (5–30)]. In the next chapter we shall show how, starting with these two conservation principles, we may obtain the solution to the equations of motion of a particle in a central force field.

If more than one charged particle acts on the charge $e$, then the total force acting on this charge, which by the superposition principle equals the vector sum of the electrical forces exerted by each of the neighboring charges on the charge $e$, is also a conservative force. Any electrical force is thus expressible as the negative gradient of a potential energy function which, in dealing with charged particles moving in electric fields, is expressed as

$$U(x, y, z) = e\Phi(x, y, z), \qquad (6\text{--}26)$$

where $\Phi(x, y, z)$ is called the *scalar electric potential* at the point $(x, y, z)$. In terms of the scalar electric potential the electric field is given by

$$\mathbf{E}(x, y, z) = -\nabla\Phi(x, y, z). \qquad (6\text{--}27)$$

If the charges exerting forces on the charged particle of interest are also in motion, then in addition to the electrical force they may also exert a magnetic force on the particle. This magnetic force is, among other things, dependent on the charge $e$ and the velocity $\mathbf{v}$ of the particle. Its dependence on these quantities is expressed by the equation

$$\mathbf{F}^m = e\mathbf{v} \times \mathbf{B}, \qquad (6\text{--}28)$$

where $\mathbf{B}$ is the magnetic induction vector produced by all the other charges at the point $(x, y, z)$.

We shall restrict ourselves essentially to the motion of charged particles in finite regions of space where the magnetic induction vector $\mathbf{B}$ has, for all practical purposes, the same magnitude and direction at all the points of that region. For such small regions of space the magnetic induction vector is found to be derivable from the *magnetic vector potential*

$$\mathbf{A} = -\tfrac{1}{2}\mathbf{r} \times \mathbf{B}. \qquad (6\text{--}29)$$

The reader should have no trouble verifying that the magnetic induction vector is equal to the curl of $\mathbf{A}$:

$$\mathbf{B} = \nabla \times \mathbf{A} = \begin{vmatrix} \mathbf{i} & \mathbf{j} & \mathbf{k} \\ \dfrac{\partial}{\partial x} & \dfrac{\partial}{\partial y} & \dfrac{\partial}{\partial z} \\ A_x & A_y & A_z \end{vmatrix}. \qquad (6\text{--}30)$$

We introduce the magnetic induction vector potential, because we shall require its use for the generalization of Lagrange's equations of motion to include the velocity-dependent magnetic forces.

We note that Eq. (6–30) is correct also for nonuniform time-dependent magnetic fields. That is, any magnetic induction vector $\mathbf{B}$ is always expressible as the curl of a magnetic vector potential $\mathbf{A}$. Only for uniform magnetic fields, however, does the magnetic vector potential assume the simple form given by Eq. (6–29).

Through a broadening of the definition of conservative forces, time-independent magnetic forces may also be considered to be conservative, but not in the same sense as the electrical forces. Along the path followed by a charged particle, the magnetic force acting on the particle does no work. This follows from the fact that a magnetic force, being always perpendicular to the velocity of the particle, is at all times normal to the path followed by the particle. We thus find that at all times the work done by the magnetic force vanishes:

$$dW^m = \mathbf{F}^m \cdot d\mathbf{s} = 0.$$

The motion of a particle in time-independent electric and magnetic fields thus always satisfies the principle of the conservation of total energy,

$$T + U = \text{const},$$

which is our reason for grouping magnetic forces with the conservative forces. In Section 6–13 we show that the magnetic force is derivable from a velocity-dependent potential energy function.

## 6–6 Motion in a uniform electric field

The equations of motion for a charged particle in a uniform electric field are identical to the equations of motion of a particle in a uniform gravitational field. Choosing the $z$-axis as the axis along which the electric field is directed, the equations of motion are

$$m\ddot{x} = m\ddot{y} = 0 \qquad \text{and} \qquad m\ddot{z} = eE.$$

The solutions to these equations were discussed in Chapter 4, and should also have been met by the reader who has had an introductory mechanics course.

The potential energy for this problem is given by

$$U = -eEz,$$

and the orbit is found to be a parabola unless, of course, the motion is confined along the $z$-direction.

## 6–7 Motion in a uniform magnetic field

The equations of motion for a charged particle in a uniform magnetic field $\mathbf{B}$ directed along the $z$-axis,

$$\mathbf{B} = B\mathbf{k}, \tag{6-31}$$

are

$$m\ddot{x} = eB\dot{y}, \tag{6-32}$$

$$m\ddot{y} = -eB\dot{x}, \tag{6-33}$$

$$m\ddot{z} = 0. \tag{6-34}$$

The magnetic field was found to do no work on the particle, wherefore it follows that the particle speed should remain constant. Since by Eq. (6–34) the $z$-component of the velocity is also a constant, the component $v_\perp$ of the velocity perpendicular to the magnetic field can be seen to remain so, too.

Considering the motion of the particle with respect to the inertial system where the particle has no $z$-component of velocity, the magnetic force on the particle will at all times be perpendicular to its path and have the constant magnitude

$$F^m = ev_\perp B. \tag{6–35}$$

From our discussion of the motion of a particle along a curve (Section 2–7), we can at any point of the path set

$$ev_\perp B = \frac{mv_\perp^2}{\rho}, \tag{6–36}$$

where $\rho$ is the radius of curvature of the path at that point. It follows that the radius of curvature has the same value at all points, which implies that the particle moves in a circle of radius

$$\rho = \frac{mv_\perp}{eB}. \tag{6–37}$$

With respect to any other inertial system moving along the $z$-axis, the particle has an additional $z$-component of velocity, and the path followed by the particle will be a circular helix.

We can, of course, arrive at the same result by solving the equations of motion directly.

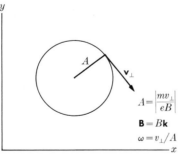

$$A = \left|\frac{mv_\perp}{eB}\right|$$
$$\mathbf{B} = B\mathbf{k}$$
$$\omega = v_\perp/A$$

FIG. 6–3. Motion of a charged particle in a plane perpendicular to a uniform magnetic field.

The first two simultaneous equations of motion for this problem, Eqs. (6–32) and (6–33), can be combined into a single equation. If we multiply the second equation by the imaginary unit $i$ and add the resulting equation to the first, we obtain

$$\frac{d^2}{dt^2}(x + iy) = -\frac{ieB}{m}\frac{d}{dt}(x + iy), \tag{6–38}$$

which has the solution

$$x + iy = C_1 e^{-i(eB/m)t} + C_2. \tag{6–39}$$

The constants $C_1$ and $C_2$ are in general complex numbers which we choose to express in the form

$$C_1 = Ae^{-i\phi} \quad \text{and} \quad C_2 = a + ib.$$

Since $x$ and $y$ are real quantities, we find that

$$x = \text{Re}\{Ae^{-i[(eB/m)t+\phi]} + a + ib\}$$

and

$$y = \text{Im}\{Ae^{-i[(eB/m)t+\phi]} + a + ib\},$$

or

$$x - a = A\cos(\omega t + \phi) \tag{6-40}$$

and

$$y - b = -A\sin(\omega t + \phi), \tag{6-41}$$

where

$$\omega = eB/m. \tag{6-42}$$

Equations (6-40) and (6-41) yield

$$(x - a)^2 + (y - b)^2 = A^2, \tag{6-43}$$

which is the equation of a circle of radius $A$ and center at the point $(a, b)$. The rotation of the position vector of constant magnitude is given by the angular velocity vector (Fig. 6-3)

$$\boldsymbol{\omega} = -\frac{eB}{m}\mathbf{k} = -\omega\mathbf{k}. \tag{6-44}$$

The magnitude of the radius of the circular orbit may be obtained from the magnitude of the velocity vector. We find that

$$\dot{x}^2 + \dot{y}^2 = v_\perp^2 = A^2\omega^2$$

or

$$A = \left|\frac{v_\perp}{\omega}\right| = \left|\frac{v_\perp m}{eB}\right|, \tag{6-45}$$

in agreement with the result arrived at above.

▶ A great number of important applications are based on the results of this section. The fact that the angular velocity [Eq. (6-44)] with which a charged particle moves in its circular orbit in a magnetic field is independent of its energy was the basic principle on which Drs. Ernest O. Lawrence and M. Stanley Livingston developed the cyclotron, an important tool for producing highly energetic beams of charged particles.

Constant magnetic fields are used extensively in order to obtain a measure of the linear momentum of a charged particle. A measure of the radius of curvature $\rho$ of the track left by a charged particle in a cloud or bubble chamber immersed in a magnetic field yields a measure of the momentum, as provided by

$$mv = e\rho B.$$

The charge on the elementary particles is equal in magnitude to the charge on the electron. Its sign is identified from the direction in which the particle is deflected. The motion of a charged particle through a uniform magnetic field combined with its passage through an electric field which yields a measure of its energy allows for a measurement of its mass. This is the principle behind the mass spectrometer. ◀

## 6–8 Motion in a uniform electric and uniform magnetic field

Choosing the plane of the magnetic and electric fields as the $xz$-plane with the $z$-axis parallel to the magnetic induction vector yields the component equations of motion

$$m\ddot{x} = e\dot{y}B + eE_x, \tag{6–46}$$

$$m\ddot{y} = -e\dot{x}B, \tag{6–47}$$

$$m\ddot{z} = eE_z. \tag{6–48}$$

This last equation for the $z$-coordinate is the same as the one-dimensional equation of motion for a particle moving with the constant acceleration

$$a_z = \frac{eE_z}{m}.$$

Its solution for the velocity and displacement in the $z$-direction is

$$\dot{z} = \dot{z}_0 + \frac{eE_z}{m} t \tag{6–49}$$

and

$$z = z_0 + \dot{z}_0 t + \frac{eE_z}{2m} t^2. \tag{6–50}$$

The first two equations of motion, on the other hand, are two coupled equations of motion. They may once more, however, as in the previous section, be combined into the single one-dimensional differential equation of motion,

$$m \frac{d^2}{dt^2} (x + iy) = -ieB \frac{d}{dt} (x + iy) + eE_x. \tag{6–51}$$

Equation (6–51) is an inhomogeneous second-order differential equation with constant coefficients. It has the solution

$$x + iy = C_1 e^{-i(eB/m)t} + C_2 - \frac{iE_x}{B} t, \tag{6–52}$$

where the constants $C_1$ and $C_2$ are generally complex. Expressing the constants in the form

$$C_1 = Ae^{-i\phi} \quad \text{and} \quad C_2 = a + ib,$$

we obtain

$$x = \text{Re}(x + iy) = A \cos(\omega t + \phi) + a \tag{6–53}$$

and

$$y = \text{Im}(x + iy) = -A \sin(\omega t + \phi) + b - \frac{E_x}{B} t, \tag{6–54}$$

where, as before, $\omega = eB/m$. The values of the constants $A$, $\phi$, $a$, and $b$ depend, of course, on the initial values of $x$, $y$, $\dot{x}$, and $\dot{y}$.

In Fig. 6–4 several possible paths which may be followed by the particle in the $xy$-plane are depicted.

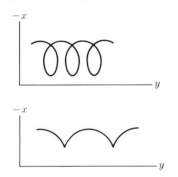

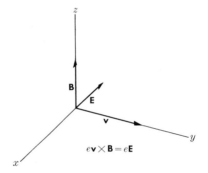

FIG. 6–4. Possible orbits of a charged particle in crossed electric and magnetic fields.

FIG. 6–5. Undeviated motion of a charged particle in crossed electric and magnetic fields.

The combination of a uniform electric field at right angles to a uniform magnetic field is used as a velocity filter. Charged particles moving perpendicularly to the two fields will generally be deflected as given by Eq. (6–52), except those particles which move with a velocity for which the electric force is balanced by the magnetic force on the particle (cf. Fig. 6–5 and Problem 6–6), which leads us to the equation

$$eE = evB \quad \text{or} \quad v = E/B.$$

Another interesting example of the motion of a charged particle under the action of a uniform electric and a uniform magnetic field is provided by the motion of the charge carriers in a conductor immersed in a uniform magnetic field, as shown in Fig. 6–6.

Positive charges, for example, moving in the increasing $y$-direction with the drift velocity $v_+$ under the action of the externally applied voltage will be deflected in the positive $x$-direction by the magnetic force due to the magnetic field along the positive $z$-direction. The charge carriers, being confined by the $x = a$ plane, will thus build up on that plane boundary of the conductor. In doing so they in turn build up an electric field normal to the surface of the conductor, which then acts on the other charge carriers within the conductor. This process continues until the resultant additional electric force on the charge carriers is equal and opposite to the magnetic force on them.

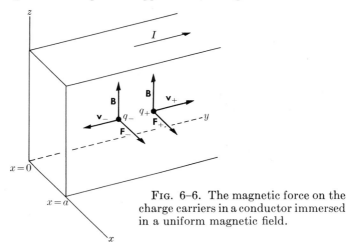

Fig. 6–6. The magnetic force on the charge carriers in a conductor immersed in a uniform magnetic field.

The final situation reached is the velocity filter mentioned, for which

$$v = E_H/B,$$

where $E_H$ is the *Hall electric field* produced by the charged carriers on the $x = a$ plane. The resultant Hall electric potential between the planes of the conductor is given by

$$\phi_H = aE_H.$$

Its direction tells us the nature of the charge on the carriers. It also permits us to obtain an estimate of the density $N$ of charge carriers. From

$$v = \frac{I/A}{eN},$$

where $A$ is the cross-sectional area of the conductor and $I$ the current in the conductor, we obtain

$$N = \frac{I/A}{ev} = \frac{IB}{AeE_H} = \frac{IBa}{Ae\phi_H}.$$

The appearance of a potential difference across the boundaries of a current-carrying conductor located in a uniform magnetic field is known as the *Hall effect*.

## 6-9 The isotropic oscillator in a magnetic field

The potential energy for the isotropic oscillator is

$$U = \tfrac{1}{2}k(x^2 + y^2 + z^2) = \tfrac{1}{2}m\omega_0^2 r^2. \tag{6-55}$$

The effect of a magnetic field on the motion of such an oscillator—or, more generally, on the motion of a charged particle under the action of a central force field—is a very important problem. The study of the response of electrons in atoms and solids to the application of magnetic fields is a very fruitful method for gathering information about the properties of their motion in such an environment. While classical physics is generally not applicable to atomic problems, we do find that in the case of the isotropic oscillator it yields an accurate qualitative description of the effect of a magnetic field on the motion in question.

Using cartesian coordinates, we find that the component equations of motion for a charged isotropic oscillator in a magnetic field directed along the $z$-axis are

$$m\ddot{x} = -m\omega_0^2 x + eB\dot{y}, \tag{6-56}$$

$$m\ddot{y} = -m\omega_0^2 y - eB\dot{x}, \tag{6-57}$$

$$m\ddot{z} = -m\omega_0^2 z. \tag{6-58}$$

The solution to these three equations of motion is once again readily obtainable. The last equation is the one-dimensional equation of motion of a simple harmonic oscillator. This component equation of motion is thus not affected by the magnetic field. The other two equations may be combined into the single one-dimensional equation for the variable $x_+ = x + iy$,

$$m\ddot{x}_+ = -m\omega_0^2 x_+ - ieB\dot{x}_+. \tag{6-59}$$

The two linearly independent solutions to this homogeneous linear differential equation are expressible in the form

$$x_+ = Ce^{i(\alpha t + \phi)}, \tag{6-60}$$

where $\alpha$ is a root of the characteristic equation

$$-m\alpha^2 - eB\alpha + m\omega_0^2 = 0. \tag{6-61}$$

The two roots of this equation are

$$\alpha = -\frac{eB}{2m} \pm \sqrt{\frac{e^2 B^2}{4m^2} + \omega_0^2}, \tag{6-62}$$

which for small magnetic fields satisfying the condition

$$\left| \frac{eB}{2m} \right| \ll \omega_0 \tag{6-63}$$

may be approximated by

$$\alpha = \pm\omega_0 - \omega_L, \tag{6-64}$$

where

$$\omega_L = \frac{eB}{2m}. \tag{6-65}$$

We shall show below that condition (6-63) is satisfied in atomic problems for all presently available magnetic fields, which is equivalent to saying that $\omega_L$ is small compared with the average angular frequency of motion of an electron in an atomic orbit.

With this approximation we obtain the two homogeneous solutions

$$x_{1+} = C_1 \exp\{i[(\omega_0 - \omega_L)t + \phi_1]\} \tag{6-66}$$

and

$$x_{2+} = C_2 \exp\{-i[(\omega_0 + \omega_L)t + \phi_2]\}. \tag{6-67}$$

The general homogeneous solution is, of course, a linear combination of these two solutions. For proper initial conditions, however, either Eq. (6-66) or (6-67) may describe a mode of the motion followed by the particle. We find that the real and imaginary parts of the first solution,

$$x_1 = C_1 \cos[(\omega_0 - \omega_L)t + \phi_1] \tag{6-68}$$

and

$$y_1 = C_1 \sin[(\omega_0 - \omega_L)t + \phi_1],$$

represent the circular motion of the particle in the $xy$-plane. The radius of the circle is $C_1$ and the angular velocity of the radius vector,

$$\boldsymbol{\omega} = (\omega_0 - \omega_L)\mathbf{k}. \tag{6-69}$$

The second homogeneous solution, which yields

$$x_2 = C_2 \cos[(\omega_0 + \omega_L)t + \phi_2] \tag{6-70}$$

and

$$y_2 = -C_2 \sin[(\omega_0 + \omega_L)t + \phi_2],$$

on the other hand, represents the circular motion of the particle in the $xy$-plane in a circle of radius $C_2$ with an angular velocity

$$\boldsymbol{\omega} = -(\omega_0 + \omega_L)\mathbf{k}. \tag{6-71}$$

We note that the introduction of a magnetic field causes the unperturbed ($\mathbf{B} = 0$) circular modes of the motion of the isotropic oscillator in a plane perpendicular to the magnetic field to precess with the additional angular velocity

$$-\omega_L\mathbf{k}.$$

This additional angular velocity is called the *Larmor precessional angular velocity* or *frequency.*

We can show that any other possible mode of the motion of the isotropic oscillator in the absence of the magnetic field is also caused to precess with this additional Larmor precessional frequency when the magnetic field is present.

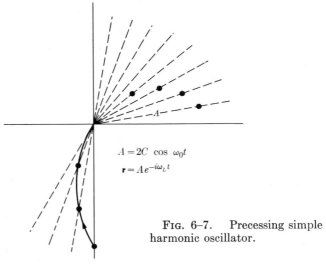

$$A = 2C \, \cos \, \omega_0 t$$

$$\mathbf{r} = A e^{-i\omega_L t}$$

FIG. 6-7.    Precessing simple harmonic oscillator.

We demonstrate this fact by considering the simple harmonic mode of motion along the $x$-axis. The linear combination of the two homogeneous solutions of Eq. (6–59), which for zero magnetic field yield the oscillatory motion of the particle along the $x$-axis, is the solution

$$x_+ = x_{1+} + x_{2+} \tag{6–72}$$

with

$$C_1 = C_2 = C \quad \text{and} \quad \phi_1 = \phi_2.$$

Choosing the initial time such that $\phi_1 = \phi_2 = 0$, we find that in the presence of the magnetic field Eq. (6–72) yields

$$x = C[\cos (\omega_0 + \omega_L)t + \cos (\omega_0 - \omega_L)t]$$

and

$$y = C[-\sin (\omega_0 + \omega_L)t + \sin (\omega_0 - \omega_L)t],$$

or

$$x = (2C \cos \omega_0 t) \cos \omega_L t \quad \text{and} \quad y = -(2C \cos \omega_0 t) \sin \omega_L t. \tag{6–73}$$

This solution may be thought of as representing a circular mode of amplitude $2C \cos \omega_0 t$, precessing with the angular velocity $-\omega_L \mathbf{k}$. From this point of view it represents the unperturbed solution which the particle follows in the absence of the magnetic field precessing, in the presence of the magnetic field, with the Larmor angular velocity (Fig. 6–7).

▶ An interesting and important application of the effect of a uniform magnetic field on the motion of an isotropic oscillator is the resultant effect it has on the response of the oscillator to the electric field of a plane polarized electromagnetic wave (Problem 6–4). We find that the presence of a magnetic field in the direction of propagation of the wave causes the left and right circularly polarized waves, into which a plane wave can be decomposed (cf. Section 12–5), to be propagated with different phase velocities. This results in the rotation of the plane of polarization of the propagating wave. This rotation of the plane of polarization by the application of a magnetic field is known as the *Faraday effect.* ◀

## 6–10 Larmor's theorem

Whenever we have a charged particle moving in a bound orbit in a finite region of space under the action of a central force field, the addition of a small magnetic field produces an additional precessional motion superimposed on the unperturbed ($\mathbf{B} = 0$) motion of the charged particle. This is known as *Larmor's theorem.*

One can prove Larmor's theorem by considering the description of the motion of a charged particle in a central field and a magnetic field with respect to the coordinate system which rotates with the constant angular velocity

$$\boldsymbol{\omega} = -\omega_L \mathbf{k}.$$

The transformation of the description of the velocity and acceleration to such a rotating coordinate system was considered in Section 3–2. Remembering that the relationship between the velocity and acceleration are

$$\mathbf{v} = \mathbf{v}' + \boldsymbol{\omega} \times \mathbf{r} \tag{6–74}$$

and

$$\mathbf{a} = \mathbf{a}' + 2\boldsymbol{\omega} \times \mathbf{v}' + \boldsymbol{\omega} \times (\boldsymbol{\omega} \times \mathbf{r}), \tag{6–75}$$

where $\mathbf{v}'$ and $\mathbf{a}'$ are the velocity and acceleration of the particle with respect to the rotating coordinate system, we find the equation of motion in terms of $\mathbf{v}'$ and $\mathbf{a}'$ to be

$$m[\mathbf{a}' + 2\boldsymbol{\omega} \times \mathbf{v}' + \boldsymbol{\omega} \times (\boldsymbol{\omega} \times \mathbf{r})] = f(r)\mathbf{e}_r + e[\mathbf{v}' + \boldsymbol{\omega} \times \mathbf{r}] \times \mathbf{B}.$$

For an angular velocity

$$\boldsymbol{\omega} = -\omega_L \mathbf{k} = -\frac{eB}{2m}\mathbf{k} = -\frac{e}{2m}\mathbf{B},$$

for which

$$2m\boldsymbol{\omega} \times \mathbf{v}' = -e\mathbf{B} \times \mathbf{v}' = e\mathbf{v}' \times \mathbf{B}$$

and

$$m\boldsymbol{\omega} \times (\boldsymbol{\omega} \times \mathbf{r}) = -\frac{e}{2}\mathbf{B} \times (\boldsymbol{\omega} \times \mathbf{r}) = -\frac{e^2}{4m}(\mathbf{B} \times \mathbf{r}) \times \mathbf{B},$$

the equation of motion reduces to

$$m\mathbf{a}' = f(r)\mathbf{e}_r - \frac{e^2}{4m}(\mathbf{B} \times \mathbf{r}) \times \mathbf{B}. \qquad (6\text{–}76)$$

For small magnetic fields for which the term in $B^2$ is negligible, we thus obtain the approximate equation of motion

$$m\mathbf{a}' = f(r)\mathbf{e}_r. \qquad (6\text{–}77)$$

The description of the motion in the rotating coordinate system is thus to a first approximation the same as the motion of the particle in the stationary system in the absence of the magnetic field. To a first approximation, then, the motion of the particle in the presence of the magnetic field will be observed to be in the same orbit as in the absence of the magnetic field, precessing, however, with the angular velocity $-\omega_L \mathbf{k}$.

## 6–11 Larmor's theorem, continued

A very interesting description of the motion of a charged particle in a central force field and a magnetic field is obtained from the equation of motion for the orbital angular momentum vector of the particle, Eq. (5–31). In the absence of the magnetic field the angular momentum vector is a constant of the motion. This follows from the fact that a central force exerts no torque on the particle, whence

$$d\mathbf{L}/dt = 0 \qquad \text{or} \qquad \mathbf{L} = \mathbf{r} \times \mathbf{p} = \text{const.}$$

By the definition of the orbital angular momentum vector,

$$\mathbf{L} = \mathbf{r} \times \mathbf{p},$$

we find that both the position vector $\mathbf{r}$ and the velocity vector $\mathbf{v}$ lie at all times in a plane perpendicular to $\mathbf{L}$. That is, under the action of a central force the orbit followed by a particle lies in a plane perpendicular to the orbital angular momentum vector.

The introduction of a magnetic field along the $z$-axis introduces a torque which destroys the conservation of the orbital angular momentum. We nevertheless find that the $z$-component of the equation of motion for the orbital angular momentum vector yields a conservation theorem. It is, as we shall show, the conservation of the $z$-component of the orbital angular momentum vector as described with respect to a coordinate system rotating with the angular velocity $-\omega_L \mathbf{k}$. This is, of course, best realized by explicitly writing out the $z$-component of the equation

$$\mathbf{N} = d\mathbf{L}/dt. \qquad (6\text{–}78)$$

In spherical or cylindrical coordinates the $z$-component equation happens to be one of Lagrange's equations of motion (Chapter 5). Utilizing cylindrical coordinates, and remembering that $\mathbf{B} = B\mathbf{k}$, we obtain for the $z$-component equation of motion of the orbital angular momentum the following:

$$\frac{d}{dt}\left(m\rho^2\dot\phi\right) = \mathbf{k} \cdot \mathbf{r} \times [e\mathbf{v} \times \mathbf{B}]$$

$$= eB(\mathbf{k} \times \mathbf{r}) \cdot (\mathbf{v} \times \mathbf{k})$$

$$= -\frac{d}{dt}\left[\frac{eB}{2}\left(\mathbf{r} \times \mathbf{k}\right)^2\right]$$

or

$$\frac{d}{dt}\left(m\rho^2\dot\phi + \frac{eB}{2}r^2\sin^2\theta\right) = 0. \tag{6–79}$$

But, for cylindrical coordinates, $\rho = r\sin\theta$, whence Eq. (6–79) may be rewritten as

$$\frac{d}{dt}\,m\rho^2(\dot\phi + \omega_L) = 0$$

or

$$m\rho^2(\dot\phi + \omega_L) = \text{const.} \tag{6–80}$$

But $\dot\phi + \omega_L$ is the $z$-component of the angular velocity vector

$$\boldsymbol{\Omega} = \dot\phi\mathbf{k} + \dot\theta\mathbf{e}_\phi + \omega_L\mathbf{k},$$

which in turn, when we recall that $\dot\phi\mathbf{k} + \dot\theta\mathbf{e}_r$ is the angular velocity of the position vector with respect to the fixed coordinate system, is the angular velocity of the position vector of the particle with respect to the coordinate system rotating with an angular velocity $-\omega_L\mathbf{k}$. It follows therefore that the conserved quantity

$$L_z' = m\rho^2(\dot\phi + \omega_L) \tag{6–81}$$

is the $z$-component of the orbital angular momentum vector with respect to the rotating coordinate system.

If

$$|\omega_L| \ll \langle\dot\phi\rangle, \tag{6–82}$$

where $|\omega_L|$ is the Larmor frequency and $\langle\dot\phi\rangle$ the magnitude of the average $z$-component of the observed angular velocity of the position vector of the particle, then to a first approximation the Larmor precession does not change the $z$-component of the orbital angular momentum appreciably, and we can set

$$L_z = L_z' = \text{const.} \tag{6–83}$$

Before proceeding to investigate the remaining component equations of motion for the angular momentum vector, we shall express the torque in a more useful form.

By a manipulation of the triple vector product,

$$\mathbf{r} \times (\mathbf{v} \times \mathbf{B}) = (\mathbf{r} \cdot \mathbf{B})\mathbf{v} - (\mathbf{r} \cdot \mathbf{v})\mathbf{B}$$
$$= (\mathbf{r} \cdot \mathbf{B})\mathbf{v} - (\mathbf{v} \cdot \mathbf{B})\mathbf{r} + (\mathbf{v} \cdot \mathbf{B})\mathbf{r} - (\mathbf{r} \cdot \mathbf{v})\mathbf{B}$$
$$= (\mathbf{r} \times \mathbf{v}) \times \mathbf{B} + \mathbf{v} \times (\mathbf{r} \times \mathbf{B}), \qquad (6\text{–}84)$$

we find that the torque

$$\mathbf{N} = e\mathbf{r} \times (\mathbf{v} \times \mathbf{B})$$

may be rewritten as

$$\mathbf{N} = e(\mathbf{r} \times \mathbf{v}) \times \mathbf{B} + e\mathbf{v} \times (\mathbf{r} \times \mathbf{B}).$$

But

$$\mathbf{v} \times (\mathbf{r} \times \mathbf{B}) = \frac{d}{dt}\,[\mathbf{r} \times (\mathbf{r} \times \mathbf{B})] - \mathbf{r} \times (\mathbf{v} \times \mathbf{B}),$$

whence it follows that

$$\mathbf{N} = e(\mathbf{r} \times \mathbf{v}) \times \mathbf{B} + \frac{d}{dt}\,[e\mathbf{r} \times (\mathbf{r} \times \mathbf{B})] - e\mathbf{r} \times (\mathbf{v} \times \mathbf{B}). \qquad (6\text{–}85)$$

This latter relation contains the torque $\mathbf{N} = e\mathbf{r} \times (\mathbf{v} \times \mathbf{B})$ on both sides of the equation. Solving for the torque yields

$$\mathbf{N} = \frac{e}{2}\,(\mathbf{r} \times \mathbf{v}) \times \mathbf{B} + \frac{d}{dt}\left[e\mathbf{r} \times \left(\frac{\mathbf{r} \times \mathbf{B}}{2}\right)\right]. \qquad (6\text{–}86)$$

With this expression for the torque, the equations of motion for the orbital angular momentum are expressible in the form

$$\frac{d}{dt}\,(\mathbf{L} + e\mathbf{r} \times \mathbf{A}) = \boldsymbol{\mu} \times \mathbf{B}, \qquad (6\text{–}87)$$

where the magnetic vector potential $\mathbf{A}$ was defined previously by the equation

$$\mathbf{A} = -\tfrac{1}{2}\mathbf{r} \times \mathbf{B},$$

and we have set

$$\boldsymbol{\mu} = \tfrac{1}{2}e\mathbf{r} \times \mathbf{v} = \frac{e}{2m}\,\mathbf{L}. \qquad (6\text{–}88)$$

The vector $\boldsymbol{\mu}$ is referred to as the *orbital magnetic moment* of the particle.

For particles moving in finite regions of space and small magnetic fields, we generally find the term $e\mathbf{r} \times \mathbf{A}$ to be negligible, in which case we are led to the solvable equation of motion

$$\frac{d}{dt}\,\mathbf{L} = \frac{e}{2m}\,\mathbf{L} \times \mathbf{B}. \qquad (6\text{–}89)$$

Fortunately this is the situation we meet in atomic problems for presently available magnetic fields.

To show that the term $e\mathbf{r} \times \mathbf{A}$ is indeed negligible requires the use of quantum mechanical results, since classical mechanics is not applicable to atomic problems. As to why we then bother to consider this problem classically at all, the answer is that a classical description of the problem, tempered by quantum mechanical results in the form of constraints, at times does lead to the correct correlation of experimental results. In such instances the classical description invariably leads to a clearer picture of the motion.

The term $e\mathbf{r} \times \mathbf{A}$ in Eq. (6–87) is negligible if the magnetic induction vector satisfies the condition

$$B \ll \frac{2L}{e\langle r^2 \rangle},\tag{6–90}$$

where $\langle r^2 \rangle$ is the average mean square radial distance. For electrons in atoms this mean square radial distance is of the order of $10^{-18}\,\mathrm{m}^2$,

$$\langle r^2 \rangle \lesssim 10^{-18}\,\mathrm{m}^2,$$

and the orbital angular momentum has a magnitude

$$L \geq h/2\pi,$$

where $h$ is *Planck's constant*. It has the value $1.05 \times 10^{-34}$ joule-sec. Using the limiting values for $L$ and $\langle r^2 \rangle$ and the value $1.6 \times 10^{-19}$ coul for the magnitude of the electronic charge, condition (6–90) becomes

$$B \ll \frac{2 \times 1.05 \times 10^{-34}}{1.6 \times 10^{-19} \times 10^{-18}}\ \text{webers/m}^2$$

or

$$B \ll 10^3\ \text{webers/m}^2.$$

The largest magnetic induction vectors which have thus far been achieved in the laboratory have been of the order of a few webers. Recently fields of the order of 10 webers/m$^2$ (100,000 gauss) have been achieved in super-conducting magnets, and fields of 50 webers/m$^2$ in pulsed magnets. Such fields are, however, still small compared to fields of $10^3$ webers/m$^2$.

Equation (6–89) is solvable. Its cartesian components are

$$\frac{dL_x}{dt} = \frac{eB}{2m}L_y, \qquad \frac{dL_y}{dt} = -\frac{eB}{2m}L_x, \qquad \frac{dL_z}{dt} = 0.\tag{6–91}$$

The last equation has already been considered. The first two may be combined into the single equation

$$\frac{dL_+}{dt} = -i\omega_L L_+,\tag{6–92}$$

where we have set

$$L_+ = L_x + iL_y.\tag{6–93}$$

This first-order differential equation has the solution

$$L_+ = Ce^{-i(\omega_L t + \phi)} \tag{6-94}$$

or

$$L_x = C \cos(\omega_L t + \phi) \quad \text{and} \quad L_y = -C \sin(\omega_L t + \phi), \tag{6-95}$$

which represents the plane vector $\mathbf{L}_\perp = L_x \mathbf{i} + L_y \mathbf{j}$, having the constant magnitude

$$L_\perp = \sqrt{L_x^2 + L_y^2} = C, \tag{6-96}$$

rotating with the angular velocity $-\omega_L \mathbf{k}$.

To a first approximation, therefore, the introduction of a magnetic field does not change the magnitude of the projection of the orbital angular momentum vector onto the $xy$-plane nor, since $L_z$ is constant, the magnitude of the orbital angular momentum vector

$$L = \sqrt{L_\perp^2 + L_z^2}. \tag{6-97}$$

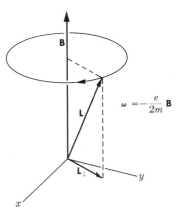

Since the orbital angular momentum vector remains constant in magnitude, it can only change in orientation, which change we have found to be expressible as a rotation about the $z$-axis (Fig. 6–8).

Having previously concluded that the motion of the particle at any instant of time takes place in a plane perpendicular to the orbital angular momentum vector, it follows that the plane of the orbit also precesses along with the angular momentum vector about the $z$-axis.

FIG. 6–8. Precessing angular momentum vector.

This is in agreement with Larmor's theorem that, with respect to a coordinate system rotating with the angular velocity $-\omega_L \mathbf{k}$, the motion of the particle is to a first approximation the same as its motion with respect to the stationary system in the absence of a magnetic field.

## 6–12 Magnetic resonance*

The foregoing analysis of the motion of a charged particle under the combined action of a central force field and a uniform magnetic field is interesting but of little use, unless it can be employed to predict experimentally observed results. In problems dealing with atomic systems it should be quite obvious that the orbit which the atomic

---

\* Charles P. Slichter, *Principles of Magnetic Resonance.* New York: Harper and Row, Chapter 2.

particle follows is not one of the physically observable attributes of the motion. What is observed is the interaction of the system with an additional time-dependent magnetic field from which it can gain (or lose) energy.

We consider therefore a magnetic moment (a charged particle traversing a bound orbit in a finite region of space)

$$\boldsymbol{\mu} = \frac{e}{2m} \, \mathbf{L} \tag{6–98}$$

which is acted on by a constant uniform magnetic field directed along the $z$-axis and a very much smaller sinusoidally varying magnetic field directed along the $y$-axis. The equation of motion for the magnetic moment is expressed by

$$\frac{d\boldsymbol{\mu}}{dt} = \frac{e}{2m} \, \boldsymbol{\mu} \times (\mathbf{B} + \mathbf{b}), \tag{6–99}$$

where the uniform magnetic field is

$$\mathbf{B} = B\mathbf{k}, \tag{6–100}$$

and the time-varying magnetic field is

$$\mathbf{b} = b \cos \omega t \mathbf{j}. \tag{6–101}$$

The cartesian components of Eq. (6–99) are

$$\frac{d\mu_x}{dt} = \frac{eB}{2m} \, \mu_y - \frac{eb}{2m} \, \mu_z \cos \omega t,$$

$$\frac{d\mu_y}{dt} = - \frac{eB}{2m} \, \mu_x, \tag{6–102}$$

$$\frac{d\mu_z}{dt} = \frac{eb\mu_x}{2m} \cos \omega t.$$

These equations are not readily solvable, since some of the coefficients of the unknown, time-dependent components $\mu_x$, $\mu_y$, and $\mu_z$ of the magnetic moment vector, are functions of time. For small $b$, however, we can attempt to obtain a solution by the method of successive approximations. We therefore set

$$\boldsymbol{\mu} = \boldsymbol{\mu}^{(0)} + \boldsymbol{\mu}^{(1)}, \tag{6–103}$$

where $\boldsymbol{\mu}^{(1)}$ is assumed to be small compared to $\boldsymbol{\mu}^{(0)}$, the zero-order approximation to the magnetic moment, which satisfies the equation

$$\frac{d\boldsymbol{\mu}^{(0)}}{dt} = \frac{e}{2m} \, \boldsymbol{\mu}^{(0)} \times \mathbf{B}. \tag{6–104}$$

In terms of $\boldsymbol{\mu}^{(0)}$ the equation for $\boldsymbol{\mu}^{(1)}$ is found to be

$$\frac{d\boldsymbol{\mu}^{(1)}}{dt} = \frac{e}{2m} \, [\boldsymbol{\mu}^{0} \times \mathbf{b} + \boldsymbol{\mu}^{(1)} \times \mathbf{B} + \boldsymbol{\mu}^{(1)} \times \mathbf{b}], \tag{6–105}$$

whose component equations, neglecting the last term on the right-hand side of this equation, are

$$\frac{du_x^{(1)}}{dt} = -\frac{eb\mu_z^{(0)}}{2m} \cos \omega t + \frac{eB}{2m} \mu_y^{(1)}, \tag{6-106}$$

$$\frac{d\mu_y^{(1)}}{dt} = -\frac{eB\mu_x^{(1)}}{2m}, \tag{6-107}$$

$$\frac{d\mu_z^{(1)}}{dt} = \frac{e\mu_x^{(0)}b}{2m} \cos \omega t. \tag{6-108}$$

The last equation has the inhomogeneous solution

$$\mu_z^{(1)} = \frac{e\mu_x^0 b}{2m} \frac{\sin \omega t}{\omega}, \tag{6-109}$$

whereas the solution for the other two component equations may readily be obtained after they are combined into the single one-dimensional first-order differential equation

$$\frac{d\mu_+^{(1)}}{dt} = -\frac{ieB}{2m} \mu_+^{(1)} - \frac{e\mu_z^{(0)}b}{2m} \cos \omega t, \tag{6-110}$$

where

$$\mu_+^{(1)} = \mu_x^{(1)} + i\mu_y^{(1)}.$$

Through the use of the integrating factor $e^{i(eB/2m)t}$, Eq. (6-110) may be rewritten as

$$\frac{d}{dt} (\mu_+^{(1)} e^{i\omega_L t}) = -\frac{eb\mu_z^{(0)}}{2m} e^{i\omega_L t} \cos \omega t, \tag{6-111}$$

which in turn may be integrated to yield the solution

$$\mu_+^{(1)} e^{i\omega_L t} = -\frac{eb\mu_z^{(0)}}{2m} \frac{e^{i\omega_L t}}{\omega^2 - \omega_L^2} (\omega \sin \omega t + i\omega_L \cos \omega t)$$

or

$$\mu_x^{(1)} = -\frac{eb\mu_z^{(0)}}{2m} \frac{\omega \sin \omega t}{\omega^2 - \omega_L^2} \tag{6-112}$$

and

$$\mu_y^{(1)} = -\frac{eb\mu_z^{(0)}}{2m} \frac{\omega_L \cos \omega t}{\omega^2 - \omega_L^2}. \tag{6-113}$$

We note that this solution has a singularity. That is, it becomes infinite when $\omega = \omega_L$. From our discussion of the simple harmonic oscillator we realize that we have here a resonance phenomenon—we have a point at which the response of the system to an external driving force is a maximum. In this problem this point is referred to as the *magnetic resonance* point.

In practice, of course, there exist damping torques which will prevent $\mu_x^{(1)}$ and $\mu_y^{(1)}$ from becoming infinite as predicted by Eqs. (6–112) and (6–113) (Problem 6–12). If they did become very large it would, of course, nullify our analysis, which assumed that

$$|\boldsymbol{\mu}^{(1)}| \ll |\boldsymbol{\mu}^{(0)}|.$$

## 6–13 Velocity-dependent potential energy functions: generalized momenta

Lagrange's equations for the motion of a particle under the action of a conservative force field and a magnetic field are, in terms of the cartesian coordinates $x_1 = x$, $x_2 = y$, and $x_3 = z$,

$$\frac{d}{dt} \frac{\partial(T - U)}{\partial \dot{x}_i} - \frac{\partial(T - U)}{\partial x_i} = e(\mathbf{v} \times \mathbf{B})_i, \qquad i = 1, 2, 3, \qquad (6\text{–}114)$$

where $e(\mathbf{v} \times \mathbf{B})_i$ is the appropriate $x$-, $y$-, or $z$-component of the magnetic force.

We find that Eq. (6–114) can be simplified by expressing the right-hand side in a form which permits it to be joined with the terms on the left-hand side. We proceed to do so.

We note that for constant magnetic fields for which

$$\mathbf{v} \times \mathbf{B} = \frac{d\mathbf{r}}{dt} \times \mathbf{B} = \frac{d}{dt}(\mathbf{r} \times \mathbf{B}) = -2\frac{d\mathbf{A}}{dt}, \qquad (6\text{–}115)$$

we can set

$$(\mathbf{v} \times \mathbf{B})_i = -2\frac{dA_i}{dt} = -2\frac{d}{dt}\frac{\partial}{\partial \dot{x}_i}(\mathbf{v} \cdot \mathbf{A}). \qquad (6\text{–}116)$$

This term is similar to the first term on the left-hand side of Eq. (6–114). We should like, however, to be able to set

$$(\mathbf{v} \times \mathbf{B})_i = -\frac{d}{dt}\frac{\partial}{\partial \dot{x}_i}(\mathbf{v} \cdot \mathbf{A}) + \frac{\partial}{\partial x_i}(\mathbf{v} \cdot \mathbf{A}). \qquad (6\text{–}117)$$

We therefore check to see what the term $(\partial/\partial x_i)(\mathbf{v} \cdot \mathbf{A})$ is equal to. We find that

$$\frac{\partial}{\partial x_i}(\mathbf{v} \cdot \mathbf{A}) = \frac{1}{2}\frac{\partial}{\partial x_i}(\mathbf{r} \cdot \mathbf{v} \times \mathbf{B}) = \tfrac{1}{2}(\mathbf{v} \times \mathbf{B})_i,$$

or by Eq. (6–116)

$$\frac{\partial}{\partial x_i}(\mathbf{v} \cdot \mathbf{A}) = -\frac{d}{dt}\frac{\partial}{\partial \dot{x}_i}(\mathbf{v} \cdot \mathbf{A}). \qquad (6\text{–}118)$$

Thus for constant magnetic fields we can set

$$(\mathbf{v} \times \mathbf{B})_i = -\frac{d}{dt}\frac{\partial}{\partial \dot{x}_i}(\mathbf{v} \cdot \mathbf{A}) + \frac{\partial}{\partial x_i}(\mathbf{v} \cdot \mathbf{A}), \qquad (6\text{–}119)$$

which permits us to reexpress Eq. (6–114) in the form

$$\frac{d}{dt}\frac{\partial}{\partial \dot{x}_i}(T - U + e\mathbf{v} \cdot \mathbf{A}) - \frac{\partial}{\partial x_i}(T - U + e\mathbf{v} \cdot \mathbf{A}) = 0. \quad (6\text{--}120)$$

Redefining the Lagrangian function as

$$L = T - U + e\mathbf{v} \cdot \mathbf{A}, \quad (6\text{--}121)$$

the equations of motion in cartesian coordinates for a particle in a conservative force field and a uniform magnetic field are thus expressed by the equation

$$\frac{d}{dt}\frac{\partial L}{\partial \dot{x}_i} - \frac{\partial L}{\partial x_i} = 0. \quad (6\text{--}122)$$

We note that the Lagrangian as defined by Eq. (6–121), derived for a particle in a uniform magnetic field, yields the correct equations of motion for a particle in any magnetic field (Problem 6–11). We further note that, in terms of the generalized coordinates $q_1$, $q_2$, $q_3$, the generalized equations of motion are

$$\sum_{i=1}^{3}\left(\frac{d}{dt}\frac{\partial L}{\partial \dot{x}_i} - \frac{\partial L}{\partial x_i}\right)\frac{dx_i}{dq_i} = 0,$$

which may readily be shown (Problem 6–23) to reduce to

$$\frac{d}{dt}\frac{\partial L}{\partial \dot{q}_i} - \frac{\partial L}{\partial q_i} = 0. \quad (6\text{--}123)$$

Indeed we find that for velocity-dependent forces which are derivable from a velocity-dependent potential energy function $U(q_i, \dot{q}_i, t)$, where the generalized forces are given by

$$Q_i = \frac{d}{dt}\frac{\partial U}{\partial \dot{q}_i} - \frac{\partial U}{\partial q_i}, \quad (6\text{--}124)$$

the equations of motion are given by Eq. (6–123), where the Lagrangian $L$ is

$$L = T - U. \quad (6\text{--}125)$$

In dealing with velocity-dependent forces derivable from a velocity-dependent potential energy function $U(q_i, \dot{q}_i, t)$, it is customary to define the *generalized* or *conjugate momentum* $p_i$ by the equation

$$p_i = \frac{\partial L}{\partial \dot{q}_i} = \frac{\partial T}{\partial \dot{q}_i} - \frac{\partial U}{\partial \dot{q}_i}. \quad (6\text{--}126)$$

This is not the same as the generalized particle momentum defined in Section 5–2. Only for velocity-independent forces for which

$$\frac{\partial L}{\partial \dot{q}_i} = \frac{\partial T}{\partial \dot{q}_i}$$

are the generalized conjugate momenta identical with the generalized particle momenta.

For problems involving magnetic forces, we find that the generalized conjugate momenta defined by Eq. (6–126) are

$$p_i = \frac{\partial L}{\partial \dot{q}_i} = (m\mathbf{v} + e\mathbf{A}) \cdot \mathbf{b}_i = mv_i + eA_i. \tag{6–127}$$

## 6–14 Conservation of energy: the Hamiltonian function

It is interesting to verify the principle of the conservation of energy directly from Lagrange's equations,

$$\frac{d}{dt} \frac{\partial (T - U)}{\partial \dot{q}_i} - \frac{\partial (T - U)}{\partial q_i} = 0, \tag{6–128}$$

for the case where the potential energy $U$ may also be a function of the velocity. The generalized forces derivable from the velocity-dependent potential energy function $U(q_i, \dot{q}_i, t)$ are

$$Q_i = \frac{d}{dt} \frac{\partial U}{\partial \dot{q}_i} - \frac{\partial U}{\partial q_i}, \tag{6–129}$$

and the work done by such generalized forces for infinitesimal changes in the generalized coordinates is

$$dW = \sum_{i=1}^{3} Q_i \, dq_i = \sum_{i=1}^{3} \left( \frac{d}{dt} \frac{\partial U}{\partial \dot{q}_i} - \frac{\partial U}{\partial q_i} \right) dq_i. \tag{6–130}$$

Equation (6–128) tells us that for any infinitesimal displacement,

$$\sum_{i=1}^{3} \left( \frac{d}{dt} \frac{\partial U}{\partial \dot{q}_i} - \frac{\partial U}{\partial q_i} \right) dq_i = \sum_{i=1}^{3} \left( \frac{d}{dt} \frac{\partial T}{\partial \dot{q}_i} - \frac{\partial T}{\partial q_i} \right) dq_i$$

or

$$\sum_{i=2}^{3} \left[ \frac{d}{dt} \left( \frac{\partial L}{\partial \dot{q}_i} \right) \frac{dq_i}{dt} \, dt - \frac{\partial L}{\partial q_i} \, dq_i \right] = 0. \tag{6–131}$$

Utilizing the relationship

$$\frac{d}{dt} \left( \frac{\partial L}{\partial \dot{q}_i} \right) \frac{dq_i}{dt} \, dt = \frac{d}{dt} \left( \frac{\partial L}{\partial \dot{q}_i} \, \dot{q}_i \right) dt - \frac{\partial L}{\partial \dot{q}_i} \, \ddot{q}_i \, dt = d \left( \frac{\partial L}{\partial \dot{q}_i} \, \dot{q}_i \right) - \frac{\partial L}{\partial \dot{q}_i} \, d\dot{q}_i, \tag{6–132}$$

we find Eq. (6–131) to be expressible in the form

$$\sum_{i=1}^{3} \left\{ d\left(\frac{\partial L}{\partial \dot{q}_i} \dot{q}_i\right) - \frac{\partial L}{\partial \dot{q}_i} d\dot{q}_i - \frac{\partial L}{\partial q_i} dq_i \right\} = 0$$

or

$$d\left(\sum_{i=1}^{3} \frac{\partial L}{\partial \dot{q}_i} d\dot{q}_i - L\right) + \frac{\partial L}{\partial t} dt = 0, \tag{6–133}$$

since

$$dL = \sum_{i=1}^{3} \left(\frac{\partial L}{\partial \dot{q}_i} d\dot{q}_i + \frac{\partial L}{\partial q_i} dq_i\right) + \frac{\partial L}{\partial t} dt. \tag{6–134}$$

If the Lagrangian $L$ does not contain time explicitly, that is, if

$$\partial L/\partial t = 0, \tag{6–135}$$

then Eq. (6–133) reduces to

$$d\left(\sum_{i=1}^{3} \frac{\partial L}{\partial \dot{q}_i} d\dot{q}_i - L\right) = 0,$$

which yields the conservation theorem

$$\sum_{i=1}^{3} \frac{\partial L}{\partial \dot{q}_i} d\dot{q}_i - L = \text{const.} \tag{6–136}$$

The partial derivative of the Lagrangian with respect to the generalized velocity was defined in the last section as the generalized momentum $p_i$. Thus, in terms of the generalized momenta, Eq. (6–136) expresses the fact that whenever Eq. (6–135) is satisfied, the quantity

$$\sum_{i=1}^{3} p_i \dot{q}_i - L$$

is a constant of the motion. That is, whenever the Lagrangian is not explicitly a function of time, the function

$$H = \sum_{i=1}^{3} p_i \dot{q}_i - L, \tag{6–137}$$

referred to as the *Hamiltonian* of the system, is a constant of the motion.

We proceed to show that for the motion of a charged particle under the combined action of a conservative force field derivable from the velocity-independent potential energy function $U(x, y, z)$ and a magnetic field, the Hamiltonian function represents the total energy.

The proof is straightforward if we realize that for this case the generalized momenta are

$$p_i = mv_i + eA_i, \tag{6-138}$$

where

$$v_i = \mathbf{v} \cdot \mathbf{b}_i \quad \text{and} \quad A_i = \mathbf{A} \cdot \mathbf{b}_i.$$

Thus if the transformation to the generalized coordinates is a time-independent coordinate transformation, for which $\dot{q}_i = v_i^\star$, then

$$H = \sum_{i=1}^{3} p_i \dot{q}_i - L$$

$$= \sum_{i=1}^{3} mv_i v_i^\star + \sum_{i=1}^{3} eA_i v_i^\star - L \tag{6-139}$$

$$= mv^2 + ev \cdot A - (\tfrac{1}{2}mv^2 - U + e\mathbf{v} \cdot \mathbf{A}) = T + U.$$

We have used the fact that

$$\sum_{i=1}^{3} mv_i v_i^\star = m\mathbf{v} \cdot \mathbf{v} \quad \text{and} \quad \sum_{i=1}^{3} eA_i v_i^\star = e\mathbf{A} \cdot \mathbf{v}.$$

That these last two equations are true follows from the expression for the scalar product of two vectors expressed in terms of their scalar product with the vectors $\mathbf{b}_i$ and their inverse vectors $\mathbf{b}_i$.

## 6–15 Hamilton's equations of motion

The Hamiltonian function defined by Eq. (6–137) is not, as it appears to be, an explicit function of the generalized velocities $\dot{q}_i$. This can be verified by considering the variation of $H$. Assuming it to be a function of $q_i$, $\dot{q}_i$, $p_i$, and $t$, we find that the variation of $H$ is

$$dH = \sum_{i=1}^{3} \left( \frac{\partial H}{\partial q_i} dq_i + \frac{\partial H}{\partial p_i} dp_i + \frac{\partial H}{\partial \dot{q}_i} d\dot{q}_i \right) + \frac{\partial H}{\partial t} dt.$$

From the definition of $H$, Eq. (6–137), it is also expressible as

$$dH = \sum_{i=1}^{3} \left( p_i d\dot{q}_i + \dot{q}_i dp_i - \frac{\partial L}{\partial \dot{q}_i} d\dot{q}_i - \frac{\partial L}{\partial q_i} dq_i \right) - \frac{\partial L}{\partial t} dt. \tag{6-140}$$

Since by definition $p_i = \partial L / \partial \dot{q}_i$, the terms

$$\sum_{i=1}^{3} \left( p_i - \frac{\partial L}{\partial \dot{q}_i} \right) d\dot{q}_i$$

in the latter equation cancel, leaving no term in $d\dot{q}_i$ on its right-hand side. Equating the two expressions for $dH$ yields

$$\frac{\partial H}{\partial \dot{q}_i} = 0, \tag{6-141}$$

$$\frac{\partial H}{\partial q_i} = -\frac{\partial L}{\partial q_i}, \tag{6-142}$$

$$\frac{\partial H}{\partial p_i} = \dot{q}_i, \tag{6-143}$$

$$\frac{\partial H}{\partial t} = \frac{\partial L}{\partial t}. \tag{6-144}$$

Equation (6–141) verifies what we set out to prove, that the Hamiltonian function is not an explicit function of the generalized velocities. It is only a function of the generalized coordinates, momenta, and time,

$$H = H(q_i, p_i, t). \tag{6-145}$$

Through the use of Lagrange's equations of motion, Eq. (6–142) may be rewritten as

$$\dot{p}_i = -\frac{\partial H}{\partial q_i}, \tag{6-146}$$

which together with Eq. (6–143), $\dot{q}_i = \partial H/\partial p_i$, constitute what are known as *Hamilton's equations of motion*. Equation (6–146) is the equivalent of Lagrange's equations of motion, whereas Eq. (6–143), which yields the generalized velocities as functions of the generalized coordinates and momenta, is the inverse of Eq. (6–126), which defines the generalized momenta as functions of the generalized coordinates and velocities. That is, Eq. (6–143) represents Eq. (6–126) solved for the $\dot{q}_i$.

For our purpose Hamilton's equations, being equivalent to Lagrange's equations, offer no obvious advantage in the solution of problems. Their importance lies in the fact that they are the basis of a more sophisticated approach to the subject of mechanics, which is important in the development of quantum mechanics and very useful in statistical mechanics. A further development of Hamiltonian mechanics is beyond the scope of this book.

As an illustration of their use and their equivalence to Lagrange's equations, we shall proceed to find the Hamiltonian and the Hamiltonian equations of motion for a charged particle in a central electric field and a uniform magnetic field, the latter being directed along the $z$-axis.

We start by obtaining the Lagrangian, since we require it for obtaining the generalized momenta. The Lagrangian for this problem we already considered in Section 6–13, where it was found to be given by

$$L = T - U + e\mathbf{v} \cdot \mathbf{A}. \tag{6-147}$$

From the Lagrangian we obtain the generalized momenta in cartesian coordinates

$$p_1 = p_x = mv_x + eA_x = mv_1 + eA_1, \tag{6-148}$$

$$p_2 = p_y = mv_2 + eA_2, \tag{6-149}$$

$$p_3 = p_z = mv_3 + eA_3, \tag{6-150}$$

which yield the generalized velocities

$$\dot{x}_i = \frac{p_i - eA_i}{m}, \qquad i = 1, 2, 3. \tag{6-151}$$

We are now in a position to construct the Hamiltonian, obtaining

$$H = \sum_{i=1}^{3} p_i \dot{x}_i - T + U - e \sum_{i=1}^{3} A_i \dot{x}_i = \frac{1}{2m} \sum_{i=1}^{3} (p_i - eA_i)^2 + U, \tag{6-152}$$

since

$$T = \frac{m}{2} \sum_{i=1}^{3} \dot{x}_i \dot{x}_i = \frac{1}{2m} \sum_{i=1}^{3} (p_i - eA_i)^2.$$

This result for the Hamiltonian function may have been obtained directly from the relation

$$m\dot{x}_i = p_i - eA_i$$

and from Eq. (6–139), which tells us that the Hamiltonian for a particle in a conservative force field and a magnetic field is the total energy,

$$H = T + U.$$

From the Hamiltonian (6–152) we obtain the cartesian equations of motion

$$\dot{p}_x = \frac{d}{dt}(m\dot{x} + eA_x) = -\frac{\partial H}{\partial x} = -\frac{\partial U}{\partial x} + e \sum_{i=1}^{3} \left(\frac{p_i - eA_i}{m}\right) \frac{\partial A_i}{\partial x}$$

or

$$\frac{d}{dt}(m_i\dot{x}_i + eA_x) = -\frac{\partial U}{\partial x} + e\mathbf{v} \cdot \frac{\partial \mathbf{A}}{\partial x}, \tag{6-153}$$

and similar equations for the $y$- and $z$-components.

Since, by Eqs. (6–116) and (6–118),

$$e\frac{dA_x}{dt} = -\frac{1}{2} e(\mathbf{v} \times \mathbf{B})_x \quad \text{and} \quad e\mathbf{v} \cdot \frac{\partial \mathbf{A}}{\partial x} = \frac{1}{2} e(\mathbf{v} \times \mathbf{B})_x,$$

it follows that Eq. (6–153) is indeed the $x$-component of Newton's equation of motion. The other components follow analogously.

The remaining Hamiltonian equations of motion yield the generalized velocities

$$\dot{x}_i = \frac{\partial H}{\partial p_i} = \frac{1}{m}\,(p_i - eA_i).$$

This is Eq. (6–151), which we recall was obtained from the equations defining the generalized momenta.

In general, for orthogonal curvilinear coordinates for which

$$\boldsymbol{b}_i = \frac{1}{h_i^2}\,\mathbf{b}_i$$

we have that

$$v_i = \mathbf{v}\cdot\mathbf{b}_i = h_i^2\mathbf{v}\cdot\boldsymbol{b}_i = h_i^2\dot{q}_i,$$

and hence

$$v^2 = \sum_{i=1}^{3} v_i\dot{q}_i = \sum_{i=1}^{3} \frac{v_i^2}{h_i^2}.$$

It follows from this that, in any problem for which the Hamiltonian equals the total energy, its expression in orthogonal curvilinear coordinates has the form

$$H = T + U = \frac{1}{2}\,mv^2 + U = \sum_{i=1}^{3} \frac{m}{2}\,\frac{v_i^2}{h_i^2} + U,$$

where the $v_i$ are to be expressed in terms of the generalized momenta. For problems involving magnetic forces for which

$$p_i = mv_i + eA_i \qquad \text{or} \qquad v_i = \frac{1}{m}\,(p_i - eA_i),$$

we thus obtain

$$H = \sum_{i=1}^{3} \frac{1}{2m}\,\frac{(p_i - eA_i)^2}{h_i^2} + U.$$

In spherical coordinates, for example, the Hamiltonian is found to have the form

$$H = \frac{(p_1 - eA_1)^2}{2m} + \frac{(p_2 - eA_2)^2}{2mr^2} + \frac{(p_3 - eA_3)^2}{2mr^2\sin^2\theta} + U,$$

where

$$p_1 - eA_1 = (\mathbf{p} - e\mathbf{A})\cdot\mathbf{e}_r,$$
$$p_2 - eA_2 = (\mathbf{p} - e\mathbf{A})\cdot(\mathbf{e}_\phi \times \mathbf{r})$$
$$= \mathbf{r}\times(\mathbf{p} - e\mathbf{A})\cdot\mathbf{e}_\phi = r[(\mathbf{p} - e\mathbf{A})\cdot\mathbf{e}_\theta],$$

and

$$p_3 - eA_3 = (\mathbf{p} - e\mathbf{A})\cdot(\mathbf{k} \times \mathbf{r})$$
$$= \mathbf{r}\times(\mathbf{p} - e\mathbf{A})\cdot\mathbf{k} = r\sin\theta[(\mathbf{p} - e\mathbf{A})\cdot\mathbf{e}_\phi].$$

## 6–16 Geometric optics and mechanics

An interesting and very important analogy exists between the trajectory of a particle under the action of a conservative force and the path followed by a light ray in a region of space where the index of refraction is a slowly varying function of position. That is, the index of refraction does not vary appreciably over a distance equal to a wavelength of the light wave in the medium. Under these circumstances the wave nature of light is not exhibited by the light wave, and its propagation through the medium is accurately described by the propagation of the points on its wavefronts along the ray trajectories normal to the wavefronts.

A light ray passing from a medium of one index of refraction into a medium having a different index of refraction satisfies Snell's law. This law states that the quantity $n \sin \theta$ remains constant where $\theta$ is the angle which the ray trajectory makes with the normal to the surface between the two media and $n$ is the index of refraction of the medium (Fig. 6–9).

This law provides us with a graphical method for determining the trajectory of a light ray through some media. By subdividing, if possible, the region through which the ray is propagating by surfaces of constant index of refraction as determined by

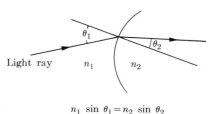

$$n_1 \sin \theta_1 = n_2 \sin \theta_2$$

Fig. 6–9. Snell's law.

$$n_m(x, y, z) = n_0(x, y, z) + m \, \Delta n, \qquad m = 0, 1, 2 \ldots,$$

(Fig. 6–10a), where $n_0(x, y, z)$ is the surface of constant index passing through the initial position of the ray and $\Delta n$ is an infinitesimal change in the index, we can approximate the index in each region by its average value over the region (Fig. 6–10b). The passage of the ray through the medium is then approximated by the discontinuous path which would be followed by the ray passing through the discontinuous region of Fig. (6–10b). This discontinuous path is determined by applying Snell's law at every discontinuous boundary.

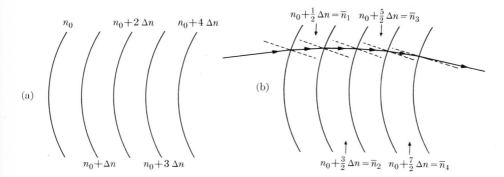

Fig. 6–10. A graphical method for tracing ray trajectories.

For the motion of a particle in a conservative force field, we find that there exists a formula analogous to Snell's law. Consider a particle moving from one region into a second region where the potential energy changes discontinuously from $U_1$ to $U_2$ as the particle crosses the boundary between the two regions (Fig. 6–11).

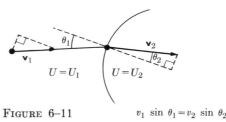

FIGURE 6–11    $v_1 \sin \theta_1 = v_2 \sin \theta_2$

A change in the potential energy of the particle entails a change in its velocity produced by a variation in the velocity component normal to the surface at which the potential energy changes discontinuously. The effect of a discontinuity in the potential energy function is equivalent to an energy impulse $Fv\Delta t$ in the direction normal to the surface of discontinuity. This impulse imparts to the particle a change in its kinetic energy, $\Delta T = Fv\Delta t = U_1 - U_2$, which results in a change in the component of the velocity normal to the surface of discontinuity. But the tangential component remains unchanged, so that

$$v_1 \sin \theta_1 = v_2 \sin \theta_2,$$

where $\theta_1$ and $\theta_2$ are the angles which the velocity vectors in the two regions make with the normal to the surface between the two media (Fig. 6–11).

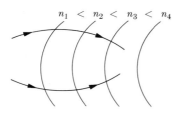

FIG. 6–12. A converging medium.

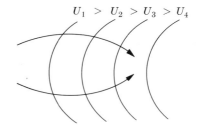

FIG. 6–13. A converging region for particle trajectories.

The magnitude of the velocity vector in the two regions may be obtained through the use of the principle of the conservation of energy, which yields the equation

$$\sqrt{E - U_1} \sin \theta_1 = \sqrt{E - U_2} \sin \theta_2.$$

It should be clear that in those problems where the index of refraction $n(x, y, z)$ and the function $\sqrt{E - U(x, y, z)}$ have the same functional dependence on position, the trajectory of a light ray which has the same initial position and direction of propagation as a particle of total energy $E$ will be the same as the path followed by the particle.

Qualitatively, for example, we find that the light rays of a wavefront propagating in a region where the surfaces of constant index of refraction are curved, and vary as shown in Fig. 6–12, will be made to curve toward each other. Such a medium is referred to as a converging medium.

Analogously, in a region wherein the surfaces of constant potential energy vary in the manner depicted in Fig. 6–13, the neighboring paths followed by particles starting out from a given point with the same speed will likewise curve toward each other. We note that this is the principle on which the design of electrostatic lenses for the focusing of beams of charged particles is based.

## 6–17 Geometric optics, mechanics, and wave mechanics

The remarkable discoveries of this century provide us with innumerable examples of phenomena inexplicable in terms of classical mechanics. The stability of atoms, the photoelectric effect, and the Davisson-Germer experiment on the diffraction of electrons, to name but a few, are such examples, all of which were instrumental in the development of our present view of the behavior of particles in small regions of space. The failure of classical physics to account for the seemingly strange behavior of particles in small regions of space is not so surprising if we realize that classical physics assumes nature to be continuous and that in dealing with the behavior of the fundamental building blocks of nature, the fundamental particles, we are investigating those parts of nature which are discontinuous. Classical physics, for this reason and for others discussed at length in books on quantum mechanics, is not applicable to the description of the creation, annihilation, and interactions of the fundamental particles.

Particles in small regions of space exhibit wave properties. Electromagnetic radiation, on the other hand, which classically is described as a wave, has been found to exhibit particle properties. The present quantum mechanical view first suggested by Louis de Broglie in 1924 is that it is natural for particles under the proper environment to exhibit wave properties and for waves to exhibit particle properties. There exists thus a particle-wave duality in nature, with the particle description representing the limit of the wave description. The particle description is good when the wave motion takes place in a region which has properties affecting the propagation of the wave which do not vary appreciably over distances equal to a wavelength of the wave. From this point of view therefore the analogy between geometric optics and mechanics is more fundamental than can be inferred from the discussion of the previous section.

Having come so close to the historical approach to the subject of wave mechanics, we cannot resist the temptation to extend our previous discussion of the analogy between optics and mechanics a little further.

A wavefront of an electromagnetic wave is defined as a surface at all of whose points the wave has the same phase. The relative phase of the wavefronts at different points along the trajectory of any ray at any given instant of time is measured by the *eikonal*, which is defined by

$$\chi = \int n \, ds, \qquad (6\text{--}154)$$

where $n$ is the index of refraction and the integral is evaluated along the ray trajectory. The surfaces of constant $\chi$ are surfaces normal to the ray trajectories.

Analogously, in dealing with the motion of a particle, we can define the function

$$\mathcal{W} = \int \mathbf{p} \cdot d\mathbf{s} = \int \sqrt{2m(E - U)}\, ds, \qquad (6\text{–}155)$$

which can be considered as a measure of the phase difference between two matter wavefronts passing through two points of the particle trajectory. While Eq. (6–155) by itself is not sufficient to specify the surfaces of constant $\mathcal{W}$, it should be clear from our analogy that such surfaces exist and that they are normal to the direction of the particle trajectory. It follows therefore from the definition of $\mathcal{W}$ that we can set

$$\mathbf{p} = \nabla \mathcal{W};$$

and hence, since

$$d\mathcal{W} = \mathbf{p} \cdot d\mathbf{s} = \sum_{i=1}^{3} p_i\, dq_i,$$

that

$$p_i = \frac{\partial \mathcal{W}}{\partial q_i}. \qquad (6\text{–}156)$$

A discussion of the analytical method for obtaining the surfaces of constant $\mathcal{W}$ is beyond the scope of this text. We should like to indicate, however, that these surfaces are the solutions of the *Hamilton-Jacobi partial differential equation* for the *Hamilton characteristic function* $\mathcal{W}$,

$$\frac{1}{2m} \sum_{i=1}^{3} \frac{1}{h_i^2} \left( \frac{\partial \mathcal{W}}{\partial q_i} \right)^2 + U(q_1, q_2, q_3) = E, \qquad (6\text{–}157)$$

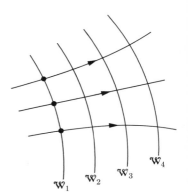

FIG. 6–14. Particle trajectories determined by the surfaces of constant $\mathcal{W}$.

which is obtained by inserting $p_i$ as provided by Eq. (6–156) into the Hamiltonian.

We note that any similar particle of the same total energy which at any time moves normal to a surface of constant $\mathcal{W}$ will continue to move along the trajectory normal to all the subsequent surfaces of constant $\mathcal{W}$ (Fig. 6–14).

In conclusion, we should like to define the De Broglie wavelength for matter waves. It is defined in analogy with the relation between the index of refraction and the wavelength of electromagnetic waves. For electromagnetic waves we have the relation

$$n = \lambda_0/\lambda, \qquad (6\text{–}158)$$

where $\lambda_0$ is the constant wavelength of the radiation in free space. For matter waves we therefore similarly set

$$\sqrt{2m(E - U)}\lambda = \text{const.}$$

Experimentally we find that

$$\lambda = h/p, \qquad (6\text{–}159)$$

where $h$ is known as *Planck's constant.* For electromagnetic waves for which the relationship between the energy of a "light particle" (called a *photon*) and the frequency $\nu$ is

$$E = h\nu, \tag{6-160}$$

and the relationship between the momentum and the energy is

$$p = E/c \tag{6-161}$$

where $c$ is the speed of light, we obtain the same relationship that is found to exist for a particle between its wavelength and momentum,

$$\lambda = \frac{c}{\nu} = \frac{h}{h\nu/c} = \frac{h}{p}. \tag{6-162}$$

## Problems

6–1. Obtain the potential energy function for the conservative forces among the following force functions:

(a)  $F_x = f_1(x)$,  $\qquad F_y = f_2(y)$,  $\qquad F_z = f_3(z)$

(b)  $F_x = \dfrac{a}{x^2 + y^2}$,  $\qquad F_y = \dfrac{b}{x^2 + y^2}$,  $\qquad F_z = 0$

(c)  $F_x = \dfrac{ax}{x^2 + y^2 + z^2}$,  $\qquad F_y = \dfrac{ay}{x^2 + y^2 + z^2}$,  $\qquad F_z = \dfrac{az}{x^2 + y^2 + z^2}$

(d)  $F_x = xy^2 z$,  $\qquad F_y = x^2 yz$,  $\qquad F_z = \frac{1}{2}x^2 y^2$

(e)  $F_x = \dfrac{a + x}{x^2 + y^2 + z^2} e^{-ax}$,  $F_y = \dfrac{b + y}{x^2 + y^2 + z^2} e^{-by}$,  $F_z = \dfrac{c + z}{x^2 + y^2 + z^2} e^{-cz}$

6–2. Find the conservative forces for which the following are the scalar potential energy functions:

(a)   $U = \frac{1}{2} \ln (x^2 + y^2 + z^2)$

(b)   $U(r, \theta, \phi) = \dfrac{a \cos \theta}{r^2}$

(c)   $U = \frac{1}{2}(k_1 x^2 + k_2 y^2 + k_3 z^2)$

(d)   $U(r, \theta, \phi) = \dfrac{e^{-kr}}{r}$

6–3. Compute the work performed by the following forces along the paths indicated:
(a) $\mathbf{F} = 4y\mathbf{i} + 2x\mathbf{j} + \mathbf{k}$ along the helix

$$x = 4 \cos \theta, \qquad y = 4 \sin \theta, \qquad z = 2\theta$$

from $\theta = 0$ to $\theta = 2\pi$.
(b) $\mathbf{F} = 2xz\mathbf{i} + 3z^2\mathbf{j} + y^2\mathbf{k}$ along the straight line $x = 2y = 4z$ from the origin to the point $(4, 2, 1)$.

6–4. Consider the isotropic two-dimensional charged harmonic oscillator in the constant uniform magnetic field $\mathbf{B} = B\mathbf{k}$ perpendicular to the plane of the motion of the oscillator under the action of the electric field

$$\mathbf{E} = E_0 \cos \omega t \mathbf{i}.$$

Show that if we express the electric field as the sum of the two rotating fields

$$\mathbf{E}_+ = \tfrac{1}{2}E_0(\cos \omega t \mathbf{i} + \sin \omega t \mathbf{j})$$

and

$$\mathbf{E}_- = \tfrac{1}{2}E_0(\cos \omega t \mathbf{i} - \sin \omega t \mathbf{j}),$$

and neglect the terms in $B^2$, resonance will be obtained for the first field, $\mathbf{E}_+$, at a frequency

$$\omega = \omega_0 - \omega_L,$$

and for the second field, $\mathbf{E}_-$, at a frequency

$$\omega = \omega_0 + \omega_L,$$

where

$$\omega_L = \frac{eB}{2m}.$$

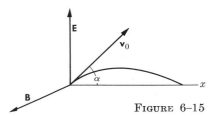

FIGURE 6–15

6–5. Repeat Problem 6–4 for the case of the damped isotropic harmonic oscillator, where

$$\mathbf{F}_{\text{damping}} = -2\mu m(\dot{x}\mathbf{i} + \dot{y}\mathbf{j}).$$

6–6. A positively charged particle of mass $m$ and charge $e$ passes through a velocity filter composed of a uniform electric field $\mathbf{E}$ directed along the $+y$-axis,

$$\mathbf{E} = E\mathbf{j},$$

and a uniform magnetic field directed along the $z$-axis,

$$\mathbf{B} = B\mathbf{k}.$$

(a) For what initial velocity directed along the $x$-axis will the charged particle pass through the velocity filter undeflected? (b) Show that any particle whose initial velocity lies in the $xy$-plane and which makes some small angle $\alpha$ with the $x$-direction will at some later time once again cross the $x$-axis. Find the point at which this crossing takes place for particles having the desired speed found in part (a) (Fig. 6–15).

6–7. In a mass spectrometer a singly charged positive ion ($q = 1.602 \times 10^{-19}$ coul) is accelerated through a potential difference of 1000 v. It then travels through a uniform magnetic field for which $B = 0.1$ weber/m$^2$, and is deflected into a circular path 0.182 m in radius. What is (a) the speed of the ion? (b) the mass of the ion, in kilograms and in atomic mass units? (c) the mass number of the ion?

6–8. A projectile shot from the ground has a range of $l$, and the highest point of its trajectory is at height $h$. What are the initial speed and the elevation angle of the projectile in terms of $h$, $l$, and $g$ (neglect air friction)?

6–9. A gun at position $x = 0$, $y = 0$, has a maximum range of $l_m$. Determine the two elevation angles which correspond to a target located at

$$x = l_m/2, \qquad y = l_m/4.$$

6–10. A positively charged particle of charge $e$ (Fig. 6–16) moves in the central electric field

$$\mathbf{E} = -\frac{\alpha}{\rho}\,\mathbf{e}_\rho$$

between the plates of a cylindrical capacitor, and the uniform magnetic field

$$\mathbf{B} = B\mathbf{k},$$

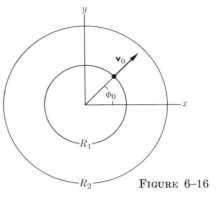

FIGURE 6–16

which is parallel to the axis of the capacitor.
  (a) Set up the equations of motion of the particle in cylindrical coordinates.  (b) Show that the equation of motion for the angle variable $\phi$, which is an ignorable coordinate, is readily solvable and yields as an integral of the motion

$$m\rho^2\dot{\phi} + \tfrac{1}{2}e\rho^2 B = h = \text{const.}$$

(c) Show that, through use of the result of part (b), the radial equation may be reduced to a one-dimensional equation of motion, yielding a second integral of the motion, expressing the conservation of the total energy.  (d) If the particle is emitted from the smaller cylinder with an initial velocity

$$\mathbf{v}_0 = v_0\mathbf{e}_\rho,$$

what must the minimum value of $v_0$ be in order that the particle reach the second cylinder of radius $R_2$? [*Hint:* For the minimum $v_0$, $R_2$ is a turning point.]
  6–11. Show that, from the fact that the magnetic induction vector is generally expressible as the curl of the magnetic vector potential,

$$\mathbf{B} = \nabla \times \mathbf{A},$$

it follows that the Lagrangian

$$L = T - U(x, y, z) + e\mathbf{v} \cdot \mathbf{A}$$

yields the correct equations of motion for the motion of a charged particle in an electromagnetic field if the electric field is

$$\mathbf{E} = -\nabla\phi - \frac{\partial \mathbf{A}}{\partial t},$$

where $U = e\phi$.
  6–12. Consider the damped motion of a magnetic moment in a uniform constant magnetic field $\mathbf{B} = B\mathbf{k}$ and a small sinusoidal magnetic field $\mathbf{b} = b_0 \cos \omega t\mathbf{j}$, where

the damping torque is accounted for by adding a damping term of the form

$$\mathbf{N}_{\text{damping}} = \alpha \left( \frac{\mu}{\mu} \right) \times \frac{d\boldsymbol{\mu}}{dt}$$

to the equations of motion for the magnetic moment $\boldsymbol{\mu}$. Obtain the steady-state solution for $\boldsymbol{\mu}^{(1)}$ of the resulting equation of motion by the method of successive approximations, where

$$\boldsymbol{\mu}^{(1)} = \boldsymbol{\mu} - \boldsymbol{\mu}^{(0)}.$$

Find the frequency for which $\boldsymbol{\mu}^{(1)}$ is a maximum.

6–13. (a) Consider the motion of the two-dimensional anisotropic harmonic oscillator whose potential energy is

$$U = \tfrac{1}{2}(k_1 x^2 + k_2 y^2).$$

For what values of $k_1$ and $k_2$ will the orbit be closed? Plot several of these orbits (Lissajous figures). (b) Obtain the Hamiltonian function for this problem, and from it Hamilton's equations of motion.

6–14. (a) Consider a charged anisotropic harmonic oscillator whose motion is confined to a plane under the additional action of a magnetic field perpendicular to the plane of its motion. Show that the equations of its motion are two homogeneous simultaneous linear differential equations of the form

$$L_1 x + L_2 y = 0 \qquad \text{and} \qquad L_3 x + L_4 y = 0,$$

where $L_1, L_2, \ldots$ are linear operators with constant coefficients. (b) Obtain the Hamiltonian function for this problem, and from it Hamilton's equations of motion.

6–15. (a) Show that two simultaneous differential equations of the form

$$L_1 x + L_2 y = 0 \qquad \text{and} \qquad L_3 x + L_4 y = 0 \qquad (A)$$

may, if the operators $L_i$ are linear operators with constant coefficients, be reduced to two one-dimensional equations of the form

$$(L_1 L_4 - L_2 L_3) x = 0 \qquad \text{and} \qquad (L_1 L_4 - L_2 L_3) y = 0. \qquad (B)$$

(b) The result of part (a) follows from the fact that linear differential operators with constant coefficients commute; that is,

$$L_i L_j = L_j L_i.$$

Can the two simultaneous equations (A) still be reduced to two one-dimensional equations if the operators $L_i$ do not commute? If so, how? (c) Show that if the $L_i$ are differential operators with constant coefficients, then the differential operator $L_1 L_4 - L_2 L_3$ is likewise a differential operator with constant coefficients. (d) From the result of part (c) we surmise that the solution to the equations (B) are expressible in the form

$$x = C_1 e^{\alpha t}, \qquad y = C_2 e^{\alpha t}.$$

Show that by using such a trial solution for $x$ and $y$ in equations (A), we find that a nontrivial solution of this form is possible only if $\alpha$ is a root of the determinantal equation

$$\begin{vmatrix} L_1(\alpha) & L_2(\alpha) \\ L_3(\alpha) & L_4(\alpha) \end{vmatrix} = 0,$$

where $L_i(\alpha)$ is $L_i(d/dt)$, with $d/dt$ replaced by $\alpha$. (e) Use this result to find the normal frequencies for the anisotropic harmonic oscillator in a magnetic field (Problem 6–14). Use

$$k_1 = 8m, \qquad k_2 = 3m, \qquad \text{and} \qquad eB = \sqrt{3}m.$$

6–16. To a first approximation, the dynamical equations of motion for an electron in a crystal are empirically found to be

$$F_x = m_1\ddot{x}, \qquad F_y = m_2\ddot{y}, \qquad \text{and} \qquad F_z = m_3\ddot{z}.$$

The effect of the crystalline periodic potential on the motion of an electron is thus representable empirically by assigning to the electron a tensor mass represented in matrix notation by

$$(\mathbf{m}) = \begin{bmatrix} m_1 & 0 & 0 \\ 0 & m_2 & 0 \\ 0 & 0 & m_3 \end{bmatrix}.$$

In terms of this tensor mass, the equations of motion are given by

$$|\mathbf{F}) = \mathbf{m}|\mathbf{a}),$$

where

$$|\mathbf{F}) \leftrightarrow \begin{bmatrix} F_x \\ F_y \\ F_z \end{bmatrix} \qquad \text{and} \qquad |\mathbf{a}) \leftrightarrow \begin{bmatrix} \ddot{x} \\ \ddot{y} \\ \ddot{z} \end{bmatrix}.$$

(a) Show that, in terms of the diagonal elements of the tensor mass, the work is

$$W_{12} = \int_1^2 \mathbf{F} \cdot d\mathbf{s} = T_2 - T_1,$$

where $T = \frac{1}{2}m_1\dot{x}^2 + \frac{1}{2}m_2\dot{y}^2 + \frac{1}{2}m_3\dot{z}^2$. (b) Show that if additional conservative forces act on the electron in a crystal, the total energy is a constant of the motion. (c) Obtain the equations of motion for an electron in a crystal under the action of a uniform electric field and a uniform magnetic field. (d) Show that the equations of motion of (c) are derivable from the Lagrangian

$$L = T - U - e\mathbf{v} \cdot \mathbf{A},$$

where $-e$ is the electronic charge. (e) Find the Hamiltonian and Hamilton's equations of motion. Show that the Hamiltonian is the total energy so long as $(\partial L/\partial t) = 0$.

6–17. Consider the plane motion of an electron in a crystal under the action of a uniform magnetic field perpendicular to the plane of its motion (see Problem 6–16). The Lagrangian for this problem is

$$L = \tfrac{1}{2}m_1\dot{x}^2 + \tfrac{1}{2}m_2\dot{y}^2 - e\mathbf{v}\cdot\mathbf{A},$$

where

$$\mathbf{v} = \dot{x}\mathbf{l} + \dot{y}\mathbf{J}, \qquad \mathbf{A} = -\frac{By}{2}\mathbf{l} + \frac{Bx}{2}\mathbf{J},$$

and $-e$ is the charge on the electron. Show that a physically meaningful solution (one for which energy is conserved) to the simultaneous equations in the form $e^{i\omega t}$ is possible only for

$$\omega = \omega_c = \pm\frac{eB}{\sqrt{m_1 m_2}},$$

where $\omega_c$ is referred to as the cyclotron frequency.

6–18. Set up and solve the equations of plane motion of an electron with tensor mass (cf. Problem 6–16) under the action of a uniform magnetic field which is perpendicular to the plane of its motion and a sinusoidal electric field directed along the $x$-axis.

6–19. Consider the three-dimensional problem of an electron in a crystal under the action of a magnetic field which lies in the $xz$-plane, making an angle $\theta$ with the $z$-axis. The kinetic energy of the electron in the crystal is given by

$$T = \tfrac{1}{2}m_1(\dot{x}^2 + \dot{y}^2) + \tfrac{1}{2}m_2\dot{z}^2.$$

Show that a physically meaningful solution of the form $e^{i\omega t}$ is possible only for

$$\omega = \frac{eB}{m^*},$$

where the effective mass $m^*$ is given by

$$\left(\frac{1}{m^*}\right)^2 = \frac{\cos^2\theta}{m_1^2} + \frac{\sin^2\theta}{m_1 m_2}.$$

6–20. Consider the motion of a charged particle in an electric field and a magnetic field subject to a damping force proportional to the first power of the velocity. Show that the steady-state current density

$$\mathbf{J} = Ne\mathbf{v}$$

is linearly related to the **E**-field as expressed by

$$|\mathbf{J}) = \boldsymbol{\sigma}\,|\,\mathbf{E}),$$

where $\boldsymbol{\sigma}$ is the d-c tensor conductivity operator. Obtain the expression for the elements of the matrix representation of the tensor conductivity.

6–21. Repeat Problem 6–20 for the complex a-c electric field $E = E_0 e^{i\omega t}$.

6–22. Consider the motion of a charged particle in a uniform magnetic field and a uniform gravitational field ($\mathbf{F} = m\mathbf{g}$) which is directed perpendicularly to the magnetic field. Show that positively and negatively charged particles have oppositely directed drift velocities in a direction perpendicular to the plane of the magnetic and gravitational fields.

6–23. Show that Eq. (6–123) follows from Eq. (6–122). [*Hint:* Remember that $L$ is a function of $x_i$ and $\dot{x}_i$ or of $q_i$ and $\dot{q}_i$, and that the time $t$ is being held fixed in $\partial L/\partial x_i$, etc.)

# 7

# *Central Force Field Motion*

The motion of a particle in a central force field is one of the most important problems in physics, for it is the type of motion which is, to a first approximation, performed by the planets with respect to the sun, satellites in their motion about the earth, and the motion of two charged particles with respect to each other.

## 7–1 General features of the motion: formal solution

Two features of the motion of a particle under the action of a central force have already been mentioned in the previous chapter. They are the two conservation theorems, the conservation of total energy and the conservation of orbital angular momentum.

Total energy is conserved since a central force,

$$\mathbf{F} = f(r)\mathbf{e}_r = f(r)\left(\frac{x}{r}\mathbf{i} + \frac{y}{r}\mathbf{j} + \frac{z}{r}\mathbf{k}\right), \tag{7-1}$$

whose magnitude is a function of the radial distance from the force center, is expressible as the negative gradient of the scalar function $U(r)$,

$$\mathbf{F} = -\boldsymbol{\nabla}U(r) = -\frac{\partial U}{\partial r}\mathbf{e}_r, \tag{7-2}$$

where $f(r) = -\partial U/\partial r$.

The curl of the gradient of a scalar function vanishes,

$$\boldsymbol{\nabla} \times \boldsymbol{\nabla}U = 0. \tag{7-3}$$

Hence $\boldsymbol{\nabla} \times \mathbf{F} = 0$, verifying that a central force whose magnitude is a function of the distance from the force center is a conservative force for which the principle of the conservation of total energy holds.

The principle of the conservation of orbital angular momentum follows from the fact that a central force does not exert any torque on the particle. For the problems in which the torque,

$$\mathbf{N} = \mathbf{r} \times \mathbf{F},$$

vanishes, the orbital angular momentum is a constant of the motion.

210

We should like to remind the reader that these conservation theorems follow directly from the equations of motion. It is therefore not necessary to attack a problem for which these conservation theorems hold by starting with the equations of motion, thereby invariably rederiving the conservation theorems all over again. The reader should acquire the habit of using conservation theorems, whenever they are applicable, as confidently as he does the equations of motion.

In the problem we are considering, it is possible to obtain a formal solution by utilizing the two conservation theorems without any further use of the equations of motion.

Since a central force is a function of the radial distance from the force center, we are inclined to utilize spherical coordinates for the kinematic description of the motion of the particle. The principle of the conservation of orbital angular momentum, $\mathbf{L} = m\mathbf{r} \times \mathbf{v}$, tells us, however, that the vectors $\mathbf{r}$ and $\mathbf{v}$ are at all times perpendicular to the angular momentum vector $\mathbf{L}$. Central force field motion thus takes place in a plane determined by the initial values of the position and velocity vectors, which also determine the direction of the angular momentum vector. If we choose the direction of $\mathbf{L}$ as the positive direction of the $z$-axis, then the motion takes place in the $xy$-plane for which the description of the motion in spherical coordinates is identical to its description in cylindrical coordinates.

The kinetic energy for $\theta = \pi/2$ is expressed by

$$T = \tfrac{1}{2}m\dot{r}^2 + \tfrac{1}{2}mr^2\dot{\phi}^2, \tag{7-4}$$

and the total energy by

$$E = \tfrac{1}{2}m\dot{r}^2 + \tfrac{1}{2}mr^2\dot{\phi}^2 + U(r), \tag{7-5}$$

where $r$ is the radial distance from the force center and $\phi$ the angle which the radius vector in the $xy$-plane makes with the fixed $x$-axis.

The $z$-component of the orbital angular momentum for this choice of $z$-axis is the magnitude of the total orbital angular momentum. We thus have

$$L_z = p_\phi = mr^2\dot{\phi} = h. \tag{7-6}$$

Solving Eq. (7–6) for $\dot{\phi}$ and inserting the dependence of $\dot{\phi}$ on $r$ into Eq. (7–5) yields

$$E = \tfrac{1}{2}m\dot{r}^2 + \frac{h^2}{2mr^2} + U(r). \tag{7-7}$$

This equation may be solved for $r$ and subsequently integrated to yield

$$\sqrt{\frac{2}{m}}\,(t - t_0) = \int_{r_0}^{r} \frac{dr}{\pm\sqrt{E - U(r) - h^2/2mr^2}}. \tag{7-8}$$

Since time is a continuously increasing variable, the positive square root must be used when $r$ increases and the negative square root when $r$ decreases.

Equation (7–8) formally yields $t$ as a function of $r$ or, when inverted, $r$ as a function of time $t$. A knowledge of $r(t)$ subsequently permits us, through the use of Eq. (7–6), to obtain $\phi(t)$. From

$$d\phi = \frac{h}{mr^2} \, dt$$

we obtain

$$\phi - \phi_0 = \int_{t_0}^{t} \frac{h \, dt}{mr^2(t)}. \tag{7–9}$$

In many applications it is not the knowledge of the dependence of the coordinates $r$ and $\phi$ on time but, rather, a knowledge of the orbit as provided by the dependence of $r$ on $\phi$ that is desired. This dependence may be obtained directly without first integrating Eqs. (7–8) and (7–9) and eliminating $t$ between them. Remembering that

$$dt = \frac{\sqrt{m/2} \, dr}{\pm\sqrt{E - U(r) - (h^2/2mr^2)}},$$

we obtain

$$d\phi = \frac{h}{mr^2} \, dt = \frac{h}{mr^2} \frac{\sqrt{m/2} \, dr}{\sqrt{E - U(r) - (h^2/2mr^2)}} \tag{7–10}$$

or

$$\phi - \phi_0 = \int_{r_0}^{r} \frac{h(dr/r^2)}{\pm\sqrt{2m[E - U(r) - (h^2/2mr^2)]}}$$

$$= \int_{u_0}^{u} \frac{h \, du}{\pm\sqrt{2m(E - U) - h^2u^2}}. \tag{7–11}$$

In the last step we have set $u = 1/r$. Since $u$ decreases as $r$ increases and vice versa—whereas for our choice of $z$-axis ($h$ positive), $\phi$ always increases [cf. Eq. (7–9)]—we must choose the plus sign for decreasing $u$ and the minus sign for increasing $u$. Equation (7–11) formally yields $\phi$ as a function of $r$ or, when inverted, the desired solution, $r$ as a function of $\phi$.

Having found $r$ as a function of $\phi$, we may in turn, if we desire, proceed to find the dependence of $r$ and $\phi$ on $t$ from

$$dt = \frac{mr^2(\phi) \, d\phi}{h}$$

or

$$t - t_0 = \int_{\phi_0}^{\phi} \frac{mr^2(\phi)}{h} \, d\phi. \tag{7–12}$$

We note that Eq. (7–10) may be rewritten in the form

$$U(r) = E - \frac{h^2}{2mr^2} - \frac{h^2}{2mr^4}\left(\frac{dr}{d\phi}\right)^2 = E - \frac{h^2}{2m} u^2 - \frac{h^2}{2m}\left(\frac{du}{d\phi}\right)^2, \tag{7–13}$$

which tells us that in general we can expect to obtain the dependence of the potential energy function on $r$ from a knowledge of the orbit, $u = u(\phi)$. An exception is the case of a circular orbit, which is a possible orbit for many different force functions.

The potential energy in turn permits us to determine the dependence of the central force on $r$ as

$$f(r) = -\frac{dU(r)}{dr}.$$

In terms of $u$ we find that

$$f(r) = -\frac{dU\left(\frac{1}{u}\right)}{du}\frac{du}{dr} = -u^2\frac{d}{du}\left[\frac{h^2u^2}{2m} + \frac{h^2}{2m}\left(\frac{du}{d\phi}\right)^2\right] \tag{7-14}$$

$$= -\frac{h^2}{m}u^3 - \frac{h^2}{m}u^2\frac{d^2u}{d\phi^2},$$

since

$$\frac{d}{du}\left(\frac{du}{d\phi}\right)^2 = \frac{d}{d\phi}\left(\frac{du}{d\phi}\right)^2\frac{d\phi}{du} = 2\frac{d^2u}{d\phi^2}.$$

Equation (7–14) is referred to as the *differential equation of the orbit*.

As an illustration, we proceed to find the central force under which a particle may move in an elliptic orbit with one of the foci of the orbit as the force center. This is the kind of orbit which the planets are observed to follow in their motion about the sun. (*Kepler's first law of planetary motion.*)

We recall that an ellipse is the locus of points the sum of whose distances from two fixed points, its foci, is a constant. If this constant is $2a$, then for the ellipse shown in Fig. 7–1 with foci along the $x$-axis, the semi-major axis is $a$ and the apsidal distances (distances of nearest and furthest approach from one of the foci) are $a(1 - \epsilon)$ and $a(1 + \epsilon)$. The semiminor axis is given by

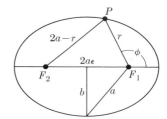

$$4a^2 - 4ar + r^2 = r^2 + 4a^2\epsilon^2 + 4a\epsilon r \cos \phi$$
or
$$r = \frac{a(1 - \epsilon^2)}{1 + \epsilon \cos \phi}$$

Fig. 7–1.     Geometry of the ellipse.

$$b = a\sqrt{1 - \epsilon^2}.$$

The equation of the ellipse in polar coordinates may be obtained by applying the law of cosines to the triangle formed by the point $P$ and the two foci. We find that

$$(2a - r)^2 = r^2 + (2a\epsilon)^2 + 2(2a\epsilon)r \cos \phi,$$

yielding

$$r = \frac{a(1 - \epsilon^2)}{1 + \epsilon \cos \phi},$$

or

$$u = \frac{1 + \epsilon \cos \phi}{a(1 - \epsilon^2)}. \tag{7-15}$$

This last equation yields

$$\left(\frac{du}{d\phi}\right)^2 = \frac{\epsilon^2 \sin^2 \phi}{a^2(1 - \epsilon^2)^2} = \frac{\epsilon^2(1 - \cos^2 \phi)}{a^2(1 - \epsilon^2)^2},$$

whence, from Eq. (7–13), we obtain

$$U\left(\frac{1}{u}\right) = E - \frac{h^2}{2m}\left[\frac{(1 + \epsilon \cos \phi)^2 + \epsilon^2(1 - \cos^2 \phi)}{a^2(1 - \epsilon^2)^2}\right]$$

$$= E + \frac{h^2}{2m}\left[\frac{1}{a^2(1 - \epsilon^2)} - \frac{2u}{a(1 - \epsilon^2)}\right]. \tag{7-16}$$

From $U(1/u) = U(r)$ we obtain the magnitude of the central force,

$$f(r) = -\frac{dU}{dr} = -\frac{h^2}{ma(1 - \epsilon^2)}\frac{1}{r^2}. \tag{7-17}$$

This in essence is *Newton's law of universal gravitation*, which states that the gravitational force with which two bodies attract each other varies inversely as the square of the distance between them.

An elliptic orbit, as we shall discuss in subsequent sections, is of course not the only orbit possible under the action of an inverse-square central force. We also note that, in dealing with atomic problems for which the orbit is not directly observable, we must find other ways for probing the fundamental law of force between atomic particles. This we shall discuss in Section 7–8.

## 7–2 General features of the orbits

In this section we shall discuss some of the qualitative features common to the possible orbits of a particle in a central force field.

We note that Eq. (7–13), expressing the principle of the conservation of total energy of the two-dimensional motion of a particle in a central force field, is also the energy conservation theorem for the one-dimensional motion of a particle in the effective potential energy field

$$U_{\text{eff}}(r) = U(r) + \frac{h^2}{2mr^2}. \tag{7-18}$$

The radial motion of a particle in a central force field is thus essentially identical to the one-dimensional motion of a particle in the effective potential energy field. The distinction between the two is that for the central force field problem the radial distance from the origin $r$ is positive definite:

$$r \geq 0.$$

Following our discussion in Section 4–7 for the one-dimensional motion of a particle, we realize that the motion in the radial direction is similarly either bounded or unbounded. It is unbounded if

$$E \geq U_{\text{eff}} \qquad (7\text{--}19)$$

for all

$$r \geq r_{\text{max}},$$

where $r_{\text{max}}$ is the maximum real root of the equation

$$E = U_{\text{eff}}(r). \qquad (7\text{--}20)$$

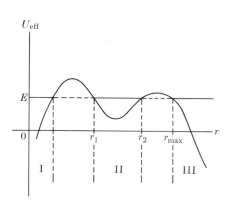

FIG. 7–2. Effective potential energy—energy diagram.

Such, for example, is the case in region III of Fig. 7–2.

Conversely, the motion is bounded if the particle is initially situated at a value of $r$ which lies between two positive real roots $r_1$ and $r_2$, $r_1 \leq r \leq r_2$, of Eq. (7–20), and the total energy satisfies the relation

$$U_{\text{eff}}(r) \leq E = U_{\text{eff}}(r_1) = U_{\text{eff}}(r_2).$$

This is the case in region II of Fig. 7–2.

If for either of the cases mentioned the particle finds itself in a physically accessible region which includes the origin, such as region I of Fig. 7–2, then it follows that the particle may pass through the origin. But if it can pass through the origin, then its angular momentum must necessarily be zero, unless of course $\dot{\phi}$ and hence $v$ becomes infinite. Classically therefore we cannot always treat a problem in which the particle passes through the origin or comes very close to the origin. For example, consider a particle moving in an attractive force field which has a singularity at the origin such that, for small values of $r$, the effective potential energy likewise becomes negatively infinite,

$$U(r) + \frac{h^2}{2mr^2} \to -\infty.$$

Such a particle will necessarily acquire a very large velocity on approaching the origin. For this reason alone, we should exclude such motion from meaningful classical considerations, for particles moving with high speeds require a relativistic description of their motion. Yet we find that a classical relativistic description is also insufficient. Highly energetic particles radiate energy and this radiation, which should somehow be included in the problem, cannot be treated classically. Finally, potential energies which have singularities at the origin yield a force acting on the particle which may vary considerably over the dimensions of the body on which it acts. Bodies which move in such rapidly varying fields cannot be treated as point particles.

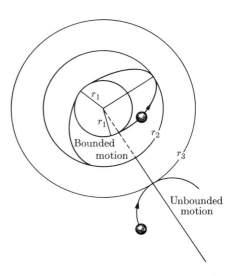

Even bodies of atomic dimensions, which we are clearly tempted to treat as particles at all times, we find, cannot be treated as particles if the force field acting on them varies considerably over their dimensions. This situation occurs when the bodies come very close to each other. Classical mechanics has indeed been found inadequate for the description of atomic problems for which quantum mechanics should be utilized.

Fig. 7–3. Illustration of the symmetry of the orbits about the turning points.

We shall therefore exercise great care in interpreting a classical description of such a problem. In general, we shall not consider them at all.

If the motion is bound, it means that the particle is confined to the region bounded by the two radial values $r_1$ and $r_2$, the turning points in the equivalent one-dimensional problem. For these apsidal radial values, the radial component of the velocity vanishes and the particle moves at those points tangentially to the circles of radii $r_1$ and $r_2$ bounding the region to which its motion is confined.

Since changing the radial component of the velocity at any point will cause the particle to retrace its radial motion yet leave the angular velocity

$$\dot{\phi} = \frac{h}{mr^2} = \frac{\mathbf{v} \cdot \mathbf{e}_\phi}{r}$$

the same, it follows that the orbits will be symmetric with respect to the position vectors of the turning points (see Fig. 7–3).

The unbounded motion of a particle in a central force field, since it has only one turning point, will have only one symmetry axis, whereas the bounded motion can have either a finite or an infinite number of symmetry axes depending on whether the orbit is closed or not. In Fig. 7–4, we indicate a number of special cases when the orbit has one, two, or three symmetry axes. If the orbit is closed, which occurs whenever the angle $\Psi$ between two successive symmetry axes satisfies the relation

$$n\Psi = 2m\pi, \qquad n, m \text{ integers},$$

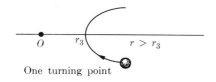

One turning point

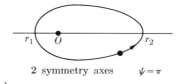

2 symmetry axes     $\psi = \pi$

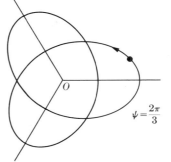

FIG. 7–4.    Examples of orbits
with one, two, and three symmetry
axes.

3 symmetry axes     $\psi = \dfrac{2\pi}{3}$

then a finite number of symmetry axes exist. When this condition is not satisfied, the motion will not repeat itself. Such aperiodic motion will contain an infinite number of symmetry axes.

In those problems where the orbit is closed, we can speak of the area of the closed orbit and a period of the motion. We find that the period of the motion $\tau$, the time for the particle to complete one closed orbit, may be obtained through the use of Eq. (7–6).

To within first-order infinitesimals, the infinitesimal area swept out by the radial vector (see Fig. 7–5) is given by

$$A = \frac{1}{2} r(r + \Delta r)\, \Delta\phi = \frac{1}{2} r^2\, \Delta\phi = \frac{h}{2m}\, \Delta t. \tag{7–21}$$

Thus we obtain for the period of the motion the relation

$$\tau = \int \frac{2m\, dA}{h} = \frac{2mA}{h}. \tag{7–22}$$

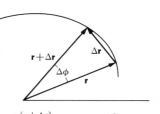

$$\Delta A = \frac{r(r + \Delta r)}{2} \sin (\Delta\phi) = \tfrac{1}{2} r^2 \Delta\phi$$

FIG. 7–5. Area swept out by
the radial vector.

Equation (7–21) states that the areal velocity swept out by the position vector is a constant:

$$\frac{dA}{dt} = \frac{h}{2m}.$$

This is *Kepler's second law of planetary motion.*

## 7–3 Stability of circular orbits

Circular orbits are possible whenever the effective potential energy

$$U_{\text{eff}}(r) = U(r) + \frac{h^2}{2mr^2}$$

has a maximum or minimum value. It should be clear from our discussion of the one-dimensional motion of a particle in a potential energy field that a circular orbit will be stable if its radial value yields a minimum value for the effective potential energy. It will be unstable if it yields a maximum.

For any circular orbit we must, of course, have

$$\frac{dU_{\text{eff}}}{dr} = \frac{dU}{dr} - \frac{h^2}{mr^3} = 0$$

or

$$f(r) = -\frac{h^2}{mr^3} = -mr\dot{\phi}^2. \tag{7–23}$$

This is the radial equation of motion, which states that, for a particle moving in a circular orbit, the force must equal the mass multiplied by the centripetal acceleration.

If we disturb a stable circular orbit, then, for small perturbations, the radial motion is expected to perform simple harmonic oscillations about the radial value of the stable circular orbit. The frequency of this oscillation, in this as in the equivalent one-dimensional problem, depends on the value of the second derivative of the effective potential energy evaluated for the radial value of the stable circular orbit. Specifically,

$$m\left(\frac{2\pi}{\tau}\right)^2 = \frac{d^2U_{\text{eff}}}{dr^2}$$

or

$$\tau = 2\pi\sqrt{\frac{m}{d^2U_{\text{eff}}/dr^2}}. \tag{7–24}$$

The problem of stable circular orbits or of stable orbits in general is of more than academic interest. It is a problem that invariably has to be considered in the design of instruments involving the motion of charged particles. As an illustration, we consider the motion of particles of charge $e$ between the plates of a cylindrical capacitor (Fig. 7–6). The electric field between the plates of such a capacitor varies inversely as the distance $r$ from the axis of the capacitor:

$$\mathbf{E} = +\frac{k}{r}\,\mathbf{e}_r. \tag{7–25}$$

The direction of the electric field is such as to yield a force $\mathbf{F} = e\mathbf{E} = (-\alpha/r)\mathbf{e}_r$

on the particle, a force which is directed toward the axis of the capacitor, that is, $\alpha > 0$.

A charged particle entering the region between the plates of the capacitor at the point $P_1$ (Fig. 7–6) perpendicular to the radius to that point, will move in a circle of radius $r$ if the radial force satisfies the equation

$$-f(r) = \frac{\alpha}{r} = mr\dot{\phi}^2, \qquad \text{where} \qquad \alpha = ek,$$

whence we obtain the relation

$$T = \tfrac{1}{2}m(r\dot{\phi})^2 = \tfrac{1}{2}\alpha \qquad (7\text{–}26)$$

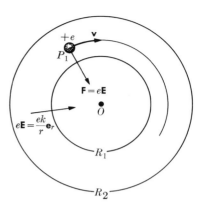

FIG. 7–6. Motion in a circular orbit in a radial electric field.

for the kinetic energy of the particle.

Any similarly charged particle of slightly different energy will not, of course, follow the same circular orbit. A sector of a cylindrical capacitor may thus be utilized as an energy filter, a device which is capable of selecting from a host of particles the ones having a specific energy.

In principle this is fine. In practice, however, it is not possible to have all the particles enter the electric field moving in the same direction or with the same energy. Most of the particles will move at a slight angle with respect to the ideal direction, and will have an energy deviating slightly from the desired energy. Quite naturally, any such particle will not be passed through the ideal filter. Such an ideal filter is thus not very practical, since the intensity of the particles passing through it will be very small. Through proper selection of the exit slit, however, we can increase the intensity by also permitting the particles which enter the slit at point $P_1$ at a slight angle from the ideal direction to come out.

That this is possible follows from the fact that the circular orbit for this problem is stable. All the particles whose velocity vector makes a slight angle with the ideal direction will oscillate about the stable circular orbit and cross the orbit a short time later (Fig. 7–7). To a first approximation, this crossing will occur at the same time and at the same point for all the particles whose entering direction makes some small angle $\beta$ with the ideal direction. By choosing the exit slit at the crossover point we can increase the intensity of the outcoming beam of particles. The widths of the entrance and exit slits will control the uncertainty in the energy and direction of the outgoing particles.

We proceed to find the angle $\Psi$ at which the exit slit should be placed. It is the angle which the position vector to the point $P_2$ at which the slightly diverging particles entering at $P_1$ will be focused makes with the radius vector to the entrance point $P_1$.

To find $\Psi$ we require the time which the particles take to go from the point $P_1$ to the point $P_2$. This time is equal to one-half the period of the oscillatory motion about the stable circular orbit, and is thus given by

$$t = \tfrac{1}{2}\tau = \pi\sqrt{\frac{m}{d^2U_{\text{eff}}/dr^2}}. \qquad (7\text{-}27)$$

For the effective potential energy which the particles have between the plates,

$$\frac{dU_{\text{eff}}}{dr} = \frac{\alpha}{r} - \frac{h^2}{mr^3}$$

and

$$\frac{d^2U_{\text{eff}}}{dr^2} = -\frac{\alpha}{r^2} + \frac{3h^2}{mr^4}. \qquad (7\text{-}28)$$

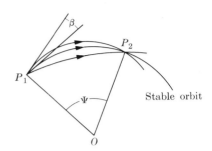

Fig. 7–7. Motion about a stable circular orbit.

By Eq. (7–26), we have

$$\frac{h^2}{mr^4} = \frac{(mr\dot\phi)^2 r^2}{mr^4} = \frac{\alpha}{r^2},$$

whence we obtain

$$\frac{d^2U_{\text{eff}}}{dr^2} = \frac{2\alpha}{r^2} = \frac{2mv^2}{r^2}, \qquad (7\text{-}29)$$

and subsequently, by Eq. (7–27),

$$t = \pi\sqrt{\frac{r^2}{2v^2}} = \frac{\pi r}{\sqrt{2}\,v}. \qquad (7\text{-}30)$$

In this period of time the particles in the circular orbit traverse a distance

$$d = vt = \pi r/\sqrt{2}.$$

Point $P_2$ is thus found to be at an angle

$$\Psi = \frac{d}{r} = \frac{\pi}{\sqrt{2}} \text{ radians} \qquad (7\text{-}31)$$

from the point $P_1$.

### 7–4 Newton's law of revolving orbits

We note that the effective potential energy for the radial motion of a particle in a central force field,

$$U_{\text{eff}}(r) = U(r) + \frac{h^2}{2mr^2},$$

is also the effective potential energy for the central-force-field motion of a particle of mass $m$ in the potential energy field,

$$U'(r) = U(r) + \frac{\kappa}{2mr^2},$$

having an orbital angular momentum $h'$, such that

$$h'^2 = h^2 - \kappa. \tag{7-32}$$

The radial solution to the latter problem is obtainable from the conservation theorem for energy,

$$E = U(r) + \frac{\kappa}{2mr^2} + \frac{1}{2}m\dot{r}^2 + \frac{h'^2}{2mr^2}, \tag{7-33}$$

and from the angular momentum,

$$mr^2\dot{\phi}' = h', \tag{7-34}$$

where $\phi'$ is the angle variable for this latter problem. So long as*

$$h'^2 + \kappa > 0, \tag{7-35}$$

this radial solution as a function of time is the same as the radial solution for a particle having orbital angular momentum $h$ moving in the potential energy field $U(r)$.

The solutions in terms of the angle variables $\phi$ and $\phi'$ will not, however, be the same. This follows from the fact that

$$d\phi' = \frac{h'\,dt}{mr^2} = \frac{h'}{h}\frac{h\,dt}{mr^2} = \frac{h'}{h}\,d\phi$$

and that $r(t)$ is the same for the two problems. Thus we have found that

$$d\phi' = \frac{h'}{h}\,d\phi$$

or

$$\phi' = \frac{h'}{h}\,\phi. \tag{7-36}$$

If the equation for the orbit of the particle moving in the potential energy field $U(r)$ with orbital angular momentum $h$ is

$$r = r(\phi),$$

then for the particle moving in the potential energy field

$$U(r) + \frac{\kappa}{2mr^2}$$

with an orbital angular momentum $h'$, where $h'^2 = h^2 - k$, the orbit equation is given by

$$r = r\left(\frac{h\phi'}{h'}\right) = r\left[\frac{\sqrt{\kappa + h'^2}}{h'}\,\phi'\right]. \tag{7-37}$$

---

* Mathematically this restriction is not necessary, for $h$ and $h'$ may be imaginary.

This can be seen by comparing Eqs. (7–13) for the two orbits, *viz:*

and

$$\frac{du}{d\phi} = \pm \frac{1}{h} \sqrt{2m \left[ E - U(u) + \frac{h^2}{2m} u^2 \right]}$$

$$\frac{du}{d\phi'} = \pm \frac{1}{h'} \sqrt{2m \left[ E - U(u) + \frac{h^2}{2m} u^2 \right]}.$$

As an example, consider the elliptical orbit which we found may be followed by a particle in an inverse-square force field. If the motion of this particle were to take place under the additional action of a central force field varying as the inverse cube of the radial distance, then the equation of the orbit for a particle having the angular momentum $h'$ would be given by

$$r = \frac{a(1 - \epsilon^2)}{1 - \epsilon \cos \left[ (\sqrt{\kappa + h'^2}/h')\phi' \right]}. \tag{7–38}$$

This orbit with respect to a coordinate system which at time $t$ is rotating with an angular velocity

$$\boldsymbol{\omega} = \lambda\dot{\phi}'\mathbf{k}, \tag{7–39}$$

where

$$\lambda = 1 - \frac{\sqrt{\kappa + h'^2}}{h'}, \tag{7–40}$$

and with respect to which the motion of the particle is described in terms of the polar coordinates $r$ and $\theta$, is the same as the orbit which the particle would follow under the action of only the inverse-square force law,

$$r = \frac{a(1 - \epsilon^2)}{1 - \epsilon \cos \theta}; \tag{7–41}$$

hence the descriptive title, *revolving orbits.*

## 7–5 Motion in an inverse-square force field

The motion of a particle in an inverse-square force field is the most important central force field problem. The gravitational force between bodies and the electrical force between charged particles are examples of such a force. While the gravitational force is always an attractive force, the electrical force may be either attractive or repulsive, depending on the charge on the interacting particles.

Before proceeding to obtain the equation for the orbit of a particle moving in an inverse-square force field, we shall investigate qualitatively the possible orbits of such motion.

For a repulsive force, the effective potential energy for the equivalent one-dimensional problem is given by

$$U_{\text{eff}} = U(r) + \frac{h^2}{2mr^2} = -\frac{k}{r} + \frac{h^2}{2mr^2}, \qquad k < 0. \tag{7–42}$$

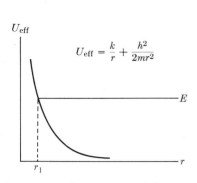

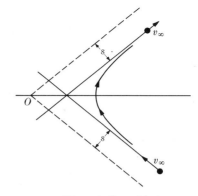

FIG. 7–8. Effective potential energy for a repulsive inverse-square force.

FIG. 7–9. Hyperbolic orbit in a repulsive inverse-square force field.

A plot of $U_{\text{eff}}(r)$ as a function of $r$ (Fig. 7–8) shows that there exists only one turning point, $r = r_1$, for which $E = U_{\text{eff}}(r)$. The motion for all possible values of the total energy, which for the effective potential energy above must be positive definite, is therefore unbounded. The orbit therefore has only one symmetry axis which passes through the point of closest approach, $r = r_1$ (Fig. 7–9). For large values of $r$, for which the magnitude of the inverse-square force approaches zero, the orbit will asymptotically approach a straight line whose distance $s$ from the center of the force is given by

$$mv_\infty s = h, \qquad (7\text{–}43)$$

which expresses the conservation of the orbital angular momentum, $v_\infty$ being the speed of the particle for large values of $r$. By the conservation of energy, $v_\infty$ is given by

$$\tfrac{1}{2}mv_\infty^2 = E. \qquad (7\text{–}44)$$

If the inverse-square central force is attractive, then the effective potential energy is

$$U_{\text{eff}}(r) = -\frac{k}{r} + \frac{h^2}{2mr^2}, \qquad k > 0. \qquad (7\text{–}45)$$

A plot of this effective potential energy function (Fig. 7–10) reveals that the motion is unbounded for all positive values of the energy, $E \geq 0$, and bounded for negative values of the total energy, $E < 0$. For the minimum value of the total energy which the particle can have, the motion follows a circular orbit. The value of the total energy for which this occurs is given by

$$E_{\text{min}} = [U_{\text{eff}}(r)]_{\text{min}} = U_{\text{eff}}(r_1),$$

where $r_1$ is the value of $r$ at which the effective potential energy has a minimum.

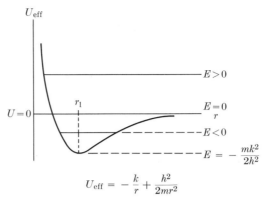

$$U_{\text{eff}} = -\frac{k}{r} + \frac{h^2}{2mr^2}$$

FIG. 7–10. Effective potential energy for an attractive inverse-square force.

We find $r_1$ to be the root of the equation

$$\frac{dU_{\text{eff}}}{dr} = 0 = \frac{k}{r^2} - \frac{h^2}{mr^3}. \tag{7–46}$$

That is,

$$r_1 = \frac{h^2}{mk}, \tag{7–47}$$

yielding, for the minimum allowed energy,

$$E_{\min} = U_{\text{eff}}\left(\frac{h^2}{mk^2}\right) = -\frac{mk^2}{2h^2}. \tag{7–48}$$

We proceed to show that the orbits which a particle may follow under the action of an inverse-square law of force are conic sections.

Specifically, we shall find that the orbit for an attractive force is

a hyperbola for $E > 0$,

a parabola for $E = 0$,

an ellipse for $-\dfrac{mk^2}{2h^2} \le E < 0.$

These results follow from the solution to the problem as provided by Eq. (7–11). For the inverse-square force for which $U(r) = -k/r$, Eq. (7–11) becomes

$$\phi - \phi_0 = \int_{u_0}^{u} \frac{h\,du}{\pm\sqrt{2m(E + ku) - h^2u^2}}$$

$$= \int_{u_0}^{u} \frac{du}{\pm\sqrt{(mk\epsilon/h^2)^2 - [u - (mk/h^2)]^2}}, \tag{7–49}$$

where we have set

$$\left(\frac{mk\epsilon}{h^2}\right)^2 = \frac{2mE}{h^2} + \frac{m^2k^2}{h^4}. \tag{7–50}$$

We now make the standard substitution in order to simplify the integrand. We set

$$u - \frac{mk}{h^2} = +\frac{mk\epsilon}{h^2}\cos\theta \quad \text{and} \quad du = -\frac{mk\epsilon}{h^2}\sin\theta\,d\theta.$$

We find that for a proper choice of $\theta_0$ (cf. Section 4–9), $\theta$ will increase continuously as $\phi$ does. With this substitution then, Eq. (7–49) reduces to

$$\phi - \phi_0 = \int_{\theta_0}^{\theta} d\theta = \theta - \theta_0$$

or

$$\cos^{-1}\left[\frac{h^2}{mk\epsilon}\left(u - \frac{mk}{h^2}\right)\right] = \phi - \phi_0 + \theta_0.$$

Solving for $u$ yields

$$u = \frac{mk}{h^2}[1 + \epsilon\cos(\phi - \phi_0 + \theta_0)], \tag{7–51}$$

where $\epsilon$ was defined in Eq. (7–50) as

$$\epsilon = \sqrt{1 + (2Eh^2/mk^2)}. \tag{7–52}$$

If we choose to measure $\phi$ from a symmetry axis, for which choice $r(\phi) = r(-\phi)$, then obviously we must have $\phi_0 = \theta_0$ such that

$$u = \frac{mk}{h^2}(1 + \epsilon\cos\phi)$$

or

$$r = \frac{h^2/mk}{1 + \epsilon\cos\phi}. \tag{7–53}$$

Equation (7–53) is the general equation of a conic* in cylindrical coordinates.

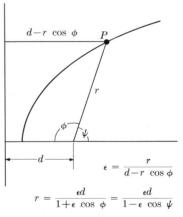

FIG. 7–11.  Geometry of a conic section.

---

* A conic section is the locus of points the ratio of whose distances from a straight line and a fixed point is a constant. From Fig. 7–11 we find this definition to yield either

$$\epsilon = \frac{r}{d - r\cos\phi} \quad \text{or} \quad r = \frac{\epsilon d}{1 + \epsilon\cos\phi},$$

depending on the definition of the angle $\phi$.

If the eccentricity $\epsilon > 1$, which occurs for $E > 0$, the orbit is a hyperbola. If $\epsilon = 1$ or $E = 0$, the orbit is a parabola, whereas for

$$0 < \epsilon < 1 \quad \text{or} \quad -mk^2/2h^2 < E < 0,$$

the orbit is an ellipse. When $E = -mk^2/2h^2$, $\epsilon = 0$ and the orbit, as previously found, is a circle.

## 7–6 Bounded motion: Kepler's third law of planetary motion

The facts that the orbits of the bounded motion of the planets about the sun are ellipses and that the radial vector sweeps out equal areas in equal times were deduced by Kepler from the observed motion of the planets. He also announced a third law of planetary motion, which we shall proceed to show is satisfied by a particle moving in an elliptical orbit under the action of an inverse-square central force field.

*Kepler's third law* states that the period of the motion is proportional to the three-half power of the semimajor axis.

The semimajor axis of an ellipse is the arithmetic mean of the minimum and maximum displacements of the particle from the force center (Fig. 7–12):

$$a = \tfrac{1}{2}(r_{\min} + r_{\max}).$$

From Eq. (7–53) for the ellipse, the semimajor axis is found to be expressible as

$$a = \frac{h^2}{2mk}\left(\frac{1}{1 + \epsilon} + \frac{1}{1 - \epsilon}\right) = \frac{h^2}{mk}\frac{1}{1 - \epsilon^2}. \tag{7–54}$$

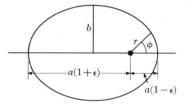

$$r = \frac{a(1 - \epsilon^2)}{1 - \epsilon \cos \phi}, \quad A = \pi ab.$$

FIG. 7–12. Geometry of an elliptical orbit.

The period of motion for a closed orbit in a central force field was found in Section 7–2 to be given by $\tau = 2mA/h$. Since the area of an ellipse is $A = \pi ab$, where the semiminor axis $b = a\sqrt{1 - \epsilon^2}$ (cf. Fig. 7–1), we indeed find, through the use of Eq. (7–54), that

$$\tau = \frac{2\pi m}{h} a^2 \sqrt{1 - \epsilon^2} = \frac{2\pi ma^2}{h}\sqrt{\frac{h^2}{mka}} = \frac{2\pi m^{1/2}}{k^{1/2}} a^{3/2}. \tag{7–55}$$

## 7–7 The virial theorem

Another very useful result for the bound motion of a particle in an inverse-square law is the fact that the magnitude of the average potential energy is twice that of the average kinetic energy. There exist several ways in which this may be shown. We shall proceed by actually evaluating the average. By Eq.

(7–13), the kinetic energy is found to be expressed by

$$T = E - U = \frac{h^2}{2mr^2}\left[1 + \frac{1}{r^2}\left(\frac{dr}{d\phi}\right)^2\right] = \frac{h^2}{2m}\left[u^2 + \left(\frac{du}{d\phi}\right)^2\right], \quad (7\text{–}56)$$

or, through the use of Eq. (7–53), by

$$T = \frac{h^2}{2m}\left(\frac{mk}{h^2}\right)^2 [(1 - \epsilon\cos\phi)^2 + \epsilon^2\sin^2\phi]. \quad (7\text{–}57)$$

The average kinetic energy $\langle T \rangle$ is defined by the equation

$$\langle T \rangle = \frac{1}{\tau}\int_0^\tau T\,dt = \frac{1}{\tau}\int_0^{2\pi} T\frac{dt}{d\phi}\,d\phi. \quad (7\text{–}58)$$

Thus since

$$\frac{d\phi}{dt} = \frac{1}{dt/d\phi} = \frac{hu^2}{m},$$

it follows that

$$\langle T \rangle = \frac{1}{\tau}\int_0^{2\pi}\frac{mT}{hu^2}\,d\phi = \frac{h}{2\tau}\int_0^{2\pi}\left[1 + \frac{e^2\sin^2\phi}{(1-\epsilon\cos\phi)^2}\right]d\phi.$$

Integrating the second term by parts yields

$$\int_0^{2\pi}\frac{\epsilon^2\sin^2\phi}{(1-\epsilon\cos\phi)^2}\,d\phi = -\left.\frac{\epsilon\sin\phi}{1-\epsilon\cos\phi}\right|_0^{2\pi} + \int_0^{2\pi}\frac{\epsilon\cos\phi}{1-\epsilon\cos\phi}\,d\phi$$

$$= \int_0^{2\pi}\left(\frac{1}{1-\epsilon\cos\phi} - 1\right)d\phi.$$

We thus obtain

$$\langle T \rangle = \frac{h}{2\tau}\int_0^{2\pi}\frac{d\phi}{1-\epsilon\cos\phi} = \frac{h}{2\tau}\frac{2\pi}{\sqrt{1-\epsilon^2}}. \quad (7\text{–}59)$$

Similarly, we find that the average potential energy

$$\langle U \rangle = \frac{1}{\tau}\int_0^\tau U\,dt = \frac{1}{\tau}\int_0^{2\pi} U\frac{dt}{d\phi}\,d\phi = -\frac{k}{\tau}\int_0^{2\pi}\frac{um}{hu^2}\,d\phi$$

$$= -\frac{h}{\tau}\int_0^{2\pi}\frac{d\phi}{1-\epsilon\cos\phi} = -\frac{h}{\tau}\frac{2\pi}{\sqrt{1-\epsilon^2}}. \quad (7\text{–}60)$$

From a comparison of Eqs. (7–59) and (7–60) we realize that

$$2\langle T \rangle = -\langle U \rangle. \quad (7\text{–}61)$$

This result follows also from the more general virial theorem which relates the average kinetic and potential energies of the motion of a particle in a finite region of space under the action of a conservative force. Equation (7–61) is known as the virial theorem for the inverse-square central force.

## 7–8 Unbounded motion: scattering

In Section 7–1 we found it possible to determine the dependence of the potential energy function on the radial distance $r$ from a knowledge of the orbit followed by a particle moving in that conservative force field. Like Newton, we deduced the dependence of the gravitational force on $r$ from a knowledge of the planetary orbits as stated by Kepler.

Unfortunately, when we deal with atomic particles, we cannot always observe the orbits. For such particles, we are thus unable to utilize the orbit method for determining the law of force. Where atomic particles are concerned, another method—*the method of scattering*—is therefore employed for probing the dependence of the potential energy function on the distance of the particle from the force or scattering center.

In a scattering experiment, a particle is fired at another particle (assumed in this discussion to be fixed) and the deflection of the first or projectile particle is measured. This particle, being initially very (infinitely) far from the force center, will naturally follow an unbounded orbit. It will thus, at some later time at the point $r_{\min}$ of closest approach to the force center, assume a zero radial velocity. The subsequent motion will carry the particle away from the force center on an orbit along which it will finally assume a velocity whose magnitude is equal to its initial magnitude, and whose direction makes an angle $\theta$ with its initial direction of motion (Fig. 7–13).

The angle $\theta$ is referred to as the *scattering angle*, and as can be seen from Fig. 7–13, which shows the orbit due to a repulsive force, it is expressible in terms of the magnitude of the angle $\phi_0$ which the initial and final radius vectors from the force center make with the symmetry axis. That is,

$$\theta = \pi - 2\phi_0. \qquad (7\text{–}62)$$

It can be shown* that a knowledge of the dependence of the scattering angle $\theta$ as a function of the angular momentum $h$ or the *impact parameter*

$$s = \frac{h}{mv_0}, \qquad (7\text{–}63)$$

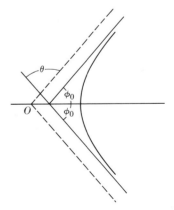

Fig. 7–13. Hyperbolic orbit in a repulsive inverse-square force field.

---

* Landau and Lifshitz, *Mechanics*. Reading, Mass.: Addison-Wesley, 1960, page 50, Problem 7.

where $v_0$ is the initial velocity of the projectile particle, is sufficient to yield the dependence of the potential energy as a function of $r$ for all values of $r > r_{\min}$.

A scattering experiment thus requires the firing of particles of the same energy but different values of impact parameter at the target particle. In any experiment, these particles are simultaneously fired at the target in the form of a beam of particles of intensity $I$ per unit area per second, which have previously been filtered to have the same kinetic energy.

When performing a scattering experiment with many particles simultaneously, it is not $\theta$ as a function of $s$ which is measured directly but rather the distribution of scattered particles per unit solid angle per unit time. This information is contained within the quantity $\sigma(\theta, \varphi)$ called the *differential scattering cross section*. It is defined as the number of particles scattered per unit solid angle per unit time in the direction specified by the spherical angles $\theta$ and $\varphi$, divided by the intensity $I$ of the incoming beam of particles.

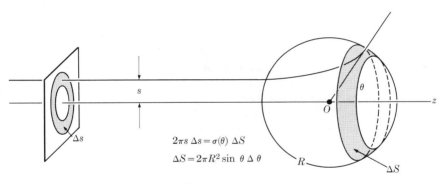

$$2\pi s \,\Delta s = \sigma(\theta)\,\Delta S$$

$$\Delta S = 2\pi R^2 \sin\,\theta\,\Delta\,\theta$$

FIGURE 7–14

For a central force the distribution, as can be seen from symmetry considerations, does not depend on $\varphi$. The distribution of scattered particles should therefore be the same within a ring of area

$$2\pi R^2 \sin\theta\,d\theta$$

on a large sphere of radius $R$ whose center is located at the scattering center (Fig. 7–14).

Assuming that the particles follow stable orbits, we should expect the particles scattered within this ring to come from a ring of radius $s$ and width $\Delta s$, that is, from an area $2\pi s\,\Delta s$ of the incident beam. We thus can set

$$I(2\pi s\,\Delta s) = -I\sigma(\theta)\,\Delta\Omega$$

or

$$\sigma(\theta) = -\frac{s}{\sin\theta}\frac{ds}{d\theta}, \qquad (7\text{–}64)$$

where $\Delta\Omega$, the solid angle subtended by the area $\Delta S$ at the origin, is

$$\Delta\Omega = \frac{\Delta S}{R^2} = \frac{2\pi R^2 \sin\theta \, \Delta\theta}{R^2}.$$

The minus sign is introduced because $\theta$ usually decreases as $s$ increases; that is, the larger the impact parameter the smaller the angle through which the particles will be scattered (see Fig. 7–15).

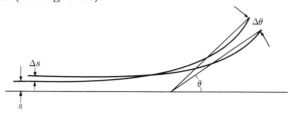

FIG. 7–15. Two orbits for slightly different values of impact parameter.

We are thus, in principle, in a position to find the impact parameter $s$ as a function of the scattering angle $\theta$ by measuring $\sigma(\theta)$.

We note as discussed previously that, for an attractive potential with a strong singularity at the origin, the $s = 0$ or $h = 0$ particles cannot be treated classically. We shall not, therefore, consider such attractive forces.

In practice, one does not obtain $s$ as a function of $\theta$ from the measured differential scattering cross section, but rather one compares the experimentally measured differential scattering cross section with the cross sections which one computes theoretically for various central forces. As an illustration, we proceed to compute the differential scattering cross section to be expected for particles moving in a repulsive inverse-square central force. Since the incoming particles have some kinetic energy, the total energy is positive definite and the resulting orbits are hyperbolas.

The equation for the orbit is provided by Eq. (7–53), from which we obtain the values of the angle $\phi_0$ for which the particle will have a very large radial distance. They are the roots of the equation

$$1 - \epsilon\cos\phi = 0;$$

that is,

$$\phi_0 = \cos^{-1}\left(\frac{1}{\epsilon}\right). \tag{7–65}$$

The relationship between the scattering angle and $\phi_0$ was previously found to be given by

$$\theta = \pi - 2\phi_0.$$

We thus find that

$$\frac{1}{\epsilon} = \cos\phi_0 = \sin\frac{\theta}{2},$$

or, through the use of Eq. (7–52), that

$$\sin \frac{\theta}{2} = \frac{k}{\sqrt{k^2 + 2mv_0^2 Es^2}} . \tag{7–66}$$

Differentiating this latter equation with respect to $\theta$ yields

$$\frac{1}{2} \cos \frac{\theta}{2} = \frac{-2kmv_0^2 Es(ds/d\theta)}{(k^2 + 2mv_0^2 Es^2)^{3/2}}$$

or

$$\frac{ds}{d\theta} = -\frac{k^2}{4s} \frac{\cos (\theta/2)}{mv_0^2 E} \epsilon^3.$$

Hence by Eq. (7–64) we obtain the differential scattering cross section

$$\sigma(\theta) = \frac{k^2 \epsilon^3}{4mv_0^2 E} \frac{\cos (\theta/2)}{2 \sin (\theta/2) \cos (\theta/2)} = \frac{k^2}{8mv_0^2 E} \frac{1}{\sin^4 (\theta/2)} . \tag{7–67}$$

Since in this problem $E = \frac{1}{2}mv_0^2$, this result reduces to

$$\sigma(\theta) = \frac{k^2}{16E^2} \csc^4 \frac{\theta}{2} . \tag{7–68}$$

This result for the differential scattering cross section was applied by Rutherford in interpreting his experiments on the scattering of $\alpha$-particles by atomic nuclei. Fortunately, the classical Rutherford scattering cross section as given by (7–68) agrees with the quantum mechanical result for the differential scattering cross section. Thus Rutherford was able to obtain agreement with his experiment, and thereby draw correct conclusions about the structure of the atom and the size of its nucleus (Problem 7–15).

## Problems

7–1. A particle follows a circular orbit under the action of an attractive central force which is directed toward a point on the circle. Show that the magnitude of the force varies as the inverse fifth power of the distance.

7–2. Find the central forces under whose action a particle will follow the following orbits:

(a)  $r = a(1 + \cos \theta)$     (b)  $r = a \exp (b\theta)$     (c)  $\dfrac{1}{r} = A \cosh \alpha(\theta - \theta_0)$

7–3. A particle moves under the action of the central force derivable from the potential energy function

$$U(r) = -\frac{k}{r} e^{-\alpha r}, \qquad k, \alpha > 0.$$

Discuss qualitatively the nature of the orbits. Investigate the existence of stable orbits.

7–4. Investigate the motion of a particle of mass $m$ in a repulsive inverse-cube law force field.

7–5. Repeat Problem 7–4 for an attractive inverse-cube law force field.

7–6. Find the differential scattering cross section $\sigma(\theta)$ for the motion of a particle in a repulsive inverse-cube force field. [*Hint:* Use Newton's law of revolving orbits.]

7–7. (a) Obtain the conditions on the $k$'s for which the circular orbits for the following central force fields will be stable.

    (i)   $U(r) = \frac{1}{2}kr^2$

    (ii)  $U(r) = (k_1/r^2) + (k_2/r^4)$

    (iii) $U(r) = -a/r^k,\ a > 0$

(b) Find the period of small oscillations about the stable circular orbits.

7–8. Find the range of a projectile having initial velocity $\mathbf{v}_0$ in the equatorial plane, taking into consideration the rotation of the earth. Consider the problem (a) in the frame of reference of a coordinate system rotating with the earth, and (b) with respect to a stationary coordinate system fixed at the center of the earth.

7–9. A particle is dropped from a height $h$ above the earth, where $h \ll R$, the radius of the earth (Fig. 7–16). Locate the point where the particle will hit the earth. (a) Consider the problem with respect to a fixed coordinate system, treating the problem as the motion of the particle in a central force field. [Note that the relative velocity of the particle with respect to the earth was initially zero.] (b) Consider the motion with respect to a coordinate system rotating with the earth.

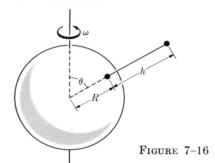

FIGURE 7–16

7–10. Find the escape velocity of a particle from the surface of the earth, given that the gravitational constant is

$$G = 6.67 \times 10^{-11}\ \frac{\text{n-m}^2}{\text{kg}^2}.$$

7–11. A small satellite of mass $m$, negligible compared with that of the earth, is projected with a speed $v$ parallel to the earth's surface at a height of 320 km. (a) Calculate the value of $v$ required to put the satellite into a circular orbit. (b) What is the escape velocity of the satellite?

Given that the satellite is projected at a height of 320 km and is observed later at a height of 1000 km when farthest from the earth's surface, calculate (c) the eccentricity of its orbit, (d) its velocity of projection, and (e) the total energy of the satellite in its elliptical orbit. Take the mass of the earth as $5.98 \times 10^{24}$ kg, its radius $6.38 \times 10^6$ m, and the gravitational constant $G$ as $6.67 \times 10^{-11}$ n-m$^2$/kg$^2$.

7–12. An artificial satellite is moving in the elliptical orbit

$$r = \frac{a(1 - \epsilon^2)}{1 - \epsilon \cos \phi}.$$

Find the minimum increase in the satellite's speed as a function of $r$ and $\phi$ that will allow the satellite to escape. For which values of $r$ and $\phi$ will this minimum escape velocity be a minimum?

7–13. (a) Find the distance of closest approach of an $\alpha$-particle of mass $m$ and initial speed $v_0$ to a nucleus of charge $Ze$. (b) What is this distance of closest approach for an $\alpha$-particle of mass $6 \times 10^{-27}$ kg and speed $v_0 = 1.6 \times 10^7$ m/sec incident on a gold foil ($Z = 79$)? [Take $e = 1.6 \times 10^{-19}$ coul, $1/4\pi\epsilon_0 = 9 \times 10^9$ n-m$^2$/coul$^2$.]

7–14. Find the distance of closest approach of a particle in a repulsive inverse-square force field as a function of the scattering angle.

7–15. Consider the motion of a simple pendulum on the surface of the earth, taking into consideration the rotation of the earth. Show that the plane of oscillation of the pendulum precesses (Foucault pendulum).

7–16. A central force potential frequently encountered in nuclear physics is the so-called rectangular well, defined by the potential:

$$U(r) = \begin{cases} 0 & r > a, \\ -U_0 & r \leq a. \end{cases}$$

Show that in classical mechanics the scattering produced by such a potential is identical with the refraction of light rays by a sphere of radius $a$ and relative index of refraction

$$n = \sqrt{(E + U_0)/E}.$$

(This equivalence demonstrates why it was possible to explain refraction phenomena both by Huygens' waves and by Newton's mechanical corpuscles.) Show also that the differential cross section $\sigma(\theta)$ is given by

$$\sigma(\theta) = \frac{n^2 a^2}{4 \cos (\theta/2)} \frac{[n \cos (\theta/2) - 1][n - \cos (\theta/2)]}{[1 + n^2 - 2n \cos (\theta/2)]^2}.$$

What is the total cross section?

# 8

# *The Dynamics of a System of Particles*

The general problem of the motion of a system of particles under their mutual interaction and the action of external forces is a very complicated one. Generally no analytical solution is obtainable unless the problem is sufficiently simplified by the introduction of additional constraints or assumptions.

In dealing with the motion of a system of particles, it is customary to distinguish between the internal forces, which the particles of the system exert on each other, and the external forces, which are due to the interaction of the system of particles under consideration with some other system or systems. It should be clear that the existence of external forces implies the existence of other particles which interact with the system of particles being studied. The motion of these other particles must be assumed to be known in order that the forces which they exert on the system of particles under consideration be specifiable.

In dealing with the problem of the motion of a large number of particles, even if such a problem were soluble, the labor involved in specifying the motion of each particle would prompt us to look for gross features of the motion.

In this and subsequent chapters we shall be concerned with the analysis of solvable constrained $N$-particle systems and with conservation theorems for such $N$-particle systems under the action of specific external forces. We begin with a study of the two-particle system, whose unconstrained motion can often be solved.

## 8–1 The two-particle system: center of mass, reduced mass

Assuming that the internal forces which the particles exert on each other satisfy Newton's third law of motion*, that is, $\mathbf{F}_2^{\text{int}} = -\mathbf{F}_1^{\text{int}} = \mathbf{F}^{\text{int}}$, the equa-

---

* We note that the magnetic force between two charged particles in motion does not obey Newton's law of action and reaction. However, in dealing with the motion of charged particles, the total linear momentum of the system includes the linear momentum of the electromagnetic field produced by the particles. From this point of view a system of two charged particles is therefore not, strictly speaking, a two-particle system. When the linear momentum of the electromagnetic field is included in the total linear momentum of a system of charged particles, then we find the results of this chapter regarding the conservation of the total linear momentum of an isolated stable system of charged particles to hold. We shall neglect the magnetic forces between charged particles, since for particle speeds that are small compared with the speed of light the magnetic forces are small compared with the electrical forces between the particles.

tions of motion for each of the two particles of mass $m_1$ and $m_2$ are, respectively,

$$\mathbf{F}_1^{\text{ext}} - \mathbf{F}^{\text{int}} = m_1\mathbf{a}_1 \qquad (8\text{-}1)$$

and

$$\mathbf{F}_2^{\text{ext}} + \mathbf{F}^{\text{int}} = m_2\mathbf{a}_2, \qquad (8\text{-}2)$$

where $\mathbf{F}_i^{\text{ext}}$ represents the external force acting on the $i$th particle.

As was the case for the motion of a single particle, a proper choice of the six coordinates in terms of which we are going to describe the motion of the two-particle system is important; and this choice of coordinates is in most instances suggested by the forces acting on the particles. A proper choice is one which simplifies the mathematical work required to arrive at a solution.

For example, in problems where each of the particles of the system moves under the action of a constant uniform external force, three coordinates which yield three independent one-dimensional equations of motion are the coordinates which describe the position of the point referred to as the *center of mass*. The position vector $\mathbf{R}$ of the center of mass of a two-particle system is defined by the equation

$$\mathbf{R} = \frac{m_1\mathbf{r}_1 + m_2\mathbf{r}_2}{m_1 + m_2}, \qquad (8\text{-}3)$$

where $\mathbf{r}_1$ and $\mathbf{r}_2$ are the position vectors of particles one and two (Fig. 8-1).

The equation of motion for the center-of-mass coordinates may be obtained by adding Eqs. (8-1) and (8-2). This step yields the equation

$$\mathbf{F}^{\text{ext}} = \mathbf{F}_1^{\text{ext}} + \mathbf{F}_2^{\text{ext}} = \frac{d^2}{dt^2}(m_1\mathbf{r}_1 + m_2\mathbf{r}_2) = M\ddot{\mathbf{R}}, \qquad (8\text{-}4)$$

where

$$M = m_1 + m_2 \qquad (8\text{-}5)$$

is the total mass of the system.

Equation (8-4) tells us that the position vector of the center of mass behaves as the position vector of a particle of mass $M$ that is acted on by a force equal to the sum of all the external forces acting on the system.

Equation (8-4) is generally not independent of the remaining three dynamical equations of motion which are also required for the complete description of the motion of a two-particle system. This is so, since the external forces and therefore also their sum are generally functions of all the six coordinates $(x_i, y_i, z_i)$ specifying the position of the particles. Equation (8-4) will thus in general contain explicitly all six coordinates that are used for the description of the motion of the particles. Only if the sum of the external forces reduces to being a function of $\mathbf{R}$, $\dot{\mathbf{R}}$, and $t$ will Eq. (8-4) be an independent equation of motion and equivalent to the equation of motion for a particle of mass $M$ under the action of a force which is a function of its position, velocity, and time.

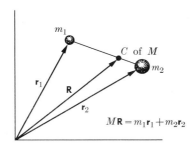

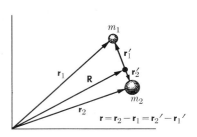

FIG. 8–1.  Center of mass for a two-particle system.

FIGURE 8–2

One example of the kind of forces for which this condition is satisfied is that of uniform external forces which are not a function of the coordinates of the particles.  Another example is provided by damping forces which are proportional to the first power of the velocity of the particles and whose damping constant is the same for both particles.  The latter forces yield a total external damping force

$$\mathbf{F}_{\text{damping}}^{\text{ext}} = -\kappa(m_1\mathbf{v}_1 + m_2\mathbf{v}_2) = -\kappa M\mathbf{V}, \tag{8–6}$$

where

$$M\mathbf{V} = m_1\mathbf{v}_1 + m_2\mathbf{v}_2.$$

In problems dealing with the motion of charged particles in uniform electric and magnetic fields, when the particles of the system have the same charge-to-mass ratio $k$, the total external force turns out to be a function of only $\mathbf{R}$ and $\dot{\mathbf{R}}$. In such cases the total external magnetic force

$$\mathbf{F}_{\text{magnetic}}^{\text{ext}} = Q_1\mathbf{v}_1 \times \mathbf{B} + Q_2\mathbf{v}_2 \times \mathbf{B} = k(m_1\mathbf{v}_1 + m_2\mathbf{v}_2) \times \mathbf{B}$$
$$= kM\mathbf{V} \times \mathbf{B} = Q\mathbf{V} \times \mathbf{B}, \tag{8–7}$$

where

$$k = \frac{Q_1}{m_1} = \frac{Q_2}{m_2}$$

and $Q = k(m_1 + m_2) = Q_1 + Q_2$ is the total charge of the system.

In problems where Eq. (8–4) is solvable independently of the remaining three equations of motion of the two-particle system, the latter three are generally the equations of motion of the coordinates which yield a description of the motion of the particles with respect to the center of mass. At times this latter description is given in terms of the relative position vector $\mathbf{r}$ of one of the particles with respect to the other.

In terms of the relative position vector

$$\mathbf{r} = \mathbf{r}_2 - \mathbf{r}_1, \tag{8–8}$$

we find the position of the particles with respect to the center of mass (cf. Fig. 8–2) to be given by

$$\mathbf{r}_1' = \mathbf{r}_1 - \mathbf{R} = -\frac{m_2}{M}\,\mathbf{r}, \qquad \mathbf{r}_2' = \mathbf{r}_2 - \mathbf{R} = \frac{m_1}{M}\,\mathbf{r}. \tag{8-9}$$

From these equations we obtain in turn the expressions for the velocities and accelerations of the particles with respect to the center of mass in terms of their own relative velocity and acceleration:

$$\mathbf{v}_1' = \mathbf{v}_1 - \dot{\mathbf{R}} = -\frac{m_2}{M}\,\dot{\mathbf{r}}, \qquad \mathbf{v}_2' = \mathbf{v}_2 - \dot{\mathbf{R}} = \frac{m_1}{M}\,\dot{\mathbf{r}}, \tag{8-10}$$

and

$$\mathbf{a}_1' = -\frac{m_2}{M}\,\ddot{\mathbf{r}}, \qquad \mathbf{a}_2' = \frac{m_1}{M}\,\ddot{\mathbf{r}}. \tag{8-11}$$

To obtain the remaining equation of motion for $\mathbf{r}$, we replace $\mathbf{a}_1$ in Eq. (8–1) by $\ddot{\mathbf{R}} - (m_2/M)\ddot{\mathbf{r}}$, and obtain the equation

$$\mathbf{F}_1^{\text{ext}} - \mathbf{F}^{\text{int}} = m_1\ddot{\mathbf{R}} - \frac{m_1 m_2}{M}\,\ddot{\mathbf{r}}$$

or, by Eq. (8–4),

$$\frac{m_1\mathbf{F}_2^{\text{ext}} - m_2\mathbf{F}_1^{\text{ext}}}{M} + \mathbf{F}^{\text{int}} = \frac{m_1 m_2}{M}\,\ddot{\mathbf{r}}. \tag{8-12}$$

We note that for the special external forces mentioned above, for which the total external force is a function of $\mathbf{R}$ and $\dot{\mathbf{R}}$ only, the term $(m_1\mathbf{F}_2^{\text{ext}} - m_2\mathbf{F}_1^{\text{ext}})/M$ in Eq. (8–12) turns out to be a function of $\mathbf{r}$ and $\dot{\mathbf{r}}$ only. Thus if the internal force between the particles is also a function of the relative position and relative velocity of the particles, Eq. (8–12) is the equation of motion for a particle of mass

$$\mu = \frac{m_1 m_2}{M} \tag{8-13}$$

under the action of the force

$$\mathbf{f}(\mathbf{r}, \dot{\mathbf{r}}) = \frac{m_1\mathbf{F}_2^{\text{ext}} - m_2\mathbf{F}_1^{\text{ext}}}{M} + \mathbf{F}^{\text{int}}.$$

The mass $\mu$ is referred to as the *reduced mass* of the two-particle system.

We have thus found that the center-of-mass coordinates and the coordinates describing the relative position of the particles with respect to each other should be appropriate for the description of the motion of a two-particle system under the action of the external forces mentioned and an internal force which depends on the relative position and relative velocity of the particles. One important example of such an internal force is the central force which is a function of the radial distance between the particles and is directed along the line joining them.

We note that, with respect to the center-of-mass coordinate system, which is the coordinate system moving with the center of mass with origin at the center of mass, the position vector $\mathbf{R}'$ of the center of mass always vanishes. That is,

$\mathbf{R}' = 0$. It follows therefore that $\dot{\mathbf{R}}' = 0$, or equivalently,

$$m_1\mathbf{v}_1' + m_2\mathbf{v}_2' = 0. \tag{8-14}$$

This equation tells us that, with respect to the center-of-mass coordinate system, the total linear momentum of the system vanishes.

## 8-2 Kinetic energy; conservation of energy

Regardless of whether the equations of motion for the center of mass and the reduced mass are independent of each other, we can apply the principle of work and energy to these equivalent single-particle equations of motion. The work performed by all the external forces on the particle of mass $M$ whose motion is identical to the motion of the center of mass will henceforth be referred to as the work on the center of mass.* It is defined by

$$W_{\mathbf{R}_1, \mathbf{R}_2} = \int_{\mathbf{R}_1}^{\mathbf{R}_2} \mathbf{F}^{\text{ext}} \cdot d\mathbf{R}, \tag{8-15}$$

which through the use of Eq. (8–4) yields

$$W_{\mathbf{R}_1, \mathbf{R}_2} = \int_{t_1}^{t_2} \frac{d}{dt} \left(\tfrac{1}{2}M\dot{R}^2\right) dt = \Delta(\tfrac{1}{2}MV^2). \tag{8-16}$$

Similarly, defining the work on the reduced mass by

$$W_{\mathbf{r}_1, \mathbf{r}_2} = \int_{\mathbf{r}_1}^{\mathbf{r}_2} \mathbf{f} \cdot d\mathbf{r} = \int_{\mathbf{r}_1}^{\mathbf{r}_2} \left(\mathbf{F}^{\text{int}} + \frac{m_1\mathbf{F}_2^{\text{ext}} - m_2\mathbf{F}_1^{\text{ext}}}{M}\right) \cdot d\mathbf{r}, \tag{8-17}$$

we find through the use of Eq. (8–12) that

$$W_{\mathbf{r}_1, \mathbf{r}_2} = \int_{t_1}^{t_2} \frac{d}{dt} \left(\frac{1}{2}\mu v^2\right) dt = \Delta\left(\frac{1}{2}\mu v^2\right). \tag{8-18}$$

The quantity

$$T_0 = \tfrac{1}{2}MV^2 \tag{8-19}$$

is referred to as the kinetic energy of the center of mass, and the quantity

$$T' = \tfrac{1}{2}\mu v^2 \tag{8-20}$$

as the kinetic energy of the reduced mass or, as shown below, the kinetic energy of the system with respect to the center of mass. We proceed to verify the appropriateness of these terms by showing that $\tfrac{1}{2}\mu v^2$ is indeed the kinetic energy with respect to the center of mass, and that $\tfrac{1}{2}MV^2 + \tfrac{1}{2}\mu v^2$ is the total kinetic energy of the system. The proof follows quite readily. For the total kinetic

---

* In the same way we shall simply refer to $\tfrac{1}{2}MV^2$ as the kinetic energy of the center of mass, $\mathbf{R} \times M\mathbf{V}$ as the angular momentum of the center of mass, etc.

energy of the system we have, through the use of Eqs. (8–10),

$$T = \tfrac{1}{2}m_1 v_1^2 + \tfrac{1}{2}m_2 v_2^2$$

$$= \frac{1}{2}\, m_1 \left| \frac{-m_2 \mathbf{v}}{M} + \mathbf{v} \right|^2 + \frac{1}{2}\, m_2 \left| \frac{m_1 \mathbf{v}}{M} + \mathbf{v} \right|^2 \tag{8–21}$$

$$= \frac{1}{2}\, \frac{m_1 m_2}{M}\, v^2 + \frac{1}{2}\, (m_1 + m_2)V^2.$$

For the kinetic energy relative to the center of mass, we find that

$$T' = \tfrac{1}{2}m_1(v_1')^2 + \tfrac{1}{2}m_2(v_2')^2$$

$$= \frac{1}{2}\, m_1 \left( \frac{-m_2 v}{M} \right)^2 + \frac{1}{2}\, m_2 \left( \frac{m_1 v}{M} \right)^2 = \frac{1}{2}\, \frac{m_1 m_2}{M}\, v^2. \tag{8–22}$$

This verifies that the total kinetic energy is separable into two parts: the kinetic energy of the center of mass and the kinetic energy with respect to the center of mass.

It is to be expected that the total energy of the system is a constant of the motion in those problems in which the external and internal forces acting on the particles are conservative and hence derivable from a potential energy function.

The forces derivable from the potential energy function

$$U = U^{\text{ext}} + U^{\text{int}} \tag{8–23}$$

are expressed by

$$\mathbf{F}_i = -\boldsymbol{\nabla}_i U = \mathbf{F}_i^{\text{ext}} + \mathbf{F}_i^{\text{int}},$$

where

$$\mathbf{F}_i^{\text{ext}} = -\boldsymbol{\nabla}_i U^{\text{ext}} = -\left( \frac{\partial U^{\text{ext}}}{\partial x_i}\, \mathbf{i} + \frac{\partial U^{\text{ext}}}{\partial y_i}\, \mathbf{j} + \frac{\partial U^{\text{ext}}}{\partial z_i}\, \mathbf{k} \right) \tag{8–24}$$

and

$$\mathbf{F}_i^{\text{int}} = -\boldsymbol{\nabla}_i U^{\text{int}}.$$

That the energy of a system of particles moving under the action of conservative forces is a constant of the motion follows from the principle of work and energy applied to Eqs. (8–1) and (8–2). We thus obtain

$$\int \mathbf{F}_1 \cdot d\mathbf{r}_1 + \int \mathbf{F}_2 \cdot d\mathbf{r}_2 = -\int (d\mathbf{r}_1 \cdot \boldsymbol{\nabla}_1 U + d\mathbf{r}_2 \cdot \boldsymbol{\nabla}_2 U)$$

$$= -\Delta U = \Delta(\tfrac{1}{2}m_1 v_1^2) + \Delta(\tfrac{1}{2}m_2 v_2^2) = \Delta T.$$

Hence $-\Delta U = \Delta T$ or

$$T + U = \text{const.} \tag{8–25}$$

We note that, in those problems for which the total conservative external force is a function of the coordinates of the center of mass only, we must have

$$\mathbf{F}^{\text{ext}} = -\boldsymbol{\nabla}_1 U^{\text{ext}} - \boldsymbol{\nabla}_2 U^{\text{ext}} = -\left( \frac{\partial U^{\text{ext}}}{\partial X}\, \mathbf{i} + \frac{\partial U^{\text{ext}}}{\partial Y}\, \mathbf{j} + \frac{\partial U^{\text{ext}}}{\partial Z}\, \mathbf{k} \right),$$

where $X$, $Y$, and $Z$ are the cartesian components of the position vector **R**. This tells us that, for such cases, the center of mass satisfies a separate energy conservation theorem as expressed by

$$T_0 + U^{\text{ext}} = \text{const.} \tag{8-26}$$

If Eqs. (8–25) and (8–26) are simultaneously satisfied, then it naturally follows that the difference between these two equations,

$$T' + U^{\text{int}} = \text{const,} \tag{8-27}$$

expresses the conservation of the total energy of the two particles with respect to the center of mass.

## 8–3 The collision of two particles

The problem of the collision of two particles is one instance in which the utilization of the center-of-mass coordinate system greatly simplifies the work involved in finding the solution.

Consider the collision of two uniform spherical particles (Fig. 8–3). We assume the particles to be spherical and uniform in order that their collision not depend on the dimension and orientation of the colliding bodies. Only in this way may they possibly be considered as particles.

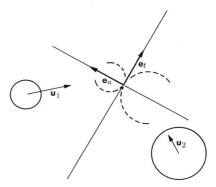

FIG. 8–3.     The collision of two particles.

In terms of the initially observed velocities **u**$_1$ and **u**$_2$ of the particles, their initial velocities with respect to the center of mass (Fig. 8–4) are

$$\mathbf{u}'_1 = \mathbf{u}_1 - \frac{m_1\mathbf{u}_1 + m_2\mathbf{u}_2}{M} = \frac{m_2(\mathbf{u}_1 - \mathbf{u}_2)}{M} \tag{8-28}$$

and

$$\mathbf{u}'_2 = \frac{m_1}{M}(\mathbf{u}_2 - \mathbf{u}_1). \tag{8-29}$$

Since, with respect to the center-of-mass coordinate system, the total linear momentum of the system vanishes, it follows that we must have

$$m_1\mathbf{u}'_1 = -m_2\mathbf{u}'_2. \tag{8-30}$$

Similarly, the velocities **v**$'_i$ which the particles have with respect to the center of mass after the collision satisfy the relation

$$m_1\mathbf{v}'_1 = -m_2\mathbf{v}'_2. \tag{8-31}$$

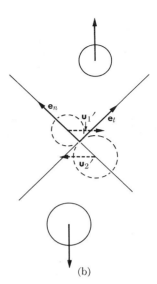

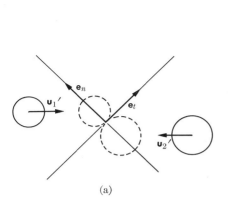

(a)

Fig. 8–4. Collision of two particles; center-of-mass coordinate system.

(b)

This relation by itself is not sufficient, however, to yield the answer we are seeking, which can only be obtained from a knowledge of the forces which the particles exert on each other—and these have not as yet been introduced. In an actual collision between two bodies, a collision in which the bodies come in contact with each other, the forces are complicated and unknown. Any further description of the motion of the particles thus depends on empirical facts about the collision.

If the collision is observed to be *elastic*, that is, if no energy is dissipated, then a second relation is provided by the equation expressing the conservation of energy,

$$\tfrac{1}{2}m_1(v_1')^2 + \tfrac{1}{2}m_2(v_2')^2 = \tfrac{1}{2}m_1(u_1')^2 + \tfrac{1}{2}m_2(u_2')^2. \qquad (8\text{--}32)$$

The four relations provided by Eqs. (8–31) and (8–32) generally are still not sufficient to yield the solution for the six components of the final velocities, $\mathbf{v}_1$ and $\mathbf{v}_2$, of the particles. If, however, we make the additional assumption that the force between the particles at contact is directed along the line joining their centers, then with respect to the center of mass the particles will remain in the plane determined by their center of mass and their initial direction of propagation with respect to the center of mass (Fig. 8–4). This takes care of two components of the final velocities and permits us to find the remaining four components of the final velocities.

We note that the only component of the velocities of the two colliding particles with respect to the center of mass, which can change under the assumption we made about the force between the uniform spherical particles, is the component of the velocities along the line joining the centers of the particles at the instant of collision; that is, the components along $\mathbf{e}_n$ in Fig. 8–4. The other components remain unchanged,

$$\mathbf{u}'_1 \cdot \mathbf{e}_t = u'_{1t} = v'_{1t} \quad \text{and} \quad u'_{2t} = v'_{2t}. \tag{8-33}$$

From the conservation of the kinetic energy in the center-of-mass coordinate system and from the equation expressing the vanishing of the component of the linear momentum with respect to the center of mass along $\mathbf{e}_n$,

$$m_1\mathbf{v}'_1 \cdot \mathbf{e}_n + m_2\mathbf{v}'_2 \cdot \mathbf{e}_n = 0 \quad \text{or} \quad m_1 v'_{1n} = -m_2 v'_{2n}, \tag{8-34}$$

we obtain the solution for an elastic collision,

$$v'_{1n} = \pm u'_{1n} \quad \text{and} \quad v'_{2n} = \pm u'_{2n}.$$

For any actual collision between two particles, it should be clear that the solution which describes the situation is given by

$$v'_{1n} = -u'_{1n} \quad \text{and} \quad v'_{2n} = -u'_{2n}. \tag{8-35}$$

With respect to the laboratory frame of reference, the velocities are subsequently found to be given by

$$\mathbf{v}_1 = u'_{1t}\mathbf{e}_t - u'_{1n}\mathbf{e}_n + \mathbf{V} \quad \text{and} \quad \mathbf{v}_2 = u'_{2t}\mathbf{e}_t - u'_{2n}\mathbf{e}_n + \mathbf{V}. \tag{8-36}$$

With the same simplifying assumption—that the force between the particles lies along the line joining the geometric centers of the bodies during the period that the bodies are in contact—we can similarly obtain an answer if either the loss in energy is provided, or the empirical constant $\epsilon$, the *coefficient of restitution*, is given. The coefficient of restitution is defined as the negative ratio of the component of the relative velocity normal to the surfaces of the colliding particles at the point of contact after and before the collision. That is,

$$\epsilon = -\frac{v'_{2n} - v'_{1n}}{u'_{2n} - u'_{1n}}. \tag{8-37}$$

In this case we likewise obtain, from the vanishing of the linear momentum with respect to the center of mass, the result that

$$m_1 v'_{1n} = -m_2 v'_{2n} \quad \text{and} \quad m_1 u'_{1n} = -m_2 u'_{2n}.$$

Hence we obtain from Eq. (8-37) the solutions

$$v'_{1n} = -\epsilon u'_{1n} \quad \text{and} \quad v'_{2n} = -\epsilon u'_{2n}. \tag{8-38}$$

The final velocities in the laboratory frame are given by

$$\mathbf{v}_1 = u'_{1t}\mathbf{e}_t - \epsilon u'_{1n}\mathbf{e}_n + \mathbf{V} \quad \text{and} \quad v_2 = u'_{2t}\mathbf{e}_t - \epsilon u'_{2n}\mathbf{e}_n + \mathbf{V}. \tag{8-39}$$

The loss in kinetic energy is readily found to be given by

$$\text{Loss in } T = \text{Loss in } T'$$

$$= \frac{m_1}{2}\left[(u'_1)^2 - (v'_1)^2\right] + \frac{m_2}{2}\left[(u'_2)^2 - (v'_2)^2\right]$$

$$= \left[\frac{m_1}{2}(u'_{1n})^2 + \frac{m_2}{2}(u'_{2n})^2\right](1 - \epsilon^2). \tag{8–40}$$

We note that our assumption regarding the direction of the force between the colliding bodies is unrealistic. In practice one expects also a tangential component which will give the bodies rotational motion (cf. Section 9–14) and change their momentum in the tangential direction. This complicates the problem considerably. We still have in that case the conservation of the linear momentum of the system and, as we shall discuss in a later section, the conservation of the angular momentum of the system. The conservation of the linear momentum is expressed by

$$m_1\mathbf{v}_1 + m_2\mathbf{v}_2 = m_1\mathbf{u}_1 + m_2\mathbf{u}_2,$$

which as already mentioned is not sufficient to yield the final velocities of the particles, given their initial velocities.

## 8–4 Rocket motion

The equations of motion of a rocket-propelled vehicle can be obtained by considering the vehicle and the ejected gas as two interacting particles. As such, the vehicle and the ejected fuel have at time $t$ a total mass $M$ moving with velocity $\mathbf{v}$ (Fig. 8–5a).

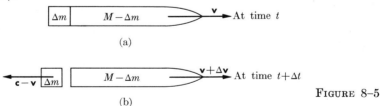

FIGURE 8–5

At some infinitesimal time $\Delta t$ later, the vehicle, after having ejected an amount of gas of mass $\Delta m$ with a velocity $-\mathbf{c}$ with respect to itself, is observed to move with the velocity $\mathbf{v} + \Delta\mathbf{v}$ and the ejected gas with the velocity $\mathbf{c} - \mathbf{v}$, as shown in Fig. 8–5(b). If no external forces are acting, the total linear momentum of the system will be conserved. It follows therefore that

$$(M - \Delta m)(\mathbf{v} + \Delta\mathbf{v}) + \Delta m(\mathbf{v} - \mathbf{c}) = M\mathbf{v},$$

or, to within first order in the infinitesimal quantities, that

$$M\,\Delta\mathbf{v} = \Delta m\mathbf{c} = -\Delta M\mathbf{c},$$

where we have set $\Delta m = -\Delta M$. In the limit as $\Delta t \to 0$ the equation of motion for rectilinear motion of the rocket is

$$M \frac{dv}{dt} = -c \frac{dM}{dt} \quad \text{or} \quad M = -c \frac{dM}{dv}. \tag{8-41}$$

This equation of motion may be readily integrated to yield

$$v - v_0 = -c \ln \frac{M(t)}{M_0}. \tag{8-42}$$

If the fuel is ejected at a uniform rate for a fixed period of time $\tau$, then the variation of the mass of the rocket as a function of time is expressed by

$$M(t) = \begin{cases} M_V + M_F \left(1 - \frac{t}{\tau}\right) & 0 \le t \le \tau, \\ M_V & \tau < t, \end{cases}$$

where $M_V$ is the mass of the vehicle and $M_F$ the mass of its fuel at the initial time $t = 0$.

A knowledge of the variation of the mass with time allows us to integrate Eq. (8–42) and thus obtain the position of the vehicle as a function of time. For any time $t < \tau$ Eq. (8–42) is

$$\frac{dx}{dt} = v_0 - c \ln \frac{M_V + M_F - M_F(t/\tau)}{M_V + M_F} = v_0 - c \ln (1 - at),$$

where

$$a = \frac{M_F}{M_V + M_F} \frac{1}{\tau}.$$

This equation has the solution

$$x = x_0 + v_0 t - c \int_0^t \ln (1 - at)\, dt$$

$$= x_0 + v_0 t - c \left[\left(t - \frac{1}{a}\right) \ln (1 - at) - t\right]. \tag{8-43}$$

If the rocket started from rest at $t = 0$, then the maximum velocity which it can obtain at time $t = \tau$ is determined by the amount of fuel $M_F$ it carried initially and the ratio of this amount to the vehicle mass at time $t = 0$. This maximum velocity may be obtained from Eq. (8–42) by setting $M(\tau) = M_V$. We thus obtain

$$v_{\max} = -c \ln \frac{M_V}{M_V + M_F} = c \ln \left(1 + \frac{M_F}{M_V}\right). \tag{8-44}$$

This equation tells us that, in order for the rocket to attain high speeds, the ratio $M_F/M_V$ should be as large as possible.

If the vehicle is also acted on by an external force, then the equation of motion of the vehicle may be obtained from a consideration of the change in linear momentum of the system's center of mass produced by the impulse of the external force over the short period of time $\Delta t$. We assume the force to be in the direction of motion of the rocket.

At time $t$, the total linear momentum of the system is

$$MV = Mv,$$

and a short time $\Delta t$ later it is found to be

$$M(V + \Delta V) = (M - \Delta m)(v + \Delta v) + \Delta m(v - c).$$

Equating the change in the momentum of the system to the impulse which it receives, we obtain to within first-order infinitesimals the equation of motion

$$F \, \Delta t = M(V + \Delta V) - MV = M \, \Delta v - c(\Delta m) = M \, \Delta v + c \, \Delta M$$

or

$$F = M \frac{dv}{dt} + c \frac{dM}{dt}. \tag{8–45}$$

## 8–5 Angular momentum

The angular momentum of a system of particles is a very important physical quantity, as is the case in the motion of a single particle. Following the definition [Eq. (5–30)] of the orbital angular momentum of a particle, we define the orbital angular momentum of the center of mass as

$$\mathbf{L}_0 = \mathbf{R} \times M\dot{\mathbf{R}}. \tag{8–46}$$

Also as for a single particle the cross product of Eq. (8–4) with $\mathbf{R}$ yields the equation of motion for the angular momentum of the center of mass,

$$\mathbf{R} \times \mathbf{F}^{\text{ext}} = \mathbf{R} \times \frac{d}{dt}(M\dot{\mathbf{R}}) = \frac{d}{dt}(\mathbf{R} \times M\dot{\mathbf{R}})$$

or

$$\mathbf{N}_0 = \frac{d}{dt}\mathbf{L}_0, \tag{8–47}$$

where the vector product

$$\mathbf{N}_0 = \mathbf{R} \times \mathbf{F}^{\text{ext}} \tag{8–48}$$

is referred to as the torque on the center of mass. Equation (8–47) tells us that the time rate of change of the angular momentum $\mathbf{L}_0$ of the center of mass equals the torque being exerted on the center of mass. Obviously if the torque on the center of mass vanishes, the angular momentum of the center of mass is a constant of the motion.

Similarly, setting

$$\mathbf{f} = \frac{m_1 \mathbf{F}_2^{\text{ext}} - m_2 \mathbf{F}_1^{\text{ext}}}{M} + \mathbf{F}^{\text{int}},$$

and taking the cross product of Eq. (8–12) and the relative position vector $\mathbf{r}$ defined by Eq. (8–8), we obtain the equation

$$\mathbf{r} \times \mathbf{f} = \mathbf{r} \times \frac{d}{dt} (\mu \dot{\mathbf{r}}) = \frac{d}{dt} (\mathbf{r} \times \mu \dot{\mathbf{r}}),$$

or

$$\mathbf{N}' = \frac{d}{dt} \mathbf{L}', \tag{8–49}$$

where

$$\mathbf{N}' = \mathbf{r} \times \mathbf{f} \tag{8–50}$$

and

$$\mathbf{L}' = \mathbf{r} \times \mu \dot{\mathbf{r}}. \tag{8–51}$$

The quantity $\mathbf{N}'$ is referred to as the total torque about the center of mass, and $\mathbf{L}'$ as the total orbital angular momentum of the system with respect to the center of mass. We proceed to show the appropriateness of these descriptions.

We begin by computing the total angular momentum about the center of mass. It is given by the sum

$$\mathbf{r}_1' \times m_1 \mathbf{v}_1' + \mathbf{r}_2' \times m_2 \mathbf{v}_2'.$$

In terms of the relative position vector $\mathbf{r}$ and relative velocity vector $\dot{\mathbf{r}}$ of particle two with respect to particle one, we indeed find this sum to be equal to the angular momentum defined by Eq. (8–51). That is,

$$m_1 \left[ -\frac{m_2 \mathbf{r}}{M} \right] \times \left[ -\frac{m_2 \mathbf{v}}{M} \right] + m_2 \left[ \frac{m_1 \mathbf{r}}{M} \right] \times \left[ \frac{m_1 \mathbf{v}}{M} \right] = \frac{m_1 m_2}{M} \mathbf{r} \times \mathbf{v} = \mathbf{L}'.$$

The torque about the center of mass is given by the sum

$$\mathbf{r}_1' \times \mathbf{F}_1 + \mathbf{r}_2' \times \mathbf{F}_2 = -\frac{m_2}{M} \mathbf{r} \times [\mathbf{F}_1^{\text{ext}} - \mathbf{F}^{\text{int}}] + \frac{m_1}{M} \mathbf{r} \times [\mathbf{F}_2^{\text{ext}} + \mathbf{F}^{\text{int}}]$$

$$= \mathbf{r} \times \mathbf{f} = \mathbf{N}'$$

The sum of Eqs. (8–47) and (8–49) yields the equation

$$\mathbf{N} = \mathbf{N}_0 + \mathbf{N}' = \frac{d}{dt} (\mathbf{L}_0 + \mathbf{L}') = \frac{d}{dt} \mathbf{L}, \tag{8–52}$$

where $\mathbf{N}$ is referred to as the total torque on the system and $\mathbf{L}$ as the total orbital angular momentum of the system. That these are correct descriptions of these vector quantities can be seen by expressing the total torque and the total orbital angular momentum in terms of the coordinates of the center of mass and the relative coordinates of the two particles.  We then find for the total torque acting on the system

$$\mathbf{N} = \mathbf{r}_1 \times \mathbf{F}_1 + \mathbf{r}_2 \times \mathbf{F}_2$$

$$= \left( -\frac{m_2}{M}\, \mathbf{r} + \mathbf{R} \right) \times (\mathbf{F}_1^{\mathrm{ext}} - \mathbf{F}^{\mathrm{int}}) + \left( \frac{m_1}{M}\, \mathbf{r} + \mathbf{R} \right) \times (\mathbf{F}_2^{\mathrm{ext}} + \mathbf{F}^{\mathrm{int}})$$

$$= \mathbf{R} \times (\mathbf{F}_1^{\mathrm{ext}} + \mathbf{F}_2^{\mathrm{ext}}) + \mathbf{r} \times \mathbf{f} = \mathbf{N}_0 + \mathbf{N}',$$

and for the total orbital angular momentum we obtain

$$\mathbf{L} = \mathbf{r}_1 \times (m_1\mathbf{v}_1) + \mathbf{r}_2 \times (m_2\mathbf{v}_2)$$

$$= m_1 \left( -\frac{m_2}{M}\, \mathbf{r} + \mathbf{R} \right) \times \left( -\frac{m_2}{M}\, \mathbf{v} + \mathbf{V} \right) + m_2 \left( \frac{m_1}{M}\, \mathbf{r} + \mathbf{R} \right) \times \left( \frac{m_1}{M}\, \mathbf{v} + \mathbf{V} \right)$$

$$= M\mathbf{R} \times \mathbf{V} + \frac{m_1 m_2}{M}\, \mathbf{r} \times \mathbf{v} = \mathbf{L}_0 + \mathbf{L}'.$$

We note that if any of the torques $\mathbf{N}$, $\mathbf{N}_0$, or $\mathbf{N}'$ vanishes, the corresponding angular momentum is a constant of the motion.

▶As an example of the application of the equation of motion for the orbital angular momentum vector, we consider the simple Atwood machine problem. This is a system of two particles connected by a light inextensible string of length $l$ passing over a pulley or radius $R$, as shown in Fig. 8–6.

For the present we neglect the effect of the pulley on the motion. That is, we assume the masses to be of such magnitude as to make the effect of the pulley on the motion negligible. The problem thus reduces to the motion of two particles being acted on by the external gravitational forces $m_1g$ and $m_2g$, as shown in Fig. 8–6, and the internal force which is transmitted from one particle to the other through the string. This is a constrained system which requires only one coordinate for the description of its motion. We thus require only one equation of motion, which we choose to obtain through use of Eq. (8–52).

Taking torques about the geometric center of the pulley, we find all the torques to be parallel to the axis of the pulley and their resultant magnitude to be given by

$$|\mathbf{N}| = (m_2 - m_1)gR, \qquad m_2 > m_1.$$

The total angular momentum of the system with respect to the center of the pulley is likewise parallel to the axis of the pulley, and has the magnitude

$$L = (m_1 + m_2)Rv,$$

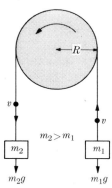

FIG. 8–6.  Atwood machine.

where $v$ is the speed of the particles. Using Eq. (8–52), we obtain the following equality:

$$(m_2 - m_1)gR = (m_1 + m_2)R\dot{v},$$

which yields for the constant acceleration of the particles

$$a = \dot{v} = \frac{m_2 - m_1}{m_1 + m_2}\,g.\,\blacktriangleleft$$

One very important problem is the motion of a system of two particles which act on each other with a force lying along the line joining the particles (central force). If in addition they move under the action of external forces which satisfy the equation

$$m_2\mathbf{F}_1^{\text{ext}} - m_1\mathbf{F}_2^{\text{ext}} = 0,$$

then we find the torque with respect to the center of mass to vanish,

$$\mathbf{N}' = \mathbf{r} \times \mathbf{F}^{\text{int}} = 0,$$

and the orbital angular momentum with respect to the center of mass to be a constant of the motion.

## 8–6 Scattering: relationship between scattering angles in the laboratory and center-of-mass coordinate systems

In Section 7–8 we discussed the scattering of a particle by a central force field, assuming at that time that the scattering center remained fixed. The solution found there with $m$ in the equations of that section replaced by the reduced mass $\mu$, represents, the scattering of particle two with respect to particle one, or since

$$\mathbf{r}_2' = \frac{m_1}{M}\,\mathbf{r} \tag{8–53}$$

and

$$\mathbf{r}_1' = -\frac{m_2}{M}\,\mathbf{r}, \tag{8–54}$$

it also represents the scattering of the two particles as observed with respect to the center-of-mass coordinate system (Fig. 8–7).

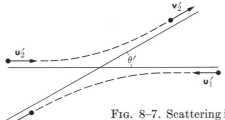

Fig. 8–7. Scattering in the center-of-mass coordinate system.

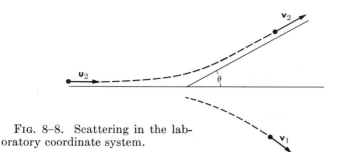

Fig. 8–8. Scattering in the laboratory coordinate system.

We let $\mathbf{u}_i$ and $\mathbf{v}_i$ represent the observed initial and final velocities of the particles in the laboratory frame of reference, and consider the case when particle one is observed to be initially at rest, $\mathbf{u}_1 = 0$, which is the usual experimental situation. Then, as can be seen from Fig. 8–8, the angle $\theta$ through which particle two, which was initially moving in the positive $x$-direction with the velocity $\mathbf{u}_2$, is scattered is given by

$$\tan \theta = \frac{v_{2y}}{v_{2x}} . \tag{8–55}$$

With respect to the center-of-mass coordinate system, on the other hand, the angle $\theta'$ through which particle two is scattered (cf. Fig. 8–7) is given by

$$\tan \theta' = \frac{v'_{2y}}{v'_{2x}} , \tag{8–56}$$

where $\mathbf{v}'_2 = \mathbf{v} - \mathbf{V}$. For the initial conditions assumed above ($\mathbf{u}_1 = 0$, $\mathbf{u}_2 = u_2\mathbf{i}$), the following relations hold:

$$\mathbf{V} = \frac{m_2 \mathbf{u}_2}{M} \tag{8–57}$$

or

$$V_x = \frac{m_2 u_2}{M} , \qquad V_y = 0, \tag{8–58}$$

and

$$\mathbf{u}'_2 = \mathbf{u}_2 - \mathbf{V} = \frac{m_1}{M} \mathbf{u}_2 \qquad \text{or} \qquad u_2 = \frac{M}{m_1} u'_2. \tag{8–59}$$

Now from the conservation of energy principle, which is applicable here, it also follows, as found in Section 8–3, that the speeds before and after the collision are the same. Hence $v'_2 = u'_2$, whence we obtain the relation between the scattering angles in the laboratory and center-of-mass coordinate systems:

$$\tan \theta = \frac{v_{2y}}{v_{2x}} = \frac{v'_{2y}}{v'_{2x} + V_x} = \frac{u'_2 \sin \theta'}{u'_2 \cos \theta' + (m_2/m_1)u'_2} ,$$

or

$$\tan \theta = \frac{\sin \theta'}{\cos \theta' + (m_2/m_1)} . \tag{8–60}$$

If the target particle, which was initially at rest in the laboratory frame of reference, is much heavier than the incident particle, then Eq. (8–60) yields the expected result that the scattering angles in the laboratory and center-of-mass coordinate systems are to a very good approximation equal:

$$\theta \approx \theta'.$$

It should be clear that in all other cases the linear momentum and kinetic energy imparted to the target nucleus may represent a large fraction of the initial momentum and energy of the projectile or scattered particle. The scattering angles and the scattering cross sections in the laboratory and center-of-mass coordinate systems will therefore be quite different.

The relationship between the scattering cross sections in the two reference frames is provided by their relationship to the impact parameter, which is the same in both coordinate systems. Thus we find that

$$\sigma(\theta) \sin \theta \, d\theta = -s \, ds = \sigma(\theta') \sin \theta' \, d\theta' \tag{8–61}$$

or

$$\sigma(\theta) = \sigma(\theta') \frac{\sin \theta'}{\sin \theta} \frac{d\theta'}{d\theta}, \tag{8–62}$$

where $\theta$ and $\theta'$ are the scattering angles in the laboratory and center-of-mass coordinate systems, respectively.

## 8–7 Dynamics of an $N$-particle system: conservation theorems

In this section we shall discuss the conservation theorems frequently employed in analyzing the motion of an $N$-particle system. They are, specifically, the conservation theorems regarding the total energy, the total linear momentum, and the total orbital angular momentum of the system.

(a) *Conservation of linear momentum: center of mass.* As for the case of two interacting particles, we begin our discussion by distinguishing between the external and internal forces of the system. With this distinction, and assuming only two-body internal forces between the particles of the system which satisfy Newton's law of action and reaction, we find the equation of motion for the $i$th particle to be

$$\mathbf{F}_i^{\text{ext}} + \sum_{j \neq i} \mathbf{F}_{ij}^{\text{int}} = m_i \mathbf{a}_i. \tag{8–63}$$

Here $\mathbf{F}_i^{\text{ext}}$ is the total external force on the $i$th particle and $\mathbf{F}_{ij}^{\text{int}}$ is the internal force which the $j$th particle exerts on the $i$th particle. When we sum Eq. (8–63) over all the particles, the sum over the internal forces vanishes,

$$\sum_{\substack{i, \, j \\ i \neq j}} \mathbf{F}_{ij}^{\text{int}} = \sum_{\substack{i, \, j \\ i \neq j}} \mathbf{F}_{ji}^{\text{int}} = \frac{1}{2} \sum_{\substack{i, \, j \\ i \neq j}} (\mathbf{F}_{ij}^{\text{int}} + \mathbf{F}_{ji}^{\text{int}}) = 0,$$

since by Newton's law $\mathbf{F}_{ij}^{\text{int}} = -\mathbf{F}_{ji}^{\text{int}}$. We are thus led to the equation

$$\mathbf{F}^{\text{ext}} = \sum_{i=1}^{N} \mathbf{F}_i^{\text{ext}} = \frac{d}{dt} \sum_{i=1}^{N} m_i \mathbf{v}_i, \tag{8–64}$$

from which we find that the total linear momentum of the system,

$$M\mathbf{V} = \sum_{i=1}^{N} m_i \mathbf{v}_i, \tag{8–65}$$

is a constant of the motion if the total external force acting on the particles vanishes. If only specific components of the total external force vanish, then of course only the corresponding components of the total linear momentum are conserved.

We note that $\mathbf{V}$ is the velocity of the center of mass whose position is defined by the equation

$$M\mathbf{R} = \sum_{i=1}^{N} m_i \mathbf{r}_i \tag{8–66}$$

with

$$M = \sum_{i=1}^{N} m_i. \tag{8–67}$$

If the sum of the external forces does not vanish, then Eq. (8–64), which can be written as

$$\mathbf{F}^{\text{ext}} = M\ddot{\mathbf{R}}, \tag{8–68}$$

expresses the fact that the equation of motion for the position vector of the center of mass is the same as the equation of motion for a particle of mass

$$M = \sum_{i=1}^{N} m_i \tag{8–69}$$

moving under the action of all the external forces. We note once again that Eq. (8–68) is an equation independent of the remaining equations of motion of the system only if the total external force reduces to being a function of $t$, $\mathbf{R}$, and its time derivatives. Under such circumstances Eq. (8–68) is in all respects the equation of motion for a particle the solution of which we were concerned with in the previous chapters. The motion of a system of particles under the action of constant uniform fields is one example of a force for which Eq. (8–68) will thus be soluble.

(b) *Conservation of energy.* Conservation of the energy of a system of particles is to be expected when the forces acting on the particles are conservative ones. Such forces were found to be derivable from a potential energy function, which in this case can be decomposed into two parts, as expressed by

$$U = U^{\text{ext}} + U^{\text{int}}, \tag{8–70}$$

such that

$$\mathbf{F}_i^{\text{ext}} = -\boldsymbol{\nabla}_i U^{\text{ext}} \quad \text{and} \quad \mathbf{F}_i^{\text{int}} = -\boldsymbol{\nabla}_i U^{\text{int}},$$

where

$$\boldsymbol{\nabla}_i = \mathbf{i}\,\frac{\partial}{\partial x_i} + \mathbf{j}\,\frac{\partial}{\partial y_i} + \mathbf{k}\,\frac{\partial}{\partial z_i}\cdot$$

The internal potential energy function, in order to yield two-body internal forces which obey Newton's law of action and reaction, must be a function of the relative distance between the two interacting particles and, since the forces between the particles are two-body forces, is expressible in the form

$$U^{\text{int}} = \frac{1}{2}\sum_{\substack{i,\,j \\ i\neq j}} U_{ij}(|\mathbf{r}_{ij}|), \tag{8–71}$$

where $\mathbf{r}_{ij} = \mathbf{r}_i - \mathbf{r}_j$. Such a potential energy function yields for the internal force which the $j$th particle exerts on the $i$th particle

$$\mathbf{F}_{ij}^{\text{int}} = -\boldsymbol{\nabla}_i U_{ij} = \boldsymbol{\nabla}_j U_{ij} = -\mathbf{F}_{ji}^{\text{int}}.$$

We note that we can set $\boldsymbol{\nabla}_i U_{ij} = \boldsymbol{\nabla}_{ij} U_{ij}$, where

$$\boldsymbol{\nabla}_{ij} = \mathbf{i}\,\frac{\partial}{\partial(x_i - x_j)} + \mathbf{j}\,\frac{\partial}{\partial(y_i - y_j)} + \mathbf{k}\,\frac{\partial}{\partial(z_i - z_j)}\cdot \tag{8–72}$$

The factor of one-half which appears in Eq. (8–71) is required, since $U_{ij} = U_{ji}$ appears twice in the summation.

Applying the principle of work and energy to Eq. (8–63), we obtain as on previous occasions

$$\mathbf{F}_i \cdot \Delta\mathbf{r}_i = \Delta(\tfrac{1}{2}m_i v_i^2),$$

whose sum yields

$$\sum_{i=1}^{N} \mathbf{F}_i^{\text{ext}} \cdot \Delta\mathbf{r}_i + \sum_{\substack{i,\,j \\ i\neq j}} \mathbf{F}_{ij}^{\text{int}} \cdot \Delta\mathbf{r}_i = \Delta\sum_{i=1}^{N} \frac{1}{2}\,m_i v_i^2 = \Delta T. \tag{8–73}$$

The first term in Eq. (8–73) is clearly the negative change in the external potential energy,

$$\sum_{i=1}^{N} \mathbf{F}_i^{\text{ext}} \cdot \Delta\mathbf{r}_i = -\sum_{i=1}^{N} \Delta\mathbf{r}_i \cdot \boldsymbol{\nabla}_i U^{\text{ext}} = -\Delta U^{\text{ext}}.$$

The second term on the left-hand side of Eq. (8–73) can be shown to be the negative of the change in the internal potential energy. We have

$$\sum_{\substack{i,\,j \\ i\neq j}} \mathbf{F}_{ij}^{\text{int}} \cdot \Delta\mathbf{r}_i = \sum_{\substack{i,\,j \\ i\neq j}} \mathbf{F}_{ji}^{\text{int}} \cdot \Delta\mathbf{r}_j = -\sum_{\substack{i,\,j \\ i\neq j}} \mathbf{F}_{ij}^{\text{int}} \cdot \Delta\mathbf{r}_j.$$

Hence it follows that

$$\sum_{\substack{i,\,j \\ i \neq j}} \mathbf{F}_{ij}^{\text{int}} \cdot \Delta \mathbf{r}_i = \frac{1}{2} \sum_{\substack{i,\,j \\ i \neq j}} \mathbf{F}_{ij}^{\text{int}} (\Delta \mathbf{r}_i - \Delta \mathbf{r}_j) = \frac{1}{2} \sum_{\substack{i,\,j \\ i \neq j}} \mathbf{F}_{ij}^{\text{int}} \cdot \Delta \mathbf{r}_{ij}$$

$$= -\frac{1}{2} \sum_{\substack{i,\,j \\ i \neq j}} \Delta \mathbf{r}_{ij} \cdot \boldsymbol{\nabla}_{ij} U_{ij}^{\text{int}} = -\Delta U^{\text{int}}.$$

Equation (8–73) thus becomes

$$\Delta(T + U^{\text{ext}} + U^{\text{int}}) = 0,$$

or, as we set out to derive, $T + U = \text{const.}$

From the fact that, for certain external forces, Eq. (8–68) may be independent of the remaining equations of motion of the system, we note that we should expect the total kinetic energy of the system to be expressible as a sum of the kinetic energy of the center of mass and the kinetic energy with respect to the center of mass. The proof is analogous to the proof for the two-particle system.

We have the relation

$$\mathbf{v}_i = \mathbf{v}_i' + \mathbf{V},$$

where $\mathbf{v}_i'$ is the velocity of the $i$th particle with respect to the center of mass. Inserting this relation into the expression for the total kinetic energy of the system, and utilizing the fact that with respect to the center of mass the total linear momentum of the system vanishes, we obtain the expected result:

$$T = \frac{1}{2} \sum_{i=1}^{N} m_i v_i^2 = \frac{1}{2} \sum_{i=1}^{N} m_i (v_i'^2 + V^2 + 2\mathbf{v}_i \cdot \mathbf{V})$$

$$= \frac{1}{2} M V^2 + \sum_{i=1}^{N} \frac{1}{2} m_i v_i'^2. \tag{8–74}$$

(c) *Conservation of orbital angular momentum.* To obtain the condition under which the total orbital angular momentum of a system is conserved, we require the equation of motion for the total orbital angular momentum of the system. Analogous to the way we handled the one-particle problem in a central force field, we take the vector product of Eq. (8–63) and $\mathbf{r}_i$ to obtain the equation of motion for the orbital angular momentum of the $i$th particle. The sum of the resulting equations then yields

$$\sum_{i} \mathbf{r}_i \times \mathbf{F}_i^{\text{ext}} + \sum_{\substack{i,\,j \\ i \neq j}} \mathbf{r}_i \times \mathbf{F}_{ij}^{\text{int}} = \frac{d}{dt} \left( \sum_{i} \mathbf{r}_i \times m_i \mathbf{v}_i \right). \tag{8–75}$$

Now if the internal force between the $i$th and $j$th particles lies along the line joining the two particles, then it follows that

$$\sum_{\substack{i,\,j \\ i \neq j}} \mathbf{r}_i \times \mathbf{F}_{ij}^{\text{int}} = \sum_{\substack{i,\,j \\ i \neq j}} \mathbf{r}_j \times \mathbf{F}_{ji}^{\text{int}} = \frac{1}{2} \sum_{\substack{i,\,j \\ i \neq j}} (\mathbf{r}_i \times \mathbf{F}_{ij}^{\text{int}} + \mathbf{r}_j \times \mathbf{F}_{ji}^{\text{int}})$$

$$= \frac{1}{2} \sum_{\substack{i,\,j \\ i \neq j}} (\mathbf{r}_i - \mathbf{r}_j) \times \mathbf{F}_{ij}^{\text{int}} = 0.$$

The last step follows from the assumption that $\mathbf{F}_{ij}^{\text{int}}$ and $\mathbf{r}_i - \mathbf{r}_j = \mathbf{r}_{ij}$ are parallel. The total torque due to the internal forces thus vanishes and Eq. (8–75) reduces to

$$\mathbf{N} = \frac{d}{dt} \mathbf{L}, \tag{8–76}$$

where

$$\mathbf{N} = \sum_{i=1}^{N} \mathbf{r}_i \times \mathbf{F}_i^{\text{ext}} \tag{8–77}$$

is the total external torque acting on the system and

$$\mathbf{L} = \sum_{i=1}^{N} \mathbf{r}_i \times m_i \mathbf{v}_i \tag{8–78}$$

is the total orbital angular momentum of the system. Equation (8–76) is the equation of motion for the total orbital angular momentum. From it we find that the total orbital angular momentum of the system is a constant of the motion if the external torque vanishes.

Here as for the two-particle system, we find that we are able to decompose the total angular momentum of a system of particles into the sum of the orbital angular momentum of the center of mass and the orbital angular momentum of the system with respect to the center of mass. Specifically, utilizing the center-of-mass coordinates and the coordinates of the particles relative to the center of mass, we find that the total orbital angular momentum is

$$\mathbf{L} = \sum_{i=1}^{N} \mathbf{r}_i \times m_i \mathbf{v}_i$$

$$= \sum_i \mathbf{r}_i' \times (m_i \mathbf{v}_i') + \sum_i m_i \mathbf{R} \times \mathbf{V} + \sum_i \mathbf{R} \times (m_i \mathbf{v}_i') + \sum_i (m_i \mathbf{r}_i') \times \mathbf{V},$$

since

$$\mathbf{r}_i = \mathbf{r}_i' + \mathbf{R} \qquad \text{and} \qquad \mathbf{v}_i = \mathbf{v}_i' + \mathbf{V}.$$

However,

$$\sum_i m_i \mathbf{r}_i' = \sum_i m_i \mathbf{v}_i' = 0;$$

the expression for the total angular momentum therefore reduces to the expected result,

$$\mathbf{L} = \sum_i \mathbf{r}'_i \times (m_i\mathbf{v}'_i) + \mathbf{R} \times M\mathbf{V} = \mathbf{L}' + \mathbf{L}_0, \qquad (8\text{--}79)$$

where

$$\mathbf{L}' = \sum_i \mathbf{r}'_i \times m_i\mathbf{v}'_i \qquad (8\text{--}80)$$

is defined as the orbital angular momentum of the system with respect to the center of mass, and $\mathbf{L}_0 = \mathbf{R} \times M\mathbf{V}$ is the orbital angular momentum of the center of mass about the origin. From Eq. (8–68) it follows that the equation of motion for the angular momentum $\mathbf{L}_0$ of the center of mass is

$$\mathbf{N}_0 = \mathbf{R} \times \mathbf{F}^{\text{ext}} = \frac{d}{dt}\,(\mathbf{R} \times M\mathbf{V}). \qquad (8\text{--}81)$$

Thus since the total torque can be expressed as

$$\mathbf{N} = \sum_i \mathbf{r}_i \times \mathbf{F}^{\text{ext}}_i = \sum_i (\mathbf{r}'_i + \mathbf{R}) \times \mathbf{F}^{\text{ext}}_i = \mathbf{N}'_i + \mathbf{N}_0, \qquad (8\text{--}82)$$

where $\mathbf{N}' = \sum_i \mathbf{r}'_i \times \mathbf{F}^{\text{ext}}_i$ is the total external torque about the center of mass, it follows from Eqs. (8–76) and (8–81) that the total orbital angular momentum about the center of mass satisfies the equation of motion

$$\mathbf{N}' = \frac{d}{dt}\,\mathbf{L}'. \qquad (8\text{--}83)$$

In dealing with the motion of a system of particles constrained to remain at fixed distances from each other, we shall find that these equations yield the equations of motion for the orientation of the rigid system, or rigid body, as such a system is called. Specifically we shall utilize Eq. (8–76) in dealing with the motion of a rigid body (Chapter 9) with one or more of its points fixed in space. Equations (8–68) and (8–83) will be utilized as the equations of motion of a rigid body with no points constrained to remain fixed in space.

## 8–8 Lagrange's equations for a two-particle system*

A two-particle system has six degrees of freedom—that is, its most general motion is describable in terms of six (three for each particle) independent coordinates. These coordinates may be the six cartesian coordinates describing the positions of the two particles in space. On the other hand, they may be any six coordinates which have a one-to-one correspondence with the sets of two points $(x_a, y_a, z_a)$ and $(x_b, y_b, z_b)$ of the two particles $a$ and $b$. That is, to each

---

* We note that the equations derived in this section for a two-particle system are equally applicable to an $N$-particle system by extending the summation from six to $3N$.

set of values of the generalized coordinates $q_1$, $q_2$, . . . , $q_6$, there exists one and only one set of values $(x_a, y_a, z_a)$ and $(x_b, y_b, z_b)$, and vice versa. This means that the cartesian coordinates of the two particles are single-valued functions of the six generalized coordinates, which in turn are single-valued functions of the cartesian coordinates of the two particles. The three coordinates describing the position of the center of mass and the three coordinates describing the relative position of the particles of a two-particle system with respect to each other are one example of a set of six frequently used generalized coordinates.

Before proceeding to discuss Lagrange's method for setting up the generalized equations of motion, we introduce a slight change in our notation. This change will indicate the analogy of our present derivation of Lagrange's equations for a two-particle system to their derivation for a single particle. It should also clarify the generalization to systems of a larger number of particles.

Notationally we shall refer to the six cartesian coordinates specifying the positions of the two particles $a$ and $b$ by $x_i$, where

$$x_1 = x_a, \quad x_2 = y_a, \quad x_3 = z_a,$$
$$x_4 = x_b, \quad x_5 = y_b, \quad x_6 = z_b. \tag{8–84}$$

We shall use a similar notation for the cartesian components of all other vectors. Thus, for example, the cartesian components of the forces $\mathbf{F}_a$ and $\mathbf{F}_b$ acting on the two particles, respectively, will be represented by $F_i$, where

$$F_1 = F_{ax}, \quad F_2 = F_{ay}, \quad F_3 = F_{az},$$
$$F_4 = F_{bx}, \quad F_5 = F_{by}, \quad F_6 = F_{bz}. \tag{8–85}$$

In specifying the cartesian components of any two similar vectors belonging, respectively, to the two particles $a$ and $b$, we shall find it convenient to arrange the six cartesian components of these two vectors in a six-element column matrix. Thus the two-position vectors $\mathbf{r}_a$ and $\mathbf{r}_b$ are simultaneously represented by the matrix

$$(\mathbf{r}) = \begin{bmatrix} x_1 \\ x_2 \\ x_3 \\ x_4 \\ x_5 \\ x_6 \end{bmatrix}, \tag{8–86}$$

and similarly the two forces $\mathbf{F}_a$ and $\mathbf{F}_b$ are simultaneously represented by the matrix

$$(\mathbf{F}) = \begin{bmatrix} F_1 \\ F_2 \\ F_3 \\ F_4 \\ F_5 \\ F_6 \end{bmatrix}. \tag{8–87}$$

In this notation the cartesian components of Newton's equations of motion for the two particles are represented by the elements of the matrix equation

$$(\mathbf{F}) = (\mathbf{m})(\mathbf{a}), \tag{8–88}$$

where $(\mathbf{m})$ is the diagonal square matrix defined by

$$(\mathbf{m}) = \begin{bmatrix} m_a & 0 & 0 & 0 & 0 & 0 \\ 0 & m_a & 0 & 0 & 0 & 0 \\ 0 & 0 & m_a & 0 & 0 & 0 \\ 0 & 0 & 0 & m_b & 0 & 0 \\ 0 & 0 & 0 & 0 & m_b & 0 \\ 0 & 0 & 0 & 0 & 0 & m_b \end{bmatrix}. \tag{8–89}$$

From a mathematical point of view, what we have done is to set up a six-dimensional vector space in which the six-dimensional vectors are represented by six-dimensional matrices. The most general vector $\mathbf{A}$ in this six-dimensional space represents simultaneously two three-dimensional vectors belonging, respectively, to each of the two particles. Such a six-dimensional vector space is referred to as the direct sum of the two three-dimensional vector spaces, a fact denoted by

$$|\mathbf{A}) = |\mathbf{A}_a \oplus \mathbf{A}_b). \tag{8–90}$$

In this notation we can also, if we so desire, refer to just one of the three-dimensional vectors. For example, the vector

$$|\mathbf{A}_a \oplus \mathbf{0}) \leftrightarrow \begin{bmatrix} A_1 \\ A_2 \\ A_3 \\ 0 \\ 0 \\ 0 \end{bmatrix}$$

specifies the three-dimensional vector $\mathbf{A}_a$ in the six-dimensional notation.

The algebra of vectors in a six-dimensional space is the same as the algebra of vectors in a three-dimensional vector space.

Two vectors $|\mathbf{A})$ and $|\mathbf{B})$ are said to be equal if the corresponding elements of their matrix representations are equal,

$$A_i = B_i. \tag{8–91}$$

The null vector is the vector whose matrix representation has zero for all its elements.

Two vectors may be added to yield a third vector. Thus if $|\mathbf{C})$ is the sum of the two vectors $|\mathbf{A})$ and $|\mathbf{B})$,

$$|\mathbf{C}) = |\mathbf{A}) + |\mathbf{B}), \tag{8–92}$$

then the elements of the matrix representing the vector $|\mathbf{C})$ are given by

$$C_i = A_i + B_i. \tag{8-93}$$

Two vectors in a six-dimensional vector space may also be multiplied. The scalar or *inner product* of two vectors, designated by $(\mathbf{A}|\mathbf{B})$, is defined by the equation

$$(\mathbf{A}|\mathbf{B}) = \sum_{i=1}^{6} A_i B_i. \tag{8-94}$$

(We note that we are dealing with a cartesian coordinate system; hence no distinction between $A_i$ and $A_i^\star$.)   Here, as in the three-dimensional case, $(\mathbf{A}| = |\widetilde{\mathbf{A}})$ refers to the same vector $\mathbf{A}$.   The matrix representation of $(\mathbf{A}|$, however, is a row matrix,

$$(\mathbf{A}| \leftrightarrow [A_1, A_2, \ldots, A_6],$$

whereas the vector $|\mathbf{A})$ is always represented by a column matrix,

$$|\mathbf{A}) \leftrightarrow \begin{bmatrix} A_1 \\ A_2 \\ A_3 \\ A_4 \\ A_5 \\ A_6 \end{bmatrix}.$$

The cartesian orthogonal unit base vectors $|\mathbf{e}_i)$ of this six-dimensional vector space have matrix representations whose elements are the Kronecker delta

$$\delta_{ij} = \begin{cases} 0 & i \neq j, \\ 1 & i = j. \end{cases} \tag{8-95}$$

Specifically,

$$|\mathbf{e}_1) \leftrightarrow \begin{bmatrix} 1 \\ 0 \\ 0 \\ 0 \\ 0 \\ 0 \end{bmatrix}, \qquad |\mathbf{e}_2) \leftrightarrow \begin{bmatrix} 0 \\ 1 \\ 0 \\ 0 \\ 0 \\ 0 \end{bmatrix}, \qquad \text{etc.} \tag{8-96}$$

In terms of any set of orthogonal unit base vectors, any vector $|\mathbf{A})$ is expressible in the form

$$|\mathbf{A}) = \sum_{i=1}^{6} A_i | \mathbf{e}_i), \tag{8-97}$$

where

$$A_i = (\mathbf{e}_i | \mathbf{A}). \tag{8-98}$$

This result is obtainable by taking the inner product of Eq. (8–97) with the unit base vectors $(e_j|$. The matrix representation of the base vector $(e_j|$ are

$$(e_1| \leftrightarrow [1, 0, 0, 0, 0, 0],$$
$$(e_2| \leftrightarrow [0, 1, 0, 0, 0, 0], \quad \text{etc.} \tag{8–99}$$

As was the case for three-dimensional vectors (cf. Section 1–5), it is of course not necessary to express a vector $|A)$ as a linear sum of the orthogonal unit base vectors $|e_i)$. Any six linearly independent vectors $|b_i)$ may be utilized. That is, we can set*

$$|A^\star) = \sum_{i=1}^{6} \alpha_i^\star |b_i), \tag{8–100}$$

where the $|b_i)$ are a set of linearly independent vectors specified by their column matrix representations

$$|b_i) \leftrightarrow \begin{bmatrix} b_{i1} \\ b_{i2} \\ b_{i3} \\ \vdots \\ b_{i6} \end{bmatrix}. \tag{8–101}$$

The elements $b_{ij}$ of the matrix representation of the vector $|b_i)$ are the inner products of the vector $|b_i)$ with the cartesian base vectors $(e_j|$. Equation (8–100) represents the six equations

$$A_j = \sum_{i=1}^{6} \alpha_i^\star b_{ij}, \quad j = 1, 2, \cdots 6, \tag{8–102}$$

which are obtainable by taking the inner product of Eq. (8–100) with $(e_j|$. Equation (8–102) may be solved for the $\alpha_i^\star$. A solution is possible only if the determinant of the coefficients of the $\alpha_i^\star$ does not vanish,

$$\det (b_{ij}) \neq 0. \tag{8–103}$$

This is also the necessary and sufficient condition for the $|b_i)$ to be linearly independent.

---

* We recall that $|A)$ and $|A^\star)$ refer to the same vector $A$ (cf. Sections 1–5 and 1–6). The star superscript indicates that we are utilizing the contravariant description of the vector $A$. If the base vectors which are utilized form an orthonormal set of base vectors, then there will of course be no distinction between $|A)$ and $|A^\star)$. We note that when the star in any inner product of two vectors is omitted, the inner product is to be evaluated by utilizing the components of the vectors along a set of cartesian orthonormal set of base vectors.

Analogous to the three-dimensional case, we find it possible to express the scalars $\alpha_i^\star$ as the scalar product of $|\mathbf{A})$ with the reciprocal base vectors $(\boldsymbol{b}_i|$,

$$\alpha_i^\star = (\boldsymbol{b}_i \mid \mathbf{A}^\star). \tag{8-104}$$

The vectors $(\boldsymbol{b}_i|$ are the vectors reciprocal to the base vectors $|\mathbf{b}_i)$. They satisfy the equation

$$(\boldsymbol{b}_i \mid \mathbf{b}_j) = \delta_{ij}, \tag{8-105}$$

whose solution yields the components of the reciprocal vectors. From the symmetry of this equation it follows that the $|\mathbf{b}_j)$'s are in turn the vectors reciprocal to the reciprocal vectors $(\boldsymbol{b}_i|$, and that therefore if we set

$$(\mathbf{A}| = \sum_{i=1}^{6} \alpha_i(\boldsymbol{b}_i|, \tag{8-106}$$

then

$$\alpha_i = (\mathbf{A} \mid \mathbf{b}_i). \tag{8-107}$$

In other words, as was the case for three-dimensional vectors, we find that a vector in a six-dimensional space (or generally an $n$-dimensional space) is specified when its inner product with six (or $n$) linearly independent vectors is known.

We are now in a position to set up the generalized equations of motion. As we do for the three-dimensional case, in dealing with the set of generalized coordinates defined by the transformation equations

$$x_i = x_i(q_1, q_2, \ldots, q_6)$$

or their inverse equations

$$q_i = q_j(x_1, x_2, \ldots, x_6), \tag{8-108}$$

we define the generalized base vectors by the equation

$$|\mathbf{b}_i) = \frac{\partial}{\partial q_i} |\mathbf{r}). \tag{8-109}$$

That is, the cartesian components of the $i$th base vector are given by

$$b_{ij} = \frac{\partial x_j}{\partial q_i}, \tag{8-110}$$

or

$$|\mathbf{b}_i) \leftrightarrow \begin{bmatrix} \dfrac{\partial x_1}{\partial q_i} \\[2mm] \dfrac{\partial x_2}{\partial q_i} \\[1mm] \vdots \\[1mm] \dfrac{\partial x_6}{\partial q_i} \end{bmatrix}. \tag{8-111}$$

Condition (8–103) that these six base vectors be linearly independent expresses the nonvanishing of the Jacobian determinant,

$$
\frac{\partial(x_1, x_2, \ldots, x_6)}{\partial(q_1, q_2, \ldots, q_6)} =
\begin{vmatrix}
\dfrac{\partial x_1}{\partial q_1} & \dfrac{\partial x_1}{\partial q_2} & \dfrac{\partial x_1}{\partial q_3} & \cdots & \dfrac{\partial x_1}{\partial q_6} \\[2mm]
\dfrac{\partial x_2}{\partial q_1} & \dfrac{\partial x_2}{\partial q_2} & \dfrac{\partial x_2}{\partial q_3} & \cdots & \dfrac{\partial x_2}{\partial q_6} \\[2mm]
\vdots & & & & \vdots \\[2mm]
\dfrac{\partial x_6}{\partial q_1} & \dfrac{\partial x_6}{\partial q_2} & & \cdots & \dfrac{\partial x_6}{\partial q_6}
\end{vmatrix}.
\tag{8–112}
$$

This is also the necessary and sufficient condition that there be a one-to-one correspondence between the set of values $(x_1, x_2, \ldots, x_6)$ of the cartesian components of the position vector and the set of values $(q_1, q_2, \ldots, q_6)$ of the six generalized coordinates.

It may be readily verified through the use of Eq. (8–105) that, for time-independent transformations to the generalized coordinates $q_i$, the reciprocal vectors are given by

$$
(b_i| \leftrightarrow \left[ \frac{\partial q_i}{\partial x_1}, \frac{\partial q_i}{\partial x_2}, \ldots, \frac{\partial q_i}{\partial x_6} \right].
\tag{8–113}
$$

In terms of the cartesian components of the generalized base vectors $|\mathbf{b}_i)$, the six-dimensional force vector is represented by the generalized forces which are the inner products of the six-dimensional force vector with the six generalized base vectors,

$$
Q_i = (\mathbf{F}|\mathbf{b}_i) = \sum_{j=1}^{6} b_{ij} F_j = \sum_{j=1}^{6} F_j \frac{\partial x_j}{\partial q_i}.
\tag{8–114}
$$

The generalized momenta $p_i$ which specify the total linear momentum of the system,

$$
\mathbf{p} = m_a \mathbf{v}_a + m_b \mathbf{v}_b,
$$

are given by

$$
p_i = (\mathbf{p}|\mathbf{b}_i) = \sum_{j=1}^{6} m_{jj} \dot{x}_j \frac{\partial x_j}{\partial q_i},
\tag{8–115}
$$

where the $m_{jj}$ are the diagonal elements of the mass matrix defined by Eq. (8–89).

Just as we did in the derivation of Eq. (2–74), we find that here, too, the relation

$$
\frac{\partial x_j}{\partial q_i} = \frac{\partial \dot{x}_j}{\partial \dot{q}_i}
\tag{8–116}
$$

holds, which permits us to express the generalized momenta in the form

$$
p_i = \sum_{j=1}^{6} m_{jj} \dot{x}_j \frac{\partial \dot{x}_j}{\partial \dot{q}_i} = \frac{\partial}{\partial \dot{q}_i} \sum_{j=1}^{6} \frac{1}{2} m_{jj} \dot{x}_j^2 = \frac{\partial}{\partial \dot{q}_i} T,
\tag{8–117}
$$

where $T$ is the total kinetic energy defined by

$$T = \sum_{j=1}^{6} \frac{1}{2} m_{jj} \dot{x}_j^2. \tag{8–118}$$

Similarly, for time-independent coordinate transformations we obtain the contravariant or generalized velocities

$$v_i^{\star} = (b_i|\mathbf{v}) = \sum_{j=1}^{6} \frac{\partial q_i}{\partial x_j} \, \dot{x}_j = \dot{q}_i. \tag{8–119}$$

Finally we obtain the generalized equations of motion which are the inner products of Newton's equation of motion,

$$(\mathbf{F}| = \frac{d}{dt} (\mathbf{p}|, \tag{8–120}$$

with the base vectors $|\mathbf{b}_i)$. We thus obtain Lagrange's equations of motion,

$$(\mathbf{F}|\mathbf{b}_i) = \frac{d}{dt} (\mathbf{p}|\mathbf{b}_i) - \left( \mathbf{p} \left| \frac{d}{dt} \, \mathbf{b}_i \right. \right),$$

or

$$Q_i = \frac{d}{dt} \frac{\partial T}{\partial \dot{q}_i} - \frac{\partial T}{\partial q_i}. \tag{8–121}$$

The last term in the previous equation follows from

$$\left( \mathbf{p} \left| \frac{d\mathbf{b}_i}{dt} \right. \right) = \sum_{j=1}^{6} m_{jj} \dot{x}_j \frac{\partial \dot{x}_j}{\partial q_i} = \frac{\partial}{\partial q_i} \sum_{j=1}^{6} \frac{1}{2} m_{jj} \dot{x}_j^2 = \frac{\partial T}{\partial q_i}. \tag{8–122}$$

In the special case of conservative forces, which are derivable from a potential energy function

$$(\mathbf{F}| \leftrightarrow - \left[ \frac{\partial U}{\partial x_1}, \frac{\partial U}{\partial x_2}, \ldots, \frac{\partial U}{\partial x_6} \right], \tag{8–123}$$

we find the generalized forces to be expressed by

$$Q_i = (\mathbf{F}|\mathbf{b}_i) = - \sum_{j=1}^{6} \frac{\partial U}{\partial x_j} \frac{\partial x_j}{\partial q_i} = - \frac{\partial U}{\partial q_i}.$$

For velocity-independent forces, this equation leads us to Lagrange's equations of motion in the form

$$\frac{d}{dt} \frac{\partial (T - U)}{\partial \dot{q}_i} - \frac{\partial (T - U)}{\partial q_i} = 0. \tag{8–124}$$

For the single-particle case, this equation also represented the equation of motion for velocity-dependent forces, such as magnetic forces, which are derivable from a velocity-dependent potential energy function as expressed by

$$F_i = \frac{d}{dt}\frac{\partial U}{\partial \dot{x}_i} - \frac{\partial U}{\partial x_i}. \tag{8–125}$$

Analogously to the three-dimensional case, for such velocity-dependent forces which yield the generalized forces (cf. Section 6–13)

$$Q_i = \frac{d}{dt}\frac{\partial U}{\partial \dot{q}_i} - \frac{\partial U}{\partial q_i}, \tag{8–126}$$

Eq. (8–124) yields the equations of motion for a system of particles.

## 8–9 Lagrange's equations and conservation theorems

Lagrange's equations are very appropriate for recognizing the constants of the motion. Quite obviously, if the Lagrangian is not a function of the generalized coordinate $q_i$, and if in addition the generalized nonconservative force $Q_i^n$ vanishes, then Lagrange's equation for this coordinate reduces to

$$\frac{d}{dt}\frac{\partial(T - U)}{\partial \dot{q}_i} = 0. \tag{8–127}$$

From this equation we find that the $i$th generalized momentum of the system is

$$p_i = \frac{\partial L}{\partial \dot{q}_i} = \text{const}, \tag{8–128}$$

where

$$L = T - U$$

is the *Lagrangian* of the system. The coordinate $q_i$ for which $\partial L/\partial q_i$ vanishes is referred to as an *ignorable coordinate*. One way of determining the existence of ignorable coordinates is to look for the coordinate symmetry operations which leave the description of the motion invariant.

The description of the motion of a system of particles is left invariant under a coordinate transformation, if the functional dependence of the Lagrangian on the new coordinates and new generalized velocities is the same as its dependence on the old coordinates and old generalized velocities.

For example, let us consider a translation of the origin of the coordinate system from the point $O$ to a new point $O'$ which is an infinitesimal distance $\Delta x_1$ from $O$ along $\mathbf{e}_1$. This translation of the coordinate system is expressed by the transformation equations

$$x'_1 = x_1 - \Delta x_1, \qquad x'_i = x_i, \qquad i \neq 1,$$

between the cartesian components $x_i$ and $x'_i$ which the position vector $\mathbf{r}$ has in the two coordinate systems. The Lagrangian expressed in terms of the new coordinates is related to the Lagrangian expressed in terms of the old in the following way:

$$L'(x_i', \dot{x}_i', t) = L(x_i' + \Delta x_i, \dot{x}_i', t) = L(x_i', \dot{x}_i', t) + \frac{\partial L}{\partial x_1} \Delta x_1,$$

since

$$\Delta x_i = 0, \quad i \neq 1.$$

Thus

$$L'(x_i', \dot{x}_i', t) = L(x_i', \dot{x}_i', t)$$

if $\partial L/\partial x_1$ vanishes. Hence we find the statement that the Lagrangian is invariant under a translation of the coordinate system along the $x_i$-axis to imply the vanishing of the partial derivative of the Lagrangian with respect to $x_i$, which in turn implies the conservation of the $i$th component of the linear momentum $p_i$.

Analogously, if a rotation of the coordinate system about an axis leaves the description of the motion of the system unaffected, then the corresponding component of the angular momentum is conserved. For spherically symmetric problems, for example, such as the motion of a system of particles under the action of a central force and internal forces whose form is independent of the orientation of the coordinate system, the total angular momentum vector is a constant of the motion. We note that this condition on the internal forces is less stringent than the requirement that they be two-body forces which satisfy Newton's third law of motion, which condition we invoked previously in order to arrive at the conservation of the angular momentum of a system of particles.

Another conservation theorem, the conservation of energy, follows from the vanishing of the derivative of the Lagrangian for a conservative system with respect to time. This result is obtainable from the work-energy theorem. Specifically, we find from the expression

$$\sum_{i=1}^{6} \left( \frac{d}{dt} \frac{\partial L}{\partial \dot{q}_i} - \frac{\partial L}{\partial q_i} \right) \Delta q_i = 0 \tag{8-129}$$

that (cf. Section 6–14)

$$\frac{d}{dt} \left( \sum_{i=1}^{6} \frac{\partial L}{\partial \dot{q}_i} \dot{q}_i \right) \Delta t - \sum_{i=1}^{6} \left( \frac{\partial L}{\partial \dot{q}_i} \ddot{q}_i + \frac{\partial L}{\partial q_i} \dot{q}_i \right) \Delta t = 0$$

or

$$\frac{d}{dt} \left( \sum_{i=1}^{6} \frac{\partial L}{\partial \dot{q}_i} \dot{q}_i - L \right) \Delta t + \frac{\partial L}{\partial t} \Delta t = 0. \tag{8-130}$$

Hence if $\partial L/\partial t = 0$, we have the Hamiltonian function

$$H(q_i, p_i) = \sum_{i=1}^{6} p_i \dot{q}_i - L \tag{8-131}$$

as a constant of the motion.

For time-independent coordinate transformations for which

$$\sum_{i=1}^{6} p_i \dot{q}_i = \sum_{i=1}^{6} p_i v_i^{\star} = (\mathbf{p}|\mathbf{v}^{\star}) = 2T,$$

the Hamiltonian represents the total energy

$$H = 2T - (T - U) = T + U. \tag{8–132}$$

We observe that the conservation theorems are intimately related to the symmetry of the system.

As an example, we consider the motion of a system of electrons in an atom under the combined action of the central electric field of the nucleus (assumed to be at rest), their own coulomb interaction, and a uniform external magnetic field directed along the $z$-axis. The Lagrangian for such a system of electrons, whose charge is $-e$, is given by

$$L = \sum_{a=1}^{z} \frac{1}{2} m v_a^2 + \sum_{a=1}^{z} \frac{Ze^2}{4\pi\epsilon_0 r_a} - \frac{1}{2}\sum_{a\neq b} \frac{e^2}{4\pi\epsilon_0 r_{ab}} + \frac{1}{2}\sum_a e\mathbf{v}_a \cdot \mathbf{r}_a \times \mathbf{B}.$$

The use of spherical coordinates for the specification of the location of each of the electrons yields, for the total kinetic energy of the system, the expression

$$\sum_a \frac{1}{2} m v_a^2 = \frac{1}{2}\sum_a m(\dot{r}_a^2 + r_a^2 \dot{\theta}_a^2 + r_a^2 \sin^2 \theta_a \dot{\phi}_a^2),$$

and for the distance between the particles the expression

$$r_{ab} = \sqrt{r_a^2 + r_b^2 + 2r_a r_b \cos\theta_{ab}},$$

where

$$\cos\theta_{ab} = \cos\theta_a \cos\theta_b + \sin\theta_a \sin\theta_b \cos(\phi_a - \phi_b).$$

For the interaction of the system with the magnetic field $\mathbf{B} = B\mathbf{k}$ we obtain

$$\sum_a \frac{1}{2} e\mathbf{v}_a \cdot \mathbf{r}_a \times \mathbf{B} = \frac{1}{2}\frac{eB}{m}\sum_a r_a^2 \sin^2 \theta_a \dot{\phi}_a.$$

The azimuthal angles $\phi$ appear only in the term $\frac{1}{2}\sum_a e^2/4\pi\epsilon_0 r_{ab}$ in the Lagrangian. They appear, however, in such a way as to leave the term invariant under a change in all the azimuthal angles by the same amount. Hence the Lagrangian is invariant to a rotation about the $z$-axis, and therefore the corresponding generalized momentum is conserved. To a first approximation, neglecting the terms containing the magnetic field, the generalized momentum is the $z$-component of the total orbital angular momentum of the system of electrons.

Also, since $L$ is not an explicit function of the time, the Hamiltonian function representing the total energy of the system is also a constant of the motion.

Another interesting observation quite readily verified through the use of the Lagrangian is the proof of Larmor's theorem (cf. Section 6–11), which states that the description of the motion of this system of negatively charged particles having the same charge-to-mass ratio in the coordinate system rotating with an angular velocity

$$\boldsymbol{\omega} = \frac{e}{2m}\, \mathbf{B}$$

is to a first approximation the same as the description in the laboratory frame of reference in the absence of the magnetic field.

The transformation to the new coordinate system which is rotating with respect to the first coordinate system with the constant angular velocity

$$\boldsymbol{\omega} = \frac{e}{2m}\, \mathbf{B}$$

is represented by the relation between the velocities in the two coordinate systems,

$$\mathbf{v}_a = \mathbf{v}_a' + \boldsymbol{\omega} \times \mathbf{r}_a.$$

Inserting this result into the Lagrangian yields the new Lagrangian for the description of the motion in the rotating coordinate system. We thus obtain

$$L' = \frac{1}{2}\sum_a mv_a'^2 + \sum_a \frac{Ze^2}{4\pi\epsilon_0 r_a} - \frac{1}{2}\sum_{a \neq b} \frac{e^2}{4\pi\epsilon_0 r_{ab}} - \frac{1}{2}\sum_a m \left| \frac{e\mathbf{B}}{2m} \times \mathbf{r}_a \right|^2.$$

For small magnetic fields and for electrons moving in bound orbits within a small region of space, which they do in their motion within an atom, the term containing $B^2$ is negligible. To within first orders in $B$, therefore, the description of the motion in the rotating coordinate system is the same as the description of the motion of the system of electrons in the atom in the absence of the magnetic field. We note that this result follows only for a system of charged particles having the same charge-to-mass ratio.

## 8–10 Lagrange's equations for constrained motion of a system

The analogy of the derivation of the generalized equations of motion of a two-particle system with the derivation of the equations of motion for a single particle appears also in the modification of Lagrange's equations of motion on the introduction of holonomic constraints having the form

$$\Phi(q_1, q_2, \ldots, q_6) = 0. \tag{8–133}$$

The justification for the introduction of a constraining force having the form expressed by

$$(\mathbf{R}| \;\leftrightarrow\; \lambda \left( \frac{\partial \Phi}{\partial x_1}, \frac{\partial \Phi}{\partial x_2}, \ldots, \frac{\partial \Phi}{\partial x_6} \right) \tag{8–134}$$

rests on the fact that, for all possible displacements consistent with the constraints, such constraining forces do no work, a fact that is expressed by the equation

$$\Delta W_c = (\mathbf{R}|\Delta\mathbf{r}) = \sum_{i=1}^{6} R_i \, \Delta x_i = 0. \tag{8–135}$$

Since for all such arbitrary displacements consistent with the constraints,

$$\Delta\Phi = \sum_{i=1}^{6} \frac{\partial\Phi}{\partial x_i} \, \Delta x_i = 0,$$

it follows that the components of the constraining force $(\mathbf{R}|$ must be proportional to the elements of the gradient of $\Phi$ as expressed by Eq. (8–134).

The generalized constraining force which is thus introduced by the constraining equation

$$\Phi(q_1, q_2, \ldots, q_6) = 0$$

is found to be given by

$$Q_i = (\mathbf{R}|\mathbf{b}_i) = \sum_{j=1}^{6} \lambda \frac{\partial\Phi}{\partial x_j} \frac{\partial x_j}{\partial q_i} = \lambda \frac{\partial\Phi}{\partial q_i}. \tag{8–136}$$

If more than one constraining equation of the form $\Phi^{(k)}(q_1, \ldots, q_6) = 0$ exists, then the total constraining force is given by

$$Q_i = \sum_{k} (\mathbf{R}^{(k)}|\mathbf{b}_i) = \sum_{k,\,j} R_j^{(k)} \frac{\partial x_j}{\partial q_i} = \sum_{k,\,j} \lambda^{(k)} \frac{\partial\Phi^{(k)}}{\partial x_j} \frac{\partial x_j}{\partial q_i} = \sum_{k} \lambda^{(k)} \frac{\partial\Phi^{(k)}}{\partial q_i}. \tag{8–137}$$

With the introduction of generalized constraining forces, Lagrange's equations for conservative forces become

$$\frac{d}{dt} \frac{\partial L}{\partial \dot{q}_i} - \frac{\partial L}{\partial q_i} = \sum_{k} \lambda^{(k)} \frac{\partial\Phi^{(k)}}{\partial q_i}. \tag{8–138}$$

We note that the argument we used to arrive at Eq. (8–134) for the constraining force introduced by a holonomic constraint can also be used to obtain the modification of Lagrange's equations when the system satisfies nondissipative nonholonomic constraints, which are expressed in the nonintegrable form

$$\sum_{i=1}^{6} \eta_i \, \Delta x_i = \sum_{j=1}^{6} \xi_j \, \Delta q_j = 0, \tag{8–139}$$

where $\eta_i$ and $\xi_j$ are functions of the coordinates and their time derivatives.

If the nonholonomic constraining forces as assumed do no work, then it follows from a comparison of Eqs. (8–139) and (8–135) that we can set

$$R_i = \lambda \eta_i. \tag{8–140}$$

In the case of the existence of several nonholonomic constraints on the system, a fact designated by the superscript $(k)$,

$$\sum_i \eta_i^{(k)} \Delta x_i = \sum_i \xi_j^{(k)} \Delta q_j = 0, \tag{8-141}$$

we express the components of the $k$th constraining force by

$$R_i^{(k)} = \lambda^{(k)} \eta_i^{(k)}. \tag{8-142}$$

We thus obtain the total generalized constraining force

$$Q_j = \sum_k \lambda^{(k)} \xi_j^{(k)}, \tag{8-143}$$

which yields Lagrange's equations in the form

$$\frac{d}{dt} \frac{\partial L}{\partial \dot{q}_i} - \frac{\partial L}{\partial q_i} = \sum_k \lambda^{(k)} \xi_i^{(k)}. \tag{8-144}$$

Our remarks in Section 5–4 concerning the reduction of the number of coordinates through use of the holonomic equations of constraint hold equally well here. If one is not interested in finding the constraining forces, then one may reduce the problem first to the minimum number of independent coordinates required for the description of the motion.

## 8–11 Applications of Lagrange's equations

In this section we shall illustrate the use of Lagrange's method for expressing the equations of motion by considering a number of important soluble $N$-particle problems involving the motion of the particles about a stable configuration. The general theory of small oscillations will be presented in Chapter 11.

(a) *The double pendulum.* To obtain the equations of motion for the double plane pendulum shown in Fig. 8–9, we first express the kinetic and potential energies in terms of the generalized coordinates and their velocities.

The potential energy in terms of the angles $\theta_1$ and $\theta_2$ which the strings make with the vertical is readily found to be given by

$$U = -m_1 g l_1 \cos \theta_1 - m_2 g (l_1 \cos \theta_1 + l_2 \cos \theta_2),$$

where we have utilized the constraining equations

$$r_1 = l_1 \quad \text{and} \quad r_2 = l_2$$

in order to eliminate $r_1$ and $r_2$ from $U$.

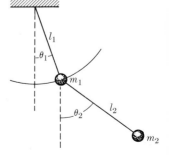

FIG. 8–9.   The double pendulum.

Similarly, when we utilize $\dot{r}_1 = \dot{r}_2 = 0$, the kinetic energy of the first particle moving in a circle of constant radius $l$ is found to be given by

$$T = \tfrac{1}{2} m_1 l_1^2 \dot{\theta}_1^2,$$

and the kinetic energy of the second particle (cf. Problem 3–11) by

$$T = \tfrac{1}{2} m_2 (l_1 \dot{\theta}_1 \sin \theta_1 + l_2 \dot{\theta}_2 \sin \theta_2)^2 + \tfrac{1}{2} m_2 (l_1 \dot{\theta}_1 \cos \theta_1 + l_2 \dot{\theta}_2 \cos \theta_2)^2.$$

The total kinetic energy of the system is thus found to be expressed by

$$T = T_1 + T_2 = \tfrac{1}{2}(m_1 + m_2) l_1^2 \dot{\theta}_1^2 + \tfrac{1}{2} m_2 l_2^2 \dot{\theta}_2^2 + m_2 l_1 l_2 \dot{\theta}_1 \dot{\theta}_2 \cos (\theta_2 - \theta_1).$$

From Eq. (8–124) there thus follow the equations of motion

$$\frac{d}{dt} [(m_1 + m_2) l_1^2 \dot{\theta}_1 + m_2 l_1 l_2 \dot{\theta}_2 \cos (\theta_2 - \theta_1)]$$
$$- (m_1 + m_2) l_1 g \sin \theta_1 - m_2 l_1 l_2 \dot{\theta}_1 \dot{\theta}_2 \sin (\theta_2 - \theta_1) = 0$$

and

$$\frac{d}{dt} [m_2 l_2^2 \dot{\theta}_2 + m_2 l_1 l_2 \dot{\theta}_1 \cos (\theta_2 - \theta_1)]$$
$$- m_2 l_2 g \sin \theta_2 + m_2 l_1 l_2 \dot{\theta}_1 \dot{\theta}_2 \sin (\theta_2 - \theta_1) = 0.$$

The interesting part of this example is the case when the angles $\theta_1$ and $\theta_2$ are small so that we can neglect all but the terms in the first power in $\theta_i$ and $\dot{\theta}_i$. To within this approximation, the equations of motion reduce to

$$(m_1 + m_2) l_1^2 \ddot{\theta}_1 + m_2 l_1 l_2 \ddot{\theta}_2 - (m_1 + m_2) l_1 g \theta_1 = 0$$

and

$$m_2 l_2^2 \ddot{\theta}_2 + m_2 l_1 l_2 \ddot{\theta}_1 - m_2 l_2 g \theta_2 = 0.$$

These are the equations of motion of a pair of coupled simple harmonic oscillators, the general equations for which have the form

$$L_1 x_1 + L_2 x_2 = 0, \qquad L_3 x_1 + L_4 x_2 = 0, \qquad (8\text{–}145)$$

where the $L_i$ in this case are linear differential operators with constant coefficients. A general method for solving such a pair of simultaneous equations is to apply the operator $L_3$ on the first equation and the operator $L_1$ on the second. Since linear operators with constant coefficients commute, that is, since

$$L_1 L_3 = L_3 L_1, \qquad (8\text{–}146)$$

it follows that, on subtracting the resulting equations, we obtain the equation

$$(L_3 L_2 - L_1 L_4) x_2 = 0. \qquad (8\text{–}147)$$

Similarly, we can obtain the equation

$$(L_3L_2 - L_1L_4)x_1 = 0. \tag{8-148}$$

[*Question:* How can one obtain the equations satisfied by $x_1$ and $x_2$ when the linear operators in Eq. (8–145) do not commute?] Since the $L_i$'s are differential operators with constant coefficients, it should be clear that the operator $(L_3L_2 - L_1L_4)$ is likewise a differential operator with constant coefficients. This means that we should expect the solutions of Eq. (8–145) to be expressible in the form

$$x_1 = Ae^{\alpha t}, \qquad x_2 = Be^{\alpha t}, \tag{8-149}$$

where $\alpha$ is a root of the characteristic equation which one obtains for the operator $L_3L_2 - L_1L_4$. To find the relation between the constants $A$ and $B$, we insert the trial solution (8–149) into Eq. (8–145), which then yields the equation

$$L_1(\alpha)A + L_2(\alpha)B = 0$$

and

$$L_3(\alpha)A + L_4(\alpha)B = 0, \tag{8-150}$$

where $L_i(\alpha)$ is the linear operator $L_i(d/dt)$ with $d/dt$ replaced by $\alpha$. These equations yield a nontrivial solution for $A$ and $B$, since $\alpha$ is a root of the equation

$$L_3(\alpha)L_2(\alpha) - L_1(\alpha)L_4(\alpha) = 0. \tag{8-151}$$

It follows therefore that

$$B = -\frac{L_1(\alpha)}{L_2(\alpha)} A, \tag{8-152}$$

yielding for nondegenerate roots the general solution

$$x_1 = \sum_i A_i e^{\alpha_i t}, \qquad x_2 = -\sum_i A_i \frac{L_1(\alpha_i)}{L_2(\alpha_i)} e^{\alpha_i t}. \tag{8-153}$$

The case with degenerate roots will be discussed in Chapter 11. There we shall also show that, for a pair of undamped coupled oscillators like the two pendulums under discussion, the roots of the secular equation are imaginary. The solutions are thus expressible as the sum of two sinusoidal terms

$$x_1 = A_1 \sin(\omega_1 t + \phi_1) + A_2 \sin(\omega_2 t + \phi_2)$$

and

$$x_2 = -A_1 \frac{L_1(i\omega_1)}{L_2(i\omega_1)} \sin(\omega_1 t + \phi_1) - A_2 \frac{L_1(i\omega_2)}{L_2(i\omega_2)} \sin(\omega_2 t + \phi_2).$$

The constants $A_1$, $A_2$, $\phi_1$, and $\phi_2$ which appear in the general solution are determined from the initial positions and velocities of the particles.

For proper initial conditions either one of the amplitudes $A_1$ or $A_2$ may vanish. In that case the pendulums will oscillate with the same single frequency. Such a mode of oscillation is referred to as a *normal mode of oscillation* of the system. The general motion is thus expressible as a linear sum of the normal modes of oscillation

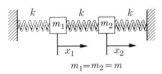

FIG. 8–10. Two coupled oscillators.     FIG. 8–11. Two coupled oscillators.

(b) *Two coupled oscillators.* Another very interesting example is the case of two equal masses joined by identical springs to each other and to two fixed walls as shown in Fig. 8–10. The motion is undamped and constrained to take place along a straight line. The kinetic energy of the system is given by

$$T = \tfrac{1}{2}m_1\dot{x}_1^2 + \tfrac{1}{2}m_2\dot{x}_2^2, \tag{8–154}$$

and the potential energy of the springs by

$$U = \tfrac{1}{2}kx_1^2 + \tfrac{1}{2}k(x_2 - x_1)^2 + \tfrac{1}{2}kx_2^2. \tag{8–155}$$

These relations for the kinetic and potential energies lead to the two equations of motion

$$m\ddot{x}_1 + m\omega_0^2 x_1 - m\omega_0^2(x_2 - x_1) = 0 \tag{8–156}$$

and

$$m\ddot{x}_2 + m\omega_0^2 x_2 + m\omega_0^2(x_2 - x_1) = 0, \tag{8–157}$$

where we have set the spring constant

$$k = m\omega_0^2 \tag{8–158}$$

and $m_1 = m_2 = m$. Assuming, as outlined above, a solution of the form

$$x_1 = Ae^{\alpha t}, \qquad x_2 = Be^{\alpha t}, \tag{8–159}$$

we obtain the equations

$$(\alpha^2 + 2\omega_0^2)A - \omega_0^2 B = 0$$

and

$$-\omega_0^2 A + (\alpha^2 + 2\omega_0^2)B = 0. \tag{8–160}$$

These are two homogeneous simultaneous equations for the constants $A$ and $B$. They have a solution only if the determinant of the coefficients vanishes,

$$\begin{vmatrix} \alpha^2 + 2\omega_0^2 & -\omega_0^2 \\ -\omega_0^2 & \alpha^2 + 2\omega_0^2 \end{vmatrix} = 0. \tag{8–161}$$

This equation has the roots

$$\alpha = \pm i\omega_0, \qquad \pm i\sqrt{3}\omega_0. \tag{8-162}$$

The general solution is thus expressible in the form

$$x_1 = A_1 \cos(\omega_0 t + \phi_1) + A_2 \cos(\sqrt{3}\omega_0 t + \phi_2)$$

and

$$x_2 = B_1 \cos(\omega_0 t + \phi_1) + B_2 \cos(\sqrt{3}\omega_0 t + \phi_2),$$

where from Eq. (1–160) it follows that

$$B_j = \frac{2\omega_0^2 + \alpha_j^2}{\omega_0^2} A_j, \qquad j = 1, 2. \tag{8-163}$$

Hence the general solution is expressed by

$$x_1 = A_1 \cos(\omega_0 t + \phi_1) + A_2 \cos(\sqrt{3}\omega_0 t + \phi_2)$$

and

$$x_2 = A_1 \cos(\omega_0 t + \phi_1) - A_2 \cos(\sqrt{3}\omega_0 t + \phi_1). \tag{8-164}$$

The constants $A_1$, $A_2$, $\phi_1$, and $\phi_2$ are obtainable from the initial values of the position and the velocity of the particles. We find that, for a proper choice of initial conditions, either $A_1$ or $A_2$ may vanish. We note that in the first mode of oscillation ($A_2 = 0$), the two particles oscillate together in phase, whereas in the second mode ($A_1 = 0$) they are $\pi$ radians out of phase. That the solutions should have this property follows from symmetry considerations of the problem.

For example, we note that in this problem an interchange of the two particles yields the same equations of motion. One way such an interchange can be accomplished is by an interchange in the numbers assigned to the particles. This would result in the configuration depicted in Fig. 8–11. The equations of motion for the new configuration being the same as before results in the identical general solutions. This means, as we shall discuss in Chapter 10, that the general solution of this problem can be decomposed into the linear sum of two solutions, one of which is even to an interchange of the particles and the other odd. In other words, the normal mode solutions are expected to be either symmetric or antisymmetric to an interchange of the subscripts on the coordinates. A choice of generalized coordinates which are symmetric and antisymmetric with respect to an interchange of the particles should thus be expected to lead to two simpler equations of motion. Indeed we find that the Lagrangian expressed in terms of the generalized coordinates

$$q_1 = \tfrac{1}{2}(x_1 + x_2) \qquad \text{and} \qquad q_2 = \tfrac{1}{2}(x_1 - x_2)$$

or

$$x_1 = q_1 + q_2 \qquad \text{and} \qquad x_2 = q_1 - q_2,$$

leads to the very much simpler independent equations of motion

$$\ddot{q}_1 + \omega_0^2 q_1 = 0 \qquad \text{and} \qquad \ddot{q}_2 + 3\omega_0^2 q_2 = 0.$$

The solutions to these equations are the normal modes found above. The coordinates $q_1$ and $q_2$ are referred to as the *normal coordinates* of the system. Symmetry considerations are very helpful in simplifying the solution of small vibration problems. They have been used extensively in the analysis of the normal vibrational modes of oscillations of molecules.* We shall discuss this more fully in Chapter 11.

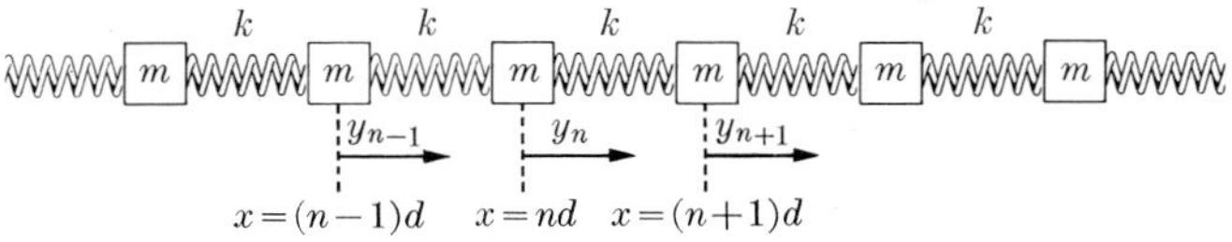

Fig. 8–12. An infinite set of coupled oscillators.

(c) *An infinite set of coupled oscillators.* In this example we consider an infinite set of identical particles connected, as shown in Fig. 8–12, by identical springs of constant

$$k = m\omega_0^2.$$

We number the particles from $-\infty$ to $\infty$ and let $y_n$ represent the displacement of the $n$th particle from its equilibrium position $x = nd$, where $d$ is the equilibrium distance between neighboring particles. The equation of motion for the $n$th particle is readily obtained from the Lagrangian

$$L = T - U,$$

where

$$T = \sum \tfrac{1}{2} m \dot{y}_n^2$$

and

$$U = \sum \tfrac{1}{2} m \omega_0^2 (y_{n+1} - y_n)^2.$$

It is found to be

$$m \frac{d^2 y_n}{dt^2} = m\omega_0^2 (y_{n+1} + y_{n-1} - 2y_n).$$

As in the previous example, it is appropriate to attempt to find a solution through the use of

$$y_n = A_n e^{i\omega t}$$

as a trial solution for the $n$th particle. This, however, would lead us to the difficult-to-solve infinite set of simultaneous equations

$$-\omega^2 A_n = \omega_0^2 (A_{n+1} + A_{n-1} - 2A_n).$$

It is therefore appropriate to investigate the symmetry of the problem and see what simplification it introduces. Among the several symmetry operations

---

* Gerhard Herzberg, *Molecular Spectra and Molecular Structure.* Princeton, N.J.: Van Nostrand, 1950.

which exist for this problem, there is the invariance of the equations of motion with respect to a change in the numbering of the particles or, equivalently, to the location of the particles along the $x$-axis. Any change by an integer in the numbers assigned to the particles will not affect the equations of motion. Furthermore, two such changes, the first increasing the numbers assigned to the particles by $m_1$ and the second by $m_2$, are equivalent to changing them in one operation by $m_1 + m_2$. This is a property exhibited by exponential functions and implies that the general solution for any particle has the same form as the general solution for any other particle and that the constants which appear in the solution differ at most by an exponential factor expressible as $e^{itnd}$.

---

We can appreciate how this exponential factor enters from the following considerations. Consider the equation of motion for the $n$th particle for large $n$. For large values of $n$ the right-hand side can be taken as an approximation for the second partial derivative of $y_n$ considered to be a continuous function of $n$. We note that $\Delta n = 1$, and that hence

$$\frac{\partial y_{n+1}}{\partial n} \approx \frac{y_{n+1} - y_n}{\Delta n} = y_{n+1} - y_n$$

and

$$\frac{\partial y_n}{\partial n} \approx \frac{y_n - y_{n-1}}{\Delta n} = y_n - y_{n-1}.$$

Therefore

$$\frac{\partial^2 y_n}{\partial n^2} \approx \frac{(\partial y_{n+1}/\partial n) - (\partial y_n/\partial n)}{\Delta n} \approx (y_{n+1} + y_{n-1} - 2y_n).$$

The equation which resulted for the trial solution

$$y_n = A_n e^{i\omega t}$$

can thus be expressed approximately as

$$-\omega^2 A_n = \omega_0^2 \frac{\partial^2 A_n}{\partial n^2} = (\omega_0 d)^2 \frac{\partial^2 A_n}{\partial (nd)^2}.$$

This equation has the solutions

$$A_n = A e^{\pm i(\omega/\omega_0 d)nd},$$

thus yielding

$$y_n = A e^{i[\omega t \pm (\omega/\omega_0 d)nd]}.$$

---

Choosing therefore

$$y_n = A e^{i(\omega t + tnd)}$$

as a new trial solution, we obtain

$$-\omega^2 A = \omega_0^2 A (e^{itd} + e^{-itd} - 2) = -\left(4\omega_0^2 \sin^2 \frac{td}{2}\right) A.$$

This equation yields the values of $\mathfrak{f}$ for which a solution is possible:

$$\pm \mathfrak{f} = \frac{2}{d} \sin^{-1}\left(\frac{\omega}{2\omega_0}\right).$$

We note that as $\omega$ increases from zero to $2\omega_0$, $|\mathfrak{f}|$ varies from zero to $\pi/d$. For values of $\omega$ larger than $2\omega_0$, $\mathfrak{f}$ becomes imaginary. This, as we shall see, means that oscillations of frequencies $\omega$ larger than $2\omega_0$ will not be propagated. Therefore $\omega = 2\omega_0$ is referred to as the *cutoff frequency*. It is the highest frequency with which one of the particles could, for example, be driven and for which all the other particles will pick up the oscillation.

We note that the real or imaginary part of

$$y_n = A e^{i(\omega t \pm \mathfrak{f} n d)}$$

represents specific values of the functions

$$y = A \cos(\omega t + \mathfrak{f}x) \quad \text{and} \quad y = A \sin(\omega t + \mathfrak{f}x),$$

which are the solutions of the wave equation

$$\frac{\partial^2 y}{\partial x^2} = \frac{1}{V^2}\frac{\partial^2 y}{\partial t^2}.$$

They represent harmonic waves traveling in the negative and positive $x$-direction with a velocity (cf. Chapter 12)

$$V = \omega/\mathfrak{f}.$$

We can thus think of the modes of oscillations found as propagating waves. For small values of $\omega$ and $\mathfrak{f}$ for which

$$\omega = 2\omega_0 \sin\frac{\mathfrak{f}d}{2} = \omega_0\mathfrak{f}d,$$

the approximate velocity of propagation is independent of the frequency, and is found to be given by

$$V = \omega/\mathfrak{f} = \omega_0 d = V_0.$$

This situation also occurs for small $d$ over a large range of frequencies.

We note that the appearance of a cutoff frequency is characteristic of any periodic structure. For example, for the frequency and incident direction for which Bragg diffraction occurs (cf. Section 1–5), that is, when

$$2d \sin\theta = m\lambda,$$

the electromagnetic wave is not propagated in the crystal.

In conclusion, we proceed to show how the most general solution for the infinite sets of coupled oscillators may be utilized to obtain the solution to the previous example. The previous problem may be considered to consist of an infinite set of particles with the $n = 0$ and $n = 3$ particles being constrained to remain at rest. This requires us to set the solutions for the $n = 0$ and $n = 3$ particles equal to zero. The general solution

$$y_n = e^{i\omega t}(Ae^{itnd} + Be^{-itnd})$$

thus yields

$$y_0 = e^{i\omega t}(A + B) = 0$$

and

$$y_3 = e^{i\omega t}(Ae^{3itd} + Be^{-3itd}) = 0.$$

The first of these two equations yields $A = -B$, and hence from the second we obtain $\sin 3fd = 0$. This equation can be satisfied only if $3fd = \pi$ or $2\pi$, which leads to

$$\omega = 2\omega_0 \sin \frac{fd}{2} = 2\omega_0 \sin \frac{\pi}{6} = \omega_0$$

or

$$\omega = 2\omega_0 \sin \frac{\pi}{3} = \omega_0\sqrt{3},$$

in agreement with the results found previously. The general solutions for particles one and two are therefore expressible as

$$y_1 = \mathrm{Re}\left(\frac{2A_1}{\sqrt{3}} e^{i\phi_1} e^{i\omega_0 t} \sin \frac{\pi}{3} + \frac{2A_2}{\sqrt{3}} e^{i\phi_2} e^{i\omega_0\sqrt{3}t} \sin \frac{2\pi}{3}\right)$$

$$= A_1 \cos (\omega_0 t + \phi_1) + A_2 \cos (\omega_0\sqrt{3}t + \phi_2)$$

and

$$y_2 = \mathrm{Re}\left(\frac{2A_1}{\sqrt{3}} e^{i\phi_1} e^{i\omega_0 t} \sin \frac{2\pi}{3} + \frac{2A_2}{\sqrt{3}} e^{i\phi_2} e^{i\omega_0\sqrt{3}t} \sin \frac{4\pi}{3}\right)$$

$$= A_1 \cos (\omega_0 t + \phi_1) - A_2 \cos (\omega_0\sqrt{3}t + \phi_2).$$

The example of this section and its extension to the more difficult two- and three-dimensional cases are important in the discussion of the vibrational modes of oscillation of crystals.

## Problems

8–1. A stationary particle of mass $3m$ kg explodes into three equal pieces. Two of the pieces fly off at right angles to each other, one with a speed of $2a$ m/sec, the other with a speed of $3a$ m/sec. What is the magnitude and direction of momentum of the third fragment? The explosion takes place in $10^{-5}$ sec. Find the average force acting on each piece during the explosion.

8–2. A nucleus, originally at rest, decays radioactively by emitting an electron of momentum 1.73 Mev/c, and at right angles to the direction of the electron a neutrino with momentum 1.00 Mev/$c$. [The *Mev* (million electron volt) is a unit of energy used in modern physics that is equal to $1.59 \times 10^{-6}$ erg. Correspondingly, Mev/$c$, where c is the speed of light, is a unit of linear momentum equal to $5.33 \times 10^{-16}$ g-cm/sec.] In what direction does the nucleus recoil? What is its momentum in Mev/$c$? If the mass of the residual nucleus is $3.90 \times 10^{-22}$ g, what is its kinetic energy in electron volts?

8–3. In a head-on collision, a particle with an initial speed $v_0$ strikes a stationary particle of the same mass. Find the velocity of the two particles after the collision if (a) half the original kinetic energy is lost, (b) the final kinetic energy is 50% greater than the original kinetic energy.

8–4. A particle of mass $M_1$ and velocity $V_1$ is captured by a nucleus at rest. A light particle of mass $M_2$ is ejected at 90° from the path of $M_1$ with a speed $V_2$, the rest of the nucleus (mass $M_3$) recoiling with the speed $V_3$. Show that the kinetic energy of $M_2$ is

$$T_2 = \frac{M_3}{M_2 + M_3}\left(Q + \frac{M_3 - M_1}{M_3}\, T_1\right),$$

where $Q$ is the energy absorbed in the reaction.

8–5. The projectile particle in an elastic collision is observed to be scattered through an angle $\theta_1$, while the path of the target particle, initially at rest, is observed to make an angle $\theta_2$ with the incident direction of the projectile particle. Find the ratio $m_1/m_2$ of the masses of the two particles.

8–6. A particle of mass $m_1$ and momentum $p_1$ collides with a particle of mass $m_2$ at rest. A reaction occurs and two particles of masses $m_3$ and $m_4$ result, which leave the scene of collision at angles $\theta_3$ and $\theta_4$ with the original path of $m_1$. Find the energy $Q$ absorbed in the reaction in terms of the masses, the angles, and $p_1$.

8–7. In a nuclear reaction whose $Q$ is known, the directions of the incident particle of mass $m_1$ and the product particles of masses $m_3$ and $m_4$ are measured. Express the energy of the incident particle in terms of the masses of the particles, the reaction energy $Q$, and the angles $\theta_3$ and $\theta_4$ of the paths of the product particles with respect to the incident direction.

8–8. A raindrop of initial mass $m_0$ gram falls from rest through a cloud whose thickness is $a$ cm. As it falls, the drop gains mass at the rate of $b$ g/sec. The droplets of the cloud are at rest relative to the ground. The motion of the drop is resisted by a force proportional to the velocity. (a) Write the differential equation for the motion of the raindrop. (b) Find the velocity of the drop as it emerges from the cloud if, during the passage, its mass has been doubled. (c) What will the limiting velocity of the drop be after it leaves the cloud, assuming that the air resistance outside the cloud is the same as that within?

8–9. A two-stage rocket is to be built capable of accelerating a 100-kg payload to a velocity of 6000 m/sec in free flight. (In a two-stage rocket, before the second stage is fired, the first stage is detached after exhausting its fuel.) Assume that the fuel used can reach an exhaust velocity of 1500 m/sec, and that structural requirements imply that an empty rocket (without fuel or payload) will weigh 10% as much as the fuel it can carry. Find the optimum choice of masses for the two stages so that the total take-off weight is a minimum. Show that it is impossible to build a single-stage rocket which will do the job.

8–10. Show that the angle of recoil of the scattering or recoil particle relative to the incident direction of the scattered particle in an elastic collision is

$$\Phi = \tfrac{1}{2}(\pi - \theta').$$

8–11. Set up Lagrange's equations for the compound Atwood machine of Fig. 8–13. (Here the body of mass $m_2$ of the simple Atwood machine is replaced by a second pulley over which passes another light string with a body of mass $m_2$ on one end and one of mass $m_3$ on the other.) Neglect the effect of the pulleys on the motion.

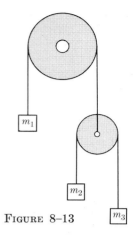

FIGURE 8–13

8–12. Two mass points of mass $m_1$ and $m_2$ are connected by a string passing through a hole in a smooth table so that $m_1$ rests on the table surface and $m_2$ hangs suspended. Assuming that $m_2$ moves only in a vertical line, what is a good set of generalized coordinates for the system? Write down Lagrange's equations for the system and, if possible, discuss the physical significance any of them might have. Reduce the problem to a single second-order differential equation, and obtain a first integral of the equation. What is its physical significance? (Consider the motion only so long as neither $m_1$ nor $m_2$ passes through the hole.) Discuss qualitatively the motion expected.

8–13. A bead of mass $3m$ is free to slide horizontally without friction on a wire, as shown in Fig. 8–14. Attached to the bead is a double pendulum. If the system is released from rest in a position near its equilibrium position, the masses oscillate, in the plane of the figure, about the vertical. (a) Write Lagrange's equations of motion for the system. (b) Find the accelerations when the displacements and velocities are small.

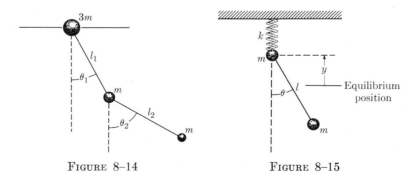

FIGURE 8–14                    FIGURE 8–15

8–14. A plane pendulum of length $l$ and bob $m$ is suspended from a second bob of mass $m$ attached to a stiff spring, as shown in Fig. 8–15. The spring constant is $k$. We neglect the mass of the support wire and of the spring in comparison with $m$. The second bob is restricted to vertical motion. (a) Write Lagrange's equations of motion for the system. (b) Interpret physically the terms in these equations.

8–15. A flyball governor for a steam engine is shown in Fig. 8–16. Two balls, each of mass $m$, are attached by means of four hinged arms, each of length $l$, to sleeves which slide on a vertical rod. The upper sleeve is fastened to the rod; the lower sleeve has the mass $M$ and is free to slide up and down the rod as the balls move out from or toward the rod. The rod-and-ball system rotates with constant angular velocity $\omega$. (a) Set up the equation for the motion, neglecting the weight of the arms and rod. Discuss the motion by the energy method (cf. Section 4–7). (b) Determine the value of the height $z$ of the lower sleeve above its lowest point as a function of $\omega$ for steady rotation of the balls, and find the frequency of small oscillations of $z$ about this steady value.

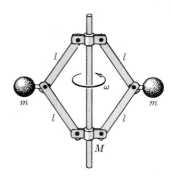

FIGURE 8–16

8–16. Discuss the motion of the governor described in Problem 8–15 if the shaft is not constrained to rotate at an angular velocity $\omega$, but is free to rotate without any externally applied torque. (a) Find the angular velocity of steady rotation for a given height $z$ of the lower sleeve. (b) Find the frequency of small vibrations about this steady motion. (c) How does this motion differ from that of Problem 8–16?

8–17. Two simple pendulums, each of mass 1 kg and length 1 m, are coupled by a light horizontal spring between the bobs. The spring has a stiffness factor $k$ of 6.2 n/m. (Fig. 8–17.) Assuming small amplitudes, find (a) the natural frequency of the pendulums before coupling, (b) the natural frequency of one coupled pendulum when the other is held at rest, (c) the frequencies for the two normal modes of vibration, and (d) the beat frequency with which energy is passed back and forth when one pendulum is set vibrating initially.

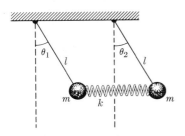

FIGURE 8–17

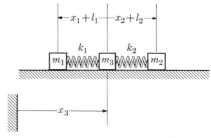

FIGURE 8–18

8–18. Set up the equations of motion for the system shown in Fig. 8–18. The relaxed lengths of the two springs are $l_1$, $l_2$. Separate the problem into two parts, one involving the motion of the center of mass, and the other involving the "internal motion" described by the two coordinates $x_1$, $x_2$. Find the normal modes of vibration.

8–19. The system of coupled oscillators shown in Fig. 8–10 is subject to a horizontal force

$$F = F_0 \cos \omega t$$

applied to mass $m_1$. Set up the equations of motion and find the steady-state solution. Sketch the amplitude and phase of the oscillations of each oscillator as functions of $\omega$.

8–20. Find the two normal modes of vibration for the pair of identically damped coupled harmonic oscillators shown in Fig. 8–19.

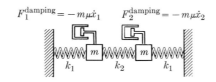

FIGURE 8–19

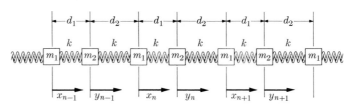

FIGURE 8–20

8–21. (a) Obtain the normal solutions for the infinite set of coupled oscillators, shown in Fig. 8–20, of the form

$$x_n = A e^{i(\omega t + \ell n d)}$$

and

$$y_n = B e^{i(\omega t + \ell n d)},$$

where $d = d_1 + d_2$. (b) What is the cutoff frequency for this set of oscillators?

8–22. Utilizing the results of the previous problem, obtain the normal modes of oscillation of the system of coupled oscillators shown in Fig. 8–21.

8–23. Consider the two semi-infinite sets of coupled oscillators coupled as shown in Fig. 8–22.

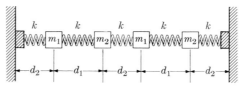

FIGURE 8–21

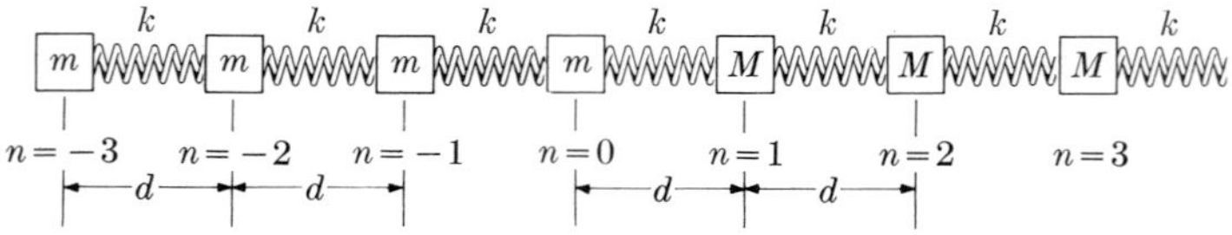

FIGURE 8–22

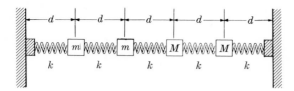

FIGURE 8–23

Show that solutions of the form

$$x_n = \begin{cases} Ae^{i(\omega t - f_1 nd)} + Be^{i(\omega t + f_1 nd)} & n \leq 0 \\ Ce^{i(\omega t + f_2 nd)} & n > 0 \end{cases}$$

and

$$x_n = \begin{cases} Fe^{i(\omega t + f_1 nd)} & n \leq 0 \\ Ee^{i(\omega t - f_2 nd)} + De^{i(\omega t + f_2 nd)} & n > 0 \end{cases}$$

exist.  Relate $B$ and $C$ to $A$, and $E$ and $F$ to $D$.

8–24.  Utilize the results of Problem 8–23 to obtain the normal modes of oscillation of the set of oscillators shown in Fig. 8–23.

# 9

# *Rigid-Body Motion*

A rigid body is a system of particles whose distances from each other do not change. Real bodies do not satisfy this restriction. But in many applications the deformations which they undergo are negligibly small. Consequently, the results we obtain here for rigid bodies are frequently good approximations for the motions of real bodies.

## 9–1 Generalized coordinates for rigid-body motion: Euler angles

The kinematic description of the general motion of a rigid body requires six independent coordinates. That six are sufficient may be seen from the fact that once the position of three noncollinear points of the body are specified, the position of all the remaining points of the body, being constrained to remain at a fixed distance from these three points, are also specified. Of the nine coordinates which would generally be required for the specification of three points, in the case of rigid bodies, due to the existence of three constraining equations expressing the constancy of the distances between any pair of these points, only six coordinates are independent.

For the unconstrained motion of a rigid body, the position of the center of mass, which was defined in the previous chapter, is customarily chosen as one of the three points.

We recall that for a discrete set of mass points the position of the center of mass was defined by the equation

$$M\mathbf{R} = \sum_i m_i \mathbf{r}_i. \tag{9–1}$$

For a continuous body, the summation in the definition of the center of mass is replaced by an integration over the volume of the body. If the mass density of the continuous body is designated by $\rho(\mathbf{r})$, the position vector $\mathbf{R}$ of the center of mass is given by

$$M\mathbf{R} = \int_V \rho(\mathbf{r})\mathbf{r}\, dV, \tag{9–2}$$

where the total mass is

$$M = \int_V \rho(\mathbf{r})\, dV \tag{9–3}$$

and

$$dV = dx\, dy\, dz.$$

282

▶As an example, we locate the center of mass of a hemisphere of uniform density (Fig. 9–1).

From the symmetry of the body, it is quite clear that the center of mass lies along the symmetry axis, which is perpendicular to the base of the hemisphere and passes through its center. Calling this axis the $z$-axis, we find the $z$-component of the position vector of the center of mass to be given by

$$Z = \frac{\int \rho z \, dV}{\int \rho \, dV}.$$

Utilizing spherical coordinates for which

$$z = r \cos \theta, \qquad dV = r^2 \, dr \sin \theta \, d\theta \, d\phi,$$

we obtain for the $z$-component of the center of mass

$$Z = \frac{\int_0^{2\pi} \int_0^{\pi/2} \int_0^R r^3 \cos \theta \sin \theta \, dr \, d\theta \, d\phi}{\int_0^{2\pi} \int_0^{\pi/2} \int_0^R r^2 \sin \theta \, dr \, d\theta \, d\phi} = \frac{2\pi (R^4/4)(\frac{1}{2} \sin^2 \theta|_0^{\pi/2})}{2\pi (R^3/3)(-\cos \theta|_0^{\pi/2})} = \frac{3R}{8}. \blacktriangleleft$$

The remaining three coordinates describe the motion of the rigid body relative to its center of mass. This motion is mathematically equivalent to that of a rigid body with one of its points fixed. The three coordinates thus describe the orientation of the body in space.

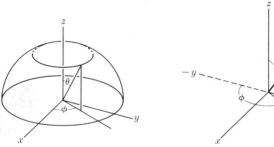

FIGURE 9–1                    FIGURE 9–2

An especially useful set of coordinates for describing the motion of a rigid body relative to one of its points, the point $O$, can be obtained if the two points whose position then specify the orientation of the body are chosen so that the position vectors $\mathbf{r}_1$ and $\mathbf{r}_2$ of these points from the first point $O$ are perpendicular to each other. To specify the position of the first point $P_1$ we require only two coordinates. This follows from the fact that the distance $|\mathbf{r}_1|$ of $P_1$ from $O$ remains constant. To specify the orientation of the vector $\mathbf{r}_1$, we utilize the two angles $\theta$ and $\phi$, where $\theta$ is the angle which $\mathbf{r}_1$ makes with the space $z$-axis, and $\phi$ is the angle which the projection of the vector $\mathbf{r}_1$ onto the $xy$-plane makes with the negative $y$-axis (Fig. 9–2). We note that the angle $\phi$ is $\pi/2$ radians

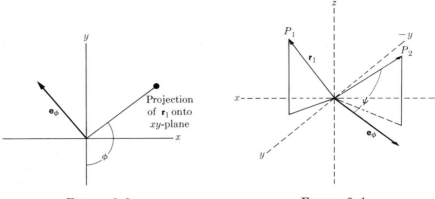

FIGURE 9–3                          FIGURE 9–4

greater than the azimuthal angle used in the description of the point $P_1$ in terms of spherical coordinates.

Also $\phi$ is the angle which the spherical unit vector $\mathbf{e}_\phi$, perpendicular to the space $z$-axis and the vector $\mathbf{r}_1$, makes with the positive $x$-axis (Fig. 9–3). This unit vector, we recall, is expressible as

$$\mathbf{e}_\phi = \frac{1}{r_1 \sin \theta} \, (\mathbf{k} \times \mathbf{r}_1).$$

Due to the existence of the two constraining equations

$$|\mathbf{r}_2| = \text{const,}$$

$$|\mathbf{r}_2 - \mathbf{r}_1| = \text{const,}$$

which express the constancy of the distance of point $P_2$ from the points $O$ and $P_1$, the point $P_2$ requires only one coordinate for the description of its position.

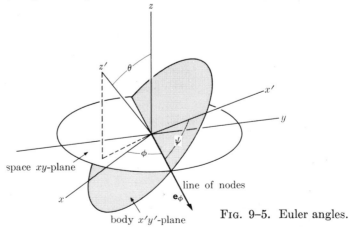

FIG. 9–5. Euler angles.

If we choose as $P_2$ a point which lies along a line perpendicular to $\mathbf{r}_1$ at $O$, then the location of the vector $\mathbf{r}_2$ in the plane perpendicular to $\mathbf{r}_1$ at $O$ is specified by the angle $\psi$ which it makes with the vector $\mathbf{e}_\phi$. We note that $\mathbf{e}_\phi$ also lies in the plane which is perpendicular to $\mathbf{r}_1$ at $O$. As shown in Fig. 9–4, the angle $\psi$ is chosen so that a rotation of $\mathbf{r}_2$ about $\mathbf{r}_1$ through an angle $-\psi$ will turn $\mathbf{r}_2$ into $\mathbf{e}_\phi$ (see figure). We shall refer to the direction of $\mathbf{r}_1$ as the positive direction of the body $z$-axis and the direction of $\mathbf{r}_2$ as the positive direction of the body $x$-axis; that is, the $z$- and $x$-axes of a coordinate system fixed in and rotating with the body. In terms of this new designation of the vectors $\mathbf{r}_1$ and $\mathbf{r}_2$, $\theta$ is the angle between the body $z$-axis and the space $z$-axis. On the other hand, $\phi$ and $\psi$ are the angles which the intersection of the body $xy$-plane and the space $xy$-plane, which lies along $\mathbf{e}_\phi$, makes with the space and body $x$-axes, respectively (Fig. 9–5).

The positive direction of the intersection of the two $xy$-planes is chosen so that a rotation of the body about this intersection through the angle $\theta$ will turn the space $z$-axis into the body $z$-axis. The intersection between the two $xy$-planes is referred to as the *line of nodes*, and the angles $\theta$, $\phi$, and $\psi$ as the Euler angles.*

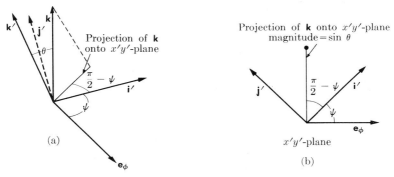

FIGURE 9–6

The relation between the body base vectors specified by $\mathbf{i}'$, $\mathbf{j}'$, and $\mathbf{k}'$ and the space base vectors $\mathbf{i}$, $\mathbf{j}$, and $\mathbf{k}$ may be obtained from the relations of the three noncoplanar vectors $\mathbf{k}$, $\mathbf{k}'$, and $\mathbf{e}_\phi$ to these base vectors. As can be seen from the choice of the vectors $\mathbf{k}'$ and $\mathbf{i}'$, we have (Figs. 9–2 and 9–3)

$$\mathbf{k}' = \sin\theta\sin\phi\mathbf{i} - \sin\theta\cos\phi\mathbf{j} + \cos\theta\mathbf{k}, \tag{9–4}$$

$$\mathbf{e}_\phi = \cos\phi\mathbf{i} + \sin\phi\mathbf{j}, \tag{9–5}$$

and, as shown in Fig. 9–6,

$$\mathbf{e}_\phi = \cos\psi\mathbf{i}' - \sin\psi\mathbf{j}', \tag{9–6}$$

$$\mathbf{k} = \sin\theta\sin\psi\mathbf{i}' + \sin\theta\cos\psi\mathbf{j}' + \cos\theta\mathbf{k}'. \tag{9–7}$$

---

* We note that this choice of Euler angles is not unique. Quite frequently, for example, the angles $\phi$ and $\psi$ are chosen as the angles which the line of nodes makes with the space and body $y$-axes.

In terms of the vectors $\mathbf{k}$, $\mathbf{k}'$, and $\mathbf{e}_\phi$ and their reciprocal vectors (cf. Problem 1–17)

$$\bar{\mathbf{k}} = -\cot\theta\sin\phi\mathbf{i} + \cot\theta\cos\phi\mathbf{j} + \mathbf{k},$$
$$\bar{\mathbf{k}}' = -\cot\theta\sin\psi\mathbf{i}' - \cot\theta\cos\psi\mathbf{j}' + \mathbf{k}', \tag{9–8}$$
$$\bar{\mathbf{e}}_\phi = \mathbf{e}_\phi,$$

we obtain

$$\mathbf{i} = (\mathbf{i}\cdot\mathbf{e}_\phi)\mathbf{e}_\phi + (\mathbf{i}\cdot\mathbf{k}')\,\bar{\mathbf{k}}' + (\mathbf{i}\cdot\mathbf{k})\bar{\mathbf{k}}$$
$$= (\cos\phi\cos\psi - \cos\theta\sin\phi\sin\psi)\mathbf{i}' - (\cos\phi\sin\psi + \cos\theta\sin\phi\cos\psi)\mathbf{j}'$$
$$+ \sin\theta\sin\phi\mathbf{k}', \tag{9–9}$$

$$\mathbf{j} = (\sin\theta\cos\psi + \cos\theta\cos\phi\sin\psi)\mathbf{i}' - (\sin\phi\sin\psi - \cos\theta\cos\phi\cos\psi)\mathbf{j}'$$
$$- \sin\theta\cos\phi\mathbf{k}'. \tag{9–10}$$

Equations (9–7), (9–9), and (9–10) relate the base vectors of the space and body coordinate systems.

The coefficients of the linear transformation relating the two sets of base vectors may be arranged to form the matrix

$$(\tilde{\mathsf{S}}) = \begin{bmatrix} \cos\psi\cos\phi - \cos\theta\sin\phi\sin\psi & -(\sin\psi\cos\phi + \cos\theta\cos\phi\cos\psi) & \sin\theta\sin\phi \\ \cos\psi\sin\phi + \cos\theta\cos\phi\sin\psi & -(\sin\psi\sin\phi - \cos\theta\cos\phi\cos\psi) & -\sin\theta\cos\phi \\ \sin\theta\sin\psi & \sin\theta\cos\psi & \cos\theta \end{bmatrix}, \tag{9–11}$$

which is the matrix which transforms the description $|\mathbf{A}')$ of any vector $\mathbf{A}$ in the body system to its description $|\mathbf{A})$ in the space coordinate system. In operator notation, this is expressed by

$$|\mathbf{A}) = \tilde{\mathsf{S}}|\mathbf{A}')$$

or (cf. Section 3–5)    (9–12)

$$|\mathbf{A}') = \mathsf{S}|\mathbf{A}).$$

The matrix representation of the latter equation is

$$\begin{bmatrix} A'_x \\ A'_y \\ A'_z \end{bmatrix} = (\mathsf{S}) \begin{bmatrix} A_x \\ A_y \\ A_z \end{bmatrix}.$$

## 9–2 Angular velocity of a rigid body

The distance between any two points of a rigid body remains fixed. This means that the position vector of any point $P$ with respect to $O$ is constant in magnitude, whence it follows (cf. Section 1–8) that the position vectors from $O$ change only in direction. The relative velocity of any point $P_i$ with respect to $O$ is thus expressible in terms of an angular velocity vector $\omega$ as expressed by

$$\mathbf{v}_i = \omega \times \mathbf{r}_i. \tag{9–13}$$

This angular velocity vector is the same as the angular velocity vector with which the body coordinate system is observed to rotate. That this is so is easily seen from the fact that the description of the position of any point $P_i$ of the body with respect to the body coordinate system (the coordinate system rotating with the body) is not a function of time.

We can express the cartesian components of the angular velocity vector in terms of the Euler angles. We recall that angular velocities add like vectors (cf. Section 1–8). Now a change in $\theta$ produces a rotation of the body about the line of nodes which is the direction of $\mathbf{e}_\phi$, a change in $\phi$ produces a rotation of the body about the space $z$-axis indicated by the vector $\mathbf{k}$, and a change in $\psi$ a rotation about the body $z$-axis indicated by the vector $\mathbf{k}'$. Hence

$$\omega = \dot{\theta}\mathbf{e}_\phi + \dot{\phi}\mathbf{k} + \dot{\psi}\mathbf{k}'. \tag{9–14}$$

This yields the following components of $\omega$ along the space axes:

$$\begin{aligned}
\omega_x &= \dot{\theta}\cos\phi + \dot{\psi}\sin\theta\sin\phi, \\
\omega_y &= \dot{\theta}\sin\phi - \dot{\psi}\sin\theta\cos\phi, \\
\omega_z &= \dot{\phi} + \dot{\psi}\cos\theta.
\end{aligned} \tag{9–15}$$

Similarly, utilizing Eqs. (9–5) and (9–7), we can obtain the components of the angular velocity vector along the body axes:

$$\begin{aligned}
\omega_{x'} &= \dot{\theta}\cos\psi + \dot{\phi}\sin\theta\sin\psi, \\
\omega_{y'} &= -\dot{\theta}\sin\psi + \dot{\phi}\sin\theta\cos\psi, \\
\omega_{z'} &= \dot{\psi} + \dot{\phi}\cos\theta.
\end{aligned} \tag{9–16}$$

## 9–3 Relation between the angular momentum and the angular velocity of a rigid body: moments and products of inertia

The angular momentum of a rigid body with respect to one of its points, the point $O$, is given by

$$\mathbf{L} = \sum_i \mathbf{r}_i \times m_i \mathbf{v}_i, \tag{9–17}$$

where $\mathbf{r}_i$ and $\mathbf{v}_i$ are the position and velocity vectors of the $i$th mass point with respect to the point $O$. For a continuous body the sum is to be replaced by an integral over the volume of the body. That is,

$$\mathbf{L} = \int \rho(\mathbf{r})\mathbf{r} \times \mathbf{v} \, dV. \tag{9–18}$$

In terms of the angular velocity vector $\omega$ with which the body is observed to rotate, the angular momentum is

$$\mathbf{L} = \sum_i m_i \mathbf{r}_i \times (\boldsymbol{\omega} \times \mathbf{r}_i) = \sum_i m_i[r_i^2 \boldsymbol{\omega} - (\mathbf{r}_i \cdot \boldsymbol{\omega})\mathbf{r}_i] \qquad (9\text{-}19)$$

or, for a continuous body,

$$\mathbf{L} = \int \rho(\mathbf{r})[r^2\boldsymbol{\omega} - (\mathbf{r} \cdot \boldsymbol{\omega})\mathbf{r}]\, dV. \qquad (9\text{-}20)$$

Explicitly stated, the cartesian components of Eq. (9–19) are

$$\begin{aligned}
L_x &= I_{xx}\omega_x + I_{xy}\omega_y + I_{xz}\omega_z, \\
L_y &= I_{yx}\omega_x + I_{yy}\omega_y + I_{yz}\omega_z, \\
L_z &= I_{zx}\omega_x + I_{zy}\omega_y + I_{zz}\omega_z,
\end{aligned} \qquad (9\text{-}21)$$

where the *moments of inertia* $I_{xx}$, $I_{yy}$, $I_{zz}$ are defined as

$$I_{xx} = \sum_i m_i(r_i^2 - x_i^2),$$

$$I_{yy} = \sum_i m_i(r_i^2 - y_i^2), \qquad (9\text{-}22)$$

$$I_{zz} = \sum_i m_i(r_i^2 - z_i^2),$$

and the *products of inertia* $I_{xy}$, $I_{xz}$, and $I_{yz}$ as

$$I_{xy} = I_{yx} = -\sum_i m_i x_i y_i,$$

$$I_{xz} = I_{zx} = -\sum_i m_i x_i z_i, \qquad (9\text{-}23)$$

$$I_{yz} = I_{zy} = -\sum_i m_i y_i z_i.$$

In matrix notation, Eqs. (9–21) are expressed by

$$\begin{bmatrix} L_x \\ L_y \\ L_z \end{bmatrix} = \begin{bmatrix} I_{xx} & I_{xy} & I_{xz} \\ I_{yx} & I_{yy} & I_{yz} \\ I_{zx} & I_{zy} & I_{zz} \end{bmatrix} \begin{bmatrix} \omega_x \\ \omega_y \\ \omega_z \end{bmatrix}. \qquad (9\text{-}24)$$

Equation (9–24) may be considered as the matrix representation of the operator equation

$$|\mathbf{L}) = \mathbf{I}|\boldsymbol{\omega}). \qquad (9\text{-}25)$$

The moments and products of inertia are thus the elements of the matrix representation of the moment-of-inertia operator $\mathbf{I}$, and as which they are referred to as the elements of the moment-of-inertia tensor.

▶ As illustrations, we shall obtain the moments and products of inertia for several rigid bodies.

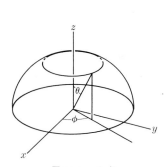

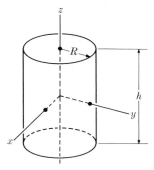

FIGURE 9–7     FIGURE 9–8

(a) *Moments of inertia of a uniform hemisphere about its symmetry axis and about an axis perpendicular to the symmetry axis through the center of the base* (Fig. 9–7)

Utilizing spherical coordinates, we find the moment of inertia about the symmetry axis, which we call the $z$-axis, to be

$$I_{zz} = \int \rho(x^2 + y^2)\, dV$$

$$= \int_0^{2\pi} \int_0^{\pi/2} \int_0^R \rho r^4 \sin^3 \theta \, dr \, d\theta \, d\phi$$

$$= \rho \frac{R^5}{5} \frac{4\pi}{3} = \frac{2}{5} M R^2,$$

where the total mass of the hemisphere is

$$M = \frac{2\pi R^3}{3} \rho.$$

Similarly, we find the moment of inertia about the $x$-axis to be

$$I_{xx} = \int \rho(y^2 + z^2)\, dV$$

$$= \int_0^{2\pi} \int_0^{\pi/2} \int_0^R \rho r^4 (\cos^2 \theta \sin \theta + \sin^3 \theta \sin^2 \phi)\, dr \, d\theta \, d\phi$$

$$= \frac{\rho R^5}{5} \left( \frac{4\pi}{3} \right) = \frac{2}{5} M R^2.$$

(b) *Moments of inertia of a uniform circular cylinder about the axis of the cylinder and about a line perpendicular to the axis passing through the center of mass* (Fig. 9–8)

Let $R$ be the radius of the cylinder and $h$ its height. Choosing the $z$-axis as the axis of the cylinder, and using cylindrical coordinates, we obtain the moment of inertia about the $z$-axis as

$$I_{zz} = \int \rho(x^2 + y^2)\, dV = \int_{-h/2}^{h/2} \int_0^{2\pi} \int_0^R \rho r^3\, dr\, d\phi\, dz$$

$$= \frac{\pi\rho h}{2} R^4 = \frac{MR^2}{2},$$

where $M$, the mass of the cylinder, is

$$M = \pi R^2 h \rho.$$

Similarly, we find the moment of inertia about the $x$-axis passing through the center of mass to be

$$I_{xx} = \int_{-h/2}^{h/2} \int_0^{2\pi} \int_0^R \rho(y^2 + z^2) r\, dr\, d\phi\, dz.$$

Integrating first with respect to $z$ yields

$$I_{xx} = \rho \int_0^{2\pi} \int_0^R \left( hr^2 \sin^2\phi + \frac{h^3}{12} \right) r\, dr\, d\phi.$$

The subsequent integrations with respect to $\phi$ and $r$ yield

$$I_{xx} = \rho \left( \frac{\pi h R^4}{4} + \frac{\pi h^3 R^2}{12} \right) = \frac{MR^2}{4} + \frac{Mh^2}{12}.$$

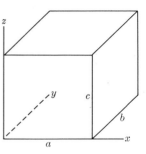

FIGURE 9–9

(c) *Moment and products of inertia of a uniform rectangular parallelepiped with respect to its edges*

Consider the rectangular parallelepiped with edges of lengths $a$, $b$, and $c$, as shown in Fig. 9–9. The moment of inertia about the $z$-axis is found to be

$$I_{zz} = \int_0^c \int_0^b \int_0^a \rho(x^2 + y^2)\, dx\, dy\, dz$$

$$= \rho c \left( \frac{ba^3}{3} + \frac{ab^3}{3} \right)$$

$$= \tfrac{1}{3} M(a^2 + b^2),$$

where

$$M = \rho abc.$$

Quite analogously from symmetry considerations we find

$$I_{xx} = \tfrac{1}{3} M(b^2 + c^2),$$
$$I_{yy} = \tfrac{1}{3} M(a^2 + c^2).$$

**Table 9–1** Moments and products of inertia about the center of mass of various bodies for the system of axes shown.

| Body | Axes | Moments and products of inertia |
|---|---|---|
| Right circular cone of height $h$ and radius of base $r$ | | $I_{xx} = I_{yy} = \dfrac{3m}{20}\left(r^2 + \dfrac{h^2}{4}\right)$<br>$I_{zz} = \tfrac{3}{10}mr^2$<br>No products of inertia |
| Rectangular parallelepiped with edges $a$, $b$, and $c$ | | $I_{xx} = \dfrac{m}{12}(b^2 + c^2)$<br>$I_{yy} = \dfrac{m}{12}(a^2 + c^2)$<br>$I_{zz} = \dfrac{m}{12}(a^2 + b^2)$<br>No products of inertia |
| Ellipsoid with semi-axes $a$, $b$, and $c$ | | $I_{xx} = \dfrac{m}{5}(b^2 + c^2)$<br>$I_{yy} = \dfrac{m}{5}(a^2 + c^2)$<br>$I_{zz} = \dfrac{m}{5}(a^2 + b^2)$<br>No products of inertia |
| Flat uniform circular ring of radii $r_1$ and $r_2$ | | $I_{xx} = I_{yy} = \dfrac{m}{4}(r_1^2 + r_2^2)$<br>$I_{zz} = \dfrac{m}{2}(r_1^2 + r_2^2)$<br>No products of inertia |
| Sphere of radius $R$ | | $I$ about any axis $= \tfrac{2}{5}mR^2$<br>No products of inertia |
| Cylindrical tube with radii $r_1$ and $r_2$ and height $h$ | | $I_{xx} = I_{yy} = \dfrac{m}{4}[r_1^2 + r_2^2 + \tfrac{1}{3}h^2]$<br>$I_{zz} = \dfrac{m}{2}(r_1^2 + r_2^2)$<br>No products of inertia |

The products of inertia in this case are also readily obtainable:

$$I_{xy} = -\int_0^c \int_0^b \int_0^a \rho xy \, dx \, dy \, dz = -\rho c \, \frac{a^2}{2} \frac{b^2}{2} = -\tfrac{1}{4} M a b,$$

and similarly,

$$I_{xz} = -\tfrac{1}{4} M a c,$$
$$I_{yz} = -\tfrac{1}{4} M b c. \blacktriangleleft$$

The moments and products of inertia for several homogeneous bodies are given in Table 9–1. We note that for the examples listed in the table the products of inertia all vanish. The coordinate axes for which this occurs are referred to as the principal axes of the body. In the next chapter, we shall show that every body has such a set of mutually orthogonal principal axes. In this so-called principal-axes coordinate system, we find that the expressions for the angular momentum and the kinetic energy of the body as functions of the angular velocity assume their simplest form. For example, the angular momentum is found to be

$$\mathbf{L} = I_1 \omega_x \mathbf{i} + I_2 \omega_y \mathbf{j} + I_3 \omega_z \mathbf{k},$$

where

$$I_1 = I_{xx}, \qquad I_2 = I_{yy}, \qquad \text{and} \qquad I_3 = I_{zz}.$$

The moments of inertia $I_1$, $I_2$, and $I_3$ about the principal axes are referred to as the *principal moments of inertia*. In the next chapter, we shall discuss a method for obtaining the principal axes and the principal moments of inertia of a rigid body.

At times it will be notationally convenient to express the moment of inertia about an axis in terms of the product of the mass of the body and the square of a quantity having the dimension of length. This quantity is referred to as the *radius of gyration*. Thus, for example, we find that the radius of gyration of the circular cylinder in terms of which

$$I_{zz} = M k_z^2$$

is

$$k_z = \frac{1}{\sqrt{2}} R.$$

For a solid homogeneous sphere we find that

$$k = \sqrt{\tfrac{2}{5}} \, R$$

for any axis passing through the center of the sphere.

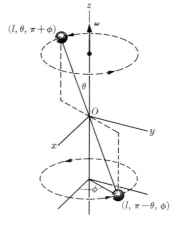

FIG. 9–10. Rotating dumbbell.

We note that the angular momentum of the body with respect to the point $O$ is a linear function of the instantaneous angular velocity vector $\boldsymbol{\omega}$ with which the body is observed to rotate, and that the angular momentum vector will generally not be parallel to the angular velocity vector. It is parallel to the angular velocity vector only when the angular velocity vector is directed along one of three special axes known as the principal axes of the rigid body. For any rigid body the three principal axes are mutually perpendicular (cf. Chapter 10). We shall therefore choose them as the body coordinate axes.

As an example of the linear relationship between the angular momentum and angular velocity vectors, we consider the rigid body composed of two particles of equal mass $m$ mounted at the ends of a rod of negligible mass and length $2l$. If we choose the $z$-axis to be along the instantaneous axis of rotation (Fig. 9–10), then

$$\omega_z = \omega \qquad \text{and} \qquad \omega_x = \omega_y = 0.$$

Utilizing Eqs. (9–21) and (9–22), we find the cartesian components of the angular momentum about the center of mass to be given by

$$
\begin{aligned}
L_x &= I_{xz}\omega = 2ml^2 \sin\theta\cos\theta\cos\phi\,\omega, \\
L_y &= I_{yz}\omega = 2ml^2 \sin\theta\cos\theta\sin\phi\,\omega, \\
L_z &= I_{zz}\omega = 2ml^2 \sin^2\theta\,\omega,
\end{aligned}
\tag{9–26}
$$

since the products of inertia of the dumbbell are

$$
\begin{aligned}
I_{xz} &= -\sum m_i x_i z_i = 2ml^2 \sin\theta\cos\theta\cos\phi, \\
I_{yz} &= -\sum m_i y_i z_i = 2ml^2 \sin\theta\cos\theta\sin\phi,
\end{aligned}
\tag{9–27}
$$

and its moment of inertia

$$I_{zz} = \sum m_i (x_i^2 + y_i^2) = 2ml^2 \sin^2\theta.$$

We indeed find that the angular momentum vector in this example is generally not parallel to the angular velocity vector. Only for the special case $\theta = \pi/2$ will the angular momentum be parallel to the angular velocity vector. In fact, for this example the angular momentum vector is at all times perpendicular to the rod joining the two particles. This can readily be verified by taking the scalar product of the angular momentum vector $\mathbf{L}$ with the position vector of one of the particles with respect to the center of mass. The position vector of the particle located at the point $(l, \pi - \theta, \phi)$ is

$$\mathbf{r} = l\sin\theta\cos\phi\mathbf{i} + l\sin\theta\sin\phi\mathbf{j} - l\cos\theta\mathbf{k}.$$

We note that a change in the orientation of the rigid body will introduce a change in the components of the position vectors of its mass particles, which in turn will change the values of the moments and products of inertia. In our example the products and moments of inertia are functions of the angles $\theta$ and $\phi$.

Even if the dumbbell is constrained to rotate about the $z$-axis, the products and moments of inertia being functions of the angle $\phi$, will vary as the body rotates about the $z$-axis.

This is a complexity which has to be taken into consideration when we consider the equation of motion of the angular momentum vector. The equations of motion contain the time derivative of $\mathbf{L}$ and hence also the time derivatives of the elements of the moment-of-inertia tensor. The direct differentiation of the elements of the moment-of-inertia tensor are usually avoided in the following manner.

Differentiating Eq. (9–17) or (9–19), which define the angular momentum vector of a system of particles, and remembering that

$$\mathbf{v} = \dot{\mathbf{r}} = \boldsymbol{\omega} \times \mathbf{r},$$

we obtain the expression

$$\frac{d\mathbf{L}}{dt} = \sum_i m_i(\boldsymbol{\omega} \times \mathbf{r}_i) \times \mathbf{v}_i + \sum_i m_i\mathbf{r}_i \times (\dot{\boldsymbol{\omega}} \times \mathbf{r}_i) + \sum_i m_i\mathbf{r}_i \times [\boldsymbol{\omega} \times (\boldsymbol{\omega} \times \mathbf{r}_i)].$$

Thus, since

$$(\boldsymbol{\omega} \times \mathbf{r}_i) \times \mathbf{v}_i = (\boldsymbol{\omega} \times \mathbf{r}_i) \times (\boldsymbol{\omega} \times \mathbf{r}_i) = 0$$

and

$$\mathbf{r}_i \times [\boldsymbol{\omega} \times (\boldsymbol{\omega} \times \mathbf{r}_i)] = -(\mathbf{r}_i \cdot \boldsymbol{\omega})(\boldsymbol{\omega} \times \mathbf{r}_i) = \boldsymbol{\omega} \times [\mathbf{r}_i \times (\boldsymbol{\omega} \times \mathbf{r}_i)],$$

the equation for the time derivative of the angular momentum vector reduces to

$$\frac{d\mathbf{L}}{dt} = \sum_i m_i\mathbf{r}_i \times (\dot{\boldsymbol{\omega}} \times \mathbf{r}_i) + \sum_i m_i\boldsymbol{\omega} \times (\mathbf{r}_i \times \mathbf{v}_i). \tag{9–28}$$

In matrix notation this latter equation is expressed by

$$\frac{d}{dt}\begin{bmatrix} L_x \\ L_y \\ L_z \end{bmatrix} = \begin{bmatrix} I_{xx} & I_{xy} & I_{xz} \\ I_{yx} & I_{yy} & I_{yz} \\ I_{zx} & I_{zy} & I_{zz} \end{bmatrix}\begin{bmatrix} \dot{\omega}_x \\ \dot{\omega}_y \\ \dot{\omega}_z \end{bmatrix} + \begin{bmatrix} (\boldsymbol{\omega} \times \mathbf{L})_x \\ (\boldsymbol{\omega} \times \mathbf{L})_y \\ (\boldsymbol{\omega} \times \mathbf{L})_z \end{bmatrix} \tag{9–29}$$

or

$$\frac{d}{dt}(\mathbf{L}) = (\mathbf{I})(\dot{\boldsymbol{\omega}}) + (\boldsymbol{\Omega})(\mathbf{L}), \tag{9–30}$$

where

$$(\boldsymbol{\Omega}) = \begin{bmatrix} 0 & -\omega_z & \omega_y \\ \omega_z & 0 & -\omega_x \\ -\omega_y & \omega_x & 0 \end{bmatrix}. \tag{9–31}$$

This result could also have been obtained in another way. We realize that with respect to the body coordinate system, which is a coordinate system rotating with the rigid body, the products and moments of inertia remain constant.

Hence with respect to such a rotating coordinate system, the time rate of change of the angular momentum vector is given by $(\mathbf{I})(\dot{\boldsymbol{\omega}})$. From Eq. (3–8), which relates the description of the time derivative of a vector in one coordinate system to the description of the time derivative of the same vector with respect to a coordinate system rotating with angular velocity $\boldsymbol{\omega}$ with respect to the first, we obtain Eq. (9–30).

## 9–4 Rotational kinetic energy of a rigid body

The rotational kinetic energy of a rigid body is likewise a function of the moments and products of inertia and the angular velocity vector. Setting

$$\mathbf{v}_i = \boldsymbol{\omega} \times \mathbf{r}_i,$$

we obtain for the rotational kinetic energy of the rigid body the relation

$$
\begin{aligned}
T &= \sum_i \tfrac{1}{2} m_i v_i^2 \\
&= \sum_i \tfrac{1}{2} m_i (\boldsymbol{\omega} \times \mathbf{r}_i) \cdot (\boldsymbol{\omega} \times \mathbf{r}_i) \\
&= \tfrac{1}{2} \sum_i m_i \boldsymbol{\omega} \cdot [\mathbf{r}_i \times (\boldsymbol{\omega} \times \mathbf{r}_i)] \\
&= \tfrac{1}{2} \boldsymbol{\omega} \cdot \mathbf{L}.
\end{aligned}
\tag{9–32}
$$

In matrix notation, Eq. (9–32) is expressible as

$$
\begin{aligned}
T &= \tfrac{1}{2} [\omega_x, \omega_y, \omega_z]
\begin{bmatrix}
I_{xx} & I_{xy} & I_{xz} \\
I_{yx} & I_{yy} & I_{yz} \\
I_{zx} & I_{zy} & I_{zz}
\end{bmatrix}
\begin{bmatrix}
\omega_x \\
\omega_y \\
\omega_z
\end{bmatrix} \\
&= \tfrac{1}{2} (\boldsymbol{\omega} \mid \mathbf{I} \mid \boldsymbol{\omega}).
\end{aligned}
\tag{9–33}
$$

## 9–5 Parallel-axis theorem

From our discussion thus far it should be quite apparent that the moments and products of inertia are functions of the point about which the body is rotating and of the orientation of the body with respect to the space coordinate axes. Fortunately the situation is not as complicated as it appears. In this section we shall show how the products and moments of inertia about any point of the body are related to the products and moments of inertia with respect to a parallel coordinate system situated at the center of mass. In the next chapter we shall investigate the dependence of the elements of the moment-of-inertia tensor on the choice of coordinate axes and their orientation with respect to the principle coordinate axes.

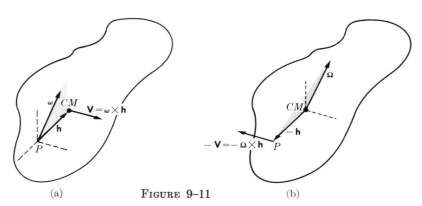

(a)                     FIGURE 9–11                    (b)

In Section 8–7 we found the total angular momentum of a system of particles about a fixed point to be expressible as the sum of the angular momentum of the system of particles about the center of mass and the angular momentum of the center of mass with respect to the fixed point. A similar result was obtained for the total kinetic energy of the system.

Now the angular velocity of the rigid body with respect to its center of mass is identical to its angular velocity with respect to any other of its points. This fact can be arrived at by expressing the relative velocities of two points of the body with respect to each other in terms of the angular velocity of the body with respect to the points. Thus, for example, the velocity of the center of mass with respect to any point $P$ of the body is given by

$$\mathbf{V} = \boldsymbol{\omega} \times \mathbf{h}, \tag{9–34}$$

where $\mathbf{h}$ is the distance of the center of mass from the point $P$, and $\boldsymbol{\omega}$ is the angular velocity of the rigid body with respect to the point $P$ (cf. Fig. 9–11). The velocity of the point $P$ with respect to the center of mass is thus $-\mathbf{V}$ and the position of $P$ with respect to the center of mass $-\mathbf{h}$. If now $\boldsymbol{\Omega}$ is the angular velocity of the rigid body with respect to the center of mass, then

$$-\mathbf{V} = \boldsymbol{\Omega} \times (-\mathbf{h}) = -\boldsymbol{\omega} \times \mathbf{h}$$

or

$$(\boldsymbol{\Omega} - \boldsymbol{\omega}) \times \mathbf{h} = 0. \tag{9–35}$$

It follows from the arbitrariness of the point $P$ or the vector $\mathbf{h}$ that

$$\boldsymbol{\omega} = \boldsymbol{\Omega}. \tag{9–36}$$

We are thus able to reexpress the angular momentum about any fixed point of the body as given by Eq. (8–79) in terms of $\boldsymbol{\omega}$ and obtain

$$\mathbf{L} = M\mathbf{R} \times (\boldsymbol{\omega} \times \mathbf{R}) + \sum_{i} m_i \mathbf{r}'_i \times (\boldsymbol{\omega} \times \mathbf{r}'_i). \tag{9–37}$$

In matrix notation, this is

$$\begin{bmatrix} L_x \\ L_y \\ L_z \end{bmatrix} = \begin{bmatrix} M(R^2 - X^2) & -MXY & -MXZ \\ -MXY & M(R^2 - Y^2) & -MYZ \\ -MZX & -MZY & M(R^2 - Z^2) \end{bmatrix} \begin{bmatrix} \omega_x \\ \omega_y \\ \omega_z \end{bmatrix}$$

$$+ \begin{bmatrix} I'_{xx} & I'_{xy} & I'_{xz} \\ I'_{yx} & I'_{yy} & I'_{yz} \\ I'_{zx} & I'_{zy} & I'_{zz} \end{bmatrix} \begin{bmatrix} \omega_x \\ \omega_y \\ \omega_z \end{bmatrix} \tag{9–38}$$

or

$$(\mathbf{L}) = (\mathbf{I}_0 + \mathbf{I}')(\boldsymbol{\omega}) = (\mathbf{I})(\boldsymbol{\omega}), \tag{9–39}$$

where $(\mathbf{I}_0)$ is the moment-of-inertia matrix of the center of mass (the moment-of-inertia matrix of a mass $M$ located at the center of mass) with respect to a point $O$, and $(\mathbf{I}')$ is the moment-of-inertia matrix of the body with respect to a coordinate system whose origin is located at the center of mass and whose base vectors are parallel to the base vectors of the coordinate system located at the point $O$.

The fact that the moment-of-inertia matrix $(\mathbf{I})$ about a point is expressible as the sum of the moment-of-inertia matrix of the center of mass and the moment-of-inertia matrix of the body with respect to the center of mass, viz.,

$$(\mathbf{I}) = (\mathbf{I}_0) + (\mathbf{I}'), \tag{9–40}$$

is known as the *parallel-axis theorem for the moment-of-inertia matrix.*

Specifically, for the case when the angular velocity of the body is constrained to have only one component, and the coordinate axes are chosen so that it is the $z$-component, we find that

$$I_{zz} = M(X^2 + Y^2) + I'_{zz}. \tag{9–41}$$

This equation states that the moment of inertia about the $z$-axis passing through a point $O$ of the body is equal to the moment of inertia of the center of mass about this $z$-axis plus the moment of inertia of the body about the $z$-axis passing through the center of mass. This is known as the parallel-axis theorem for the moment of inertia about an axis.

## 9–6 Equations of motion for a rigid body

The equations of motion for the description of the general motion of a rigid body were already obtained in the last chapter when we discussed the conservation theorems for an $N$-particle system. Equation (8–68), $\mathbf{F} = M\mathbf{A}$, yields the equations of motion for the position vector of the center of mass; and appropriate components of Eq. (8–83),

$$\mathbf{N}' = \frac{d}{dt}\,\mathbf{L}',$$

yield the generalized equations of motion for the angle variables describing the orientation of the rigid body with respect to a space coordinate system at the center of mass.

If the motion of the body is constrained to take place with one or more collinear points of the body remaining fixed, then Eq. (8–76), $\mathbf{N} = \dot{\mathbf{L}}$, will yield the generalized equations of motion for the angle variables used to describe the orientation of the body with respect to a space coordinate system located at one of the constrained points. We now proceed to present the form assumed by specific components of the equation of motion for the angular momentum vector.

(a) *Components along the instantaneous directions of the mutually perpendicular principal axes of the body: Euler's equations*

The relation between the angular momentum vector and the angular velocity vector assumes its simplest form when expressed in terms of the unit vectors of the body coordinate system which point along the principal axes of the body:

$$\mathbf{L} = I_1\omega_x\,\mathbf{i}' + I_2\omega_{y'}\mathbf{j}' + I_3\omega_{z'}\mathbf{k}', \qquad (9\text{–}42)$$

where $\omega_{x'}$, $\omega_{y'}$, and $\omega_{z'}$ are the components of the angular velocity vector along the principal axes. To obtain the components of the equation

$$\mathbf{N} = \frac{d}{dt}\,\mathbf{L} \qquad (9\text{–}43)$$

along the instantaneous directions of the principal axes, we express the time derivative of $\mathbf{L}$ as given by Eq. (9–30) by

$$\frac{d}{dt}\,\mathbf{L} = \left(\frac{d}{dt}\,\mathbf{L}\right)' + \boldsymbol{\omega} \times \mathbf{L}, \qquad (9\text{–}44)$$

where $(d\mathbf{L}/dt)'$ refers to the time derivative of $\mathbf{L}$ with respect to the body set of coordinate axes.

From Eq. (9–42) and remembering that the principal moments of inertia and the body base vectors are constant with respect to the body coordinate system, we find that the time derivative of $\mathbf{L}$ with respect to the rotating-body coordinate system is

$$\left(\frac{d\mathbf{L}}{dt}\right)' = I_1\dot{\omega}_{x'}\mathbf{i}' + I_2\dot{\omega}_{y'}\mathbf{j}' + I_3\dot{\omega}_{z'}\mathbf{k}'. \qquad (9\text{–}45)$$

The scalar products of Eq. (9–43), where (9–44) is substituted for $(d\mathbf{L}/dt)$, with the vectors $\mathbf{i}'$, $\mathbf{j}'$, and $\mathbf{k}'$ thus yield the equations of motion

$$N_{x'} = I_1\dot{\omega}_{x'} - (I_2 - I_3)\omega_{y'}\omega_{z'}, \qquad (9\text{–}46)$$

$$N_{y'} = I_2\dot{\omega}_{y'} - (I_3 - I_1)\omega_{z'}\omega_{x'}, \qquad (9\text{–}47)$$

$$N_{z'} = I_z\dot{\omega}_{z'} - (I_1 - I_2)\omega_{y'}\omega_{x'}. \qquad (9\text{–}48)$$

These three equations are known as the Euler equations of motion for the rotation of a rigid body.

(b) *Generalized equations of motion for the Euler angles*

Of the three Euler equations of motion, the component equation (9–48) along the body z-axis happens to be the generalized equation of motion for the angle $\psi$, since a change in $\psi$ produces a rotation of the body about $\mathbf{k}'$, which points along the body z-axis. Through use of Eq. (9–16), which relates the components of the angular velocity vector along the body axes to the Euler angles, Eq. (9–48) assumes the form

$$N_{z'} = \frac{d}{dt}\,[I_3(\dot\psi + \dot\phi\cos\theta)] - (I_1 - I_2)(\dot\phi^2\sin^2\theta - \dot\theta^2)\sin\psi\cos\psi$$

$$- (I_1 - I_2)(\dot\theta\dot\phi\sin\theta)(\cos^2\psi - \sin^2\psi). \tag{9–49}$$

The remaining generalized equations of motion can similarly be obtained by taking the scalar products of Eq. (9–43) with $\mathbf{k}$ and $\mathbf{e}_\phi$, which are the axes of rotation for a change in $\phi$ and $\theta$ respectively. It is simpler, however, to obtain them from the Lagrangian, utilizing the expression for the rotational kinetic energy which in terms of the principal moments of inertia is given by

$$T = \tfrac{1}{2}(I_1\omega_{x'}^2 + I_2\omega_{y'}^2 + I_3\omega_{z'}^2)$$

$$= \tfrac{1}{2}I_1(\dot\theta\cos\psi + \dot\phi\sin\psi\sin\theta)^2 + \tfrac{1}{2}I_2(-\dot\theta\sin\psi + \dot\phi\sin\theta\cos\psi)^2$$

$$+ \tfrac{1}{2}I_3(\dot\psi + \dot\phi\cos\theta)^2. \tag{9–50}$$

The derivation of the remaining two generalized equations of motion is left as an exercise for the reader (Problem 9–22).

## 9–7 Motion of a rigid body about a fixed axis of rotation

The simplest rigid-body problems deal with the rotational motion of a rigid body about an axis whose orientation in space remains fixed or unchanged. In mathematical language this fact is expressed by the equations

$$\omega_x = \omega_y = 0,$$

where we have chosen the z-axis to lie along the fixed axis of rotation. With this choice of space axes we have at all times only a z-component of the angular velocity vector; therefore we drop the subscript, setting

$$\omega_z = \omega. \tag{9–51}$$

In problems in which the rigid body is constrained to rotate about a fixed axis, it is customary to take components of the equation of motion for the angular momentum of the rigid body along the cartesian space axes. We thus obtain the three component equations

$$N_x = \dot L_x, \qquad N_y = \dot L_y, \qquad N_z = \dot L_z, \tag{9–52}$$

where the relations of $\dot{L}_x$, $\dot{L}_y$, and $\dot{L}_z$ to the components of the angular velocity $\omega$ and the angular acceleration $\dot{\omega}$ are given by Eq. (9–29). Remembering that $\omega_x = \omega_y = \dot{\omega}_x = \dot{\omega}_y = 0$, we can reduce (9–52) to

$$N_x = I_{xz}\dot{\omega} + I_{yz}\omega^2,$$
$$N_y = I_{yz}\dot{\omega} - I_{xz}\omega^2, \qquad (9\text{–}53)$$
$$N_z = I_{zz}\dot{\omega}.$$

The last equation is the one which determines the rotational motion of the rigid body, whereas the other two component equations of motion for the angular momentum of the body determine the constraining torques which are required to prevent the axis of rotation from changing its direction. If the axis of rotation happens to lie along one of the principal axes of the rigid body, then we obtain the equations

$$N_x = N_y = 0$$

and $\qquad\qquad\qquad\qquad\qquad\qquad\qquad\qquad\qquad\qquad\qquad (9\text{–}54)$

$$N_z = I_{zz}\dot{\omega} = I\dot{\omega},$$

where we have set

$$I_{zz} = I.$$

In either case we find the kinetic energy to be given by

$$T = \tfrac{1}{2}\boldsymbol{\omega} \cdot \mathbf{L} = \tfrac{1}{2}I_{zz}\omega^2, \qquad (9\text{–}55)$$

and the rate at which work is done on the body by

$$P = \mathbf{N} \cdot \boldsymbol{\omega} = N_z\omega. \qquad (9\text{–}56)$$

▶As a first example, we consider the Atwood machine problem (Fig. 9–12), which involves the rotational motion of a pulley about its fixed axis. For the

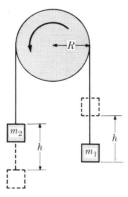

FIG. 9–12. Atwood machine.

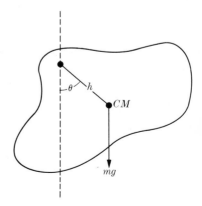

FIG. 9–13. A physical pendulum.

case where the string does not slip the acceleration with which the particles move is related to the angular acceleration $\alpha$ of the pulley, as expressed by

$$R\alpha = a.$$

We are thus confronted with a problem which has only one degree of freedom and for which, if we are not interested in the constraining torques, only one equation of motion is required. This may be taken to be the equation expressing the conservation of energy

$$\tfrac{1}{2}m_1v^2 + \tfrac{1}{2}m_2v^2 + \tfrac{1}{2}I\omega^2 - (m_2 - m_1)gh = \text{const},$$

where $h$ is the distance traversed by the mass $m_2$; or it may be taken as the equation of motion for the $z$-component of the total angular momentum of the system,

$$(m_2 - m_1)gR = \frac{d}{dt}[m_1vR + m_2vR + I\omega].$$

This latter relation yields for the acceleration of the particles

$$a = \frac{m_2 - m_1}{m_1 + m_2 + I/R^2}\,g.$$

If we are interested in the tension in the string, then Newton's equations of motion for the particles,

$$m_2g - T = m_2a, \qquad T_1 - m_1g = m_1a,$$

and the equation of motion for the angular momentum of the pulley

$$(T_2 - T_1)R = I\alpha$$

are appropriate. ◄

▶ As a second example, we consider the physical pendulum. Any rigid body free to move about a fixed horizontal axis under the action of a uniform gravitational field is referred to as a physical pendulum (cf. Fig. 9–13). The component along the axis of rotation of the torque due to the gravitational force is found to have the magnitude $Mgh \sin\theta$, where $h$ is the distance of the center of mass from the axis of rotation, and $\theta$ is the angle which the line drawn from the center of mass perpendicular to the axis of rotation makes with the vertical. If a counterclockwise rotation about the axis of rotation, as shown in Fig. 9–13, is taken as positive, then the equation of motion for the $z$-component of the angular momentum is

$$I\ddot{\theta} = -Mgh \sin\theta.$$

This is a one-dimensional equation of motion for which the equation expressing the conservation of energy,

$$\tfrac{1}{2}I\omega^2 - Mgh \cos\theta = \text{const},$$

holds.  Following the method outlined in Chapter 4, this equation may be utilized to obtain $\theta$ as a function of time.

Of special interest is the case when $\theta$ is small so that $\sin \theta$ may be approximated by $\theta$.  The equation of motion for the $z$-component of the angular momentum then reduces to the equation of motion of a simple harmonic oscillator whose natural frequency of oscillation is given by

$$\omega^2 = \frac{Mgh}{I}.$$

The moment of inertia may be expressed by the parallel-axis theorem as

$$I = Mk^2 + Mh^2,$$

where $k$ is the radius of gyration of the body about a parallel axis through its center of mass.  In terms of the radius of gyration, the frequency of oscillation is given by the equation

$$\omega^2 = \frac{gh}{k^2 + h^2}.$$

This latter relation answers the question as to the location of the point at which one has to suspend the body in order that it oscillate with a given frequency of oscillation.  We find this answer to be given by the roots of the equation

$$h^2 - \frac{g}{\omega^2} h + k^2 = 0. \tag{9–57}$$

So long as

$$k^2 \leq \frac{g^2}{4\omega^2},$$

this equation yields two roots,

$$h_1 = \frac{g}{2\omega^2} + \sqrt{\frac{g^2}{4\omega^4} - k^2}, \qquad h_2 = \frac{g}{2\omega^2} - \sqrt{\frac{g^2}{4\omega^4} - k^2},$$

whose sum is

$$l = h_1 + h_2 = \frac{g}{\omega^2}.$$

There thus exist two different distances of the axis of rotation from the center of mass about which the body oscillates with a given frequency $\omega$.  We note that the length $l$ defined by the previous equation happens to be the length of a simple pendulum having the same frequency of small oscillations $\omega$.

It should be clear that the period

$$\tau = 2\pi \sqrt{\frac{k^2 + h^2}{gh}},$$

having extremely large values both for very small and for very large values of

$h$, assumes for some value of $h$ a minimum value. We find this minimum value to be

$$\tau_{\min} = 2\pi\sqrt{\frac{2k}{g}} .$$

At frequency

$$\omega = \frac{2\pi}{\tau_{\min}} ,$$

for which $g/2\omega^2 = k$,

$$h_1 = h_2 = \frac{g}{2\omega^2}.$$

From the relation for the product of the roots of Eq. (9–57)

$$h_1 h_2 = k^2,$$

we obtain another relation for $l$,

$$l = h_1 + h_2 = h_1 + \frac{k^2}{h_1} = h_2 + \frac{k^2}{h_2}.\blacktriangleleft$$

## 9–8 The plane motion of a rigid body: instantaneous axis of rotation

If the motion of the center of mass of a rigid body takes place in a plane which is perpendicular to the constrained axis of rotation of the body, then the motion is called plane or laminar motion of the rigid body. Even if the center of mass does not move in a plane perpendicular to the axis of rotation, we can obtain by a change of coordinates a description of the motion with respect to a coordinate system moving parallel to the axis of rotation, and with respect to which the center of mass does move in a plane perpendicular to the axis of rotation.

For the plane motion of a rigid body there exists an instantaneous axis of rotation, which is the axis determined by the points whose instantaneous velocity vanishes. That such a set of points exists can be seen as follows.

Consider a rigid body rotating with an angular velocity $\omega$ and whose center of mass for the plane motion of the rigid body has a velocity perpendicular to $\omega$ (Fig. 9–14).

There exists a set of points whose speed with respect to the center of mass is $V$. They lie at a distance $h$ from the axis through the center of mass which is parallel to the axis of rotation. That is, the magnitude of the velocity $\mathbf{v}'$ of these points is

$$|\mathbf{v}'| = h\omega = V. \tag{9–58}$$

The points whose speed with respect to the center of mass is $V$ lie on a circular cylinder of radius $h$, whose axis is collinear with the axis of rotation through the center of mass. This set of points contains a subset of points whose velocity with respect to the center of mass is parallel to the observed velocity $\mathbf{V}$ of the center

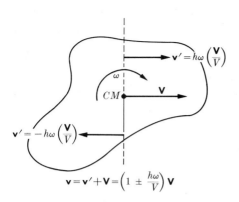

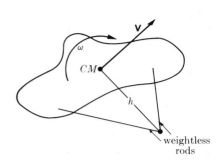

FIG. 9–14.   Instantaneous axis of rotation.

FIG. 9–15.   Instantaneous axis of rotation.

of mass.  This latter set of points lie along the intersection of the cylinder of radius $h$ and the plane which contains the axis of rotation through the center of mass and which is perpendicular to the velocity vector $\mathbf{V}$.  Of the two lines of intersection, one line has a velocity $-\mathbf{V}$ with respect to the center of mass. With respect to the observer, the velocity of the points on this line vanishes.

This set of points which are momentarily observed to be at rest determine the line which is referred to as the instantaneous axis of rotation.  Even if these points happen to lie outside the body, we may consider them as part of the body, being attached to the body by means of weightless rods (Fig. 9–15).

The important equations of motion for the plane motion of a rigid body are the equations of motion for the center of mass,

$$\mathbf{F} = M\mathbf{A}, \tag{9–59}$$

and the component of the equation of motion for the angular momentum along the axis of rotation (the $z$-axis) through the center of mass,

$$N'_z = I\dot{\omega}. \tag{9–60}$$

At times it is convenient to replace the latter equation by the equation of motion for the $z$-component of the angular momentum about the instantaneous axis of rotation.

## 9–9 The plane motion of a rigid body: rolling motion

A body is said to be rolling on a surface $S$ if its point of contact with the surface has zero velocity with respect to the surface on which the body rolls.  For example, consider a rolling cylinder or sphere (Fig. 9–16).  The condition of rolling for these bodies is expressed by the vanishing of the velocity of the contact point $P$,

$$\mathbf{v}_P = \mathbf{v} + \boldsymbol{\omega} \times \mathbf{R} = \mathbf{0}. \tag{9–61}$$

In this equation **v** is the velocity of the geometric center of the cylinder or sphere with respect to the surface on which they roll, **R** the radius vector from the geometric center to the point $P$, $\omega$ the angular velocity of the body, and $\mathbf{v}_P$ the velocity of the point of contact with respect to the surface.

For a uniform cylinder which is rolling on top of an incline (Fig. 9–17), which in turn is moving with a velocity **V** as shown, the equation of constraint reduces in component form to

$$\dot{x} - \dot{X} - r\omega \cos \theta = 0,$$

$$\dot{y} - r\omega \sin \theta = 0.$$

The constraint of rolling is generally not integrable. It is a *nonholonomic constraint*. For the plane motion of a rigid body, however, the equation expressing the condition of rolling can be integrated, and the constraint of rolling is holonomic.

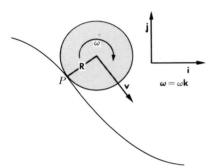

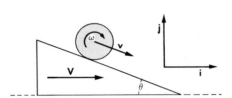

FIG. 9–16. A rolling body.          FIG. 9–17. Cylinder rolling on a moving incline.

A constraint necessarily implies the existence of constraining forces. The constraining forces which are necessary to keep a body rolling on a surface are directed tangential to the surface. Since a smooth surface can exert forces only in a direction normal to itself, it is clear that rolling is generally not possible on a smooth frictionless surface. Frictional forces are complicated. In the case of rolling bodies, however, we need only insist that the constraining force required to keep the body rolling does not exceed the maximum frictional force which the surface can exert on the body. This maximum frictional force is empirically found to be proportional to the normal force $\mathfrak{N}$ between the surface and the body,

$$f_{\max} = \mu_s F_n = \mu_s \mathfrak{N}, \tag{9–62}$$

where $\mu_s$ is known as the *coefficient of static friction*. For rolling the constraining frictional force $f$ required to keep the body rolling must be less than this maximum frictional force which the surface can apply,

$$f \leq \mu_s \mathfrak{N}. \tag{9–63}$$

If this condition is not satisfied, the body will not roll but rather perform a motion referred to as rolling and sliding. When sliding occurs the frictional force with which the surface acts on the body is found empirically to be expressed by

$$f = \mu_{sl}\mathfrak{N}, \tag{9-64}$$

where $\mu_{sl}$ is the *coefficient of sliding friction*.

Frictional forces acting on a body are always directed opposite to the direction of the relative velocity of the point of contact of the body with respect to the surface on which it moves.

▶ As an example, consider the problem of a uniform cylinder of radius $r$ rolling under the action of gravity on top of a larger stationary cylinder of radius $R$ (Fig. 9–18).

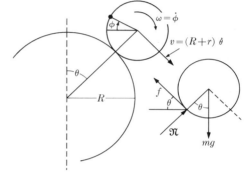

FIG. 9–18. Cylinder rolling on a stationary cylinder.

The center of mass of the smaller cylinder moves in a circle of constant radius $R + r$ and has therefore at all times a tangential speed given by

$$v = (R + r)\dot{\theta},$$

where $\theta$ is the angle which the radius vector makes with the vertical as shown. The condition of rolling is expressed by

$$v_P = (R + r)\dot{\theta} - r\dot{\phi} = 0.$$

Assuming the frictional force to act as shown in Fig. 9–18, we find the tangential and normal components of the equations of motion for the center of mass to be

$$mg \sin \theta - f = m(r + R)\ddot{\theta}$$

and

$$mg \cos \theta - \mathfrak{N} = m(r + R)\dot{\theta}^2.$$

The equation of motion for the angular momentum about the center of mass is

$$rf = I\ddot{\phi}, \tag{9-65}$$

where $I$ is the moment of inertia of the cylinder about the axis of rotation through the center of mass.

These equations may be solved to yield the differential equation for $\theta$. Its solution may subsequently be used to yield $f$, $\mathfrak{N}$, and $\phi$ as functions of time $t$.

It should be apparent that the smaller cylinder will not continue to roll on top of the larger one, but that it will leave the larger cylinder at some point. Even before this point is reached, slipping should occur (why?)

Neglecting the occurrence of slipping, we find that the smaller cylinder will separate from the larger one when the normal force $\mathfrak{N}$ between the cylinders vanishes. ◄

## 9–10 Conservation of energy in rolling

We note that the frictional forces present in problems of rolling bodies do not dissipate energy. This can be seen quite readily by considering the motion of the rolling body with respect to its instantaneous axis of rotation. For bodies rolling on surfaces at rest, the instantaneous axis happens to pass through the point or points of contact between the rolling body and the surface. The contact between the surface and the body being along the instantaneous axis, the frictional forces acting at those points do not contribute to the torque about the instantaneous axis. They therefore do not contribute to the change in the rotational kinetic energy about the instantaneous axis. Since the rotational kinetic energy about the instantaneous axis represents the total kinetic energy of the body, we conclude that the frictional force of rolling does not do any net work on the rolling body.

► For example, in the illustration of the last section, the differential equation for $\theta$ is

$$mg \sin \theta = \left[ \frac{I}{r^2} (R + r) + m(r + R) \right] \ddot{\theta},$$

which, upon using the condition of rolling to replace

$$\left( \frac{r + R}{r} \right)^2 \dot{\theta}^2 \qquad \text{by} \qquad \dot{\phi}^2,$$

yields the following equation expressing the conservation of total energy:

$$\tfrac{1}{2}m(r + R)^2\dot{\theta}^2 + \tfrac{1}{2}I\dot{\phi}^2 + mg(r + R) \cos \theta = \text{const.}$$

Hence we have demonstrated that in this example the frictional force of rolling does not dissipate any energy. ◄

► As a second example, we consider the motion of a uniform cylinder rolling down an incline, which is free to move on a frictionless horizontal plane (Fig. 9–19a). In this problem, the equations of motion for the cylinder are somewhat more easily obtained if we describe its motion with respect to the incline. Since the incline moves to the left with an acceleration **A**, the equations of motion of the cylinder with respect to the incline are identical to the equations of motion

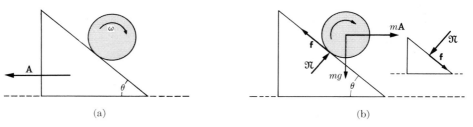

FIG. 9–19. Cylinder rolling on a sliding incline.

for a cylinder rolling on a stationary incline under the action of an additional force of magnitude $mA$ directed to the right as shown in Fig. (9–19b). The normal and tangential components of the equations of motion for the center of mass of the cylinder are thus

$$mg \sin \theta + mA \cos \theta - f = ma$$

and

$$mg \cos \theta - mA \sin \theta - \mathfrak{N} = 0,$$

where $a$ is the acceleration of the center of mass of the cylinder with respect to the incline. The equation of motion for the rotation of the cylinder about its center of mass is

$$rf = I\ddot{\phi} = \frac{Ia}{r},$$

where we have used the equation of constraint

$$r\dot{\phi} = v$$

to obtain

$$r\ddot{\phi} = a.$$

The equation of motion for the horizontal motion of the incline is

$$\mathfrak{N} \sin \theta - f \cos \theta = MA,$$

where the positive direction of motion for the incline is defined towards the left as shown in Fig. (9–19a).

We note that we have five unknown quantities, $\phi$, $a$, $A$, $f$ and $\mathfrak{N}$, for which we have found five equations of motion. In addition to (or from) these equations, we find that we also have the conservation of the total energy as expressed by

$$\tfrac{1}{2}I\dot{\phi}^2 + \tfrac{1}{2}MV^2 + \tfrac{1}{2}m(v_x - V)^2 + \tfrac{1}{2}mv_y^2 + mgh = \text{const},$$

where $v_x$ and $v_y$ are the $x$- and $y$-components of the velocity of the center of the cylinder relative to the incline, and $h$ is the vertical height of the center of mass of the cylinder. ◀

## 9–11 The plane motion of a rigid body: rolling and sliding

Rolling and sliding or the slipping of a rigid body on a surface occurs if either the frictional force required to keep the body rolling exceeds the maximum frictional force which the surface can exert on the body, or if the initial conditions with which the body is set into motion on the surface do not satisfy the condition of rolling.

In either case the frictional force exerted on the body is the maximum kinetic frictional force given by

$$f = \mu_{sl}\mathfrak{N}.$$

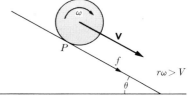

The direction of the frictional force is opposite to the direction of the relative velocity of the point of contact of the body with respect to the surface.

FIG. 9–20. Cylinder rolling and sliding down an incline.

For example, if for the cylinder on the fixed incline of angle $\theta$ depicted in Fig. 9–20 for the directions of $\omega$ and $V$ indicated we have

$$r\omega > V,$$

then the frictional force would be directed down the plane, as the relative velocity of the point of contact $P$ with respect to the incline is then directed up the plane. Conversely, if

$$r\omega < V,$$

then the frictional force will be directed up the plane.

The equations of motion for the cylinder in this case are identical to the equations which are appropriate when rolling occurs except for the fact that the constraining force $f$ is replaced by the frictional force $\pm\mu_{sl}\mathfrak{N}$. The sign depends on the direction of the frictional force. For the example under consideration the equations of motion are

$$Mg \sin\theta \pm \mu_{sl}\mathfrak{N} = MA \quad\text{and}\quad \pm\mu_{sl}\mathfrak{N}_r = I\ddot{\phi}.$$

In this case, of course, $A \neq r\ddot{\phi}$.

We note that the frictional force will always attempt to get the cylinder to roll. If the maximum kinetic frictional force $\mu_{sl}\mathfrak{N}$ is less than the constraining force required to keep the cylinder rolling, then the attempt will not succeed and the cylinder will continue to roll and slide.

The case may occur (cf. Problem 9–16) where due to the initial conditions with which the cylinder was placed on the surface the condition of rolling will be assumed by the cylinder at some later time. However, if the frictional force required to keep it rolling is larger than $f_{\max}$, the body will not continue to roll. In solving problems involving rolling and sliding care must be exercised, since the frictional force may change direction abruptly at the instant that rolling momentarily occurs.

Since the frictional force may change direction in problems where the condition of rolling is assumed momentarily, such problems should be done in two parts. The first part is confined to the motion before the condition of rolling is momentarily satisfied. The second part continues from that moment. It should be clear that when a body rolls and slides, energy is not conserved.

## 9–12 Static equilibrium of rigid bodies

In Section 9–8 we discussed the equations of motion for a rigid body. From these we find that a rigid body which is at rest will continue to remain at rest, if the total external force acting on it and the total external torque about its center of mass vanish. Such a body is said to be in *static equilibrium.*

The equations expressing the vanishing of the total external force and torque,

$$\sum_i \mathbf{F}_i^{\text{ext}} = 0, \tag{9–66}$$

$$\sum_i \mathbf{N}_i' = 0, \tag{9–67}$$

yield in general six independent equations of equilibrium, which permit us to solve for a maximum of six of the quantities which appear in these equations. If the forces or torques or both are coplanar or collinear, then the number of independent equations are less than six, and correspondingly, fewer than six unknown quantities may be obtained through the use of the equations of equilibrium.

It may appear that the equation of motion for the angular momentum about any fixed point yields additional equations of equilibrium, which will permit us to solve for more unknowns. This is not so, since by Eq. (8–142)

$$\mathbf{N}^{\text{ext}} = \mathbf{N}_0 + \mathbf{N}', \tag{9–68}$$

where

$$\mathbf{N}_0 = \mathbf{R} \times \sum_i \mathbf{F}_i^{\text{ext}}.$$

That is, the torque about any other point is not independent of Eqs. (9–66) and (9–67). Equation (9–68) does give us the additional freedom, however, to take torques about any point or points. In doing so, we must be cognizant of the number of independent equations which we can have, and exercise care not to exceed that number.

▶ To demonstrate the use of Eqs. (9–66) and (9–67), we consider the problem of the ladder shown in Fig. 9–21 which is standing on a frictionless horizontal surface. (Why must we assume the surface to be frictionless?) We desire to find the normal reactions of the floor on the ladder and the tension in the strut which prevents the ladder from collapsing. The legs of the ladder weigh $W_1$ and $W_3$ newtons, respectively, and a man of weight $W_2$ newtons is standing on the ladder, a distance $l_2$ from the foot of one leg as shown. The legs of the ladder are equally long. Considering the ladder as a rigid body, we can have only

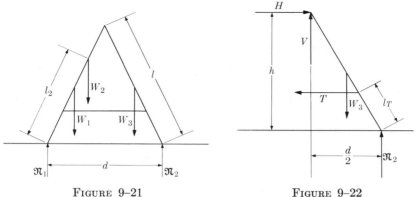

FIGURE 9–21                    FIGURE 9–22

two unknown quantities in this problem, since the torques and also the forces are collinear. These unknown quantities are $\mathfrak{N}_1$ and $\mathfrak{N}_2$. Taking torques about the feet of the ladder, we obtain the two equations

$$\mathfrak{N}_1 d - W_3 \frac{d}{4} - W_1 \left(\frac{d}{2} + \frac{d}{4}\right) - W_2 \left(\frac{d}{2} + \frac{l - l_2}{l}\frac{d}{2}\right) = 0$$

and

$$\mathfrak{N}_2 d - W_1 \frac{d}{2} - W_2 \frac{l_2}{l} d - W_3 \left(\frac{d}{2} + \frac{d}{4}\right) = 0,$$

from which we may obtain $\mathfrak{N}_1$ and $\mathfrak{N}_2$ in terms of the remaining known quantities.

At times we shall also be interested in the internal force as, for example, the tension in the strut. To solve for the tension in the strut, we consider one leg of the ladder (Fig. 9–22) on which are acting the strut, the floor, and the other leg of the ladder. Having removed the strut and the other leg, we must introduce the internal forces which these exert on the leg under consideration. We note that the forces are now coplanar and the torques are still collinear. We can thus have only three independent equations of equilibrium, permitting us to solve for $H$, $V$, and $T$.

To solve for $T$ we take moments about the top of the ladder. This eliminates $H$ and $V$ from the resulting equation, yielding

$$\mathfrak{N}_2 \frac{d}{2} - Th\frac{l - l_T}{l} = 0,$$

where

$$h = \sqrt{l^2 - \frac{d^2}{4}}.$$

The use of Eq. (9–66) then gives us

$$H = T \quad \text{and} \quad V = \mathfrak{N}_2 - W_3. \blacktriangleleft$$

## 9–13 Equilibrium of a system of particles: the principle of virtual work

While the method outlined in the previous section will always succeed in yielding the required number of equations for an solvable static equilibrium problem, it does not necessarily yield the equations from which one may obtain the answer with a minimum of effort.

Consider, for example, the problem depicted in Fig. 9–23. In this problem we have three uniform logs of equal cross section and weight, placed between two vertical walls as shown. We wish to find the horizontal forces which the logs exert on the vertical walls.

The method which yields a more general set of equilibrium equations is based on the principle of virtual work. Since there exists a maximum number of independent equilibrium equations, any equation obtained from the principle of virtual work must necessarily be a function of Eqs. (9–66) and (9–67).

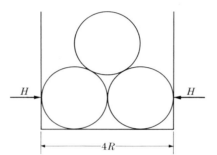

FIGURE 9–23

To obtain the principle of virtual work we consider a system of particles in static equilibrium. This means that each particle is in equilibrium, and that therefore the total force on the $i$th particle vanishes,

$$\mathbf{F}_i = \mathbf{F}_i^{\text{ext}} + \mathbf{F}_i^{\text{int}} + \mathbf{R}_i = 0, \tag{9–69}$$

where $\mathbf{R}_i$ represents the constraining force that may be acting on the $i$th particle. But this means that the scalar product of (9–69) with any vector will also vanish,

$$\mathbf{F}_i \cdot \mathbf{u} = 0. \tag{9–70}$$

Suppose we let

$$\mathbf{u} = \Delta\mathbf{r}_i,$$

where $\Delta\mathbf{r}_i$ is any small vector which could represent a possible displacement of the $i$th particle if it were set into motion. Hence

$$\mathbf{F}_i \cdot \Delta\mathbf{r}_i = 0$$

or

$$\sum_i \mathbf{F}_i \cdot \Delta\mathbf{r}_i = 0.$$

If the $\Delta\mathbf{r}_i$'s are chosen so that any constraints which exist between the coordinates of the particles are satisfied, then the constraining forces $\mathbf{R}_i$ acting on the particles will be perpendicular to the displacements $\Delta\mathbf{r}_i$, and thus

$$\sum_i \mathbf{R}_i \cdot \Delta\mathbf{r}_i = 0.$$

In any case $\mathbf{F}_i \cdot \Delta\mathbf{r}_i$ represents the infinitesimal work $\Delta W_i$ which the force $\mathbf{F}_i$ does on the $i$th particle over the possible infinitesimal displacement $\Delta\mathbf{r}_i$ of the particle. If a particle is situated at a point where the total force on it vanishes, then there will be no work performed on it; that is,

$$\Delta W_i = \mathbf{F}_i \cdot \Delta\mathbf{r}_i = 0$$

or

$$\Delta W = \sum_i \Delta W_i = 0. \tag{9–71}$$

Since this is the work which would be performed by all the forces acting on the system in equilibrium if the particles were displaced by the small amounts $\Delta\mathbf{r}_i$ from their equilibrium positions, $\Delta W$ is referred to as the virtual work. Equation (9–71) expresses the fact that for a system of particles in static equilibrium the virtual work vanishes.

▶ Let us apply the principle of virtual work towards finding the forces which the walls exert on the logs of Fig. 9–23. Due to the symmetry of the problem, it can be surmised that the magnitudes of the forces are equal. Consider thus the effect of moving the right-hand wall a distance $\Delta x$. It is to be expected that in that case the upper log will push the two lower logs apart and descend a distance $\Delta y$, which is a function of $\Delta x$. From Fig. 9–24, which depicts the triangle formed by the centers of the logs, and calling the distance between the centers of the two lower logs $2x$, we find that

$$x^2 + y^2 = 4R^2,$$

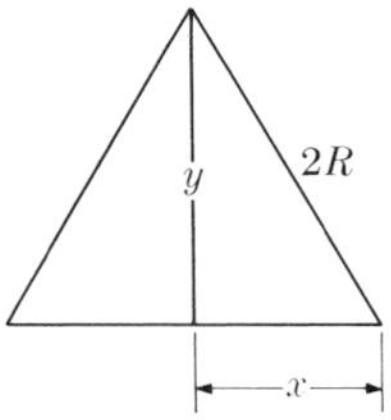

whence we obtain

$$2x\,\Delta x + 2y\,\Delta y = 0 \quad\text{or}\quad |\Delta y| = \frac{x}{y}\,|\Delta x|.$$

For our example in which the logs remain in contact

$$x = R, \quad y = R\sqrt{3}, \quad\text{and}\quad |\Delta y| = \frac{1}{\sqrt{3}}\,|\Delta x|.$$

FIGURE 9–24

The virtual displacements which we have made are consistent with the constraints between the logs. The virtual work is therefore the sum of the virtual work performed by the gravitational forces and the horizontal force of the displaced wall acting on the logs. That is,

$$\Delta W = mg|\Delta y| - H|\Delta x|.$$

Setting the virtual work equal to zero yields the desired solution

$$H = mg\sqrt{3}/3. \blacktriangleleft$$

In terms of the generalized coordinates $q_j$, which may be utilized for the kinematic description of a system of particles, we find that the virtual displacements $\Delta q_j$ give

$$\Delta W = \sum_j Q_j \, \Delta q_j. \tag{9-72}$$

Since the generalized coordinates, and therefore their virtual displacements, are independent, it follows that the conditions for equilibrium are

$$Q_j = 0. \tag{9-73}$$

Specifically, if we have a system of particles under the action of conservative internal and external forces, then the conditions of equilibrium are expressed by

$$Q_j = -\frac{\partial U}{\partial q_j} = -\left(\frac{\partial U^{\text{ext}}}{\partial q_j} + \frac{\partial U^{\text{int}}}{\partial q_j}\right) = 0. \tag{9-74}$$

This equation, we note, expresses a necessary condition for the potential energy function $U(q_1, q_2, \ldots, q_n)$ to be an extremum. In Chapter 11, which deals with the theory of small vibrations, we shall discuss the conditions on the second-order derivatives which classify the extrema as maximum or minimum. It should be clear from our discussion on the stability of one-dimensional equilibrium points that a stable equilibrium point for an $N$-particle system should likewise be expected to be one of minimum potential energy.

### 9–14 The collision of rigid bodies

In Section 8–3 we discussed the collision of two particles and found the total linear momentum of the system to be conserved. In dealing with the collision of two rigid bodies, we encounter an additional conservation theorem, the conservation of the total angular momentum of the system.

Thus, for example, in the collision of the two rigid bodies shown in Fig. 9–25, from the vanishing of the total linear momentum of the system with respect to its center of mass $C$, we once again find that

$$M_2\mathbf{U}_2' = -M_1\mathbf{U}_1' \quad \text{and} \quad M_2\mathbf{V}_2' = -M_1\mathbf{V}_1', \tag{9-75}$$

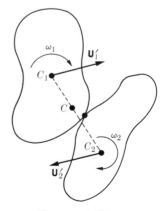

FIGURE 9–25

where $\mathbf{U}_i'$ and $\mathbf{V}_i'$ are the relative velocities before and after the collision of the centers of mass $C_i$ of the two colliding bodies with respect to the center of mass of the system.

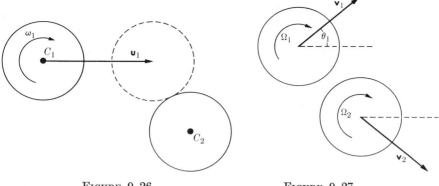

FIGURE 9–26          FIGURE 9–27

In addition, we also have the conservation of the angular momentum as expressed by

$$\mathbf{L}_1 + \mathbf{L}_2 = \mathbf{J}_1 + \mathbf{J}_2, \tag{9–76}$$

where $\mathbf{L}_i$ and $\mathbf{J}_i$ represent the total angular momenta of the bodies before and after the collision with respect to any fixed point $O$.

The application of these conservation theorems to the collision between two arbitrary rigid bodies can be quite complicated. To elucidate the principles involved, we consider the relatively simple case of the collision of two identical ice hockey pucks of mass $M$ which are free to slide on a frictionless horizontal plane. We consider the case when the first puck having an initial angular velocity $\omega_1$ and initial velocity $\mathbf{u}_1$ collides with the second identical puck initially at rest as shown in Fig. 9–26. After the collision the first puck has an angular velocity $\Omega_1$ and moves with a velocity of magnitude $v_1$ directed with an angle $\theta_1$ from its incident direction (Fig. 9–27). This information is sufficient to yield the final linear velocity $\mathbf{v}_2$ and the final angular velocity $\Omega_2$ of the second puck. The final velocity of the second puck is obtained from the conservation of the linear momentum of the system. From

$$M\mathbf{u}_1 - M\mathbf{v}_1 = M\mathbf{v}_2$$

we find that (cf. Fig. 9–28)

$$M^2 v_2^2 = M^2(u_1^2 + v_1^2 - 2u_1 v_1 \cos \theta_1)$$

and

$$\sin \theta_1 = \frac{v_2}{v_1} \sin \theta_2.$$

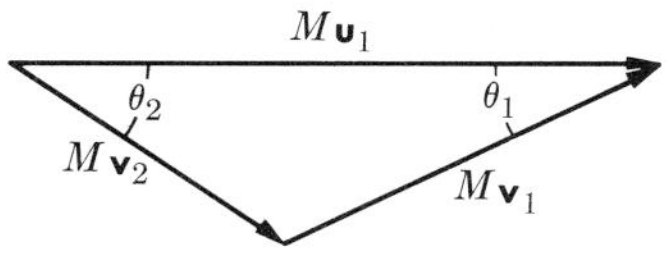

FIGURE 9–28

The final angular velocity of the second puck is obtained from the conservation of the total angular momentum of the system. In this problem the angular momenta with respect to the point at which the center of mass of the system is located at the instant of collision, that is, with respect to the point of contact between the pucks, are directed perpendicularly to the horizontal plane. Their magnitudes before the collision are $L_1 = I\omega_1 + Mu_1 R \sin \alpha$ and $L_2 = 0$, where $\alpha$ is the angle between $\mathbf{u}_1$ and the line joining the two centers of the pucks at the instant of contact (Fig. 9–29), and $R$ is the radius of the pucks.

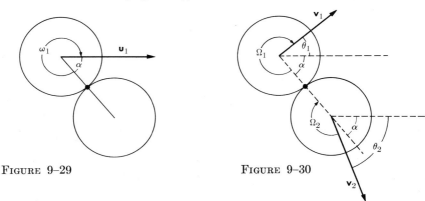

FIGURE 9–29                              FIGURE 9–30

After the collision the magnitudes of the angular momenta are (cf. Fig. 9–30)

$$J_1 = I\Omega_1 + MRv_1 \sin (\alpha + \theta_1), \qquad J_2 = I\Omega_2 + MRv_2 \sin (\theta_2 - \alpha).$$

The principle of the conservation of angular momentum thus yields

$$\begin{aligned} I\Omega_2 = I\omega_1 &- I\Omega_1 - Mv_1 R \sin (\alpha + \theta_1) \\ &+ Mu_1 R \sin \alpha - Mv_2 R \sin (\theta_2 - \alpha). \end{aligned}$$

We note that the conservation of the angular momentum plays an important role in the analysis of scattering problems and nuclear reactions. For example, simply from a consideration of the conservation of the total angular momentum of the system it follows that in the decay of the neutron a proton and an electron could not be the only decay products. At least one additional particle is theoretically required to satisfy the conservation of the angular momentum, linear momentum, and total energy of the system. This third particle is the neutrino.

## 9–15 The torque-free motion of a rigid body

As an example of the application of Euler's equations of motion, we consider the torque-free motion of a rigid body with one point fixed. This example also includes the unconstrained motion of a torque-free rigid body with respect to its center of mass.

Before proceeding with an analysis of this problem, we shall present an illuminating geometric description of the motion due to Poinsot.*

For the torque-free motion of a rigid body with one point fixed we have the conservation of the angular momentum and the total energy of the body. The latter in this case is equal to the kinetic energy of the body. These conservation theorems are expressed by

$$\mathbf{L} = \text{const} \qquad (9\text{-}77)$$

and

$$T = \tfrac{1}{2}\boldsymbol{\omega} \cdot \mathbf{L} = \tfrac{1}{2}(\boldsymbol{\omega}|\mathbf{I}|\boldsymbol{\omega}) = \text{const}. \qquad (9\text{-}78)$$

Considering that $\mathbf{L}$ is constant,

$$\boldsymbol{\omega} \cdot \mathbf{L} = 2T \qquad (9\text{-}79)$$

tells us that the component of $\boldsymbol{\omega}$ along the constant angular momentum vector is constant. In an $\omega$-space whose $\omega_x$-, $\omega_y$-, and $\omega_z$-axes coincide with the space $x$-, $y$-, and $z$-axes, (9-79) is the equation of a plane which is perpendicular to the angular momentum vector and is at a distance $2T/L$ from the origin.

On the other hand, in the same $\omega$-space

$$\phi(\boldsymbol{\omega}) = (\boldsymbol{\omega}|\mathbf{I}|\boldsymbol{\omega}) = 2T \qquad (9\text{-}80)$$

is the equation of an ellipsoid whose axes coincide with the principal axes of the body. Equation (9-78) thus tells us that the plane represented by Eq. (9-79) and referred to as the *invariable plane* and the ellipsoid represented by Eq. (9-80) have at any instant one point in common. Hence the invariable plane

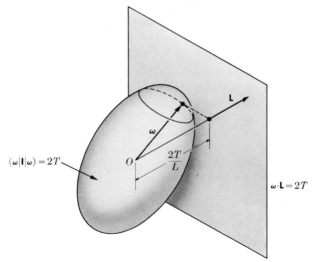

FIGURE 9-31

---

* Poinsot, *Théorie Nouvelle de la Rotation des Corps*, 1834.

should at all times be tangential to the *Poinsot ellipsoid* (Fig. 9–31). That this is so can be verified by finding the normal to the Poinsot ellipsoid at the point $(\omega_x, \omega_y, \omega_z)$. We find the unit normal to be given by

$$\mathbf{n} = \frac{\nabla_\omega \phi(\omega)}{|\nabla_\omega \phi(\omega)|}, \tag{9–81}$$

where

$$\nabla_\omega \phi(\omega) = \frac{\partial \phi}{\partial \omega_x} \mathbf{i} + \frac{\partial \phi}{\partial \omega_y} \mathbf{j} + \frac{\partial \phi}{\partial \omega_z} \mathbf{k} = 2\mathbf{L}. \tag{9–82}$$

Since the points of the body which lie along the instantaneous angular velocity vector have zero instantaneous velocity, it follows that the point of contact between the Poinsot ellipsoid and the invariable plane has zero velocity with respect to the plane.

The motion of the rigid body can thus be described as the rolling of the Poinsot ellipsoid on the invariable plane.

Even with this simplifying description the motion of an asymmetrical body is still quite complicated to visualize. Its analytical description is also complicated and involves the use of elliptic integrals. We shall therefore restrict ourselves to the simpler torque-free motion of a symmetric rigid body.

For a symmetric rigid body for which $I_1 = I_2 = I$ the Poinsot ellipsoid is an ellipsoid of revolution. The angular velocity vector will thus remain constant in magnitude and be observed to precess about the invariable line, which is the line through the fixed point of the body, perpendicular to the invariable plane (Fig. 9–32). In precessing, the angular velocity vector traces out a cone in space, referred to as the space cone.

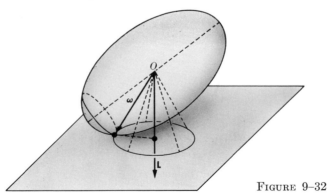

Figure 9–32

With respect to the body coordinate system, the angular velocity vector is also constant in magnitude, and its tip will trace out a circle on the Poinsot ellipsoid. That is, the angular velocity vector precesses about the body symmetry axis, and will similarly trace out a cone with respect to the rigid body, which is referred to as the body cone. The two cones are tangent to each other along the instantaneous axis of rotation. The motion of the symmetric body will thus appear as the rolling of the body cone on the space cone (Fig. 9–33). Conversely, with respect to the body the space cone will appear to roll on the body cone.

We proceed to verify these conclusions by an analytical treatment of the torque-free motion for a symmetric rigid body. For a symmetric body for which $I_1 = I_2 = I$, Euler's equations of motion [(9–46) through (9–48)] reduce to

$$I\dot{\omega}_1 - (I - I_3)\omega_2\omega_3 = 0, \tag{9–83}$$

$$I\dot{\omega}_2 - (I_3 - I)\omega_1\omega_3 = 0, \tag{9–84}$$

and

$$I\dot{\omega}_3 = 0, \tag{9–85}$$

where we have set

$$\omega_{x'} = \omega_1, \qquad \omega_{y'} = \omega_2, \qquad \text{and} \qquad \omega_{z'} = \omega_3.$$

Equation (9–85) yields the result that $\omega_3$, the component of the angular velocity along the symmetry axis of the rigid body, is a constant.

Inserting this result in the other two Euler equations yields a pair of simultaneous differential equations with constant coefficients,

$$\dot{\omega}_1 + \left(\frac{I_3 - I}{I}\omega_3\right)\omega_2 = 0, \tag{9–86}$$

$$\dot{\omega}_2 - \left(\frac{I_3 - I}{I}\omega_3\right)\omega_1 = 0.$$

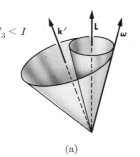

Assuming a solution of the form

$$\omega_1 = Ae^{i\alpha t} \qquad \text{and} \qquad \omega_2 = Be^{i\alpha t},$$

we obtain

$$i\alpha A + kB = 0, \qquad -kA + i\alpha B = 0, \tag{9–87}$$

where

$$k = \frac{I_3 - I}{I}\omega_3. \tag{9–88}$$

The homogeneous simultaneous equations for the amplitudes $A$ and $B$ have a nontrivial solution only if

$$\alpha^2 = k^2 \qquad \text{or} \qquad \alpha = \pm k, \tag{9–89}$$

for which

$$B = \mp iA. \tag{9–90}$$

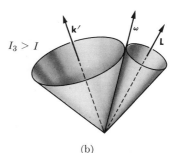

Fig. 9–33. Space and body cones.

Since $\omega_1$ and $\omega_2$ are real, the general solution for $\omega_1$ and $\omega_2$ is thus found to be expressed by

$$\omega_1 = C \cos (kt + \phi), \qquad \omega_2 = C \sin (kt + \phi), \tag{9-91}$$

where

$$2A = Ce^{i\phi}.$$

These expressions for $\omega_1$ and $\omega_2$ represent the vector

$$\boldsymbol{\omega}_\perp = \omega_1 \mathbf{i}' + \omega_2 \mathbf{j}' \tag{9-92}$$

of constant magnitude

$$\omega_\perp = C,$$

rotating about the body $z$-axis with the constant angular velocity

$$\Omega = k. \tag{9-93}$$

The total angular-velocity vector

$$\boldsymbol{\omega} = \omega_1 \mathbf{i}' + \omega_2 \mathbf{j}' + \omega_3 \mathbf{k}' \tag{9-94}$$

thus has the constant magnitude

$$\omega = \sqrt{\omega_1^2 + \omega_2^2 + \omega_3^2} = \sqrt{C^2 + \omega_3^2}, \tag{9-95}$$

and it too precesses about the body $z$-axis with the constant precessional angular velocity $\Omega$.

For example, our earth may be considered, to a first approximation, to be a torque-free rigid body. The axis of rotation of the earth is known to make a small angle with its symmetry axis, and is observed to precess about the symmetry axis approximately once every 447 days. To a first approximation, $(I_3 - I)/I$ is very nearly equal to $33 \times 10^{-4}$, and hence we would expect to find the period of precession of the axis of rotation about the symmetry axis to be

$$\tau = \frac{2\pi}{\Omega} = \frac{2\pi}{\omega_3} \frac{I}{I_3 - I} = \frac{10^4}{33} \times 1 \text{ day} = 300 \text{ days.}$$

The discrepancy between the observed and computed period is attributed to the nonrigid character of the earth.

Returning to the problem under discussion, and choosing the direction of $\mathbf{L}$ as the space $z$-axis, we find as inferred from the Poinsot construction that

$$L_{z'} = I_3 \omega_3 = L \cos \theta, \tag{9-96}$$

or that the angle between $\boldsymbol{\omega}$ and $\mathbf{L}$ remains constant,

$$\cos \theta = \frac{I_3 \omega_3}{L} = \text{const.} \tag{9-97}$$

Also from [cf. Eq. (9–12)]

$$L_{x'} = L \sin \theta \sin \psi = I\omega_1, \tag{9-98}$$
$$L_{y'} = L \sin \theta \cos \psi = I\omega_2,$$

we find that

$$\tan \psi = \frac{L_{x'}}{L_{y'}} = \frac{\omega_1}{\omega_2} = \cot (kt + \phi) \tag{9-99}$$

or

$$\psi = \frac{\pi}{2} - (kt + \phi). \tag{9-100}$$

This value of $\psi$ ensures that $\sin \psi$ has at all times the same sign as $\omega_1$ and $\cos \psi$ the same sign as $\omega_2$.

Finally, utilizing the fact that $\dot{\theta} = 0$, the last of Eqs. (9–16) tells us that

$$\dot{\phi} \cos \theta = \omega_3 - \dot{\psi} = \omega_3 + k = \frac{I_3 \omega_3}{I},$$

or

$$\dot{\phi} = \frac{I_3 \omega_3}{I \cos \theta} = \frac{L}{I} = \dot{\phi}_0 = \text{const}, \tag{9-101}$$

where $\dot{\phi}_0$ is the constant rate of precession of the body $z$-axis about the space $z$-axis.

Another interesting example is the force-free motion of a rigid body whose angular velocity vector makes a very small angle with one of the principal axes of the body. Choosing this principal axis as the body $z$-axis, Euler's equations of motion are, to a first approximation,

$$I_1 \dot{\omega}_1 - (I_2 - I_3)\omega_2\omega_3 = 0,$$
$$I_2 \dot{\omega}_2 - (I_3 - I_1)\omega_1\omega_3 = 0, \tag{9-102}$$

and

$$I_3 \dot{\omega}_3 = 0.$$

We have assumed that $\omega_1$ and $\omega_2$ are small, and have neglected the term in $\omega_1\omega_2$. These equations yield

$$I_3 \omega_3 = \text{const}, \tag{9-103}$$

which in turn reduces the first two equations of motion to the two simultaneous differential equations with constant coefficients,

$$\dot{\omega}_1 - \left(\frac{I_2 - I_3}{I_1} \omega_3\right) \omega_2 = 0$$

and

$$\tag{9-104}$$

$$\dot{\omega}_2 - \left(\frac{I_3 - I_1}{I_2} \omega_3\right) \omega_1 = 0.$$

Assuming a trial solution of the form

$$\omega_1 = Ae^{i\alpha t}, \qquad \omega_2 = Be^{i\alpha t}, \tag{9-105}$$

we find a solution to be possible only if

$$\alpha^2 = \left(\frac{I_3 - I_2}{I_1}\right)\left(\frac{I_3 - I_1}{I_2}\right)\omega_3^2. \tag{9-106}$$

Interestingly, we find that we can obtain a real value for $\alpha$ only if $I_3$ is either the largest or the smallest principal moment of inertia. If $I_3$ is the intermediate principal moment of inertia, that is if

$$I_1 < I_3 < I_2,$$

then $\alpha$ is imaginary.

A real value of $\alpha$ yields the solution

$$\omega_1 = C \cos(\alpha t + \phi),$$

$$\omega_2 = C\sqrt{\frac{I_3 - I_1}{I_3 - I_2}\left(\frac{I_1}{I_2}\right)} \sin(\alpha t + \phi), \tag{9-107}$$

which means that the angular velocity vector will remain in the neighborhood of the body $z$-axis.

On the other hand, an imaginary value of $\alpha$ yields a solution of the form

$$\omega_1 = A_1 e^{\beta t} + A_2 e^{-\beta t}, \qquad \omega_2 = B_1 e^{\beta t} + B_2 e^{-\beta t}, \tag{9-108}$$

which indicates that $\omega_1$ and $\omega_2$ increase exponentially with time. For this latter case then $\omega_1$ and $\omega_2$ will not remain small, and hence our analysis based on the approximate equations of motion, Eq. (9–102), is not appropriate. We note therefore that the force-free rotational motion of a rigid body having an angular velocity vector directed along the principal axis which has the largest or smallest value of the principal moments of inertia is stable, whereas the motion in the neighborhood of the principal axis having the intermediate value of the moment of inertia is unstable.

## 9–16 The motion of a symmetric top under the action of gravity

In this section we shall discuss the motion of a symmetric rigid body with one point on its symmetry axis fixed under the action of gravity (cf. Fig. 9–34). Choosing the symmetry axis as the body $z$-axis and setting

$$I_1 = I_2 = I,$$

we find the Lagrangian function for the rigid body to be

$$L = \tfrac{1}{2}I\dot\theta^2 + \tfrac{1}{2}I\dot\phi^2 \sin^2\theta + \tfrac{1}{2}I_3(\dot\psi + \dot\phi \cos\theta)^2 - Mgh \cos\theta, \tag{9-109}$$

where we have used Eq. (9–50) for the kinetic energy and

$$U = Mgh \cos \theta \qquad (9\text{–}110)$$

for its potential energy.

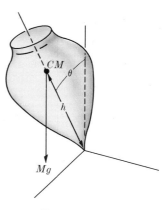

Since the Lagrangian is not an explicit function of the Euler angles $\psi$ and $\phi$ and the time $t$, three integrals of the motion are the constancy of the generalized momenta $p_\psi$ and $p_\phi$, and the conservation of the total energy $E$. These three integrals of the motion are expressed by

$$p_\psi = \frac{\partial L}{\partial \dot\psi} = I_3(\dot\psi + \dot\phi \cos \theta) = Ia,$$

$$(9\text{–}111)$$

FIGURE 9–34

where $a$ is a constant,

$$p_\phi = \frac{\partial L}{\partial \dot\phi} = I\dot\phi \sin^2 \theta + I_3 \cos \theta(\dot\psi + \dot\phi \cos \theta) = Ib, \qquad (9\text{–}112)$$

where $b$ is a constant, and

$$T + U = \tfrac{1}{2}I\dot\theta^2 + \tfrac{1}{2}I\dot\phi^2 \sin^2 \theta + \tfrac{1}{2}I_3(\dot\psi + \dot\phi \cos \theta)^2 + Mgh \cos \theta$$
$$= E. \qquad (9\text{–}113)$$

We find that $p_\psi$ is the component of the angular momentum along the body $z$-axis, and $p_\phi$ is the component of the angular momentum along the space $z$-axis.

In principle the solution to the problem may be obtained from these three integrals of the motion without any further use of the equations of motion for the rigid body.

For example, Eqs. (9–111) and (9–112) may be solved for $\dot\psi$ and $\dot\phi$, yielding

$$\dot\phi = \frac{b - a \cos \theta}{\sin^2 \theta} \qquad (9\text{–}114)$$

and

$$\dot\psi = \frac{I_1 a}{I_3} - \frac{b - a \cos \theta}{\sin^2 \theta} \cos \theta. \qquad (9\text{–}115)$$

These expressions in turn, when used in Eq. (9–113), yield the equation

$$E' = E - \frac{(Ia)^2}{2I_3} = \frac{1}{2}\,I\dot\theta^2 + \frac{1}{2}\,I\left(\frac{b - a \cos \theta}{\sin \theta}\right)^2 + Mgh \cos \theta, \qquad (9\text{–}116)$$

from which we may obtain the time dependence of the angle $\theta$ between the body and space $z$-axes. A knowledge of the time dependence of $\theta$ in turn provides us with the time dependence of $\phi$ and $\psi$ through the integration of Eqs. (9–114) and (9–115).

Except under special circumstances for which simplifying approximations can be introduced, the general solution expressing $\theta$ as a function of time

involves elliptic integrals,* which tend to
obscure the physics of the problem. We therefore proceed with a qualitative discussion of
the motion.

Equation (9–116) expressing the conservation of energy also expresses the conservation
of total energy for the plane motion of a physical pendulum of moment of inertia $I$ about the
axis of rotation in the effective potential-
energy field

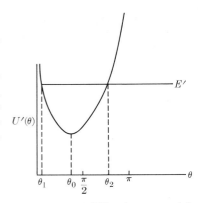

FIG. 9–35. Effective potential
energy function for the $\theta$-motion
of the top.

$$U'(\theta) = Mgh \cos \theta + \frac{1}{2} I \left( \frac{b - a \cos \theta}{\sin \theta} \right)^2. \tag{9–117}$$

This is a one-dimensional problem for which the
discussion of Sections 4–7 and 4–8 applies. Since
$U'$ assumes infinite values for $\theta = 0$ or $\pi$, and finite values for all other values
of $\theta$, it follows that for some value of $\theta$ between 0 and $\pi$ $U'(\theta)$ assumes a minimum value (cf. Fig. 9–35). This occurs at the value $\theta_0$, which is the root of the
equation

$$\frac{dU'}{d\theta} = -Mgh \sin \theta + Ia \left( \frac{b - a \cos \theta}{\sin \theta} \right) - I \frac{(b - a \cos \theta)^2}{\sin^3 \theta} \cos \theta$$

$$= -Mgh \sin \theta + \frac{I(b - a \cos \theta)(a - b \cos \theta)}{\sin^3 \theta} = 0. \tag{9–118}$$

In general, therefore, the $\theta$-motion is a bound motion, confined between the
two values $\theta_1$ and $\theta_2$ of $\theta$, which are the roots of the equation

$$E' = U'(\theta)$$

or

$$E' = Mgh \cos \theta + \frac{1}{2} I \left( \frac{b - a \cos \theta}{\sin \theta} \right)^2. \tag{9–119}$$

The variation in the angle $\theta$ is referred to as the nutation of the symmetry axis
of the top.

If

$$E' = U'(\theta_0), \tag{9–120}$$

then $\theta$ remains fixed at $\theta_0$, and the top precesses about the space $z$-axis with the
constant angular velocity

$$\dot{\phi} = \frac{b - a \cos \theta_0}{\sin^2 \theta_0}. \tag{9–121}$$

---

* For a detailed integration, see W. D. MacMillan, *Theoretical Mechanics*, Vol. 3
(*Dynamics of Rigid Bodies*), pp. 216 ff. New York: McGraw Hill.

Now, we find that for a given value of $\theta_0$ there exist two values of $\dot{\phi}$ which will satisfy Eq. (9–118), which is a quadratic in $(b - a \cos \theta)/\sin^2 \theta$, as may be seen by rewriting it as

$$I\dot{\phi}_0^2 \cos \theta_0 - \dot{\phi}_0(I_3\dot{\psi} + I_3\dot{\phi}_0 \cos \theta_0) + Mgh = 0. \qquad (9–122)$$

The two values of $\dot{\phi}_0$ which satisfy this equation are

$$\dot{\phi}_0 = \frac{I_3\dot{\psi} \pm \sqrt{I_3^2\dot{\psi}^2 - 4Mgh(I - I_3) \cos \theta_0}}{2I \cos \theta_0}. \qquad (9–123)$$

These two values of $\dot{\phi}_0$ for which the symmetry axis of the top will precess uniformly at the constant angle $\theta_0$ are referred to as the "fast" and "slow" precessional angular velocities.

Since $\dot{\phi}_0$ must be real, it should be clear that the quantity under the square-root sign in Eq. (9–123) must be positive definite,

$$I_3^2\dot{\psi}^2 - 4Mgh(I - I_3) \cos \theta_0 \geq 0. \qquad (9–124)$$

This limits the values of $\dot{\psi}$ for which steady precession may occur at the angle $\theta_0$.

The effective potential energy $U'(\theta)$ given by Eq. (9–117) was found to have a minimum. It follows therefore that situations exist for which the nutational motion of the axis of the top can be described as a small simple harmonic oscillation about the value $\theta = \theta_0$, at which $U'(\theta)$ assumes its minimum value. The frequency of these small oscillations is given by

$$\omega = \sqrt{\frac{1}{I} \frac{d^2U'(\theta_0)}{d\theta_0^2}}. \qquad (9–125)$$

We find that

$$\frac{d^2U'(\theta_0)}{d\theta_0^2} = I(a^2 - 4a\dot{\phi}_0 \cos \theta_0 + 3\dot{\phi}_0^2 \cos^2 \theta_0 + \dot{\phi}_0^2). \qquad (9–126)$$

An important example of such a situation is the fast top, which is a top spinning very rapidly about its symmetry axis with angular velocity $\dot{\psi}_0$, and which is initially at rest at an angle $\theta_1$ and then released. For this case we find that

$$a = \frac{I_3\dot{\psi}_0}{I}, \qquad (9–127)$$

$$b = \frac{I_3\dot{\psi}_0 \cos \theta_1}{I}, \qquad (9–128)$$

and

$$E' = Mgh \cos \theta_1. \qquad (9–129)$$

If now

$$Ia^2 \gg 2Mgh,$$

that is, if the rotational kinetic energy about the symmetry axis is much larger than the maximum possible change in the potential energy, then we find that $\dot{\phi}$ is small and that to a first approximation we can set

$$\frac{d^2 U'(\theta_0)}{d\theta_0^2} = Ia^2$$

or

$$\omega = a = \frac{I_3 \dot{\psi}_0}{I}. \tag{9-130}$$

With this approximation we find that we can set

$$\theta = \theta_1 + A - A \cos \omega t, \tag{9-131}$$

where $A$ is a small quantity.  The average angle $\theta_0$ is

$$\theta_0 = \theta_1 + A. \tag{9-132}$$

This solution for $\theta$ in turn yields

$$\dot{\phi} = \frac{b - a \cos \theta}{\sin^2 \theta} \approx \frac{b - a[\cos \theta_1 - \sin \theta_1 (A - A \cos \omega t)]}{\sin^2 \theta_1 + 2 \sin \theta_1 \cos \theta_1 (A - A \cos \omega t)}$$

or

$$\dot{\phi} = \frac{a}{\sin \theta_1} (A - A \cos \omega t). \tag{9-133}$$

The average angular velocity of precession is

$$\langle \dot{\phi} \rangle = \frac{I_3 \dot{\psi}_0 A}{I \sin \theta_1}.$$

To find the amplitude of the nutation we note that the second root of Eq. (9–119) is

$$\theta_2 = \theta_1 + 2A.$$

Setting this value of $\theta_2$ into Eq. (9–119) yields

$$Mgh \cos \theta_1 = Mgh \cos (\theta_1 + 2A) + \frac{1}{2} I \left[ \frac{b - a \cos (\theta_1 + 2A)}{\sin (\theta_1 + 2A)} \right]^2,$$

from which we find that

$$A = \frac{Mgh \sin \theta_1}{Ia^2}, \tag{9-134}$$

and thus

$$\langle \dot{\phi} \rangle = \frac{Mgh}{I_3 \dot{\psi}_0}. \tag{9-135}$$

In summary then we find that a fast top released from rest precesses slowly and nutates sinusoidally with a large frequency and small amplitude.

## Problems

9–1. (a) Work out a formula for the moments of inertia of a cone of mass $m$, height $h$, and generating angle $\alpha$, about its axis of symmetry, and about an axis through the apex perpendicular to the axis of symmetry. Find the center of mass of the cone.

(b) Explain how these results may be used to determine the center of mass of the frustum of the cone (Fig. 9–36) and the moments of inertia about the horizontal axes through each base. The mass of the frustum is $M$.

(c) Utilize the principal moments of inertia about the center of mass listed in Table 9–1 and the parallel-axis theorem to check your answer to Part (a).

9–2. Find a formula for the radius of gyration of a uniform rod of length $l$ about an axis through one end making an angle $\theta$ with the rod.

9–3. Determine the principal moments of inertia of the ellipsoid with semiaxes $a$, $b$, $c$.

9–4. Through the use of Eqs. (9–21) we find that a rigid body rotating about one of its principal axes has an angular momentum vector which is parallel to its angular velocity vector:

$$|\mathbf{L}) = \mathbf{I}|\boldsymbol{\omega}) = \lambda|\boldsymbol{\omega}),$$

where $\lambda$ is the principal moment of inertia about the principal axis. This equation yields a set of homogeneous simultaneous equations for the components of $\boldsymbol{\omega}$ which has a nontrivial solution for only specific values of $\lambda$.

(a) Use this equation to obtain the principal moments of inertia (i.e., find $\lambda$) about the center of mass of a flat rigid body in the shape of a 45° right triangle with uniform mass density.

(b) What are the directions of the principal axes?

9–5. (a) Three mass points are located at the points $(a, 0, 0)$, $(0, a, 2a)$, and $(0, 2a, a)$. Obtain the moments and products of inertia with respect to the coordinate axes at the origin.

(b) Utilize the equation (cf. Problem 9–4)

$$\mathbf{I}|\boldsymbol{\omega}) = \lambda|\boldsymbol{\omega})$$

to obtain the principal moments of inertia and the directions of the principal axes of the system at the origin.

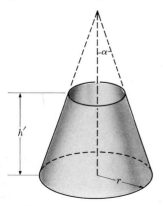

FIG. 9–36. Frustum of a cone.

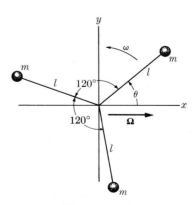

FIGURE 9–37

9–6. Three equal masses are mounted on rigid weightless rods, making angles of 120° as shown in Fig. 9–37. The system rotates with constant angular velocity $\omega = \dot\theta$ about the $z$-axis, which is perpendicular to the plane of the paper and directed upward. The direction of rotation is indicated by the arrow. At the same time, the system turns about the $x$-axis in such a way that the $y$-axis moves out of the plane of the page. This rotation is at a constant angular velocity $\Omega \ll \omega$. (a) Establish principal axes for the system, and (b) by means of Euler's equations compute the torques about $Ox$, $Oy$, and $Oz$. (c) Would the same analysis be valid if the origin $O$ were describing a curve in space?

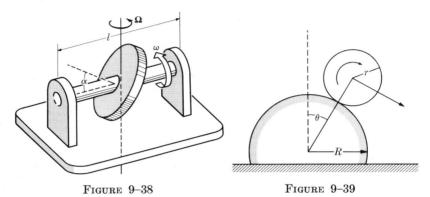

FIGURE 9–38                          FIGURE 9–39

9–7. A symmetrical disk of axial moment of inertia $I_3$ and transverse moment of inertia $I$ rotates with angular speed $\omega$ on a shaft of length $l$, as shown in Fig. 9–38. The axis of symmetry of the disk makes a small angle $\alpha$ with the shaft. The disk is mounted at the middle of the shaft. By the use of Euler's angles $\theta$, $\psi$, and $\phi$, and Lagrange's equations, (a) find the torque on the shaft and the forces exerted on the bearings. (b) Investigate also the torques if the entire support system rotates with angular speed $\Omega$ about the vertical. Neglect the motion of the shaft.

9–8. A wire hoop of radius $r$ and mass $m$ rolls without slipping over the curved surface of a cylinder of radius $R$, as shown in Fig. 9–39. (a) Obtain the Lagrangian equations of motion for the hoop. (b) At what angle $\theta$ will the hoop leave the cylinder? [*Hint:* Utilize the principle of conservation of energy.]

9–9. A pendulum bob, mounted on a light stiff rod, is supported on a rotating table, as shown in Fig. 9–40. The plane of the pendulum motion is always perpendicular to the plane of the suporting framework. Let the mass of the bob be $m$, length of pendulum $l$, moment of inertia of turntable about its axis $I$. Let $\theta$ be the angular displacement of the pendulum from the vertical at time $t$. The rod supporting the bob has negligible mass compared with $m$. The moment of inertia $I$ is large compared with the moment of inertia of the bob about the vertical.

Initially $\theta = 0$ and $v = v_0$ for the bob, where $v$ is the velocity of the bob, and $\omega = \omega_0$, where $\omega$ is the angular velocity of the turntable at time $t$.

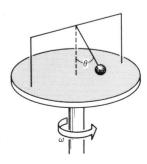

FIGURE 9–40

From the laws for the conservation of energy and angular momentum, together with an energy diagram, discuss the motion of the system. [*Hint:* Expand $\sin \theta$ and $\cos \theta$ where necessary in a Maclaurin series and retain only terms to the fourth order in $\theta$.] Distinguish between the situations when $\theta$ is small and when $\theta$ is large. Investigate the critical angular velocity $\omega_0 = \sqrt{g/l}$; i.e., state what happens when $\omega_0 < \sqrt{g/l}$ and when $\omega_0 > \sqrt{g/l}$.

9–10. A uniform bar of mass $M$ and length $2l$ is suspended from one end by a spring of force constant $k$. The bar can swing freely only in one vertical plane, and the spring is constrained to move only in the vertical direction. Set up the equations of motion in the Lagrangian formulation.

9–11. A uniform rod slides with its ends on a smooth vertical circle. If the rod subtends an angle of 120° at the center of the circle, show that the equivalent simple pendulum has a length equal to the radius of the circle.

9–12. An automobile is started from rest with one of its doors initially at right angles. If the hinges of the door are toward the front of the car, the door will slam shut as the automobile picks up speed. Obtain a formula for the time needed for the door to close if the acceleration $A$ of the car is constant, the radius of gyration of the door about the axis of rotation is $k_0$, and the center of mass is at a distance $d$ from the hinges. Show that if $A$ is 1 ft/sec$^2$ and the door is a uniform rectangle 4 ft wide, the time will be approximately 3.04 seconds.

9–13. (a) Obtain the kinetic energy of a rolling cylinder of radius $R$ whose center of mass is at a distance $h$ from its geometric center and one of whose principal axes is parallel to the axis of the cylinder when the cylinder is rolling on a horizontal plane. Express $T$ in terms of the principal moment of inertia $I$ about this axis.

(b) Obtain the equations of motion of the cylinder and the period of small oscillations of the cylinder about its equilibrium position.

9–14. (a) Obtain the kinetic energy of a homogeneous cylinder of radius $r$ which is rolling inside a fixed cylindrical shell of radius $R$.

(b) Repeat Part (a) for the case when the cylindrical shell of mass $M$ is free to roll on a horizontal surface.

(c) Obtain Lagrange's equations of motion and from them the period of small oscillations about the equilibrium position.

9–15. A solid right circular cone whose vertex angle is $2\alpha$ rolls without slipping on a plane inclined at an angle $\beta$ to the horizontal. The cone has a mass $M$ and a slant height $L$.

(a) Write the Lagrangian equations of motion for the cone, using as generalized coordinate the angle $\theta$ between its line of contact with the plane and the line of steepest descent.

(b) What is the frequency of small oscillations about this equilibrium position? [*Hint:* Use the line of contact as the instantaneous axis of rotation and remember that the vertex of the cone remains fixed.]

9–16. A ball is initially projected at a speed $v_0$ up an inclined plane of inclination angle $\theta$ and coefficient of friction $\mu$ such that motion in a vertical plane results. Find the position of the ball as a function of the time, if the ball had no initial rotational motion, (a) when $\mu > \frac{2}{7} \tan \theta$; (b) when $\mu < \frac{2}{7} \tan \theta$.

9–17. (a) A uniform rod of length $2l$ is balanced vertically on the floor and then allowed to fall. Find its angular acceleration and angular velocity at the time when it makes an angle $\theta$ with the vertical, if the floor is so rough that the lower end cannot slip.

(b) Repeat Part (a) for the case when the floor is smooth and slipping occurs.

(c) Obtain the equations of motion for the case when the coefficient of friction is $\mu$.

9–18. A cylindrically symmetric wheel of mass $M$ and radius of gyration $k$ about the symmetry axis spins smoothly on a fixed horizontal axle of radius $a$ which passes through a hole of slightly larger radius at the hub of the wheel. The coefficient of friction between the bearing surfaces is $\mu$. If the wheel is initially spinning with angular velocity $\omega_0$, what are the time and the number of turns that it takes to stop? [*Hint:* Axle and hub touch at only one point.]

9–19. A horizontal rod of mass $m$ and length $2l$ falls under gravity and strikes a knife-edge located one half of the way from the center to the end of the rod (Fig. 9–41). Its velocity just before the impact is **V**. The coefficient of restitution between the rod and the knife-edge is $\epsilon$. Calculate (a) the velocity of the center of mass of the rod and (b) its angular velocity immediately after it strikes the obstruction.

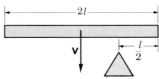

FIGURE 9–41

9–20. A symmetrical top of axial moment of inertia $I_3$ is started with its axis in the vertical position, that is $\theta = 0$ and $\dot\theta = 0$.

(a) Establish the effective potential $V'(\theta)$ for this case.

(b) Show that if $\dot\psi^2 > 4mghI/I_3^2$, the angle will remain zero.

(c) Show also that if $\dot\psi$ is less than the above value, the top will, after a slight disturbance, oscillate between $\theta$ nearly equal to zero and

$$\theta = \cos^{-1}\left(\frac{\dot\psi^2 I_3^2}{2mghI} - 1\right).$$

9–21. A symmetrical top of axial moment of inertia $I_3$ is set in motion at $t = 0$, with $\dot\theta = 0$, $\theta = \pi/2$, and $\dot\phi = I_3\dot\psi/I$. Investigate the behavior of the top for $t > 0$ if

$$\dot\psi^2 = 2mghI/I_3^2.$$

9–22. (a) Show that Eq. (9–49) follows from Eq. (9–50) for the rotational kinetic energy of a rigid body.

(b) Obtain the remaining two generalized equations of motion for the angles $\theta$ and $\phi$.

# 10

# *Elements of Linear Transformation Theory*

In previous chapters, whenever we thought it appropriate, we chose to acquaint the reader with the matrix representation of vectors and linear vector equations, which related the components of one vector linearly to the components of another, or which related two different but equivalent descriptions of the same vector. Linear relations occur frequently in physics, and invariably their representation and the algebraic manipulation of them are expressed more concisely in matrix or its equivalent operator notation. We have reached the point in our study of mechanics where the introduction and use of some of the basic elements of matrix algebra is appropriate. Since, however, the use of matrix algebra is so indispensable in, for example, the quantum mechanical descriptions of the results of measurements on a system and of the relations which exist between different measurable physical quantities, we shall give a more complete discussion of the elements of linear transformation theory than would otherwise be required. The reader will find the material of this chapter extremely useful.

We shall begin with a review of the matrix representation of vectors and operators in a real three-dimensional vector space introduced previously, and we shall subsequently generalize the three-dimensional results to real and complex $n$-dimensional vector spaces.

## 10–1 Review of the matrix representation of three-dimensional vectors

In Chapter 1* we found a three-dimensional vector to be specifiable in terms of its scalar product with three noncoplanar vectors. Thus given the scalar products

$$\alpha_i = \mathbf{A} \cdot \mathbf{b}_i \qquad (10\text{–}1)$$

---

* A review of Section 1–5 may be helpful at this point.

of the vector $\mathbf{A}$ with the three known noncoplanar vectors $\mathbf{b}_i$, the vector $\mathbf{A}$ was found to be expressed by

$$\mathbf{A} = \sum_{i=1}^{3} \alpha_i \mathbf{b}_i, \qquad (10\text{--}2)$$

where the $\mathbf{b}_i$'s are the three vectors reciprocal to the vectors $\mathbf{b}_i$. Two sets of base vectors are said to be reciprocal if their scalar products satisfy the relation

$$\mathbf{b}_i \cdot \mathbf{b}_i = \delta_{ij} = \begin{cases} 0 & i \neq j, \\ 1 & i = j. \end{cases} \qquad (10\text{--}3)$$

The base vectors $\mathbf{b}_i$ reciprocal to the base vectors $\mathbf{b}_i$ can readily be found by solving the nine equations contained within Eq. (10–3) for the nine components of the three reciprocal base vectors. The solution for three-dimensional vectors was found in Section 1–5.

We furthermore found it convenient to utilize the specification of a vector $\mathbf{A}$ in terms of its scalar products

$$\alpha_i^{\star} = \mathbf{A} \cdot \mathbf{b}_i \qquad (10\text{--}4)$$

with the reciprocal vectors $\mathbf{b}_i$. In terms of the $\alpha_i^{\star}$'s the vector $\mathbf{A}$ was found to be expressed by

$$\mathbf{A} = \sum_{i=1}^{3} \alpha_i^{\star} \mathbf{b}_i. \qquad (10\text{--}5)$$

We distinguished the two ways of expressing the vector $\mathbf{A}$ by placing a star superscript on the symbol representing the vector $\mathbf{A}$ whenever we wished it to be expressed as given by Eq. (10–5). That is, we let

$$\mathbf{A}^{\star} = \sum_{i=1}^{3} \alpha_i^{\star} \mathbf{b}_i. \qquad (10\text{--}6)$$

The scalar product of two vectors $\mathbf{A}$ and $\mathbf{B}$ was thus found to be expressible most efficiently in the form

$$\mathbf{A}^{\star} \cdot \mathbf{B} = \sum_{i=1}^{3} \alpha_i^{\star} \beta_i = \sum_{i=1}^{3} \alpha_i \beta_i^{\star} = \mathbf{A} \cdot \mathbf{B}^{\star}, \qquad (10\text{--}7)$$

where

$$\beta_i = \mathbf{B} \cdot \mathbf{b}_i$$

and

$$\beta_i^{\star} = \mathbf{B} \cdot \mathbf{b}_i.$$

Once the base vectors $\mathbf{b}_i$ and their reciprocal vectors $\mathbf{b}_i$ have been selected, the specification of the vector $\mathbf{A}$ may be provided either by the $\alpha_i$'s or the $\alpha_i^{\star}$'s. It is customary to utilize matrix notation for the specification of a vector; and such a specification is referred to as the *matrix representation* of the vector.

The matrix representation of a vector is the orderly arrangement of its scalar products with the base vectors or the reciprocal base vectors in a row or column matrix. Thus

$$[\alpha_1, \alpha_2, \alpha_3] \quad \text{and} \quad \begin{bmatrix} \alpha_1 \\ \alpha_2 \\ \alpha_3 \end{bmatrix}$$

are the matrix representations of the vector **A**, and

$$[\alpha_1^\star, \alpha_2^\star, \alpha_3^\star] \quad \text{and} \quad \begin{bmatrix} \alpha_1^\star \\ \alpha_2^\star \\ \alpha_3^\star \end{bmatrix}$$

are the matrix representations of the vector **A**⋆. Since both the column and row matrix representations of a vector are useful, we introduced an additional notation with which we could distinguish the particular representation that is desired. Thus the vector **A** is indicated by |**A**) when its representation is to be a column matrix, and by (**A**| when its representation is to be a row matrix. That is,

$$|\mathbf{A}) \leftrightarrow \begin{bmatrix} \alpha_1 \\ \alpha_2 \\ \alpha_3 \end{bmatrix},$$

$$(\mathbf{A}| \leftrightarrow [\alpha_1, \alpha_2, \alpha_3]. \tag{10–8}$$

Similarly, for the same vector **A** expressed in terms of its scalar products with the reciprocal base vectors, we have

$$|\mathbf{A}^\star) \leftrightarrow \begin{bmatrix} \alpha_1^\star \\ \alpha_2^\star \\ \alpha_3^\star \end{bmatrix} \tag{10–9}$$

and

$$(\mathbf{A}^\star| \leftrightarrow [\alpha_1^\star, \alpha_2^\star, \alpha_3^\star].$$

One refers to the row matrix $[\alpha_1, \alpha_2, \alpha_3]$ as the transpose of the column matrix

$$\begin{bmatrix} \alpha_1 \\ \alpha_2 \\ \alpha_3 \end{bmatrix}.$$

Symbolically this is expressed by

$$[\alpha_1, \alpha_2, \alpha_3] = \widetilde{\begin{bmatrix} \alpha_1 \\ \alpha_2 \\ \alpha_3 \end{bmatrix}}.$$

Analogously, we refer to the vector (**A**| as the transpose of the vector |**A**), and vice versa. We express this fact by the equation

$$(\mathbf{A}| = \widetilde{|\mathbf{A})} \quad \text{or} \quad |\mathbf{A}) = \widetilde{(\mathbf{A}|}. \tag{10–10}$$

## 10–2 Matrix algebra*

Column and row matrices are only two examples of matrices in general. A matrix is defined as an orderly array of numbers arranged in a table of rows and columns, the elements of which may be combined with those of another similar matrix according to specific rules for their addition and multiplication. These rules are very much like the rules for the combination of vectors, hence the usefulness of matrices in the representation and handling of vector operations.

A matrix of $m$ rows and $n$ columns is referred to as an $m \times n$ matrix. The matrix

$$\begin{bmatrix} 3 & 2 & -1 \\ 2 & 0 & 5 \end{bmatrix}$$

is thus an example of a $2 \times 3$ matrix.

Two matrices are said to be equal if and only if they have the same number of rows and columns, and if the elements of one matrix are equal to the corresponding elements of the second matrix. Thus if the matrix (**S**) is equal to the matrix (**T**), then the element $S_{ij}$ belonging to the $i$th row and $j$th column of (**S**) is equal to $T_{ij}$, the element belonging to the $i$th row and $j$th column of (**T**),

$$S_{ij} = T_{ij}.$$

Two $m \times n$ matrices may be added to yield a third $m \times n$ matrix. The matrix (**R**) which is equal to the sum or difference of the matrices (**S**) and (**T**),

$$(\mathbf{R}) = (\mathbf{S}) \pm (\mathbf{T}), \tag{10–11}$$

is defined as the matrix whose elements are equal to the sum or difference of the elements of (**S**) and (**T**):

$$R_{ij} = S_{ij} \pm T_{ij}. \tag{10–12}$$

Thus, for example, the sum of the two matrices

$$(\mathbf{S}) = \begin{bmatrix} 1 & 0 \\ -2 & 3 \end{bmatrix} \quad \text{and} \quad (\mathbf{T}) = \begin{bmatrix} 2 & -1 \\ 1 & -1 \end{bmatrix}$$

is the matrix

$$(\mathbf{R}) = \begin{bmatrix} 1+2 & 0-1 \\ -2+1 & 3-1 \end{bmatrix} = \begin{bmatrix} 3 & -1 \\ -1 & 2 \end{bmatrix}.$$

---

* Most of the material in this section was introduced in earlier sections (cf. Sections 1–6 and 3–5).

The multiplication of a matrix $(S)$ by a scalar $c$ yields a similar matrix whose elements are $c$ times those of $(S)$. That is,

$$(R) = c(S) \tag{10–13}$$

implies

$$R_{ij} = cS_{ij}. \tag{10–14}$$

Two matrices may also be multiplied, as was first introduced in Section 3–5. The multiplication of two arbitrary matrices $(S)$ and $(T)$, denoted by $(S)(T)$, is defined, however, only if the number of columns of $(S)$ are the same as the number of rows of $(T)$. Thus if $(S)$ is an $m \times p$ matrix and $(T)$ a $p \times n$ matrix, then the product matrix

$$(R) = (S)(T) \tag{10–15}$$

is defined. It is an $m \times n$ matrix whose elements $R_{ij}$ are given by

$$R_{ij} = \sum_{k=1}^{p} S_{ik}T_{kj}. \tag{10–16}$$

For example, the matrix product of the two matrices

$$(S) = \begin{bmatrix} 1 & 2 & 3 \\ 2 & 1 & 0 \\ 4 & 3 & -1 \end{bmatrix} \quad \text{and} \quad (T) = \begin{bmatrix} 2 & -1 \\ 1 & 2 \\ 0 & 1 \end{bmatrix}$$

is found to be the matrix

$$(R) = \begin{bmatrix} 1 & 2 & 3 \\ 2 & 1 & 0 \\ 4 & 3 & -1 \end{bmatrix}\begin{bmatrix} 2 & -1 \\ 1 & 2 \\ 0 & 1 \end{bmatrix}$$

$$= \begin{bmatrix} 1\cdot2+2\cdot1+3\cdot0 & -1\cdot1+2\cdot2\ \cdot\ 3\cdot1 \\ 2\cdot2+1\cdot1+0\cdot0 & -2\cdot1+1\cdot2+0\cdot1 \\ 4\cdot2+3\cdot1-1\cdot0 & -4\cdot1+3\cdot2-1\cdot1 \end{bmatrix} = \begin{bmatrix} 4 & 6 \\ 5 & 0 \\ 11 & 1 \end{bmatrix}.$$

The scalar product of two vectors is expressible in terms of the matrix product of their row and column matrix representations. That is,

$$\mathbf{A}^{\star} \cdot \mathbf{B} = (\mathbf{A}^{\star}|\mathbf{B}) = [\alpha_1^{\star}, \alpha_2^{\star}, \alpha_3^{\star}]\begin{bmatrix} \beta_1 \\ \beta_2 \\ \beta_3 \end{bmatrix} = \sum_{i=1}^{3} \alpha_i^{\star}\beta_i, \tag{10–17}$$

and from this equation we find that

$$(\mathbf{A}^\star|\mathbf{B}) = (\mathbf{B}^\star|\mathbf{A}) = (\mathbf{A}|\mathbf{B}^\star). \tag{10-18}$$

We note that the multiplication of an $m \times p$ matrix by an $p \times m$ matrix may be performed in either order. That is, we can form either the product $(\mathbf{S})(\mathbf{T})$ or the product $(\mathbf{T})(\mathbf{S})$. We find, however, that even in the case of square matrices for which $m = p$, the two matrix products are in general not equal:

$$(\mathbf{S})(\mathbf{T}) \neq (\mathbf{T})(\mathbf{S}).$$

In other words, matrix multiplication does not in general commute. Two square matrices for which the ordering of the matrices in the matrix product does not matter, that is, for which

$$(\mathbf{S})(\mathbf{T}) = (\mathbf{T})(\mathbf{S}), \tag{10-19}$$

are said to be *commuting matrices*. For example, the matrices

$$(\mathbf{S}) = \begin{bmatrix} 0 & 1 \\ -1 & 0 \end{bmatrix} \quad \text{and} \quad (\mathbf{T}) = \begin{bmatrix} 0 & 1 \\ 1 & 0 \end{bmatrix}$$

do not commute, for we find that

$$(\mathbf{S})(\mathbf{T}) = \begin{bmatrix} 0 & 1 \\ -1 & 0 \end{bmatrix}\begin{bmatrix} 0 & 1 \\ 1 & 0 \end{bmatrix} = \begin{bmatrix} 1 & 0 \\ 0 & -1 \end{bmatrix},$$

whereas

$$(\mathbf{T})(\mathbf{S}) = \begin{bmatrix} 0 & 1 \\ 1 & 0 \end{bmatrix}\begin{bmatrix} 0 & 1 \\ -1 & 0 \end{bmatrix} = \begin{bmatrix} -1 & 0 \\ 0 & 1 \end{bmatrix} = -(\mathbf{S})(\mathbf{T}). \tag{10-20}$$

Matrices for which this last relationship holds are said to *anticommute*.

As may readily be verified, matrix multiplication is associative:

$$[(\mathbf{R})(\mathbf{S})](\mathbf{T}) = (\mathbf{R})[(\mathbf{S})(\mathbf{T})] = (\mathbf{R})(\mathbf{S})(\mathbf{T}). \tag{10-21}$$

It is also distributive:

$$(\mathbf{R})[(\mathbf{S}) + (\mathbf{T})] = (\mathbf{R})(\mathbf{S}) + (\mathbf{R})(\mathbf{T}). \tag{10-22}$$

The *zero* or *null matrix* $(\mathbf{0})$ is the matrix all of whose elements are zero. It satisfies the following matrix equations:

$$(\mathbf{S}) + (\mathbf{0}) = (\mathbf{S}),$$
$$(\mathbf{S})(\mathbf{0}_1) = (\mathbf{0}_2)(\mathbf{S}) = (\mathbf{0}_3), \tag{10-23}$$

where the subscripts on the null matrices indicate that they are not necessarily of the same dimensions.

The *unit* or *identity matrix* **(1)** was introduced previously in Section 3–5. It is the matrix which satisfies the matrix equations

$$\mathbf{(1)(S)} = \mathbf{(S)},$$
$$\mathbf{(S)(1)} = \mathbf{(S)}. \tag{10–24}$$

It follows from the rule for the multiplication of two matrices that the unit matrix must be a square matrix whose elements are given by

$$\mathbf{(1)}_{ij} = \delta_{ij}. \tag{10–25}$$

That is, the unit matrix has vanishing off-diagonal elements and diagonal elements of unit magnitude,

$$\mathbf{(1)} = \begin{bmatrix} 1 & 0 & 0 & \cdot & \cdot & \cdot \\ 0 & 1 & 0 & 0 & & \cdot \\ 0 & 0 & 1 & 0 & & \cdot \\ \cdot & & 0 & 1 & & \cdot \\ \cdot & & & & & \cdot \\ \cdot & \cdot & \cdot & \cdot & \cdot & \cdot \end{bmatrix}. \tag{10–26}$$

A matrix having zero off-diagonal elements is referred to as a *diagonal matrix*. Its elements are expressed by

$$S_{ij} = \lambda_i \delta_{ij}. \tag{10–27}$$

We thus find that the multiplication of a matrix by a scalar $c$ is equivalent to its multiplication by the *scalar matrix*

$$\mathbf{(C)} = c\mathbf{(1)}.$$

The *transpose* $\widetilde{\mathbf{(S)}}$ of the matrix **(S)** is the matrix formed by interchanging the rows and columns of **(S)**. Thus if **(S)** is a $m \times n$ matrix, then its transpose $\widetilde{\mathbf{(S)}}$ is a $n \times m$ matrix whose elements are

$$\widetilde{S}_{ij} = S_{ji}. \tag{10–28}$$

For example, the transpose of the matrix

$$\mathbf{(S)} = \begin{bmatrix} 1 & 2 & -3 \\ 4 & 1 & 0 \\ 3 & 2 & -1 \end{bmatrix}$$

is the matrix

$$\widetilde{\mathbf{(S)}} = \begin{bmatrix} 1 & 4 & 3 \\ 2 & 1 & 2 \\ -3 & 0 & -1 \end{bmatrix}.$$

If it happens that

$$\widetilde{(\mathsf{S})} = (\mathsf{S}), \tag{10-29}$$

then the matrix is said to be a symmetric matrix. On the other hand, if

$$\widetilde{S}_{ij} = -S_{ji}, \tag{10-30}$$

that is, if

$$\widetilde{(\mathsf{S})} = -(\mathsf{S}), \tag{10-31}$$

then the matrix is said to be an *antisymmetric* matrix.

We note that any matrix can always be decomposed into a symmetric and an antisymmetric part. Thus letting $(\mathsf{S}_s)$ and $(\mathsf{S}_a)$ represent the symmetric and antisymmetric parts of the matrix $(\mathsf{S})$, we find that setting

$$(\mathsf{S}) = (\mathsf{S}_s) + (\mathsf{S}_a) \qquad \text{and} \qquad \widetilde{(\mathsf{S})} = (\mathsf{S}_s) - (\mathsf{S}_a)$$

yields

$$(\mathsf{S}_s) = \tfrac{1}{2}[(\mathsf{S}) + \widetilde{(\mathsf{S})}] \tag{10-32}$$

and

$$(\mathsf{S}_a) = \tfrac{1}{2}[(\mathsf{S}) - \widetilde{(\mathsf{S})}], \tag{10-33}$$

or

$$(\mathsf{S}) = \tfrac{1}{2}[\widetilde{(\mathsf{S})} + (\mathsf{S})] + \tfrac{1}{2}[(\mathsf{S}) - \widetilde{(\mathsf{S})}]. \tag{10-34}$$

For example, from the matrix

$$(\mathsf{S}) = \begin{bmatrix} 1 & 2 & -3 \\ 4 & 1 & 0 \\ 3 & 2 & -1 \end{bmatrix}$$

and its transpose

$$\widetilde{(\mathsf{S})} = \begin{bmatrix} 1 & 4 & 3 \\ 2 & 1 & 2 \\ -3 & 0 & -1 \end{bmatrix}$$

we can construct the symmetric part of $(\mathsf{S})$,

$$(\mathsf{S}_s) = \tfrac{1}{2}[(\mathsf{S}) + \widetilde{(\mathsf{S})}] = \begin{bmatrix} 1 & 3 & 0 \\ 3 & 1 & 1 \\ 0 & 1 & -1 \end{bmatrix},$$

and the antisymmetric part

$$(\mathsf{S}_a) = \tfrac{1}{2}[(\mathsf{S}) - \widetilde{(\mathsf{S})}] = \begin{bmatrix} 0 & -1 & -3 \\ 1 & 0 & -1 \\ 3 & 1 & 0 \end{bmatrix}.$$

We note that since for an antisymmetric matrix,

$$S_{ij} = -S_{ji},$$

a $3 \times 3$ antisymmetric matrix is specified if its three off-diagonal elements

$$S_{23} = S_1, \qquad S_{31} = S_2, \qquad \text{and} \qquad S_{12} = S_3$$

are known.

The transpose of the product of two matrices $(S)$ and $(T)$ equals the product of the transpose of $(T)$ with the transpose of $(S)$,

$$[\widetilde{(S)(T)}] = (\widetilde{T})(\widetilde{S}). \tag{10–35}$$

This result can be verified quite readily. From the definition of the product of two matrices and the definition of the transpose of a matrix we find that

$$[(S)(T)]_{ij} = \sum_k S_{ik} T_{kj},$$

and hence

$$[\widetilde{(S)(T)}]_{ji} = [(S)(T)]_{ij} = \sum_k S_{ik} T_{kj} = \sum_k \widetilde{T}_{jk} \widetilde{S}_{ki} = [(\widetilde{T})(\widetilde{S})]_{ji}.$$

For example, consider the transpose of the product of the two matrices

$$(S) = \begin{bmatrix} 1 & 2 & 3 \\ 2 & 1 & 0 \\ 4 & 3 & -1 \end{bmatrix} \qquad \text{and} \qquad (T) = \begin{bmatrix} 2 & -1 & 0 \\ 1 & 2 & 2 \\ 0 & 1 & 1 \end{bmatrix}.$$

We find that

$$(S)(T) = \begin{bmatrix} 4 & 6 & 7 \\ 5 & 0 & 2 \\ 11 & 1 & 5 \end{bmatrix},$$

and thus

$$[\widetilde{(S)(T)}] = \begin{bmatrix} 4 & 5 & 11 \\ 6 & 0 & 1 \\ 7 & 2 & 5 \end{bmatrix},$$

which we find is equal to

$$(\widetilde{T})(\widetilde{S}) = \begin{bmatrix} 2 & 1 & 0 \\ -1 & 2 & 1 \\ 0 & 2 & 1 \end{bmatrix} \begin{bmatrix} 1 & 2 & 4 \\ 2 & 1 & 3 \\ 3 & 0 & -1 \end{bmatrix} = \begin{bmatrix} 4 & 5 & 11 \\ 6 & 0 & 1 \\ 7 & 2 & 5 \end{bmatrix}.$$

Another important matrix is the *inverse* or *reciprocal* of a square matrix. The inverse $(S^{-1})$ of the square matrix $(S)$ is the matrix whose product with $(S)$

yields the unit matrix. That is,

$$(\mathbf{S}^{-1})(\mathbf{S}) = (\mathbf{1}) \qquad (10\text{–}36)$$

or, equivalently,

$$(\mathbf{S})(\mathbf{S}^{-1}) = (\mathbf{1}). \qquad (10\text{–}37)$$

That Eqs. (10–36) and (10–37) are equivalent, and that either is sufficient for the definition of a unique inverse follows from the definition of the unit matrix, Eq. (10–24). Multiplying Eq. (10–36) by $(\mathbf{S})$, we find that

$$[(\mathbf{S})(\mathbf{S}^{-1})](\mathbf{S}) = (\mathbf{S}),$$

which implies that

$$(\mathbf{S})(\mathbf{S}^{-1}) = (\mathbf{1}).$$

For the $n \times n$ square matrix $(\mathbf{S})$ an inverse can be obtained if and only if the $n^2$ simultaneous equations

$$\sum_{k=1}^{n} S_{ik}^{-1} S_{kj} = \delta_{ij} \qquad (10\text{–}38)$$

representing the elements of Eq. (10–36) can be solved for the $S_{ij}^{-1}$'s. The necessary and sufficient condition that this be possible is the nonvanishing of the determinant formed by the elements of the matrix $(\mathbf{S})$; that is, det $(\mathbf{S}) \neq 0$. A square matrix whose determinant does not vanish is called a *nonsingular* square matrix. On the other hand, if the determinant does vanish, it is called a *singular* square matrix.

## 10–3 The direct product: operators

There is yet another way in which two matrices may be multiplied. It is the *direct product* of two matrices $(\mathbf{S})$ and $(\mathbf{T})$, which is defined as the matrix whose elements are the products of the elements of $(\mathbf{S})$ and $(\mathbf{T})$. Thus if $(\mathbf{S})$ is an $m \times n$ matrix of $m \cdot n$ elements and $(\mathbf{T})$ an $o \times p$ matrix of $o \cdot p$ elements, then the direct product, designated by

$$(\mathbf{R}) = (\mathbf{S}) \otimes (\mathbf{T}), \qquad (10\text{–}39)$$

is an $(m \cdot o) \times (n \cdot p)$ matrix with $(m \cdot o \cdot n \cdot p)$ matrix elements arranged in a suitable order. In order to distinguish the direct product of a row and a column matrix from the matrix product of the same matrices, we shall denote the former by placing the column matrix to the left of the row matrix. The direct product of the matrices $(\mathbf{A})$ and $(\mathbf{B})$ is thus defined by

$$(\mathbf{A}) \otimes (\mathbf{B}) = \begin{bmatrix} A_1 \\ A_2 \\ A_3 \end{bmatrix} [B_1, B_2, B_3] = \begin{bmatrix} A_1B_1 & A_1B_2 & A_1B_3 \\ A_2B_1 & A_2B_2 & A_2B_3 \\ A_3B_1 & A_3B_2 & A_3B_3 \end{bmatrix}. \qquad (10\text{–}40)$$

We can think of the direct-product matrix $(\mathbf{A}) \otimes (\mathbf{B})$ as the matrix representation of the direct product of the two vectors $|\mathbf{A})$ and $(\mathbf{B}|$. We shall find this interpretation of the direct product of the column matrix $(\mathbf{A})$ and the row matrix $(\mathbf{B})$ extremely useful. We indicate such a product of the two vectors $|\mathbf{A})$ and $(\mathbf{B}|$ by $|\mathbf{A})(\mathbf{B}|$, and the above interpretation of the direct product of the two matrices $(\mathbf{A})$ and $(\mathbf{B})$ is expressed by

$$|\mathbf{A})(\mathbf{B}| \leftrightarrow \begin{bmatrix} A_1B_1 & A_1B_2 & A_1B_3 \\ A_2B_1 & A_2B_2 & A_2B_3 \\ A_3B_1 & A_3B_2 & A_3B_3 \end{bmatrix}. \tag{10–41}$$

As an example of the usefulness of the direct product of a column and a row matrix, we consider the matrix product of the square matrix $(\mathbf{A}) \otimes (\mathbf{B}^\star)$ with the column matrix

$$(\mathbf{C}) = \begin{bmatrix} C_1 \\ C_2 \\ C_3 \end{bmatrix}.$$

The result is the column matrix

$$(\mathbf{D}) = \begin{bmatrix} A_1(B_1^\star C_1 + B_2^\star C_2 + B_3^\star C_3) \\ A_2(B_1^\star C_1 + B_2^\star C_2 + B_3^\star C_3) \\ A_3(B_1^\star C_1 + B_2^\star C_2 + B_3^\star C_3) \end{bmatrix} = (\mathbf{A})(\mathbf{B}^\star|\mathbf{C}), \tag{10–42}$$

which can readily be seen to be the matrix representation of the vector

$$\mathbf{D} = (\mathbf{B} \cdot \mathbf{C})\mathbf{A}. \tag{10–43}$$

Thus we started out by multiplying the matrix representation of the direct product $|\mathbf{A})(\mathbf{B}^\star|$ with the matrix representation of the vector $|\mathbf{C})$, and we ended up with the matrix representation of the vector $|\mathbf{D}) = |\mathbf{A})\{(\mathbf{B}^\star|\mathbf{C})\}$. It follows therefore that we can set

$$\{|\mathbf{A})(\mathbf{B}^\star|\}|\mathbf{C}) = |\mathbf{A})\{(\mathbf{B}^\star|\mathbf{C})\}, \tag{10–44}$$

and similarly,

$$(\mathbf{C}|\{|\mathbf{A}^\star)(\mathbf{B}|\} = \{(\mathbf{C}|\mathbf{A}^\star)\}(\mathbf{B}|. \tag{10–45}$$

Equation (10–43) is a linear equation relating the components of the vector $|\mathbf{D})$ to the components of the vector $|\mathbf{A})$. From Eq. (10–42) we see that we can also interpret it as a linear vector equation relating the components of the vector $|\mathbf{D})$ to the components of the vector $|\mathbf{C})$. In this sense, we think of the direct product

$$\mathbf{P} = |\mathbf{A})(\mathbf{B}^\star| \tag{10–46}$$

as an operator which, when operating on the vector $|\mathbf{C})$, produces the vector $|\mathbf{D})$, as expressed by

$$|\mathbf{D}) = \mathbf{P}|\mathbf{C}). \tag{10–47}$$

With this notation, we are able to express, for example, the relationship between the angular momentum and angular velocity vectors of a rigid body (cf. Section 9–3) as

$$|\mathbf{L}) = \mathbf{I}|\omega),$$

where the moments of inertia and products of inertia are in this sense considered to be the elements of the matrix representation of the moment-of-inertia operator $\mathbf{I}$. Similarly, one can express the most general relationship between the electric-field and the electric-displacement vectors at any point in an anisotropic medium as

$$|\mathbf{D}) = \epsilon|\mathbf{E}),$$

and the relationship between $\mathbf{B}$ and $\mathbf{H}$ as

$$|\mathbf{B}) = \mu|\mathbf{H}).$$

Innumerable other examples can be quoted in which we have two vector quantities linearly related to each other. For all of these, the notation and the mathematical manipulation of their equations, which will be discussed in the following sections, are the same. Consequently, the subsequent sections of this chapter are very important. The simplicity and usefulness of the notation which we introduced should become apparent as we continue to use it in the subsequent sections and chapters.

---

As a final example* (cf. Problem 1–19), we consider the relationship between the matrix representations of the vectors

$$|\mathbf{A}) = \sum_j \alpha_j |\boldsymbol{b}_j) \qquad \text{and} \qquad |\mathbf{A}^\star) = \sum_j \alpha_j^\star |\boldsymbol{b}_j^\star).$$

The column matrix representations of the base vectors $\boldsymbol{b}_i$ are found to be given by

$$|\mathbf{b}_1^\star) \leftrightarrow \begin{bmatrix} 1 \\ 0 \\ 0 \end{bmatrix}, \qquad |\mathbf{b}_2^\star) \leftrightarrow \begin{bmatrix} 0 \\ 1 \\ 0 \end{bmatrix}, \qquad |\mathbf{b}_3^\star) \leftrightarrow \begin{bmatrix} 0 \\ 0 \\ 1 \end{bmatrix}, \qquad (10\text{–}48)$$

and

$$|\mathbf{b}_1) \leftrightarrow \begin{bmatrix} g_{11} \\ g_{12} \\ g_{13} \end{bmatrix}, \qquad |\mathbf{b}_2) \leftrightarrow \begin{bmatrix} g_{21} \\ g_{22} \\ g_{23} \end{bmatrix}, \qquad |\mathbf{b}_3) \leftrightarrow \begin{bmatrix} g_{31} \\ g_{32} \\ g_{33} \end{bmatrix}, \qquad (10\text{–}49)$$

where

$$g_{ij} = \mathbf{b}_i \cdot \mathbf{b}_j = (\mathbf{b}_i|\mathbf{b}_j^\star). \qquad (10\text{–}50)$$

---

* In this example, the elements of the matrix representations of a vector are the scalar products of the vector and the base vectors $\boldsymbol{b}_i$ or the reciprocal base vectors $\boldsymbol{b}_i$ whose cartesian components are assumed to be known. The awkwardness of the notation should make it clear why one prefers to choose orthonormal base vectors for which there is no distinction between the covariant and contravariant components.

Similarly, the matrix representation of the reciprocal base vectors $b_i$ are given by

$$|b_1) \leftrightarrow \begin{bmatrix} 1 \\ 0 \\ 0 \end{bmatrix}, \qquad |b_2) \leftrightarrow \begin{bmatrix} 0 \\ 1 \\ 0 \end{bmatrix}, \qquad |b_3) \leftrightarrow \begin{bmatrix} 0 \\ 0 \\ 1 \end{bmatrix}, \qquad (10\text{--}51)$$

and

$$|b_1^\star) \leftrightarrow \begin{bmatrix} \overset{\star}{g}_{11} \\ \overset{\star}{g}_{12} \\ \overset{\star}{g}_{13} \end{bmatrix}, \qquad |b_2^\star) \leftrightarrow \begin{bmatrix} \overset{\star}{g}_{21} \\ \overset{\star}{g}_{22} \\ \overset{\star}{g}_{23} \end{bmatrix}, \qquad |b_3^\star) \leftrightarrow \begin{bmatrix} \overset{\star}{g}_{31} \\ \overset{\star}{g}_{32} \\ \overset{\star}{g}_{33} \end{bmatrix}, \qquad (10\text{--}52)$$

where

$$\overset{\star}{g}_{ij} = b_i \cdot b_j = (b_i | b_j^\star). \qquad (10\text{--}53)$$

From the definition of the $\alpha_j^\star$ we obtain

$$\alpha_j^\star = (b_j^\star | A) = \sum_i (b_j^\star | b_i) \alpha_i = \sum_i \overset{\star}{g}_{ji} \alpha_i. \qquad (10\text{--}54)$$

But (10–54) may be interpreted as the equation expressing the relationship which exists between the elements of the matrix equation

$$\begin{bmatrix} \alpha_1^\star \\ \alpha_2^\star \\ \alpha_3^\star \end{bmatrix} = \begin{bmatrix} \overset{\star}{g}_{11} & \overset{\star}{g}_{12} & \overset{\star}{g}_{13} \\ \overset{\star}{g}_{21} & \overset{\star}{g}_{22} & \overset{\star}{g}_{23} \\ \overset{\star}{g}_{31} & \overset{\star}{g}_{32} & \overset{\star}{g}_{33} \end{bmatrix} \begin{bmatrix} \alpha_1 \\ \alpha_2 \\ \alpha_3 \end{bmatrix}, \qquad (10\text{--}55)$$

which in turn may be considered to be the matrix representation of the equation

$$|A^\star) = g^\star | A), \qquad (10\text{--}56)$$

where the operator $g^\star$ is

$$g^\star = \sum_i |b_i^\star)(b_i^\star|, \qquad (10\text{--}57)$$

as may be verified by operating with it on

$$|A) = \sum_j \alpha_j | b_j).$$

In terms of $g^\star$, the scalar product of two vectors is expressible in the form

$$(B|A^\star) = (B|g^\star|A). \qquad (10\text{--}58)$$

Analogously, we find that

$$\alpha_i = (b_i | A^\star) = \sum_j (b_i | b_j^\star) \alpha_j^\star, \qquad (10\text{--}59)$$

which yields

$$|A) = g|A^\star), \qquad (10\text{--}60)$$

where the operator $g$ is found to be given by

$$g = \sum_i |b_i)(b_i|. \qquad (10\text{--}61)$$

In terms of **g**, the scalar product between two vectors is expressible as

$$(\mathbf{A}^\star|\mathbf{B}) = (\mathbf{A}^\star|\mathbf{g}|\mathbf{B}^\star). \tag{10-62}$$

The operator **g** is referred to as the *metric operator,* and the elements $g_{ij}$ of its matrix representation as the *covariant elements of the metric tensor.*

Combining Eqs. (10–56) and (10–60), we find that

$$|\mathbf{A}) = \mathbf{gg}^\star|\mathbf{A}) \qquad \text{and} \qquad |\mathbf{A}^\star) = \mathbf{g}^\star\mathbf{g}|\mathbf{A}^\star),$$

whence it follows that

$$\mathbf{g}^\star\mathbf{g} = \mathbf{gg}^\star = \mathbf{1}, \tag{10-63}$$

where **1** is the unit operator whose matrix representation is the unit matrix. From the definition of the inverse of a matrix, we realize that we can call **g**$^\star$ the inverse metric operator,

$$\mathbf{g}^\star = \mathbf{g}^{-1}. \tag{10-64}$$

Since the matrix representation of **g**$^\star$ is inverse to the matrix representation of **g**, we obtain the important relation

$$\sum_k g^\star_{ik}g_{kj} = \delta_{ij}. \tag{10-65}$$

Through the use of Eqs. (10–57), (10–60), and (10–63), we find the unit operator **1** that satisfies the relations

$$\mathbf{1}|\mathbf{A}) = |\mathbf{A}) \qquad \text{and} \qquad (\mathbf{A}^\star|\mathbf{1} = (\mathbf{A}^\star|$$

to be given by

$$\mathbf{1} = \mathbf{gg}^\star = \mathbf{g}\sum_i |\mathbf{b}^\star_i)(\mathbf{b}^\star_i| = \sum_i |\mathbf{b}_i)(\mathbf{b}^\star_i|, \tag{10-66}$$

since

$$\mathbf{g}|\mathbf{b}^\star_i) = |\mathbf{b}_i). \tag{10-67}$$

Equivalently, the unit operator satisfying the relations

$$\mathbf{1}|\mathbf{A}^\star) = |\mathbf{A}^\star) \qquad \text{and} \qquad (\mathbf{A}|\mathbf{1} = (\mathbf{A}| \tag{10-68}$$

is given by

$$\mathbf{1} = \mathbf{g}^\star\mathbf{g} = \mathbf{g}^\star\sum_i |b_i)(\mathbf{b}_i| = \sum_i |b^\star_i)(\mathbf{b}_i|, \tag{10-69}$$

since

$$\mathbf{g}^\star|b_i) = |b^\star_i).$$

The choice of which of the two apparently different expansions of the unit operator to use depends on the vector on which the unit operator operates. We must always choose the one which will form a scalar product with the vector being operated on. Thus, for example, when operating on the vectors $|\mathbf{A})$ or $(\mathbf{A}^\star|$, we must choose the form given by Eq. (10–66).

In conclusion, we present a suitable way of arranging the elements of the direct-product matrix $(\mathbf{R}) = (\mathbf{S}) \otimes (\mathbf{T})$. We first express $(\mathbf{R})$ as a matrix whose elements themselves are matrices, that is

$$(\mathbf{R}) = \begin{bmatrix} S_{11}(\mathbf{T}) & S_{12}(\mathbf{T}) & S_{13}(\mathbf{T}) & \cdots \\ S_{21}(\mathbf{T}) & S_{22}(\mathbf{T}) & & \cdot \\ S_{31}(\mathbf{T}) & S_{32}(\mathbf{T}) & & \vdots \\ \vdots & & \cdot & \\ \vdots & \cdot & & \cdots \end{bmatrix}, \tag{10–70}$$

and we subsequently expand the matrix $(\mathbf{T})$, obtaining

$$(\mathbf{R}) = \begin{bmatrix} S_{11}T_{11} & S_{11}T_{12} & \cdots & S_{12}T_{11} & S_{12}T_{12} & \cdots \\ S_{11}T_{21} & S_{11}T_{22} & \cdots & S_{12}T_{21} & S_{12}T_{22} & \cdots \\ \vdots & \vdots & & \vdots & \vdots & \\ S_{21}T_{11} & S_{21}T_{12} & \cdots & S_{22}T_{11} & S_{22}T_{12} & \cdots \\ S_{21}T_{21} & S_{21}T_{22} & \cdots & S_{22}T_{21} & S_{22}T_{22} & \cdots \\ \vdots & \vdots & & \vdots & \vdots & \end{bmatrix}. \tag{10–71}$$

As an example, we obtain the direct product of the two column matrices

$$(\mathbf{A}) = \begin{bmatrix} A_1 \\ A_2 \\ A_3 \end{bmatrix} \quad \text{and} \quad (\mathbf{B}) = \begin{bmatrix} B_1 \\ B_2 \\ B_3 \end{bmatrix}.$$

It is the nine-element column matrix

$$(\mathbf{R}) = (\mathbf{A}) \otimes (\mathbf{B}) = \begin{bmatrix} A_1(\mathbf{B}) \\ A_2(\mathbf{B}) \\ A_3(\mathbf{B}) \end{bmatrix} = \begin{bmatrix} A_1 B_1 \\ A_1 B_2 \\ A_1 B_3 \\ A_2 B_1 \\ A_2 B_2 \\ A_2 B_3 \\ A_3 B_1 \\ A_3 B_2 \\ A_3 B_3 \end{bmatrix},$$

which, as we shall discuss in the next section, can be thought of as the matrix representation of the vector $|\mathbf{R})$ in a nine-dimensional space. This matrix representation is obtained by forming the direct product of the matrix representations of the vectors $|A\rangle$ and $|B\rangle$. We express this fact by setting

$$|R\rangle = |A\rangle \otimes |B\rangle = |A \otimes B\rangle. \tag{10–72}$$

Finally, we note that utilizing cartesian base vectors, the elements of the matrix representation of the vector product of two vectors $A$ and $B$ form the elements of the $3 \times 3$ antisymmetric matrix representation of the operator

$$|A\rangle\langle B| - |B\rangle\langle A|,$$

that is, the matrix

$$\begin{bmatrix} 0 & A_1 B_2 - A_2 B_1 & A_1 B_3 - A_3 B_1 \\ A_2 B_1 - A_1 B_2 & 0 & A_2 B_3 - A_3 B_2 \\ A_3 B_1 - A_1 B_3 & A_3 B_2 - A_2 B_3 & 0 \end{bmatrix}.$$

The vector $C$, whose components are

$$\begin{aligned} C_1 &= A_2 B_3 - A_3 B_2, \\ C_2 &= A_3 B_1 - A_1 B_3, \\ C_3 &= A_1 B_2 - A_2 B_1, \end{aligned}$$

has, of course, the rotational properties of a vector. However, under an inversion of the coordinate system for which the vectors $A$ and $B$ change sign in the manner of the position vector $r$, the vector $C$ does not change sign. This vector $C$ does not therefore behave like an ordinary vector under an inversion of the coordinate system. Such vectors are referred to as *pseudovectors* or *axial vectors*, whereas the vectors which do change sign under an inversion of the coordinate system are referred to as *polar vectors*.

Similarly, the scalar product of an axial and a polar vector forms what is referred to as a *pseudoscalar*. It is a scalar which changes sign under an inversion.

## 10–4 Linear vector spaces

The concept of a $n$-dimensional linear vector space is a generalization of the more familiar two- and three-dimensional vector spaces, for which we defined the matrix representation of a vector in the space in question as the matrix array of the scalar products of the vector with the base vectors or their reciprocal vectors. We now generalize this idea by considering any row or column matrix of two or three elements as the matrix representation of a two- or three-dimensional vector. This also suggests the further generalization that any $n$-dimensional row or column matrix be considered as the matrix representation of an $n$-dimensional vector.

At times the base vectors of such an $n$-dimensional space will be known. Such was the case, for example, for the six-dimensional vector space we constructed for representing the motion of a two-particle system (Section 8–7).

This six-dimensional space was the *direct sum* of the three-dimensional vector space used for the description of the motion of particle $a$ and the three-dimensional vector space of particle $b$, as expressed by

$$|\mathbf{A}) = |\mathbf{A}_a \oplus \mathbf{A}_b), \tag{10–73}$$

where $\mathbf{A}_a$ is a three-dimensional vector associated with particle $a$ and $\mathbf{A}_b$ a similar vector associated with particle $b$. The base vectors of this six-dimensional vector space were defined as follows:

$$|\mathbf{b}_i) = \left|\frac{\partial \mathbf{r}}{\partial q_i}\right) = \left|\frac{\partial \mathbf{r}_a}{\partial q_i} \oplus \frac{\partial \mathbf{r}_b}{\partial q_i}\right). \tag{10–74}$$

Their reciprocal vectors for time-independent coordinate transformations were shown to be the vectors

$$|b_i) = |\nabla_a q_i \oplus \nabla_b q_i), \tag{10–75}$$

where

$$\nabla_a = \mathbf{i}\,\frac{\partial}{\partial x_a} + \mathbf{j}\,\frac{\partial}{\partial y_a} + \mathbf{k}\,\frac{\partial}{\partial z_a}$$

and

$$\nabla_b = \mathbf{i}\,\frac{\partial}{\partial x_b} + \mathbf{j}\,\frac{\partial}{\partial y_b} + \mathbf{k}\,\frac{\partial}{\partial z_b}.$$

At other times, we shall simply have a matrix (or array) of numbers which satisfy the necessary rules for addition and multiplication with the elements of other matrices of the same dimension, and which combinations yield meaningful new matrices or scalars without the existence of any base vectors. This nonexistence of base vectors is all right so long as similar $n$-dimensional matrices can be added meaningfully and so long as the rule for the multiplication of their elements to form meaningful scalars is known. Such meaningful multiplication may require the introduction of a metric (tensor) operator of the space.

For example, let us in anticipation consider the relativistic description of a particle to be discussed in Chapter 13. We shall find that the complete description of the motion of the particle requires not only the specification of its cartesian components, but also the time at which the particle was observed to be at the point $(x, y, z)$. We shall furthermore find that the four scalar quantities $x, y, z$, and $ct$, where $c$ is the speed of light, satisfy the rules for the combination of the elements of a matrix. We shall therefore arrange them in the four-dimensional matrix

$$(\mathbf{r}) = [x, y, z, ct],$$

which shall then be considered to be the matrix representation of the position vector $(\mathbf{r}|$ in a four-dimensional space.

A meaningful scalar product in this four-dimensional space is the scalar

$$\Delta s^2 = -\Delta x^2 - \Delta y^2 - \Delta z^2 + c^2\,\Delta t^2,$$

which can be considered as the square of the magnitude of the vector $(\Delta s|$. If the matrix representation of the metric operator $\mathbf{g}$ is taken to be

$$\mathbf{g} = \mathbf{g}^{-1} \leftrightarrow \begin{bmatrix} -1 & 0 & 0 & 0 \\ 0 & -1 & 0 & 0 \\ 0 & 0 & -1 & 0 \\ 0 & 0 & 0 & 1 \end{bmatrix},$$

then we obtain

$$\Delta s^2 = (\Delta s|\mathbf{g}^{-1}|\Delta s)$$

$$= [\Delta x, \Delta y, \Delta z, c\,\Delta t] \begin{bmatrix} -1 & 0 & 0 & 0 \\ 0 & -1 & 0 & 0 \\ 0 & 0 & -1 & 0 \\ 0 & 0 & 0 & 1 \end{bmatrix} \begin{bmatrix} \Delta x \\ \Delta y \\ \Delta z \\ c\,\Delta t \end{bmatrix}$$

$$= -\Delta x^2 - \Delta y^2 - \Delta z^2 + c^2\,\Delta t^2.$$

In the relativistic description of the motion of a particle, it is also possible to construct a different four-dimensional vector space in which the metric is the unit operator whose matrix representation is the unit matrix. In this space, the fourth component of the position vector or any other vector is imaginary,

$$(\mathbf{r}| \leftrightarrow [x, y, z, ict],$$

and the scalar $\Delta s^2$ is given by

$$-\Delta s^2 = (\Delta \mathbf{r}|\Delta \mathbf{r})$$

$$= [\Delta x, \Delta y, \Delta z, ic\,\Delta t] \begin{bmatrix} \Delta x \\ \Delta y \\ \Delta z \\ ic\,\Delta t \end{bmatrix}$$

$$= \Delta x^2 + \Delta y^2 + \Delta z^2 - c^2\,\Delta t^2.$$

We shall utilize the latter representation in which the metric is the unit operator. In quantum mechanics where confusion may arise between the relativistic $i$ which appears in the fourth component of any four vectors and the so-called quantum mechanical $i$, the former representation is notationally more convenient. The fact that the scalar product of two vectors in this space is expressible as $(\mathbf{A}|\mathbf{B})$ means that we are dealing with a set of orthonormal (orthogonal unit) base vectors which are their own reciprocal vectors. Hence there is no distinction between the vector $|\mathbf{A})$ and the vector $|\mathbf{A}^\star)$, and

$$(\mathbf{A}^\star|\mathbf{B}) = (\mathbf{A}|\mathbf{B}).$$

We shall henceforth restrict ourselves to the description of vectors in terms of such orthonormal sets of base vectors $\mathbf{e}_i$, that is, in terms of coordinate systems whose metric operator is equal to the unit operator.

Mathematically, a vector space is defined as a set of vectors, in our case a set of matrices, whose addition and multiplication by a scalar obey the following rules:

(a) Two vectors may be added, and their sum yields a unique vector.

(b) The addition of vectors is associative and commutative.

(c) There exists a null vector $\mathbf{0}$ such that

$$|\mathbf{A}) + |\mathbf{0}) = |\mathbf{A}),$$

which defines the negative of a vector $|\mathbf{A})$ as the vector whose sum with $|\mathbf{A})$ yields the null vector:

$$|\mathbf{A}) + |-\mathbf{A}) = |\mathbf{0}) \qquad \text{or} \qquad |-\mathbf{A}) = -|\mathbf{A}).$$

(d) The multiplication of a vector $|\mathbf{A})$ by a scalar $c$ defines a unique vector $c|\mathbf{A})$, and such a multiplication has the following properties:

$$c_1|c_2\mathbf{A}) = c_1 c_2 |\mathbf{A}),$$
$$(c_1 + c_2)|\mathbf{A}) = c_1|\mathbf{A}) + c_2|\mathbf{A}),$$
$$c[|\mathbf{A}) + |\mathbf{B})] = c|\mathbf{A}) + c|\mathbf{B}),$$
$$\mathbf{1}|\mathbf{A}) = |\mathbf{A}).$$

Since matrices satisfy these rules, any set of similar $m \times n$ matrices can be considered to be the matrix representations of vectors of a vector space whose dimensionality is equal to the number of elements in each matrix, that is $m \cdot n$. It is customary, however, to represent vectors by column or row matrices.

## 10–5 Base vectors of an $n$-dimensional vector space

Quite analogously to our discussion of the representation of a vector in a three-dimensional space, we find that any $n$-dimensional vector ($n$-dimensional column matrix) may be expressed as the linear sum of $n$ linearly independent base vectors. A set of $n$ vectors $\mathbf{b}_1, \mathbf{b}_2, \ldots, \mathbf{b}_n$ are said to be linearly independent if only the set of numbers $c_1, c_2, \ldots, c_n$, where

$$c_1 = c_2 = c_3 = \cdots = c_n = 0,$$

satisfy the condition

$$\sum_{i=1}^{n} c_i \mathbf{b}_i = \mathbf{0}$$

If a set of $c$'s containing at least one nonzero element can be found for which the linear sum of the base vectors can be made equal to zero, then the set of vectors $\mathbf{b}_i$ is said to be linearly dependent. This means that one or more of the vectors is expressible as a linear sum of the remaining vectors.

The necessary and sufficient condition that $n$ $n$-dimensional vectors $\mathbf{b}_i$ be linearly independent is the nonvanishing of the determinant formed by the elements of their matrix representations, that is,

$$
\begin{vmatrix}
b_{11} & b_{12} & \cdots & b_{1n} \\
b_{21} & b_{22} & \cdots & b_{2n} \\
b_{31} & b_{32} & \cdots & b_{3n} \\
\vdots & \vdots & & \vdots \\
b_{n1} & b_{n2} & \cdots & b_{nn}
\end{vmatrix} \neq 0. \tag{10-76}
$$

A most convenient choice notationally for the set of base vectors is a set of $n$ linearly independent orthogonal unit base vectors $\mathbf{e}_i$ which satisfy the equations

$$
(\mathbf{e}_i|\mathbf{e}_j) = \delta_{ij}. \tag{10-77}
$$

With this choice, there is no distinction between the $\mathbf{e}_i$'s and their reciprocal vectors $\mathfrak{c}_i$'s, for then the reciprocal vectors

$$
\mathfrak{c}_i = \mathbf{e}_i. \tag{10-78}
$$

Hence there is also no distinction between $|\mathbf{A})$ and $|\mathbf{A}^\star)$.

It should be quite clear that the base vectors $\mathbf{e}_i$ expressed in terms of their scalar products with themselves have the matrix representations

$$
\begin{aligned}
(\mathbf{e}_1| &\leftrightarrow [1, 0, 0, 0, \ldots], \\
(\mathbf{e}_2| &\leftrightarrow [0, 1, 0, 0, \ldots], \\
(\mathbf{e}_3| &\leftrightarrow [0, 0, 1, 0, \ldots], \\
&\quad \text{etc.}
\end{aligned} \tag{10-79}
$$

Now any $n$-dimensional vector $\mathbf{A}$ is specified if its scalar product with the $n$ base vectors are known. This follows from the fact that if the base vectors are linearly independent, we can set

$$
|\mathbf{A}) = \sum_{i=1}^{n} \alpha_i|\mathbf{e}_i), \tag{10-80}
$$

and solve the $n$ simultaneous equations that result for the $\alpha_i$'s. We find these to be given by

$$
\alpha_i = (\mathbf{e}_i|\mathbf{A}). \tag{10-81}
$$

This result is obvious, considering that

$$
|\mathbf{A}) \leftrightarrow \begin{bmatrix} \alpha_1 \\ \alpha_2 \\ \alpha_3 \\ \vdots \\ \alpha_n \end{bmatrix},
$$

and hence by the rules for the multiplication of a matrix by a scalar and for matrix addition that

$$|\mathbf{A}) \leftrightarrow \alpha_1 \begin{bmatrix} 1 \\ 0 \\ 0 \\ 0 \\ \vdots \end{bmatrix} + \alpha_2 \begin{bmatrix} 0 \\ 1 \\ 0 \\ 0 \\ \vdots \end{bmatrix} + \alpha_3 \begin{bmatrix} 0 \\ 0 \\ 1 \\ 0 \\ \vdots \end{bmatrix} + \cdots$$

## 10–6 Linear transformations

Basically any set of $n$ linear equations of the form

$$y_i = \sum_{j=1}^{n} t_{ij} x_j, \tag{10–82}$$

which relate the $n$ variables $y_i$ to the $n$ variables $x_j$, and where the $t_{ij}$, are constants, define a linear transformation. Of special importance to us are the instances when the $n$ $y_i$'s and the $n$ $x_j$'s may respectively be considered to be the elements of the matrix representations of the two vectors $|\mathbf{y})$ and $|\mathbf{x})$ in an $n$-dimensional vector space. Equation (10–82) may then be considered to be the elements of the matrix representation of the vector equation

$$|\mathbf{y}) = \mathbf{T}|\mathbf{x}), \tag{10–83}$$

where the $t_{ij}$'s are considered to be elements of the matrix representation of the operator $\mathbf{T}$.

The operator $\mathbf{T}$ is an example of a *linear operator* $\mathbf{L}$ defined as an operator which satisfies the equation

$$\mathbf{L}[c_1|\mathbf{A}) + c_2|\mathbf{B})] = c_1\mathbf{L}|\mathbf{A}) + c_2\mathbf{L}|\mathbf{B}). \tag{10–84}$$

Now we find that we can express the operator $\mathbf{T}$ as a linear sum of operators

$$|\mathbf{e}_i)(\mathbf{e}_j|,$$

which are the direct products of the base vectors $|\mathbf{e}_i)$ with the base vectors $(\mathbf{e}_j|$. These $n^2$ operators, each of which has only one nonvanishing element, are linearly independent operators in terms of which any linear operator in the $n$-dimensional vector space may be expanded. This follows from the fact that an operator in an $n$-dimensional space has $n^2$ elements in its $n \times n$ matrix representation which can always be expressed as the linear sum of $n^2$ linearly independent $n \times n$ matrices.

The set above is the simplest set of $n^2$ linearly independent $n \times n$ matrices. It yields a set of matrices each of which has only one nonvanishing matrix element, and that one equal to unity. It is, however, not always the most useful set. For example, consider a two-dimensional vector space in which any linear operator has four elements in its matrix representation. Any such operator is expressible as a linear sum of the four linearly independent operators

$$|\mathbf{e}_1)(\mathbf{e}_1| \leftrightarrow \begin{bmatrix} 1 & 0 \\ 0 & 0 \end{bmatrix}, \qquad |\mathbf{e}_1)(\mathbf{e}_2| \leftrightarrow \begin{bmatrix} 0 & 1 \\ 0 & 0 \end{bmatrix},$$

$$|\mathbf{e}_2)(\mathbf{e}_1| \leftrightarrow \begin{bmatrix} 0 & 0 \\ 1 & 0 \end{bmatrix}, \qquad |\mathbf{e}_2)(\mathbf{e}_2| \leftrightarrow \begin{bmatrix} 0 & 0 \\ 0 & 1 \end{bmatrix}.$$

In quantum mechanics, we find that the four linearly independent operators

$$\mathbf{1} \leftrightarrow \begin{bmatrix} 1 & 0 \\ 0 & 1 \end{bmatrix}, \qquad \boldsymbol{\sigma}_2 \leftrightarrow i\begin{bmatrix} 0 & -1 \\ 1 & 0 \end{bmatrix},$$

$$\boldsymbol{\sigma}_1 \leftrightarrow \begin{bmatrix} 0 & 1 \\ 1 & 0 \end{bmatrix}, \qquad \boldsymbol{\sigma}_3 \leftrightarrow \begin{bmatrix} 1 & 0 \\ 0 & -1 \end{bmatrix}$$

are more useful for representing the effect of a linear operator on a vector of a two-dimensional vector space as, for example, the spin space of the electron. The $\sigma_i$ operators are known as the *Pauli spin operators*.

We note that the two-dimensional spin vector space is not the same as the usual two-dimensional vector space of plane vectors with which the reader is familiar. In Chapter 12 we shall show how the state of polarization of a harmonic plane wave can be denoted by a vector in such a two-dimensional vector space. The effect of a polarization filter or the effect of a transmitting medium on the state of polarization of the plane harmonic wave which it transmits is thus representable by an operator on the incident two-dimensional polarization vector.

In terms of the operators $|\mathbf{e}_i)(\mathbf{e}_j|$ we find the operator $\mathbf{T}$ to be expressed by

$$\mathbf{T} = \sum_{i,\,j=1}^{n} t_{ij}|\mathbf{e}_i)(\mathbf{e}_j|, \tag{10-85}$$

which indeed yields

$$\mathbf{T}|\mathbf{x}) = \mathbf{T}\sum_{k=1}^{n} x_k|\mathbf{e}_k) = \sum_{ijk} x_k t_{ij}|\mathbf{e}_i)(\mathbf{e}_j|\mathbf{e}_k)$$

$$= \sum_{ik} x_k t_{ik}|\mathbf{e}_i) = \sum_{i} y_i|\mathbf{e}_i) = |\mathbf{y}).$$

A very useful representation of the unit operator is

$$\mathbf{1} = \sum_{i=1}^{n} |\mathbf{e}_i)(\mathbf{e}_i|, \tag{10-86}$$

which follows from the fact that $\delta_{ij}$ are the elements of the unit matrix which is the matrix representation of **1**.

Interestingly, we note that the matrix elements $t_{ij}$ of the matrix representation of the operator **T** are expressed symbolically by

$$(\mathbf{e}_i|\mathbf{T}|\mathbf{e}_j) = \sum_{kl} (\mathbf{e}_i|\mathbf{e}_k)(\mathbf{e}_l|\mathbf{e}_j)t_{kl} = t_{ij}. \qquad (10\text{–}87)$$

At times we shall be interested in relating the components of the vector

$$|\mathbf{z}) = \mathbf{S}|\mathbf{y})$$

to the components of the vector $|\mathbf{x})$, where

$$|\mathbf{y}) = \mathbf{T}|\mathbf{x}).$$

This relationship is readily obtained by inserting the latter equation into the previous one to yield

$$|\mathbf{z}) = \mathbf{ST}|\mathbf{x}). \qquad (10\text{–}88)$$

The component form of Eq. (10–88) expresses the fact that

$$z_i = \sum_{jk} S_{ij}T_{jk}x_k = \sum_k \left( \sum_j S_{ij}T_{jk} \right) x_k, \qquad (10\text{–}89)$$

which in turn reveals that the matrix representation of the operator **ST** is the matrix product of the matrices (**S**) and (**T**),

$$(\mathbf{ST})_{ik} = \sum_j S_{ij}T_{jk}. \qquad (10\text{–}90)$$

As a special example, we consider the case when

$$|\mathbf{z}) = \mathbf{S}|\mathbf{y}) \qquad (10\text{–}91)$$

is the equation inverse to

$$|\mathbf{y}) = \mathbf{T}|\mathbf{x}); \qquad (10\text{–}92)$$

that is, when

$$|\mathbf{z}) = |\mathbf{x}).$$

Equation (10–91) represents the set of simultaneous equations represented by Eq. (10–92) solved for the $x_i$. It is well known that such solutions exist only if the determinant of **T** (the determinant value of its matrix representation) does not vanish; in other words, if the matrix representation of **T** is nonsingular. This means that a matrix exists which represents the operator inverse to **T**.

Since

$$\mathbf{T}^{-1}\mathbf{T} = \mathbf{1},$$

we find that

$$\mathbf{S} = \mathbf{T}^{-1},$$

so that

$$\mathbf{S}|\mathbf{y}) = \mathbf{T}^{-1}\mathbf{T}|\mathbf{x}).$$

We can obtain the matrix elements of the inverse operator from the determinant solution of the equations

$$y_i = \sum_j t_{ij} x_j.$$

That is,

$$x_i = \frac{\begin{vmatrix} y_1 & t_{1,i+1} & t_{1,i+2} \cdots t_{1n} & t_{11} \cdots t_{1,i-1} \\ y_2 & t_{2,i+1} & t_{2,i+2} \cdots t_{1n} & t_{21} \cdots t_{1,i-1} \\ \vdots & & & \vdots \\ y_n & t_{n,i+1} & t_{n,i+2} \cdots t_{nn} & t_{n1} \cdots t_{1,i-1} \end{vmatrix}}{\det(t_{kl})}$$

$$= \sum_j \frac{y_j \, \text{cofactor} \, t_{ji}}{\det(t_{kl})}$$

$$= \sum_j t_{ij}^{-1} y_j.$$

(10–93)

The determinant, cofactor $t_{ji}$, is formed from the det $(t_{kl})$. It is det $(t_{kl})$ with its $j$th row and $i$th column removed and the result multiplied by $(-1)^{i+j}$. We can check that $t_{ij}^{-1}$ so defined yields the matrix inverse to the matrix representation of **T**. We find that

$$(\mathbf{T}\mathbf{T}^{-1})_{ij} = \sum_k t_{ik} t_{kj}^{-1} = \sum_k \frac{t_{ik}(\text{cofactor} \, t_{jk})}{\det(t_{rs})}$$

(10–94)

$$= \frac{\det(t_{rs})}{\det(t_{rs})} \delta_{ij} = \delta_{ij}.$$

That

$$\sum_k t_{ik} \, \text{cofactor} \, t_{jk} = \begin{cases} \det(t_{ij}) & i = j \\ 0 & i \neq j \end{cases}$$

(10–95)

can be seen as follows. By definition

$$\det(t_{ij}) = \sum_k t_{jk} \, \text{cofactor} \, t_{jk}, \qquad j = \text{const.}$$

In the case in question we use the elements of the $j$th column for the expansion of the determinant. If we replace the $j$th column in the determinant by the $i$th column, there results a new determinant which has two equal columns and which therefore vanishes. This fact is expressed by the $\delta_{ij}$ in Eq. (10–94).

As an example, we shall determine the inverse of the nonsingular matrix

$$(\mathbf{T}) = \begin{bmatrix} 2 & -1 & 3 \\ 1 & 2 & 0 \\ 1 & 4 & 5 \end{bmatrix}$$

whose determinant value is

$$\det (t_{ij}) = \begin{vmatrix} 2 & -1 & 3 \\ 1 & 2 & 0 \\ 1 & 4 & 5 \end{vmatrix} = 31.$$

We find that

$$t_{11}^{-1} = \frac{\begin{vmatrix} 2 & 0 \\ 4 & 5 \end{vmatrix}}{31} = \frac{10}{31}, \qquad t_{21}^{-1} = \frac{\begin{vmatrix} 0 & 1 \\ 5 & 1 \end{vmatrix}}{31} = -\frac{5}{31}, \qquad \text{etc.},$$

which yield the following as the inverse matrix

$$(\mathbf{T}^{-1}) = \frac{1}{31} \begin{bmatrix} 10 & 17 & -6 \\ -5 & 7 & 3 \\ 2 & -9 & 5 \end{bmatrix}.$$

We can readily verify that this is in fact the inverse of the matrix ($\mathbf{T}$) above.

## 10–7 Coordinate transformations*

In this section we shall consider the relationship between the descriptions of a vector or a linear operator with respect to different sets of orthonormal base vectors. Consider two sets of orthonormal base vectors $\mathbf{e}_i$ and $\mathbf{e}'_i$ related by

$$|\mathbf{e}'_i) = \sum_j |\mathbf{e}_j)(\mathbf{e}_j|\mathbf{e}'_i) \qquad (10\text{–}96)$$

or by the equation

$$|\mathbf{e}_i) = \sum_j |\mathbf{e}'_j)(\mathbf{e}'_j|\mathbf{e}_i). \qquad (10\text{–}97)$$

We note that in operator form, these equations are

$$|\mathbf{e}'_i) = \mathbf{1}|\mathbf{e}'_i), \qquad (10\text{–}98)$$

and

$$|\mathbf{e}_i) = \mathbf{1}'|\mathbf{e}_i) \qquad (10\text{–}99)$$

where $\mathbf{1}$ is the unit operator in the unprimed coordinate system and $\mathbf{1}'$ the unit operator expressed in terms of the primed base vectors. It thus appears that the operation with a unit operator on a vector yields the expansion of the vector in terms of the unit base vectors which appear in the expansion of the unit

---

* Cf. Sections 3–5.

operator. We find this indeed to be so. For example, we have

$$|\mathbf{A}) = \mathbf{1}|\mathbf{A}) = \sum_i |\mathbf{e}_i)(\mathbf{e}_i|\mathbf{A}) = \sum_i \alpha_i|\mathbf{e}_i)$$

and

$$|\mathbf{A}) = \mathbf{1}'|\mathbf{A}) = \sum_i |\mathbf{e}_i')(\mathbf{e}_i'|\mathbf{A}) = \sum \alpha_i'|\mathbf{e}_i').$$

We thus find that using

$$|\mathbf{A}) = \sum_j \alpha_j|\mathbf{e}_j),$$

we can obtain

$$|\mathbf{A}') = \mathbf{1}'|\mathbf{A}) = \sum_{ij} |\mathbf{e}_i')(\mathbf{e}_i'|\mathbf{e}_j)\alpha_j = \sum_i \left[\sum_j (\mathbf{e}_i'|\mathbf{e}_j)\alpha_j\right]|\mathbf{e}_i'),$$

which yields the relation

$$\alpha_j' = \sum_j (\mathbf{e}_j'|\mathbf{e}_j)\alpha_j. \tag{10-100}$$

Similarly, we obtain

$$\alpha_i = \sum_j (\mathbf{e}_i|\mathbf{e}_j')\alpha_j'. \tag{10-101}$$

Referring to the vector $|\mathbf{A})$ expressed in terms of the primed base vectors as $|\mathbf{A}')$, we find that the last two equations are expressed in operator notation by

$$|\mathbf{A}') = \mathbf{S}|\mathbf{A}) \quad \text{and} \quad |\mathbf{A}) = \mathbf{S}^{-1}|\mathbf{A}'), \tag{10-102}$$

where $\mathbf{S}$ is the transformation operator whose matrix representation has the elements

$$S_{ij} = (\mathbf{e}_i'|\mathbf{e}_j).$$

Its inverse has the elements

$$S_{ji}^{-1} = (\mathbf{e}_j|\mathbf{e}_i') = (\mathbf{e}_i'|\mathbf{e}_j) = S_{ij} = \widetilde{S}_{ji}.$$

That is,

$$\mathbf{S}^{-1} = \widetilde{\mathbf{S}}. \tag{10-103}$$

A transformation whose matrix satisfies condition (10–103) is referred to as an *orthogonal transformation*.

A note of explanation is in order at this point. We started with a given vector $|\mathbf{A})$, and obtained the relation between the matrix representations of the vector with respect to two different sets of orthonormal base vectors. We then ended up with the transformation equations relating the descriptions of a vector $|\mathbf{A}')$ to the description of the vector $|\mathbf{A})$. The reason for our being able to do this lies in the fact that the important equations are after all (10–100) and (10–101), which relate the $\alpha$'s and define the transformation we are considering. Now it happens that we obtain the same set of transformation equations for two

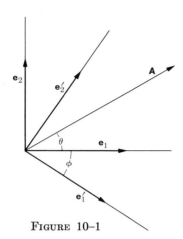

FIGURE 10–1

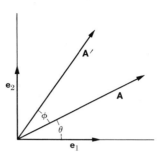

FIGURE 10–2

different geometrical operations.  To understand this better, let us consider a change of the base vectors of a two-dimensional vector space (cf. Fig. 10–1), such as a rotation of the base vectors through an angle $-\phi$.  Equation (10–100) then relate the descriptions of a vector **A** with respect to the two sets of base vectors.  On the other hand, consider a fixed coordinate system and a rotation of the vector **A** through an angle $+\phi$ (Fig. 10–2).  Since the new vector **A**′ makes the same angle with $\mathbf{e}_1$ as **A** makes with the vector $\mathbf{e}'_1$, it follows that the description of **A**′ in the unprimed coordinate system is the same as the description of **A** in the primed coordinate system.

Given the transformation equations (10–100) and (10–101), we are of course at liberty to give to them either of the two interpretations.  To derive the transformation equations, we use the first.  In the end, it was notationally simpler to use the second interpretation of the change of the vector $|\mathbf{A})$ to the vector $|\mathbf{A}')$ as expressed by Eqs. (10–102).  This latter interpretation is notationally less confusing.

We see that the determinant value of

$$\mathbf{S}\mathbf{S}^{-1} = \mathbf{1}$$

is one.  Hence for an orthogonal transformation for which

$$\det(\mathbf{S}) = \det(\tilde{\mathbf{S}}) = \det(\mathbf{S}^{-1}),$$

we find that

$$[\det(\mathbf{S})]^2 = 1 \quad \text{or} \quad \det(\mathbf{S}) = \pm 1.$$

For an ordinary rotation of the coordinate system, referred to as a *proper rotation*, the determinant value will be $+1$.  An orthogonal transformation whose transformation matrix has the determinant value $-1$ can always be expressed as

$$\mathbf{S} = -\mathbf{1T},$$

where **T** is a proper rotation operator. The operator $-\mathbf{1}$ is the *inversion operator*. An orthogonal transformation whose transformation matrix has the determinant value $-1$ thus involves a proper rotation and an inversion of the coordinate system. Such an orthogonal transformation is referred to as an *improper rotation*.

In a similar fashion, we can obtain the transformation equations for the elements of the matrix representation of an operator **K**. From our discussion of operators in the previous section we realize that in terms of the unprimed base vectors, the operator **K** is expressed by

$$\mathbf{K} = \sum_{ij} k_{ij} |\mathbf{e}_i)(\mathbf{e}_j|. \tag{10-104}$$

In terms of the primed base vectors, it is expressed by

$$\mathbf{K}' = \sum_{ij} k'_{ij} |\mathbf{e}'_i)(\mathbf{e}'_j|. \tag{10-105}$$

As was the case with the vector $|\mathbf{A})$ we can change the vectors $|\mathbf{e}_i)$ to the vectors $|\mathbf{e}'_i)$ by multiplying by the unit operator expressed in terms of the primed base vectors. We thus find

$$\mathbf{K}' = \mathbf{1}'\mathbf{K}\mathbf{1}'$$

$$= \left[\sum_i |\mathbf{e}'_i)(\mathbf{e}'_i|\right]\left[\sum_{lm} k_{lm}|\mathbf{e}_l)(\mathbf{e}_m|\right]\left[\sum_j |\mathbf{e}'_j)(\mathbf{e}'_j|\right]$$

$$= \sum_{ij}\left[\sum_{lm} (\mathbf{e}'_i|\mathbf{e}_l)k_{lm}(\mathbf{e}_m|\mathbf{e}_{j'})\right]|\mathbf{e}'_i)(\mathbf{e}'_j|,$$

which yield the transformation equation we are seeking for the elements of the matrix representation of an operator,

$$k'_{ij} = \sum_{lm} (\mathbf{e}'_i|\mathbf{e}_l)k_{lm}(\mathbf{e}_m|\mathbf{e}'_j) = (\mathbf{e}'_i|\mathbf{K}|\mathbf{e}'_j). \tag{10-106}$$

Once again we consider this equation as one that relates the elements of the matrix representation of the operator equation

$$\mathbf{K}' = \mathbf{S}\mathbf{K}\widetilde{\mathbf{S}} = \mathbf{S}\mathbf{K}\mathbf{S}^{-1}. \tag{10-107}$$

As an example, we consider the transformation of the moment-of-inertia operator from the unprimed coordinate system in which its matrix representation is

$$(\mathbf{I}) = \begin{bmatrix} \frac{7}{3} & -\frac{2}{3} & 0 \\ -\frac{2}{3} & 2 & -\frac{2}{3} \\ 0 & -\frac{2}{3} & \frac{5}{3} \end{bmatrix}$$

to a primed coordinate system whose direction cosines with the unprimed co-ordinate system $S_{ij} = (\mathbf{e}'_i|\mathbf{e}_j)$ are the elements of the orthogonal transformation matrix

$$(\mathbf{S}) = \begin{bmatrix} -\frac{1}{3} & -\frac{2}{3} & -\frac{2}{3} \\ -\frac{2}{3} & -\frac{1}{3} & \frac{2}{3} \\ -\frac{2}{3} & \frac{2}{3} & -\frac{1}{3} \end{bmatrix}.$$

The representation of the moment-of-inertia operator in the primed coordinate system is given by

$$(\mathbf{I}') = (\mathbf{S})(\mathbf{I})(\tilde{\mathbf{S}})$$

$$= \begin{bmatrix} -\frac{1}{3} & -\frac{2}{3} & -\frac{2}{3} \\ -\frac{2}{3} & -\frac{1}{3} & \frac{2}{3} \\ -\frac{2}{3} & \frac{2}{3} & -\frac{1}{3} \end{bmatrix} \begin{bmatrix} \frac{7}{3} & -\frac{2}{3} & 0 \\ -\frac{2}{3} & 2 & -\frac{2}{3} \\ 0 & -\frac{2}{3} & \frac{5}{3} \end{bmatrix} \begin{bmatrix} -\frac{1}{3} & -\frac{2}{3} & -\frac{2}{3} \\ -\frac{2}{3} & -\frac{1}{3} & \frac{2}{3} \\ -\frac{2}{3} & \frac{2}{3} & -\frac{1}{3} \end{bmatrix}$$

$$= \begin{bmatrix} -\frac{1}{3} & -\frac{2}{3} & -\frac{2}{3} \\ -\frac{2}{3} & -\frac{1}{3} & \frac{2}{3} \\ -\frac{2}{3} & \frac{2}{3} & -\frac{1}{3} \end{bmatrix} \begin{bmatrix} -\frac{1}{3} & -\frac{4}{3} & -2 \\ -\frac{2}{3} & -\frac{2}{3} & 2 \\ -\frac{2}{3} & \frac{4}{3} & -1 \end{bmatrix}$$

$$= \begin{bmatrix} 1 & 0 & 0 \\ 0 & 2 & 0 \\ 0 & 0 & 3 \end{bmatrix}.$$

In Section 10–9 we shall show that there always exists a coordinate system in which the moment-of-inertia matrix is diagonal.

Another interesting and important example is the transformation of the angular momentum vector. This vector, being the vector product of two polar vectors, as was discussed previously, transforms under a rotation like an axial vector whose components are the elements of the matrix representation of an antisymmetric operator. Specifically, the components of the angular momentum vector are the nonvanishing elements of the matrix representing the operator

$$\mathbf{L} = |\mathbf{r})(\mathbf{p}| - |\mathbf{p})(\mathbf{r}|.$$

This matrix representation is

$$(\mathbf{L}) = \begin{bmatrix} 0 & L_z & -L_y \\ -L_z & 0 & L_x \\ L_y & -L_x & 0 \end{bmatrix}.$$

Let us investigate the transformation properties of this vector and satisfy ourselves that under a proper rotation, $L_x$, $L_y$, and $L_z$ transform like the components of a polar vector. We leave it as an exercise for the reader to verify that under an improper rotation, $L_x$, $L_y$, and $L_z$ do not transform like the components of a polar vector.

The transformation matrix for a rotation of the coordinate system through an angle $-\phi$ (Fig. 10–1) about the $z$-axis is

$$(\mathbf{S}) = \begin{bmatrix} \cos\phi & -\sin\phi & 0 \\ \sin\phi & \cos\phi & 0 \\ 0 & 0 & 1 \end{bmatrix}.$$

Hence we obtain

$$(\mathbf{L'}) = (\mathbf{S})(\mathbf{L})(\tilde{\mathbf{S}})$$

$$= \begin{bmatrix} \cos\phi & -\sin\phi & 0 \\ \sin\phi & \cos\phi & 0 \\ 0 & 0 & 1 \end{bmatrix} \begin{bmatrix} 0 & L_z & -L_y \\ -L_z & 0 & L_x \\ L_y & -L_x & 0 \end{bmatrix} \begin{bmatrix} \cos\phi & \sin\phi & 0 \\ -\sin\phi & \cos\phi & 0 \\ 0 & 0 & 1 \end{bmatrix}$$

$$= \begin{bmatrix} \cos\phi & -\sin\phi & 0 \\ \sin\phi & \cos\phi & 0 \\ 0 & 0 & 1 \end{bmatrix} \begin{bmatrix} -L_z\sin\phi & L_z\cos\phi & -L_y \\ -L_z\cos\phi & -L_z\sin\phi & L_x \\ L_y\cos\phi + L_x\sin\phi & L_y\sin\phi - L_x\cos\phi & 0 \end{bmatrix}$$

$$= \begin{bmatrix} 0 & L_z & -(L_y\cos\phi + L_x\sin\phi) \\ -L'_z & 0 & -(L_y\sin\phi - L_x\cos\phi) \\ L'_y & -L'_x & 0 \end{bmatrix},$$

which yields the transformation equations

$$L'_x = L_x\cos\phi - L_y\sin\phi,$$
$$L'_y = L_x\sin\phi + L_y\cos\phi,$$
$$L'_z = L_z.$$

These being identical to the transformation equations of the components of a vector, we have shown that the elements $L_{23}$, $L_{31}$, and $L_{12}$ of the matrix representation of the operator $\mathbf{L} = |\mathbf{r})(\mathbf{p}| - |\mathbf{p})(\mathbf{r}|$ transform under a proper rotation like the components of a polar vector.

The rotation vector is another example of an axial vector. As shown in Section 3–5, its components also form the nonvanishing elements of an antisymmetric matrix representing the operator

$$\mathbf{\Omega} \leftrightarrow \begin{bmatrix} 0 & -\omega_z & \omega_y \\ \omega_z & 0 & -\omega_x \\ -\omega_y & \omega_x & 0 \end{bmatrix}.$$

That $\boldsymbol{\omega}$ is indeed an axial vector may also be inferred from Eq. (3–5) which yields for the time derivative of a vector of constant magnitude

$$\dot{\mathbf{A}} = \boldsymbol{\omega} \times \mathbf{A}.$$

Clearly $\mathbf{A}$ and $\dot{\mathbf{A}}$ are both polar vectors or both axial vectors. Thus in order that this equation transform correctly under an inversion, $\boldsymbol{\omega}$ should not change sign—that is, $\boldsymbol{\omega}$ must be an axial vector.

The magnetic induction vector is a third example of a pseudovector. This can be seen from the equation of motion of a charged particle in a magnetic field,

$$\dot{\mathbf{p}} = q\mathbf{v} \times \mathbf{B}.$$

Clearly since $\dot{\mathbf{p}}$ and $\mathbf{v}$ change sign under an inversion of the coordinate system, $\mathbf{B}$ must not change sign. We note that in matrix notation the latter equation is expressible as

$$(\mathbf{F}) = q(\mathbf{B})(\mathbf{v}),$$

where $(\mathbf{B})$ is the antisymmetric square matrix

$$\begin{bmatrix} 0 & B_z & -B_y \\ -B_z & 0 & B_x \\ B_y & -B_x & 0 \end{bmatrix}.$$

In Chapter 13 we shall find that the electromagnetic field components form the elements of an antisymmetric $4 \times 4$ matrix.

## 10–8 Complex vector space

If the elements of the $n$-dimensional column matrices are complex numbers, then we have a complex vector space. The addition of two vectors in this space and the multiplication of vectors by scalars follow the rules that define a vector space; these rules were listed in Section 10–4. The definition of a scalar product of two vectors in a complex space, however, is no longer unique. For example, we may define the scalar product as we did the scalar product of two real vectors by

$$(\mathbf{A}|\mathbf{B}) = [\alpha_1, \alpha_2, \ldots, \alpha_n]\begin{bmatrix} \beta_1 \\ \beta_2 \\ \vdots \\ \beta_n \end{bmatrix} = (\mathbf{B}|\mathbf{A}). \tag{10–108}$$

On the other hand, we can also define a scalar product of two complex vectors by

$$(\mathbf{A}^*|\mathbf{B}) = [\alpha_1^*, \alpha_2^*, \ldots, \alpha_n^*]\begin{bmatrix} \beta_1 \\ \beta_2 \\ \vdots \\ \beta_n \end{bmatrix} = (\mathbf{B}^*|\mathbf{A})^*, \tag{10–109}$$

where the asterisk indicates the complex conjugate of the vector or scalar.

We find use for both definitions of the scalar product of two complex vectors. For example, as already mentioned, we employ at times in the special theory of relativity complex four-dimensional vectors whose fourth component is imaginary. The position vector in the relativistic four-dimensional vector space is

$$(\mathbf{r}| \leftrightarrow [x, y, z, ict].$$

The scalar product of two vectors in this relativistic complex vector space is defined by the first definition of the scalar product $(\mathbf{A}|\mathbf{B})$, since this yields for the vector $|\Delta\mathbf{r})$ the required magnitude

$$\Delta r^2 = \Delta x^2 + \Delta y^2 + \Delta z^2 - c^2\,\Delta t^2 = -\Delta s^2.$$

On the other hand, for most applications we shall require the magnitude of nonzero vectors to be positive definite. This property is assured if the scalar product of two vectors is defined by $(\mathbf{A}^*|\mathbf{B})$, which yields

$$A^2 = (\mathbf{A}^*|\mathbf{A}) = \sum_{i=1}^{n} |\alpha_i|^2.$$

As an illustration, the complex matrix representation

$$|\mathbf{A}) \leftrightarrow
\begin{bmatrix}
-\dfrac{1}{\sqrt{2}}\,(A_x + iA_y) \\[2ex]
A_z \\[2ex]
\dfrac{1}{\sqrt{2}}\,(A_x - iA_y)
\end{bmatrix}
=
\begin{bmatrix}
-\dfrac{1}{\sqrt{2}}\,A_+ \\[2ex]
A_z \\[2ex]
\dfrac{1}{\sqrt{2}}\,A_-
\end{bmatrix}$$

of a vector $|\mathbf{A})$ is extremely important in quantum mechanics. We also note that the complex coordinate $x_+ = x + iy$ was used by us in the solution of the isotropic oscillator problem and in the problem of a charged harmonic oscillator in a magnetic field. The magnitude of the vector is given by

$$A^2 = (\mathbf{A}^*|\mathbf{A}) = \left[-\dfrac{1}{\sqrt{2}}\,A_-,\ A_z,\ \dfrac{1}{\sqrt{2}}\,A_+\right]
\begin{bmatrix}
-\dfrac{1}{\sqrt{2}}\,A_+ \\[2ex]
A_z \\[2ex]
\dfrac{1}{\sqrt{2}}\,A_-
\end{bmatrix}$$

$$= A_x^2 + A_y^2 + A_z^2.$$

Whenever in dealing with complex vector spaces we assume this latter definition for the scalar product, we shall remind ourselves of the fact that this definition is being used by notationally replacing the symbols $|\mathbf{A})$ and $(\mathbf{A}^*|$ by the symbols $|\mathbf{A}\rangle$ and $\langle\mathbf{A}|$. That is,

$$|\mathbf{A}\rangle = |\mathbf{A})$$

and                                                                                    (10–110)

$$\langle\mathbf{A}| = (\mathbf{A}^*|.$$

In the new notation, the scalar product $(\mathbf{A}^*|\mathbf{B})$ is indicated by

$$\langle\mathbf{A}|\mathbf{B}\rangle.$$

Since the matrix representations of $\langle\mathbf{A}|$ and $|\mathbf{A}\rangle$ satisfy the equation

$$[\alpha_1^*, \alpha_2^*, \ldots, \alpha_n^*] = \begin{bmatrix} \widetilde{\alpha_1} \\ \alpha_2 \\ \vdots \\ \alpha_n \end{bmatrix}^*$$

we shall similarly relate the vectors. That is, we set

$$\langle\mathbf{A}| = |\widetilde{\mathbf{A}}\rangle^* = |\mathbf{A}\rangle^\dagger.$$         (10–111)

The transpose complex conjugate of a vector $|\mathbf{A}\rangle$ or of an operator $\mathbf{L}$ is referred to as the *Hermitian adjoint* of the vector or operator. The Hermitian adjoint of an operator is indicated by a dagger superscript,

$$\mathbf{L}^\dagger = \widetilde{\mathbf{L}}^*.$$                                        (10–112)

It should be clear that in dealing with complex vector spaces the linear operators which operate on the vectors are likewise complex. That is, their matrix representations have complex elements.

Complex matrices whose Hermitian adjoint is equal to the matrix, as expressed by

$$\mathbf{S}^\dagger = \mathbf{S},$$                                                    (10–113)

are referred to as *Hermitian* matrices. It should be clear that all real operators are Hermitian operators. Hermitian operators play a very important role in quantum mechanics. On the other hand, operators which satisfy the equation

$$\mathbf{S}^\dagger = -\mathbf{S}$$                                                    (10–114)

are referred to as *anti-Hermitian*. It follows that all real antisymmetric operators are anti-Hermitian.

Similarly to the decomposition of an operator into a symmetric and an antisymmetric part, a complex operator can be decomposed into a Hermitian and an anti-Hermitian part. We find that we can express any operator as

$$\mathbf{S} = \tfrac{1}{2}(\mathbf{S} + \mathbf{S}^\dagger) + \tfrac{1}{2}(\mathbf{S} - \mathbf{S}^\dagger).$$   (10–115)

The reader should have no trouble verifying that the first part, $\frac{1}{2}(\mathbf{S} + \mathbf{S}^\dagger)$, is Hermitian and the second part, $\frac{1}{2}(\mathbf{S} - \mathbf{S}^\dagger)$, anti-Hermitian.

It can also be readily verified that if we decompose a Hermitian operator into a real part $\mathbf{R}$ and an imaginary part $\mathbf{I}$,

$$\mathbf{S} = \mathbf{R} + \mathbf{I},$$

the real part is symmetric,

$$\mathbf{R} = \widetilde{\mathbf{R}},$$

and the imaginary part antisymmetric,

$$\mathbf{I} = -\widetilde{\mathbf{I}}.$$

The derivations of the remaining equations in this section follow exactly the derivations of the analogous equations for real vectors and operators in a real vector space. In terms of the unit orthogonal base vectors $|\mathbf{e}_i\rangle$ of a complex vector space, any vector $|\mathbf{A}\rangle$ is expressible as

$$|\mathbf{A}\rangle = \sum_{i=1}^{n} \alpha_i |\mathbf{e}_i\rangle, \tag{10–116}$$

where

$$\alpha_i = \langle \mathbf{e}_i | \mathbf{A} \rangle, \tag{10–117}$$

and any operator $\mathbf{T}$ is expressible as

$$\mathbf{T} = \sum_{ij} T_{ij} |\mathbf{e}_i\rangle\langle\mathbf{e}_j|, \tag{10–118}$$

where the matrix elements $T_{ij}$ are expressible as

$$T_{ij} = \langle \mathbf{e}_i | \mathbf{T} | \mathbf{e}_j \rangle. \tag{10–119}$$

The unit operator $\mathbf{1}$ is given by

$$\mathbf{1} = \sum_{i} |\mathbf{e}_i\rangle\langle\mathbf{e}_i|. \tag{10–120}$$

The change in the description of a vector $|\mathbf{A}\rangle$ under a coordinate transformation from the unit orthogonal base vectors $|\mathbf{e}_i\rangle$ to the orthonormal base vectors $|\mathbf{e}_i'\rangle$ can be expressed in terms of the transformation matrix $(\mathbf{S})$, which has the elements

$$S_{ij} = \langle \mathbf{e}_i' | \mathbf{e}_j \rangle. \tag{10–121}$$

In terms of the operator $\mathbf{S}$ we find that the transformation, interpreted as a transformation of the vector $|\mathbf{A}\rangle$, is expressed by

$$|\mathbf{A}'\rangle = \mathbf{S}|\mathbf{A}\rangle. \tag{10–122}$$

Similarly, for an operator $\mathbf{L}$ we obtain

$$\mathbf{L'} = \mathbf{SLS}^{-1}, \tag{10–123}$$

where $\mathbf{S}^{-1}$ is the inverse transformation operator. For this operator $\mathbf{S}^{-1}$ we obtain the matrix elements

$$S_{ji}^{-1} = \langle \mathbf{e}_j | \mathbf{e}_i' \rangle = \widetilde{S}_{ij}^*. \tag{10–124}$$

A transformation for which the inverse of the transformation operator is its Hermitian adjoint,

$$\mathbf{S}^{-1} = \widetilde{\mathbf{S}}^* = \mathbf{S}^\dagger, \tag{10–125}$$

is referred to as a *unitary transformation*, and any operator whose inverse equals its Hermitian adjoint,

$$\mathbf{U}^{-1} = \mathbf{U}^\dagger, \tag{10–126}$$

is referred to as a *unitary operator*. A unitary transformation leaves the scalar product $\langle \mathbf{A} | \mathbf{B} \rangle$ of two vectors invariant.

As an illustration, we consider the complex representation of a three-dimensional vector for which the base vectors are

$$\mathbf{e}_1 = -\frac{1}{\sqrt{2}}\,(\mathbf{e}_x + i\mathbf{e}_y),$$

$$\mathbf{e}_2 = \mathbf{e}_z,$$

and

$$\mathbf{e}_3 = \frac{1}{\sqrt{2}}\,(\mathbf{e}_x - i\mathbf{e}_y).$$

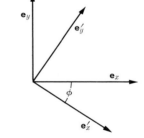

FIGURE 10–3

For a rotation of the coordinate axes about the $z$-axis through an angle $-\phi$, we have (cf. Fig. 10–3)

$$\langle \mathbf{e}_x' | \mathbf{e}_x \rangle = \cos\phi, \qquad \langle \mathbf{e}_x' | \mathbf{e}_y \rangle = -\sin\phi,$$

$$\langle \mathbf{e}_y' | \mathbf{e}_x \rangle = \sin\phi, \qquad \langle \mathbf{e}_y' | \mathbf{e}_y \rangle = \cos\phi,$$

from which we obtain

$$\mathbf{e}_1' = -\frac{1}{\sqrt{2}}\,(\mathbf{e}_x' + i\mathbf{e}_y')$$

$$= -\frac{1}{\sqrt{2}}\,[\cos\phi\,\mathbf{e}_x - \sin\phi\,\mathbf{e}_y + i(\sin\phi\,\mathbf{e}_x + \cos\phi\,\mathbf{e}_y)] = e^{i\phi}\mathbf{e}_1,$$

$$\mathbf{e}_2' = \mathbf{e}_2, \quad \text{and} \quad \mathbf{e}_3' = e^{-i\phi}\mathbf{e}_3.$$

Hence the transformation matrix is

$$(\mathbf{S}) = \begin{bmatrix} e^{i\phi} & 0 & 0 \\ 0 & 1 & 0 \\ 0 & 0 & e^{-i\phi} \end{bmatrix}.$$

The inverse matrix is clearly the matrix $(\mathbf{S})$ with $\phi$ replaced by $-\phi$, or

$$(\mathbf{S}^{-1}) = (\widetilde{\mathbf{S}})^*.$$

For the sinusoidally varying vectors

$$|\mathbf{A}) \leftrightarrow \begin{bmatrix} -\dfrac{1}{\sqrt{2}}\,A_+ \\[2mm] A_z \\[2mm] \dfrac{1}{\sqrt{2}}\,A_- \end{bmatrix} e^{i\omega t},$$

we note that

$$\begin{bmatrix} A_+ \\ 0 \\ 0 \end{bmatrix}$$

represents a vector rotating counterclockwise in the $xy$-plane, and

$$\begin{bmatrix} 0 \\ 0 \\ A_- \end{bmatrix}$$

a vector rotating clockwise in the $xy$-plane as shown in Fig. 10–4 (cf. Section 1–9). That this is so can be seen from the transformation matrix which tells us that with respect to a coordinate system rotating with the angular velocity $\omega$

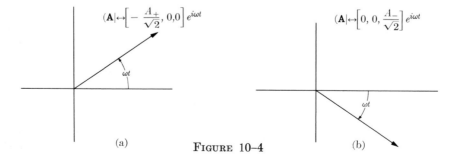

$$(\mathbf{A}| \leftrightarrow \left[ -\frac{A_+}{\sqrt{2}},\, 0, 0 \right] e^{i\omega t}$$

$$(\mathbf{A}| \leftrightarrow \left[ 0,\, 0,\, \frac{A_-}{\sqrt{2}} \right] e^{i\omega t}$$

(a)    FIGURE 10–4    (b)

about the $z$-axis for which $\phi = -\omega t$ (note $\phi$ represents a rotation of the coordinate system through $-\phi$ about the $z$-axis),

$$A'_+ = A_+ e^{i\omega t} e^{i\phi} = A_+.$$

That is, with respect to the rotating coordinate system the vector represented by $A'_+$ is a constant. Similarly, with respect to a coordinate system rotating with an angular velocity $-\omega$ about the $z$-axis, $\phi = \omega t$ and

$$A'_- = A_- e^{i\phi} e^{-i\phi} = A_-$$

remains fixed.

This result has an important application. For example, in dealing with the propagation of a plane harmonic electromagnetic wave,

$$E_+ = E_x + iE_y \qquad \text{and} \qquad E_- = E_x - iE_y$$

are utilized for the mathematical representation of the circular polarized modes.

## 10–9 Eigenvalues and eigenvectors of an operator: diagonalization of normal operators

Of special importance is the operator eigenvalue equation

$$\mathbf{L}|\mathbf{u}\rangle = \lambda|\mathbf{u}\rangle, \tag{10–127}$$

where $\lambda$ is a constant. This equation for a given operator $\mathbf{L}$ has a solution for only specific values of $\lambda$ referred to as the *eigenvalues* of the operator $\mathbf{L}$. With each of the eigenvalues $\lambda_i$ there is usually associated only one vector $|\mathbf{u}_i\rangle$ which satisfies the eigenvalue equation. The vectors $|\mathbf{u}_i\rangle$ are referred to as the *eigenvectors* of the operator $\mathbf{L}$.

To find the eigenvalues, we rewrite Eq. (10–127) as

$$(\mathbf{L} - \lambda\mathbf{1})|\mathbf{u}\rangle = 0, \tag{10–128}$$

which yields the $n$ homogeneous simultaneous equations

$$\sum_{j=1}^{n} (L_{ij} - \lambda\delta_{ij})u_j = 0. \tag{10–129}$$

These homogeneous simultaneous equations are solvable only if the determinant of the coefficients of the components $u_j$'s of the vector $|\mathbf{u}\rangle$ vanish. This determinantal equation,

$$\det (L_{ij} - \lambda\delta_{ij}) = 0,$$

is referred to as the *secular equation*. Since it is of the $n$th order in $\lambda$, it can be satisfied for $n$ values of $\lambda$. We shall assume for the moment that the roots of the secular equation are distinct. In that case we are in a position to find a $|\mathbf{u}_i\rangle$ for each of the roots $\lambda_i$. This is accomplished by solving $n - 1$ of the simultaneous equation for $n - 1$ components of the vector $|\mathbf{u}_i\rangle$ in terms of the $n$th component. Since the magnitude of the vector $|\mathbf{u}_i\rangle$ satisfying Eq. (10–128) is arbitrary, we are at liberty to adjust it to be one, thereby fixing the magnitude of the $n$th component, too.

As an example, consider the symmetric operator whose matrix representation is given by

$$\mathbf{L} \leftrightarrow \begin{bmatrix} 1 & 0 & 5 \\ 0 & -2 & 0 \\ 5 & 0 & 1 \end{bmatrix}.$$

The secular equation for this operator is

$$\begin{vmatrix} 1 - \lambda & 0 & 5 \\ 0 & -2 - \lambda & 0 \\ 5 & 0 & 1 - \lambda \end{vmatrix} = (1 - \lambda)^2(-2 - \lambda) + 25(2 + \lambda) = 0.$$

Its roots are

$$\lambda = -2, -4, 6.$$

For the eigenvalue $\lambda_1 = -2$ we subsequently obtain two independent equations for the components of the eigenvector $|\mathbf{u}_1\rangle$. They are the equations

$$3u_{11} + 5u_{13} = 0 \quad \text{and} \quad 5u_{11} + 3u_{13} = 0,$$

which can be satisfied only if $u_{11} = u_{13} = 0$. Hence

$$|\mathbf{u}_1\rangle \leftrightarrow \begin{bmatrix} 0 \\ 1 \\ 0 \end{bmatrix}.$$

Similarly, we find for the second eigenvalue $\lambda_2 = -4$ the eigenvector $|\mathbf{u}_2\rangle$, whose components are obtained from the equations

$$5u_{21} + 5u_{23} = 0,$$
$$0u_{21} + (-2 + 4)u_{22} + 0u_{23} = 0.$$

The solution to these equations is $u_{22} = 0$ and $u_{23} = -u_{21}$, which leads to the normalized eigenvector

$$|\mathbf{u}_2\rangle \leftrightarrow \frac{1}{\sqrt{2}} \begin{bmatrix} 1 \\ 0 \\ -1 \end{bmatrix}.$$

The normalized eigenvector belonging to the third eigenvalue is found to be

$$|\mathbf{u}_3\rangle \leftrightarrow \frac{1}{\sqrt{2}}\begin{bmatrix} 1 \\ 0 \\ 1 \end{bmatrix}.$$

If the roots of the secular equation are not distinct, we have what is referred to as a *degeneracy*. To see how one handles such degeneracies, let us consider the case when one of the eigenvalues is a double root of the secular equation. This means that only $n-2$ of the simultaneous equations for the components of its eigenvector are linearly independent, which suggests that we solve for $n-2$ of its components in terms of the remaining two components. Let us choose these to be the components $u_{\lambda 1}$ and $u_{\lambda 2}$. We then find that any set of values of $u_{\lambda 1}$ and $u_{\lambda 2}$ yields an eigenvector of $\mathbf{L}$ associated with the degenerate eigenvalue $\lambda$. In any $n$-dimensional eigenvalue problem, we seek $n$ eigenvectors. Two of these eigenvectors obviously belong to the degenerate eigenvalue, which is a double root of the secular equation. These two may be taken as the normalized eigenvectors which are obtained when we first set $u_{\lambda 1}$ and then $u_{\lambda 2}$ equal to zero, or any normalized linear combination of these. The extension to triply and higher-multiple degenerate eigenvalues should thus be clear.

As an example, we proceed to find the principle moments of inertia of a uniform cube with respect to one of its corners. The principal moments of inertia are the moments of inertia about the principal set of axes passing through the point in question. They are in turn the axes about which the rigid body must rotate in order to have its angular momentum vector parallel to its angular velocity vector; that is, to have the angular momentum vector be

$$\mathbf{L} = \lambda\boldsymbol{\omega}.$$

This leads us to the eigenvalue equation

$$\mathbf{I}|\mathbf{u}\rangle = \lambda|\mathbf{u}\rangle.$$

The roots of the resultant secular equation are the principal moments of inertia, and the eigenvectors designate the directions of the principal axes. Utilizing the results for the moment of inertia and products of inertia of a rectangular parallelepiped found in Section 9–3, we obtain for $a = b = c$ the moment-of-inertia matrix

$$(\mathbf{I}) = Ma^2 \begin{bmatrix} \frac{2}{3} & -\frac{1}{4} & -\frac{1}{4} \\ -\frac{1}{4} & \frac{2}{3} & -\frac{1}{4} \\ -\frac{1}{4} & -\frac{1}{4} & \frac{2}{3} \end{bmatrix}.$$

Setting $\lambda = Ma^2 K$, we obtain the secular equation

$$Ma^2 \begin{vmatrix} \frac{2}{3} - K & -\frac{1}{4} & -\frac{1}{4} \\ -\frac{1}{4} & \frac{2}{3} - K & -\frac{1}{4} \\ -\frac{1}{4} & -\frac{1}{4} & \frac{2}{3} - K \end{vmatrix} = 0$$

or

$$(K - \tfrac{11}{12})^2 (K - \tfrac{1}{6}) = 0.$$

The principal moments of inertia are thus

$$I_1 = I_2 = \tfrac{11}{12}Ma^2 \quad \text{and} \quad I_3 = \tfrac{1}{6}Ma^2.$$

For $K = \frac{1}{6}$ the components of the eigenvector are obtainable from the equations

$$(\tfrac{2}{3} - \tfrac{1}{6})u_1 - \tfrac{1}{4}u_2 = \tfrac{1}{4}u_3$$

and

$$-\tfrac{1}{4}u_1 + (\tfrac{2}{3} - \tfrac{1}{6})u_2 = \tfrac{1}{4}u_3.$$

These yield

$$u_1 = u_2 = u_3,$$

which means that the principal axis lies along the [1, 1, 1]-direction.

The other eigenvectors are determined from

$$(\tfrac{2}{3} - \tfrac{11}{12})u_1 = \tfrac{1}{4}u_2 + \tfrac{1}{4}u_3.$$

That is, the principal axes are directed along the vectors designated by

$$[-(u_2 + u_3), u_2, u_3]$$

for any value of $u_2$ and $u_3$. All these vectors lie in a plane normal to the [1,1,1]-direction as can be verified by taking the vector product of the latter principal axes with the vector lying along the [1, 1, 1]-direction. Any two linearly independent vectors in the [1, 1, 1]-plane may thus be chosen as the principal axes. It is customary, however, to choose two vectors which are orthogonal. If two vectors obtained for arbitrary values of $u_2$ and $u_3$ are not orthogonal, then a new orthogonal set may readily be obtained through the use of the *Schmidt orthogonalization method* to be discussed below.

This eigenvalue problem is analogous to the mathematical problem of finding the coordinate system with respect to which the ellipsoid

$$I_{xx}x^2 + I_{yy}y^2 + I_{zz}z^2 + 2I_{xy}xy + 2I_{xz}xz + 2I_{yz}yz = C \qquad (10\text{--}130)$$

has the simpler form

$$I_1 x'^2 + I_2 y'^2 + I_3 z'^2 = C. \qquad (10\text{--}131)$$

The surface generated by Eq. (10–130) is referred to as the *moment-of-inertia ellipsoid.* We can now understand that the coincidence of two of the principal moments of inertia implies that the moment-of-inertia ellipsoid is an ellipsoid of revolution. Any axis perpendicular to the principal axis associated with the discrete principal moment of inertia can thus be taken as another principal axis.

▶ As a second example, we refer to the problem of the two coupled harmonic oscillators discussed in Section 8–11. We found this problem to be invariant under a permutation of the two particles, which operation is mathematically expressed by the permutation operator

$$\mathbf{P} \leftrightarrow \begin{bmatrix} 0 & 1 \\ 1 & 0 \end{bmatrix}$$

operating on the two-dimensional position vector

$$|\mathbf{r}\rangle \leftrightarrow \begin{bmatrix} x_1 \\ x_2 \end{bmatrix}$$

of the particles:

$$(\mathbf{P}) \begin{bmatrix} x_1 \\ x_2 \end{bmatrix} = \begin{bmatrix} x_2 \\ x_1 \end{bmatrix}.$$

The eigenvalue equation for this permutation operator is

$$\mathbf{P}|\mathbf{u}\rangle = \lambda|\mathbf{u}\rangle,$$

which yields the secular equation

$$\begin{vmatrix} -\lambda & 1 \\ 1 & -\lambda \end{vmatrix} = 0$$

having the roots

$$\lambda = \pm 1.$$

The normalized eigenvectors of the permutation operator associated with the eigenvalue $\lambda_1 = +1$ is

$$|\mathbf{u}_1\rangle \leftrightarrow \frac{1}{\sqrt{2}} \begin{bmatrix} 1 \\ 1 \end{bmatrix}.$$

The normalized eigenvector associated with the eigenvalue $\lambda_2 = -1$ is

$$|\mathbf{u}_2\rangle \leftrightarrow \frac{1}{\sqrt{2}} \begin{bmatrix} 1 \\ -1 \end{bmatrix}.$$

In terms of these eigenvectors, we find the position vector to be

$$|\mathbf{r}\rangle = \xi_1|\mathbf{u}_1\rangle + \xi_2|\mathbf{u}_2\rangle$$

or

$$\begin{bmatrix} x_1 \\ x_2 \end{bmatrix} = \frac{\xi_1}{\sqrt{2}} \begin{bmatrix} 1 \\ 1 \end{bmatrix} + \frac{\xi_2}{\sqrt{2}} \begin{bmatrix} 1 \\ -1 \end{bmatrix}.$$

This yields

$$x_1 = \frac{1}{\sqrt{2}} (\xi_1 + \xi_2) \quad \text{and} \quad x_2 = \frac{1}{\sqrt{2}} (\xi_1 - \xi_2)$$

or

$$\xi_1 = \frac{1}{\sqrt{2}} (x_1 + x_2) \quad \text{and} \quad \xi_2 = \frac{1}{\sqrt{2}} (x_1 - x_2),$$

which are the even and odd normal coordinates. ◀

Of special interest are the eigenvalues and eigenvectors of the *normal operators*, which are operators which commute with their Hermitian adjoint:

$$\mathbf{L}\mathbf{L}^\dagger = \mathbf{L}^\dagger\mathbf{L}. \tag{10–132}$$

These operators are important in that their normalized eigenvectors, as shall be shown, are orthogonal to each other and satisfy the equation

$$\langle \mathbf{u}_i | \mathbf{u}_j \rangle = \delta_{ij}. \tag{10–133}$$

They may therefore be chosen as the orthonormal set of base vectors. If they are used as base vectors, then the matrix representation of the normal operator **L**, whose eigenvectors they are, assumes its simplest form, which is diagonal. This may be readily recognized by finding the matrix elements of **L**, which by Eq. (10–119) are given as

$$L_{ij} = \langle \mathbf{u}_i | \mathbf{L} | \mathbf{u}_j \rangle = \lambda_j \langle \mathbf{u}_i | \mathbf{u}_j \rangle. \tag{10–134}$$

We now proceed to prove Eq. (10–133). Operating on the eigenvalue equation

$$\mathbf{L} | \mathbf{u}_i \rangle = \lambda_i | \mathbf{u}_i \rangle$$

by $\mathbf{L}^\dagger$, we obtain the equation

$$\mathbf{L}^\dagger \mathbf{L} | \mathbf{u}_i \rangle = \lambda_i \mathbf{L}^\dagger | \mathbf{u}_i \rangle \tag{10–135}$$

or by Eq. (10–132),

$$\mathbf{L}\mathbf{L}^\dagger | \mathbf{u}_i \rangle = \lambda_i \mathbf{L}^\dagger | \mathbf{u}_i \rangle. \tag{10–136}$$

We have thus found that the vector $\mathbf{L}^\dagger | \mathbf{u}_i \rangle$ is also an eigenvector of the operator **L**, associated with the same eigenvalue $\lambda_i$ as the vector $| \mathbf{u}_i \rangle$. But if the $\lambda_i$'s are distinct, then only one eigenvector is associated with each $\lambda_i$. Hence it follows that for discrete eigenvalues we can set

$$\mathbf{L}^\dagger | \mathbf{u}_i \rangle = c_i | \mathbf{u}_i \rangle, \tag{10–137}$$

which yields

$$\langle \mathbf{u}_i | \mathbf{L}^\dagger \mathbf{L} | \mathbf{u}_i \rangle = \langle \mathbf{u}_i | \lambda_i \mathbf{L}^\dagger | \mathbf{u}_i \rangle = \lambda_i c_i \langle \mathbf{u}_i | \mathbf{u}_i \rangle. \tag{10–138}$$

The Hermitian adjoint of this equation yields the result

$$\langle \mathbf{u}_i | \mathbf{L}^\dagger \mathbf{L} | \mathbf{u}_i \rangle^\dagger = \langle \mathbf{u}_i | \mathbf{L}\mathbf{L}^\dagger | \mathbf{u}_i \rangle = \lambda_i^* c_i^* \langle \mathbf{u}_i | \mathbf{u}_i \rangle. \tag{10–139}$$

Equations (10–138) and (10–139) tell us that

$$\lambda_i c_i = \lambda_i^* c_i^*,$$

which implies that $\lambda_i c_i$ is real or that

$$c_i = \lambda_i^*. \tag{10–140}$$

Hence we obtain the result

$$\lambda_i c_i = |\lambda_i|^2.$$

Having found that $\mathbf{L}^\dagger \mathbf{L}|\mathbf{u}_j\rangle = |\lambda_j|^2|\mathbf{u}_j\rangle$, it follows that

$$\langle\mathbf{u}_i|\mathbf{L}^\dagger\mathbf{L}|\mathbf{u}_j\rangle = |\lambda_j|^2\langle\mathbf{u}_i|\mathbf{u}_j\rangle,$$

whose Hermitian adjoint is

$$|\lambda_j|^2\langle\mathbf{u}_j|\mathbf{u}_i\rangle = \langle\mathbf{u}_j|\mathbf{L}^\dagger\mathbf{L}|\mathbf{u}_i\rangle = |\lambda_i|^2\langle\mathbf{u}_j|\mathbf{u}_i\rangle$$

or

$$[|\lambda_i|^2 - |\lambda_j|^2]\langle\mathbf{u}_j|\mathbf{u}_i\rangle = 0.$$

If $\lambda_i \neq \lambda_j$, we obtain the result we set out to prove,

$$\langle\mathbf{u}_j|\mathbf{u}_i\rangle = 0. \tag{10–141}$$

Since the $|\mathbf{u}_j\rangle$'s were assumed to have been normalized, Eq. (10–133) follows. We have thus shown the normalized eigenvectors associated with different eigenvalues of a normal operator to form an orthonormal set of vectors.

We note that a Hermitian operator is a normal operator, whence it follows that the normalized eigenvectors of a Hermitian operator form an orthonormal set of vectors, and a Hermitian operator can be expressed as

$$\mathbf{H} = \sum_i h_i|\mathbf{u}_i\rangle\langle\mathbf{u}_i|, \tag{10–142}$$

where the $h_i$'s are its eigenvalues.

We proceed to show that the eigenvalues of a Hermitian operator are real. This follows quite readily from

$$\langle\mathbf{u}_i|\mathbf{H}|\mathbf{u}_i\rangle = \langle\mathbf{u}_i|\mathbf{H}^\dagger|\mathbf{u}_i\rangle,$$

and from the fact that the eigenvalues of the Hermitian adjoint of a normal operator are the complex conjugates of the eigenvalues of the operator (cf. Eq. 10–140). Hence

$$h_i = h_i^*, \tag{10–143}$$

which proves that the $h_i$'s are real.

In the case of a degeneracy, that is, if two or more eigenvectors of a normal operator are associated with the same eigenvalue, we see clearly that the eigenvectors associated with different eigenvalues are still orthogonal to each other.

As for the $k$ eigenvectors associated with a $k$-fold degenerate eigenvalue $\lambda_i$ (a $k$th-order root of the secular equation), it is always possible to construct from these $k$ linearly independent eigenvectors $k$ linear combinations which are orthogonal to each other and also, of course, to the eigenvectors of the normal operator which are associated with the eigenvalue $\lambda_j \neq \lambda_i$. The method for constructing these mutually orthogonal vectors is known as the Schmidt orthogonalization process for a set of linearly independent unit vectors $|\mathbf{u}_i\rangle$. We assume that the vectors $|\mathbf{u}_i\rangle$ are unit vectors. If they are not, they can readily be made so.

The Schmidt orthogonalization method consists of setting

$$|\mathbf{u}_1'\rangle = |\mathbf{u}_1\rangle,$$
$$|\mathbf{u}_2'\rangle = \alpha_2[|\mathbf{u}_1\rangle + \beta_2|\mathbf{u}_2\rangle],$$
$$|\mathbf{u}_3'\rangle = \alpha_3[|\mathbf{u}_1\rangle + \beta_3|\mathbf{u}_2\rangle + \gamma_3|\mathbf{u}_3\rangle]$$

and then adjusting $\alpha_2$ and $\beta_2$ so that

$$\langle \mathbf{u}_2'|\mathbf{u}_2'\rangle = 1 \quad \text{and} \quad \langle \mathbf{u}_2|\mathbf{u}_1\rangle = 0.$$

This gives us two equations which we can solve for $\alpha_2$ and $\beta_2$, yielding

$$\beta_2 = -\frac{1}{\langle \mathbf{u}_1'|\mathbf{u}_2\rangle} \quad \text{and} \quad \alpha_2 = (\beta^2 - 1)^{-1/2}.$$

The values of $\alpha_3$, $\beta_3$, and $\gamma_3$ are in turn obtained from the three equations

$$\langle \mathbf{u}_3'|\mathbf{u}_3'\rangle = 1, \quad \langle \mathbf{u}_3'|\mathbf{u}_2'\rangle = 0, \quad \langle \mathbf{u}_3'|\mathbf{u}_1'\rangle = 0.$$

This process can be continued until we obtain $k$ new unit vectors which are orthogonal to each other and, of course, also to the eigenvectors associated with different eigenvalues. The general formula for the $i$th vector can be written as

$$|\mathbf{u}_i'\rangle = \alpha_i\left[ \mathbf{1} - \sum_{j=1}^{i-1} |\mathbf{u}_j'\rangle\langle \mathbf{u}_j'| \right]|\mathbf{u}_i\rangle, \tag{10–144}$$

where $\alpha_i$ is the normalization constant which makes

$$\langle \mathbf{u}_i'|\mathbf{u}_i'\rangle = 1.$$

For the degenerate eigenvalues of the moment-of-inertia operator of the uniform cube considered above, we find the two eigenvectors

$$\langle \mathbf{u}_1| \leftrightarrow \frac{1}{\sqrt{2}}[-1, 1, 0]$$

and

$$\langle \mathbf{u}_2| \leftrightarrow \frac{1}{\sqrt{2}}[-1, 0, 1]$$

by setting first $u_3$ and then $u_2$ equal to zero.

These two vectors are not orthogonal to each other. We can, however, obtain the two eigenvectors

$$\langle \mathbf{u}_1'| = \langle \mathbf{u}_1| \leftrightarrow \frac{1}{\sqrt{2}}[-1, 1, 0]$$

and

$$\langle \mathbf{u}_2'| = \alpha[\langle \mathbf{u}_1| + \beta\langle \mathbf{u}_2|],$$

which, for the proper value of $\beta$, are orthogonal to each other. We find

$$\beta = -\frac{1}{\langle \mathbf{u}_2|\mathbf{u}_1\rangle} = -2$$

to be such a value. For $\langle \mathbf{u}_2'|$ to be normalized $\alpha$ must then have the value $1/\sqrt{3}$. Hence

$$\langle \mathbf{u}_2'| \leftrightarrow \frac{1}{\sqrt{3}}\left[\frac{1}{\sqrt{2}}, \frac{1}{\sqrt{2}}, -\frac{2}{\sqrt{2}}\right].$$

We note that the moment-of-inertia operator of a rigid body, being a real symmetric operator, is Hermitian. There always exist therefore three mutually perpendicular vectors for which

$$\mathbf{I}|\mathbf{u}_i\rangle = I_i|\mathbf{u}_i\rangle,$$

where the $I_i$'s are referred to as principal moments of inertia, and where the unit vectors $|\mathbf{u}_i\rangle$ determine the principal axes of the rigid body. With respect to the principal axes, the moment-of-inertia matrix (tensor) assumes its simplest form whose off-diagonal elements, which are the products of inertia, vanish.

## 10–10 Simultaneous diagonalization of commuting normal operators

Two or more commuting operators which operate on vectors of the same vector space can be shown to have a common set of eigenvectors.

If the eigenvectors of the operators are nondegenerate, the proof of the above statement follows readily. Consider the two commuting operators $\mathbf{L}_1$ and $\mathbf{L}_2$. Letting $|\mathbf{u}_i\rangle$ represent the eigenvectors associated with the nondegenerate eigenvalues of the operator $\mathbf{L}_1$ such that

$$\mathbf{L}_1|\mathbf{u}_i\rangle = \lambda_i|\mathbf{u}_i\rangle,$$

we find that when we operate on this equation with $\mathbf{L}_2$ we obtain

$$\mathbf{L}_2\mathbf{L}_1|\mathbf{u}_i\rangle = \mathbf{L}_1\mathbf{L}_2|\mathbf{u}_i\rangle = \lambda_i\mathbf{L}_2|\mathbf{u}_i\rangle.$$

Thus we see that $\mathbf{L}_2|\mathbf{u}_i\rangle$ is also an eigenvector of the operator $\mathbf{L}_1$ associated with the eigenvalue $\lambda_i$. Since $\lambda_i$ is a nondegenerate eigenvalue, it follows that

$$\mathbf{L}_2|\mathbf{u}_i\rangle = c_i|\mathbf{u}_i\rangle,$$

which proves that $|\mathbf{u}_i\rangle$ is also an eigenvector of $\mathbf{L}_2$.

If $\lambda_i$ has more than one eigenvector associated with it, the eigenvectors $|u_i^{(k)}\rangle$, then the eigenvector $L_2|u_i^{(1)}\rangle$ of $L_1$ is expressible as a linear sum of the eigenvectors $|u_i^{(k)}\rangle$ of $L_1$ associated with the eigenvalue $\lambda_i$, that is,

$$L_2|u_i^{(1)}\rangle = \sum_j \alpha_j^{(1)}|u_i^{(j)}\rangle.$$

Similarly,

$$L_2|u_i^{(k)}\rangle = \sum_j \alpha_j^{(k)}|u_i^{(j)}\rangle.$$

For simplicity, let us assume that there are two eigenvectors associated with the eigenvalue $\lambda_i$. We then have

$$L_2|u_i^{(1)}\rangle = \alpha_1^{(1)}|u_i^{(1)}\rangle + \alpha_2^{(1)}|u_i^{(2)}\rangle \tag{10-145}$$

and

$$L_2|u_i^{(2)}\rangle = \alpha_1^{(2)}|u_i^{(1)}\rangle + \alpha_2^{(2)}|u_i^{(2)}\rangle.$$

We can now inquire into the existence of a linear combination of $|u_i^{(1)}\rangle$ and $|u_i^{(2)}\rangle$ which are eigenvectors of $L_2$. That is, we seek

$$|v_i\rangle = A|u_i^{(1)}\rangle + B|u_i^{(2)}\rangle$$

which satisfies the equation

$$L_2|v_i\rangle = K|v_i\rangle,$$

or

$$L_2[A|u_i^{(1)}\rangle + B|u_i^{(2)}\rangle] = K[A|u_i^{(1)}\rangle + B|u_i^{(2)}\rangle].$$

This is an eigenvalue equation which, through the use of Eq. (10-145), leads to

$$\{A[\alpha_1^{(1)} - K] + B\alpha_1^{(2)}\}|u_i^{(1)}\rangle + \{A\alpha_2^{(1)} + B[\alpha_2^{(2)} - K]\}|u_i^{(2)}\rangle = 0.$$

If the eigenvectors $|u_i^{(k)}\rangle$ were chosen to be orthogonal to each other, then their coefficients in the previous equation vanish,

$$A(\alpha_1^{(1)} - K) + B\alpha_1^{(2)} = 0$$

and

$$A\alpha_2^{(1)} + B(\alpha_2^{(2)} - K) = 0.$$

These simultaneous equations can be solved for $A$ and $B$ only if the determinant of their coefficients vanishes,

$$\begin{vmatrix} \alpha_1^{(1)} - K & \alpha_1^{(2)} \\ \alpha_2^{(1)} & \alpha_2^{(2)} - K \end{vmatrix} = 0.$$

This determinantal equation yields two roots or two eigenvalues of $L_2$, and hence two eigenvectors of $L_2$. In this fashion, all the eigenvectors of $L_1$ can be adjusted to be also simultaneous eigenvectors of $L_2$. Conversely, all the eigenvectors of $L_2$ can be adjusted to be simultaneous eigenvectors of $L_1$, which proves the initial statement.

The extension of this theorem to three or more commuting operators is left as an exercise for the reader. The use of the set of simultaneous orthonormal eigenvectors of a set of commuting normal operators as base vectors of the vector space will yield diagonal representations for the normal commuting operators.

What we have found is a very important and useful result. As an example, we refer once more to the two coupled harmonic oscillator problem of Section 8–11. The equations of motion for the two particles are expressible in terms of the differential operator $L$ whose matrix representation is given by

$$L \leftrightarrow \begin{bmatrix} m\,\dfrac{d^2}{dt^2} + 2k & -k \\[2mm] -k & m\,\dfrac{d^2}{dt^2} + 2k \end{bmatrix}.$$

That is, Eqs. (8–156) and (8–157) are expressible as

$$L|x\rangle = 0,$$

where

$$|x\rangle \leftrightarrow \begin{bmatrix} x_1 \\ x_2 \end{bmatrix}.$$

Now, we found that the permutation operation leaves the equations of motions invariant,

$$PL|x\rangle = PLP^{-1}P|x\rangle = LP|x\rangle.$$

This means that

$$PLP^{-1} = L \quad \text{or} \quad PL = LP.$$

That is, the permutation operator commutes with the differential operator $L$ as can also be verified directly. It follows therefore that there is a linear combination of the eigenvectors of $L$ associated with the eigenvalue zero which are simultaneously eigenvectors of the permutation operator $P$. In fact, the solutions we obtained were themselves the simultaneous eigenvectors. Conversely, the nondegenerate eigenvectors of $P$ are simultaneously eigenvectors of $L$. Indeed the eigenvectors

$$|v_1\rangle \leftrightarrow \frac{x_1 + x_2}{2} \begin{bmatrix} 1 \\ 1 \end{bmatrix}, \qquad |v_2\rangle \leftrightarrow \frac{x_1 - x_2}{2} \begin{bmatrix} 1 \\ -1 \end{bmatrix}$$

of $P$ are also eigenvectors of $L$. Such symmetry considerations are very helpful and are used extensively for simplifying the solution of the equations of motion of a system of coupled oscillators (cf. Problem 11–23).

## Problems

10–1. Compute each of the following matrix products:

(a) $\begin{bmatrix} 3 & 2 & 1 \\ 6 & 2 & 1 \\ 1 & 0 & 1 \end{bmatrix} \begin{bmatrix} -1 & 0 & 0 \\ 1 & 2 & 1 \\ 0 & 1 & 1 \end{bmatrix}$

(b) $\begin{bmatrix} 2 & 3 & 1 & 4 \end{bmatrix} \begin{bmatrix} -2 & 1 \\ 1 & 1 \\ 1 & 2 \\ -1 & 1 \end{bmatrix}$

(c) $\begin{bmatrix} 3 & 1 & 2 & 0 \\ 0 & 6 & 0 & 1 \\ 4 & 1 & 3 & 2 \\ 1 & 1 & 1 & 1 \end{bmatrix} \begin{bmatrix} 1 \\ 1 \\ -1 \\ -1 \end{bmatrix}$

(d) $\begin{bmatrix} 1 & 0 & 3 \\ 2 & 0 & 1 \\ 1 & -1 & 0 \end{bmatrix} \begin{bmatrix} -1 & 0 & 2 \\ 1 & 1 & 0 \\ 3 & 0 & 0 \end{bmatrix} \begin{bmatrix} 0 & 1 & 0 \\ 0 & 2 & 0 \\ 1 & 0 & 2 \end{bmatrix}$

10–2. Identify the nonsingular matrices among the following, and find their inverse matrices.

(a) $\begin{bmatrix} 2 & 0 & 1 \\ 1 & 1 & -1 \\ 0 & 3 & 1 \end{bmatrix}$

(b) $\begin{bmatrix} 0 & 3 & 3 \\ -1 & 0 & 2 \\ 2 & 1 & 1 \end{bmatrix}$

(c) $\begin{bmatrix} 1 & 1 & 0 \\ 1 & 2 & 1 \\ -1 & 1 & 2 \end{bmatrix}$

10–3. Express each of the matrices of the previous problem as a sum of a symmetric and an antisymmetric matrix.

10–4. (a) Obtain the vectors reciprocal to the set of vectors represented by the following matrices:

$$[3, 2, 1], \quad [4, 3, -4], \quad \text{and} \quad [-7, 3, 1].$$

(b) Express the vector $[6, 8, 1]$ as a linear combination of the vectors of Part (a).

10–5. (a) Utilize the Schmidt orthogonalization method to obtain a set of orthonormal vectors from the vectors of Problem 10–4(a).

(b) Repeat part (a) for the vectors $[1, 0, 0]$, $[1, 1, 0]$ and $[1, 1, 1]$.

10–6. (a) Show that the nonvanishing of the determinant

$$\begin{vmatrix} M_{11}^{(1)} & M_{11}^{(2)} & \cdots & \cdots & M_{11}^{(n^2)} \\ M_{12}^{(1)} & M_{12}^{(2)} & & & M_{12}^{(n^2)} \\ \vdots & \vdots & & & \vdots \\ M_{1n}^{(1)} & M_{1n}^{(2)} & & & \\ M_{21}^{(1)} & M_{21}^{(2)} & & & \\ \vdots & & & & \\ M_{2n}^{(1)} & & & & \\ M_{31}^{(1)} & & & & \\ \vdots & & & & \vdots \\ M_{nn}^{(1)} & M_{nn}^{(2)} & \cdots & \cdots & M_{nn}^{(n^2)} \end{vmatrix}$$

formed from the elements of the $n^2$ $n \times n$ matrices $(\mathbf{M}^{(k)})$ is a necessary and sufficient condition for linear independence of the $n^2$ matrices.

(b) Show that the Pauli matrices

$$(\mathbf{M}^{(1)}) = \begin{bmatrix} 0 & 1 \\ 1 & 0 \end{bmatrix}, \qquad (\mathbf{M}^{(2)}) = i \begin{bmatrix} 0 & 1 \\ -1 & 0 \end{bmatrix}, \qquad (\mathbf{M}^{(3)}) = \begin{bmatrix} 1 & 0 \\ 0 & -1 \end{bmatrix},$$

and the unit matrix

$$(\mathbf{M}^{(4)}) = \begin{bmatrix} 1 & 0 \\ 0 & 1 \end{bmatrix}$$

are four linearly independent $2 \times 2$ matrices.

(c) Express the matrix

$$\begin{bmatrix} 2 & 1 \\ 0 & -3 \end{bmatrix}$$

as a linear combination of the four matrices $(\mathbf{M}^{(i)})$ of Part (b).

10-7. Form the direct products $(\mathbf{A}) \otimes (\mathbf{B})$ of the following matrices:

(a)   $(\mathbf{A}) = \begin{bmatrix} 1 \\ 3 \\ -1 \end{bmatrix}$   and   $(\mathbf{B}) = [2, 2, -1]$

(b)   $(\mathbf{A}) = \begin{bmatrix} 1 \\ 3 \\ -1 \end{bmatrix}$   and   $(\mathbf{B}) = \begin{bmatrix} 2 \\ 2 \\ -1 \end{bmatrix}$

(c)   $(\mathbf{A}) = \begin{bmatrix} 2 & 3 \\ 1 & 2 \\ -1 & 4 \end{bmatrix}$   and   $(\mathbf{B}) = [3, 0, 2]$

10-8. (a) Transform the operator $\mathbf{M} = |A)(B| + |B)(A|$, where $(A| \leftrightarrow [5, -3, 2]$ and $(B| \leftrightarrow [0, 5, 10]$, into a coordinate system rotated $45°$ about the $z$-axis by using Eq. (10–107).

(b) Transform the vectors $|A)$ and $|B)$ by using Eq. (10–102), and show that $\mathbf{M}' = |A')(B'| - |B')(A'|$ agrees with $\mathbf{M}'$ as obtained in Part (a).

10-9. (a) Obtain the inverse of the Lorentz transformation matrix

$$\begin{bmatrix} \dfrac{1}{\sqrt{1 - V^2/c^2}} & 0 & 0 & -\dfrac{iV}{c}\dfrac{1}{\sqrt{1 - V^2/c^2}} \\[2ex] 0 & 1 & 0 & 0 \\[1ex] 0 & 0 & 1 & 0 \\[1ex] \dfrac{iV}{c}\dfrac{1}{\sqrt{1 - V^2/c^2}} & 0 & 0 & \dfrac{1}{\sqrt{1 - V^2/c^2}} \end{bmatrix}$$

which transforms the description of a relativistic event (a vector in relativistic four-space) of a particle from one (primed) inertial coordinate system to another (unprimed), where the first system is moving with speed $V$ along the positive $x$-axis with respect to the second system.

(b) Given that under a Lorentz transformation the electromagnetic field transforms like the matrix elements of an operator, obtain the Lorentz transformation equations of the electric- and magnetic-field vectors whose components constitute the elements of the electromagnetic-field matrix

$$(\mathbf{F}) = \begin{bmatrix} 0 & cB_z & -cB_y & -iE_x \\ -cB_z & 0 & cB_x & -iE_y \\ cB_y & -cB_x & 0 & -iE_z \\ iE_x & iE_y & iE_z & 0 \end{bmatrix}.$$

10–10. The trace of a square matrix $(\mathbf{M})$ is defined by the equation

$$\text{Trace } (\mathbf{M}) = \sum_i M_{ii}.$$

(a) Show that the trace of the matrix representation of an operator is invariant under a unitary transformation.

(b) Show that the sum $\sum_{ij} M_{ij} N_{ji}$ formed from the matrix elements of the square matrices $(\mathbf{M})$ and $(\mathbf{N})$ is invariant under a unitary transformation.

(c) Show that from the matrix elements of the electromagnetic-field matrix of the previous problem we can form the invariant $(c^2 B^2 - E^2)$.

(d) Show that the eigenvalues of a square matrix are invariant under a unitary transformation.

(e) Show that hence the determinant value of a square matrix is an invariant under a unitary transformation.

(f) Show that with the result of part (e) we can obtain the Lorentz invariant expression $\mathbf{B} \cdot \mathbf{E}$ from the electromagnetic-field matrix of Problem 10–9.

10–11. Diagonalize the following matrices

(a) $\begin{bmatrix} 3 & -1 \\ -1 & 3 \end{bmatrix}$

(b) $\begin{bmatrix} 0 & 5 & 10 \\ 0 & -3 & 6 \\ 0 & -3 & 4 \end{bmatrix}$

(c) $\begin{bmatrix} 7 & \sqrt{6} & -\sqrt{3} \\ \sqrt{6} & 2 & -5\sqrt{2} \\ -\sqrt{3} & -5\sqrt{2} & -3 \end{bmatrix}$

(d) $\begin{bmatrix} 2 & 2 & 3 \\ 1 & 3 & 3 \\ 1 & 2 & 4 \end{bmatrix}$

(e) $\begin{bmatrix} 20 & 0 & 16 \\ 0 & 9 & 0 \\ 16 & 0 & 20 \end{bmatrix}$

(f) $\begin{bmatrix} 1 & i \\ -i & 1 \end{bmatrix}$

10–12. (a) Show that the eigenvalues of an antisymmetric matrix are imaginary or zero.

(b) Obtain the eigenvalues and a set of eigenvectors of the antisymmetric angular velocity matrix

$$\begin{bmatrix} 0 & -\omega_z & \omega_y \\ \omega_z & 0 & -\omega_x \\ -\omega_y & \omega_x & 0 \end{bmatrix}.$$

10–13. (a) Do Problem 9–4. (b) Do Problem 9–5.

10–14. Utilize the results of Problem 9–1(a) to obtain the moment of inertia of a circular cone about a slant height.

10–15. Solve the matrix equation

$$(R)(X) = (S)$$

for the matrix $(X)$, given that

$$(R) = \begin{bmatrix} 2 & 2 \\ 1 & 3 \end{bmatrix}, \qquad (S) = \begin{bmatrix} 2 & -1 \\ 3 & 5 \end{bmatrix}.$$

10–16. Given that the definition of the $n$th power of a square matrix $(M)$, where $n$ is an integer, is expressed by $(M)^n = (M)(M)(M) \cdots [n \text{ factors}]$, show that:

(a) The transformation which diagonalizes $(M)$ also diagonalizes $(M)^n$.

(b) The eigenvalues of $(M)^n$ are the eigenvalues of $(M)$ raised to the power $n$.

(c) If

$$\sum_{i=0}^{n} C_i(M)^2 = 0, \qquad \text{then} \qquad \sum_{i=1}^{n} C_i\lambda^2 = 0,$$

where $\lambda$ is an eigenvalue of $(M)$.

(d) $\dfrac{1}{(1) - (M)} \equiv \{(1) - (M)\}^{-1} = (1) + (M) + (M)^2 + \cdots$

10–17. The definition of $(M)^{1/n}$, where $n$ an integer, for a square matrix $(M)$ is expressed by

$$\{(M)^{1/n}\}^n = (M).$$

(a) Show that the eigenvalues of $(M)^{1/n}$ are $\lambda^{1/n}$ where $\lambda$ are the eigenvalues of $(M)$.

(b) Obtain the matrix $(M)$ which satisfies the equation

$$(M)^2 = \begin{bmatrix} 1 & 0 & 5 \\ 0 & -2 & 0 \\ 5 & 0 & 1 \end{bmatrix}.$$

10–18. If $f(x)$ is a continuous function of $x$ which is expandable in a power series in $x$, that is, if

$$f(x) = \sum_n a_n x^n,$$

then by the function $f(\mathbf{M})$ of the operator $\mathbf{M}$, we understand the following:

$$f(\mathbf{M}) = \sum_n a_n \mathbf{M}^n.$$

Show that the transformation operator

$$\mathbf{R}_z(\phi_3) \leftrightarrow \begin{bmatrix} \cos\phi_3 & -\sin\phi_3 & 0 \\ \sin\phi_3 & \cos\phi_3 & 0 \\ 0 & 0 & 1 \end{bmatrix}$$

for the rotation of a vector about the $z$-axis through an angle $\phi_3$, such that $|\mathbf{r}') = \mathbf{R}|\mathbf{r})$, is expressible as

$$\mathbf{R}_z(\phi_3) = 1 + \{-i\phi_3\mathbf{M}_3\} + \frac{1}{2!}\{-i\phi_3\mathbf{M}_3^2\} + \cdots$$
$$= e^{i\phi_3\mathbf{M}_3},$$

where

$$\mathbf{M}_3 \leftrightarrow \begin{bmatrix} 0 & -i & 0 \\ i & 0 & 0 \\ 0 & 0 & 0 \end{bmatrix}.$$

Similarly, show that

$$\mathbf{R}_x(\phi_1) = e^{-i\phi_1\mathbf{M}_1} \qquad \text{and} \qquad \mathbf{R}_y(\phi_2) = e^{-i\phi_2\mathbf{M}_2},$$

where

$$\mathbf{M}_1 \leftrightarrow \begin{bmatrix} 0 & 0 & 0 \\ 0 & 0 & -i \\ 0 & i & 0 \end{bmatrix}, \qquad \mathbf{M}_2 \leftrightarrow \begin{bmatrix} 0 & 0 & i \\ 0 & 0 & 0 \\ -i & 0 & 0 \end{bmatrix}.$$

10–19. A matrix group is defined as a set of square matrices satisfying the following properties.

(a) The unit matrix is a member of the group.

(b) For every member of the group there is another member in the group which is its inverse.

(c) The matrix product of two members of the group yields a matrix which is also a member of the group.

Show that the set of matrices

$$(\mathbf{M}_1) = \begin{bmatrix} 1 & 0 \\ 0 & 1 \end{bmatrix}, \qquad (\mathbf{M}_2) = \begin{bmatrix} -\frac{1}{2} & \sqrt{3}/2 \\ -\sqrt{3}/2 & -\frac{1}{2} \end{bmatrix},$$

$$(\mathbf{M}_3) = \begin{bmatrix} -\frac{1}{2} & -\sqrt{3}/2 \\ \sqrt{3}/2 & -\frac{1}{2} \end{bmatrix}, \qquad (\mathbf{M}_4) = \begin{bmatrix} -1 & 0 \\ 0 & 1 \end{bmatrix},$$

$$(\mathbf{M}_5) = \begin{bmatrix} \frac{1}{2} & -\sqrt{3}/2 \\ -\sqrt{3}/2 & -\frac{1}{2} \end{bmatrix}, \qquad (\mathbf{M}_6) = \begin{bmatrix} 1 & 0 \\ 0 & 1 \end{bmatrix}$$

form a matrix group.

10–20. (a) Obtain the simultaneous eigenvectors of the two commuting matrices

$$(\mathbf{A}) = \begin{bmatrix} 7 & 5 & 0 \\ -1 & 1 & 0 \\ -2 & -2 & 1 \end{bmatrix} \quad \text{and} \quad (\mathbf{B}) = \begin{bmatrix} 3 & -5 & 0 \\ 1 & 9 & 0 \\ 2 & 2 & 8 \end{bmatrix}$$

and their eigenvalues.

(b) Obtain the transformation matrix which diagonalizes the two matrices simultaneously.

10–21. Prove that

(a) $\{\mathbf{AB}\}^{-1} = \mathbf{B}^{-1}\mathbf{A}^{-1}$,

(b) $\{\mathbf{AB}\}^{\dagger} = \mathbf{B}^{\dagger}\mathbf{A}^{\dagger}$,

where $\mathbf{A}$ and $\mathbf{B}$ are two operators.

10–22. The derivative of a matrix $(\mathbf{M})$ is defined as the matrix whose elements are the derivatives of the matrix elements of $(\mathbf{M})$. Thus, if

$$(\mathbf{N}) = \frac{d(\mathbf{M})}{dt},$$

then

$$N_{ij} = \frac{d}{dt} M_{ij}.$$

(a) Show that the derivative with respect to $t$ of the matrix representation of an operator $\mathbf{M}$ represents the operator $d\mathbf{M}/dt$, if the orthonormal base vectors of the vector space do not depend on $t$.

(b) Show that if the base vectors do change with $t$, and if we can set

$$\frac{d|\mathbf{e})}{dt} = \Omega|\mathbf{e})$$

(we are assuming the base vectors to remain orthonormal), then the derivative $d\mathbf{M}/dt$ of the operator $\mathbf{M}$ is given by

$$\frac{d\mathbf{M}}{dt} = \frac{d'\mathbf{M}}{dt} + \Omega\mathbf{M} + \mathbf{M}\widetilde{\Omega},$$

where $d'\mathbf{M}/dt$ is the derivative of $\mathbf{M}$ with respect to the rotating coordinate system.

(c) Show that the matrix representation of $d\mathbf{M}/dt$ is given by

$$\left(\frac{d\mathbf{M}}{dt}\right) = \frac{d}{dt}(\mathbf{M}) + (\Omega)(\mathbf{M}) + (\mathbf{M})(\widetilde{\Omega}).$$

10–23. (a) Show that

$$P(a) = e^{a(d/dx)} = \sum_{n=0}^{\infty} \frac{1}{n!} a^n \frac{d^n}{dx^n}$$

is the differential operator which represents the effect on any function $\psi(x)$ of a translation of the origin of coordinates from the point $(0, 0, 0)$ to the point $(-a, 0, 0)$. That is,

$$P(a)\psi(x) = \psi(x + a).$$

(b) Show that the translation operator $P(a)$ commutes with the differential operator $d/dx$.

(c) Show that the eigenfunctions of $d/dx$ satisfying the eigenvalue equation

$$\frac{d}{dx}\psi_\lambda(x) = \lambda\psi(x)$$

are simultaneously eigenfunctions of the operator $P(a)$. Obtain the eigenvalues of $P(a)$ to which they belong. To what values are the $\lambda$'s restricted if the eigenfunctions of $P(a)$ are required to remain finite for all $x$?

(d) Show that the eigenfunctions of $d/dx$ belonging to the eigenvalue

$$\lambda = \kappa + i\left(\frac{2\pi n}{a}\right)$$

are degenerate eigenfunctions of the operator $P(a)$ belonging to the same eigenvalue. Hence show that the eigenfunctions of the operator $P(a)$ are expressible in the form

$$\Psi(\kappa, x) = e^{\kappa x}\phi(x),$$

where $\phi(x)$ is a periodic function of $x$ with period $a$.

# 11

# *The Theory of Small Oscillations*

We met the problem of coupled oscillators in Chapter 8, but postponed at that time the general treatment of the oscillatory motion of a system of particles about their configurations of stable equilibrium until after our treatment of the theory of linear transformations. Our reason for this postponement was that not until Chapter 10 did we discuss the appropriate techniques for efficiently handling the sets of simultaneous linear differential equations which occur in the problem of small oscillations of a system about a stable equilibrium configuration.

The ideal situation occurs when the coordinates chosen for the description of the motion of the system lead to a set of independent or uncoupled differential equations, whose solution can be obtained by the methods outlined in Chapter 4. While this ideal situation is not to be expected, we do find that in many problems we shall be able to obtain a set of coordinates for which the ideal situation is met. The coordinates for which the equations of motion for the system performing small oscillations about the equilibrium points are uncoupled are referred to as *normal coordinates*, and the solution to the uncoupled equations as the *normal modes of oscillation* of the system.

We shall begin by discussing the stability of the equilibrium configurations of a system of particles.

## 11–1 Conditions for the stability of an equilibrium configuration of a conservative system of particles

A system of particles is said to be in static equilibrium if all the particles are and remain at rest. This situation can occur only if the sum of the forces acting on each of the particles of the system vanishes. For a conservative system whose forces are derivable from a potential-energy function this fact is expressed by the vanishing of the generalized forces (cf. Section 9–13),

$$Q_i = -\frac{\partial U}{\partial q_i} = 0. \tag{11–1}$$

This equation yields the values $q_i^0$ of the generalized coordinates for the equilibrium configurations. While this condition is sufficient for the identification

385

of the equilibrium configurations, it is not sufficient for the determination of the stability of an equilibrium configuration. Whether or not an equilibrium configuration is stable is determined from the second-order derivatives of the potential-energy function evaluated for $q_i = q_i^0$. The general definition of a stable equilibrium is very much the same as that for the one-dimensional case. We define an equilibrium configuration as stable if for any small value of the total energy, taking the potential energy of the equilibrium configuration as zero, the kinetic energy of the system is bounded for all nearby configurations. In other words,

$$T \leq E.$$

For all nearby configurations the potential-energy function may be approximated by the first nonvanishing term in its Taylor-series expansion about the points

$$q_i = q_i^0.$$

The Taylor-series expansion of the potential-energy function is given by

$$U(q_1, q_2, \ldots, q_n) = U(q_1^0, q_2^0, \ldots, q_n^0) + \sum_i \frac{\partial U(q_1^0, q_2^0, \ldots, q_n^0)}{\partial q_i^0} x_i$$

$$+ \frac{1}{2!} \sum_{i,j} \frac{\partial^2 U(q_1^0, q_2^0, \ldots, q_n^0)}{\partial q_i^0 \, \partial q_j^0} x_i x_j + \cdots, \qquad (11\text{-}2)$$

where we have set

$$x_i = \Delta q_i = q_i - q_i^0.$$

Now by choice we make the first term $U(q_1^0, q_2^0, \ldots, q_n^0)$ in Eq. (11–2) vanish. By Eq. (11–1) the second term is found to vanish, too, whence to a first approximation we obtain

$$U(q_1, q_2, \ldots, q_n) = \mathfrak{U}(x_1, x_2, \ldots, x_n),$$

where

$$\mathfrak{U}(x_1, x_2, \ldots, x_n) = \tfrac{1}{2} \sum_{i,j} k_{ij} x_i x_j \qquad (11\text{-}3)$$

with

$$k_{ij} = \frac{\partial^2 U(q_1^0, q_2^0, \ldots, q_n^0)}{\partial q_i^0 \, \partial q_j^0} = k_{ji}. \qquad (11\text{-}4)$$

In order for the kinetic energy $T = E - \mathfrak{U}$ to be less than the total energy $E$, the potential energy for nearby configurations must be positive definite. Indeed, if for small displacements from equilibrium

$$\mathfrak{U} \geq 0, \qquad (11\text{-}5)$$

then

$$T \leq E.$$

The condition for an equilibrium configuration of an $N$-particle system to be stable is thus the same as the condition found for the one-dimensional case—that is, that the potential energy for an equilibrium configuration be a minimum with respect to the potential energy for any nearby configurations.

The conditions on the constants $k_{ij}$ which ensure that the quadratic expressions for $\mathfrak{U}(x_1, x_2, \ldots, x_n)$ be positive definite are*

$$k_{11} > 0, \qquad \begin{vmatrix} k_{11} & k_{12} \\ k_{21} & k_{22} \end{vmatrix} > 0, \qquad \begin{vmatrix} k_{11} & k_{12} & k_{13} \\ k_{21} & k_{22} & k_{23} \\ k_{31} & k_{32} & k_{33} \end{vmatrix} > 0, \qquad \text{etc.} \qquad (11\text{–}6)$$

As an example, consider the potential-energy function

$$U = -m_1 g l_1 \cos \theta_1 - m_2 g (l_1 \cos \theta_1 + l_2 \cos \theta_2) + m_1 g l_1 + m_2 g (l_1 + l_2)$$

of the double pendulum of Section 8–11. By Eq. (11–1), we must have

$$\frac{\partial U}{\partial \theta_1} = (m_1 g l_1 + m_2 g l_1) \sin \theta_1 = 0$$

and

$$\frac{\partial U}{\partial \theta_2} = m_2 g l_2 \sin \theta_2 = 0$$

for equilibrium. These conditions are satisfied by

$$\theta_1 = 0 \quad \text{or} \quad \pi \qquad \text{and} \qquad \theta_2 = 0 \quad \text{or} \quad \pi.$$

Obviously, we realize from experience that the stable equilibrium configuration occurs for $\theta_1 = \theta_2 = 0$. Let us check to see if Eq. (11–6) is satisfied only for these values of $\theta_1$ and $\theta_2$.

We find that

$$k_{11} = \frac{\partial^2 U}{\partial \theta_1^2} = (m_1 g l_1 + m_2 g l_1) \cos \theta_1$$

is positive definite only for $\theta_1 = 0$, and that since

$$k_{12} = k_{21} = 0,$$

the determinant det $(k_{ij})$ is positive definite only if $k_{22}$ is positive definite too. This leads us to $\theta_2$ being zero at the point of stable equilibrium.

---

* Cf. W. F. Osgood, *Advanced Calculus*, p. 179. New York: Macmillan, 1925.

## 11-2 The equations of motion for small displacements from equilibrium: undamped motion

In order to obtain the equations of motion from the Lagrangian, we require the kinetic energy to be expressed in terms of the $x_i$'s and their time derivatives. In general the kinetic energy is a function of the generalized coordinates and velocities. It is, however, at all times a quadratic function of the generalized velocities. The kinetic energy is thus expressible in the form

$$T = \frac{1}{2} \sum_{i,j} m_{ij}(q_1, q_2, \ldots, q_n)\dot{q}_i\dot{q}_j, \tag{11-7}$$

where the $m_{ij}$'s express the functional dependence of the kinetic energy on the generalized coordinates.

For small displacements from equilibrium the functions $m_{ij}(q_1, q_2, \ldots, q_n)$ may be expanded in a Taylor series about the equilibrium configuration, yielding

$$T = \frac{1}{2} \sum_{i,j} m_{ij}(q_1^0, q_2^0, \ldots, q_n^0)\dot{x}_i\dot{x}_j$$
$$+ \frac{1}{2} \sum_{i,j} \left[ \sum_{\alpha} \frac{\partial m_{ij}(q_1^0, q_2^0, \ldots, q_n^0)}{\partial q_\alpha^0} x_\alpha \right] \dot{x}_i\dot{x}_j + \cdots. \tag{11-8}$$

Since the kinetic energy for the motion about a stable-equilibrium configuration is bounded, it follows that the generalized velocities $\dot{q}_i = \dot{x}_i$ are likewise bounded. We assume them to be small, thereby allowing us to neglect all except the first term in the Taylor-series expansion for the kinetic energy.

We thus obtain the approximate Lagrangian

$$L = T - U = \frac{1}{2} \sum_{i,j} (m_{ij}\dot{x}_i\dot{x}_j - k_{ij}x_ix_j), \tag{11-9}$$

where we have set

$$m_{ij} = m_{ij}(q_1^0, q_2^0, \ldots, q_n^0) = m_{ji}. \tag{11-10}$$

This Lagrangian yields the simultaneous differential equations of motion

$$\frac{d}{dt} \frac{\partial L}{\partial \dot{x}_i} - \frac{\partial L}{\partial x_i} = 0,$$

or

$$\sum_j m_{ij}\ddot{x}_j + k_{ij}x_j = 0. \tag{11-11}$$

These are $n$ homogeneous simultaneous linear differential equations which can be considered as the $n$ components of the matrix equation

$$(\mathbf{M})(\ddot{\mathbf{x}}) + (\mathbf{K})(\mathbf{x}) = 0, \tag{11-12}$$

where the matrices $(\mathbf{M})$, $(\mathbf{K})$, $(\ddot{\mathbf{x}})$, and $(\mathbf{x})$ are defined by

$$(\mathbf{M}) = \begin{bmatrix} m_{11} & m_{12} & \cdots & m_{1n} \\ m_{21} & m_{22} & \cdots & m_{2n} \\ \vdots & & & \vdots \\ m_{n1} & m_{n2} & \cdots & m_{nn} \end{bmatrix}, \tag{11–13}$$

$$(\mathbf{K}) = \begin{bmatrix} k_{11} & k_{12} & \cdots & k_{1n} \\ k_{21} & k_{22} & \cdots & k_{2n} \\ \vdots & & & \vdots \\ k_{n1} & k_{n2} & \cdots & k_{nn} \end{bmatrix}, \tag{11–14}$$

$$(\ddot{\mathbf{x}}) = \begin{bmatrix} \ddot{x}_1 \\ \ddot{x}_2 \\ \vdots \\ \ddot{x}_n \end{bmatrix} = \frac{d^2}{dt^2} \begin{bmatrix} x_1 \\ x_2 \\ \vdots \\ x_n \end{bmatrix}, \tag{11–15}$$

and

$$(\mathbf{x}) = \begin{bmatrix} x_1 \\ x_2 \\ \vdots \\ x_n \end{bmatrix}. \tag{11–16}$$

Equation (11–12) may in turn be considered to be the matrix representation of the operator equation

$$\mathbf{M}|\ddot{\mathbf{x}}\rangle + \mathbf{K}|\mathbf{x}\rangle = 0, \tag{11–17}$$

where $|\mathbf{x}\rangle$ is the $n$-dimensional vector whose matrix representation is $(\mathbf{x})$, and $\mathbf{M}$ and $\mathbf{K}$ are two operators having the matrix representations $(\mathbf{M})$ and $(\mathbf{K})$. Since the kinetic energy is at all times a positive definite quantity, it follows from Eq. (11–6) that $\mathbf{M}$ is a symmetric nonsingular operator for which the inverse operator $\mathbf{M}^{-1}$ and the operators $\mathbf{M}^{1/2}$ and $\mathbf{M}^{-1/2}$ exist (cf. Problem 10–17). Hence we can express Eq. (11–17) in the form

or

$$\frac{d^2}{dt^2} \mathbf{M}^{1/2}|\mathbf{x}\rangle = -\mathbf{M}^{-1/2}\mathbf{K}\mathbf{M}^{-1/2}\mathbf{M}^{1/2}|\mathbf{x}\rangle$$

$$\frac{d^2}{dt^2} |\bar{\mathbf{x}}\rangle = -\lambda|\bar{\mathbf{x}}\rangle, \tag{11–18}$$

where

$$|\bar{\mathbf{x}}\rangle = \mathbf{M}^{1/2}|\mathbf{x}\rangle.$$

We note that $\mathbf{M}^{-1/2}$ and $\mathbf{K}$ are symmetric operators, whence it follows that the operator

$$\lambda = \mathbf{M}^{-1/2}\mathbf{K}\mathbf{M}^{-1/2}$$

is likewise symmetric.

As an example, we reconsider the double pendulum which we met in Section 8–11. The potential energy for the double pendulum,

$$U = m_1 g l_1 (1 - \cos\theta_1) + m_2 g l_1 (1 - \cos\theta_1) + m_2 g l_2 (1 - \cos\theta_2),$$

has about the equilibrium configuration $(\theta_1 = \theta_2 = 0)$ the Taylor-series expansion

$$U = \tfrac{1}{2}(m_1 + m_2) g l_1 \theta_1^2 + \tfrac{1}{2} m_2 g l_2 \theta_2^2,$$

yielding

$$k_{11} = (m_1 + m_2) g l_1, \qquad k_{12} = k_{21} = 0, \qquad k_{22} = m_2 g l_2.$$

The kinetic energy was previously found to be given by (cf. Section 8–11)

$$T = \tfrac{1}{2}(m_1 + m_2) l_1^2 \dot\theta_1^2 + \tfrac{1}{2} m_2 l_2^2 \dot\theta_2^2 + m_2 l_1 l_2 \dot\theta_1 \dot\theta_2 \cos(\theta_1 - \theta_2)$$
$$= \tfrac{1}{2}(m_1 + m_2) l_1^2 \dot\theta_1^2 + \tfrac{1}{2} m_2 l_2^2 \dot\theta_2^2 + m_2 l_1 l_2 \dot\theta_1 \dot\theta_2,$$

from which we obtain

$$m_{11} = (m_1 + m_2) l_1^2,$$
$$m_{12} = m_{21} = m_2 l_1 l_2,$$
$$m_{22} = m_2 l_2^2.$$

The two equations of motion for small displacements from equilibrium are thus obtainable from the Lagrangian

$$L = \tfrac{1}{2} m_{11} \dot\theta_1^2 + \tfrac{1}{2} m_{22} \dot\theta_2^2 + \tfrac{1}{2}(m_{12} + m_{21}) \dot\theta_1 \dot\theta_2 - \tfrac{1}{2} k_{11} \theta_1^2 - \tfrac{1}{2} k_{22} \theta_2^2.$$

They are expressed by

$$\begin{bmatrix} m_{11} & m_{12} \\ m_{21} & m_{22} \end{bmatrix} \begin{bmatrix} \ddot\theta_1 \\ \ddot\theta_2 \end{bmatrix} + \begin{bmatrix} k_{11} & 0 \\ 0 & k_{22} \end{bmatrix} \begin{bmatrix} \theta_1 \\ \theta_2 \end{bmatrix} = 0.$$

In this example it turns out to be algebraically simpler to rewrite this latter equation as

$$(\mathbf{K}^{1/2})(\ddot{\boldsymbol\theta}) + (\mathbf{K}^{1/2})(\mathbf{M}^{-1})(\mathbf{K}^{1/2})(\mathbf{K}^{1/2})(\boldsymbol\theta) = 0$$

or

$$\frac{d^2}{dt^2}(\bar{\boldsymbol\theta}) + (\boldsymbol\lambda)(\bar{\boldsymbol\theta}) = 0,$$

where

$$(\mathbf{K}^{1/2}) = \begin{bmatrix} k_{11}^{1/2} & 0 \\ 0 & k_{22}^{1/2} \end{bmatrix},$$

$$(\bar{\boldsymbol\theta}) = (\mathbf{K}^{1/2})(\boldsymbol\theta)$$

and

$$(\boldsymbol\lambda) = (\mathbf{K}^{1/2})(\mathbf{M}^{-1})(\mathbf{K}^{1/2}).$$

The elements of the matrix $(\mathbf{M}^{-1})$ are (cf. Section 10–6)

$$m_{11}^{-1} = \frac{m_{22}}{\det(m_{ij})},$$

$$m_{22}^{-1} = \frac{m_{11}}{\det(m_{ij})},$$

$$m_{21}^{-1} = m_{12}^{-1} = \frac{-m_{12}}{\det(m_{ij})},$$

where

$$\det(m_{ij}) = m_{11}m_{22} - m_{12}^2 = m_1 m_2 l_1^2 l_2^2.$$

This casts the equation of motion into the form of Eq. (11–18).

## 11–3 Normal coordinates

Having found it possible to express in operator notation, the equations of motion of a system for small displacements from equilibrium, we are in a position to utilize the efficient language of the previous chapter to discuss the simplification and subsequent solution of the equations of motion.

In the language of the previous chapter (11–18) represents a vector equation which states that the second time derivative of the vector $|\bar{\mathbf{x}}\rangle$ is equal to the vector produced by operating with $-\boldsymbol{\lambda}$ on the vector $|\bar{\mathbf{x}}\rangle$. Since the operator

$$\boldsymbol{\lambda} = \mathbf{M}^{-1/2}\mathbf{K}\mathbf{M}^{-1/2}$$

is a real symmetric operator, its simplest description is the diagonal description, which is obtained if we use its orthonormal eigenvectors as base vectors. The simplest description of $\boldsymbol{\lambda}$ will likewise yield the simplest equations of motion, which is a set of independent one-dimensional equations. We therefore consider first the eigenvalue problem

$$\boldsymbol{\lambda}|\boldsymbol{\rho}_i\rangle = \lambda_i|\boldsymbol{\rho}_i\rangle, \tag{11–19}$$

which is equivalent to the operator equation

$$\mathbf{M}^{-1/2}\mathbf{K}\mathbf{M}^{-1/2}|\boldsymbol{\rho}_i\rangle = \lambda_i|\boldsymbol{\rho}_i\rangle. \tag{11–20}$$

From (11–20) we obtain the result that the eigenvalues of $\boldsymbol{\lambda}$ are given by the equation

$$\lambda_i = \frac{\langle\boldsymbol{\rho}_i|\mathbf{M}^{-1/2}\mathbf{K}\mathbf{M}^{-1/2}|\boldsymbol{\rho}_i\rangle}{\langle\boldsymbol{\rho}_i|\boldsymbol{\rho}_i\rangle}. \tag{11–21}$$

Since both the kinetic and the potential energies are positive definite quantities, it follows that

$$\langle\boldsymbol{\rho}_i|\mathbf{M}^{-1/2}\mathbf{K}\mathbf{M}^{-1/2}|\boldsymbol{\rho}_i\rangle > 0,$$

and hence that

$$\lambda_i > 0.$$

This allows us to set

$$\lambda_i = \omega_i^2. \tag{11-22}$$

In terms of the orthonormal eigenvectors $|\boldsymbol{\rho}_i\rangle$ of $\boldsymbol{\lambda}$, the vector $|\overline{\mathbf{x}}\rangle$ is expressible as

$$|\overline{\mathbf{x}}\rangle = \sum_i y_i|\boldsymbol{\rho}_i\rangle, \tag{11-23}$$

where

$$y_i = \langle\boldsymbol{\rho}_i|\overline{\mathbf{x}}\rangle. \tag{11-24}$$

Inserting this result into the equation of motion, Eq. (11–18), yields

$$\frac{d^2}{dt^2}\sum_i y_i|\boldsymbol{\rho}_i\rangle = -\boldsymbol{\lambda}|\overline{\mathbf{x}}\rangle = -\sum_i \lambda_i y_i|\boldsymbol{\rho}_i\rangle. \tag{11-25}$$

The scalar product of the previous equation with the constant eigenvector $\langle\boldsymbol{\rho}_j|$ subsequently yields the equation of motion for the generalized coordinate $y_j$,

$$\frac{d^2 y_j}{dt^2} = -\omega_j^2 y_j. \tag{11-26}$$

The solution of this equation was discussed in Chapter 4, and was found to be

$$y_j = A_j \cos(\omega_j t + \phi_j). \tag{11-27}$$

We have thus shown that for the undamped motion of a system of particles about a stable configuration we can always find a set of coordinates $y_j$, which yields a set of independent generalized equations of motion.

The linear relation of the $y_j$'s to the $\overline{x}_i$'s is given by Eq. (11–24), which in terms of the components of the vectors $\langle\boldsymbol{\rho}_j|$ and $|\overline{\mathbf{x}}\rangle$ are expressed by

$$y_j = \rho_{j1}\overline{x}_1 + \rho_{j2}\overline{x}_2 + \cdots + \rho_{jn}\overline{x}_n. \tag{11-28}$$

The components $\rho_{jl}$ of the $j$th eigenvector are obtained from the solution of (11–19), the eigenvalue problem for $\boldsymbol{\lambda}$.

The coordinates $y_j$ are referred to as the *normal coordinates*, and the $\omega_j$'s as the *normal frequencies*. The solutions

$$y_j = A_j \cos(\omega_j t + \phi_j) \tag{11-29}$$

or, equivalently,

$$\begin{bmatrix} \overline{x}_1^{(j)} \\ \overline{x}_2^{(j)} \\ \vdots \\ \overline{x}_n^{(j)} \end{bmatrix} = A_j \cos(\omega_j t + \phi_j)\begin{bmatrix} \rho_{j1} \\ \rho_{j2} \\ \vdots \\ \rho_{jn} \end{bmatrix} \tag{11-30}$$

are referred to as the *normal modes of vibration* of the system.

As an example, we consider the solution of the set of simultaneous linear differential equations with constant coefficients,

$$
\begin{bmatrix} \ddot{x}_1 \\ \ddot{x}_2 \\ \ddot{x}_3 \end{bmatrix} = - \begin{bmatrix} 5 & 0 & 1 \\ 0 & 2 & 0 \\ 1 & 0 & 5 \end{bmatrix} \begin{bmatrix} x_1 \\ x_2 \\ x_3 \end{bmatrix}.
$$

From the matrix representation of $\lambda$,

$$
(\lambda) = \begin{bmatrix} 5 & 0 & 1 \\ 0 & 2 & 0 \\ 1 & 0 & 5 \end{bmatrix},
$$

we obtain the eigenvalue equation

$$
\begin{bmatrix} 5 & 0 & 1 \\ 0 & 2 & 0 \\ 1 & 0 & 5 \end{bmatrix} \begin{bmatrix} \rho_1 \\ \rho_2 \\ \rho_3 \end{bmatrix} = \lambda \begin{bmatrix} \rho_1 \\ \rho_2 \\ \rho_3 \end{bmatrix},
$$

which has a solution only if

$$
\begin{vmatrix} 5 - \lambda & 0 & 1 \\ 0 & 2 - \lambda & 0 \\ 1 & 0 & 5 - \lambda \end{vmatrix} = 0.
$$

This secular equation has the three roots

$$
\lambda_1 = 2, \qquad \lambda_2 = 4, \qquad \lambda_3 = 6.
$$

For $\lambda_2 = 4$ we obtain the eigenvector $|\rho_2\rangle$ whose components are related by the equations

$$
(5 - 4)\rho_{21} + \rho_{23} = 0,
$$
$$
(2 - 4)\rho_{22} = 0,
$$
$$
\rho_{21} + (5 - 4)\rho_{23} = 0.
$$

Thus we obtain

$$
\rho_{21} = -\rho_{23}, \qquad \rho_{22} = 0
$$

or

$$
|\rho_2\rangle \leftrightarrow \frac{1}{\sqrt{2}} \begin{bmatrix} 1 \\ 0 \\ -1 \end{bmatrix}.
$$

Similarly, we obtain the eigenvectors

$$|\boldsymbol{\rho}_1\rangle \leftrightarrow \begin{bmatrix} 0 \\ 1 \\ 0 \end{bmatrix} \quad \text{and} \quad |\boldsymbol{\rho}_3\rangle \leftrightarrow \frac{1}{\sqrt{2}} \begin{bmatrix} 1 \\ 0 \\ 1 \end{bmatrix},$$

which yield the normal coordinates

$$y_j = \langle \boldsymbol{\rho}_j | \bar{\mathbf{x}} \rangle = \sum_{i=1}^{3} \rho_{ji} \bar{x}_i.$$

In matrix notation this latter equation is expressed by

$$\begin{bmatrix} y_1 \\ y_2 \\ y_3 \end{bmatrix} = \begin{bmatrix} 0 & 1 & 0 \\ \dfrac{1}{\sqrt{2}} & 0 & -\dfrac{1}{\sqrt{2}} \\ \dfrac{1}{\sqrt{2}} & 0 & \dfrac{1}{\sqrt{2}} \end{bmatrix} \begin{bmatrix} \bar{x}_1 \\ \bar{x}_2 \\ \bar{x}_3 \end{bmatrix},$$

which may be considered as the matrix representation of the operator equation

$$|\mathbf{y}\rangle = \mathbf{S}|\bar{\mathbf{x}}\rangle.$$

As was shown above, the $y_j$'s so defined satisfy the equations

$$\ddot{y}_j + \lambda_j y_j = 0, \quad j = 1, 2, 3, \dots, n.$$

That they do may be seen from the fact that by operating on the equation of motion for the vector $|\bar{\mathbf{x}}\rangle$,

$$\frac{d^2}{dt^2}|\bar{\mathbf{x}}\rangle + \boldsymbol{\lambda}|\bar{\mathbf{x}}\rangle = 0,$$

with the transformation operator $\mathbf{S}$, we obtain

$$\frac{d^2}{dt^2}\mathbf{S}|\bar{\mathbf{x}}\rangle + \mathbf{S}\boldsymbol{\lambda}\mathbf{S}^{-1}\mathbf{S}|\bar{\mathbf{x}}\rangle = 0 \quad \text{or} \quad \frac{d^2}{dt^2}|\mathbf{y}\rangle + \boldsymbol{\lambda}'|\mathbf{y}\rangle = 0,$$

where $\boldsymbol{\lambda}' = \mathbf{S}\boldsymbol{\lambda}\mathbf{S}^{-1}$. For our example, the matrix representation of $\boldsymbol{\lambda}'$ is

$$(\boldsymbol{\lambda}') = \begin{bmatrix} 0 & 1 & 0 \\ \dfrac{1}{\sqrt{2}} & 0 & -\dfrac{1}{\sqrt{2}} \\ \dfrac{1}{\sqrt{2}} & 0 & \dfrac{1}{\sqrt{2}} \end{bmatrix} \begin{bmatrix} 5 & 0 & 1 \\ 0 & 2 & 0 \\ 1 & 0 & 5 \end{bmatrix} \begin{bmatrix} 0 & \dfrac{1}{\sqrt{2}} & \dfrac{1}{\sqrt{2}} \\ 1 & 0 & 0 \\ 0 & -\dfrac{1}{\sqrt{2}} & \dfrac{1}{\sqrt{2}} \end{bmatrix} = \begin{bmatrix} 2 & 0 & 0 \\ 0 & 4 & 0 \\ 0 & 0 & 6 \end{bmatrix}.$$

Thus $(\boldsymbol{\lambda}')$ is found to be the diagonal form of $(\boldsymbol{\lambda})$. What we have shown is that the transformation matrix formed from the matrix representations of the eigenvectors of a symmetric operator diagonalizes the matrix representation of the operator.

We note that if the operator $\boldsymbol{\lambda}$ has two or more identical eigenvalues, we can still obtain a set of orthonormal eigenvectors as noted in the previous chapter. As for the normal modes of oscillation of the system, this just means that the normal mode for the corresponding frequency is not unique. Any linear combination of the two or more normal modes having the same normal frequency is also a normal mode of that frequency.

## 11–4 Damped motion

We next turn our attention to the more realistic case when dissipative forces are present. Once again we consider only the effect of dissipative forces which are proportional to the first power of the velocity of the particles of the system. The motion under the action of such dissipative forces is referred to as *damped motion*.

The damped motion of a system of particles about a point of stable equilibrium is mathematically more complicated than the undamped case, because normal coordinates which satisfy independent uncoupled equations of motion do not always exist for this type of motion. The existence of normal modes in any problem is a welcomed simplification. This is especially true if one wishes to consider the effect of additional forces on the motion. If these additional forces are small, such as, for example, the forces introduced when additional terms in the Taylor-series expansion of the potential energy are retained, then for those problems for which normal-mode solutions exist there exists a systematic method for approximating the effect of the perturbing forces on the system (cf. Section 11–7). When normal modes are not available, the situation is mathematically much more complicated.

Assuming for simplicity the dissipative forces on the $l$th particle to be of the form

$$\mathbf{F}^{(l)} = -\mu^{(l)}\mathbf{v}^{(l)}, \qquad (11\text{–}31)$$

the total generalized dissipative forces are found to be expressed by

$$Q_i = -\sum_j \mu_{ij}(q_1, q_2, \ldots, q_n)\dot{q}_j$$

$$\simeq -\sum_j \mu_{ij}(q_1^0, q_2^0, \ldots, q_n^0)\dot{q}_j = -\sum_j \mu_{ij}\dot{x}_j. \qquad (11\text{–}32)$$

The $\mu_{ij}(q_1, q_2, \ldots, q_n)$'s are generally functions of the generalized coordinates $q_j$, and satisfy the condition

$$\mu_{ij}(q_1, q_2, \ldots, q_n) = \mu_{ji}(q_1, q_2, \ldots, q_n).$$

This fact may be ascertained by comparing the expression for the generalized damping force

$$Q_i = \sum_l \mathbf{F}^{(l)} \cdot \frac{\partial \mathbf{r}^{(l)}}{\partial q_i} = -\sum_l \mu^{(l)} \mathbf{v}^{(l)} \cdot \frac{\partial \mathbf{r}^{(l)}}{\partial q_i}$$

with the expression for the generalized momentum

$$p_i = \sum_l m^{(l)} \mathbf{v}^{(l)} \cdot \frac{\partial \mathbf{r}^{(l)}}{\partial q_i} = \frac{\partial T}{\partial \dot{q}_i} = \sum_j m_{ij} \dot{q}_j.$$

For small displacements from equilibrium we replace $\mu_{ij}(q_1, q_2, \ldots, q_n)$ by its value for the coordinates $q_i^0$ of the equilibrium configuration,

$$\mu_{ij} = \mu_{ij}(q_1^0, q_2^0, \ldots, q_n^0). \tag{11-33}$$

The inclusion of dissipative forces modifies the equations of motion, which are then expressed generally by

$$\sum_j m_{ij}\ddot{x}_j + \mu_{ij}\dot{x}_j + k_{ij}x_j = 0 \tag{11-34}$$

or in operator form by

$$\mathbf{M}|\ddot{\mathbf{x}}\rangle + \mu|\dot{\mathbf{x}}\rangle + \mathbf{K}|\mathbf{x}\rangle = 0. \tag{11-35}$$

As already mentioned, except in special cases no linear transformation of the generalized coordinates exists which will yield a set of uncoupled differential equations of motion.

Such exceptional cases do occur. An example is the case for which the two symmetric operators $\mathbf{M}^{-1/2}\mu\mathbf{M}^{-1/2}$ and $\mathbf{M}^{-1/2}\mathbf{K}\mathbf{M}^{-1/2}$ can be simultaneously diagonalized. This can always be done if these operators commute, or if one of the operators, $\mu$ or $\mathbf{K}$, is a scalar multiple of the operator $\mathbf{M}$. Thus, for example, we may have

$$\mu_{ij} = 2\mu m_{ij},$$

in which case we obtain for $|\bar{\mathbf{x}}\rangle = \mathbf{M}^{1/2}|\mathbf{x}\rangle$ the equation of motion

$$\frac{d^2}{dt^2}|\bar{\mathbf{x}}\rangle + 2\mu \frac{d}{dt}|\bar{\mathbf{x}}\rangle + \mathbf{M}^{-1/2}\mathbf{K}\mathbf{M}^{-1/2}|\bar{\mathbf{x}}\rangle = 0. \tag{11-36}$$

The operator $\mathbf{M}^{-1/2}\mathbf{K}\mathbf{M}^{-1/2}$ may now be diagonalized by the transformation operator $\mathbf{S}$ in the manner discussed in the previous section, where the matrix elements $S_{ij}$ of $\mathbf{S}$ are the elements of the matrix representations of the eigenvectors $|\rho_i\rangle$ of the operator $\lambda = \mathbf{M}^{-1/2}\mathbf{K}\mathbf{M}^{-1/2}$; that is,

$$(\mathbf{S}) = \begin{bmatrix} \rho_{11} & \rho_{12} & \cdots & \rho_{1n} \\ \rho_{21} & \rho_{22} & \cdots & \rho_{2n} \\ \vdots & & & \vdots \\ \rho_{n1} & \rho_{n2} & \cdots & \rho_{nn} \end{bmatrix}.$$

Operating with **S** on Eq. (11–36) then yields the uncoupled equations of motion represented by

$$\frac{d^2}{dt^2}|\mathbf{y}\rangle + 2\mu \frac{d}{dt}|\mathbf{y}\rangle + \lambda'|\mathbf{y}\rangle = 0, \tag{11–37}$$

where

$$|\mathbf{y}\rangle = \mathbf{S}|\bar{\mathbf{x}}\rangle = \mathbf{S}\mathbf{M}^{1/2}|\mathbf{x}\rangle \tag{11–38}$$

and

$$\lambda' = \mathbf{S}\lambda\mathbf{S}^{-1}. \tag{11–39}$$

The uncoupled equations are the one-dimensional equations of motion for a damped harmonic oscillator.

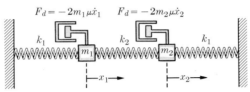

FIGURE 11–1

▶ As an illustration, we consider the damped motion of the coupled oscillators shown in Fig. 11–1 which are acted upon by the damping forces

$$F_i = -2m_i\mu\dot{x}_i, \qquad i = 1, 2.$$

Lagrange's equations of motion for this system of particles are

$$m_1\ddot{x}_1 + 2m_1\mu\dot{x}_1 + (k_1 + k_2)x_1 - k_2x_2 = 0$$

and

$$m_2\ddot{x}_2 + 2m_2\mu\dot{x}_2 + (k_1 + k_2)x_2 - k_2x_1 = 0,$$

or

$$\frac{d^2}{dt^2}\begin{bmatrix}\bar{x}_1\\\bar{x}_2\end{bmatrix} + 2\mu\frac{d}{dt}\begin{bmatrix}\bar{x}_1\\\bar{x}_2\end{bmatrix} + (\lambda)\begin{bmatrix}\bar{x}_1\\\bar{x}_2\end{bmatrix} = 0,$$

where

$$\begin{bmatrix}\bar{x}_1\\\bar{x}_2\end{bmatrix} = \begin{bmatrix}m_1^{1/2} & 0\\0 & m_2^{1/2}\end{bmatrix}\begin{bmatrix}x_1\\x_2\end{bmatrix} = \begin{bmatrix}m_1^{1/2}x_1\\m_2^{1/2}x_2\end{bmatrix}$$

and

$$(\lambda) = (\mathbf{M}^{-1/2})(\mathbf{K})(\mathbf{M}^{-1/2}) = \begin{bmatrix}\dfrac{k_1+k_2}{m_1} & -\dfrac{k_2}{\sqrt{m_1m_2}}\\[3mm] -\dfrac{k_2}{\sqrt{m_1m_2}} & \dfrac{k_1+k_2}{m_2}\end{bmatrix}.$$

For the case where $m_1 = m_2 = m$,

$$(\lambda) = \frac{1}{m}\begin{bmatrix}k_1+k_2 & -k_2\\-k_2 & k_1+k_2\end{bmatrix}.$$

The eigenvalues of this matrix are

$$\lambda_1 = \frac{k_1}{m} \quad \text{and} \quad \lambda_2 = \frac{2k_2 + k_1}{m},$$

and the matrix representations of the eigenvectors $|\boldsymbol{\rho}_1\rangle$ and $|\boldsymbol{\rho}_2\rangle$ belonging to these eigenvalues are

$$|\boldsymbol{\rho}_1\rangle \leftrightarrow \frac{1}{\sqrt{2}} \begin{bmatrix} 1 \\ 1 \end{bmatrix} \quad \text{and} \quad |\boldsymbol{\rho}_2\rangle \leftrightarrow \frac{1}{\sqrt{2}} \begin{bmatrix} 1 \\ -1 \end{bmatrix}.$$

Hence the matrix representation of the operator $\mathbf{S}$ which diagonalizes $\boldsymbol{\lambda}$ is

$$(\mathbf{S}) = \frac{1}{\sqrt{2}} \begin{bmatrix} 1 & 1 \\ 1 & -1 \end{bmatrix}.$$

This $(\mathbf{S})$ yields the normal coordinates

$$y_1 = \frac{1}{\sqrt{2}} (\bar{x}_1 + \bar{x}_2) \quad \text{and} \quad y_2 = \frac{1}{\sqrt{2}} (\bar{x}_1 - \bar{x}_2),$$

which satisfy the uncoupled set of differential equations

$$\ddot{y}_1 + 2\mu\dot{y}_1 + \frac{k_1}{m} y_1 = 0,$$

$$\ddot{y}_2 + 2\mu\dot{y}_2 + \frac{2k_2 + k_1}{m} y_2 = 0.$$

The solutions of these equations were discussed in Chapter 4. ◀

Usually the equations of motion for a damped system cannot be uncoupled by a linear transformation. In such cases we attempt to obtain a solution by guessing and seeing if the trial solution can be made to satisfy the equations of motion. Since they are linear differential equations with constant coefficients, we anticipate that they may have solutions of the form

$$x_i = A_i e^{\alpha t}.$$

When we insert this trial solution into Eq. (11–34), we obtain the homogeneous set of simultaneous equations

$$\sum_j (\alpha^2 m_{ij} + \alpha\mu_{ij} + k_{ij}) A_j = 0 \tag{11–40}$$

or the equivalent operator equation

$$(\alpha^2 \mathbf{M} + \alpha\boldsymbol{\mu} + \mathbf{K})|\mathbf{x}\rangle = 0. \tag{11–41}$$

A nontrivial solution to these equations is possible only if the determinant of the coefficients vanishes:

$$\det\left(\alpha^2 M_{ij} + \alpha\mu_{ij} + k_{ij}\right) = 0. \tag{11–42}$$

This determinant yields a polynomial of order $2n$ in $\alpha$. Equation (11–42) therefore has $2n$ roots, which, if distinct, yield $2n$ unique solutions of the form

$$\begin{bmatrix} x_1 \\ x_2 \\ \vdots \\ x_n \end{bmatrix} = \begin{bmatrix} A_1 \\ A_2 \\ \vdots \\ A_n \end{bmatrix} e^{\alpha t} \tag{11–43}$$

for the $n$ second-order differential equations of motion.

▶ As an example, we consider the two damped coupled oscillators shown in Fig. 11–2, whose rectilinear motion is described by the equations of motion

$$2\ddot{x}_1 + 3\dot{x}_1 + 6x_1 - 4x_2 = 0,$$
$$\ddot{x}_2 + 6\dot{x}_2 + 4x_2 - 4x_1 = 0.$$

Since the two matrices

$$(\mathbf{M}^{-1/2})(\boldsymbol{\mu})(\mathbf{M}^{-1/2}) = \begin{bmatrix} \dfrac{1}{\sqrt{2}} & 0 \\ 0 & 1 \end{bmatrix}\begin{bmatrix} 3 & 0 \\ 0 & 6 \end{bmatrix}\begin{bmatrix} \dfrac{1}{\sqrt{2}} & 0 \\ 0 & 1 \end{bmatrix} = \begin{bmatrix} \dfrac{3}{2} & 0 \\ 0 & 6 \end{bmatrix}$$

and

$$(\mathbf{M}^{-1/2})(\mathbf{K})(\mathbf{M}^{-1/2}) = \begin{bmatrix} \dfrac{1}{\sqrt{2}} & 0 \\ 0 & 1 \end{bmatrix}\begin{bmatrix} 6 & -4 \\ -4 & 4 \end{bmatrix}\begin{bmatrix} \dfrac{1}{\sqrt{2}} & 0 \\ 0 & 1 \end{bmatrix} = \begin{bmatrix} 3 & -2\sqrt{2} \\ -2\sqrt{2} & 4 \end{bmatrix}$$

do not commute, normal coordinates do not exist. We therefore attempt to find a solution having the form

$$x_1 = Ae^{\alpha t} \quad\text{and}\quad x_2 = Be^{\alpha t}.$$

This trial solution leads to the two homogeneous simultaneous equations

$$(2\alpha^2 + 3\alpha + 6)A - 4B = 0,$$
$$-4A + (\alpha^2 + 6\alpha + 4)B = 0.$$

These equations can be satisfied only if $\alpha$ is a root of the determinantal equation

$$\begin{vmatrix} 2\alpha^2 + 3\alpha + 6 & -4 \\ -4 & \alpha^2 + 6\alpha + 0 \end{vmatrix} = 0.$$

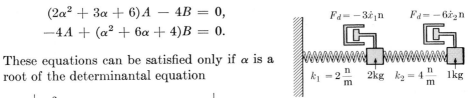

$F_d = -3\dot{x}_1 \text{n}$    $F_d = -6\dot{x}_2 \text{n}$

$k_1 = 2\dfrac{\text{n}}{\text{m}}$   2kg   $k_2 = 4\dfrac{\text{n}}{\text{m}}$   1kg

FIGURE 11–2

The values of $\alpha$ which satisfy the above equation are

$$\alpha_{1,2} = -1 \pm i\sqrt{3}, \qquad \alpha_{3,4} = \frac{-11 \pm \sqrt{105}}{4}.$$

The general homogeneous solution is thus expressible as

$$x_1 = \sum_{i=1}^{4} A_i e^{\alpha_i t} \qquad \text{and} \qquad x_2 = \sum_{i=1}^{4} B_i e^{\alpha_i t},$$

where

$$B_i = \frac{2\alpha_i^2 + 3\alpha_i + 6}{4} A_i. \blacktriangleleft$$

If the roots are degenerate, then a trial solution having the form

$$x_j = (A_j + B_j t + \cdots + G_j t^{m-1})e^{\alpha t}, \tag{11–44}$$

where $m$ is the order of the root, is substituted into the equations of motion. For a second-order root, the trial solution

$$x_j = (A_j + B_j t)e^{\alpha t} \tag{11–45}$$

inserted into Eq. (11–34) yields, for example, the equations

$$e^{\alpha t}\left[\sum_j (m_{ij}\alpha^2 + \mu_{ij}\alpha + k_{ij})(A_j + B_j t) + \sum_j (2\alpha m_{ij} + \mu_{ij})B_j\right] = 0.$$

Since the functions $te^{\alpha t}$ and $e^{\alpha t}$ are linearly independent, the last equation can be satisfied for all $t$ only if the coefficients of these functions vanish. We thus obtain the $2n$ homogeneous simultaneous equations

$$\sum_j (\alpha^2 m_{ij} + \alpha\mu_{ij} + k_{ij})B_j = 0 \tag{11–46}$$

and

$$\sum_j (2\alpha m_{ij} + \mu_{ij})B_j + \sum_j (\alpha^2 m_{ij} + \alpha\mu_{ij} + k_{ij})A_j = 0. \tag{11–47}$$

Since the determinant formed by the coefficients of Eqs. (11–46) and (11–47) vanishes for the value of $\alpha$ which is a double root of Eq. (11–42), these equations may be solved for $2n - 2$ of the coefficients $A_j$ and $B_j$ in terms of the remaining two constants.

For simplicity we shall restrict ourselves to the case when the roots of Eq. (11–42) are discrete, and refer the reader to the very useful and more direct operational Laplace-transform method for obtaining the homogeneous solutions to any set of simultaneous linear differential equations with constant coefficients.*

---

* H. S. Carlslaw and J. C. Jaeger, *Operational Methods in Applied Mathematics.* New York: Oxford University Press, 1941, and R. V. Churchill, *Modern Operational Mathematics in Engineering.* New York: McGraw Hill, 1944.

This method circumvents some of the difficulties we may encounter in attempting to solve by the method of trial solution outlined here the simultaneous equations of motion when degenerate roots exist.

The roots of Eq. (11–42) will usually be complex, and will therefore occur in complex conjugate pairs. From a physical point of view the real part of the roots is expected to be negative in order that they yield a damped solution of the form

$$x_j = A_j e^{-\beta t \pm i\gamma t}.$$

Such a solution expresses the fact that energy is being dissipated and, as is to be expected, the oscillations die out after a sufficiently long period of time.

We can show this to be indeed the case. Consider the operator

$$\mathfrak{L} = \alpha^2 \mathbf{M} + \alpha \boldsymbol{\mu} + \mathbf{K}, \tag{11–48}$$

whose Hermitian adjoint is

$$\mathfrak{L}^\dagger = \alpha^{*2} \mathbf{M} + \alpha^* \boldsymbol{\mu} + \mathbf{K} = \mathfrak{L}^*. \tag{11–49}$$

From Eq. (11–41) we obtain

$$\langle \mathbf{x} | \mathfrak{L} | \mathbf{x} \rangle = 0.$$

The Hermitian adjoint of this expression also vanishes,

$$\langle \mathbf{x} | \mathfrak{L} | \mathbf{x} \rangle^\dagger = \langle \mathbf{x} | \mathfrak{L}^\dagger | \mathbf{x} \rangle = 0.$$

Hence we obtain

$$\langle \mathbf{x} | \mathfrak{L} - \mathfrak{L}^* | \mathbf{x} \rangle = 0$$

or

$$(\alpha^2 - \alpha^{*2}) \langle \mathbf{x} | \mathbf{M} | \mathbf{x} \rangle + (\alpha - \alpha^*) \langle \mathbf{x} | \boldsymbol{\mu} | \mathbf{x} \rangle = 0. \tag{11–50}$$

Setting

$$\alpha = -\beta + i\gamma, \tag{11–51}$$

we obtain

$$-4i\beta\gamma \langle \mathbf{x} | \mathbf{M} | \mathbf{x} \rangle + 2i\gamma \langle \mathbf{x} | \boldsymbol{\mu} | \mathbf{x} \rangle = 0$$

or

$$\beta = \frac{1}{2} \frac{\langle \mathbf{x} | \boldsymbol{\mu} | \mathbf{x} \rangle}{\langle \mathbf{x} | \mathbf{M} | \mathbf{x} \rangle}. \tag{11–52}$$

Now, the kinetic energy is positive definite. Hence it follows that the scalar $\langle \mathbf{x} | \mathbf{M} | \mathbf{x} \rangle$ is positive definite. Furthermore, realizing that the dissipation of energy results in a decrease in the energy of the system, that is,

$$\frac{d\mathcal{E}}{dt} = \langle \dot{\mathbf{x}} | \mathbf{F}_{\text{damping}} \rangle = -\langle \dot{\mathbf{x}} | \boldsymbol{\mu} | \dot{\mathbf{x}} \rangle \tag{11–53}$$

is a negative quantity, we see that for the case under discussion the scalar quantity $\langle \mathbf{x} | \boldsymbol{\mu} | \mathbf{x} \rangle$ is also positive definite. We have thus succeeded in showing $\beta$ to be a positive constant.

We note that the equations of motion for a system of charged coupled oscillators in a magnetic field have the same form as that given by Eq. (11–35). In such a case, however, since magnetic forces do no work,

$$\langle \dot{\mathbf{x}} | \boldsymbol{\mu} | \dot{\mathbf{x}} \rangle = 0$$

for all $|\dot{\mathbf{x}}\rangle$. Hence for magnetic forces

$$\langle \mathbf{x} | \boldsymbol{\mu} | \mathbf{x} \rangle = 0,$$

and $\beta$ also vanishes. This means that for this problem we should expect only imaginary roots and no dissipation of energy.

## 11–5 Forced oscillations: sinusoidal driving force

Once again in dealing with time-dependent driving forces we consider, as we did in the one-dimensional case discussed in Chapter 4, only sinusoidal and impulsive forces, as the solution for any other force can be obtained by summing solutions for these time-dependent forces. We further subdivide our discussion into the cases when normal modes do and do not exist. In this section we consider the effect of sinusoidal driving forces of the form

$$\mathbf{F}^{(l)} = \mathbf{F}_0^{(l)} e^{i\omega t} \tag{11–54}$$

on the $l$th particle of a coupled system of oscillators. For these driving forces we obtain the generalized equations of motion

$$\sum_j (m_{ij}\ddot{x}_j + \mu_{ij}\dot{x}_j + k_{ij}x_j) = Q_i e^{i\omega t}. \tag{11–55}$$

The amplitude of the generalized driving force is given by

$$Q_i = \sum_l \mathbf{F}_0^{(l)} \cdot \frac{\partial \mathbf{r}^{(l)}}{\partial q_i}, \tag{11–56}$$

where $\mathbf{F}_0^{(l)}$ specifies the amplitude and direction of the external driving force acting on the $l$th particle of the system.

The existence of normal modes implies the existence of a coordinate transformation operator $\mathbf{S}$, which transforms the vector $|\mathbf{M}|^{1/2}|\mathbf{x}\rangle$ into the vector $|\mathbf{y}\rangle$, as expressed by

$$|\mathbf{y}\rangle = \mathbf{S}\mathbf{M}^{1/2}|\mathbf{x}\rangle, \tag{11–57}$$

and whose components satisfy independent equations of motion. This means that the transformation operator $\mathbf{S}$ simultaneously diagonalizes the operators $\mathbf{M}^{-1/2}\boldsymbol{\mu}\mathbf{M}^{-1/2}$ and $\mathbf{M}^{-1/2}\mathbf{K}\mathbf{M}^{-1/2}$, yielding the equations

$$\ddot{y}_j + 2\mu_j \dot{y}_j + \omega_j^2 y_j = \mathcal{F}_j e^{i\omega t}, \tag{11–58}$$

where

$$|\mathcal{F}\rangle = \mathbf{S}\mathbf{M}^{-1/2}|\mathbf{Q}\rangle, \tag{11–59}$$

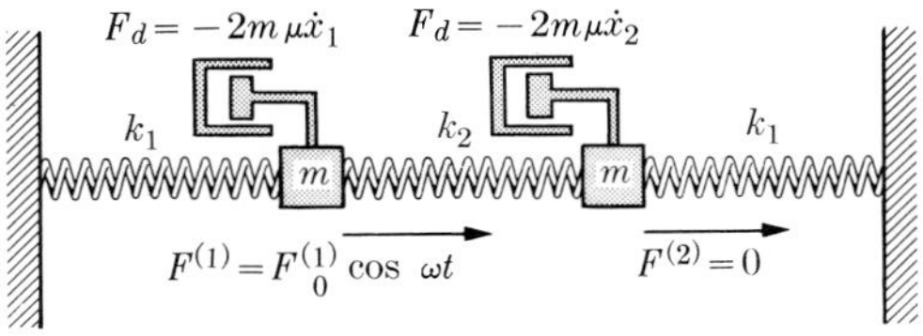

$$F_d = -2m\mu\dot{x}_1 \qquad F_d = -2m\mu\dot{x}_2$$

$$F^{(1)} = F_0^{(1)} \cos \omega t \qquad F^{(2)} = 0$$

FIGURE 11–3

and $2\mu_j$ and $\omega_j^2$ are respectively the diagonal elements of the simultaneously diagonalized matrix representations of the operators $\mathbf{M}^{-1/2}\boldsymbol{\mu}\mathbf{M}^{-1/2}$ and $\mathbf{M}^{-1/2}\mathbf{K}\mathbf{M}^{-1/2}$. As mentioned above, this simultaneous diagonalization is possible only under very special circumstances.

Equation (11–58) is the equation of motion for a one-dimensional forced harmonic oscillator. Its solution is

$$y_j = \frac{\mathscr{F}_j e^{i(\omega t - \phi_j)}}{\sqrt{(\omega_j^2 - \omega^2)^2 + 4\mu_j^2\omega^2}}, \tag{11–60}$$

where

$$\tan \phi_j = \frac{2\mu_j\omega}{\omega_j^2 - \omega^2}. \tag{11–61}$$

The case where normal modes exist is thus the simplest, yielding the result that the excitation of any mode is independent of any other. The excitation of any mode is a function of the amplitude of the generalized force $\mathscr{F}_j$ and the driving frequency $\omega$. It is a maximum at the resonant frequency

$$\omega_j^{\text{res}} = \sqrt{\omega_j^2 - 2\mu_j^2}. \tag{11–62}$$

▶ As an example, we obtain the equations of motion for the normal coordinates of the forced vibration of the first system of coupled oscillators considered in the previous section. We consider the case when $m_1 = m_2 = m$ and the first mass is forced by a sinusoidal driving force (Fig. 11–3), for which

$$\mathbf{F}^{(1)} = \mathbf{F}_0^{(1)} e^{i\omega t}, \qquad \mathbf{F}^{(2)} = 0.$$

This force gives us the equations of motion

$$\mathbf{M}|\ddot{\mathbf{x}}\rangle + \boldsymbol{\mu}|\dot{\mathbf{x}}\rangle + \mathbf{K}|\mathbf{x}\rangle = |\mathbf{F}_0\rangle e^{i\omega t},$$

where

$$\mathbf{M} \leftrightarrow \begin{bmatrix} m & 0 \\ 0 & m \end{bmatrix} = m\begin{bmatrix} 1 & 0 \\ 0 & 1 \end{bmatrix},$$

$$\boldsymbol{\mu} \leftrightarrow \begin{bmatrix} 2m\mu & 0 \\ 0 & 2m\mu \end{bmatrix} = 2m\mu\begin{bmatrix} 1 & 0 \\ 0 & 1 \end{bmatrix},$$

$$\mathbf{K} = \begin{bmatrix} k_1 + k_2 & -k_2 \\ -k_2 & k_1 + k_2 \end{bmatrix}, \qquad |\mathbf{F}_0\rangle \leftrightarrow \begin{bmatrix} F_0^{(1)} \\ 0 \end{bmatrix}.$$

Operating on the equation of motion with the operator

$$\mathbf{SM}^{-1/2} \leftrightarrow \frac{1}{\sqrt{2}} \begin{bmatrix} 1 & 1 \\ 1 & -1 \end{bmatrix} \begin{bmatrix} \dfrac{1}{\sqrt{m}} & 0 \\ 0 & \dfrac{1}{\sqrt{m}} \end{bmatrix} = \frac{1}{\sqrt{2m}} \begin{bmatrix} 1 & 1 \\ 1 & -1 \end{bmatrix}$$

yields for the normal coordinates

$$|\mathbf{y}\rangle = \mathbf{SM}^{1/2}|\mathbf{x}\rangle$$

or

$$y_1 = \sqrt{\frac{m}{2}}\,(x_1 + x_2), \qquad y_2 = \sqrt{\frac{m}{2}}\,(x_1 - x_2),$$

the equations of motion

$$\ddot{y}_1 + 2\mu\dot{y}_1 + \frac{k_1}{m}\,y_1 = \frac{F_0}{\sqrt{2m}}\,e^{i\omega t},$$

$$\ddot{y}_2 + 2\mu\dot{y}_2 + \frac{(k_1 + 2k_2)}{m}\,y_2 = \frac{F_0}{\sqrt{2m}}\,e^{i\omega t}.$$

The solutions to these independent equations were discussed in Chapter 4. ◀

When normal modes do not exist, we attempt to solve Eq. (11–55) directly by assuming a particular solution of the form

$$x_j = A_j e^{i\omega t}. \tag{11–63}$$

For this trial solution we obtain the equations

$$e^{i\omega t} \sum_j (-\omega^2 m_{ij} + i\omega\mu_{ij} + k_{ij}) A_j = Q_i e^{i\omega t}, \tag{11–64}$$

which are expressed in operator notation by

$$\mathbf{P}|\mathbf{A}\rangle = |\mathbf{Q}\rangle, \tag{11–65}$$

where the operator $\mathbf{P}$ is

$$\mathbf{P} = -\omega^2\mathbf{M} + i\omega\boldsymbol{\mu} + \mathbf{K}. \tag{11–66}$$

Since $\omega$ is not equal to one of the generally complex roots of Eq. (11–42), it follows that $\mathbf{P}$ is nonsingular. There exists thus the inverse operator $\mathbf{P}^{-1}$. Operating with $\mathbf{P}^{-1}$ on Eq. (11–65) yields the solution

$$|\mathbf{A}\rangle = \mathbf{P}^{-1}|\mathbf{Q}\rangle. \tag{11–67}$$

The inverse of an operator was discussed in Section 10–6. There it was shown that its matrix representation contains the determinant value of the operator $\mathbf{P}$

as a denominator. This determinant value may be factored. In terms of the roots of Eq. (11–42), which are the values for $i\omega$ which make det $[\mathbf{P}(i\omega)]$ vanish,

$$\det(\mathbf{P}) = \prod_{j=1}^{n} (i\omega + \beta_j + i\gamma_j)(i\omega + \beta_j - i\gamma_j). \tag{11–68}$$

The solution may thus be expanded as a sum of partial fractions which contain the factors of det $(\mathbf{P})$ as denominators. That is, the solution is expressible as a sum of terms containing the fractions

$$\frac{1}{\omega_j^2 - \omega^2 + 2i\omega\beta_j}, \tag{11–69}$$

where in this case

$$\omega_j^2 = \gamma_j^2 + \beta_j^2 = |\alpha_j|^2.$$

Once again, as in the one-dimensional case, we notice the presence of resonance denominators which determine the response of the system to the external sinusoidal driving forces.

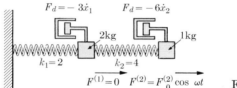

Figure 11–4

▶ As an example, we obtain the particular solution for the forced motion of the second coupled system of the previous section for which normal coordinates do not exist (Fig. 11–4). The application of a sinusoidal driving force to the second particle yields the equations of motion

$$2\ddot{x}_1 + 3\dot{x}_1 + 6x_1 - 4x_2 = 0,$$
$$\ddot{x}_2 + 6\dot{x}_2 + 4x_2 - 4x_1 = F_0^{(2)} e^{i\omega t}.$$

Assuming a solution of the form

$$x_1 = Ae^{i\omega t}$$

and

$$x_2 = Be^{i\omega t},$$

we obtain the simultaneous equations

$$(-2\omega^2 + 3i\omega + 6)A - 4B = 0$$

and

$$-4A + (-\omega^2 + 6i\omega + 4)B = F_0^{(2)}.$$

The solution of these equations is

$$A = \frac{\begin{vmatrix} 0 & -4 \\ F_0^{(2)} & -\omega^2 + 6i\omega + 4 \end{vmatrix}}{\begin{vmatrix} -2\omega^2 + 3i\omega + 6 & -4 \\ -4 & -\omega^2 + 6i\omega + 4 \end{vmatrix}},$$

and

$$B = \frac{\begin{vmatrix} -2\omega^2 + 3i\omega + 6 & 0 \\ -4 & F_0^{(2)} \end{vmatrix}}{(i\omega - \alpha_1)(i\omega - \alpha_2)(i\omega - \alpha_3)(i\omega - \alpha_4)},$$

where the $\alpha_i$'s are the values of $i\omega$, which are the roots of the determinant of the coefficients of $A$ and $B$. They were previously found to be

$$\alpha_{1,2} = -1 \pm i\sqrt{3}, \qquad \alpha_{3,4} = \frac{-11 \pm \sqrt{105}}{4}. \blacktriangleleft$$

## 11–6 Forced oscillation: impulsive forces, tensor Green's function

The solution to the problem of impulsive forces acting on a system for the case when normal modes exist results once again in the solution of a set of one-dimensional equations of motion. For the generalized impulsive force

$$\mathcal{F}_l = \delta_{lm}\delta(t - t') \tag{11–70}$$

acting on the $m$th normal mode (cf. Eq. 11–58) we have for the normal coordinates the equations of motion

$$\ddot{y}_l + 2\mu_l\dot{y}_l + \omega_l^2 y_l = \delta_{lm}\delta(t - t'), \tag{11–71}$$

whose solution was obtained in Section 4–12. The normal mode solution $y_m$ for such an impulsive force is referred to as *Green's function*, and is generally represented by the symbol $G_m(t|t')$. That is, for the impulsive force above the particular solution to Eq. (11–71) is

$$y_l(t) = G_l(t|t')\delta_{lm}. \tag{11–72}$$

In terms of the Green function the general solution which has a zero displacement and a zero first-order time derivative at the initial time $t = 0$ for any generalized time-dependent driving force $|\mathbf{Q}(t)\rangle$ is given by

$$y_l(t) = \int_0^t G_l(t|t')\mathcal{F}_l(t')\, dt', \tag{11–73}$$

or in operator notation by

$$|\mathbf{y}\rangle = \int_0^t \mathbf{G}(t|t')\mathbf{S}\mathbf{M}^{-1/2}|\mathbf{Q}(t')\rangle\, dt', \tag{11–74}$$

where $\mathbf{G}(t|t')$ is the operator whose matrix representation, referred to as the *tensor Green function*, is the diagonal matrix

$$
\begin{bmatrix}
G_1(t|t') & 0 & 0 & \cdots & 0 \\
0 & G_2(t|t') & 0 & & \cdot \\
0 & 0 & G_3(t|t') & & \vdots \\
\vdots & & & & \vdots \\
0 & \cdot & \cdot & \cdots & G_n(t|t')
\end{bmatrix}.
$$

The solution for the coordinates of the vector

$$
|\mathbf{x}\rangle = \mathbf{M}^{-1/2}\mathbf{S}^{-1}|\mathbf{y}\rangle
$$

is given in operator notation by

$$
|\mathbf{x}\rangle = \mathbf{M}^{-1/2}\mathbf{S}^{-1}|\mathbf{y}\rangle = \int_0^t \mathbf{M}^{-1/2}\mathbf{S}^{-1}\mathbf{G}(t|t')\mathbf{S}\mathbf{M}^{-1/2}|\mathbf{Q}(t')\rangle \, dt'
$$

$$
= \int_0^t \overline{\mathbf{G}}(t|t')|\mathbf{Q}(t')\rangle \, dt', \tag{11–75}
$$

where the operator

$$
\overline{\mathbf{G}}(t|t') = \mathbf{M}^{-1/2}\mathbf{S}^{-1}\mathbf{G}(t|t')\mathbf{S}\mathbf{M}^{-1/2} \tag{11–76}
$$

has a matrix representation involving off-diagonal matrix elements. That is,

$$
\overline{\mathbf{G}}(t|t') \leftrightarrow
\begin{bmatrix}
\overline{G}_{11}(t|t') & \overline{G}_{12}(t|t') & \cdots \\
\overline{G}_{21}(t|t') & \overline{G}_{22}(t|t') & \vdots \\
\vdots & & \cdots
\end{bmatrix}, \tag{11–77}
$$

where

$$
\overline{G}_{ij}(t|t') = \sum_{klm} M_{ik}^{-1/2}S_{kl}^{-1}G_l(t|t')S_{lm}M_{mj}^{-1/2}. \tag{11–78}
$$

If normal coordinates do not exist, then the solution for an impulsive force may be obtained by expanding the impulsive force as a Fourier integral (a Fourier series containing all frequencies) and utilizing the results of the previous section and the superposition principle satisfied by solutions to linear differential equations.

The Fourier integral for the Dirac delta function is readily obtained. We proceed to show that

$$
\delta(t - t') = \frac{1}{2\pi}\int_{-\infty}^{\infty} e^{i\omega(t-t')} \, d\omega. \tag{11–79}
$$

To obtain this expression we expand the delta function between the times $-\tau$ and $\tau$ as a Fourier series, and then take its limit as $\tau$ becomes very large. We find that if we set

$$
\delta(t - t') = \sum_{n=0}^{\infty} a_n \cos \frac{n\pi t}{\tau} + \sum_{n=1}^{\infty} b_n \sin \frac{n\pi t}{\tau},
$$

then we must have

$$a_0 = \frac{1}{2\tau},$$

$$a_n = \frac{1}{\tau} \cos \frac{n\pi t'}{\tau}, \qquad n \neq 0,$$

$$b_n = \frac{1}{\tau} \sin \frac{n\pi t'}{\tau}.$$

Thus for any time $t$ between the times $-\tau$ and $\tau$ we can set

$$\delta(t - t') = \frac{1}{2\tau} + \sum_{n=1}^{\infty} \frac{1}{\tau} \cos \frac{n\pi(t - t')}{\tau} = \frac{1}{2} \sum_{-\infty}^{\infty} \frac{e^{i(n\pi/\tau)(t-t')}}{\tau}. \qquad (11\text{--}80)$$

In the limit as we let $\tau$ approach infinity, and setting

$$\omega_n = \frac{n\pi}{\tau}, \qquad \Delta\omega = \frac{\pi}{\tau},$$

we find that indeed

$$\delta(t - t') = \frac{1}{2\pi} \lim_{\Delta\omega \to 0} \sum_{-\infty}^{\infty} e^{i\omega_n(t-t')} \Delta\omega$$

$$= \frac{1}{2\pi} \int_{-\infty}^{\infty} e^{i\omega(t-t')} \, d\omega. \qquad (11\text{--}81)$$

Utilizing Eq. (11–80), the Fourier-series expansion for the Dirac delta function between the times $-\tau$ and $\tau$ we obtain for the generalized force

$$Q_j = \delta_{jl}\,\delta(t - t') \qquad (11\text{--}82)$$

the equations of motion

$$\sum_j m_{ij}\ddot{x}_j^{(l)} + \mu_{ij}\dot{x}_j^{(l)} + k_{ij}x_j^{(l)} = \delta_{il}\,\delta(t - t')$$

$$= \delta_{il} \sum_{-\infty}^{\infty} \frac{1}{2\tau} e^{i(n\pi/\tau)(t-t')}. \qquad (11\text{--}83)$$

Utilizing Eq. (11–67), the solution to this set of simultaneous differential equations is given by

$$x_j^{(l)} = \sum_{n=-\infty}^{\infty} \frac{1}{2\tau} e^{i(n\pi/\tau)(t-t')} P_{jl}^{-1}\left(\frac{in\pi}{\tau}\right). \qquad (11\text{--}84)$$

Setting

$$x_j^{(l)} = \overline{G}_{jl}(t|t'),$$

we find that in the limit as we let $\tau$ approach infinity, we can set

$$\overline{G}_{jl}(t|t') = \frac{1}{2\pi} \int_{-\infty}^{\infty} e^{i\omega(t-t')} P_{jl}^{-1}(i\omega) \, d\omega, \qquad (11\text{--}85)$$

where $\overline{G}_{jl}(t|t')$ is the $jl$th element of the Green function matrix, referred to as the tensor Green function. It is the matrix representation of the Green function operator $\overline{\mathbf{G}}(t|t')$. In terms of this Green function operator the solution which for any generalized time-dependent force $|\mathbf{Q}(t)\rangle$ has zero initial displacement and vanishing initial velocity may be shown to be expressed by

$$|\mathbf{x}(t)\rangle = \int_{t_0}^{t} \overline{\mathbf{G}}(t|t')|\mathbf{Q}(t')\rangle \, dt'. \tag{11–86}$$

## 11–7 Perturbation theory

The physical description of the motion of a system in terms of normal modes is so much simpler than the case when normal modes do not exist that one usually attempts to express solutions for the latter case in the language of the normal-mode framework. Such attempts can be successful whenever the equations of motion can be expressed in the form

$$\left(\mathbf{M}^{(0)}\frac{d^2}{dt^2} + \boldsymbol{\mu}^{(0)}\frac{d}{dt} + \mathbf{K}^{(0)}\right)|\mathbf{x}\rangle = \left(\mathbf{M}^{(1)}\frac{d^2}{dt^2} + \boldsymbol{\mu}^{(1)}\frac{d}{dt} + \mathbf{K}^{(1)}\right)|\mathbf{x}\rangle, \tag{11–87}$$

where $\mathbf{M}^{(0)-1/2}\boldsymbol{\mu}^{(0)}\mathbf{M}^{(0)-1/2}$ and $\mathbf{M}^{(0)-1/2}\mathbf{K}^{(0)}\mathbf{M}^{(0)-1/2}$ are commuting operators which may be diagonalized simultaneously, and

$$\mathbf{M}^{(1)} = \mathbf{M} - \mathbf{M}^{(0)}, \tag{11–88}$$

$$\boldsymbol{\mu}^{(1)} = \boldsymbol{\mu} - \boldsymbol{\mu}^{(0)}, \tag{11–89}$$

$$\mathbf{K}^{(1)} = \mathbf{K} - \mathbf{K}^{(0)} \tag{11–90}$$

are small operators such that the terms on the right-hand side of Eq. (11–87) may be considered as small perturbations of the system whose motion is described by the equation

$$\left(\mathbf{M}^{(0)}\frac{d^2}{dt^2} + \boldsymbol{\mu}^{(0)}\frac{d}{dt} + \mathbf{K}^{(0)}\right)|\mathbf{x}^{(0)}\rangle = 0. \tag{11–91}$$

Let $\boldsymbol{\mathcal{L}}^{(0)}$ represent the operator whose diagonal matrix representation has the elements

$$\mathcal{L}_{ij}^{(0)} = \left(\frac{d^2}{dt^2} + 2\mu_i\frac{d}{dt} + \omega_i^2\right)\delta_{ij}, \tag{11–92}$$

where $2\mu_i$ and $\omega_i^2$ are the diagonal elements of the diagonal matrix representations of the operators $\mathbf{M}^{(0)-1/2}\boldsymbol{\mu}^{(0)}\mathbf{M}^{(0)-1/2}$ and $\mathbf{M}^{(0)-1/2}\mathbf{K}^{(0)}\mathbf{M}^{(0)-1/2}$. Thus $\boldsymbol{\mathcal{L}}^{(0)}$ operating on the normal-mode vector $|\mathbf{y}^{(0)}\rangle = \mathbf{S}\mathbf{M}^{(0)1/2}|\mathbf{x}^0\rangle$, yields for the unperturbed system the normal-mode equation

$$\boldsymbol{\mathcal{L}}^{(0)}|\mathbf{y}^{(0)}\rangle = 0 \tag{11–93}$$

for Eq. (11–91).

The perturbed system satisfies the equations

$$\left(\frac{d^2}{dt^2} + 2\mu_i \frac{d}{dt} + \omega_i^2\right) y_i = \sum_j \left(\bar{m}_{ij} \frac{d^2}{dt^2} + \bar{\mu}_{ij} \frac{d}{dt} + \bar{k}_{ij}\right) y_j. \quad (11\text{--}94)$$

In operator notation these equations are expressed by

$$\mathcal{L}^{(0)}|\mathbf{y}\rangle = \mathcal{L}^{(1)}|\mathbf{y}\rangle. \quad (11\text{--}95)$$

The solution to this operator equation can be expressed in terms of the Green function operator by considering the right-hand side of Eq. (11–94) as an inhomogeneous term. We thus find the particular solution to be expressed formally by

$$|\mathbf{y}\rangle = \int^t \mathbf{G}(t|t')\mathcal{L}^{(1)}|\mathbf{y}(t')\rangle \, dt'. \quad (11\text{--}96)$$

Equation (11–96) is an integral equation which we may attempt to solve by an iterative procedure (cf. Section 4–14). If this iterative procedure works, then it yields the same solution as the method of successive approximation applied to the original differential equations.

We note that Eq. (11–94) can be generalized to include the perturbation of the system by small nonlinear terms in $y_j$ and $\dot{y}_j$.

Thus, for example, if Eq. (11–95) assumed the nonlinear form

$$\sum_j \mathcal{L}_{ij}^{(0)} y_j = \sum_j \mathcal{L}_{ij}^{(1)} y_j + \sum_{jk} \mathcal{L}_{ijk}^{(2)} y_j y_k + \cdots, \quad (11\text{--}97)$$

the solution is formally expressed by

$$y_i(t) = \int^t G_i(t|t') \left[ \sum_j \mathcal{L}_{ij}^{(1)} y_j(t') + \sum_{jk} \mathcal{L}_{ijk}^{(2)} y_j(t') y_k(t') + \cdots \right]. \quad (11\text{--}98)$$

We should like to note that the iterative method does not work well unless the damping forces are very small, so that the damping terms may all be considered as small perturbations, i.e., $\boldsymbol{\mu}^0 = \mathbf{0}$.

## Problems

11–1. (a) A mass $m$ is subjected to a conservative force whose potential energy is

$$U = U_0 \exp \frac{1}{a^2} [5x^2 + 3y^2 + 3z^2 - 2yz - 7ya - 3za],$$

where $U_0$ and $a$ are positive constants. Show that $U$ has one minimum point; and find the normal frequencies of vibration about this minimum point.

(b) If the mass is subjected to an additional force whose components are

$$F_x = F_y = F_z = Be^{-at},$$

what is its motion about the equilibrium point?

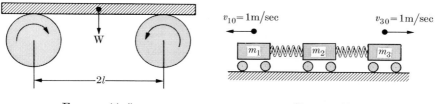

FIGURE 11-5                    FIGURE 11-6

11-2. A bar of weight $W$ rests on top of two wheels whose centers are a distance $2l$ apart and which are driven with the same constant angular velocities $\omega$ in the opposite directions, as shown in Fig. 11-5. The coefficient of friction between the wheels and the bar is $\mu$. The bar is set in motion from equilibrium by a slight push which gives it an initial velocity $v_0$. Obtain and solve the differential equation for its subsequent motion.

11-3. A mass $m$ hangs on the end of a spring whose spring constant is $k$ and whose mass per unit length is $\lambda$. The natural length of the spring is $l$. Each point of the spring oscillates vertically over a distance proportional to the natural distance of the point from the fixed support.

(a) Find the kinetic energy of the system, including the mass of the spring.

(b) Write the Lagrangian equation of motion, solve it, and show that the period of oscillation is

$$\tau = 2\pi\sqrt{(3m + \lambda l)/3k}.$$

11-4. The equilibrium configuration of a molecule is represented by three atoms of equal mass at the vertices of a 45° right triangle connected by springs of equal force constant. Obtain the secular determinant whose roots are normal frequencies of vibration in the plane, and show that the secular equation has the triple root $\omega = 0$. Obtain the nonvanishing frequencies of free vibration. [*Hint:* This problem has reflection symmetry about the altitude to the hypotenuse.]

11-5. Consider the three-mass system of Fig. 11-6. (a) Write the differential equations of motion. (b) For $m_1 = 1$ kg, $m_2 = 3$ kg, $m_3 = 2$ kg, and $k = 6$n/m, find the natural frequencies of the system. (c) For the initial conditions of unstretched springs, the center mass $m_2$ stationary, and the end masses moving as shown at a speed $v_{i0} = 1$ m/sec, find the expression for the motion of mass $m_2$ as a function of time.

11-6. Show that the total energy of a system with three degrees of freedom, oscillating about its equilibrium configuration, is equal to the sum of the energies of its principal modes of oscillation. Show that the time average of the kinetic energy of a principal mode of oscillation is equal to its average potential energy when the averages are taken over a long interval of time.

11-7. Do Problem 6-15(e).

11-8. Do Problems 6-16 and 6-17.

11-9. Do Problem 6-19.

11-10. Derive the equations of motion of the two simple pendulums connected by a relatively light linear spring, as shown in Fig. 11-7. Assume that the motion takes place only in the plane of the diagram, and evaluate the natural frequencies of vibration for small displacements from equilibrium which characterize this system.

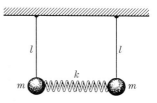

FIGURE 11-7

11–11. Derive and solve the differential equations for the motion of a uniform rigid bar of length $L$ supported elastically as shown in Fig. 11–8. Consider only the motion in the plane of the diagram.

11–12. Two equal masses on a frictionless surface are connected by a viscous damper, and each is restrained by a spring, as shown in Fig. 11–9. Find the motion of the system which starts from rest with the left-hand mass initially displaced by a distance $x_{10}$ from its equilibrium position, and the other mass initially at its equilibrium position. Consider only simple rectilinear motion.

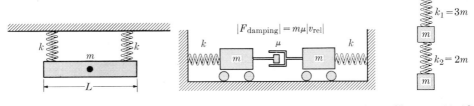

FIGURE 11–8          FIGURE 11–9          FIGURE 11–10

11–13. The mass-spring system illustrated in Fig. 11–10 is free to move only linearly in the vertical direction. When the system is in static equilibrium under the action of gravity, the springs, of course, are under some tension. Suppose that the lower mass is raised until the lower spring has no tension. If the lower mass is then suddenly released, what will be the expression for the subsequent motion of the upper mass. (*Note:* Define the origins of your coordinates carefully.)

11–14. The masses illustrated in Fig. 8–10 are coupled together with a damper as shown in Fig. 11–11. The mass on the left-hand side is driven with a force

$$F = F_0 \cos \omega t.$$

The displacements from equilibrium are $q_1$ and $q_2$.

(a) Write expressions for the kinetic energy and the potential energy for the system.

(b) Assuming that the damping force is proportional to the difference in velocity between the two masses, set up the equations of motion for $q_1$ and $q_2$. Obtain the characteristic equation and solve it for the frequencies of free vibration. How do these frequencies compare with those of the undamped motion?

(c) Find the steady-state motion of the system under the action of the force $F = F_0 \cos \omega t$ acting on the mass on the left-hand side as shown.

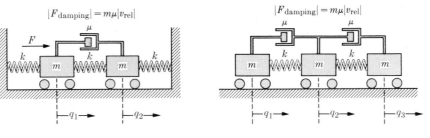

FIGURE 11–11                    FIGURE 11–12

11–15. Three equal masses are connected by springs, as shown in Fig. 11–12, with dampers of coefficient $\mu$ between them.

(a) Set up the expressions of $T$ and $U$ for this sytem, and obtain the equations of motion.

(b) Using trial solutions of the form $q_1 = Ae^{\lambda t}$, $q_2 = Be^{\lambda t}$, and $q_3 = Ce^{\lambda t}$, obtain the characteristic equation of the system.

(c) Show that the characteristic equation may be written in the form

$$m\lambda^2(m\lambda^2 + m\mu\lambda + k)(m\lambda^2 + 3m\mu\lambda + 3k) = 0.$$

If this system is to have nonoscillatory motion, the discriminant of each of the last two quadratic factors must be $\geq 0$. Show that $\mu \geq 2\sqrt{k/m}$ will satisfy the condition for nonoscillatory motion.

11–16. In Fig. 11–13 the four masses move only along a horizontal straight line under the action of four identical springs of spring constant $k$, and a weak spring of spring constant $k' \ll k$. Find, to first order in $k'$, an approximate solution for the normal modes of vibration of the system.

11–17. Do Problems 8–21 and 8–22.

11–18. Do Problem 8–23.

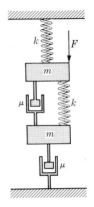

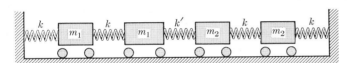

FIGURE 11–13                    FIGURE 11–14

11–19. Derive and obtain the steady-state solution of the equations for the vertical motion of the system illustrated in Fig. 11–14. Define carefully the origins for your coordinates. The applied force is $F = F_0(1 - e^{-t})$.

11–20. A triple pendulum is formed by suspending a mass $M$ by a string of length $l$ from a fixed support. A mass $m$ is hung from $M$ by a string of length $l$, and from this second mass a third mass $m$ is hung by a third string of length $l$. The masses swing in a single vertical plane. Set up the equations for small oscillations of the system, using as coordinates the angles $\theta_1$, $\theta_2$, $\theta_3$ made by the three strings with the vertical. Show that if $M \gg m$, the normal coordinates may readily be found if terms of order $(m/M)^{1/2}$ are neglected. Find the approximate normal frequencies to order $m/M$.

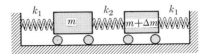

FIGURE 11–15

11–21. Obtain a first-order estimate in $\Delta m/m$ for the normal frequencies of vibration of the system of masses shown in Fig. 11–15.

11–22. Obtain a first-order estimate in $\Delta k/k$ for the resonant frequencies of the system of particles shown in Fig. 11–16.

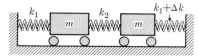

FIGURE 11–16

11–23. The equilibrium configuration of an $X_3$ molecule is represented by three atoms of equal mass at the vertices of an equilateral triangle connected by springs of equal force constant (Fig. 11–17).

(a) Utilizing cartesian coordinates as indicated, obtain the Lagrangian for the system of particles whose motion is constrained to the plane of their equilibrium configuration.

(b) Show that the Lagrangian is invariant under the six operations of the permutation group of three elements, the operations $\mathbf{1}$, $\mathbf{P}_{12}$, $\mathbf{P}_{13}$, $\mathbf{P}_{23}$, $(\mathbf{P}_{12}\mathbf{P}_{31})$, and $(\mathbf{P}_{12}\mathbf{P}_{23})$, where $\mathbf{P}_{ij}$ refers to the interchange of the $i$th and $j$th particles.

(c) Show that the six permutation operations do not commute.

(d) Obtain the $6 \times 6$ matrix representation of the commutative permutation operations

$$\mathbf{O}_1 = \mathbf{P}_{23}\mathbf{P}_{12} \quad \text{and} \quad \mathbf{O}_2 = \mathbf{P}_{13}\mathbf{P}_{12}.$$

These matrices, when operating on the six-element column matrix $(\mathbf{r})$ whose elements represent in succession the coordinates of the system and whose transpose is

$$(\tilde{\mathbf{r}}) = [x_1, y_1, x_2, y_2, x_3, y_3],$$

yields the new assignment of the coordinates of the particles.

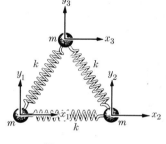

FIGURE 11–17

(e) Obtain the matrix representations of the simultaneous eigenvectors of the two commutative operators of Part (b) and the transformation matrix which simultaneously diagonalizes their commuting matrix representations.

(f) Express the six-dimensional vector $|\mathbf{r}\rangle$ as a linear sum of the eigenvectors found in Part (e) and subsequently show that the Lagrangian expressed in terms of the eigenvectors of $\mathbf{O}_1$ and $\mathbf{O}_2$ yield simpler equations of motion.

(g) Obtain the normal frequencies of vibration of the system.

<h1 style="text-align: center">12</h1>

<h1 style="text-align: center">Wave Propagation Along a String</h1>

In this chapter we consider the dynamic behavior of a string under tension. For small displacements of the string from its equilibrium position we shall find the kinematic description of small portions of the string about their equilibrium position to be represented by the propagation of a transverse wave along the string. We shall subsequently acquaint ourselves with such salient features of wave motion as reflection, transmission, interference, and the polarization of transverse waves by considering a number of problems involving discontinuities in the density of the string and constraints on the motion of some of its points. These are features which are generally associated with any wave motion and not just with the motion of waves along a string.

By restricting ourselves to the motion of waves along a string, we are restricting ourselves to the simplest case—the one-dimensional propagation of a wave. This restriction, however, does not detract from the importance and general applicability of our discussion. One-dimensional plane waves are good approximations to all waves at large distances from the source producing them. By restricting ourselves to the one-dimensional motion of waves, we have the advantage of being able to discuss the important features of wave motion unemcumbered by mathematical difficulties.

## 12–1 Mathematical representation of plane waves, the principle of superposition, wave equations

In this section we shall obtain the general formal mathematical dependence on the coordinates and the time of a physical quantity $\Psi$, observed to be propagating with a velocity $v$ in a given direction.

Consider, for example, a very long string under tension, one end of which was momentarily displaced at time $t = 0$ from its equilibrium position. Pictures of the string taken at periodic time intervals will, if no dissipation is present, reveal a situation as depicted in Fig. 12–1. That is, the picture of the string at a time $t_2$, showing the displacements of the points of the string as a function

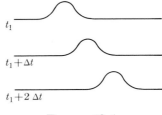

$t_1$

$t_1 + \Delta t$

$t_1 + 2\,\Delta t$

FIGURE 12–1

415

of position at that time, appears to be the same as the picture at some previous time $t_1$ with the string seemingly displaced to the right by a distance (Fig. 12–2)

$$d = v(t_2 - t_1).$$

Mathematically this fact is expressed by

$$\Psi = \Psi(z - vt), \tag{12–1}$$

where $\Psi$ represents the displacement of the string from its equilibrium position.

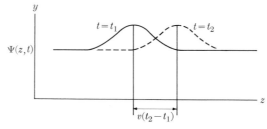

FIGURE 12–2

Similarly, we find that a disturbance in the string that is propagated to the left (decreasing $z$-direction) with the same velocity is mathematically expressed by the equation

$$\Psi = \Psi(z + vt). \tag{12–2}$$

Equations (12–1) and (12–2) quite generally describe the propagation of any wave in the increasing or decreasing $z$-direction in a nondissipative, nondispersive medium. Here $\Psi$ could just as well represent the magnitude of the electric vector of a plane polarized electromagnetic wave, the pressure in a medium through which a sound wave is propagating, or the probability amplitude of a matter wave from which the probability for finding a particle within a given volume of space may be determined.

There is an additional condition, the principle of superposition, which we shall require the propagating physical quantity to satisfy. The principle of superposition states that if two independent waves are simultaneously propagated through a medium, then the resultant physical quantity at any point is the linear sum of the two waves,

$$\Psi = \Psi_1 + \Psi_2. \tag{12–3}$$

This condition is satisfied only by the solutions to linear partial differential equations. We are thereby restricting ourselves to waves whose equation is a linear partial differential equation. A shock wave is an example of a wave which does not satisfy the principle of superposition.

Many linear partial differential equations exist whose solutions are functions having the form of Eqs. (12–1) and (12–2). For example, we find that the function

$$\Psi = \Psi(z \pm vt) \tag{12–4}$$

satisfies any of the following wave equations

$$\frac{\partial \Psi}{\partial z} = \pm \frac{1}{v} \frac{\partial \Psi}{\partial t},$$

$$\frac{\partial^2 \Psi}{\partial z^2} = \frac{1}{v^2} \frac{\partial^2 \Psi}{\partial t^2},$$

$$\frac{\partial^4 \Psi}{\partial z^4} = \frac{1}{v^4} \frac{\partial^4 \Psi}{\partial t^4}.$$

Specific functions of $z \pm vt$ satisfy still more complicated wave equations. In the next section we shall show that the very frequently occurring equation

$$\frac{\partial^2 \Psi}{\partial z^2} = \frac{1}{v^2} \frac{\partial^2 \Psi}{\partial t^2} \tag{12–5}$$

is the wave equation satisfied by waves along a vibrating string.

The question arises whether functions of the form given by Eq. (12–4) are the only possible solutions of Eq. (12–5). That they are can be seen by making the coordinate transformation

$$\xi_1 = z + vt \qquad \text{and} \qquad \xi_2 = z - vt$$

or

$$z = \tfrac{1}{2}(\xi_1 + \xi_2) \qquad \text{and} \qquad vt = \tfrac{1}{2}(\xi_1 - \xi_2).$$

This transformation yields

$$\frac{\partial^2 \Psi}{\partial z^2} = \frac{\partial^2 \Psi}{\partial \xi_1^2} + 2 \frac{\partial^2 \Psi}{\partial \xi_1 \partial \xi_2} + \frac{\partial^2 \Psi}{\partial \xi_2^2}$$

and

$$\frac{1}{v^2} \frac{\partial^2 \Psi}{\partial t^2} = \frac{\partial^2 \Psi}{\partial \xi_1^2} - 2 \frac{\partial^2 \Psi}{\partial \xi_1 \partial \xi_2} + \frac{\partial^2 \Psi}{\partial \xi_2^2}$$

or

$$\frac{\partial^2 \Psi}{\partial z^2} - \frac{1}{v^2} \frac{\partial^2 \Psi}{\partial t^2} = 4 \frac{\partial^2 \Psi}{\partial \xi_1 \partial \xi_2} = 0.$$

The solutions to the equation

$$\frac{\partial^2 \Psi}{\partial \xi_1 \partial \xi_2} = 0$$

are expressible only as the linear sum of a function $\Psi_1(\xi_1)$ of $\xi_1$ only and a function $\Psi_2(\xi_2)$ of $\xi_2$ only. That is,

$$\Psi = \Psi_1(\xi_1) + \Psi_2(\xi_2) = \Psi_1(z + vt) + \Psi_2(z - vt).$$

## 12–2 The wave equation for the vibrating string

In order to obtain the wave equation for a vibrating string under tension, we concentrate our attention on a small portion of the string (Fig. 12–3). We shall assume the horizontal position of the string along the $z$-axis to be its equilibrium position. We note that by making this assumption we are neglecting the effect of gravity on the string. In other words, we assume the tension in the string to be sufficiently large so as to make the gravitational effect negligible.

Consider now an infinitesimal portion of the string of length $\Delta s$ which is displaced in the vertical plane by a small amount from its equilibrium position along the horizontal $z$-axis.

The forces acting on this small portion of the string are the tensions $T(z)$ and $T(z + \Delta z)$ as shown in Fig. 12–3. These forces act at the two endpoints of the small piece of string, the points whose projections onto the $z$-axis have the coordinates $z$ and $z + \Delta z$. The resultant force on the small section has a vertical and a horizontal component, which are given by

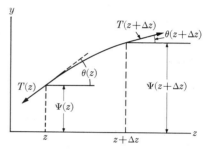

FIGURE 12–3

$$R_{\text{horizontal}} = T(z + \Delta z) \cos \theta(z + \Delta z) - T(z) \cos \theta(z)$$

and

$$R_{\text{vertical}} = T(z + \Delta z) \sin \theta(z + \Delta z) - T(z) \sin \theta(z).$$

For small displacements $\Psi$ from equilibrium the angle $\theta$ which the tangents to the string at any point make with the $z$-axis will likewise be small. We shall restrict ourselves to small displacements which allow us to approximate the sine of the angles involved by their tangent and the cosine by unity. For this approximation and the further assumption that for such small displacements the tension in the string does not vary appreciably from point to point, so that we can set

$$T(z + \Delta z) = T(z) = T,$$

it follows that

$$R_{\text{horizontal}} = 0,$$

and

$$R_{\text{vertical}} = T[\tan \theta(z + \Delta z) - \tan \theta(z)] = T\Delta \frac{\partial \Psi}{\partial z} = T \frac{\partial^2 \Psi}{\partial z^2} \Delta z. \qquad (12\text{–}6)$$

By Newton's law of motion this yields the equation of motion

$$T \frac{\partial^2 \Psi}{\partial z^2} \Delta z = m \frac{\partial^2 \Psi}{\partial t^2}. \qquad (12\text{–}7)$$

The mass $m$ of the small piece of string is to within the same approximation given by

$$m = \mu \, \Delta z, \tag{12–8}$$

where $\mu$ is the linear mass density of the string. Newton's equation of motion for the small piece of string is thus the wave equation

$$\frac{\partial^2 \Psi}{\partial z^2} = \frac{1}{v^2} \frac{\partial^2 \Psi}{\partial t^2}, \tag{12–9}$$

where

$$v^2 = \frac{T}{\mu}. \tag{12–10}$$

From our discussion in the previous section it should be clear that the motion of the string as a whole is thus expressible by the superposition of solutions of the form

$$\Psi = \Psi(z \pm vt),$$

all propagating with the same speed

$$v = \sqrt{\frac{T}{\mu}}.$$

The specific functional dependence of the displacement $\Psi$ on the position variable $z$ and the time $t$ is, as we shall see, determined by the displacement and velocity of the string as a function of $z$ at some initial time $t_0$.

For the present we shall consider the propagation of harmonic waves along the string which have the functional form

$$\Psi = A \cos \left[ k(z \pm vt) + \phi \right]. \tag{12–11}$$

Their importance lies in the fact that any function of $z$ and $t$ which describes the propagation of a wave along the string is expressible as a linear sum of such harmonic waves. By the principle of superposition therefore any complicated vibrational motion of the string can be analyzed by independent considerations of the independent harmonic waves which describe its motion.

## 12–3 Harmonic waves

By far the simplest wave is a harmonic wave having the form

$$\Psi = A \cos \left[ k(z \pm vt) + \phi \right], \tag{12–12}$$

where $k$ is a constant referred to as the *wave number* of the wave. Dimensionally it must be expressed in radians per unit length in order that $k(z \pm vt)$ have the dimension of radians. Therefore $k$ is conveniently expressed by

$$k = \frac{2\pi}{\lambda}, \tag{12–13}$$

where $\lambda$ has the dimension of length and is referred to as the *wavelength* of the harmonic wave. In terms of the wavelength, the displacement of the string is given by

$$\Psi(z, t) = A \cos\left[2\pi\left(\frac{z}{\lambda} \pm \frac{v}{\lambda} t\right) + \phi\right]. \tag{12-14}$$

The ratio $v/\lambda$ is referred to as the *frequency* of the wave,

$$\nu = \frac{v}{\lambda} = \frac{1}{\tau}. \tag{12-15}$$

Hence other equivalent ways of expressing a harmonic wave are

$$\Psi = A \cos\left[2\pi\left(\frac{z}{\lambda} \pm \frac{t}{\tau}\right) + \phi\right], \tag{12-16}$$

and

$$\Psi = A \cos(kz \pm \omega t + \phi),$$

where

$$\omega = 2\pi\nu. \tag{12-17}$$

The angular frequency $\omega$ of the wave is customarily also referred to as simply the frequency.

In dealing with harmonic waves it is algebraically simpler to consider them as a superposition of the complex harmonic waves

$$\psi = A e^{i\omega t} e^{\pm i(kz + \phi)} \tag{12-18}$$

and their complex conjugates, which are mathematically linearly independent. Since, however, the displacements of the string will at all times be real quantities, we can economize our formulas and considerations by concentrating only on the complex waves given by Eq. (12–18). It must follow that the waves

$$\psi = B e^{-i\omega t} e^{\mp i(kz + \phi)},$$

which are the complex conjugates of the complex harmonic waves of Eq. (12–18) and which would also appear in any general solution, must necessarily have an amplitude

$$B = A^*.$$

We shall therefore consider only the complex harmonic waves expressed by Eq. (12–18) which have the exponential time factor $e^{+i\omega t}$.

The complex harmonic wave

$$\psi = A e^{i(kz + \phi)} e^{i\omega t} \tag{12-19}$$

will thus be understood to represent the real harmonic wave

$$\Psi = \operatorname{Re} \psi = A \cos(kz + \omega t + \phi)$$

travelling in the negative $z$-direction; and the complex harmonic wave

$$\psi = Ae^{-i(kz+\phi)}e^{i\omega t} \tag{12-20}$$

to represent the real harmonic wave

$$\Psi = \mathrm{Re}\,\psi = A\cos(kz - \omega t + \phi)$$

travelling in the increasing $z$-direction.

## 12–4 Energy flow in a harmonic wave

Waves transmit energy. It is therefore appropriate to discuss the average energy which is transmitted by a harmonic wave per unit time. To obtain this energy flow per unit time we consider the total energy per wavelength of the string transmitted along the string with speed $v$. The total energy of the string contains a kinetic and a potential part. The kinetic energy of any small section $\Delta z$ oscillating in the vertical direction is given by

$$K.E. = \frac{1}{2}(\mu\,\Delta z)\left(\frac{\partial\Psi}{\partial t}\right)^2. \tag{12-21}$$

The potential energy of the string can be obtained by finding the work which was performed in displacing it from its equilibrium position. The work performed on a small section is given by

$$W = \int_0^\Psi R_{\mathrm{vertical}}\,d\Psi = \Delta z\int_0^\Psi T\frac{\partial^2\Psi}{\partial z^2}\,d\Psi$$

or, for a harmonic wave for which $(\partial^2\Psi/\partial z^2) = -k^2\Psi$, by

$$W = \Delta z\int_0^\Psi - Tk^2\Psi\,d\Psi = -\tfrac{1}{2}Tk^2\Psi^2\,\Delta z. \tag{12-22}$$

The potential energy, being the negative of this work, is given by

$$U = \tfrac{1}{2}Tk^2\Psi^2\,\Delta z. \tag{12-23}$$

Furthermore,

$$Tk^2 = \mu v^2\left(\frac{2\pi}{\lambda}\right)^2 = \mu\omega^2,$$

whence for the harmonic wave

$$\Psi = A\cos k(z \pm vt)$$

the average energy per unit length of the string is found to be

$$\begin{aligned}\mathcal{E} &= \tfrac{1}{2}\mu\omega^2 A^2\sin^2 k(z \pm vt) + \tfrac{1}{2}Tk^2A^2\cos^2 k(z \pm vt)\\ &= \tfrac{1}{2}\mu\omega^2 A^2.\end{aligned} \tag{12-24}$$

Having found the average energy per unit length of the string, it is a simple matter to obtain the average energy flow per unit time in the $z$-direction. Since all the energy in a piece of the string of length $v \times 1$ will pass any fixed point in unit time, it follows that the average energy flow $S$ past any given point in the direction in which the wave is being propagated is given by

$$S = \frac{dE}{dt} = v\mathcal{E} = \frac{1}{2}\,\mu\omega^2 A^2 v = \frac{1}{2}\,T\omega k A^2. \tag{12-25}$$

## 12–5 Polarization

In our discussion thus far we have restricted the vibrational motion of the string to take place in the vertical plane. Under ordinary circumstances, however, a string under tension could just as well be made to oscillate in the horizontal or any other plane. More complicated oscillatory modes could also be envisioned. Whatever oscillation the string does perform, the displacement of any point of the string in the $xy$-plane is specified by its components along the horizontal $x$-direction and the vertical $y$-direction. For small displacements from equilibrium we now obtain the two equations of motion

$$R_y = \mu\,\frac{\partial^2\Psi_y}{\partial t^2}\,\Delta z \quad \text{and} \quad R_x = \mu\,\frac{\partial^2\Psi_x}{\partial t^2}\,\Delta z, \tag{12-26}$$

where $\Psi_x$ and $\Psi_y$ are the $x$- and $y$-components of the displacement of the points on the string. The resultant forces in the $x$- and $y$-directions are found to be

$$R_x = T\Delta\left(\frac{\partial\Psi_x}{\partial s}\right) \quad \text{and} \quad R_y = T\Delta\left(\frac{\partial\Psi_y}{\partial s}\right).$$

For small displacement from equilibrium, for which as before we assume that $\Delta s$ may be replaced by $\Delta z$, etc., we obtain

$$R_x = T\,\frac{\partial^2\Psi_x}{\partial z^2}\,\Delta z \quad \text{and} \quad R_y = T\,\frac{\partial^2\Psi_y}{\partial z^2}\,\Delta z.$$

This results in the two independent wave equations

$$\frac{\partial^2\Psi_x}{\partial z^2} - \frac{1}{v^2}\frac{\partial^2\Psi_x}{\partial t^2} = 0, \quad \frac{\partial^2\Psi_y}{\partial z^2} - \frac{1}{v^2}\frac{\partial^2\Psi_y}{\partial t^2} = 0. \tag{12-27}$$

The most general solution describing the vibrational motion of the string is thus given by the transverse displacement vector

$$\boldsymbol{\Psi}(z, t) = \Psi_x(z, t)\mathbf{i} + \Psi_y(z, t)\mathbf{j}, \tag{12-28}$$

where $\Psi_x$ and $\Psi_y$ are the solutions to the two-component wave equations for the string. The solutions which describe the displacement of the string in the

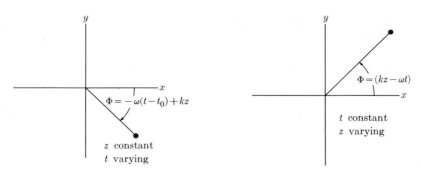

FIGURE 12–4                                FIGURE 12–5

vertical or horizontal plane or, for that matter, any other plane are referred to as *plane polarized* solutions.

The resultant vibrational motion of a string may, however, have other very interesting modes. Consider, for example, the superposition of the two plane polarized harmonic waves

$$\Psi_x = \text{Re } (Ae^{-ikz}e^{i\omega t}) = A \cos (kz - \omega t),$$
$$\Psi_y = \text{Re } (iAe^{-ikz}e^{i\omega t}) = A \sin (kz - \omega t). \tag{12-29}$$

The resultant displacement of any point of the string, when both waves are simultaneously propagating along the string, is found to have the constant magnitude $A$, and the displacement vector at any point $z$ is found to make the angle

$$\Phi = -\omega(t - t_0) + kz$$

with the positive $x$-axis (Fig. 12–4).

The displacement vector at any point $z$ will thus be observed to rotate about the positive $z$-axis with the angular velocity $-\omega$. For any given time $t$, the string as a function of $z$ will assume the shape of a circular helix, where the angle which the displacement vector makes with the positive $x$-axis increases as $z$ increases (Figs. 12–5, 6). Such a wave is referred to as a *left circularly polarized wave*.

On the other hand, the resultant wave produced by the superposition of the two plane polarized waves

$$\Psi_x = \text{Re } (Ae^{-ikz}e^{i\omega t}) = A \cos (kz - \omega t),$$
$$\Psi_y = \text{Re } (-iAe^{-ikz}e^{i\omega t}) = -A \sin (kz - \omega t) \tag{12-30}$$

is a *right circularly polarized wave* (Fig. 12–7). It is so named, because the displacement vector at any point $z$ rotates in time about the direction of propagation of the wave according to the right-hand rule. We note that for the left circularly polarized wave the displacement vector rotates about the direction of propagation according to the left-hand rule.

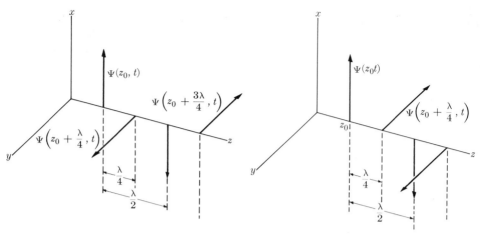

FIG. 12–6.  Left circularly polarized wave.    FIG. 12–7. Right circularly polarized wave.

The polarization is referred to as circular, since the magnitude of the displacement vector at any point remains fixed and the points of the string move in circles.

The shape which the string will assume under the different circular polarizations can be obtained by winding a string on a circular cylinder about the positive or negative $z$-axis while moving the cylinder in the positive $z$-direction (Fig. 12–8).

We note that the linear combination of a left- and a right-handed circularly polarized wave of equal amplitude but arbitrary phase difference leads to a plane polarized wave. More explicitly, we find that the superposition of two such waves yields

$$\Psi_x = \text{Re}\,[(Ae^{-ikz} + Ae^{-ikz+i\phi})e^{i\omega t}],$$

$$\Psi_y = \text{Re}\,[(iAe^{-ikz} - iAe^{-ikz+i\phi})e^{i\omega t}],$$

$$(12\text{–}31)$$

or

$$\Psi_x = 2A\,\cos\left(kz - \omega t - \frac{\phi}{2}\right)\cos\frac{\phi}{2},$$

$$\Psi_y = 2A\,\cos\left(kz - \omega t - \frac{\phi}{2}\right)\sin\frac{\phi}{2},$$

$$(12\text{–}32)$$

which are the equations of a harmonic wave polarized in a plane making an angle $\phi/2$ with the positive $x$-axis.

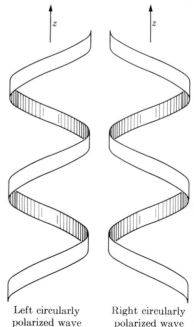

Left circularly          Right circularly
polarized wave          polarized wave

FIGURE 12–8

Similarly, we find that the linear combination of a left and a right circularly polarized wave with different amplitude and arbitrary phase generally leads to an *elliptically polarized wave*. Specifically, if the time $t = 0$ is chosen when the left circularly polarized wave has at the point $z = 0$ a displacement along the positive $x$-axis, and the right circularly polarized wave has at the point $z = 0$ and time $t = 0$ a displacement vector making an angle $\phi$ with the positive $x$-axis, then the resultant wave is given by

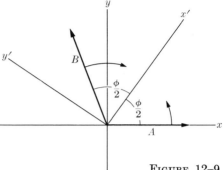

Figure 12–9

$$\Psi_x = \mathrm{Re}\,[(A + Be^{i\phi})e^{-i(kz-\omega t)}],$$
$$\Psi_y = \mathrm{Re}\,[i(A - Be^{i\phi})e^{-i(kz-\omega t)}].$$

$$(12\text{–}33)$$

These may be rewritten as

$$\Psi_x = \mathrm{Re}\,[(Ae^{-i\phi/2} + Be^{i\phi/2})e^{i\phi/2}e^{-i(kz-\omega t)}],$$

$$(12\text{–}34)$$

$$\Psi_y = \mathrm{Re}\,[i(Ae^{-i\phi/2} - Be^{i\phi/2})e^{i\phi/2}e^{-i(kz-\omega t)}].$$

The components of the resultant displacements along the $x'$- and $y'$-axes (cf. Fig. 12–9) which are related to the $x$- and $y$-axes by the transformation equations

$$x' = x\cos\frac{\phi}{2} + y\sin\frac{\phi}{2}, \qquad y' = -x\sin\frac{\phi}{2} + y\cos\frac{\phi}{2},$$

are described by

$$\Psi_{x'} = \mathrm{Re}\,[(A + B)e^{i\phi/2}e^{-i(kz-\omega t)}] = (A + B)\cos\left(kz - \omega t - \frac{\phi}{2}\right)$$

and

$$(12\text{–}35)$$

$$\Psi_{y'} = \mathrm{Re}\,[i(A - B)e^{i\phi/2}e^{-i(kz-\omega t)}] = (A - B)\sin\left(kz - \omega t - \frac{\phi}{2}\right).$$

Since

$$\left(\frac{\Psi_{x'}}{A + B}\right)^2 + \left(\frac{\Psi_{y'}}{A - B}\right)^2 = 1,$$

the displacement of the string at any point $z$ is found at all times to be along the ellipse having a semimajor axis of magnitude $(A + B)$ lying along the $x'$-axis, and a semiminor axis of magnitude $|A - B|$ along the $y'$-axis. Hence the name *elliptic polarization*. Whether the wave is left or right elliptically polarized depends on the amplitudes of the circularly polarized waves into which it can be decomposed. It will assume the same sense of polarization as the circularly polarized wave having the larger amplitude.

The complex description of the propagation of a transverse wave along a string, combined with the matrix representation of the displacement vector, gives us a very convenient and useful notation for representing the propagation of polarized transverse waves along a string. Thus, for example, if we let

$$|\Psi\rangle \leftrightarrow \mathrm{Re} \begin{bmatrix} \psi_x \\ \psi_y \end{bmatrix},$$

we find that the real part of the complex harmonic wave

$$|\psi\rangle \leftrightarrow (\psi) = \begin{bmatrix} 1 \\ 0 \end{bmatrix} e^{-i(kz-\omega t)}$$

represents a harmonic wave plane polarized in the $xz$-plane, whereas the real part of the complex harmonic wave

$$|\psi\rangle \leftrightarrow (\psi) = \begin{bmatrix} 0 \\ i \end{bmatrix} e^{-i(kz-\omega t)} \tag{12-36}$$

represents a harmonic wave plane polarized in the $yz$-plane. Similarly, the waves

$$|\psi\rangle \leftrightarrow (\psi) = \begin{bmatrix} 1 \\ i \end{bmatrix} e^{-i(kz-\omega t)} \tag{12-37}$$

and

$$|\psi\rangle \leftrightarrow (\psi) = \begin{bmatrix} 1 \\ -i \end{bmatrix} e^{-i(kz-\omega t)} \tag{12-38}$$

represent, respectively, left and right circularly polarized waves propagating in the increasing $z$-direction. In this notation the matrix contains the information about the state of polarization of the wave, whereas the exponential gives us the frequency, wave number, and direction of propagation.

Regarding the energy in these waves, the two modes of plane polarization being independent, the total energy propagated is equal to the sum of the energy in each. That is, the wave

$$|\psi\rangle \leftrightarrow (\psi) = \begin{bmatrix} A \\ B \end{bmatrix} e^{-i(kz-\omega t)}$$

has an average energy flow per unit time given by

$$S = \frac{\mu\omega^2 v}{2} \left( |A|^2 + |B|^2 \right) \tag{12-39}$$

or

$$S = \frac{1}{2}\mu\omega^2 \langle\psi|\psi\rangle = \frac{1}{2} Tk\omega\langle\psi|\psi\rangle = -\frac{T}{2} \left\langle \frac{\partial\psi}{\partial t} \Big| \frac{\partial\psi}{\partial z} \right\rangle, \tag{12-40}$$

where $\langle\psi| = |\psi\rangle^\dagger$.

## 12–6 Reflection and transmission of harmonic waves

Having discussed the propagation of a harmonic wave along a uniform string under tension, we next turn our attention to the propagation of a plane polarized harmonic wave along a string in a region where the linear mass density of the string changes discontinuously at a certain point. (Fig. 12–10.) We choose this point as the origin of the horizontal $z$-axis.

Since the mass per unit length is no longer a constant for the entire string, the linear mass density appearing in the wave equation

$$\frac{\partial^2 \Psi}{\partial z^2} - \frac{\mu}{T}\frac{\partial^2 \Psi}{\partial t^2} = 0 \qquad (12\text{–}41)$$

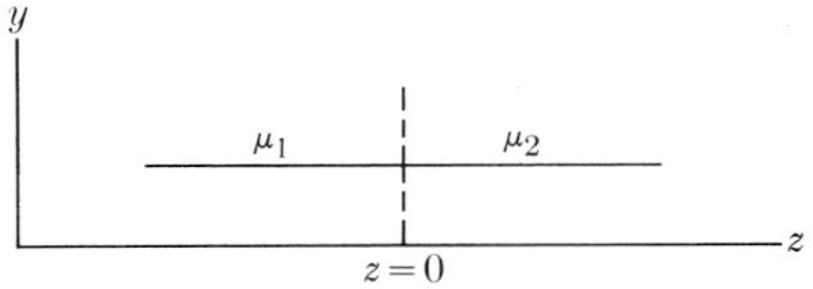

FIGURE 12–10

must now be considered as a function of position. For the case under consideration we have

$$\mu = \begin{cases} \mu_1 & z < 0, \\ \mu_2 & z > 0. \end{cases} \qquad (12\text{–}42)$$

Problems involving discontinuities can be handled by solving the wave equation in each of the continuous regions and then attempting to match the solutions in each region at the point of discontinuity through the application of boundary conditions.

For the problem of a vibrating string two boundary conditions are quite obvious. Clearly as long as the two parts of the string remain connected we must have the same displacment $\Psi$, and hence the same $\partial\Psi/\partial t$ in both regions. Mathematically this fact is expressed by

$$\Psi_1(0, t) = \Psi_2(0, t)$$

and

$$\frac{\partial\Psi_1(0, t)}{\partial t} = \frac{\partial\Psi_2(0, t)}{\partial t}. \qquad (12\text{–}43)$$

The latter equation requires that the frequency of the harmonic waves in each of the two regions be the same. Another condition which must be satisfied is the conservation of energy. That is, if the two parts of the string are smoothly joined so that no loss of energy occurs at the coupling point, then as much energy must leave the point $z = 0$ as approaches it. This condition (see below) is satisfied only if the slope of the string at the junction is continuous,

$$\left.\frac{\partial\Psi_1(z, t)}{\partial z}\right|_{z=0} = \left.\frac{\partial\Psi_2(z, t)}{\partial z}\right|_{z=0}. \qquad (12\text{–}44)$$

Equations (12–43) and (12–44) are referred to as the boundary conditions at the junction.

It should be clear that any solutions in the two parts of the string are also dependent on the boundary conditions which must be met at the ends of the string. Let us assume for the moment that the ends have no effect, either because they are so far away that for a sufficiently long period of time their effect will not be felt in the region of the discontinuity, or because the ends absorb all the energy that approaches them without reflecting any (cf. Problem 12–4). We thus have the situation where a harmonic wave produced in one region of the string is propagated towards the junction and possibly split up into a reflected and a transmitted wave. If the harmonic wave is incident from the first region, the region $z < 0$, then we expect two waves in the first region, one moving to the right and the other to the left. Expressed in terms of complex waves, we thus have

$$\psi_1(z, t) = A e^{i(-k_1 z + \omega t)} + B e^{i(k_1 z + \omega t)}, \tag{12-45}$$

in the first region, where

$$k_1 = \frac{\omega}{v_1} = \omega \sqrt{\frac{\mu_1}{T}}. \tag{12-46}$$

(Note that the same exponential time dependence $e^{i\omega t}$ is used for both waves.)

In the second region we have only one wave moving to the right as expressed by

$$\psi_2(z, t) = C e^{i(-k_2 z + \omega t)}, \tag{12-47}$$

where

$$k_2 = \frac{\omega}{v_2} = \omega \sqrt{\frac{\mu_2}{T}}. \tag{12-48}$$

Imposing the boundary conditions at the point $z = 0$, we obtain the relations which must exist between the amplitudes of the three waves. That is, from Eq. (12–43) we obtain

$$A + B = C, \tag{12-49}$$

and from Eq. (12–44)

$$i(-A + B)k_1 = -ik_2 C. \tag{12-50}$$

We note that multiplication of these two equations yields

$$k_1(A^2 - B^2) = k_2 C^2, \tag{12-51}$$

which ensures that we have conservation of energy.

In terms of the propagation constants $k_1$ and $k_2$, we find the relationships between the amplitudes of the waves to be

$$B = \frac{k_1 - k_2}{k_1 + k_2} A = \frac{\sqrt{\mu_1} - \sqrt{\mu_2}}{\sqrt{\mu_1} + \sqrt{\mu_2}} A \tag{12-52}$$

and

$$C = \frac{2k_1}{k_1 + k_2} A = \frac{2\sqrt{\mu_1}}{\sqrt{\mu_1} + \sqrt{\mu_2}} A. \tag{12-53}$$

We note that when $\mu_1 < \mu_2$, there is a change in phase upon reflection. The reflected wave is then $\pi$ radians out of phase with the incident wave. In terms of the velocity in the two sections, we find that for a wave incident upon a region in which its velocity is less than the velocity in the first region, the reflected wave is $\pi$ radians out of phase with the incident wave. The transmitted wave is at all times in phase with the incident wave.

A second interesting problem is the case of a string whose linear mass density changes discontinuously at two points, the points $z = \pm a$, as shown in Fig. 12–11.

Calling the linear mass densities respectively $\mu_1$, $\mu_2$, and $\mu_3$, we find that for a harmonic wave originating in the first section we will obtain a reflected wave in the first section, two waves one moving to the right the other to the left in the second section, and a transmitted wave moving to the right in the third section. These facts are expressed by the complex harmonic waves

$$\psi_1(z, t) = (Ae^{-ik_1 z} + Be^{ik_2 z})e^{i\omega t},$$
$$\psi_2(z, t) = (Ce^{-ik_2 z} + De^{ik_2 z})e^{i\omega t}, \quad (12\text{–}54)$$
$$\psi_3(z, t) = Ee^{-ik_3 z}e^{i\omega t},$$

where

$$k_i = \omega\sqrt{\frac{\mu_i}{T}}. \quad (12\text{–}55)$$

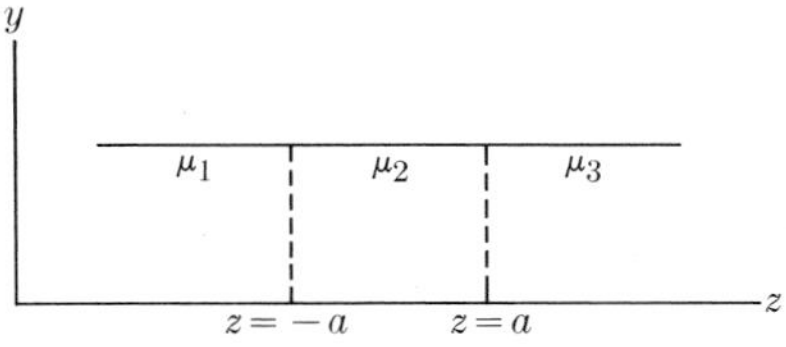

FIGURE 12–11

Applying the boundary conditions at the point $z = -a$ yields the equations

$$Ae^{ik_1 a} + Be^{-ik_1 a} = Ce^{ik_2 a} + De^{-ik_2 a},$$
$$k_1(Ae^{ik_1 a} - Be^{-ik_1 a}) = k_2(Ce^{ik_2 a} - De^{-ik_2 a}), \quad (12\text{–}56)$$

whereas at the point $z = +a$ the boundary conditions yield

$$Ce^{-ik_2 a} + De^{ik_2 a} = Ee^{-ik_3 a},$$
$$k_2(Ce^{-ik_2 a} - De^{ik_2 a}) = k_3 Ee^{-ik_3 a}. \quad (12\text{–}57)$$

Equations (15–56) and (15–57) are four simultaneous equations which we may solve for the four constants $B$, $C$, $D$, and $E$ in terms of the amplitude $A$ of the incoming wave. The equations relating the amplitudes of the waves are somewhat simpler to solve, however, when expressed in terms of the *reflection coefficients* (cf. Eq. 12–52)

$$r_{ij} = \frac{k_i - k_j}{k_i + k_j} \quad (12\text{–}58)$$

and the *transmission coefficients* (cf. Eq. 12–53)

$$t_{ij} = \frac{2k_i}{k_i + k_j} \quad (12\text{–}59)$$

for the reflection and transmission of a wave incident from the $i$th medium onto the $j$th medium. In terms of these coefficients the relationship between the amplitudes of the waves are expressed at the point $z = -a$ by the relations

$$Be^{-ik_1a} = r_{12}Ae^{ik_1a} + t_{21}De^{-ik_2a},$$
$$Ce^{ik_2a} = t_{12}Ae^{ik_1a} + r_{21}De^{-ik_2a}, \tag{12-60}$$

and at the point $z = a$ by

$$Ee^{-ik_3a} = t_{23}Ce^{-ik_2a},$$
$$De^{ik_2a} = r_{23}Ce^{-ik_2a}. \tag{12-61}$$

Of special interest are generally only the constants $B$ and $E$ which are respectively the amplitude of the reflected wave and the amplitude of the wave transmitted into the third region. Solving the latter simultaneous equations for $B$, we obtain

$$\frac{Be^{-ik_1a}}{Ae^{ik_1a}} = r_{12} + \frac{t_{21}t_{12}r_{23}}{e^{4ik_2a} - r_{21}r_{23}}. \tag{12-62}$$

We note that the amplitude of the reflected wave is a complicated function of the width $2a$ of the second medium and the relative magnitudes of the propagation constants in each portion of the string. Interestingly, we find that under certain conditions the amplitude of the reflected wave can be made to vanish (see Problem 12–13). This is the principle used, for example, to reduce the reflection of light waves by camera lenses and other optical instruments.

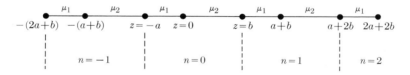

FIGURE 12–12

Another very interesting and important example is the problem of the propagation of waves along a string whose linear mass density alternates between the values $\mu_1$ and $\mu_2$ as shown in Fig. 12–12. The string thus forms a periodic structure and the problem is an example of the propagation of waves in a periodic medium.

The wave equation satisfied by the different sections of the string of linear mass density $\mu_1$ is

$$\frac{\partial^2 \Psi}{\partial z^2} - \frac{1}{v_1^2}\frac{\partial^2 \Psi}{\partial t^2} = 0. \tag{12-63}$$

The wave equation satisfied by the other sections is

$$\frac{\partial^2 \Psi}{\partial z^2} - \frac{1}{v_2^2} \frac{\partial^2 \Psi}{\partial t^2} = 0. \tag{12-64}$$

These equations have the complex solution

$$\psi_n = e^{i\omega t} \begin{cases} A_n e^{ik_1 z} + B_n e^{-ik_1 z} & \text{region 1} \\ C_n e^{ik_2 z} + D_n e^{-ik_2 z} & \text{region 2} \end{cases} \tag{12-65}$$

in the $n$th section of the string. It now remains for us to apply the boundary conditions at each point where the mass density changes. This would lead us to an infinite set of homogeneous simultaneous equations. Obviously we must look for some way of simplifying the problem. Just as for the problem of the infinite set of identical coupled oscillators which we considered in Section 8–11, we find that the equations of motion and their solutions are invariant either to a change by an integer in the numbers assigned to the sections or to a shift of the origin of coordinates by an integer multiple of $(a + b)$. From symmetry considerations we are thus led to seek solutions of the form (cf. Problem 10–23)

$$\psi(z) = e^{i\kappa z}\phi(z), \tag{12-66}$$

where $\phi(z)$ is a periodic function of period $(a + b)$. That the solutions of linear differential equations whose differential operator commutes with the operator which translates the origin of coordinates by integer multiples of a given length are expressible in this form is known as *Bloch's theorem*. In terms of the constants $A_n$, $B_n$, $C_n$, and $D_n$ appearing in Eq. (12–65), $\phi(z)$ is found to be expressed by

$$\phi_n(z) = \begin{cases} A_n e^{i(k_1 - \kappa)z} + B_n e^{-i(k_1 + \kappa)z} & \text{region 1} \\ C_n e^{i(k_2 - \kappa)z} + D_n e^{-i(k_2 + \kappa)z} & \text{region 2.} \end{cases} \tag{12-67}$$

From the boundary conditions satisfied by the string at $z = 0$ we obtain

$$A_0 + B_0 = C_0 + D_0$$

and

$$k_1(A_0 - B_0) = k_2(C_0 - D_0). \tag{12-68}$$

The boundary conditions at $z = -a$ yield

$$e^{-i\kappa a}[A_0 e^{-i(k_1 - \kappa)a} + B_0 e^{i(k_1 + \kappa)a}] = e^{-i\kappa a}[C_{-1} e^{-i(k_2 - \kappa)a} + D_{-1} e^{i(k_2 + \kappa)a}]$$

and

$$k_1 e^{-i\kappa a}[A_0 e^{-i(k_1 - \kappa)a} - B_0 e^{i(k_1 + \kappa)a}] = k_2 e^{-i\kappa a}[C_{-1} e^{-i(k_2 - \kappa)a} - D_{-1} e^{i(k_2 + \kappa)a}]. \tag{12-69}$$

The symmetry property, $\phi(z + a + b) = \phi(z)$, of the function $\phi(z)$ allows us to set

$$\phi_{-1}(-a) = \phi_0(b) \quad \text{and} \quad \left.\frac{\partial\phi_{-1}}{\partial z}\right|_{z=-a} = \left.\frac{\partial\phi_0}{\partial z}\right|_{z=b}, \qquad (12\text{-}70)$$

or by Eq. (12–67),

$$C_{-1}e^{-i(k_2-\kappa)a} + D_{-1}e^{i(k_2+\kappa)a} = C_0 e^{i(k_2-\kappa)b} + D_0 e^{-i(k_2+\kappa)b}$$

and
$$\qquad (12\text{-}71)$$

$$C_{-1}e^{-i(k_2-\kappa)a} - D_{-1}e^{i(k_2+\kappa)a} = C_0 e^{i(k_2-\kappa)b} - D_0 e^{-i(k_2+\kappa)b}.$$

We are then able to simplify Eq. (12–69) to obtain together with Eq. (12–68) the four linear homogeneous equations

$$A_0 + B_0 - C_0 - D_0 = 0,$$

$$k_1 A_0 - k_1 B_0 - k_2 C_0 + k_2 D_0 = 0,$$

$$A_0 e^{-i(k_1-\kappa)a} + B_0 e^{i(k_1+\kappa)a} - C_0 e^{i(k_2-\kappa)b} - D_0 e^{-i(k_2+\kappa)b} = 0,$$

$$k_1 A_0 e^{-i(k_1-\kappa)a} - k_1 B_0 e^{i(k_1+\kappa)a} - k_2 C_0 e^{i(k_2-\kappa)b} + k_2 D_0 e^{-i(k_2+\kappa)b} = 0.$$

$$\qquad (12\text{-}72)$$

These four simultaneous equations for the four constants $A_0$, $B_0$, $C_0$, and $D_0$ have a solution only if the determinant of their coefficients vanishes:

$$\begin{vmatrix} 1 & 1 & -1 & -1 \\ k_1 & -k_1 & -k_2 & k_2 \\ e^{-i(k_1-\kappa)a} & e^{i(k_1+\kappa)a} & -e^{i(k_2-\kappa)b} & -e^{-i(k_2+\kappa)b} \\ k_1 e^{-i(k_1-\kappa)a} & -k_1 e^{i(k_1+\kappa)a} & -k_2 e^{i(k_2-\kappa)b} & k_2 e^{-i(k_2+\kappa)b} \end{vmatrix} = 0 \qquad (12\text{-}73)$$

or

$$\cos \kappa(a + b) = \cos k_1 a \cos k_2 b - \frac{k_1^2 + k_2^2}{2k_1 k_2} \sin k_1 a \sin k_2 b. \qquad (12\text{-}74)$$

This transcendental equation yields $\kappa$ as a function of $\omega = k_i v_i$. We note that for certain ranges of $\omega$ the absolute value of the right-hand side of Eq. (12–74) will be less than one while for other ranges it will exceed one. The latter case yields a complex value for $\kappa$, which means that waves of that frequency will not propagate along the string. We thus obtain ranges of the frequency $\omega$ of the waves for which propagation occurs (*transmission bands*) and ranges for which propagation does not occur or is forbidden. This, for example, is what takes place in the case of electron matter waves which describe the motion of electrons in the periodic electric potential of a crystal. There, too, we find the existence of *allowed* and *forbidden bands* of propagation for the electron matter waves. In quantum mechanics the energy associated with a beam of electrons is related to the frequency of the matter wave describing their motion. Hence we find that only electrons which have an energy within one of the allowed energy bands can propagate in a periodic potential.

## 12-7 Vibrating string with fixed ends

In this section we investigate the effect which constraints on the endpoints of the string have on the propagation of harmonic waves along the string. Specifically, we shall consider the case of a string with fixed endpoints.

It should be clear that a single harmonic wave moving in one direction cannot represent the vibrating string with both ends fixed, for such a single wave will require every point of the string, including the endpoints, to perform simple harmonic oscillation with the same amplitude. We can, however, combine the two harmonic waves

$$\psi_1 = A e^{-i(kz-\omega t-\phi)},$$
$$\psi_2 = A e^{i(kz+\omega t+\phi)} \tag{12-75}$$

to yield a zero displacement of the string at the $z = 0$ end of the string. This is the linear combination

$$\Psi = \mathrm{Re}\,(\psi_1 - \psi_2) = \mathrm{Re}\,[-2iA \sin kz e^{i(\omega t+\phi)}]$$
$$= 2A \sin kz \sin (\omega t + \phi). \tag{12-76}$$

But this solution will not satisfy the boundary condition at the $z = l$ end of the string unless the propagation constant assumes the specific values

$$k = \frac{n\pi}{l}, \quad n \text{ integer.} \tag{12-77}$$

We have thus found that only very special harmonic waves can exist on a string with fixed ends. These are the standing harmonic waves with wavelength

$$\lambda_n = \frac{2l}{n} \tag{12-78}$$

or frequency

$$\omega_n = \frac{\pi n}{l} \sqrt{\frac{T}{\mu}}. \tag{12-79}$$

The solutions given by Eq. (12-76) with these values of $k$ and $\omega$ are known as

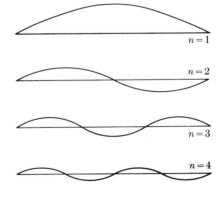

FIG. 12-13.  Normal modes of the vibrating string.

the *normal modes of vibration* of a string with fixed ends. The solution for $n = 1$ yields the fundamental mode. This mode of vibration is shown in Fig. 12-13. All the other modes, or *harmonics* of the vibrating string, vibrate with one or more points, in addition to the endpoints, remaining fixed at all times. These points are referred to as *nodes*. Figure 12-13 also shows the mode of vibration of the first few harmonics. We note that the first harmonic has one node between the endpoints, the second harmonic two, etc. This is quite characteristic of the solutions of the wave equation subject to homogeneous boundary conditions. That is, we find the existence of characteristic solutions which have no nodes, one node, two nodes, etc. The larger the number of nodes, the larger the characteristic frequency of the characteristic solution.

These solutions have the further very useful property that they form a complete set of orthogonal functions in terms of which any complicated motion of the string with fixed ends is expressible. That is, any solution describing the vibrational motion of the string can be expressed as a linear sum of the normal modes $\Psi_n(z, t)$,

$$\Psi(z, t) = \sum_{n=1}^{\infty} a_n \Psi_n(z, t). \tag{12–80}$$

We proceed with a discussion which shows how the coefficients $a_n$ in the expansion and the phase $\phi_n$ of the normal modes are determined by the initial values of $\Psi$ and $\partial\Psi/\partial t$.

## 12–8 The general motion of a vibrating string

Having discussed the characteristic vibrations of a string with fixed ends, we now turn our attention to the general motion of such a string. Specifically, we are interested in showing how the amplitudes of the characteristic modes in terms of which the general motion is expressible are determined.

We find that the coefficient $a_n$ and the phase $\phi_n$ of the $n$th normal mode in the normal-mode expansion of the general solution

$$\Psi(z, t) = \sum_{n=1}^{\infty} a_n \sin \frac{n\pi z}{l} \sin (\omega_n t + \phi_n) \tag{12–81}$$

are determined if at some initial time $t_0$ the shape $\Psi(z, t_0)$ of the string and the velocity $\partial\Psi(z, t_0)/\partial t_0$ of the points of the string are known. Choosing $t_0 = 0$, we find that in order for $\Psi(z, t)$ as given by Eq. (12–81) to satisfy the initial conditions, we must have

$$\Psi(z, 0) = \sum_{n=1}^{\infty} a_n \sin \phi_n \sin \frac{n\pi z}{l} \tag{12–82}$$

and

$$v(z, 0) = \frac{\partial\Psi(z, t)}{\partial t}\Big|_{t=0} = \sum_{n=1}^{\infty} a_n \omega_n \cos \phi_n \sin \frac{n\pi z}{l}. \tag{12–83}$$

Equations (12–82) and (12–83) are Fourier-series expansions of $\Psi(z, 0)$ and $v(z, 0)$, which we have met previously in our discussion of the forced motion of the simple harmonic oscillator (Chapter 4). Following the method outlined there, we can obtain the coefficients of $\sin (n\pi z/l)$ in each of the expansions above. We thus find that

$$A_n = a_n \sin \phi_n = \frac{2}{l} \int_0^l \Psi(\xi, 0) \sin \frac{n\pi\xi}{l} \, d\xi, \tag{12-84}$$

$$\omega_n B_n = \omega_n a_n \cos \phi_n = \frac{2}{l} \int_0^l v(\xi, 0) \sin \frac{n\pi\xi}{l} \, d\xi, \tag{12-85}$$

from which we obtain

$$a_n = \sqrt{A_n^2 + B_n^2} \tag{12-86}$$

and

$$\tan \phi_n = \frac{A_n}{B_n}. \tag{12-87}$$

Equation (12–81) provides us with a function of $z$ and $t$ which satisfies the wave equation and the initial conditions satisfied by the string. It is therefore the solution we are seeking.

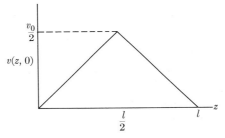

FIGURE 12–14

▶ As an example, we consider a string of length $l$ which has a mass per unit length $\mu$ and is under a tension $T$. At time $t = 0$ the string is given an impulsive blow which gives it an initial velocity as expressed by (Fig. 12–14)

$$v(z, 0) = \begin{cases} \dfrac{v_0}{l} z & 0 \leq z \leq \dfrac{l}{2}, \\[2mm] \dfrac{v_0}{l}(l - z) & \dfrac{l}{2} \leq z \leq l, \end{cases}$$

while

$$\Psi(z, 0) = 0.$$

Obviously in this case $A_n$ as given by Eq. (12-84) vanishes and

$$\omega_n B_n = \frac{2}{l} \left[ \int_0^{l/2} \frac{v_0}{l} \xi \sin \frac{n\pi\xi}{l} \, d\xi + \int_{l/2}^l \frac{v_0}{l}(l - \xi) \sin \frac{n\pi\xi}{l} \, d\xi \right]$$

$$= \frac{4v_0}{n^2\pi^2} \sin \frac{n\pi}{2}.$$

Thus we obtain

$$a_n = B_n = \frac{4v_0}{\omega_n n^2 \pi^2} \sin \frac{n\pi}{2},$$

yielding

$$\tan \phi_n = 0 \quad \text{or} \quad \phi_n = 0.$$

The general solution is thus

$$\Psi(z, t) = \frac{4v_0}{\pi^2} \sum_{m=1}^{\infty} \frac{(-1)^{m+1}}{(2m-1)^2 \omega_{2m-1}} \sin \frac{2m-1}{l} \pi z \sin \omega_{2m-1} t,$$

where

$$\omega_{2m-1} = \frac{2m-1}{l} \pi v = \frac{2m-1}{l} \pi \sqrt{\frac{T}{\mu}}.$$

Explicitly,

$$\Psi(z, t) = \frac{4v_0 l}{\pi^3 v} \left[ \sin \frac{\pi z}{l} \sin \frac{\pi v t}{l} - \frac{1}{3^3} \sin \frac{3\pi z}{l} \sin \frac{3\pi v t}{l} \right.$$
$$\left. + \frac{1}{5^3} \sin \frac{5\pi z}{l} \sin \frac{5\pi v t}{l} - \cdots \right]. \blacktriangleleft$$

Our method for obtaining the general solution for the vibrating string has been somewhat indirect, and depended on our recognition of the fact that the different harmonic waves which can exist on the string constituted a complete set of functions in terms of which any solution for the vibrating string was expressible. We shall now proceed to show that we can obtain the same solution by the separation of variables which is customarily the first method used in attempting to solve a partial differential equation. This method, if successfully applied, requires us eventually to solve a set of independent ordinary differential equations, which are inherently simpler to solve than the original partial differential equation. Unfortunately not all partial differential equations are solvable by this method.

In the method of separation of variables, we seek solutions to the partial differential equation which are expressed as the product of a number of functions, each of which is a function of only one of the independent variables. Thus, for the wave equation

$$\frac{\partial^2 \psi}{\partial z^2} = \frac{1}{v^2} \frac{\partial^2 \psi}{\partial t^2}, \tag{12-88}$$

we seek solutions of the form

$$\psi(z, t) = Z(z) T(t). \tag{12-89}$$

When a solution of this form is inserted into the wave equation, it yields

$$\frac{1}{Z} \frac{\partial^2 Z}{\partial z^2} = \frac{1}{v^2} \frac{1}{T} \frac{\partial^2 T}{\partial t^2}. \tag{12-90}$$

The left-hand side of (12–90) is a function only of $z$ and the right-hand side a function only of $t$. But since $z$ and $t$ are independent variables, this equality can hold for all values of $z$ and $t$ only if the functions on both sides of the equation have the same value for all values of $z$ and $t$. That is, Eq. (12–90) can be satisfied only if

$$\frac{1}{Z}\frac{\partial^2 Z}{\partial z^2} = -k^2 \quad \text{and} \quad \frac{1}{v^2}\frac{1}{T}\frac{\partial^2 T}{\partial t^2} = -k^2, \tag{12–91}$$

where $k^2$ is referred to as the separation constant. These differential equations have the solutions

$$Z(z) = A e^{\pm ikz} \quad \text{and} \quad T(t) = B e^{\pm i\omega t},$$

where

$$\omega^2 = k^2 v^2.$$

They yield

$$\psi(z, t) = C e^{\pm ikz \pm i\omega t}, \tag{12–92}$$

which are the complex harmonic waves with which we started our discussion.

## 12–9 Forced vibration of a string: resonance, Green's function

A string in free motion must have been acted upon by a force at some previous time from which it obtained its vibrational energy. In this section we shall consider the effect of a sinusoidal driving force on the vibrational motion of a string. Once again as in the case of the simple harmonic oscillator, we shall find the existence of resonant frequencies for which the response of the string to the driving force is large.

A sinusoidal driving force acting at different points of the string is expressed by

$$F(z, t) = \text{Re}\,[Tf(z)e^{i(\omega t + \phi)}]. \tag{12–93}$$

The constraint at the ends of the string require that $f(0) = f(l) = 0$. Just as for the case of the simple harmonic oscillator, we choose to consider the effect of the complex force

$$F(z, t) = Tf(z)e^{i(\omega t + \phi)} \tag{12–94}$$

on the string. The solution we seek will once more be the real part of the particular solution of the inhomogeneous wave equation

$$\frac{\partial^2 \psi}{\partial z^2} - \frac{1}{v^2}\frac{\partial^2 \psi}{\partial t^2} = -f(z)e^{i(\omega t + \phi)}. \tag{12–95}$$

As for all linear differential equations, the general solution will be the linear sum of the particular solution and the general homogeneous solution which we discussed in the last section.

It is to be expected that the particular solution will have the same exponential time dependence as the driving force. Thus setting

$$\psi(z, t) = g(z)e^{i(\omega t + \phi)}, \tag{12-96}$$

we obtain the result that $g(z)$ must satisfy the differential equation

$$\frac{d^2 g(z)}{dz^2} + \frac{\omega^2}{v^2} g(z) = -f(z), \tag{12-97}$$

subject of course to the boundary condition

$$g(0) = g(l) = 0.$$

Expanding $g(z)$ and $f(z)$ in a Fourier sine series between $z = 0$ and $z = l$, that is, letting

$$g(z) = \sum_{n=1}^{\infty} g_n \sin \frac{n\pi z}{l}, \qquad f(z) = \sum_{n=1}^{\infty} f_n \sin \frac{n\pi z}{l}, \tag{12-98}$$

we obtain

$$\sum_{n=1}^{\infty} g_n \left[ \frac{\omega^2}{v^2} - \left( \frac{n\pi}{l} \right)^2 \right] \sin \frac{n\pi z}{l} = - \sum_{n=1}^{\infty} f_n \sin \frac{n\pi z}{l} \tag{12-99}$$

or

$$g_n = \frac{f_n}{k_n^2 - k^2}, \tag{12-100}$$

where

$$k^2 = \frac{\omega^2}{v^2} \quad \text{and} \quad k_n^2 = \left( \frac{n\pi}{l} \right)^2. \tag{12-101}$$

The coefficients $g_n$ of the space part of the particular solution are thus related to the coefficients $f_n$ of the Fourier-series expansion of $f(z)$. Specifically, since

$$f_n = \frac{2}{l} \int_0^l f(\xi) \sin \frac{n\pi \xi}{l} \, d\xi, \tag{12-102}$$

we find that we can express the solution in the form

$$\Psi(z, t) = \frac{2}{l} \cos{(\omega t + \phi)} \sum_{n=1}^{\infty} \frac{\sin{(n\pi z/l)}}{k_n^2 - k^2} \int_0^l f(\xi) \sin \frac{n\pi \xi}{l} \, d\xi. \tag{12-103}$$

We note the existence of a resonance denominator in the particular solution. It tells us that the mode most excited is the one whose frequency $\omega_n = vk_n$ is closest to the driving frequency. This is so, of course, only if

$$f_n \neq 0$$

for that mode. For $k = k_n$ Eq. (12–103) predicts an infinite amplitude for that mode. This is due to our neglect of damping forces.

When damping forces of the form

$$F_{\text{damping}} = -\frac{2T}{v}\lambda\frac{\partial\Psi}{\partial t}$$   (12–104)

are present, the particular solution has the form (cf. Problem 12–9)

$$\Psi(z, t) = \frac{2}{l}\operatorname{Re} e^{i(\omega t+\phi)}\sum_{n=1}^{\infty}\frac{f_n\sin\,(n\pi z/l)}{k_n^2 - k^2 + 2ik\lambda},$$   (12–105)

which leads to finite amplitudes at resonance.

It is interesting to note that a sinusoidal driving force of the form

$$F_\omega(z, t) = Tf(z)e^{i\omega t}$$   (12–106)

is expressible in terms of the Dirac delta function,

$$F_\omega(z, t) = Te^{i\omega t}\int_0^l f(\xi)\delta(\xi - z)\,d\xi.$$   (12–107)

Hence the response of the system to a sinusoidal driving force of frequency $\omega$ should be expected to be expressible in terms of the response of the system to a sinusoidal driving force of frequency $\omega$ applied to the string only at the point $z = z'$. This response for which we shall use the symbol $G_\omega(z|z')$ satisfies the inhomogeneous equation

$$\frac{\partial^2 G_\omega(z|z')}{\partial z^2} + \frac{\omega^2}{v^2}\,G_\omega(z|z') = -\delta(z - z').$$   (12–108)

We met this equation previously in Section 4–12. We referred to the function $G_\omega(z|z')$ as the *Green function* for the simple harmonic oscillator, and we obtained for it a closed-form expression which vanished at $z = 0$.

Here we are interested in obtaining the Green function which also vanishes at $z = l$. Replacing $f(\xi)$ in Eq. (12–103) by $\delta(\xi - z')$, we find the normal-mode expansion for the Green function $G_\omega(z|z')$ to be:

$$G_\omega(z|z') = \frac{2}{l}\sum_{n=1}^{\infty}\frac{\sin\,(n\pi z/l)\sin\,(n\pi z'/l)}{k_n^2 - k^2}.$$   (12–109)

In terms of $G_\omega(z|z')$, Eq. (12–103) may be reexpressed as

$$\Psi(z, t) = \cos\,(\omega t + \phi)\int_0^l G_\omega(z|z')f(z')\,dz'.$$   (12–110)

Another very useful closed-form expression for $G_\omega(z|z')$ can be obtained by solving Eq. (12–108) in the two regions $0 \leq z \leq z'$ and $z' \leq z \leq l$, and applying the boundary conditions which $G_\omega(z|z')$ must satisfy at $z = z'$. These conditions are the continuity of $G_\omega(z|z')$ at $z = z'$ and the discontinuity in its slope which must satisfy the equation

$$\frac{\partial G_\omega(z|z')}{\partial z}\bigg|_{z=z'+} - \frac{\partial G_\omega(z|z')}{\partial z}\bigg|_{z=z'-} = -1.$$
(12–111)

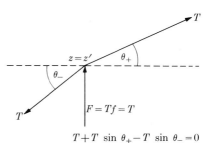

$$T + T \sin \theta_+ - T \sin \theta_- = 0$$

FIG. 12–15.    Application of Newton's equations of motion to a massless point.

This latter condition follows from an integration of Eq. (12–108) over an infinitesimal interval including the point $z = z'$. It can also be obtained from Newton's law of motion for the point $z = z'$. Since a point has no mass, this law states that the sum of all the forces acting on that point must vanish. Obviously if a force is applied at a single point of the string, the slope of the string will not be continuous. Assuming the tension on both sides of the string nevertheless to remain the same, we obtain Eq. (12–111) (cf. Fig. 12–15).

The solution to Eq. (12–108) in the first region satisfying the boundary condition at $z = 0$ is

$$G_\omega(z|z') = A(z') \sin kz,$$

whereas in the second region it is

$$G_\omega(z|z') = B(z') \sin k(l - z).$$

Symmetry of the Green function $G_\omega(z|z')$ and the requirement that the two solutions yield the same result at $z = z'$ suggest that we express $G_\omega(z|z')$ as

$$G_\omega(z|z') = C \begin{cases} \sin kz \sin k(l - z') & z < z', \\ \sin k(l - z) \sin kz' & z > z'. \end{cases}$$
(12–112)

The constant $C$ is chosen so that $G_\omega(z|z')$ satisfy Eq. (12–111). This yields

$$-Ck[\cos k(l - z') \sin kz' + \cos kz' \sin k(l - z')] = -1$$

or

$$C = \frac{1}{k \sin kl}.$$
(12–113)

Hence we have obtained the closed-form solution

$$G_\omega(z|z') = \frac{1}{k \sin kl} \begin{cases} \sin kz \sin k(l - z') & z < z', \\ \sin k(l - z) \sin kz' & z > z'. \end{cases}$$
(12–114)

For computational purposes this response function is more convenient than the normal-mode expansion of the Green function.

▶ We shall now demonstrate the usefulness of Green's functions for obtaining approximate solutions for a perturbed string. We consider the problem of a string of length $l$, with fixed ends, which is composed of two parts of different linear mass density as shown in Fig. 12–16. The exact solution may readily be obtained. The space part of the solution is

$$Z(z) = \begin{cases} A \sin k_1 z & 0 < z < a, \\ B \sin k_2(l - z) & a < z < l. \end{cases} \tag{12–115}$$

The boundary conditions at $z = a$ lead to the transcendental equation

$$\frac{1}{k_1} \tan k_1 a = \frac{1}{k_2} \tan k_2(l - a)$$

or

$$\sqrt{\frac{\mu_2}{\mu_1}} \tan \omega \sqrt{\frac{\mu_1}{T}}\, a = \tan \omega \sqrt{\frac{\mu_2}{T}}\, (l - a), \tag{12–116}$$

whose roots yield the normal frequencies of vibration of the composite string.

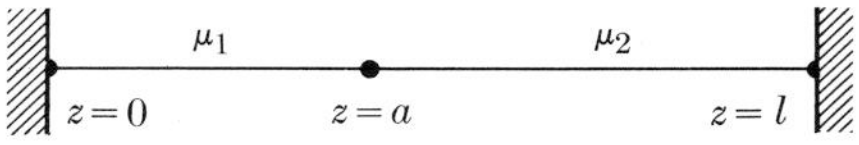

FIGURE 12–16

An approximate estimate of the normal frequencies of vibration may be obtained from the solution expressed in terms of the normal mode expansion of the Green function. This solution may be obtained by first expressing the wave equation satisfied by the string as

$$\frac{\partial^2 \Psi(z, t)}{\partial z^2} - \frac{1}{v_2^2} \frac{\partial^2 \Psi(z, t)}{\partial t^2} = \frac{\mu'}{T} \frac{\partial^2 \Psi(z, t)}{\partial t^2},$$

or assuming an $e^{i\omega t}$ time dependence, $\Psi(z, t) = Z(z)e^{i\omega t}$, by

$$\frac{d^2 Z(z)}{dz^2} + \frac{\omega^2}{v_2^2} Z(z) = -\frac{\omega^2 \mu'}{T} Z(z),$$

where

$$\mu' = \begin{cases} \mu_1 - \mu_2 & 0 < z < a, \\ 0 & a < z < l. \end{cases}$$

Treating the right-hand side of the above equation as an inhomogeneous term of the wave equation, the solution by Eq. (12–110) is

$$Z(z) = \int_0^l \frac{\mu' \omega^2}{T} Z(z') G_\omega(z|z')\, dz',$$

If $\mu'$ or $a$ is small, then we can expect

$$Z(z) = Z_n(z)$$

to be a good first approximation to the correct solution, where $Z_n$ is one of the normal modes of the string of linear mass density $\mu_2$. Utilizing only the $n$th term in the normal-mode expansion for the Green function, we obtain the approximate result

$$Z_n(z) = \left[ \frac{\mu_1 - \mu_2}{T} \omega^2 \frac{2}{l} \int_0^a Z_n(\xi)^2 \, d\xi \right] \frac{Z_n(z)}{k_n^2 - k^2},$$

where

$$k_n^2 = \frac{\omega_n^2}{v_2^2} \quad \text{and} \quad k^2 = \frac{\omega^2}{v_2^2}.$$

We have thus obtained the first-order perturbation formula for the shift in the resonant frequency of the $n$th normal mode as

$$k_n^2 - k^2 = \frac{\mu_1 - \mu_2}{T} \omega^2 \int_0^a \Psi_n(\xi)^2 \, d\xi.$$

Setting

$$k_n^2 - k^2 \approx 2k_n(k_n - k) = 2k_n \, \Delta k_n$$

and

$$\omega^2 \approx \omega_n^2,$$

we find that

$$\Delta k_n = \frac{\mu_1 - \mu_2}{T} \frac{\omega_n}{k_n l} \int_0^a Z_n(\xi)^2 \, d\xi. \blacktriangleleft$$

## 12–10 Impulsive force: Green's function

As a final example, we consider formally the response of the string to the impulsive force

$$F(z, t) = T\delta(z - z')\delta(t - t') = I(z, t|z', t') \qquad (12\text{–}117)$$

which is applied at the point $z = z'$ at time $t = t'$. The resulting equation of motion of the string for this force is

$$\frac{\partial^2 G(z, t|z', t')}{\partial z^2} - \frac{1}{v^2} \frac{\partial^2 G(z, t|z', t')}{\partial t^2} = -\delta(z - z')\delta(t - t'), \qquad (12\text{–}118)$$

where we have set $\Psi(z, t) = G(z, t|z', t')$. The usefulness of the impulsive force $I(z, t|z', t')$ lies in the fact that any other force $Tf(z, t)$ is expressible as an integral involving the impulsive force,

$$Tf(z, t) = \int_0^l \int_0^\infty f(z', t')I(z, t|z', t') \, dt' \, dz'. \qquad (12\text{–}119)$$

It follows therefore that the response $\Psi(z, t)$ to the force $Tf(z, t)$ should be expressible in terms of the Green function $G(z, t|z't')$, which is the response of the string to the impulsive force $I(z, t|z', t')$. Formally we find the particular solution for the general time-dependent force $F(z, t) = Tf(z, t)$ to be

$$\Psi(z, t) = \int_0^l \int_0^t G(z, t|z', t')f(z', t') \, dt' \, dz'. \tag{12-120}$$

In order to find the Green function $G(z, t|z', t')$, we require the Fourier-integral representation of the Dirac delta function,

$$\delta(t - t') = \frac{1}{2\pi} \int_{-\infty}^{\infty} e^{i\omega(t-t')} \, d\omega, \tag{12-121}$$

which we found in Section 11–6. What this means is that we are able to express the impulsive force $I(z, t|z', t')$ as a sum of simple harmonic impulsive forces,

$$I(z, t|z', t') = \frac{T}{2\pi} \delta(z - z') \lim_{\Delta\omega \to 0} \sum_{-\infty}^{\infty} e^{i\omega_n(t-t')} \Delta\omega. \tag{12-117}$$

Hence by the results of the previous section we find that

$$G(z, t|z', t') = \frac{1}{2\pi} \int_{-\infty}^{\infty} e^{i\omega(t-t')}G_\omega(z|z') \, d\omega, \tag{12-118}$$

where $G_\omega(z|z')$ is the response to the sinusoidal force $T\delta(z - z')e^{i\omega t}$ applied at the point $z = z'$.

## Problems

12–1. A 1 m long string of mass density $\mu = 4 \times 10^{-4}$ kg/m, with fixed ends, is under a tension of 1 newton. At time $t = 0$ the center of the string is displaced by 0.1 m, as shown in Fig. 12–17, and released from rest. Find the displacement of the points of the string at subsequent times.

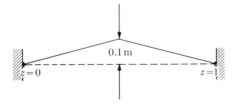

FIGURE 12–17

12–2. A horizontal string of length $l$ is under tension $T$. Its $z = 0$ end is fixed, and its $z = l$ end is attached to a bead of negligible size and mass which is free to slide on a frictionless vertical wire. Assuming that the vertical displacement of the bead is small, (a) obtain the boundary condition which must be satisfied by any vibrational mode of the string at its $z = l$ end; (b) obtain the normal modes of vibration of the string.

12–3. (a) Repeat part (a) of the previous problem for the case when the bead's motion is impeded by a frictional force proportional to its velocity.

(b) Obtain the transcendental equation whose roots yield the normal modes of vibration of the string.

12–4. Consider a semi-infinite horizontal string, under tension $T$, one of whose ends, the $z = 0$ end, is terminated by a bead of negligible mass free to slide on a vertical wire. The motion of the bead is impeded by a force which is proportional to its speed:

$$F_{\text{damping}} = -\frac{2T}{v} \lambda \frac{\partial \Psi(0, t)}{\partial t}.$$

A harmonic wave is incident upon the $z = 0$ end. Find the reflected wave as a function of the constant of proportionality $\lambda$. For what value of $\lambda$ is there no reflected wave?

12–5. Repeat Problem 12–2 for the case when the bead has a mass $m$.

12–6. Repeat Problem 12–3 for the case when the bead has a mass $m$.

12–7. The $z = l$ end of a string of length $l$ under tension $T$ is fixed and the $z = 0$ end is forced to move sinusoidally as expressed by

$$\psi(0, t) = A \sin \omega t.$$

Find the steady-state solution of the string.

12–8. Assume the damping force exerted by the air on a vibrating string at any point of the string to be proportional to the velocity of the point of the string,

$$F_{\text{damping}} = -\frac{2T}{v} \lambda \frac{\partial \Psi}{\partial t}.$$

Set up the equations of motion for a string of length $l$ with fixed ends under tension $T$ and under the action of such a damping force. Obtain the normal modes of vibration of the string by utilizing the method of separation of variables.

12–9. Obtain the steady-state solution for the string of the previous problem under the action of the sinusoidal driving force

$$F(z, t) = Tf(z) \cos (\omega t + \phi).$$

12–10. Apply the method of separation of variables (Section 12–8) to the three-dimensional wave equation

$$\frac{\partial^2 \psi}{\partial x^2} + \frac{\partial^2 \psi}{\partial y^2} + \frac{\partial^2 \psi}{\partial z^2} = \frac{1}{v^2} \frac{\partial^2 \psi}{\partial t^2}.$$

This equation is satisfied, for example, by the pressure increment of a sound wave. Find the normal modes of vibration of sound waves in a rectangular box of sides $a$, $b$, and $c$ by using the boundary condition—the vanishing of the normal derivative of $\psi$,

$$\mathbf{n} \cdot \nabla \psi = 0$$

—which must be satisfied by the pressure (sound) wave at a rigid boundary.

12–11. The $z$-component $E_3$ of the electric-field vector of a transverse magnetic electromagnetic wave ($TM$ wave) propagated in a wave guide, whose sides are parallel to the $z$-axis, satisfies the wave equation

$$\frac{\partial^2 E_3}{\partial x^2} + \frac{\partial^2 E_3}{\partial y^2} + \frac{\partial^2 E_3}{\partial z^2} = \frac{1}{v^2}\frac{\partial^2 E_3}{\partial t^2},$$

and is subject to the boundary condition

$$E_3 = 0$$

at the boundary of the guide. Show that a solution for a guide of rectangular cross-section of sides $a$ and $b$ of the form

$$E_3(x, y, z, t) = X(x)\,Y(y)e^{i\gamma z}e^{i\omega t},$$

with $\gamma$ real, is possible only for certain values of $\omega$. Find the smallest frequency (*cutoff frequency*) for which unattenuated propagation of a wave down the rectangular guide will occur. Obtain the cutoff frequencies for the various $TM$ modes.

12–12. Show that the total energy contained within the vibrational motion of a string of length $l$ with fixed ends is equal to the sum of the total energy contained within each of the normal modes which appear in the normal-mode expansion (Eq. 12–81) of $\Psi(z, t)$.

12–13. (a) The electric-field component of a plane polarized electromagnetic wave propagating along the $z$-axis in an isotropic medium satisfies the wave equation

$$\frac{\partial^2 E}{\partial z^2} = \mu\epsilon\frac{\partial^2 E}{\partial t^2},$$

where $\mu$ and $\epsilon$ are respectively the magnetic permeability and the electric permittivity of the medium. Suppose this wave is incident normally upon the interface between two regions in which the phase velocities of the wave are respectively $v_1$ and $v_2$, where

$$v_i = \frac{1}{\sqrt{\mu_i\epsilon_i}}.$$

Obtain the reflection and transmission coefficients $r_{12}$ and $t_{12}$ for a plane polarized harmonic wave, given that

$$E_1 = E_2 \quad \text{and} \quad \frac{\partial E_1}{\partial z} = \frac{\partial E_2}{\partial z}$$

are the boundary conditions satisfied by the electric-field component of the wave at the interface. Express $r_{12}$ and $t_{12}$ in terms of the relative index of refraction

$$n_{12} = \frac{v_2}{v_1} = \frac{n_1}{n_2}$$

of the two media, where $n_1$ is the index of refraction assigned to medium 1 and $n_2$ the index hence assigned to region 2.

(b) Referring to Fig. 12–11, obtain for the case $2ak_2 = \pi$ the relation which must be satisfied by the propagation constants $k_1$, $k_2$, and $k_3$ of a harmonic wave in the three media in order that there be no reflected wave (cf. Eq. 12–62). Express this relation in terms of the indices of refraction $n_i$ of the three media.

12–14. An optically active medium is one in which a right circularly polarized wave has a phase velocity different from that of a left circularly polarized wave. As a result of this difference in phase velocity, the superposition of a right and a left circularly polarized wave having the same amplitude and travelling in the same direction will yield an electric field vector which as a function of $z$ will appear to precess. If therefore we concentrate on one point of a wavefront of the combined wave, we will find that the plane of polarization of the electric field vector at that point rotates as the wave passes through the medium. Express the angle of rotation of the plane of polarization as a function of the indices of refraction $n_+$ and $n_-$ for the right- and left-handed polarized waves, and of the thickness of the medium $d$.

12–15. Consider the string of length $2l$ with fixed ends as shown in Fig. 12–18. The center point of this string is attached to a spring of spring constant $\kappa$.

(a) Show that only the symmetric modes of the freely vibrating string are changed by the presence of the spring.

(b) Obtain the boundary condition which must be satisfied by the solutions describing the motion of the string at the point $z = 0$.

(c) Obtain the transcendental equation whose roots yield the normal frequencies of the new symmetric modes.

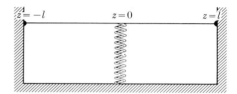

FIGURE 12–18

(d) Obtain both from the answer to part (c) and through use of the normal-mode expansion of the Green function for the string an approximate formula for the change in the normal frequencies introduced by a spring of very small spring constant.

12–16. Consider the string of length $2l$ with fixed ends, as shown in Fig. 12–19, at whose center there is attached a bead of mass $m$.

(a) Consider the string to be composed of the two sections defined by $-l \leq z \leq 0$ and $0 \leq z \leq l$, and obtain the boundary conditions which must be satisfied by the solution for the vibrating string at the point $z = 0$.

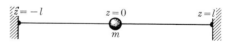

FIGURE 12–19

(b) Obtain the transcendental equation whose roots yield the normal frequencies of vibration of the system.

(c) Obtain an estimate of the shift in the normal frequency for small $m$.

(d) Consider the string with the bead as a string with linear mass density

$$\bar{\mu} = \mu + m\delta(z),$$

and consider the contribution to the wave equation by the $m\delta(z)$ term in $\bar{\mu}$ as an inhomogeneous term. Utilize the closed-form Green function for this problem to obtain a solution. Show that the solution thus obtained yields for $z = 0$ the transcendental equation of part (b).

(e) Utilize the normal-mode expansion of the Green function for this problem to obtain an estimate of the change in the resonant frequency for small $m$. Compare the result with the answer to part (c).

12–17. Consider two identical strings of length $2l$ both with fixed ends and under tension $T$, and coupled as shown in Fig. 12–20 by a spring of spring constant $\kappa$ joining their centers.

(a) Set up the wave equations satisfied by the strings and obtain the boundary conditions satisfied by the solutions at the midpoints of the strings.

(b) Show that the antisymmetric solutions

$$\psi_i = A \sin \frac{\pi z}{l} \, e^{i\omega t}, \qquad i = 1, 2$$

for the isolated strings are also normal solutions for the coupled strings.

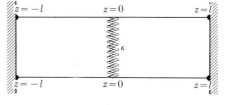

FIGURE 12–20

(c) Since the partial differential equations satisfied by the strings are invariant to a permutation of the numbers assigned to the strings, we can expect that the transformation

$$\phi_1 = \psi_1 + \psi_2, \qquad \phi_2 = \psi_1 - \psi_2$$

will simplify the equations of motion and the boundary conditions. Show that this transformation yields a pair of uncoupled partial differential equations for $\phi_1$ and $\phi_2$ with simpler boundary conditions at $z = 0$.

(d) Obtain the transcendental equation whose roots yield the normal frequencies of the symmetric modes of vibration (symmetric in $z$) of the system.

# 13

# *The Special Theory of Relativity*

In our introduction of the classical equations of motion, we made it clear that they were sufficient only for the description of the motion of particles whose speed is small compared with the speed of light in vacuum. Our discussions in the previous chapters have thus been confined to the application of Newton's equations of motion to the motion of a system of slowly moving particles. When the observed velocities of the particles have magnitudes which are comparable to $c$, the speed of light, the results obtained through the use of Newton's equations of motion are in disagreement with experimental observations. For example, an electron of mass $m_0$ and electric charge $-e$ which was accelerated from rest through the electric potential difference $\phi$ should, according to classical mechanics, be observed to move with a speed

$$v = \sqrt{\frac{2e\phi}{m_0}}.$$

Instead the relationship between the observed speed of the electron and the accelerating potential is found to be expressed by the equation

$$m_0 c^2 \left[ \frac{1}{\sqrt{1 - v^2/c^2}} - 1 \right] = e\phi.$$

We note that this latter expression reduces to the classical result for speeds $v \ll c$.

There are innumerable other examples which illustrate the discrepancy between the actual motion of particles at speeds comparable to the speed of light and the motion predicted by classical Newtonian mechanics. Obviously we require a modification in our fundamental formulation of mechanics and in the basic equations of motion, which will yield results in agreement with experimental observations of such rapidly moving particles.

In this chapter we shall be concerned with the modification of Newtonian mechanics, which is known as the *special theory of relativity*, and with the application of the relativistic equations of motion to the electrodynamics of relativistic (fast moving) particles. The special theory of relativity concerns

448

itself with, among other things, the relationships between the results of measurements of observable physical quantities performed by different inertial observers and their mathematical formulation of basic physical laws.

Interestingly enough, it was the failure of classical physics to explain the experimentally observed fact that the speed of light in vacuum is a constant irrespective of the motion of the observer* which led Einstein to extend the classical principle of relativity to include also all other laws of nature. This classical principle of relativity states that the laws of mechanics have the same form with respect to all inertial observers. It was Einstein's genius which recognized the impossibility of the detection of absolute motion, and which led him to postulate this extended "principle of relativity" and to the assumption that the velocity of light in vacuum is a constant, the same for all inertial observers.

This assumed constancy of the observed speed of light and its consequences are at variance with our common-sense understanding of nature, which has been distilled from our day-to-day experiences with phenomena explainable by classical physics. Nonetheless, agreement between experimental observations and the theoretical predictions based on the assumed fundamental equations of any theory is the only yardstick with which to measure the validity of the theory, and the many experimental corroborations of the predictions of the special theory of relativity have by now erased any doubt as to its fundamental validity.

## 13–1 The Lorentz transformation

The assumed constancy of the velocity of light requires us to change our classical concept of time as an absolute physical quantity which is independent of the motion of the observer. That time intervals $\Delta t$ and $\Delta t'$ as measured by two different inertial observers can no longer be equated can be seen by considering the mathematical description of a wavefront emitted at some instant of time, chosen to be the time $t = t' = 0$, from a point which is chosen as the instantaneously coincident origins of the two different inertial observers. Since the speed of light is the same in all directions to all inertial observers, each observer will find the wavefront to be a sphere with center located at the origin of his coordinate system, since this is the point from which the observer finds the wave to have been emitted. This conclusion is contrary to our classical experience, on the basis of which we would anticipate each observer to see the same spherical wavefront with its center located at the point from which it was emitted, the point at which the origin of the observer's coordinate system was located at the times $t = t' = 0$. The constancy of the speed of light thus leads us to the conclusion that the two inertial observers see different spherical

---

* A. A. Michelson and E. W. Morley, *Am. J. Sci.*, **34,** 333 (1887); *Phil. Mag.*, **24,** 449 (1887).

wavefronts which are respectively described by the equations

$$x^2 + y^2 + z^2 = c^2 t^2 \quad \text{and} \quad x'^2 + y'^2 + z'^2 = c'^2 t'^2. \quad (13\text{--}1)$$

Clearly the two observers may utilize the wavefront emitted at time $t = t' = 0$ in order to locate the position of a particle $P$ at rest, say, with respect to the first (unprimed) inertial observer and observed to move with a velocity $-\mathbf{v}$ with respect to a second (primed) inertial observer. This may be accomplished by each observer measuring the time at which the wave reflected or scattered by the particle reaches the origin of his coordinate system. If this time is respectively $2t$ and $2t'$, then the unprimed observer will conclude the particle to have been located at time $t$ at a distance

$$r = ct$$

from his origin $O$, while the primed observer will conclude the particle to have been at time $t'$ at a distance

$$r' = ct'$$

from his origin $O'$.

Clearly

$$r \neq r',$$

and hence we must conclude that similarly

$$t \neq t'.$$

We thus see that the assumption of the constancy of the speed of light leads us to the fact that different inertial observers each utilizing a uniformly running clock calibrated to measure time intervals in the same unit of time will in general, as in the case just discussed, obtain different measurements of the time it takes for a light wave to go from one point to another. Thus since the determination of the position of a particle invariably involves the use of light waves or other signals assumed to propagate with the speed of light, it follows that two different inertial observers will give different kinematic descriptions of the motion of particles. It is therefore natural for us to seek the relationships which may exist between such different kinematical descriptions of the motion of a particle by different inertial observers.

The Lorentz transformation equations relate the coordinates $(x, y, z, t)$ of space and time which one observer utilizes in his description of the motion of a particle to the coordinates $(x', y', z', t')$ of space and time which a second inertial observer utilizes in his description of the motion of the same particle. The specification of the four coordinates $x$, $y$, $z$, and $t$, determined as described above through the use of light waves, is referred to as an *event*.

Before proceeding with the derivation of the Lorentz transformation equations we stop to consider the mathematical form which we expect to obtain for the transformation equations. We naturally assume that each inertial observer has set up for himself an isotropic cartesian coordinate system and that he utilizes a clock which has been calibrated to measure the passing of time at a uniform rate. The calibration of a clock may readily be checked by a measurement of the time which elapses for a light signal to reach a series of points equally spaced along a straight line. A small change $(\Delta x, \Delta y, \Delta z, \Delta t)$ in the space and time coordinates of an event observed by one observer is equivalent to a change $(\Delta x', \Delta y', \Delta z', \Delta t')$ in the space and time coordinates of the same event as observed by a second observer. Since the speed of light is found to be the same in all directions, and space is therefore isotropic, it is plausible to assume that the relationship between the observed changes $(\Delta x, \Delta y, \Delta z, \Delta t)$ and $(\Delta x', \Delta y', \Delta z', \Delta t')$ in an event are independent of the coordinates $(x, y, z, t)$. After all, the choice of the origins of the coordinate systems, the times $t = 0$ and $t' = 0$ and the orientation of the coordinate axes are really quite arbitrary. The only transformation between coordinates for which the differential changes have this property is the linear transformation which, in operator notation, is expressed by

$$|\mathbf{r}) = \mathsf{S}|\mathbf{r}'), \tag{13-2}$$

where having set

$$x_1 = x, \qquad x_2 = y, \qquad x_3 = z, \qquad x_4 = ict,$$

$$|\mathbf{r}) \leftrightarrow \begin{bmatrix} x_1 \\ x_2 \\ x_3 \\ x_4 \end{bmatrix}, \tag{13-3}$$

$$|\mathbf{r}') \leftrightarrow \begin{bmatrix} x_1' \\ x_2' \\ x_3' \\ x_4' \end{bmatrix}, \tag{13-4}$$

and $\mathsf{S}$ is the Lorentz transformation operator, which is represented by a sixteen-element $4 \times 4$ matrix with matrix elements $S_{ij}$.

Having assumed the transformation to be linear, we proceed to an evaluation of the matrix elements of the Lorentz transformation matrix. In doing so, we shall restrict ourselves to the case where the cartesian coordinate axes of the coordinate systems of the two inertial observers are chosen respectively parallel to each other, and the relative velocity vector of the two observers lies along the $x$-axes of the two coordinate systems (Fig. 13–1). The vector $\mathbf{V}$ in the figure represents the relative velocity of $O'$ with respect to $O$. Clearly for this choice of coordinate axes a change in the $x$-coordinate or the time $t$ of an event observed by the unprimed observer cannot produce a change in the $y'$- and $z'$-coordinates of the same event described by the primed observer, and vice versa. We note

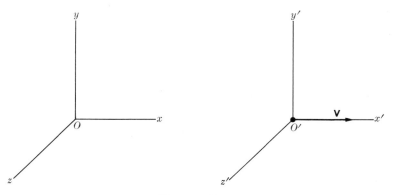

FIGURE 13–1

that if one observer observes a particle to be in motion along the $x$-axis, the other observer will likewise observe the particle to be moving along the $x$-axis. Hence we conclude that the transformation equations reduce to

$$
\begin{aligned}
x_1 &= S_{11}x_1' + S_{14}x_4', \\
x_2 &= S_{22}x_2' + S_{23}x_3', \\
x_3 &= S_{33}x_3' + S_{32}x_2', \\
x_4 &= S_{41}x_1' + S_{44}x_4',
\end{aligned}
\tag{13–5}
$$

where clearly $S_{22} = S_{33}$ and by a similar argument $S_{23} = S_{32} = 0$.

Below we shall find the constant $S_{22}$ to have the value 1. The Lorentz transformation matrix thus reduces to

$$
(\mathbf{S}) =
\begin{bmatrix}
S_{11} & 0 & 0 & S_{14} \\
0 & 1 & 0 & 0 \\
0 & 0 & 1 & 0 \\
S_{41} & 0 & 0 & S_{44}
\end{bmatrix}.
\tag{13–6}
$$

We can further simplify the Lorentz transformation matrix by noting that in each coordinate system the description of the wavefront of light emitted at time $t = t' = 0$ is given by Eq. (13–1) or

$$
(\mathbf{r}|\mathbf{r}) = (\mathbf{r}'|\mathbf{r}') = 0,
$$

where

$$
(\mathbf{r}|\mathbf{r}) = \sum_{i=1}^{4} x_i^2.
$$

Thus utilizing

$$
|\mathbf{r}) = \mathbf{S}|\mathbf{r}'),
$$

and its transpose

$$
(\mathbf{r}| = (\mathbf{r}'|\widetilde{\mathbf{S}},
$$

we find that

$$(\mathbf{r}|\mathbf{r}) = (\mathbf{r}'|\widetilde{\mathbf{S}}\mathbf{S}|\mathbf{r}') = \sum_{ikj} x_i' \widetilde{S}_{ik} S_{kj} x_j' = 0. \qquad (13\text{–}7)$$

Since this latter equation is satisfied at any time for all points along the wave-front, it necessarily follows that the coefficient of the $x_1' x_4'$ term, vanishes:

$$\sum_{k=1}^{4} \widetilde{S}_{1k} S_{k4} = \sum_{k=1}^{4} S_{k1} S_{k4} = 0$$

or

$$S_{11} S_{14} + S_{41} S_{44} = 0. \qquad (13\text{–}8)$$

Two other relations between the elements of the Lorentz transformation matrix may be obtained as follows. We note that the events of the origin $O$ of the un-primed observer are specified respectively by

$$x_1 = 0, \qquad x_4 = ict,$$

and $\qquad (13\text{–}9)$

$$x_1' = -Vt', \qquad x_4' = ict'$$

by the two observers. Similarly, for the origin $O'$ of the primed observer the events are specified respectively by

$$x_1' = 0, \qquad x_4' = ict',$$

and

$$x_1 = Vt, \qquad x_4 = ict. \qquad (13\text{–}10)$$

Inserting Eq. (13–9) into the transformation equations (13–5) yields

$$0 = S_{11}(-Vt') + S_{14}(ict') \qquad \text{or} \qquad S_{14} = -\frac{iV}{c} S_{11}, \qquad (13\text{–}11)$$

and inserting Eq. (13–10) into (13–5) yields

$$Vt = S_{14}(ict') \qquad \text{and} \qquad ict = S_{44}(ict').$$

Hence we obtain

$$S_{14} = -\frac{iV}{c} S_{44}. \qquad (13\text{–}12)$$

Equations (13–8), (13–11), and (13–12) yield the solution

$$S_{11} = S_{44} \qquad \text{and} \qquad S_{14} = -S_{41}. \qquad (13\text{–}13)$$

We now proceed to show that a fourth relation between the elements of the Lorentz transformation matrix is

$$S_{11}^2 + S_{14}^2 = 1, \qquad (13\text{–}14)$$

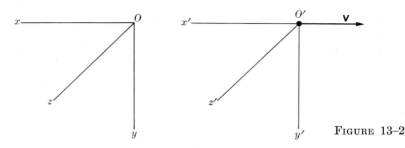

FIGURE 13–2

which is sufficient to provide us with the values of the matrix elements $S_{ij}$:

$$S_{11} = S_{44} = \frac{1}{\sqrt{1 - V^2/c^2}} \tag{13–15}$$

$$S_{14} = -S_{41} = \frac{-iV/c}{\sqrt{1 - V^2/c^2}}. \tag{13–16}$$

In the process we shall also find that

$$S_{22} = S_{33} = 1. \tag{13–17}$$

Hence we shall find the Lorentz transformation equations to be

$$x_1 = \frac{x_1' - (iV/c)x_4'}{\sqrt{1 - V^2/c^2}}, \qquad x_2 = x_2',$$

$$x_3 = x_3', \qquad x_4 = \frac{x_4' + (iV/c)x_1'}{\sqrt{1 - V^2/c^2}}. \tag{13–18}$$

Interestingly, we note that the requirement that the coordinates $x$, $y$, $z$, $t$ obtained through the use of these transformation equations for any real values of $x'$, $y'$, $z'$, and $t'$ be real means that $\sqrt{1 - (V^2/c^2)}$ must be real. This restricts the magnitude of the observed relative velocity $V$ of one inertial observer with respect to another to be less than the speed of light. In Section 13–3 we shall find this restriction to hold for the magnitude of any observed velocity.

To obtain Eq. (13–14) we note that a rotation of the coordinate axes about the respective $z$-axes through an angle of 180° inverts the $x$- and $y$-axes to the positions shown in Fig. 13–2. The transformation matrix for this orientation of the coordinate axes is clearly

$$(\bar{\mathsf{S}}) = \begin{bmatrix} S_{11} & 0 & 0 & -S_{14} \\ 0 & S_{22} & 0 & 0 \\ 0 & 0 & S_{33} & 0 \\ -S_{41} & 0 & 0 & S_{44} \end{bmatrix}, \tag{13–19}$$

where $S_{ij}$ are the elements of the original Lorentz transformation matrix. But the new orientation of the coordinate axes tells us that $(\bar{\mathsf{S}})$ is the Lorentz trans-

formation matrix which transforms the coordinates of an event in the primed
inertial system to the coordinates of the event in the unprimed system with
respect to which the primed system is moving with a velocity of magnitude $V$
directed along the negative $x$-axis. But this is the transformation matrix which
transforms the description of an event in the primed coordinate system to the
unprimed coordinate system for the original orientation of their coordinate
axes (Fig. 13–1). Hence [cf. Eq. (13–13)] $(\widetilde{\mathbf{S}}) = (\widetilde{\mathbf{S}})$ is the Lorentz transformation
matrix which is the inverse of $(\mathbf{S})$, that is,

$$(\widetilde{\mathbf{S}})(\mathbf{S}) = (\mathbf{1}).\tag{13–20}$$

From (13–20) we readily obtain Eqs. (13–14) and (13–17).

Interestingly enough, we have found the Lorentz transformation to be an
orthogonal transformation. Thus if we consider events to be vectors in a four-
dimensional vector space, and $|\mathbf{r})$ and $|\mathbf{r}')$ two different descriptions of the same
event with respect to differently oriented coordinate axes in this four-dimensional
vector space, then we find that the four-dimensional coordinate systems of
different inertial observers have different orientations in this four-dimensional
space, and that the Lorentz transformation represents a proper rotation* in
this four-dimensional vector space. The four-dimensional vector space is known
as *world space* or *Minkowski space*.

A general rotation in a four-dimensional space is, of course, difficult to visualize. For the special case under consideration, however, when the relative
velocity of the two observers lies along their parallel $x$-axes, the Lorentz transformation represents a rotation in the $x_1x_4$-plane. To see that this is indeed so
we consider an event of the point $O'$, the origin of the primed observer's space
coordinate system. To the unprimed observer $I$ the events of $O'$ are specified
by the four-position vector

$$|\mathbf{r}) \leftrightarrow \begin{bmatrix} Vt \\ 0 \\ 0 \\ ict \end{bmatrix},\tag{13–21}$$

whereas to the primed observer $I'$ they are specified by

$$|\mathbf{r}') \leftrightarrow \begin{bmatrix} 0 \\ 0 \\ 0 \\ ict' \end{bmatrix}.\tag{13–22}$$

Thus the $x_4'$-coordinate axis of $I'$ lies along the event vector in four-space, whereas
with respect to the unprimed observer the event vector lies in the $x_1x_4$-plane,

---

* A proper rotation is defined as an orthogonal transformation whose transformation
matrix has the determinant value $+1$.

making an angle $\theta$ with the $x_4$-axis (cf. Fig. 13–3), where

$$\tan \theta = \frac{-iV}{c}. \qquad (13\text{–}23)$$

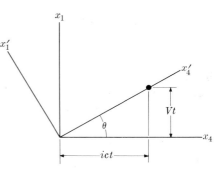

FIGURE 13–3

As can be seen from Fig. 13–3, the components of the event vector along the $x_1$-, $x_4$-, $x_1'$-, and $x_4'$-axes are related by

$$x_1 = x_1' \cos \theta + x_4' \sin \theta,$$
$$x_4 = -x_1' \sin \theta + x_4' \cos \theta. \qquad (13\text{–}24)$$

Now in order to obtain results consistent with the choice of positive axes, we must choose

$$\cos \theta = [1 + \tan^2 \theta]^{-1/2} = \frac{1}{\sqrt{1 - V^2/c^2}}, \qquad (13\text{–}25)$$

$$\sin \theta = -[1 - \cos^2 \theta]^{1/2} = \frac{-iV/c}{\sqrt{1 - V^2/c^2}}. \qquad (13\text{–}26)$$

We thus obtain the equations

$$x_1 = \frac{x_1' - (iV/c)x_4'}{\sqrt{1 - V^2/c^2}}, \qquad x_4 = \frac{x_4' + (iV/c)x_1'}{\sqrt{1 - V^2/c^2}}, \qquad (13\text{–}27)$$

which are in agreement with Eqs. (13–18).

The Lorentz transformation, being an orthogonal linear transformation, thus leaves the magnitude of any four-dimensional position vector invariant. For any event, we thus have

$$(\mathbf{r}|\mathbf{r}) = (\mathbf{r}'|\widetilde{\mathbf{S}}\mathbf{S}|\mathbf{r}') = (\mathbf{r}'|\mathbf{r}'). \qquad (13\text{–}28)$$

The events of the motion of a particle trace out in the four-space a curve which is referred to as the particle's *world line*.

From the change $|\Delta\mathbf{r})$ in the four-position vector of an event of a particle we can obtain another important invariant, the quantity $\Delta\tau$, defined by

$$\Delta\tau^2 = -\frac{1}{c^2}(\Delta\mathbf{r}|\Delta\mathbf{r}), \qquad (13\text{–}29)$$

which yields

$$\Delta\tau = \sqrt{1 - \frac{v^2}{c^2}}\,\Delta t, \qquad (13\text{–}30)$$

where

$$v = \lim_{\Delta t \to 0} \sqrt{\left(\frac{\Delta x}{\Delta t}\right)^2 + \left(\frac{\Delta y}{\Delta t}\right)^2 + \left(\frac{\Delta z}{\Delta t}\right)^2} \qquad (13\text{–}31)$$

is the observed speed of the particle.

The invariant quantity

$$\tau = \int d\tau = \int \sqrt{1 - \frac{v^2}{c^2}}\, dt \qquad (13\text{–}32)$$

is referred to as the *proper time*. In the next Section we shall find $\tau$ to be the time measured by a clock attached to the coordinate system which is moving at all times with the particle.

## 13–2 Time dilation and the Lorentz-Fitzgerald contraction

In the previous section we concluded that the assumption of the constancy of the speed of light results in different specifications of events by different inertial observers. As a result, events (measurements of position and time) which are observed to occur simultaneously by one observer will not be observed to occur simultaneously by a different inertial observer; and the time intervals between two events will also be observed to be different by different inertial observers.

Similarly different observers will assign different space components to an event and thereby obtain different measurements for the distance between two space points. Thus, without a proper understanding of the measurement of an event, we may come up with seemingly paradoxical results. A careful, explicit analysis of the way measurements are performed, as assumed by the special theory of relativity, points out that results which appear to be paradoxical are found to be so only because they were obtained as a result of measurements which were not the same. Since discussions of such apparent paradoxes are readily available elsewhere* we shall not dwell on them here.

In this section we would like to touch upon briefly the topics of time dilation and Lorentz-Fitzgerald contraction.

Time dilation refers to the relationship between the time of the events of a clock observed by an observer $I$ to be moving with constant velocity **V** along the $x$-axis and the time of the events of the same clock as measured by an observer $I'$ moving with the clock—more specifically, by an observer with respect to whom the clock is at rest and located at the origin $O'$ of his coordinate system. To this latter observer the events of the clock are the same as the events of $O'$, and they are specified by

$$x'_1 = x'_2 = x'_3 = 0 \qquad \text{and} \qquad x'_4 = ict'.$$

Observer $I$, on the other hand, measuring the events of $O'$ and utilizing a clock which was synchronized to read

$$t = t' = 0$$

* R. P. Feynman et al., *The Feynman Lectures on Physics*. Vol. 1, p. 16–3. Reading, Mass.: Addison-Wesley, 1963. Edwin F. Taylor, *Introductory Mechanics*. New York: Wiley, 1963.

at the instant the origins $O$ and $O'$ of the coordinate systems of the observers coincided, will describe the events of $O'$ by

$$x_1 = Vt, \qquad x_2 = x_3 = 0, \qquad x_4 = ict.$$

Thus by Eqs. (13–18) we find the relationship between $t$ and $t'$ to be

$$t = \frac{t'}{\sqrt{1 - V^2/c^2}}. \qquad (13\text{--}33)$$

That is, observer $I$ will find his clock to yield a larger measurement of the time of the events of $O'$ than the clock of observer $I'$ moving with $O'$. Observer $I$ will therefore claim the clock which he observes to be moving to be running slower than his clock.

We should like to point out that this time dilation has been observed experimentally in cosmic rays which contain fast moving, unstable $\mu$-mesons. The mean life time of a $\mu$-meson at rest being only $2.2 \times 10^{-6}$ second, the average distance covered by a fast moving meson is classically not expected to exceed

$$d = 2.2 \times 10^{-6}\, c = 6.6 \times 10^2 \,\text{m}.$$

Yet these $\mu$-mesons are created in the outer atmosphere, and a sizeable number of them appear in the laboratory after having traversed a distance of some $10^4$ meters. This is possible only because the measured lifetimes of fast moving mesons are longer than the measured lifetimes of the mesons at rest. The relation between the lifetime of a meson at rest and a meson in motion is found to be consistent with the prediction of Eq. (13–33).

We note that with respect to the rest system of a particle—the coordinate system with respect to which the particle is instantaneously at rest—the rate of the clock attached to and moving with the particle and the rate of the clock attached to the rest system are the same: $\Delta t' = \Delta t_0$, where $\Delta t'$ is an infinitesimal time interval between events of the particle measured by the clock of the rest system, and $\Delta t_0$ the corresponding infinitesimal time interval measured by the particle's clock. Thus for any other observer, with respect to whom the particle is moving with instantaneous speed $v$, we find from Eq. (13–33) that

$$\Delta t_0 = \Delta t \sqrt{1 - v^2/c^2}. \qquad (13\text{--}34)$$

If we continue to equate [Eq. (13–34)] the infinitesimal time intervals $\Delta t_0$ of the particle's clock to the time intervals $\Delta t$ as measured by the observer who observes the particle to move with the speed $v(t)$, then upon summing we will find that

$$\sum \Delta t_0 = \sum \sqrt{1 - \frac{v^2}{c^2}}\, \Delta t$$

or that

$$\tau = \int \Delta t_0 = \int \sqrt{1 - \frac{v^2}{c^2}}\, dt. \qquad (13\text{--}35)$$

Hence the proper time $\tau$ for a particle, defined previously by Eq. (13–32), is the time of the events of the particle as read by the clock moving with the particle.

Another interesting consequence of the constancy of the speed of light is the phenomenon of the *Lorentz-Fitzgerald contraction*, or the apparent shortening of the length of a rod which is in motion with respect to an observer. We find that the distance between two space points whose events are measured simultaneously by one observer is less than the distance between these same space points which is obtained from the determination of the space components of the same events measured by a different inertial observer. Specifically, it is the difference in the components of the space position vector of the events of the two endpoints of the rod along the direction of the relative velocity vector of the two observers which appears to be contracted.

To obtain the relationship between the $x$-components of two events which are measured as described we let

$$l = x_2 - x_1$$

be the projection of the distance between the points $(x_1, y_1, z_1)$ and $(x_2, y_2, z_2)$, measured simultaneously at time $t$ by observer $I$. Another observer, utilizing a coordinate system and a clock which reads $t' = 0$ when $t = 0$, as described previously, will find the events of the two points to be specified by

$$x_1' = (x_1 - Vt)\left(1 - \frac{V^2}{c^2}\right)^{-1/2},$$

$$t_1' = \left(t - \frac{V}{c^2}x_1\right)\left(1 - \frac{V^2}{c^2}\right)^{-1/2},$$

$$x_2' = (x_2 - Vt)\left(1 - \frac{V^2}{c^2}\right)^{-1/2}, \tag{13–36}$$

$$t_2' = \left(t - \frac{V}{c^2}x_2\right)\left(1 - \frac{V^2}{c^2}\right)^{-1/2}.$$

He will thus obtain

$$l' = x_2' - x_1' = \frac{x_2 - x_1}{\sqrt{1 - V^2/c^2}}$$

or

$$l = l'\sqrt{1 - V^2/c^2}. \tag{13–37}$$

We note that since $t_1' \neq t_2'$, $l'$ is not a meaningful measurement of the distance between the two points. Only a simultaneous measurement of the distance between two points can be meaningful. On the other hand, if the points $x_2'$ and $x_1'$ were to be at rest with respect to $O'$, then of course a simultaneous measurement is no longer necessary. $I'$ will then obtain at all times the same result $l_0$ for the distance between the points. Thus

$$l' = l_0$$

no matter at what time the measurements are performed. We thus obtain the Lorentz-Fitzgerald contraction formula

$$l = l_0 \sqrt{1 - V^2/c^2}, \tag{13-38}$$

which states that the simultaneous measurement of the endpoints of a rod observed to be moving with a speed $V$ in the direction of its length will make the rod appear to be contracted by the factor $\sqrt{1 - (V^2/c^2)}$.

We note that the apparent contraction of the length of a body in the direction of its motion excludes rigid-body motion from relativistic considerations. Relativistically bodies all of whose points remain at fixed distances from each other do not exist.

## 13–3 Transformation of velocities

In this section we shall proceed to obtain the transformation equations for the velocity of a particle. These are readily obtained through the use of the Lorentz transformation equations for the coordinates of an event. From Eqs. (13–18) we find

$$\frac{dx}{dt} = \left( \frac{dx'}{dt'} \frac{dt'}{dt} + V \frac{dt'}{dt} \right) \left( 1 - \frac{V^2}{c^2} \right)^{-1/2},$$

$$\frac{dy}{dt} = \frac{dy'}{dt'} \frac{dt'}{dt}, \qquad \frac{dz}{dt} = \frac{dz'}{dt'} \frac{dt'}{dt},$$

$$\frac{dt'}{dt} = \frac{1}{dt/dt'} = \frac{\sqrt{1 - V^2/c^2}}{1 + (dx'/dt')(V/c^2)}. \tag{13-39}$$

The last equation allows us to reexpress the other equations of (13–39) in the form

$$v_x = \frac{dx}{dt} = \frac{v_x' + V}{1 + v_x' V/c^2},$$

$$v_y = v_y' \frac{\sqrt{1 - V^2/c^2}}{1 + v_x' V/c^2}, \tag{13-40}$$

$$v_z = v_z' \frac{\sqrt{1 - V^2/c^2}}{1 + v_x' V/c^2}.$$

These are the desired transformation equations relating the cartesian components of the velocity of a point as measured by two different inertial observers.

We note that since it is logical to require the temporal sequence of events to be the same with respect to all inertial observers, at no time should the denominator of the last equation of Eq. (13–39) be negative. This leads us to conclude that no observed velocity should ever be found to have a magnitude which exceeds the speed of light.

It is readily shown that this conclusion is not inconsistent with the velocity transformation equations derived above. To verify that Eqs. (13–40) are in agreement with the statement that no particle can be observed to move with a speed exceeding the speed of light, let us obtain the velocity of a particle with respect to observer $I$ given that its velocity with respect to $I'$ is

$$v'_x = ac, \qquad v'_y = v'_z = 0,$$

where $a$ is a constant less than one in magnitude. Setting

$$V = bc,$$

where $|b| < 1$, as we have previously concluded, Eq. (13–40) yields

$$v_x = \frac{(a + b)c}{1 + ab}.$$

Since for values of $a$ and $b$ less than or equal to one the fraction $(a + b)/(1 + ab)$ is at a maximum at $a = b = 1$, it follows that for all values of $a$ and $b$ less than one,

$$\frac{a + b}{1 + ab} < \frac{1 + 1}{1 + 1 \cdot 1} = 1.$$

Hence $v_x$ is also less than $c$.

## 13–4 Four-velocity and four-acceleration

In dealing with the relativistic motion of a particle, we find it mathematically more convenient to introduce the concept of the four-velocity. The instantaneous four-velocity $|u)$ of a particle is defined as the particle's proper-time rate of change of its four-position vector $|r)$:

$$|u) = \frac{d}{d\tau} |r). \tag{13–41}$$

Since the proper time of a particle is a Lorentz-invariant quantity, it follows that the four components of the four-velocity transform under a Lorentz transformation like the four components of the four-position vector $|r)$. Clearly then the four-velocity vector which like the four-position vector is a vector in the world space, behaves like $|r)$ under all rotations in that space.

In terms of the components $x_i$ specifying the four-position vector in the world space, the components of the four-velocity are defined by

$$u_i = \frac{dx_i}{d\tau}. \tag{13–42}$$

We note that since for a particle moving with speed $v$

$$d\tau = \sqrt{1 - v^2/c^2}\, dt,$$

the first three (or space) components of the four-velocity are related to the cartesian components

$$v_i = \frac{dx_i}{dt}$$

of the ordinary velocity. These relations are expressed by

$$v_i = \mathfrak{u}_i\sqrt{1 - v^2/c^2}, \qquad i = 1, 2, 3. \tag{13–43}$$

The fourth component of the four-velocity is

$$\mathfrak{u}_4 = \frac{d(ict)}{d\tau} = \frac{ic}{\sqrt{1 - v^2/c^2}}. \tag{13–44}$$

One immediate advantage of the four-dimensional velocity is that its mathematical transformation property from one coordinate system to another is identical to the transformation property of the four-position vector. The Lorentz transformation equations of the four-velocity are thus easier to remember. Under a Lorentz transformation we have

$$|\mathfrak{u}) = \mathsf{S}|\mathfrak{u}'), \tag{13–45}$$

where $\mathsf{S}$ is the Lorentz transformation operator or, more explicitly,

$$\mathfrak{u}_1 = \frac{\mathfrak{u}'_1 - (iV/c)\mathfrak{u}'_4}{\sqrt{1 - V^2/c^2}}, \qquad \mathfrak{u}_2 = \mathfrak{u}'_2,$$

$$\mathfrak{u}_3 = \mathfrak{u}'_3, \qquad \mathfrak{u}_4 = \frac{\mathfrak{u}'_4 + (iV/c)\mathfrak{u}'_1}{\sqrt{1 - V^2/c^2}}. \tag{13–46}$$

The last equation yields

$$\frac{ic}{\sqrt{1 - v^2/c^2}} = \frac{\dfrac{ic}{\sqrt{1 - v'^2/c^2}} + \dfrac{iV}{c}\dfrac{v'_x}{\sqrt{1 - v'^2/c^2}}}{\sqrt{1 - V^2/c^2}}$$

or

$$\sqrt{1 - \frac{V^2}{c^2}}\sqrt{1 - \frac{v'^2}{c^2}} = \left(1 + \frac{v'_x V}{c^2}\right)\sqrt{1 - \frac{v^2}{c^2}}, \tag{13–47}$$

which when inserted into the other equations of (13–46) yields Eqs. (13–40). For example, we find that

$$v_1 = \mathfrak{u}_1\sqrt{1 - v^2/c^2} = \frac{(v'_1 + V)\sqrt{1 - v^2/c^2}}{\sqrt{1 - v'^2/c^2}\sqrt{1 - V^2/c^2}}$$

or

$$v_1 = \frac{v'_1 + V}{1 + v'_1 V/c^2}.$$

Since $|\mathfrak{u})$ is a four-vector in world space, it follows that its magnitude remains invariant under any orthogonal transformation in that space. Hence $\mathfrak{u}^2 = (\mathfrak{u}|\mathfrak{u})$ is invariant under a Lorentz transformation. Indeed we find $\mathfrak{u}^2$ to have the constant value $-c^2$:

$$\mathfrak{u}^2 = \sum_{i=1}^{4} \mathfrak{u}_i^2 = \frac{v^2}{1 - v^2/c^2} - \frac{c^2}{1 - v^2/c^2} = -c^2. \tag{13–48}$$

This is another example of the usefulness of the four-dimensional language in relativity. We find that if we are able to express different physical quantities and their relations in four-vector language, then the Lorentz transformation properties of these physical quantities and their relationships are automatically known. Furthermore, all equations expressed in four-vector language will automatically retain their mathematical form under a Lorentz transformation and hence satisfy the condition placed on the fundamental physical laws by the theory of relativity: that their mathematical form be invariant under a Lorentz transformation.

Analogously to the four-velocity we define the four-acceleration $|\mathfrak{a})$ of a particle as the particle's proper-time rate of change of the four velocity $|\mathfrak{u})$

$$|\mathfrak{a}) = \frac{d}{d\tau} |\mathfrak{u}). \tag{13–49}$$

In this case the relationship between the classical definition of the acceleration $\mathbf{a} = d\mathbf{v}/dt$ and the space part of the relativistic acceleration $|\mathfrak{a})$, is not a simple mathematical relation. Only in the rest frame of the particle, the inertial frame with respect to which the particle is momentarily at rest, are the space components of $|\mathfrak{a})$ simply related to the cartesian components of the ordinary acceleration $\mathbf{a}$. In fact, in the rest frame we find

$$\mathfrak{a}_i = a_i \quad (i = 1, 2, 3) \qquad \text{and} \qquad \mathfrak{a}_4 = 0. \tag{13–50}$$

Equations (13–50), which relates the components of the four-acceleration to the ordinary acceleration in the particle's rest frame and the transformation equations for the ordinary and the four-accelerations could in principle be utilized to obtain the relationship between the $a_i$ and the $\mathfrak{a}_i$ in any other inertial frame. We find, however, that this step is unnecessary, for the relativistically correct dynamical equations of motion, which we shall consider in the following section, assume a very simple form when expressed in terms of the four-acceleration, and solutions of the equations of motion are readily obtained in terms of the four-vector description of the motion of a particle.

Interestingly, we note that the inner product of the velocity four-vector and the acceleration four-vector vanishes:

$$(\mathfrak{u}|\mathfrak{a}) = 0, \tag{13–51}$$

since

$$(\mathfrak{u}|\mathfrak{a}) = \frac{1}{2} \frac{d}{d\tau} (\mathfrak{u}|\mathfrak{u}) = -\frac{1}{2} \frac{d}{d\tau} c^2.$$

## 13–5 Relativistic dynamics, relativistic equations of motion, relativistic mass, linear momentum

Realizing that Newton's equations of motion, which satisfactorily relate the time rate of change of the linear momentum of a slowly moving particle to the force acting on it, are not Lorentz invariant and hence do not satisfy the extended principle of relativity, we find it necessary to obtain a suitable generalization of Newton's equations which is Lorentz invariant. Whatever form this generalization may assume, we must require the relativistic Lorentz-invariant equations of motion to reduce to Newton's equations for slow moving particles. In fact, we shall arrive at a generalization by noting that in the rest frame of the particle Newton's equations are expressible in four-vector language. In this way we will obtain a generalization which reduces to Newton's equations of motion in the particle's rest frame and which automatically satisfies the relativistic requirement that the basic equations of motion be Lorentz invariant. We shall therefore assume the new equations to be the correct relativistic dynamical equations of motion and proceed to investigate the consistency of its consequences and their agreement with experimental observations.

In the previous section we found that in the rest frame of the particle there is no distinction between the ordinary acceleration and the three nonvanishing components of the four-accelerations. Now in the rest frame of the particle, Newton's equation of motion

$$\mathbf{F} = m_0\mathbf{a},$$

where $m_0$ is the mass assigned to the particle by an observer with respect to whom the particle is at rest, has certainly been found to be satisfactory. It is natural therefore to assume the existence of a four-force $|\mathbf{K})$, which in the rest frame of the particle has only three nonvanishing components, which are identical to the cartesian components of the force $\mathbf{F}$ acting on the particle. In the rest frame of the particle we thus set

$$K_i = F_i, \qquad i = 1, 2, 3,$$
$$K_4 = 0.$$

What we have thus assumed is the existence of a four-force vector $|\mathbf{K})$ which is related to the four-acceleration vector as expressed by,

$$|\mathbf{K}) = m_0|\mathbf{a}). \tag{13–52}$$

Equation (13–52) certainly yields the correct equation of motion in the particle's rest frame and is automatically Lorentz invariant. We thus make the assumption that it is the correct relativistic equation of motion, and proceed to investigate the consequences of this assumption.

In any other inertial system with respect to which the particle is observed to move with velocity $\mathbf{v}$ along the positive $x$-axis, the components of the four-

force vector are related to the components $(F_1, F_2, F_3, 0)$ of the force acting
on the particle in its rest frame as given by

$$
\begin{bmatrix} K_1 \\ K_2 \\ K_3 \\ K_4 \end{bmatrix} = \begin{bmatrix} \gamma & 0 & 0 & -i\beta\gamma \\ 0 & 1 & 0 & 0 \\ 0 & 0 & 1 & 0 \\ i\beta\gamma & 0 & 0 & \gamma \end{bmatrix} \begin{bmatrix} F_1 \\ F_2 \\ F_3 \\ 0 \end{bmatrix}, \tag{13-53}
$$

where $\beta = v/c$ and $\gamma = (1 - v^2/c^2)^{-1/2}$. From this matrix equation we find
that the first three (or space) components of the four-force are related to the
force acting on the particle in its rest frame, and the fourth component of the
four-force is related to the scalar product of the space components of the four-
force and the particle's velocity.

Furthermore, from Eq. (13–52) we find that

$$
K_i = m_0 \frac{d}{d\tau} \frac{dx_i}{d\tau} = \frac{1}{\sqrt{1 - v^2/c^2}} \frac{d}{dt} \frac{m_0}{\sqrt{1 - v^2/c^2}} \frac{dx_i}{dt}. \tag{13-54}
$$

Hence if we continue to use the classical definition of the force as the time rate
of change of the linear momentum of the particle, we find that the classical
force should be defined by

$$
\mathbf{F} = \frac{d}{dt}(m_0\gamma\mathbf{v}). \tag{13-55}
$$

This equation then yields the relation between the space components of the
four-force and the cartesian components of the classical force $\mathbf{F}$ acting on a
particle observed to be moving with speed $v$:

$$
K_i = \gamma F_i, \qquad i = 1, 2, 3, \tag{13-56}
$$

where

$$
\gamma = (1 - v^2/c^2)^{-1/2}. \tag{13-57}
$$

Equation (13–55) also yields the relativistic definition of the classical linear
momentum $\mathbf{p}$ of the particle:

$$
\mathbf{p} = m_0\gamma\mathbf{v}. \tag{13-58}
$$

We note that this definition of the linear momentum of the particle reduces to
the familiar classical definition when the particle's speed is small compared to
the speed of light. Expanding $\gamma$ in Eq. (13–58) and keeping only the terms within
$v^2/c^2$, we find Eq. (13–58) to yield

$$
\mathbf{p} = m_0\mathbf{v}.
$$

We also note that we can keep the classical definition of the linear momentum
as the product of the mass times the velocity of the particle by defining the

mass $m$ of a particle observed to be moving with speed $v$ by

$$m = m_0\gamma, \tag{13–59}$$

where $m_0$ is referred to as the *rest mass* of the particle and $m$ as its *relativistic mass*.

We note that this variation of the mass of a particle with its speed has been verified experimentally for electrons and other fast moving particles, and is the only modification of Newton's laws we require to be able to correctly describe the relativistic motion of particles.

We prefer, however, to continue describing the relativistic motion of a particle in the four-vector language, for not only, as we have seen, does it simplify the transformation of the observations made in one inertial system to the observations made in another system, but it is also the most efficient mathematical way for expressing the equations of motion and obtaining their solution.

## 13–6 Four-force, relativistic kinetic energy, four–momentum

In the previous section we related the space components of the four-force $|\mathbf{K})$ to the cartesian components of the classical force $\mathbf{F}$, and found that

$$K_i = \gamma F_i, \qquad i = 1, 2, 3. \tag{13–60}$$

We can rewrite Eq. (13–51) as

$$(\mathbf{u}|m_0\mathbf{a}) = (\mathbf{u}|\mathbf{K}) = 0$$

or

$$\gamma^2\mathbf{v} \cdot \mathbf{F} + ic\gamma K_4 = 0.$$

From this equation we find the fourth component of the four-force to be explicitly given by

$$K_4 = \frac{i\mathbf{F} \cdot \mathbf{v}\gamma}{c} = \frac{i}{c}\frac{d\mathfrak{I}}{d\tau}, \tag{13–61}$$

where, as in the classical case, we have set

$$\mathbf{F} \cdot \mathbf{v} = \frac{d\mathfrak{I}}{dt}, \tag{13–62}$$

and shall refer to $\mathfrak{I}$ as the kinetic energy. Let us check if this definition of the kinetic energy is consistent with its classical definition. From Eqs. (13–52) and (13–49) we find that

$$K_4 = m_0 \frac{d}{d\tau}\, \mathfrak{u}_4 = m_0\gamma \frac{d}{dt}\, (ic\gamma). \tag{13–63}$$

Hence equating Eqs. (13–61) and (13–63) yields

$$\frac{d\mathfrak{I}}{dt} = \frac{d}{dt}\, (m_0c^2\gamma), \tag{13–64}$$

which has the solution

$$\mathfrak{J} = m_0 c^2 \gamma + \mu, \tag{13–65}$$

where $\mu$ is a constant.

For small particle velocities we find that to within second-order terms in $v^2/c^2$,

$$\mathfrak{J} \approx m_0 c^2 + \tfrac{1}{2} m_0 v^2 + \mu.$$

Thus if we wish $\mathfrak{J}$ to yield the classical result for the kinetic energy, we should choose $\mu = -m_0 c^2$. However, in any application in which the kinetic energy appears it is the difference in the kinetic energy of a particle at two different points along its trajectory or two different instances that appears. The choice of the constant $\mu$ is thus really immaterial. Relativistically, however, we find the choice $\mu = 0$ to be notationally preferable.* In this manner the kinetic energy is related to the fourth component of a four-vector, the four-momentum vector, defined by

$$\mathfrak{p}_i = m_0 \mathfrak{u}_i. \tag{13–66}$$

The space components of this four-momentum vector are equal to the components of the ordinary linear momentum $\mathbf{p}$ defined by Eq. (13–58),

$$\mathfrak{p}_i = p_i, \qquad i = 1, 2, 3. \tag{13–67}$$

The fourth component of the four-momentum is

$$\mathfrak{p}_4 = \frac{i}{c} \mathfrak{J}. \tag{13–68}$$

We note the Lorentz invariant magnitude of the four-momentum vector,

$$\mathfrak{p}^2 = \sum_{i=1}^{4} \mathfrak{p}_i^2 = p^2 - \frac{\mathfrak{J}^2}{c^2} = \sum_{i=1}^{4} m_0^2 \mathfrak{u}_i^2 = -m_0^2 c^2, \tag{13–69}$$

yields the relation

$$\mathfrak{J}^2 = p^2 c^2 + m_0^2 c^4, \tag{13–70}$$

which is in agreement with the definition of the relativistic kinetic energy of the particle defined by Eq. (13–65) with $\mu = 0$. From

$$\mathfrak{J} = m_0 c^2 \gamma \tag{13–71}$$

we obtain

$$m = m_0 \gamma = \frac{1}{c^2} \mathfrak{J},$$

---

* We should like to point out that in many books, the choice $\mu = -m_0 c^2$ is made, and the quantity $T = m_0 c^2 (\gamma - 1)$ is referred to as the particle's kinetic energy, while $\mathfrak{J} = m_0 c^2 \gamma$ is called the total energy.

which permits us to obtain the very useful relation between the linear momentum and the relativistic kinetic energy

$$\mathbf{p} = \frac{\mathfrak{I}}{c^2}\,\mathbf{v}.$$ (13–72)

We note that the relativistic mass of a particle is a measure of its relativistic kinetic energy, and that a change in the kinetic energy of a particle appears as a change in its relativistic mass,

$$\Delta\mathfrak{I} = (\Delta m)c^2.$$ (13–73)

This seemingly startling result implies that mass is but another form of energy and that we should accordingly modify the principle of the conservation of energy to include the possible conversion of mass energy into some other form of energy, and vice versa. This conversion of mass into energy or energy into mass has by now been amply demonstrated by nuclear reactions, nuclear fission, and the creation and destruction of elementary particles.

A most direct, often quoted example is the observed annihilation of an electron-positron pair at rest and the resultant appearance of two photons each with an energy equal to the rest energy of the electron or positron. Two photons are required in order to conserve the total linear momentum of the system (cf. Section 13–16).

———————

A *photon* is the name associated with the discrete bundle of electromagnetic energy in which form such energy is radiated. Quantum mechanically we find the photon to be a particle of zero mass observed to be moving, as do all particles of zero mass, with the speed of light. (The neutrino is another example of a particle having zero mass.) The total kinetic energy of a particle of zero rest mass is of course indeterminate on the basis of the equation

$$\mathfrak{I} = mc^2 = \frac{m_0 c^2}{\sqrt{1 - v^2/c^2}}.$$

Its kinetic energy must therefore be found by some other means. For a photon we find the kinetic energy to be related to the frequency of the emitted radiation. Specifically, we find

$$\mathfrak{I} = h\nu,$$ (13–74)

where $h$ is Planck's constant and $\nu$ the frequency of the radiation.

Now from Eq. (13–72), which holds for all particles, we find the definition of the classical linear momentum $\mathbf{p}$ of the photon to be

$$\mathbf{p} = \frac{h\nu}{c^2}\,\mathbf{c} = \frac{h}{\lambda}\,\frac{\mathbf{c}}{c}.$$

Its magnitude is

$$p = \frac{h}{\lambda}.$$ (13–75)

We note that this relation between $p$ and $\lambda$ is the same as the relation between the De Broglie wavelength and the linear momentum of a particle which we found in Section 6–17.

The four-momentum associated with a photon is given by

$$|\mathfrak{p}) \leftrightarrow \begin{bmatrix} p_1 \\ p_2 \\ p_3 \\ ih\nu/c \end{bmatrix} = \frac{h}{2\pi} \begin{bmatrix} k_1 \\ k_2 \\ k_3 \\ ik \end{bmatrix},$$

where, in terms of $\mathbf{e}_x$, $\mathbf{e}_y$, and $\mathbf{e}_z$, the unit vectors directed along the $x$-, $y$-, $z$-axes, the vector

$$\mathbf{k} = k_1\mathbf{e}_x + k_2\mathbf{e}_y + k_3\mathbf{e}_z$$

is the propagation vector of the wave (cf. Section 3–2 and 12–3). It has the magnitude

$$k = 2\pi/\lambda,$$

and is directed in the direction of propagation of the photon. We note that the Lorentz-invariant magnitude of the four-momentum of the photon (Eq. 13–69) indeed vanishes:

$$\sum_{i=1}^{4} \mathfrak{p}_i^2 = \left(\frac{h}{2\pi}\right)^2 \left[\sum_{i=1}^{3} k_i^2 - k^2\right] = 0. \tag{13–76}$$

Interestingly, having found the photon four-momentum, we are in a position to relate, through use of the Lorentz transformation, the wavelength $\lambda$ or the frequency

$$\nu = c/\lambda$$

of an electromagnetic wave in one inertial frame to its frequency in any other inertial frames. The change which occurs in the frequency of a wave when we transform its description from one inertial frame to another is known as the *Doppler effect*. The use of the momentum four-vector of the wave or the four-propagation vector

$$|\mathfrak{f}) \leftrightarrow \begin{bmatrix} k_1 \\ k_2 \\ k_3 \\ ik \end{bmatrix}$$

yields the result quite readily (Problem 13–6). Finally we note that the phase of a harmonic wave, defined by

$$\varphi = \mathbf{k} \cdot \mathbf{r} - \omega t \tag{13–77a}$$

is expressible as the inner product of two four-vectors, and is therefore a scalar invariant. Specifically we find that

$$\varphi = \sum_{i=1}^{3} k_i x_i + \left(\frac{i\omega}{c}\right)(ict) = \sum_{j=1}^{4} k_j x_j = (\mathfrak{f}|\mathfrak{r}). \tag{13–77b}$$

### 13–7 Transformation properties of the electromagnetic field

In this section we shall express the Lorentz force acting on a charged particle moving in an electromagnetic field in the four-vector language. The possibility of doing this (not all known forces can be expressed in covariant four-vector language) permits us to infer the transformation equations for the electromagnetic-field vectors **E** and **B**.

The Lorentz force on a charged particle moving with velocity **v** is given by

$$\mathbf{F} = q(\mathbf{v} \times \mathbf{B} + \mathbf{E}). \tag{13–78}$$

The work which this Lorentz force performs per unit time on the charged particle is

$$\mathbf{F} \cdot \mathbf{v} = q\mathbf{E} \cdot \mathbf{v}. \tag{13–79}$$

The Lorentz force four-vector is thus by Eqs. (13–60) and (13–61) found to be defined by

$$K_i = \gamma F_i \quad (i = 1, 2, 3), \qquad K_4 = \frac{iq\gamma}{c} \mathbf{E} \cdot \mathbf{v}. \tag{13–80}$$

From the Lorentz transformation equations for the four-force it is not difficult to deduce the Lorentz transformation properties of the electromagnetic-field vectors. It is simpler, however, to attempt to express the Lorentz force acting on a charged particle in four-vector language. We recall that in Section 10–7 we were able to express the magnetic force acting on a charged particle in matrix notation. There we found a $3 \times 3$ magnetic-field matrix which when operating on the matrix representation of the particle's velocity vector yielded the matrix representation of the force vector. We therefore naturally seek as the extension into the world space a $4 \times 4$ electromagnetic-field matrix which when operating on the particle's four-velocity yields the Lorentz four-force.

From the rotational and space inversion properties of the magnetic-induction vector **B**, we suspect that in the absence of an electric field, the relation between the space components of the four-force and the space components of the four-velocity should be, as found previously,

$$\begin{bmatrix} F^m_1 \\ F^m_2 \\ F^m_3 \end{bmatrix} = q \begin{bmatrix} 0 & B_3 & -B_2 \\ -B_3 & 0 & B_1 \\ B_2 & -B_1 & 0 \end{bmatrix} \begin{bmatrix} v_1 \\ v_2 \\ v_3 \end{bmatrix}.$$

Since a magnetic force does no work on a charged particle, the fourth component of the magnetic four-force vanishes. In four-vector language the relationship between the four-force and the four-velocity is thus found to be

$$\begin{bmatrix} K^m_1 \\ K^m_2 \\ K^m_3 \\ K^m_4 \end{bmatrix} = q \begin{bmatrix} 0 & B_3 & -B_2 & 0 \\ -B_3 & 0 & B_1 & 0 \\ B_2 & -B_1 & 0 & 0 \\ 0 & 0 & 0 & 0 \end{bmatrix} \begin{bmatrix} u_1 \\ u_2 \\ u_3 \\ u_4 \end{bmatrix}. \tag{13–81}$$

The electric force acting on a particle is additive to the magnetic force. Hence we may consider it independently. If the electric force acting on a charged particle is expressible as the matrix product of a $4 \times 4$ electric-field matrix and the four-velocity, then clearly, since only the fourth component of the electric four-force depends on the velocity of the particle, the electric-field components may appear only in the fourth row or fourth column of the $4 \times 4$ electric-field matrix. We indeed find the electric four-force $|\mathbf{K}^e)$ to be expressible in the form

$$\begin{bmatrix} K_1^e \\ K_2^e \\ K_3^e \\ K_4^e \end{bmatrix} = \frac{q}{c} \begin{bmatrix} 0 & 0 & 0 & -iE_1 \\ 0 & 0 & 0 & -iE_2 \\ 0 & 0 & 0 & -iE_3 \\ iE_1 & iE_2 & iE_3 & 0 \end{bmatrix} \begin{bmatrix} u_1 \\ u_2 \\ u_3 \\ u_4 \end{bmatrix}. \tag{13-82}$$

The total electromagnetic four-force acting on a charged particle is thus found to be expressed by

$$\begin{bmatrix} K_1 \\ K_2 \\ K_3 \\ K_4 \end{bmatrix} = \frac{q}{c} \begin{bmatrix} 0 & cB_3 & -cB_2 & -iE_1 \\ -cB_3 & 0 & cB_1 & -iE_2 \\ cB_2 & -cB_1 & 0 & -iE_3 \\ iE_1 & iE_2 & iE_3 & 0 \end{bmatrix} \begin{bmatrix} u_1 \\ u_2 \\ u_3 \\ u_4 \end{bmatrix} \tag{13-83}$$

or, in operator notation,

$$|\mathbf{K}) = \frac{q}{c}\, \mathfrak{F}|\mathbf{u}), \tag{13-84}$$

where $\mathfrak{F}$ is referred to as the electromagnetic-field operator.

Since both $|\mathbf{K})$ and $|\mathbf{u})$ are four-vectors, which behave similarly under a Lorentz transformation, the Lorentz transformation of the field operator $\mathfrak{F}$ is determined. Thus, since under the Lorentz transformation from a primed coordinate system $I'$ to an unprimed system $I$, whose proper Lorentz transformation operator is $\mathbf{S}$,

$$|\mathbf{K}) = \mathbf{S}|\mathbf{K}') \qquad \text{and} \qquad |\mathbf{u}) = \mathbf{S}|\mathbf{u}'), \tag{13-85}$$

we find that the electromagnetic-field operator transforms in the following manner:

$$\mathfrak{F} = \mathbf{S}\mathfrak{F}\mathbf{S}^{-1}. \tag{13-86}$$

For the Lorentz transformation from a primed inertial system moving with speed $V$ along the positive $x$-axis with respect to an unprimed inertial system for which

$$(\mathbf{S}) = \begin{bmatrix} \Gamma & 0 & 0 & -i(V/c)\Gamma \\ 0 & 1 & 0 & 0 \\ 0 & 0 & 1 & 0 \\ i(V/c)\Gamma & 0 & 0 & \Gamma \end{bmatrix},$$

where $\Gamma = (1 - V/c)^{-1/2}$, we find Eq. (13–86) to yield for the electromagnetic field the transformation equations (cf. Problem 10–9):

$$E_1 = E'_1, \qquad\qquad B_1 = B'_1,$$

$$E_2 = \Gamma(E'_2 + VB'_3), \qquad B_2 = \Gamma\left(B'_2 - \frac{V}{c^2}E_3\right), \qquad (13\text{–}87)$$

$$E_3 = \Gamma(E'_3 - VB'_2), \qquad B_3 = \Gamma\left(B'_3 + \frac{V}{c^2}E_2\right).$$

In subsequent sections we shall consider the relativistic motion of a charged particle in time-independent electromagnetic fields, while neglecting the effect of the radiation reaction on the motion of the particle. By a proper choice of the inertial coordinate system with respect to which to describe the motion, we can reduce the relativistic motion in uniform time-independent fields to one of four special cases. They are motion in a uniform electric field, a uniform magnetic field, parallel electric and magnetic fields, and perpendicular electric and magnetic fields. This fact follows from the field invariants

$$E^2 - c^2B^2 \qquad \text{and} \qquad \mathbf{E} \cdot \mathbf{B}$$

(cf. Problem 10–10), which can be constructed from the electromagnetic field matrix. Thus if $\mathbf{E} \cdot \mathbf{B}$ does not vanish in one inertial system in which the fields are $\mathbf{E}_0$ and $\mathbf{B}_0$, then the scalar product of $\mathbf{E}$ and $\mathbf{B}$ does not vanish in any other inertial system. Hence we can always find an inertial system (Problem 13–15) in which the fields $\mathbf{E}$ and $\mathbf{B}$ are parallel and hence satisfy the equations

$$\begin{aligned} \mathbf{E} \cdot \mathbf{B} = EB = \mathbf{E}_0 \cdot \mathbf{B}_0, \\ E^2 - c^2B^2 = E_0^2 - c^2B_0^2. \end{aligned} \qquad (13\text{–}88)$$

On the other hand, if $\mathbf{E}_0$ is perpendicular to $\mathbf{B}_0$, such that

$$\mathbf{E}_0 \cdot \mathbf{B}_0 = 0,$$

and if in addition

$$E_0^2 - c^2B_0^2 > 0,$$

then there exists an inertial system in which $\mathbf{B}$ vanishes. Thirdly, if

$$\mathbf{E}_0 \cdot \mathbf{B}_0 = 0 \qquad \text{and} \qquad E_0^2 - c^2B_0^2 < 0,$$

then we can find an inertial system in which $\mathbf{E}$ vanishes.

Finally, if

$$\mathbf{E}_0 \cdot \mathbf{B}_0 = 0 \qquad \text{and} \qquad E_0^2 - c^2B_0^2 = 0,$$

then we find that $\mathbf{E}$ and $\mathbf{B}$ are mutually perpendicular in all inertial frames of reference.

## 13–8 The motion of a charged particle in a uniform electric field

The four relativistic equations of motion for a charged particle in a uniform electric field directed along the $x$-axis are

$$\frac{dp_x}{d\tau} = q\gamma E, \qquad \frac{dp_y}{d\tau} = \frac{dp_z}{d\tau} = 0,$$

$$\frac{d\Im}{d\tau} = q\gamma v_x E = qE \frac{dx}{d\tau}.$$

From the last equation we obtain the equation that expresses the conservation of the total energy of the particle. Its integration yields

$$\Im = qEx + \lambda, \tag{13–89}$$

where $\lambda$ is a constant. We thus find that we can set

$$\Im + q\phi = \lambda = \Im_0 + q\phi_0, \tag{13–90}$$

where we have set the electric potential

$$\phi = -Ex. \tag{13–91}$$

By a proper choice of the origin of the coordinates, we can make the total energy vanish. This we can do for the choice of origin which yields

$$x_0 = \frac{\Im_0}{qE}. \tag{13–92}$$

The other equations yield

$$p_y = p_{y0}, \qquad p_z = p_{z0}, \qquad p_x = qEt + \mu, \tag{13–93}$$

where $\mu$ is a constant of integration. The last equation was obtained by first setting

$$\gamma = \frac{1}{\sqrt{1 - v^2/c^2}} = \frac{dt}{d\tau}$$

in the first component of the equation of motion.

By a proper choice of the initial time we can also reduce this constant of integration to zero. Thus, setting

$$t_0 = \frac{p_{x0}}{qE}, \tag{13–94}$$

we find that $\mu = 0$.

To obtain $x$ as a function of time we now utilize the relation

$$p_x = m_0\gamma \frac{dx}{dt} = \frac{\Im}{c^2} \frac{dx}{dt} = \frac{qEx}{c^2} \frac{dx}{dt}. \tag{13–95}$$

The last step in the previous equation follows from Eq. (13–89). We have therefore obtained the equation

$$\frac{x}{c^2} \frac{dx}{dt} = t \quad \text{or} \quad \frac{d}{dt}\left(\frac{1}{2} x^2\right) = c^2 t,$$

whose solution is

$$x^2 = (ct)^2 + \nu. \tag{13–96}$$

The constant of integration

$$\nu = [x(0)]^2, \tag{13–97}$$

where $x(0)$ is the position of the particle at time $t = 0$.

Analogously, setting

$$p_y = \frac{\Im}{c^2} \frac{dy}{dt} = \frac{qEx}{c^2} \frac{dy}{dt} = \frac{qE}{c^2} \sqrt{(ct)^2 + [x(0)]^2} \frac{dy}{dt} = p_{y0},$$

we obtain

$$\frac{dy}{dt} = \frac{p_{y0}c^2}{qE\sqrt{(ct)^2 + [x(0)]^2}}. \tag{13–98}$$

The solution of this equation is

$$y = \frac{p_{y0}c}{qE} \sinh^{-1} \frac{ct}{x(0)}. \tag{13–99}$$

By a proper choice of the $y$-, and $z$-axes, we can confine the motion to the $xy$-plane. Thus through the use of Eq. (13–96) and a little algebra we obtain the equation for the particles trajectory

$$x = x(0) \cosh \frac{qEy}{p_{y0}c}, \tag{13–100}$$

which is the equation of a catenary.

## 13–9 Motion in a uniform magnetic field

The motion of a charged particle in a uniform time-independent magnetic field directed along the $z$-axis is governed by the four relativistic equations of motion

$$\frac{d\mathbf{p}}{d\tau} = q\gamma \mathbf{v} \times \mathbf{B} \tag{13–101}$$

and

$$\gamma \mathbf{v} \cdot \mathbf{F} = \frac{d\Im}{d\tau} = 0. \tag{13–102}$$

The last equation tells us that the magnetic force does no work on the particle and that hence its kinetic energy

$$\Im = mc^2$$

remains constant.   This means that the particle's relativistic mass, which is expressible as

$$m = \frac{\mathfrak{J}}{c^2},$$

and hence its speed $v$ are likewise constant.

That the speed remains fixed may also be ascertained by rewriting Eq. (13–101) in the form

$$\frac{d}{dt}(m\mathbf{v}) = m\frac{d\mathbf{v}}{dt} + \mathbf{v}\frac{dm}{dt} = q\mathbf{v} \times \mathbf{B}. \qquad (13\text{–}103)$$

Since $dm/dt = 0$, this equation is identical to the classical equation of motion for a charged particle in a uniform time-independent magnetic field.   The solution of such an equation we considered in Section 6–7.

The trajectory of the relativistic particle in a magnetic field is thus likewise a helix whose axis lies along the direction of the magnetic field and along which the particle moves with constant speed.

## 13–10 Motion under the action of parallel electric and magnetic fields

The relativistic equations of motion for a charged particle moving in uniform and parallel electric and magnetic fields directed along the $z$-axis are

$$m_0 \frac{d^2 x}{d\tau^2} = qB\frac{dy}{d\tau}, \qquad (13\text{–}104)$$

$$m_0 \frac{d^2 y}{d\tau^2} = -qB\frac{dx}{d\tau}, \qquad (13\text{–}105)$$

$$m_0 \frac{d^2 z}{d\tau^2} = qE\gamma, \qquad (13\text{–}106)$$

$$icm_0 \frac{d^2 t}{d\tau^2} = \frac{iqE}{c}\frac{dz}{d\tau}. \qquad (13\text{–}107)$$

Equations (13–104) and (13–105) are independent of the remaining two.   They are also identical to the classical equations (6–33) and (6–34) of the motion of a particle in a uniform magnetic field but with the time $t$ replaced by the particle's proper time $\tau$.

Their solutions are thus similar to the classical solutions.   Specifically, we find (cf. Section 6–7)

$$x - a = A \cos[\omega\tau + \phi_0],$$
$$y - b = -A \sin[\omega\tau + \phi_0], \qquad (13\text{–}108)$$

where

$$\omega = \frac{qB}{m_0}. \qquad (13\text{–}109)$$

The other two equations, with $\gamma$ replaced by $dt/d\tau$, reduce to the simultaneous differential equations with constant coefficients:

$$\frac{d^2z}{d\tau^2} = \frac{qE}{m_0}\frac{dt}{d\tau} \quad \text{and} \quad \frac{d^2t}{d\tau^2} = \frac{qE}{m_0c^2}\frac{dz}{d\tau}. \tag{13–110}$$

The solution of these simultaneous differential equations are

$$z - g = D\cosh\frac{qE}{m_0c}(\tau - \phi'),$$

$$c(t - h) = D\sinh\frac{qE}{m_0c}(\tau - \phi'). \tag{13–111}$$

By a proper choice of the origin of the coordinates, the orientation of the $x$-, $y$-coordinate axes, and the initial value of the proper time, we can make the constants of integration $a$, $b$, $g$, and $h$ vanish. Remembering further that the magnitude of the four-velocity is a constant,

$$\sum_{i=1}^{4} u_i^2 = -c^2,$$

we find $A$ and $D$ to be related:

$$D = \sqrt{\left(\frac{m_0c^2}{qE}\right)^2 + \left(\frac{B}{E}\right)^2 A^2}. \tag{13–112}$$

The trajectory is a spiral.

## 13–11 Generalized coordinates, Lagrange's equations of motion

Until now we have confined our description of the relativistic motion of a particle in terms of the cartesian components $(x_1, x_2, x_3)$ of its space position vector and in terms of the time as represented by $x_4 = ict$. This, however, is unnecessarily restrictive. At times we find it appropriate to utilize another set of four generalized coordinates $q_i$ which have a one-to-one correspondence with the $x_i$ as expressed by the transformation equations

$$x_i = x_i(q_1, q_2, q_3, q_4), \quad i = 1, 2, 3, 4. \tag{13–113}$$

The method for handling the relativistic motion of a particle in terms of generalized coordinates is quite analogous to our approach to setting up the generalized equations of motion for a slowly moving particle. We find, however, that there are two different approaches which are used to obtain generalized equations of motion for a relativistic particle. The distinction between the two methods lies essentially in a difference in the choice of generalized base vectors and in the fact that one approach restricts itself to coordinate transformations which keep $x_4$ as one of the generalized coordinates. That is, the approach restricts itself to time-dependent coordinate transformations of the form

$$x_i = x_i(q_1, q_2, q_3, t), \qquad i = 1, 2, 3,$$

and

$$x_4 = q_4.$$

(13–114)

Since the method for dealing with such transformations is already familiar to us (we introduced it in Sections 3–2 and 5–3 to handle time-dependent coordinate transformations), we shall discuss it first.

This first approach utilizes a description of the motion of a particle in the three-dimensional space as functions of time; it also utilizes the three vectors

$$\mathbf{b}_i = \frac{\partial \mathbf{r}}{\partial q_i} = \frac{\partial x_1}{\partial q_i} \mathbf{e}_1 + \frac{\partial x_2}{\partial q_i} \mathbf{e}_2 + \frac{\partial x_3}{\partial q_i} \mathbf{e}_3, \qquad i = 1, 2, 3, \qquad (13\text{–}115)$$

($\mathbf{e}_1 = \mathbf{i}$, $\mathbf{e}_2 = \mathbf{j}$, $\mathbf{e}_3 = \mathbf{k}$) as base vectors. As before, the *generalized forces* are defined as the scalar products of the force vector and the base vectors,

$$Q_i = \mathbf{F} \cdot \mathbf{b}_i = \sum_{j=1}^{3} F_j \frac{\partial x_j}{\partial q_i}, \qquad (13\text{–}116)$$

and the *generalized relativistic particle momenta* as the scalar product of the relativistic linear momentum of the particle and the base vectors,

$$p_i = \mathbf{p} \cdot \mathbf{b}_i = \frac{m_0}{\sqrt{1 - v^2/c^2}} \mathbf{v} \cdot \mathbf{b}_i. \qquad (13\text{–}117)$$

We can rewrite this expression for the generalized momenta as

$$p_i = \frac{\partial}{\partial \dot{q}_i} [-m_0 c^2 \sqrt{1 - v^2/c^2}] \qquad (13\text{–}118)$$

by noting once again (cf. Section 2–5) that

$$\frac{\partial x_j}{\partial q_i} = \frac{\partial \dot{x}_j}{\partial \dot{q}_i},$$

and hence that

$$p_i = \frac{m_0}{\sqrt{1 - v^2/c^2}} \sum_{j=1}^{3} \dot{x}_j \frac{\partial x_j}{\partial q_i}$$

$$= \frac{m_0}{\sqrt{1 - v^2/c^2}} \frac{\partial}{\partial \dot{q}_i} \sum_{j=1}^{3} \frac{1}{2} \dot{x}_j^2 = -\frac{\partial}{\partial \dot{q}_i} (m_0 c^2 \sqrt{1 - v^2/c^2}).$$

We note that for a relativistic particle,

$$p_i \neq \frac{\partial \mathfrak{J}}{\partial \dot{q}_i}$$

as was the case for a Newtonian particle.

The $\dot{q}_j$'s are referred to as the *generalized velocities*. For time-dependent coordinate transformations they are not the scalar products of the velocity vector and the inverse base vectors.

The generalized or *Lagrange's equations* of motion are the scalar products of the relativistic equation of motion,

$$\mathbf{F} = \frac{d}{dt}\left[\frac{m_0\mathbf{v}}{\sqrt{1 - v^2/c^2}}\right], \tag{13-119}$$

and the base vectors. Thus we find the generalized equations of motion to be

$$\mathbf{F} \cdot \mathbf{b}_i = \frac{d\mathbf{p}}{dt} \cdot \mathbf{b}_i$$

$$= \frac{d}{dt}(\mathbf{p} \cdot \mathbf{b}_i) - \mathbf{p} \cdot \frac{d}{dt}\mathbf{b}_i$$

$$= \frac{d}{dt}(p_i) - \frac{m_0}{\sqrt{1 - v^2/c^2}}\mathbf{v} \cdot \frac{\partial}{\partial q_i}\frac{d\mathbf{r}}{dt}$$

$$= \frac{dp_i}{dt} + m_0c^2\frac{\partial}{\partial q_i}\sqrt{1 - v^2/c^2}$$

or

$$Q_i = \frac{d}{dt}\frac{\partial}{\partial \dot{q}_i}(-m_0c^2\sqrt{1 - v^2/c^2}) - \frac{\partial}{\partial q_i}(-m_0c^2\sqrt{1 - v^2/c^2}). \tag{13-120}$$

If the force **F** is derivable from a velocity-dependent potential energy function $U(\mathbf{r}, \mathbf{v}, t)$ as expressed by

$$\mathbf{F}_i = \frac{d}{dt}\frac{\partial U}{\partial \dot{x}_i} - \frac{\partial U}{\partial x_i}, \tag{13-121}$$

then the generalized forces are given by (cf. Section 6-13)

$$Q_i = \frac{d}{dt}\frac{\partial U}{\partial \dot{q}_i} - \frac{\partial U}{\partial q_i}, \tag{13-122}$$

and Lagrange's equations are expressed by

$$\frac{d}{dt}\frac{\partial \mathcal{L}}{\partial \dot{q}_i} - \frac{\partial \mathcal{L}}{\partial q_i} = 0, \tag{13-123}$$

where the Lagrangian is

$$\mathcal{L} = -m_0c^2\sqrt{1 - v^2/c^2} - U(\mathbf{r}, \mathbf{v}, t). \tag{13-124}$$

Unfortunately we do not know the correct relativistic interation energy for all known forces. For electromagnetic forces we do know the potential energy function, which is

$$U = q\phi - q(\mathbf{A} \cdot \mathbf{v}). \tag{13–125}$$

Hence the relativistic Lagrangian for a charged particle in an electromagnetic field is found to be

$$\mathcal{L} = -m_0 c^2 \sqrt{1 - v^2/c^2} - q\phi + q\mathbf{A} \cdot \mathbf{v}. \tag{13–126}$$

For the motion of a particle in a velocity-dependent force field derivable from a potential energy function, it is customary to refer to

$$P_i = \frac{\partial \mathcal{L}}{\partial \dot{q}_i} \tag{13–127}$$

as the *conjugate momentum*.

## 13–12 Covariant Lagrangian formulation

In the covariant Lagrangian formulation of the relativistic equations of motion of a particle, we consider the description of the motion in terms of the events of the particle in four-space. The description of the events of a particle in terms of the four generalized coordinates $q_i$ utilizes the four linearly independent base vectors defined by

$$|\mathfrak{b}_i) = \frac{\partial |\mathbf{r})}{\partial q_i}. \tag{13–128}$$

The four components of these base vectors are given by

$$\mathfrak{b}_{ij} = \frac{\partial x_j}{\partial q_i}, \tag{13–129}$$

where

$$x_j = x_j(q_1, q_2, q_3, q_4), \qquad j = 1, 2, 3, 4. \tag{13–130}$$

Any other four-vector in the world space may be specified in terms of its inner products with these four base vectors. Thus the four-force is expressed in terms of the *four generalized forces*

$$\mathfrak{Q}_i = (\mathbf{K}|\mathfrak{b}_i) = \sum_{j=1}^{4} K_j \frac{\partial x_j}{\partial q_i}. \tag{13–131}$$

The four *covariant generalized particle momenta* are defined analogously as the inner products of the four-momentum vector and the four-base vectors

$$\mathfrak{p}_i = (\mathfrak{p}|\mathfrak{b}_i). \tag{13–132}$$

From the definition (Eq. 13–66) of the four-momentum and the four-base vectors, we find that

$$\mathfrak{p}_i = \sum_{j=1}^{4} m_0 \mathfrak{u}_j \frac{\partial x_j}{\partial q_i}. \tag{13–133}$$

From the coordinate transformation equations

$$x_j = x_j(q_1, q_2, q_3, q_4),$$

it follows that

$$\mathfrak{u}_j = \frac{\partial x_j}{\partial \tau} = \sum_{i=1}^{4} \frac{\partial x_j}{\partial q_i} \frac{\partial q_i}{\partial \tau}$$

and hence that

$$\frac{\partial \mathfrak{u}_j}{\partial \mathring{q}_i} = \frac{\partial x_j}{\partial q_j}, \tag{13-134}$$

where we have set

$$\mathring{q}_i = \frac{\partial q_i}{\partial \tau}. \tag{13-135}$$

Utilizing this result in Eq. (13-133) yields in turn

$$\mathfrak{p}_i = \sum_{j=1}^{4} m_0 \mathfrak{u}_j \frac{\partial \mu_j}{\partial \mathring{q}_i} = \frac{\partial}{\partial \mathring{q}_i} \left( \frac{1}{2} m_0 \mathfrak{u}^2 \right), \tag{13-136}$$

where the square of the four-velocity $\mathfrak{u}^2$ is to be expressed in terms of the generalized coordinates $q_i$ and their proper-time derivatives $\mathring{q}_i$. That is, the value $-c^2$ is not to be utilized.

The generalized equations of motion are the scalar products of the relativisitic equation of motion

$$|\mathbf{K}) = \frac{d}{d\tau} |\mathfrak{p}) \tag{13-137}$$

with the base vectors. We thus obtain the four covariant generalized equations of motion

$$(\mathfrak{b}_i | \mathbf{K}) = \left( \mathfrak{b}_i \left| \frac{d}{d\tau} \mathfrak{p} \right. \right) = \frac{d}{d\tau} (\mathfrak{b}_i | \mathfrak{p}) - \left( \frac{d\mathfrak{b}_i}{d\tau} \middle| \mathfrak{p} \right),$$

which, since

$$\left( \frac{d\mathfrak{b}_i}{d\tau} \middle| \mathfrak{p} \right) = \sum_j \frac{\partial \mathring{x}_j}{\partial q_i} m_0 \mathfrak{u}_j = \frac{\partial}{\partial q_i} \frac{1}{2} m_0 \mathfrak{u}^2,$$

are expressed by

$$\mathfrak{Q}_i = \frac{d}{d\tau} \frac{\partial}{\partial \mathring{q}_i} \left( \frac{1}{2} m \mathfrak{u}^2 \right) - \frac{\partial}{\partial q_i} \left( \frac{1}{2} m_0 \mathfrak{u}^2 \right). \tag{13-138}$$

The electromagnetic four-forces acting on a charged particle are derivable from the Lorentz-invariant interaction potential energy function*

$$U(x_i, \mathfrak{u}_i) = -\frac{q}{c} \sum_{i=1}^{4} \mathfrak{u}_i A_i, \tag{13-139}$$

---

* From electromagnetic theory we find that the $A_i$'s are the components of an electromagnetic four-vector potential.

where

$$A_1 = A_x c, \qquad A_2 = A_y c,$$
$$A_3 = A_z c, \qquad A_4 = i\phi.$$

In terms of $U$, we can express the components of the four-force by

$$K_i = \frac{d}{d\tau} \frac{\partial U}{\partial \mathring{x}_i} - \frac{\partial U}{\partial x_i}. \tag{13–140}$$

The generalized electromagnetic forces are thus found to be given by

$$\mathfrak{Q}_i = \frac{d}{d\tau} \frac{\partial U}{\partial \mathring{q}_i} - \frac{\partial U}{\partial q_i}. \tag{13–141}$$

The generalized covariant equations of motion are thus

$$\frac{d}{d\tau} \frac{\partial \mathfrak{L}}{\partial \mathring{q}_i} - \frac{\partial \mathfrak{L}}{\partial q_i} = 0, \tag{13–142}$$

where the covariant Lagrangian for a particle in an electromagnetic field is

$$\mathfrak{L} = \sum_{i=1}^{4} \left( \frac{1}{2} m_0 u_i^2 + \frac{q}{c} u_i A_i \right). \tag{13–143}$$

The generalized conjugate momenta for a particle in an electromagnetic field are defined by

$$\mathfrak{P}_i = \frac{\partial \mathfrak{L}}{\partial \mathring{q}_i}. \tag{13–144}$$

For the coordinates $x_i$ we find the conjugate four-momentum to be

$$\mathfrak{P}_i = \frac{\partial \mathfrak{L}}{\partial u_i} = m_0 u_i + \frac{q}{c} A_i, \qquad i = 1, 2, 3. \tag{13–145}$$

The fourth component of the conjugate momentum is

$$\mathfrak{P}_4 = i \left( \frac{m_0 c}{\sqrt{1 - v^2/c^2}} + \frac{q\phi}{c} \right) = \frac{i\mathcal{E}}{c}, \tag{13–146}$$

where

$$\mathcal{E} = \mathfrak{T} + q\phi \tag{13–147}$$

is the total relativistic energy of a charged particle in an electromagnetic field. The total energy of a particle multipled by $i/c$ has thus been found to be the momentum canonical to the fourth component of the four-position vector, that is, the time multiplied by the factor $ic$.

## 13–13 Motion of a charged particle in a Coulomb field

As an example of the application of the generalized covariant formulation discussed in the previous section, we shall consider the motion of a particle of of rest mass $m_0$ and charge $q$ under the action of the force produced by the charge $q'$ of another charged particle fixed at the origin of the coordinates. Since for this case $A_1 = A_2 = A_3 = 0$ and

$$A_4 = i\phi = \frac{iq'}{4\pi\epsilon_0 r},$$    (13–148)

the covariant potential energy is given by

$$U = -\frac{q}{c}\, u_4 A_4 = \frac{qq'}{4\pi\epsilon_0 r}\, \gamma,$$    (13–149)

where $r$ is the distance of the charge $q$ from the origin. As in the classical motion of a charged particle in a Coulomb field, we find the relativistic motion likewise to take place in the plane determined by the particle's initial velocity and position vectors.

Thus, utilizing the cylindrical coordinates $r$ and $\theta$ for the description of the motion of the particle in the plane, and referring to the plane as the $xy$-plane, we find that

$$\begin{aligned}
\mathrm{u}^2 &= \left(\frac{dx}{d\tau}\right)^2 + \left(\frac{dy}{d\tau}\right)^2 - c^2\left(\frac{dt}{d\tau}\right)^2 \\
&= \left(\frac{dr}{d\tau}\right)^2 + r^2\left(\frac{d\theta}{d\tau}\right)^2 - c^2\left(\frac{dt}{d\tau}\right)^2.
\end{aligned}$$    (13–150)

Hence the covariant Lagrangian for this problem

$$\mathcal{L} = \tfrac{1}{2}m_0 \mathrm{u}^2 - U$$    (13–151)

yields the equations of motion

$$m_0\frac{d^2 r}{d\tau^2} - m_0 r\left(\frac{d\theta}{d\tau}\right)^2 - \frac{qq'\gamma}{4\pi\epsilon_0 r^2} = 0,$$    (13–152)

$$\frac{d}{d\tau}\left(m_0 r^2\frac{d\theta}{d\tau}\right) = 0,$$    (13–153)

$$\frac{d}{d\tau}\left(m_0 \mathrm{u}_4 + \frac{q}{c}\, A_4\right) = 0.$$    (13–154)

The last two equations are readily integrated to yield

$$m_0 r^2\frac{d\theta}{d\tau} = l$$    (13–155)

and

$$m_0 \mathrm{u}_4 + \frac{q}{c}\, A_4 = \frac{i\lambda}{c},$$    (13–156)

where $\lambda$ is a constant. Equation (13–156), expressed as

$$\frac{i}{c}\left(\frac{m_0 c^2}{\sqrt{1 - v^2/c^2}} + \frac{qq'}{4\pi\epsilon_0 r}\right) = \frac{i}{c}\,\lambda,$$

tells us that

$$\lambda = 3 + q\phi = \mathcal{E} \qquad (13\text{--}157)$$

is the total energy of the particle. We have now obtained two first integrals of the motion: the conservation of the angular momentum $l$ and the total energy $\mathcal{E}$ of the particle.

Also, expressing Eq. (13–156) in the form

$$im_0 c\,\frac{dt}{d\tau} = \frac{i\mathcal{E}}{c} - \frac{iqq'}{4\pi\epsilon_0 cr}\,,$$

we find that

$$\gamma = \frac{dt}{d\tau} = \frac{\mathcal{E}}{m_0 c^2} - \frac{qq'}{4\pi\epsilon_0 m_0 c^2 r}\,, \qquad (13\text{--}158)$$

which when inserted into Eq. (13–152) yields the equation

$$m_0\frac{d^2 r}{d\tau^2} - m_0 r\left(\frac{d\theta}{d\tau}\right)^2 = \frac{qq'}{4\pi\epsilon_0 r^2}\left(\frac{\mathcal{E}}{m_0 c^2} - \frac{qq'}{4\pi\epsilon_0 m_0 c^2 r}\right). \qquad (13\text{--}159)$$

But this equation together with Eq. (13–153) with $\tau$ replaced by $t$ are the classical equations of motion of a particle under the combined action of a central force of magnitude $(qq'\mathcal{E}/4\pi\epsilon_0 m_0 c^2)(1/r^2)$ and an inverse-cube central force of magnitude $(qq'/4\pi\epsilon_0)^2(1/m_0 c^2 r^3)$. We considered this problem in Section 7–4 under the title, "Newton's theory of revolving orbits."

We can therefore utilize either the results of Section 7–4 or otherwise proceed to integrate the differential equation (7–14) for the orbit in order to find the trajectory of the particle. We leave it as an exercise (cf. Problem 13–11) for the reader to show that when a proper choice is made of the line from which $\theta$ is measured, it is possible to express the solutions of the differential equation for the orbits by

$$(c^2 l^2 - k^2)\frac{1}{r} = c\sqrt{(l\mathcal{E})^2 - m_0^2 c^2(l^2 c^2 - k^2)}\,\cos\phi\sqrt{1 - \frac{k^2}{l^2 c^2}} - \mathcal{E}k,$$

$$(13\text{--}160)$$

if $lc > |k|$, where $k = qq'/4\pi\epsilon_0$, and

$$(k^2 - l^2 c^2)\frac{1}{r} = \pm c\sqrt{(l\mathcal{E})^2 + m_0^2 c^2(k^2 - l^2 c^2)}\,\cosh\phi\sqrt{\frac{k^2}{l^2 c^2} - 1} + \mathcal{E}k,$$

$$(13\text{--}161)$$

if $lc < |k|$, and where the plus sign is used for particles of like charges, and the minus sign for particles of opposite charges. If $lc = |k|$, then the equation of the orbit is

$$\frac{2\mathcal{E}k}{r} = \mathcal{E}^2 - m_0^2 c^4 - \phi^2 \left(\frac{\mathcal{E}k}{lc}\right)^2.$$    (13–162)

There are a number of interesting trajectories. For example, for an attractive potential ($k < 0$), the solutions to Eqs. (13–161) and (13–162) are spirals along which paths the particle approaches and finally reaches the origin with increasing $\theta$.

### 13–14 Angular momentum

As in the three-dimensional case, we find the generalized momentum conjugate to an angle variable to be a specific element of the matrix representation of the operator (cf. Section 10–7)

$$\mathfrak{L} = |\mathbf{r})(\mathfrak{p}| - |\mathfrak{p})(\mathbf{r}|.$$    (13–163)

This antisymmetric operator has only six distinct elements $\mathfrak{L}_{ij}$ in its $4 \times 4$ matrix representation. They are the generalized momenta conjugate to the angle variables $\theta_{ij}$, which are the angles made by the projection of the four-position vector onto the $x_i x_j$-plane and the $x_i$-axis. That is,

$$\tan \theta_{ij} = \frac{x_j}{x_i} = \cot \theta_{ji}.$$    (13–164)

Let us see that this is indeed so. We note that the definition of the angles $\theta_{ij}$ leads us to conclude that for small changes in the orientation of the four-position vector of a particle,

$$\Delta\theta_{ij} = -\Delta\theta_{ji}.$$    (13–165)

These $\theta_{ij}$'s, which by the way are not independent, thus lead us to the six elements of the antisymmetric angular velocity matrix. They are the elements defined by

$$\Omega_{ij} = \frac{d\theta_{ij}}{d\tau} = -\frac{d\theta_{ji}}{d\tau} = -\Omega_{ji}.$$    (13–166)

If the four-position vector of a particle changes only in direction, then the four-velocity of the particle is given by

$$\mathfrak{u}_i = -\sum_{j=1}^{4} \Omega_{ij} x_j.$$    (13–167)

The inner product of Eq. (13–167) and the four-position vector vanishes as it should. If the four-position vector also changes in magnitude, then the part of the four-velocity given by Eq. (13–167) contributes to the total $\mathfrak{u}^2$ only the term

$$\sum_{ijk} \Omega_{ij}\Omega_{ik} x_j x_k.$$    (13–168)

Hence the generalized momentum associated with the angle $\theta_{ij}$ is

$$\mathfrak{L}_{ij} = \frac{\partial m_0 \mathfrak{u}^2 / 2}{\partial \Omega_{ij}}.$$    (13–169)

From (13–168) and (13–169) we indeed find that

$$\mathfrak{L}_{ij} = m_0 \sum_k (\Omega_{ik} x_j x_k - \Omega_{jk} x_i x_k)$$

or

$$\mathfrak{L}_{ij} = -\mathfrak{p}_i x_j + x_i \mathfrak{p}_j. \tag{13–170}$$

These $\mathfrak{L}_{ij}$'s are the elements of the matrix representation of the operator $\mathfrak{L}$ of (13–163).

As is the case of the antisymmetric electromagnetic-field matrix ($\mathfrak{F}$), we find that from the six elements of the angular momentum matrix ($\mathfrak{L}$) we can form two sets of three elements, each of which transform under a rotation of the spatial coordinate axes like the three components of a vector. These are the sets ($\mathfrak{L}_{23}, \mathfrak{L}_{31}, \mathfrak{L}_{12}$) and $(c/i)(\mathfrak{L}_{41}, \mathfrak{L}_{42}, \mathfrak{L}_{43})$. The first set defines the relativistic three-dimensional angular momentum vector.

## 13–15 The collision of particles: reactions, threshold energy

In this section we shall consider the collision of particles in which we allow for a possible change in the internal structure of the particles. That is, we allow for a reaction to take place, so that the outgoing particles are not necessarily the same as the original colliding particles. We shall, however, restrict ourselves to a system for which the total relativistic four-momentum is a constant of the motion. For a closed system of particles we will also find the angular momentum of the system to be conserved. But, we shall be concerned only with the consequences of the conservation of the four-momentum.

By far the simplest reaction is the collision of two particles of rest masses $m_1$ and $m_2$ which results in the formation of a single particle of rest mass $M$, or the reverse problem, the decay of a particle of rest mass $M$ into two particles of rest masses $m_3$ and $m_4$. The decay into more than two particles is, of course, also possible. Since, however, the introduction of additional particles only complicates the application of the conservation of the four-momentum, we shall restrict our discussion essentially to the case when at most only two different particles appear as a result of the collision.

We note that a reaction in which the collision of particles one and two results in the appearance of particles three and four may be considered to occur in two steps as follows: first, the formation of a single compound particle of rest mass $M$, and then the decay of the compound particle into particles three and four. This picture of a reaction was first introduced by Niels Bohr.*

---

The reaction in which more than two reaction particles appear may similarly be decomposed into intermediate steps. Such a reaction may, for example, be considered to occur as follows:

$$m_1 + m_2 \rightarrow M_1 \rightarrow m_3 + M_2 \rightarrow m_3 + m_4 + M_3 \rightarrow \cdots$$

where $M_1$, $M_2$, $M_3$, etc. are intermediate compound particles.

---

* N. Bohr, *Nature*, **137**, 344, 351 (1936).

In the usual problem the momenta $\mathbf{p}_1$ and $\mathbf{p}_2$ and the energies $\mathfrak{I}_1$ and $\mathfrak{I}_2$ of the incoming particles of rest masses $m_1$ and $m_2$, which combine to form the compound particle, are furnished. From this information we readily find the energy

$$\mathfrak{I} = \mathfrak{I}_1 + \mathfrak{I}_2 \tag{13-171}$$

of the compound particle, its linear momentum

$$\mathbf{P} = \mathbf{p}_1 + \mathbf{p}_2, \tag{13-172}$$

its velocity

$$\mathbf{V} = \frac{c^2}{\mathfrak{I}}\,\mathbf{P}, \tag{13-173}$$

and its rest mass

$$M = \frac{1}{c^2}\,\sqrt{\mathfrak{I}^2 - P^2 c^2}. \tag{13-174}$$

In the second step of the reaction the compound particle of rest mass $M$ and velocity $\mathbf{V}$ decays into the two particles of rest masses $m_3$ and $m_4$. In this part the momenta $\mathbf{p}_3$ and $\mathbf{p}_4$ of the emerging particles are unknown. Furthermore, the four equations provided by the conservation of the four-momentum are not sufficient to permit us to determine the linear momenta of the outgoing particles.

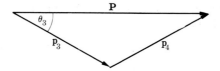

FIGURE 13–4

We may introduce the additional simplifying assumption that the motion of all the particles take place in a plane. This reduces the total number of unknown components of the momenta of the outgoing particles to four and the number of equations introduced by the conservation of the four-momentum to three. The additional information we require so as to be able to solve for the momenta and energies of the outgoing particles is customarily the experimentally determined angle which the momentum of one of the outgoing particles makes with the total linear momentum of the system. From Fig. 13–4 we find that in term of the angle $\theta_3$ which $\mathbf{p}_3$ makes with $\mathbf{P}$,

$$p_4^2 = p_3^2 + P^2 - 2p_3 P \cos\theta_3, \tag{13-175}$$

which, together with the energy equation

$$\mathfrak{I}_3 + \mathfrak{I}_4 = \mathfrak{I}$$

or

$$\sqrt{p_4^2 c^2 + m_4^2 c^4} + \sqrt{p_3^2 c^2 + m_3^2 c^4} = \sqrt{P^2 c^2 + M^2 c^4}, \tag{13-176}$$

provides us with sufficient information to determine $p_3$ and $p_4$. A knowledge of $p_3$ and $p_4$ in turn allows us to find $\Im_3$ and $\Im_4$, and the angle $\theta_4$ which $\mathbf{p}_4$ makes with $\mathbf{P}$.

We note that in case the sum of the rest masses of the outgoing particles exceeds the sum of the rest masses of the initial particles, that is, if

$$\sum_{i=3}^{N} m_i > m_1 + m_2,$$

the reaction is energetically possible only if the energy of the incoming particles exceeds a certain minimum value $\Im_{\min}$. Considering the usual case in which particle two is initially at rest and the total incoming energy is

$$\Im = \Im_1 + m_2 c^2, \tag{13–177}$$

we find for

$$\Im = \Im_{\min} \tag{13–178}$$

that the rest mass of the compound particle is

$$M = \sum_{i=3}^{N} m_i,$$

and that the outgoing particles all move together with the velocity $\mathbf{V}$ of the compound particle. Hence

$$\Im_{\min} = \Im_{1,\min} + m_2 c^2 = \sqrt{P^2 c^2 + M^2 c^4}$$

$$= \sqrt{p_1^2 c^2 + M^2 c^4} \tag{13–179}$$

or

$$\Im_{1,\min} + m_2 c^2 = \sqrt{\Im_{1,\min}^2 + (M^2 - m_1^2) c^4}. \tag{13–180}$$

This equation yields

$$\Im_{1,\min} = \frac{M^2 - m_1^2 - m_2^2}{2 m_2} c^2. \tag{13–181}$$

The *threshold energy* of a reaction is defined as the minimum energy above the rest energy of the incoming particles which is required to energetically permit the reaction to take place. For the case under discussion, that is, for $m_2$ initially at rest, we find the threshold energy to be

$$\Im_{\text{th}} = \Im_{\min} - (m_1 + m_2) c^2 = \Im_{1,\min} - m_1 c^2$$

or

$$\Im_{\text{th}} = \frac{M^2 - (m_1 + m_2)^2}{2 m_2} c^2. \tag{13–182}$$

As an example, we shall consider the threshold energy for the production of a proton-antiproton pair in a proton-proton collision. The reaction is schematically represented by

$$p + p \rightarrow p + p + p + \overline{p},$$

where $p$ represents a proton and $\overline{p}$ the antiproton. For this reaction,

$$M = 4m_p,$$

where $m_p$ is the rest mass of the proton, and hence we find

$$\mathfrak{I}_{th} = \frac{16m_p^2 - 4m_p^2}{2m_p} c^2 = 6m_p c^2.$$

The rest mass of a proton is 938 Mev. Hence the threshold energy for this reaction is

$$\mathfrak{I}_{th} = 6 \times 938 \text{ Mev} = 5630 \text{ Mev}.$$

## Problems

13–1. The average lifetime of a muon at rest is $2.21 \times 10^{-6}$ second. If the muons formed high in the atmosphere travel with a speed $v = 0.99c$, what is the average distance which they will be observed to traverse before decaying?

13–2. The maximum energy of the electrons produced in the decay of a muon at rest is found to be 55 Mev. The decay is represented by

$$\mu^- \rightarrow e^- + \nu_e + \overline{\nu}_\mu,$$

where $\nu_e$ and $\overline{\nu}_\mu$ represent respectively the electron's neutrino and the muon's antineutrino. Given that the rest mass of the electron is 0.51 Mev and that the neutrino and antineutrino have zero rest masses, find the rest mass of the muon. Find the minimum energy carried away by the two neutrinos.

13–3. A pion whose rest mass is 273 times the rest mass $m_e$ of an electron decays while at rest into a muon of rest mass 207 $m_e$ and a muon's neutrino;

$$\pi^+ \rightarrow \mu^+ + \nu_\mu,$$
$$\pi^- \rightarrow \mu^- + \overline{\nu}_\mu.$$

Find the energy and linear momentum received by the muon.

13–4. The velocities of the points $P_1$ and $P_2$ are respectively observed to be

$$\mathbf{v}_1 = v\mathbf{i} \quad \text{and} \quad \mathbf{v}_2 = v_{2x}\mathbf{i} + v_{2y}\mathbf{j}$$

by an observer $I$. Find the relative velocity of $P_2$ with respect to $P_1$ (a) in the rest frame of $P_1$, (b) in the rest frame of $P_2$. We note that the descriptions of the relative velocity of $P_2$ with respect to $P_1$ in these two rest frames, each of which has its coordinate axes parallel to the coordinate axes of $I$, are not the same. Hence it follows that the coordinate axes of the rest frame of $P_2$, which are parallel to the coordinate axes of the rest frame of $P_1$, are not in turn parallel to the coordinate axes of the rest frame of $P_2$, whose coordinate axes are parallel to the axes of observer $I$.

By comparing the two descriptions of $\mathbf{v}_{21} = \mathbf{v}_2 - \mathbf{v}_1$ with respect to the two rest frames of $P_2$, show that for an infinitesimal relative velocity, that is, for

$$v_{2x} = v + \Delta v_x \qquad \text{and} \qquad v_{2y} = \Delta v_y,$$

where $\Delta v_x$ and $\Delta v_y$ are infinitesimal velocities, the two $x$-axes of the rest frames of $P_2$ described above make an infinitesimal angle with each other which is given by

$$\Delta\theta = \frac{v\,\Delta v_y}{c^2},$$

and represents a rotation about their parallel $z$-axes. Hence we can set

$$\Delta\boldsymbol{\theta} = \frac{\mathbf{v} \times \Delta\mathbf{v}}{c^2},$$

from which we conclude that the coordinate system attached to an accelerated particle which remains at all times parallel to itself will be observed to rotate with the angular velocity

$$\boldsymbol{\omega} = \frac{\Delta\boldsymbol{\theta}}{\Delta t} = \frac{1}{c^2}\,\mathbf{v} \times \frac{\Delta\mathbf{v}}{\Delta t} = \frac{1}{c^2}\,\mathbf{v} \times \mathbf{a}$$

by an observer with respect to whom the particle moves with velocity $\mathbf{v}$ and acceleration $\mathbf{a}$. This phenomenon is important in atomic physics and is known as the *Thomas precession*.

13–5. Show that a general Lorentz transformation between two inertial coordinate systems $I$ and $I'$ with $I'$ moving with a velocity $\mathbf{V} = V_x\mathbf{i} + V_y\mathbf{j} + V_z\mathbf{k}$ with respect to $I$ is

$$\mathbf{r} = \mathbf{r}' + (\gamma - 1)\,\frac{\mathbf{r}' \cdot \mathbf{V}}{V^2}\,\mathbf{V} + \gamma t\mathbf{V}$$

and

$$t = \left(t' + \frac{\mathbf{r}' \cdot \mathbf{V}}{c^2}\right)\gamma, \qquad \text{where} \qquad \gamma = \left(1 - \frac{V^2}{c^2}\right)^{-1/2}.$$

Obtain the Lorentz transformation matrix for these equations.

13–6. (a) Utilizing the four-momentum vector of a photon (cf. Section 13–6), obtain the relation between the frequencies of the photon as observed by two different inertial observers $I$ and $I'$, where $I'$ is moving with a velocity $V$ along the positive $x$-axis with respect to observer $I$, which is also the direction of propagation of the photon.

(b) Find the change in the frequency of a plane electromagnetic wave reflected normally from a plane mirror which is moving in a direction normal to itself with velocity $\mathbf{V} = \pm V\mathbf{i}$.

13–7. Do Problem 10–9.

13–8. Do Problems 10–10.

13–9. Given that the electric field of a stationary charge $q$ is

$$\mathbf{E} = \frac{q}{4\pi\epsilon_0 r^3}\,\mathbf{r} = -\nabla\left(\frac{q}{4\pi\epsilon_0 r}\right),$$

obtain the electromagnetic field produced by a charge $q$ which is observed to be moving with a velocity $\mathbf{V} = V\mathbf{i}$.

13–10. Show that from the equations of motion and for the proper choice of the origin of a coordinate system we find the differential equation for the orbit of a charged particle moving in a uniform electric field to be

$$\frac{d^2 x}{dy^2} - \frac{q^2 E^2}{c^2 p_{y0}^2} x = 0.$$

Utilize this equation to obtain the orbit of a particle moving in a uniform electric field.

13–11. Obtain the differential equation for the orbit of a relativistic particle in an inverse-square central-force field, and show that Eqs. (13–160), (13–161), and (13–162) describe its possible orbits.

13–12. Discuss qualitatively the motion of a relativistic charged particle under the action of the axially symmetric magnetic field derivable from the vector potential

$$\mathbf{A} = \alpha \ln \rho \; \mathbf{k},$$

where $\rho$ is the distance of the particle from the $z$-axis.

13–13. Determine the relativistic motion of a charged particle under the action of mutually perpendicular electric and magnetic fields.

13–14. A photon may be described as a particle of zero mass possessing nevertheless a linear momentum $p = h/\lambda = h\nu/c$ and a kinetic energy $h\nu$. If the photon collides with an electron of mass $m$ at rest, it will be scattered off at some angle $\theta$ with a new energy $h\nu'$. Show that the change in the wavelength of the photon is related to the scattering angle $\theta$ by the formula

$$\lambda' - \lambda = 2\lambda_c \sin^2 \frac{\theta}{2},$$

where $\lambda_c = h/mc$ is known as the *Compton wavelength*. Show also that the kinetic energy gained by the recoiling electron is

$$\Im - m_0 c^2 = \Delta \Im = h\nu \, \frac{2(\lambda_c/\lambda) \sin^2 (\theta/2)}{1 + 2(\lambda_c/\lambda) \sin^2 (\theta/2)}.$$

13–15. Given that in one inertial system $\mathbf{E}_0 \cdot \mathbf{B}_0 \neq 0$ and that $\mathbf{E}_0$ is not parallel to $\mathbf{B}_0$, find the speed $V$ of the inertial system which is moving in a direction perpendicular to $\mathbf{E}_0$ and $\mathbf{B}_0$, with respect to which the electric and magnetic fields $\mathbf{E}$ and $\mathbf{B}$ are parallel.

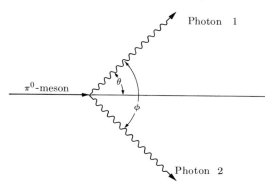

FIGURE 13–5

13–16. A $\pi^0$-meson of rest energy $\mathfrak{I}_0$, moving with a velocity $\mathbf{v}$ in the laboratory, disintegrates into two $\gamma$-rays. Find (a) the energy of the $\gamma$-ray observed at an angle $\theta$ with the direction of motion of the $\pi^0$-meson; (b) the energy of the second $\gamma$-ray and the angle $\phi$ which the direction in which the second $\gamma$-ray is observed to propagate makes with the direction of propagation of the first (cf. Fig. 13–5).

13–17. If a particle of initial kinetic energy $\mathfrak{I}_0$ and rest energy $m_0c^2$ strikes a like particle at rest, what is the kinetic energy $\mathfrak{I}$ of the particle scattered elastically at an angle $\theta$?

13–18. An energy of $2m_pc^2 = 1862$ Mev is required to produce a "proton pair" in the center-of-mass system. What is the threshold energy required for an electron to produce a "proton-pair" by striking a proton at rest?

# Suggested References

## Intermediate Mechanics Texts

BECKER, R. A., *Introduction to Theoretical Mechanics*. New York: McGraw-Hill, 1954.

McCUSKEY, S. W., *An Introduction to Advanced Dynamics*. Reading, Mass.: Addison-Wesley, 1959.

LINDSAY, R. B., *Physical Mechanics*. Princeton, N.J.: Van-Nostrand, 1961.

OSGOOD, W. F., *Mechanics*. New York: Macmillan, 1937.

SYMON, K. R., *Mechanics*. Reading, Mass.: Addison-Wesley, 1960.

SYNGE, J. L., and GRIFFITH, B. A., *Principles of Mechanics*. New York: McGraw-Hill, 1959.

## Advanced Mechanics and Relativity Texts

BERGMANN, P. G., *Introduction to the Theory of Relativity*. New York: Prentice-Hall, 1942.

BRILLOUIN, L., *Wave Propagation in Periodic Structures*. New York: McGraw-Hill, 1946 (New York: Dover, 1953).

CORBEN, H. C., and STEHLE, P., *Classical Mechanics*. New York: Wiley, 1950.

GOLDSTEIN, H., *Classical Mechanics*. Reading, Mass.: Addison-Wesley, 1950.

LANCZOS, C., *The Variation Principles of Mechanics*. Toronto: University of Toronto Press, 1949.

LANDAU, L. D., and LIFSHITZ, E. M., *Mechanics*. London: Permagon Press, 1960 (Reading, Mass.: Addison-Wesley, 1960).

SLATER, J. C., and FRANK, N. H., *Mechanics*. New York: McGraw-Hill, 1947.

SOMMERFELD, A., *Mechanics* (Lectures on Theoretical Physics). New York: Academic Press, 1949.

WEBSTER, A. G., *The Dynamics of Particles and of Rigid, Elastic, and Fluid Bodies*. Leipzig: B. G. Teubner, 1904.

WHITTAKER, E. T., *A Treatise on the Analytical Dynamics of Particles and Rigid Bodies*. Cambridge: Cambridge University Press, 1937 (New York: Dover, 1944).

## Mathematics Texts

CHURCHILL, R. V., *Fourier Series and Boundary Value Problems*. New York: McGraw-Hill, 1963.

KAPLAN, W., *Advanced Calculus*. Reading, Mass.: Addison-Wesley, 1952.

LASS, H., *Vector and Tensor Analysis*. New York: McGraw-Hill, 1950.

OSGOOD, W. F., *Advanced Calculus*. New York: Macmillan, 1925.

PHILLIPS, H. B., *Vector Analysis*. New York: Wiley, 1933.

SOKOLNIKOFF, I. S., and REDHEFFER, R. M., *Mathematics of Physics and Modern Engineering*. New York: McGraw-Hill, 1958.

# Answers to
# Odd-Numbered Problems

## Chapter 1

1-1. (a) $9\mathbf{j} + 2\mathbf{k}$  (b) $A = 5\sqrt{2}, B = \sqrt{21}, C = \sqrt{6}$

(d) $\mathbf{A} \cdot \mathbf{B} = 3, \mathbf{A} \cdot \mathbf{C} = 7, \mathbf{B} \cdot \mathbf{C} = -8, \cos \theta_{AB} = 3/5\sqrt{42},$
$\cos \theta_{AC} = 7/5\sqrt{12}, \cos \theta_{BC} = -8/3\sqrt{14}$

(e) $\mathbf{A} \times \mathbf{B} = -28\mathbf{i} + \mathbf{j} + 16\mathbf{k}, \mathbf{A} \times \mathbf{C} = 9\mathbf{i} + 7\mathbf{j} - 11\mathbf{k},$
$\mathbf{B} \times \mathbf{C} = 2\mathbf{i} - 3\mathbf{j} - 7\mathbf{k}$

(f) $\mathbf{A} \cdot \mathbf{B} \times \mathbf{C} = -41$, no  (g) zero

1-3. $c = -2$  1-5. $-13\mathbf{i} + 31\mathbf{j} - 17\mathbf{k}$

1-11. $\mathbf{b}_1 = (6\mathbf{i} + \mathbf{j} + 11\mathbf{k})/41, \mathbf{b}_2 = (-\mathbf{i} - 7\mathbf{j} + 5\mathbf{k})/41,$
$\mathbf{b}_3 = (16\mathbf{i} - 11\mathbf{j} + 2\mathbf{k})/41$

1-13. $\mathbf{r} = x\mathbf{i} + y\mathbf{j} + z\mathbf{k}$, where $x + 7y + 18z = 13$

1-17. (a) $\bar{\mathbf{k}} = \sin \psi \csc \theta \mathbf{i}' + \cos \psi \csc \theta \mathbf{j}', \bar{\mathbf{k}}' = -\cot \theta \sin \psi \mathbf{i}' - \cot \theta \cos \psi \mathbf{j}' + \mathbf{k}$
$\bar{\mathbf{e}}_\phi' = \cos \psi \mathbf{i}' - \sin \psi \mathbf{j}' = \mathbf{e}_\phi'$

(b) $\mathbf{i} = (\mathbf{i} \cdot \mathbf{k})\bar{\mathbf{k}} + (\mathbf{i} \cdot \mathbf{k}')\bar{\mathbf{k}}' + (\mathbf{i} \cdot \mathbf{e}_\phi')\bar{\mathbf{e}}_\phi' = \sin \theta \sin \phi \bar{\mathbf{k}}' + \cos \phi \bar{\mathbf{e}}_\phi'$
$\mathbf{j} = (\mathbf{j} \cdot \mathbf{k})\bar{\mathbf{k}} + (\mathbf{j} \cdot \mathbf{k}')\bar{\mathbf{k}}' + (\mathbf{j} \cdot \mathbf{e}_\phi')\bar{\mathbf{e}}_\phi'$

See Eqs. 9–9 and 9–10 for solution.

1-19. (a) $\left(\dfrac{x}{A}\right)^2 + \left(\dfrac{y}{B}\right)^2 = 1$

(b) $x = (A + B) \cos \omega t, y = (A - B) \sin \omega t, A > B$ counterclockwise,
$A < B$ clockwise

## Chapter 2

2-1. (a) $\mathbf{v} = -n\omega A \sin n\omega t \mathbf{i} + m\omega B \cos m\omega t \mathbf{j}$
$\mathbf{a} = -(n\omega)^2 A \cos n\omega t \mathbf{i} - (m\omega)^2 B \sin m\omega t \mathbf{j}$

(b) $\mathbf{v} = 3\mathbf{i} - 4\mathbf{j} + 2t\mathbf{k}, \mathbf{a} = 2\mathbf{k}$

(c) $\mathbf{v} = a(1 - \omega \cos \omega t)\mathbf{i} + a\omega \sin \omega t \mathbf{j}, \mathbf{a} = a\omega^2 \sin \omega t \mathbf{i} + a\omega^2 \cos \omega t \mathbf{j}$

(d) $\mathbf{v} = (b_1 + 2c_1 t)\mathbf{i} - kd_2 e^{-kt}\mathbf{j}, \mathbf{a} = 2c_1\mathbf{i} + k^2 d_2 e^{-kt}\mathbf{j}$

2-3. $\mathbf{v} = \dot{\rho}\mathbf{e}_\rho + \rho\dot{\phi}\mathbf{e}_\phi + \dot{z}\mathbf{k} = ab\mathbf{e}_\phi - c\mathbf{k},$
$\mathbf{a} = (\ddot{\rho} - \rho\dot{\phi}^2)\mathbf{e}_\rho + (\rho\ddot{\phi} + 2\dot{\rho}\dot{\phi})\mathbf{e}_\phi + \ddot{z}\mathbf{k} = -ab^2\mathbf{e}_\rho$

493

2–5.  $\mathbf{b}_1 = \dfrac{a}{2}\,(\sinh q_1 \cos q_2\mathbf{i} + \cosh q_1 \sin q_2\mathbf{j})$

$\mathbf{b}_2 = \dfrac{a}{2}\,(-\cosh q_1 \sin q_2\mathbf{i} + \sinh q_1 \cos q_2\mathbf{j}),\ \mathbf{b}_3 = \mathbf{k}$

Vectors are orthogonal with magnitudes

$$h_1 = h_2 = \frac{a}{2}\sqrt{\cosh^2 q_1 - \cos^2 q_2},\qquad h_3 = 1.$$

$$\boldsymbol{b}_i = \frac{1}{h_i^2}\,\mathbf{b}_i$$

2–7.  $v_1 = \tfrac{1}{2}bx\dot\phi \sin \phi,\ v_2 = \tfrac{1}{2}bx\dot x \sin \phi + cx^2\dot\phi$

$a_1 = \dfrac{d}{dt}\,v_1 - (ax + \tfrac{1}{2}b\dot x\dot\phi \sin \phi + cx\dot\phi^2)$

$a_2 = \dfrac{d}{dt}\,v_2 - (bx\dot x\dot\phi \cos \phi)$

2–11. (a)  $\rho = \left[1 + \left(\dfrac{dy}{dx}\right)^2\right]^{3/2} \Big/ \dfrac{d^2 y}{dx^2}$

(b) For polar coordinates $r$ and $\phi$,

$$\rho = \left[r^2 + \left(\frac{dr}{d\phi}\right)^2\right]^{3/2} \Big/ \left[2\left(\frac{dr}{d\phi}\right)^2 + r^2 - r\frac{d^2 r}{d\phi^2}\right]$$

2–15.  $\mathbf{e}_t = \dfrac{1}{\sqrt{2}}\,(\mathbf{j} - \mathbf{k})$

# Chapter 3

3–1.  $\mathbf{v} = (20\mathbf{i} - 20\mathbf{j} - 10\mathbf{k})$, speed $= 30$ knots

3–3.  (a) 4 m/sec$^2$ vertically up      (b) zero

3–5.  $V = R\omega - v_B,\ A = R\alpha - a_B$

3–7.  Utilizing cylindrical base vectors,

$\mathbf{r} = A \sin \omega t\,\mathbf{e}_r$

$\mathbf{v} = A\omega \cos \omega t\,\mathbf{e}_r - A\Omega \sin \omega t\,\mathbf{e}_\phi$

$\mathbf{a} = (-A\omega^2 \sin \omega t - A\Omega^2 \sin \omega t)\mathbf{e}_r - 2A\omega\Omega \cos \omega t\,\mathbf{e}_\phi$

3–9.  (a) $-2gt\Omega \sin \theta\,\mathbf{e}_\phi$      (b) $d = r_0 g\Omega \sin \theta \sqrt{2h/g},\ r_0 =$ radius of earth

3–11. (a) $v_{1x} = l_1\dot\theta_1 \cos \theta_1,\ v_{1y} = l_1\dot\theta_1 \sin \theta_1$

$v_{2x} = l_2\dot\theta_2 \cos \theta_2 + v_{1x},\ v_{2y} = l_2\dot\theta_2 \sin \theta_2 + v_{2x}$

$a_{1x} = l_1\ddot\theta_1 \cos \theta_1 - l_1\dot\theta_1^2 \sin \theta_1,\ a_{1y} = l_1\ddot\theta_1 \sin \theta_1 + l_1\dot\theta_1^2 \cos \theta_1$

$a_{2x} = l_2\ddot\theta_2 \cos \theta_2 - l_2\dot\theta_2^2 \sin \theta_2 + a_{1x},$

$a_{2y} = l_2\ddot\theta_2 \sin \theta_2 + l_2\dot\theta_2^2 \cos \theta_2 + a_{1y}$

3–13.  $\begin{bmatrix} 11 & 11 & -2 \\ 10 & 3 & 0 \\ 46 & 40 & 6 \end{bmatrix}$      3–15. See Section 10–6, Eq. (10–93).

# Chapter 4

4-1. (a) $t_{up} = \dfrac{v_0}{g(\sin\theta + \mu\cos\theta)}$, $t_{down} = \sqrt{\dfrac{v_0^2}{g^2(\sin^2\theta - \mu^2\cos^2\theta)}}$,

$t = t_{up} + t_{down}$

(b) $\mu_{min} = \tan\theta$

4-3. $x_p = \dfrac{(F_0/m)e^{-\alpha t}\sin(\omega t + \phi)}{(\alpha^2 + \omega^2)^{1/2}}$, where $\phi = \tan^{-1}\dfrac{2\alpha\omega}{\alpha^2 - \omega^2}$

$x(t) = At + B + x_p$. $A$ and $B$ are determined from $x(0)$ and $\dot{x}(0)$.

4-5. $e^{-\mu x} = \dfrac{a}{\mu t + b}$, $\dot{x} = \dfrac{1}{\mu t + b}$.

4-7. (a) $E = \frac{1}{2}m\dot{x}^2 + \frac{1}{3}kx^3 = \frac{1}{2}mv_0^2$     (b) $\dot{x} = 0$ at $x = (3mv_0^2/2k)^{1/3}$

(c) $\dot{x} = \sqrt{v_0^2 - (2kx^3/3m)}$

4-9. (a) $F(x) = -\dfrac{a}{x} + \dfrac{2b}{x^3}$, $x > 0$     (b) $x = \sqrt{\dfrac{2b}{a}}$

(c) yes, $\omega = \sqrt{\dfrac{a^2}{mb}}$

4-11. Bounded for $E < 0$, unbounded for $E > 0$; $\tau = -\dfrac{\pi a}{E}\sqrt{\dfrac{m}{-2E}}$

4-13. For $\mu < \omega_0$,

$$x = Ae^{-\mu t}\sin(\nu t + \phi) + Ct + D,$$

where $C = F_0/m\omega^2$, $D = -2\mu F_0/m\omega_0$ and $A$ and $\phi$ are the solution of the equations

$$x(0) - D = A\sin\phi, \qquad \dot{x}(0) - C = A\nu\cos\phi - \mu A\sin\phi.$$

4-15. $\sigma = \dfrac{Ne^2}{m}\dfrac{2\mu - i\omega}{\omega^2 + 4\mu^2}$

4-17. $\omega_r = \omega_0$, $\Delta \approx \mu\sqrt{3}$

4-23. (a) $\omega_0 = \sqrt{gl}$     (b) $\omega_0 = \sqrt{gb/a^2}$

4-25. Assuming $x_1 = a_1\cos\omega t + a_3\cos 3\omega t$, we find

$$(\omega_0^2 - \omega^2)a_1 = F_0/m - \beta(\tfrac{3}{4}a_1^3 + \tfrac{3}{4}a_1^2 a_3 + \tfrac{3}{2}a_1 a_3^3),$$
$$(\omega_0^2 - 9\omega^2)a_3 = -\beta(\tfrac{1}{4}a_1^3 + \tfrac{3}{4}a_3^3 + \tfrac{3}{2}a_1^2 a_3),$$

which are to be solved for $a_1$ and $a_3$.

4-27. Assumed solution yields

$$(\omega_0^2 - \omega^2)a_1 = F_0/m - \beta(\tfrac{3}{4}a_1^3 + \tfrac{1}{4}a_{1/3}^3 + \tfrac{3}{2}a_1 a_{1/3}^2),$$
$$(\omega_0^2 - \tfrac{1}{9}\omega^2)a_{1/3} = -\beta(\tfrac{3}{4}a_{1/3}^3 + \tfrac{3}{2}a_1^2 a_{1/3} + \tfrac{3}{4}a_1 a_{1/3}^2).$$

The latter equation is quadratic in $a_{1/3}$ ($a_{1/3}$ is a factor),

$$(\omega_0^2 - \tfrac{1}{9}\omega^2) = -\beta(\tfrac{3}{4}a_{1/3}^2 + \tfrac{3}{2}a_1 + \tfrac{3}{4}a_1 a_{1/3}).$$

A solution is possible if $a_{1/3}$ is real. This is satisfied if the discriminant of the latter equation is positive definite.

## Chapter 5

5-3.   (a) along $\mathbf{e}_1$, $mg \cos \theta + m\ddot{y} \cos \theta - R = -ml\dot{\theta}^2$

along $\mathbf{e}_2$, $-mg \sin \theta - m\ddot{y} \sin \theta = ml\ddot{\theta}$

$R$ = tension in the string

5-5.   $T = l^2\dot{\theta}^2 + v^2 + 2vl\dot{\theta} \sin (\theta - \phi)$, where $\phi = (v/a)t$ is the angle which the radius vector of the point of support makes with the $x$-axis; $U = mga \sin \phi - mgl \cos \theta$

5-7.   (a) $T = \frac{1}{2}m(\dot{\rho}^2 + \rho^2\dot{\phi}^2 + \dot{z}^2)$, $U = mg\rho \cos \phi$, constraint $\rho - a = 0$

(b) $R = 3mg \cos \phi - 2mg$        (c) $R = 0$ or $\cos \phi = \frac{2}{3}$

5-9.   (a) $T = \frac{1}{2}m(\dot{\rho}^2 + \rho^2\dot{\phi}^2 + \dot{z}^2)$, $U = mgz$, $\rho - z \tan \alpha = 0$

(b) $v^2 = gz$

5-11.  (a) along $\mathbf{e}_1$: $-R_1 + R_2 \cos (\theta_2 - \theta_1) + m_1g \cos \theta_1 = -m_1l_1\dot{\theta}_1^2$,

where $R_i$ = tension in the $i$th string

along $\mathbf{e}_2$: $R_2 \sin (\theta_2 - \theta_1) - m_1g \cos \theta_1 = m_1l_1\ddot{\theta}_1$

along $\mathbf{e}_3$: $m_2g \cos \theta_2 - R_2 = -m_2l_2\ddot{\theta}_2 + m_2l_1\ddot{\theta}_1 \sin (\theta_2 - \theta_1)$

$\qquad\qquad\qquad -m_2l_1\dot{\theta}_1^2 \cos (\theta_2 - \theta_1)$

along $\mathbf{e}_4$: $-m_2g \sin \theta_2 = m_2l_2\ddot{\theta}_2 + m_2l_1\ddot{\theta}_1 \cos (\theta_2 - \theta_1)$

$\qquad\qquad\qquad + m_2l_1\dot{\theta}_1^2 \sin (\theta_2 - \theta_1)$

(b) $T = \frac{1}{2}m_1l_1^2\dot{\theta}_1^2 + \frac{1}{2}m_2(l_2^2\dot{\theta}_2^2 + l_1^2\dot{\theta}_1^2) + m_2l_1l_2\dot{\theta}_1\dot{\theta}_2 \cos (\theta_2 - \theta_1)$

5-15.  (a) $T = \frac{1}{2}m(q_1^2 + q_2^2)(\dot{q}_1^2 + \dot{q}_2^2)$, $p_1 = m(q_1^2 + q_2^2)\dot{q}_1$, $p_2 = m(q_1^2 + q_2^2)\dot{q}_2$

(c) $Q_1 = -mq_1\dot{q}_2^2 = -mcu_0^2$, $Q_2 = mq_2\dot{q}_2^2 = mu_0^3t$

(d) $F_x = Q_1b_{1x} + Q_2b_{2x}$, $F_y = Q_1b_{1y} + Q_2b_{2y}$, where

$$b_1 = \nabla q_1 = \frac{1}{h_1^2}\,\mathbf{b}_1 = \frac{1}{h_1^2}\,(q_1\mathbf{i} + q_2\mathbf{j}),$$

$$b_2 = \frac{1}{h_2^2}\,\mathbf{b}_2 = \frac{1}{h_2^2}\,(-q_2\mathbf{i} + q_1\mathbf{j});$$

$$h_1^2 = h_2^2 = q_1^2 + q_2^2 = c^2 + u_0^2t^2$$

## Chapter 6

6-1.   (a), (c), and (d) are conservative

(a) $U = -\left[\int f(x)\, dx + \int f(y)\, dy + \int f(z)\, dz\right]$

(c) $U = -a \ln r = -\frac{a}{2} \ln (x^2 + y^2 + z^2)$        (d) $U = -\dfrac{x^2y^2z^2}{2}$

6-3.   (a) $4\pi - 16$        (b) $13\frac{1}{3}$

6-5.   For $\mu^2 \ll \omega_0^2$ and small $\omega_L$,

$$(\omega_{\text{res}} \pm \omega_L)^2 = \omega_0^2 - 2\mu^2.$$

6-7.   (a) $v_0 = 2\phi/qB = 1.1 \times 10^5$ m/sec

(b) $m = 2T/v_0^2 = 2.45 \times 10^{-23}$ g $= 14.7$ amu        (c) $A = 15$

6-9.  $\theta = 84°, 58°$

6-13.  (a) $x = A \cos(\omega_1 t + \phi_1)$, $y = B \sin(\omega_2 t + \phi_2)$, where $m\omega_1^2 = k_1$, $m\omega_2^2 = k_2$; orbit closed if $n_1\omega_1 = n_2\omega_2$, where $n_1$ and $n_2$ are integers

(b) $H = \dfrac{p_1^2}{2m} + \dfrac{p_2^2}{2m} + \frac{1}{2}(k_1 x^2 + k_2 y^2)$, $\dot{x} = \dfrac{p_1}{m}$, $\dot{y} = \dfrac{p_2}{m}$

$\dot{p}_1 = -k_1 x$, $\dot{p}_2 = -k_2 y$

6-15.  (c) $\alpha = i\omega = \pm i\sqrt{2}, \pm 2i\sqrt{3}$

6-21.  With **B** along the $z$-axis,

$$\sigma_{xx} = \sigma_{yy} = \frac{Nq^2}{m} \frac{2\mu + i\omega}{(2\mu + i\omega)^2 + q^2 B^2/m^2}$$

$$\sigma_{xy} = -\sigma_{yx} = \frac{Nq^2}{m} \frac{qB/m}{(2\mu + i\omega)^2 + q^2 B^2/m^2}$$

$$\sigma_{xz} = \sigma_{zx} = \sigma_{yz} = \sigma_{zy} = 0, \ \sigma_{zz} = \frac{Nq^2}{m} \frac{1}{2\mu + i\omega}$$

# Chapter 7

7-3.  $U_{\text{eff}} = \dfrac{k}{r^2}\left[ \dfrac{h^2}{2mk} - re^{-\alpha r} \right]$

Bounded orbit possible if for some value of $r$, $re^{-\alpha r} > h^2/2mk$. This is possible if the maximum value of $re^{-\alpha r}$ exceeds $h^2/2mk$ or $1/\alpha e > h^2/2mk$. For this case two circular orbits are possible. The one having a negative total energy is stable. Hence we must have

$$E = U_{\text{eff}} < 0 \quad \text{or} \quad \frac{k}{r^2}\left[ \frac{h^2}{2mk} - re^{-\alpha r} \right] < 0.$$

But for a circular orbit

$$\frac{h^2}{2mr^3} = -F_r = \frac{k(1 + \alpha r)}{r^2} e^{-\alpha r}.$$

Hence $(k/r)[\alpha r - 1]e^{-\alpha r} < 0$ or $\alpha a < 1$ for the stable orbit of radius $a$.

7-5.  By Newton's law of revolving orbits we expect the orbits to be straight-line motion described with respect to a precessing coordinate system; that is, spirals. Specifically, for

$$h^2 > mk, \quad \frac{1}{r} = A \cos \sqrt{1 - \frac{mk}{h^2}}\,(\phi - \phi_0),$$

$$h^2 < mk, \quad \frac{1}{r} = A \cosh \sqrt{\frac{mk}{h^2} - 1}\,(\phi - \phi_0),$$

(or a linear combination of $e^{\pm\sqrt{mk/h^2 - 1}\,\phi}$),

$$h^2 = mk, \quad \frac{1}{r} = A\phi + B.$$

7–7.   (a) $k > 0, m\omega^2 = 4k$

  (b) $k_2 > 0, k_1 < 0, m\omega^2 = |k_1|^3/4k_2^2$

  (c) $k < 2, m\omega^2 = (2 - k)h^2/m$

7–9.   approximately $\frac{1}{3}\Omega \sin \theta \sqrt{8h^3/g}$ eastward

7–11.  (a) $v = \sqrt{GM/r}$      (b) $v = \sqrt{2GM/r}$

  (c) $a = \frac{1}{2}(r_{\max} + r_{\min}), \epsilon = \dfrac{1}{2a}(r_{\max} - r_{\min})$

  (d) $v_0 = \sqrt{\dfrac{GM}{2a}\dfrac{r_{\max}}{r_{\min}}}$      (e) $E = -\dfrac{GMm}{2a}$

7–13. $r_{\min} = \dfrac{2Ze^2}{4\pi\epsilon_0 mv_0^2}$

# Chapter 8

8–1.   If $\mathbf{p}_1 = 3a\mathbf{i}, \mathbf{p}_2 = 2a\mathbf{j}$, then

$$\mathbf{p}_3 = -(3a\mathbf{i} + 2a\mathbf{j}), \qquad \mathbf{F}_i = \mathbf{p}_i \times 10^5.$$

8–3.   (a) $v_1 = v_2 = \frac{1}{2}v_0$      (b) $v_1 = \frac{1}{2}v_0(1 + \sqrt{2}), v_2 = \frac{1}{2}v_0(1 - \sqrt{2})$

8–5.   $\dfrac{m_1}{m_2} = 1 + 2\dfrac{\sin\theta_2}{\sin\theta_1}\cos(\theta_1 + \theta_2) = \dfrac{\sin^2(\theta_2 + \theta_1) - \sin^2\theta_1}{\sin^2\theta_1}$

8–7.   $T_1 = Q\left[\dfrac{1}{m_1} - \dfrac{m_1}{m_3}\dfrac{\sin^2\theta_4}{\sin^2(\theta_3 + \theta_4)} - \dfrac{m_1}{m_4}\dfrac{\sin^2\theta_3}{\sin^2(\theta_3 + \theta_4)}\right]$

8–9.   $M_1 = 36{,}200$ kg, $M_2 = 1770$ kg

8–11.  Measuring, $x_1, x_2, x$ from the horizontal line passing through the center of the fixed pulley,

$$T = \frac{1}{2}(m_1\dot{x}_1^2 + m_2\dot{x}_2^2 + m_3\dot{x}_3^2),$$
$$U = -m_1gx_1 - m_2gx_2 - m_3gx_3.$$

The constraint is $x_2 + x_3 + 2x_1 = $ const, which introduces the tensions in the strings connecting the masses into the equations of motion.

8–13.  (a) $T = \frac{3}{2}m\dot{x}^2 + \frac{1}{2}ml_1^2\dot{\theta}_1^2\sin^2\theta_1 + \frac{1}{2}m(l_1\dot{\theta}_1\cos\theta_1 + \dot{x})^2$

  $\qquad + \frac{1}{2}m(l_1\dot{\theta}_1\sin\theta_1 + l_2\dot{\theta}_2\sin\theta_2)^2$

  $\qquad + \frac{1}{2}m(l_1\dot{\theta}_1\cos\theta_1 + l_2\dot{\theta}_2\cos\theta_2 + \dot{x})^2$

  $U = -2mgl_1\cos\theta_1 - mgl_2\cos\theta_2$

  (b) For small $\theta$,

  $T = \frac{3}{2}m\dot{x}^2 + \frac{1}{2}m(l_1\dot{\theta}_1 + \dot{x})^2 + \frac{1}{2}m(l_1\dot{\theta}_1 + l_2\dot{\theta}_2 + \dot{x})^2$

  $U = mgl_1\theta_1^2 + \frac{1}{2}mgl_2\theta_2^2$

8–15. (a) With spherical coordinates specifying the position of the balls,

$$T = m(l^2\dot{\theta}^2 + l^2 \sin^2 \theta\dot{\phi}^2) + \tfrac{1}{2}M(2l \sin \theta\dot{\theta})^2$$
$$U = -2mgl \cos \theta - 2Mgl \cos \theta$$

(b) height $z = 2l - 2\,\dfrac{m + M}{m\omega^2}\,g$

equilibrium at $l \cos \theta_0 = \dfrac{m + M}{m\omega^2}\,g$

frequency of small oscillations $\Omega$ given by

$$\Omega^2 = \frac{m\omega^2 \sin^2 \theta_0}{m + 2M \sin^2 \theta_0} = \frac{(m + M)g/l \cos \theta_0}{m + 2M \sin^2 \theta_0}$$

8–17. (a) $\omega = \sqrt{\dfrac{l}{g}}$   (b) $\omega^2 = \dfrac{k}{m} + \dfrac{g}{l}$   (c) $\omega^2 = \dfrac{g}{l} + \dfrac{2k}{m}, \dfrac{g}{l}$

(d) $\omega_{\text{beat}} = \sqrt{\dfrac{k}{m}}$

8–19. $x_1 = A \cos \omega t$, $x_2 = B \cos \omega t$, where $A = F_0(2k - m\omega^2)/mD$,
$B = kF_0/mD$, $D = (3k - m\omega)(k - m\omega)$

8–21. The relation between $f$ and $\omega$ is

$$\omega^4 - 2k\left(\frac{1}{m} + \frac{1}{M}\right)\omega^2 + \frac{4k^2}{mM} \sin^2 \frac{fd}{2} = 0.$$

For propagation,

$$\frac{4k^2}{mM} \sin^2 \frac{fd}{d} = \frac{2k}{mM} (m + M)\omega^2 - \omega^4 \geq 0;$$

hence $\omega^2 \leq (2k/mM)(m + M)$.

For all values of $fd$ between zero and $\pi$ there are two roots for $\omega^2$. The larger root lies between $2k/m$ and $(2k/mM)(m + M)$, whereas the smaller root lies between zero and $2k/M$, where $M > m$. Hence propagation also does not occur for $2k/M < \omega^2 < 2k/m$.

8–23. For $m\omega_1^2 = k$ and $M\omega_2^2 = k$ we find that

$$\sin^2 \frac{f_1 d}{2} = \frac{\omega^2}{4\omega_1^2}, \qquad \sin^2 \frac{f_2 d}{2} = \frac{\omega^2}{4\omega_2^2}.$$

For the $n = 0$ and $n = 1$ masses we obtain the equations

$$-m\omega^2(A + B) = -2k(A + B) + k(Ce^{if_2 d} + Ae^{if_1 d} + Be^{-if_1 d}],$$
$$-M\omega^2 Ce^{if_2 d} = -2kC + k(e^{2if_2 d} + A + B),$$

which can be solved for $B$ and $C$ in terms of $A$. Similar equations are obtained for the constants $D$, $E$, and $F$.

## Chapter 9

9–1. (a) $\tfrac{3}{10}mr^2$, $\tfrac{3}{20}mr^2 + \tfrac{3}{5}mh^2$, $\tfrac{1}{4}h$ from the base

9–3. See Table 9–1.

9-5. (a) $I_{xx} = 10Ma^2$, $I_{yy} = I_{zz} = 6Ma^2$, $I_{yz} = 4Ma^2$, $I_{xz} = I_{xy} = 0$
(b) $I_1 = I_2 = 5$, $I_3 = 1$

$$\mathbf{e}_{1,2} = (a^2 + b^2)^{-1/2}[a\mathbf{i} + b(\mathbf{j} - \mathbf{k})], \quad \mathbf{e}_3 = \frac{1}{\sqrt{2}}(\mathbf{j} + \mathbf{k})$$

9-7. (a) Choosing $\mathbf{k}$ along the axis of rotation ($\boldsymbol{\omega} = \omega\mathbf{k}$), $\mathbf{k}'$ along the disk's symmetry axis and $\mathbf{i}$ vertically upward yields $\dot{\psi} = \dot{\theta} = 0$, $\dot{\phi} = \omega$, $N_\psi = N_\phi = 0$, and

$$N_\theta = \tfrac{1}{4}I_3\omega^2 \sin 2\alpha,$$

$$\mathbf{F} = \frac{W}{2}\mathbf{i} \pm \frac{N_\theta}{l}[\sin(\omega t + \phi_0)\mathbf{i} - \cos(\omega t + \phi_0)\mathbf{j}].$$

(b) Choosing $\mathbf{k}$ vertically upward, $t = 0$ when the plane of $\mathbf{k}$ and $\mathbf{k}'$ is vertical, and the $\mathbf{i}$-axis along the initial direction of $\boldsymbol{\omega}$ yields

$$\boldsymbol{\omega} = \omega(\cos\Omega t\,\mathbf{i} + \sin\Omega t\,\mathbf{j}), \qquad \boldsymbol{\Omega} = \Omega\mathbf{k},$$

whence

$$\dot{\psi} = (\boldsymbol{\omega} + \boldsymbol{\Omega})\cdot\overline{\mathbf{k}}' = -\frac{\omega}{\sin\theta}\sin(\Omega t - \phi),$$

$$\dot{\theta} = (\boldsymbol{\omega} + \boldsymbol{\Omega})\cdot\mathbf{e}_\phi = \omega\cos(\Omega t - \phi),$$

$$\dot{\phi} = (\boldsymbol{\omega} + \boldsymbol{\Omega})\cdot\overline{\mathbf{k}} = \Omega + \omega\cot\theta\sin(\Omega t - \phi),$$

and

$$N_\psi = \frac{d}{dt}I_3(\dot{\psi} + \dot{\phi}\cos\theta),$$

$$N_\theta = \frac{d}{dt}(I_1\dot{\theta}) - I\dot{\phi}^2\sin\theta\cos\theta + I_3(\dot{\psi} + \dot{\phi}\cos\theta)\dot{\phi}\sin\theta,$$

$$N_\phi = \frac{d}{dt}[I_1\dot{\phi}\sin^2\theta + I_3(\dot{\psi} + \dot{\phi}\cos\theta)\cos\theta].$$

9-9. For small angles the equation of motion for $\theta$ is

$$\ddot{\theta} = -\left[\frac{g}{l} - \omega_0^2\right]\theta,$$

which yields oscillatory motion for $g/l > \omega_0^2$. (Expansion not valid for $g/l < \omega_0^2$)

9-13. (a) $T = \tfrac{1}{2}I\dot{\phi}^2 + \tfrac{1}{2}Mh^2\dot{\phi}^2 - MRh\dot{\phi}^2\cos\phi + MR^2\dot{\phi}^2$, $U = -Mgh\cos\phi$
(b) $(I + Mh^2 - 2MRh\cos\phi + MR^2)\ddot{\phi} = -Mgh\sin\phi$, which for small $\phi$ reduces to

$$\ddot{\phi} = -\frac{Mgh}{I + M(R - h)^2}\phi.$$

Hence $\omega^2 = Mgh/I + M(R - h)^2$.

9-15. (a) $T = \tfrac{3}{40}ML^2\dot{\theta}^2[1 + 5\cos^2\alpha]$
$U = -\tfrac{3}{4}MgL\cos^2\alpha\cos\beta\cos\theta + \text{const}$
(b) $\omega^2 = 10g\cos^2\alpha\cos\beta/L(1 + 5\cos^2\alpha)$

9-17. (a) $\tfrac{1}{2}I\dot{\theta}^2 + \tfrac{1}{2}Mgl\cos\theta = \tfrac{1}{2}Mgl$, $I = \tfrac{1}{3}Ml^2$
(b) $\tfrac{1}{2}I\dot{\theta}^2 + \tfrac{1}{2}Mv^2 + \tfrac{1}{2}Mgl\cos\theta = \tfrac{1}{2}Mgl$, where $v^2 = \tfrac{1}{2}l\dot{\theta}\sin\theta$

(c) $I\ddot{\theta} = \dfrac{\Re l}{2}\sin\theta - \dfrac{\mu\Re l}{2}\cos\theta,\ M\ddot{y} = Mg - \Re,\ M\ddot{x} = -\mu\Re$

$\ddot{y} = \dfrac{l}{2}\dot\theta\sin\theta$ and $\Re$ = normal reaction force

9–19. $v_{CM} = \dfrac{3 - 4\epsilon}{7} v,\ l\omega = \dfrac{12}{7}(1 + \epsilon)v$

9–21. Top will precess uniformly without nutating.

## Chapter 10

10–1. (a) $\begin{bmatrix} -1 & 5 & 3 \\ -4 & 5 & 3 \\ -1 & 1 & 1 \end{bmatrix}$ (b) $[-4 \quad 11]$ (c) $\begin{bmatrix} 2 \\ 5 \\ 0 \\ 0 \end{bmatrix}$ (d) $\begin{bmatrix} 2 & 8 & 4 \\ 4 & 1 & 8 \\ 2 & -1 & 4 \end{bmatrix}$

10–3. (a) $(\mathbf{S_s}) = \begin{bmatrix} 2 & \frac{1}{2} & \frac{1}{2} \\ \frac{1}{2} & 1 & 1 \\ \frac{1}{2} & 1 & 1 \end{bmatrix},\ (\mathbf{S_a}) = \begin{bmatrix} 0 & -\frac{1}{2} & \frac{1}{2} \\ \frac{1}{2} & 0 & -2 \\ -\frac{1}{2} & 2 & 0 \end{bmatrix}$

(b) $(\mathbf{S_s}) = \begin{bmatrix} 0 & 1 & \frac{5}{2} \\ 1 & 0 & \frac{3}{2} \\ \frac{5}{2} & \frac{3}{2} & 1 \end{bmatrix},\ (\mathbf{S_a}) = \begin{bmatrix} 0 & 2 & \frac{1}{2} \\ -2 & 0 & \frac{1}{2} \\ -\frac{1}{2} & -\frac{1}{2} & 0 \end{bmatrix}$

(c) $(\mathbf{S_s}) = \begin{bmatrix} 1 & 1 & -\frac{1}{2} \\ 1 & 2 & 1 \\ -\frac{1}{2} & 1 & 2 \end{bmatrix},\ (\mathbf{S_a}) = \begin{bmatrix} 1 & 0 & \frac{1}{2} \\ 0 & 0 & 0 \\ -\frac{1}{2} & 0 & 0 \end{bmatrix}$

10–5. (a) $\mathbf{u}_1 \leftrightarrow \dfrac{1}{\sqrt{14}}[3, 2, 1],\ \mathbf{u}_2 \leftrightarrow \dfrac{1}{\sqrt{27}}[-1, -1, 5],\ \mathbf{u}_3 \leftrightarrow \dfrac{1}{3\sqrt{42}}[-11, 16, 1]$

10–7. (a) $\begin{bmatrix} 2 & 2 & -1 \\ 6 & 6 & -3 \\ -2 & -2 & 1 \end{bmatrix}$ (b) $\begin{bmatrix} 2 \\ 2 \\ -1 \\ 6 \\ 6 \\ -3 \\ -2 \\ -2 \\ 1 \end{bmatrix}$ (c) $\begin{bmatrix} 6 & 0 & 4 & 9 & 0 & 6 \\ 3 & 0 & 2 & 6 & 0 & 4 \\ -3 & 0 & -2 & 12 & 0 & 8 \end{bmatrix}$

10-9.  (a)
$$\begin{bmatrix} \gamma & 0 & 0 & \dfrac{iV}{c}\gamma \\[2mm] 0 & 1 & 0 & 0 \\[2mm] 0 & 0 & 1 & 0 \\[2mm] -\dfrac{iV}{c}\gamma & 0 & 0 & \gamma \end{bmatrix}, \text{ where } \gamma = \left[1 - \dfrac{V^2}{c^2}\right]^{-1/2}$$

(b) See Eq. (13–87).

10-11. Diagonal elements are
  (a) 2, 4          (b) −1, 3, −2          (c) 4, 10, −8
  (d) 1, 7, 1       (e) 9, 4, 36          (f) 0, 2

10-15. $(\mathbf{X}) = \dfrac{1}{4}\begin{bmatrix} 0 & -13 \\ 4 & 12 \end{bmatrix}$     10-17. $(\mathbf{M}) = \begin{bmatrix} \sqrt{\tfrac{3}{2}} \pm i & 0 & \sqrt{\tfrac{3}{2}} \mp i \\[2mm] 0 & \pm i\sqrt{2} & 0 \\[2mm] \sqrt{\tfrac{3}{2}} \mp i & 0 & \sqrt{\tfrac{3}{2}} \pm i \end{bmatrix}$

## Chapter 11

11-1.  (a) Equilibrium at $(0, \tfrac{3}{2}a, a)$, $m\omega^2 = 10U/a^2$, $4U/a^2$, $2U/a^2$, where
$$U = U(0, \tfrac{3}{2}a, a) = U_0 e^{-27/4}$$

11-3.  (a) $T = \tfrac{1}{2}m\dot{x}^2 + \tfrac{1}{6}\lambda l\dot{x}^2$

11-5.  (b) $\omega = 0, \pm 2, \pm 9$
  (c) General solution:
$$x_1 = 3A \cos(2\omega t + \phi_1) + 4B \cos(3\omega t + \phi_2) + \alpha t + \beta,$$
$$x_2 = A \cos(2\omega t + \phi_1) - 2B \cos(3\omega t + \phi_2) + \alpha t + \beta,$$
$$x_3 = -3A \cos(2\omega t + \phi_1) + B \cos(3\omega t + \phi_2) + \alpha t + \beta,$$
  $A$, $B$, $\alpha$, $\beta$ determined from the initial conditions

11-11. $T = \tfrac{1}{2}M\left(\dfrac{\dot{x}_1 + \dot{x}_2}{2}\right)^2 + \tfrac{1}{2}I\omega^2$, where $l\omega = \dot{x}_2 - \dot{x}_1$
$$U = -\tfrac{1}{2}Mg(x_1 + x_2) + \tfrac{1}{2}k(x_1^2 + x_2^2)$$

11-13. Initial conditions: $\dot{x}_1 = \dot{x}_2 = 0$, $k_1 x_1 = m_2 g$, $k_2|x_2 - x_1| = m_2 g$, or
$$k_2(x_2 - x_1) = m_2 g \quad \text{if} \quad k_1 > k_2,$$
$$k_2(x_1 - x_2) = m_2 g \quad \text{if} \quad k_1 < k_2,$$

where $x_1$ and $x_2$ are measured from the respective equilibrium positions of the masses.

General solution:

$$x_1 = 2A \cos (\sqrt{6}\, t + \phi_1) + B \cos (t + \phi_2)$$
$$x_2 = -A \cos (\sqrt{6}\, t + \phi_1) + 2B \cos (t + \phi_2)$$

11-15. (a) $T = \frac{1}{2}m(\dot{x}_1^2 + \dot{x}_2^2 + \dot{x}_3^2),\ U = \frac{1}{2}k(x_2 - x_1)^2 + \frac{1}{2}k(x_3 - x_2)^2$

$m\ddot{x}_1 = k(x_2 - x_1) + m\mu(\dot{x}_2 - \dot{x}_1)$

$m\ddot{x}_2 = k(x_3 - x_2) - k(x_2 - x_1) - m\mu(\dot{x}_2 - \dot{x}_1) - m\mu(\dot{x}_3 - \dot{x}_2)$

$m\ddot{x}_3 = -k(x_3 - x_2) - m\mu(\dot{x}_3 - \dot{x}_2)$

11-19. $x_1 = A + Be^{-t}, x_2 = C + De^{-t}$, where

$$A = C = F_0/m\omega_0^2, \qquad m\omega_0^2 = k,$$

and

$$B = \frac{1 - 2\mu + \omega_0^2}{\omega_0^2 - \mu} \qquad D = \frac{(F_0/m)(1 - 2\mu + \omega_0^2)}{(\mu - \omega_0^2)^2 - (1 - \mu + 2\omega_0^2)(1 - 2\mu + \omega_0^2)}$$

11-21. $\omega_1 = \sqrt{\dfrac{k_1 + 2k_2}{m}}\left(1 - \dfrac{\Delta m}{4m}\right),\ \omega_2 = \sqrt{\dfrac{k_1}{m}}\left(1 - \dfrac{\Delta m}{4m}\right)$

11-23. (a) $L = \frac{1}{2}m \sum\limits_{i=1}^{6} \dot{x}_i^2 - \dfrac{k}{2}[(x_1 - x_2)^2 + (x_2 - x_3)^2 + (x_3 - x_1)^2$

$$+ (x_4 - x_5)^2 + (x_5 - x_6)^2 + (x_6 - x_4)^2],$$

where

$$x_1 = x_a, \quad x_2 = x_b, \quad x_3 = x_c, \quad x_4 = y_a, \quad x_5 = y_b, \quad x_6 = y_c,$$

$a, b, c,$ designating the three particles.

(d) $\mathbf{O}_1 = \begin{bmatrix} 0 & 1 & 0 & 0 & 0 & 0 \\ 0 & 0 & 1 & 0 & 0 & 0 \\ 1 & 0 & 0 & 0 & 0 & 0 \\ 0 & 0 & 0 & 0 & 1 & 0 \\ 0 & 0 & 0 & 0 & 0 & 1 \\ 0 & 0 & 0 & 1 & 0 & 0 \end{bmatrix}, \mathbf{O}_2 = \begin{bmatrix} 0 & 0 & 1 & 0 & 0 & 0 \\ 1 & 0 & 0 & 0 & 0 & 0 \\ 0 & 1 & 0 & 0 & 0 & 0 \\ 0 & 0 & 0 & 0 & 0 & 1 \\ 0 & 0 & 0 & 1 & 0 & 0 \\ 0 & 0 & 0 & 0 & 1 & 0 \end{bmatrix}$

(e) Eigenvalues are $\lambda = 1,\ e^{2\pi i/3},\ e^{4\pi i/3}$

Eigenvectors for

$\lambda = 1:$ $\mathbf{e}_1 \leftrightarrow \dfrac{1}{\sqrt{3}}[1, 1, 1, 0, 0, 0],\ \mathbf{e}_4 \leftrightarrow \dfrac{1}{\sqrt{3}}[0, 0, 0, 1, 1, 1]$

$\lambda = e^{2\pi i/3}: \mathbf{e}_2 \leftrightarrow \dfrac{1}{\sqrt{3}}[1, \epsilon, \epsilon^2, 0, 0, 0],\ \mathbf{e}_5 \leftrightarrow \dfrac{1}{\sqrt{3}}[0, 0, 0, 1, \epsilon, \epsilon^2]$

$\lambda = e^{4\pi i/3}: \mathbf{e}_3 \leftrightarrow \dfrac{1}{\sqrt{3}}[1, \epsilon^2, \epsilon, 0, 0, 0],\ \mathbf{e}_6 \leftrightarrow \dfrac{1}{\sqrt{3}}[0, 0, 0, 1, \epsilon^2, \epsilon],$

where $\epsilon = -\frac{1}{2}(1 - i\sqrt{3})$, $\epsilon^2 = -\frac{1}{2}(1 + i\sqrt{3}) = \epsilon^*$, $\epsilon^{*2} = \epsilon$

$$(\mathbf{S}) = \frac{1}{\sqrt{3}} \begin{bmatrix} 1 & 1 & 1 & 0 & 0 & 0 \\ 1 & \epsilon & \epsilon^2 & 0 & 0 & 0 \\ 1 & \epsilon^2 & \epsilon & 0 & 0 & 0 \\ 0 & 0 & 0 & 1 & 1 & 1 \\ 0 & 0 & 0 & 1 & \epsilon & \epsilon^2 \\ 0 & 0 & 0 & 1 & \epsilon^2 & \epsilon \end{bmatrix}$$

(f) $|\bar{\mathbf{r}}\rangle = \mathbf{S}|\mathbf{r}\rangle$, $\bar{x}_1 = \dfrac{1}{\sqrt{3}}(x_1 + x_2 + x_3)$, $\bar{x}_2 = \dfrac{1}{\sqrt{3}}(x_1 + \epsilon x_2 + \epsilon^2 x_3)$

$\bar{x}_3 = \dfrac{1}{\sqrt{3}}(x_1 + \epsilon^2 x_2 + \epsilon x_3)$, etc.

(g) $\omega^2 = 0, 3k/m, 3k/m$.

## Chapter 12

12-1.  $\psi(z, t) = \sum_{n=1}^{\infty} a_n \sin k_n z \cos \omega_n t$,  where  $k_n = (2n - 1)\pi$,  $\omega_n = \sqrt{T/\mu}\, k_n$, $a_n = 0.8(-1)^{n+1}/k_n^2$

12-3.  (a) $T \dfrac{\partial \psi}{\partial z} + \dfrac{T\lambda}{v} \dfrac{\partial \psi}{\partial t} = 0$, where $T\lambda/v$ is the damping constant

(b) $\psi_n(z, t) = A e^{-k_n vt} \sinh k_n z$, where the $k_n$'s are the roots of the equation

$$\tan kl = 1/\lambda$$

12-5.  (a) $-T \dfrac{\partial \psi}{\partial z} = m \dfrac{\partial^2 \psi}{\partial t^2}$

(b) $\psi_n(z, t) = A \sin k_n l \sin \omega_n t$, where $\omega_n = k_n \sqrt{T/\mu}$, and $k_n$ is a root of the equation

$$k_n \tan k_n l = \mu/m$$

12-7.  $\psi(z, t) = A \sin \omega t \, \dfrac{\sin k(l - z)}{\sin kl}$, where $k = \omega \sqrt{\dfrac{\mu}{T}}$

12-9.  $\psi(z, t) = \mathrm{Re} \displaystyle\sum_{n=1}^{\infty} \dfrac{f_n e^{i(\omega t + \phi)} \sin (n\pi z/l)}{(k_n^2 - k^2) + 2i\lambda k}$, where $k_n = \omega_n \sqrt{\dfrac{\mu}{T}} = \dfrac{n\pi}{l}$,

$k = \omega \sqrt{\dfrac{\mu}{T}}$, $f_n = \dfrac{2}{l} \displaystyle\int_0^l f(z) \sin k_n z \, dz$

12-11.  $\gamma = \sqrt{k^2 - \left(\dfrac{n\pi}{a}\right)^2 - \left(\dfrac{m\pi}{b}\right)^2}$

Cutoff frequency is $\omega = kv = \pi v/a$, where $a$ is the larger dimension of the cross section. For the $nm$ TM mode the cutoff frequency is

$$\omega = v \sqrt{\left(\frac{n\pi}{a}\right)^2 + \left(\frac{m\pi}{b}\right)^2}.$$

12–13. (a) $r_{12} = \dfrac{n_{12} - 1}{n_{12} + 1}$, $t_{12} = \dfrac{2n_{12}}{n_{12} - 1}$    (b) $k_2 = \sqrt{k_1 k_3}$, $n_2 = \sqrt{n_1 n_3}$

12–15. (b) $T\left(\dfrac{\partial \psi}{\partial z}\bigg|_{0+} - \dfrac{\partial \psi}{\partial z}\bigg|_{0-}\right) = \kappa \psi$    (c) $\tan kl = -\dfrac{2Tk}{\kappa}$

(d) $\left(\dfrac{n\pi}{l} - k_n\right) = \dfrac{\kappa}{n\pi T}$

12–17. (a) $\dfrac{\partial^2 \psi_1}{\partial z^2} - \dfrac{1}{v^2} \dfrac{\partial^2 \psi_1}{\partial t^2} = -\kappa(\psi_2 - \psi_1)\delta(z)$, $\dfrac{\partial^2 \psi_2}{\partial z^2} - \dfrac{1}{v^2} \dfrac{\partial^2 \psi_2}{\partial t^2} = \kappa(\psi_2 - \psi_1)\delta(z)$

or

$$\frac{\partial^2 \psi_i}{\partial z^2} - \frac{1}{v^2} \frac{\partial^2 \psi_i}{\partial t^2} = 0$$

with

$$T\left(\frac{\partial \psi_1}{\partial z}\bigg|_{0+} - \frac{\partial \psi_1}{\partial z}\bigg|_{0-}\right) = -\kappa(\psi_2 - \psi_1) \quad \text{at} \quad z = 0,$$

$$T\left(\frac{\partial \psi_2}{\partial z}\bigg|_{0+} - \frac{\partial \psi_2}{\partial z}\bigg|_{0-}\right) = \kappa(\psi_2 - \psi_1) \quad \text{at} \quad z = 0$$

(d) For the even solution $\phi_1$ the eigenfrequencies are obtained from the equation $\cos kl = 0$. The eigenfrequencies for the odd solution $\phi_2$ are obtained from the equation $\tan kl = -Tk/\kappa$.

## Chapter 13

13–1.  $d = 2.55 \times 10^4 \text{m}$

13–3.  $pc = 79.5 m_e$, $\mathfrak{I} = 193.5 m_e$

13–9.  $E_x = \dfrac{q}{4\pi\epsilon_0} \dfrac{(x - Vt)(1 - V^2/c^2)}{\bar{r}^3}$, $E_y = \dfrac{q}{4\pi\epsilon_0} \dfrac{y(1 - V^2/c^2)}{\bar{r}^3}$

$E_z = \dfrac{q}{4\pi\epsilon_0} \dfrac{z(1 - V^2/c^2)}{\bar{r}^3}$

where $\bar{r}^2 = (x - Vt)^2 + y^2 + z^2$.

$\mathbf{B} = \gamma \dfrac{\mathbf{V}}{c^2} \times \mathbf{E}'$,    $\mathbf{B} = \dfrac{\mathbf{V} \times \mathbf{E}}{c^2}$

or

$B_x = 0$,    $B_y = -\dfrac{q}{4\pi\epsilon_0} \dfrac{V}{c^2} E_z$,    $B_z = \dfrac{q}{4\pi\epsilon_0} \dfrac{V}{c^2} E_y$

13-11. $\dfrac{d^2u}{d\theta^2} + \lambda u = -\dfrac{k\mathcal{E}}{l^2c^2}$ , where $f(r) = \dfrac{k}{r}$, $\lambda = 1 - \dfrac{k^2}{l^2c^2}$

13-13. Equations of motion are:

$$m\overset{\circ\circ}{x} = \gamma qE + q\overset{\circ}{y}B = qE\overset{\circ}{t} + qB\overset{\circ}{y},$$

$$m\overset{\circ\circ}{y} = -q\overset{\circ}{x}B,$$

$$m\overset{\circ\circ}{z} = 0, \qquad mc\overset{\circ\circ}{t} = \dfrac{qE}{c}\overset{\circ}{x}$$

These are simultaneous differential equations with constant coefficients. The trial solution $x = Ae^{\alpha\tau}$, etc., yields a secular equation whose roots are

$$\alpha^2 = 0, \dfrac{q^2}{m^2c^2}(E^2 - c^2B^2),$$

where zero is a fourth-order root. For a proper choice of origin, the solution which satisfies the condition $u^2 = -c^2$ for $E^2 < c^2B^2$ is

$$x = A_1 \cos(\omega\tau + \phi),$$

$$y = \dfrac{qB}{m\omega} A_1 \sin(\omega\tau + \phi) + \dfrac{qE}{mc} A_2\tau,$$

$$ct = \dfrac{qE}{mc\omega} A_1 \sin\omega\tau + \dfrac{Bq}{m} A_2\tau,$$

$$z = A_3\omega\tau,$$

where

$$A_2^2 - A_1^2 - A_3^2 = \dfrac{1}{\omega^2}, \qquad \omega^2 = \dfrac{q^2}{m^2c^2}(c^2B^2 - E^2).$$

13-15. $V$ is the root of the equation

$$\dfrac{V/c}{1 - V^2/c^2} = \dfrac{|\mathbf{E} \times \mathbf{B}|}{c^2B^2 + E^2}$$

which is less than $c$ in magnitude.

13-17. It is the solution of

$$\dfrac{\mathfrak{I}_1 - mc^2}{\mathfrak{I}_1 + mc^2} = \dfrac{\mathfrak{I}_0 - mc^2}{\mathfrak{I}_0 + mc^2} \cos^2\theta.$$

# Index